Y0-BOF-098

PARTY GOVERNMENT IN 48 DEMOCRACIES (1945-1998)

PARTY GOVERNMENT IN 48 DEMOCRACIES (1945-1998)

Composition – Duration – Personnel

by

Jaap Woldendorp
Hans Keman
*Department of Political Science and Government Administration,
Vrije Universiteit Amsterdam*

and

Ian Budge
*Department of Government,
Essex University*

KLUWER ACADEMIC PUBLISHERS
DORDRECHT / BOSTON / LONDON

A C.I.P. Catalogue record for this book is available from the Library of Congress.

ISBN 0-7923-6727-8

Published by Kluwer Academic Publishers,
P.O. Box 17, 3300 AA Dordrecht, The Netherlands.

Sold and distributed in North, Central and South America
by Kluwer Academic Publishers,
101 Philip Drive, Norwell, MA 02061, U.S.A.

In all other countries, sold and distributed
by Kluwer Academic Publishers,
P.O. Box 322, 3300 AH Dordrecht, The Netherlands.

Printed on acid-free paper

All Rights Reserved
© 2000 Kluwer Academic Publishers
No part of the material protected by this copyright notice may be reproduced or
utilized in any form or by any means, electronic or mechanical,
including photocopying, recording or by any information storage and
retrieval system, without written permission from the copyright owner.

Printed in the Netherlands.

CONTENTS

vi

FOREWORD

Since the 1980s, political scientists have developed a renewed interest in the study of political institutions, based on the assumption that "institutions matter" - that is, that formal governmental institutions and constitutional-legal rules (as well as informal institutions like parties and interest groups) are crucial determinants of the shape of politics and policy outcomes. In this respect, the "new institutionalism" resembles the "old institutionalism" of pre-behaviorist days, but the crucial difference between the two is that the new institutionalists are committed to systematic empirical testing of their hypotheses, at least in principle. In practice, however, especially in comparative analyses, this goal has often been frustrated by the lack of reliable data for a large number of countries. Researchers have therefore usually been limited to testing their hypotheses with modest data sets collected for their own particular purposes.

Of all of the political institutions, the executive branch of the government is by far the most important; it can be regarded as the irreducible core of government and the principal embodiment of political authority with specific powers that are not lodged elsewhere in the political system. Almost all countries in the world, and certainly all modern democracies, have an executive body called "government", "cabinet", or "administration" (as in the term "the Clinton administration") that has the main responsibility for running the country's public affairs.

Of the many types and forms of government, the most widespread is party government – that is, government in which parties make and shape the composition of government. Parties also exist in different types and forms, but their roles and functions are invariably crucial in any democratic system. Parties are particularly important for the formation and viability of government in parliamentary democracies where parties decide which of them will participate in government, who is to become the prime minister, who will be the other ministers, and how the portfolios will be distributed. And parties are also responsible for the life of a government by their actions in parliament and/or by their results in the electoral arena. In short, parties are the key actors for the study of government in parliamentary democracies.

It is surprising therefore how few large-scale systematic studies exist concerning the life and times of party government. There are relatively few comparative studies that go beyond a handful, or sometimes a couple of handfuls, of countries. And those that do exist tend to be limited with regard to the variables used. It is equally surprising to observe how little effort has been made to systematically collect data on the core variables representing the potential room for maneuver that governments have vis-à-vis the legislatures – how much leeway they have and to what extent they are constrained. In other words, the study of democratic party-government has been hampered by the lack of well-conceived variables and comprehensive coverage. This has been an unfortunate situation especially in view of the rapid extension of liberal democracies around the world and the concomitant need to study the political institutionalization of party government (in particular in parliamentary settings).

This new data handbook therefore represents a huge and most welcome improvement in our ability to test the many institutionalist hypotheses. It fills many of the gaps that I have mentioned. It contains the party composition and duration of no less than 46 parliamentary (including a few semi-presidential) and two presidential democracies. Furthermore, the book presents, for all 48 countries, both the government composition at the level of the ministries and each of the ministers (name, gender, and party affiliation). Any student of government can now define his or her research questions, develop his or her operationalizations, and select the number of cases needed to conduct a truly systematic and comparative analysis of party government. An additional extremely helpful contribution is that the authors have gathered relevant institutional and constitutional information for all 48 democracies and provide variables that can be used comparatively and that enable the interested student of party government to conduct his or her analysis much efficiently and effectively than until now.

I believe that this data collection will be a vital asset to the study of government in general and to the comparative study of party government in parliamentary democracies in particular. A database like this handbook has been long overdue, and is bound to significantly further the comparative study of party government.

September 2000
AREND LIJPHART
Research Professor Emeritus of Political Science
University of California, La Jolla

PREFACE AND ACKNOWLEDGEMENTS

This work derives from the data assembled for Ian Budge and Hans Keman *Parties and Democracy: Coalition formation and government functioning in twenty states* (Oxford, Oxford University Press, 1990; 1993). The concerns of that book with party pursuit of policy, government formation and termination, the distribution of ministries and the consequences of sectoral domination of parties in particular policy areas, remain unique. The data published here enables further exploration of these questions - along with many other aspects of government functioning - which are coming to the forefront of coalition theory and policy analysis today. The information we have collected goes further than the original set in terms of the government characteristics recorded, the time-span covered and in particular the range of countries included. In this book 51 parliamentary systems are covered representing 48 nations for the whole post-war period (1945-1998).

Collecting so much data as we have done would be an impossible task had we not been able to draw on the help of so many friends and colleagues. It is only a small recompense for these devoted efforts to list them here. But we would like to thank them publicly as we have already done privately for checking, collating, correcting and supplementing our information in so many countries. We hope that they, along with other readers, will find the information useful for their research. They are Attila Agh, Peter Aimer, Klaus Armingeon, Judith Bara, Stefano Bartolini, Thomas Bauer, Ali Çarkoglu, Frank Castles, Josep Colomer, Lieven De Winter, Patrick Dumont, Svante Ersson, Gillian Evans, Joseph Farrugia, Danica Fink-Hafner, Markus Freitag, Natasha Gaber, Michael Gallagher, Mike Ghasemi, Joyce Hamilton, Hans Hirter, Rob Hoppe, Efthalia Kalogeropoulou, Anthony King, Peter Kloos, Peter Kopecki, Svannur Kristjánsson, Sándor Kurtán, Arend Lijphart, Peter Mair, Michael McDonald, Evald Mikkel, Subrata Mitra, Peter Nannestad, Ian Neary, Herbert Obinger, Hans Oversloot, François Pétry, Sven Quenter, Feliciana Rajevska, Vitold Rajevskis, Bas Rijkers, Manfred Schmidt, Mat Shugart, Roos Siwalette, Inka Slodkowska, and Noël Vergunst.

We came into contact with many of these colleagues through the meetings, workshops, and research groups of the *European Consortium for Political Research* (ECPR), the enduring basis for comparative investigations on Europe, whose journal first published our preliminary data set in 1993 and later in 1998.[1] Without the stimulus of the ECPR, indeed the idea of us undertaking or others using a handbook such as this would be hardly conceivable. Indeed the authors might not even have met each other in the first place.

---

[1] Woldendorp, J., H. Keman, I. Budge (1993) 'Political Data 1945-1990. Party Government in 20 Democracies' *European Journal of Political Research*, 24/1 (July): 1-120; Woldendorp, J., H. Keman, I. Budge (1998) 'Party Government in 20 Democracies: an Update (1990-1995)' *European Journal of Political Research*, 33/1 (January): 125-164.

Apart from colleagues we also received valuable assistance from civil servants in many countries. We are especially grateful for the help of *Aliki Boef*, Press and Information Officer of the Embassy of Greece in The Hague who showed us the way through the intricate vicissitudes of post-war Greek governments. *Adrième Austin*, Attachée of Embassy of Jamaica in Brussels supplied us with the most recent and updated information on Jamaican governments.

We also would like to thank Sabine Wesseldijk and her staff of Kluwer Academic Publishers, who were most helpful in seeing this book through its final stage.

Finally our gratitude goes to our universities: University of *Essex* and the *Vrije Universiteit* (Amsterdam) which supported us throughout and provided our infrastructure. Without all the help we received this book would not have been possible.

Whilst we gratefully acknowledge the assistance of all these, we ourselves of course remain responsible for any remaining errors or misinterpretations. In fact, we would appreciate it if mistakes or errors found would be communicated to us since we endeavour to keep the information contained in this data handbook not only up-to-date, but also as correct as possible.

Amsterdam & Colchester, January 2000
JAAP WOLDENDORP and HANS KEMAN
Department of Political Science, Vrije Universiteit, Amsterdam, the Netherlands
IAN BUDGE
Department of Government, University of Essex, England

Correspondence to email: JJ.Woldendorp@scw.vu.nl

LIST OF FIGURES

LIST OF TABLES

CHAPTER 1

PARTY GOVERNMENT AND PARLIAMENTARY DEMOCRACY

1.1   Introduction

This book is an attempt to provide a compact and comprehensive data collection, which *simultaneously* provides *comparative* and *complete* information on the composition of governments in terms of parties, ministries, portfolios and parliamentary support, as well as on their duration and reasons for termination. Of course, such information is gradually becoming available (e.g. Paloheimo, 1984; Von Beyme, 1985; Laver and Schofield, 1990: Appendix; Schmidt, 1992, Woldendorp, Keman, Budge, 1993, 1993a; and more recently Lane et al. 1997), but most of these data are still *fragmentary* in scope, range of countries and periods covered.

The data collection presented in this book grew out of our investigation of the relation between *parties and governments in parliamentary democracies* (see: Budge and Keman, 1990, 1993). In order to make the data collection available to the political science community (and beyond) we decided to update the information for the period 1945-1990, covering 20 parliamentary democracies. In addition, we had the original data cross-checked and added a number of variables that would be helpful for cross-national research on government composition, the ideological colour of governments, the size and duration of governments, etc. (see also section 3 of this chapter). These data were published in the *European Journal of Political Research* (volume 24/1) as well as separately as a book (Woldendorp, Keman and Budge, 1993). This endeavour has met with considerable success among fellow-comparativists, as is demonstrated by the widespread use of the collection since its publication.

In 1997 therefore, we decided to have the data collection updated and rechecked and published the results (again) in the *European Journal of Political Research* (volume 33/2: 125-164). In the process we came to the conclusion that the data set could and should be extended beyond its original frame and supplemented with contextual information. On the one hand, because there are obviously (and in particular after the developments in Central and Eastern Europe since 1989) many more parliamentary democracies than the original 20 countries which form the core of the OECD-world. On the other hand, comprehensive, constitutional information is lacking with respect to the institutional setting in which *parliamentary governments* operate as a *type* of democracy (see: Lijphart, 1992; Schmidt, 1995a). This information presented in an accessible way and comparative fashion is much needed. Yet, as with data on government composition *per se*, this information is not widely available for other countries than the 20 established democracies (but see: Lijphart, 1991; Huber et al., 1993). Hence, this data-collection — although developed on the basis of our earlier work — can be considered as providing a genuinely new coverage of 51 parliamentary democracies, together with an extensive survey of their institutional features. These latter features are broadly similar to those covered in Lijphart's seminal work on democracies (1984 and 1999; but see also: Bingham Powell, 1982; Lijphart, 1994; Laver and Shepsle, 1994; Colomer, 1996; Budge et al., 1997; Keman, 1997).

In summary: this databook provides comparatively organised information on the composition of parliamentary governments in 51 democracies as well as comprehensive information on the institutional framework in which these democratic governments operate.

The presentation of the data on party government is organised in such a way that every researcher can use the information as a *basic data set*, ready to be transformed according to his or her needs in the light of research undertaken at whatever level of analysis (e.g. individual ministers and separate ministries, or specific parties and governments, or countries), both cross-nationally and across time.

In the remainder of this introductory chapter we shall discuss the *substantive* grounds for the choice of variables in relation both to the existing literature and the data currently available (section 2). This concise discussion is intended to demonstrate — among other things — how the data can be used and hence its value for research in comparative politics. In section 3, the *reliability* of sources and the conceptual *validity* of the variables will be discussed in more detail. Finally, in section 4, the *format* used and the *presentation* of the data in the countrytables as well as in the chapter on the institutional framework will be explained. In addition to the data-presentation for each country two chapters have been included in which the analytical value and empirical usefulness of some variables will be discussed. One chapter is devoted to the constitutional features of the countries under review (Chapter 2). This information will be helpful for understanding under what institutional conditions parliamentary governments operate. The other chapter demonstrates the use of the data in relation to government duration and stability in view of party system characteristics and reasons of termination (Chapter 3). The comparative presentation of these features and discussion of these variables will demonstrate the added value of these data for studies of government functioning in parliamentary democracies.

1.2   Government in Parliamentary Democracies

One of the basic features of any parliamentary democracy is that there is a (freely) elected government, which can be held accountable for its actions.

Hence elections are an essential element of democracy and of paramount interest to political scientists. The same observation can be made with respect to the formation and subsequent composition and termination of government. Political parties play a key role in both elections and governments, shaping the actual process of democratic decision-making. There is, however, little consistent and reliable information in the shape of standardised data for governments as opposed to elections. Therefore we have sought not only to collect these data, but also to present them in such a way that any student of comparative or national politics can use them for their own research purposes. Before going into the choice of variables and the cases under review, we shall briefly elaborate what is meant by democratic government *per se*, and by parliamentary government in particular.

In principle democratic governance entails, as Abraham Lincoln put it in 1861: "Government by the people, for the people, of the people". In fact elections play a major role in the relationship between the people and its government. Hence, the most prevalent form of democracy is *indirect* (possibly, with certain features of direct democracy; Budge, 1996). To put it differently, democratic governance is basically *representative* government shaped by an institutional arrangement (which is almost always constitutionally driven; Schumpeter, 1950: 265-268). In addition, representative government is seen as establishing the legitimate authority of the state within a democratic society (Cf. Weber, in: Schmidt, 1995a: 205-206). Finally, this institutional arrangement provides the basis for the mutual obligations between the democratic leadership or government, and the population within the nation-state. These obligations ultimately define the conditions that have to be met in order to delineate the concept of democratic government. These are (Held, 1987; Beetham, 1994):
   (a) popular representation by means of elections (freely and regularly held)
   (b) fully guaranteed civil rights for all citizens (in practice)
   (c) supremacy of the Rule of Law (by means of a constitution).

In Table 1.1 information will be presented for all the countries included in the data-collection to show how far these conditions are indeed met (see also: Schmidt, 1995b: 264-292).

Having said what democratic government is, let us now turn to the question of what a *parliamentary democracy* is (or is not). This type of democracy is essentially characterised by the fact that the *ultimate* power of the state to decide, act, appoint, etc. rests with parliament. Hence, in the final analysis a parliamentary system is characterised by how the relationship between the executive and legislative has been prescribed in its constitution (Cf. Lijphart, 1992). Contrary to other types of democratic government, such as plebiscitary and direct democracy, on the one hand, and (semi-) presidential democracy, on the other hand, it is not the separation of powers that defines parliamentary government but the fact that parliament and government are characterised by *power-sharing*. From this it follows that parliamentary government can be considered as a mode of democratic government in which co-operation between representatives (of parties) in parliament and government is almost compulsory. In addition, government action is dependent on consensus and concertation in parliament, in particular regarding the mode of interaction between government and opposition (Budge and Keman, 1990; Linz, 1990).

Parliamentary government – the principal subject of our data – is by and large produced by the constitutional organisation of representative democracy. Its principal feature is that the executive and legislative powers are *shared* by crucial functionaries, like the Head of State, (Head of) Government, and to a variable extent are *fused* with parliament (leading to oscillating developments in power relationships, often described as a developments towards 'monism' or 'dualism'; see: Lijphart, 1984; Blondel, 1987).

It is precisely this type of government for which information is mostly presented in this book and variables have been developed to enhance the study of this type of democratic governance (see further: Budge and Keman, 1990; Woldendorp et al., 1993). The conceptual discussion of parliamentary governments helps to clarify which democratic systems are included and which are not. Obviously *presidential democracies* are not included (see for a clear description of the differences of the two types: Verney, 1992). Apart from the fact that in a presidential democracy the Head of State or President is the sole executive and only responsible to the constitution, there is no government consisting of ministers who are *individually* responsible to parliament and are *collectively* responsible for governmental action at the same time. However, we did include *semi-presidential democracies*. The reason being that this type of democratic government is considered in general to be responsible to parliament and is often seen as a form of *dual* leadership (mostly shared between the Head of the State and the Prime Minister; Blondel, 1987; Duverger, 1992). Instead of sheer power *division* – as in a presidential system – or of power *sharing* – as in parliamentary systems – one could argue (cf. Blondel, 1987) that in a semi-presidential system the relationship between the executive and legislative is *alternating* due to the constitutional features of such a system. Hence, depending on the actual power division *in* parliament and *between* parliament and president (e.g. as is manifested in the case of "divided government"; Weaver and Rockman, 1993), either the parliamentary government or the president directs government actions (see also: Gallagher et al., 1995: 18-21; Budge, et al., 1997: ch. 10).

Since parliament and government are considered by most authors as crucial actors with respect to the functioning of this type of democracy, we have decided to include semi-presidential democracies in our data-collection. Of course, there are not many cases of semi-presidentialism among the 51 countries that figure in this book. In Europe there is France, Finland, Poland and, as some would argue, Portugal. In Eastern Europe: Romania and Slovakia. Outside Europe, we have Botswana, South Africa, Sri Lanka and (perhaps) Pakistan (see also: Lijphart, 1992: 8-10).

In sum: the basic unit of analysis in this data-collection is a parliamentary system with representative government. These governments are ultimately responsible to parliament for their actions. This feature is also apparent in what are labelled "semi-presidential democracies". This brings us to a discussion of the selection of countries and the period of investigation covered in this databook.

1.3   The Choice of Countries and Period under Investigation

As most comparative analyses of representative government concentrate on post-war developments, the *period* covered will be *1945-1998*. As will become clear this implies a shorter period for those countries that became independent after 1945, experienced an interruption of democracy, or where a democratic constitution was only recently introduced (as is the case in post-communist countries). As detailed above, we have included only those democracies that can be characterised as *parliamentary* or *semi-presidential*. Hence, only those political systems are included that fulfil the criteria of 'democraticness' (as discussed in the previous section) and where government is (fully) *responsible to Parliament*, with or without features of dual leadership and alternating dominance of either the Executive or the Legislature. Table 1.1 lists the countries included. In addition, some general information has been reported which indicates the constitutional age (1), if and when the constitution has been drastically revised (2), the introduction of universal suffrage (for men and women) (3), the degree of 'democraticness' (4 & 5), and finally a categorisation in terms of: the absence of interrupted democracy; originated as a democracy after 1945; experienced non democraticness between 1945-1998; having experienced a drastic change of the democratic system.

All in all *51 cases* are included in the data-collection, representing 48 countries. France is treated as two cases, South Africa as three. According to the literature (Lijphart, 1984; Gallagher et al., 1995) both countries changed their constitution from parliamentary government in the direction of semi-presidentialism. Yet, this development is not comparable to the situation prevailing in the United States of America and the Russian Federation. The administration there (note the term!) is only indirectly responsible to parliament (Lijphart, 1992: Part II). Switzerland must be considered as a special case too: its governing committee is elected by its parliament but cannot be dismissed during the parliamentary period. In addition its 'president' is an office that circulates annually among the members of the Federal Council, i.e. among the four parties that have formed the government since 1959 (the 'magic formula', see: Steiner, 1986: 124-126; Kerr, 1987: 124-126; Lijphart, 1992: 237-241). However, parliament is predominant and thus Switzerland is deviant but certainly not presidential.

Table 1.1: Democracy Scores of Countries and Cases

Countries	(1)	(2)	(3)	(4)	(5)	Cat
Australia	1901	1986	1902	10	1	I
Austria	1867	1945	1918	10	1	I
Bangladesh	1972	1991	1972	9	2	II
Belgium	1831	1970-93	1948	10	1	I
Botswana	1966	1997	1966	10	2	II
Bulgaria	1879	1991	1944	8	2	IV
Canada	1867	1982	1918	10	1	I
Czech Rep.	1920	1993	1920/1993	10	1	IV
Czechoslovakia	1920	1989	1920	-	-	IV
Denmark	1849	1953	1915	10	1	I
Estonia	1992	1992	1918	8	3	IV
Finland	1906	1919	1906	10	1	I
France IV	1791	1946	1944	9	1	I
France V	1946	1958*	1944	8	1	IV
Germany	1871	1949	1918	10	1	IV
Greece	1952	1975	1952	10	1	III
Guyana	1980	1995	1953	5	2	II
Hungary .	1949	1989	1953	10	1	IV
Iceland	1874	1944	1915	10	1	I
India	1950	1994	1950	8	4	II
Ireland	1922	1937	1928	10	1	I
Israel	Unwritten		1948	9	1	II
Italy	1861	1948	1945	10	1	I
Jamaica	1962	1962	1944	6	NA	II
Japan	1889	1947	1945	10	2	IV
Latvia	1922	1991	1918	8	3	IV
Lithuania	1990	1991	1944	10	1	IV
Luxembourg	1918	1956	1919	10	1	I
Macedonia	1991	1997	1946	8	4	II
Malta	1964	1982	1947	7	1	II
Namibia	1990	1990	1989	NA	1	II
Netherlands	1814	1983	1919	10	1	I
New Zealand	Unwritten		1893	10	1	I
Norway	1814	1998	1913	10	1	I
Pakistan	1973	1985	1947	8	3	III
Poland	1815	1992	1945	8	2	IV
Portugal	1822	1976	1974	10	1	IV
Romania	1861	1991	1946	5	4	IV
Slovakia	1920	1993	1920/1993	8	2	IV
Slovenia	1991	1991	1945	10	1	IV
South Africa 1+2	1909	1961/1984	-	3	3	IV
South Africa 3*	1961	1994*	1984/1993	7	2	IV
Spain	1873	1978	1931	9	1	IV
Sri Lanka	1947	1978	1931	5	4	III
Sweden	1809	1975	1921	10	1	I
Switzerland	1874	1978	1971	10	1	I
Turkey	1921	1982	1930	10	5	III
United Kingdom	Unwritten		1928	10	1	I
Russian Federation	1905	1993	1918	7	3	IV**
United States	1781	1789	1920	10	1	I**

(1) *Year* of Introduction of Constitution
(2) *Year* of most recent Revision of Constitution
(3) *Universal Suffrage*: Introduction of the Right to Vote for *both* men and women (*year*)
(4) *Democracy Scale*: 10 = optimal; 1 = completely absent (Jaggers/Gurr, 1995; Vanhanen, 1997)

(5) *Political and Civil Rights*: 1 = good performance; 7 = bad performance (Freedom House)
Cat:

   I = Uninterrupted Parliamentarism *before*1945;
   II = Idem since Independence *after* 1945;
   III = Interrupted Democracy *between* 1945-1996;
   IV = Drastic *change* of the Polity.

* = In *France* the constitutional change of 1958 meant a change from pure parliamentarism to semi-presidentialism. *South Africa* adopted in 1994 its present constitution which transformed the polity from semi-polyarchy to a fully fledged one; in 1984 it changed its mode of representation but this did not imply a genuine development towards more polyarchy.
** = *Presidential* Democracy

NA = Not Available; - = not applicable.
Sources: Inter-Parliamentary Union = IPU (1986), Schmidt (1995, Table 12: 285-292), Maddex (1996)
N.B: if the information in the sources mentioned was conflicting IPU information was followed.

As stated above, almost all countries in Table 1.1 are characterised by similar systematic features, i.e. by being a constitutional parliamentary democracy (for some period) between 1945 and 1996. Neither the Russian Federation nor the United States of America belongs to this type of democracy. They have been included for the simple reason that they are too important to be omitted and are usually included in cross-national analyses of democratic performance.

In our view then, the remaining cases listed in Table 1.1 are parliamentary democracies, albeit with a wide variation in constitutional features and related institutional practices (Lijphart, 1994; Schmidt, 1995b; Hague et al. 1998). Some of this cross-national and cross-temporal variation is manifested in Table 1.1. First of all, one can clearly distinguish between "older" and "younger" systems of parliamentary government: 25 countries emerged as such before 1914 and 14 after 1945. In terms of the *practice* of party government and relations with parliament, these established systems are not only grounded more deeply, but also have more in common than the "younger" systems. Yet, it is also obvious that one-third of the cases grouped in *category I* have experienced a (more or less) drastic revision of the constitution after 1945. In this respect the differences with other countries are not that striking (this will be elaborated in Chapter 2). Some of the constitutional changes are related to the right to the vote (universal suffrage) and to the organisation of representation (electoral system). Most striking is the (relatively) late introduction of *female* participation: before 1914 only one-third of all systems had introduced universal suffrage. The laggards in this respect are more often than not Catholic countries.

The degree of 'democraticness' (4 & 5 in Table 1.1) is represented by two indexes:

1. Jaggers and Gurr (1995) is the most recent index that measures *"Polyarchy"* (Cf. Dahl, 1971), hence the possibilities of public participation, political concertation and party competition.

2. The index published regularly by Freedom House (1995) indicates the

prevalence of *political* and *civil* rights at the level of the individual citizen in various political systems across the world.

Taking the score of ≥ 8 on Polyarchy as a cut-off point (10 being the maximum), only 15% of cases fall below this point. They are either "young" new democracies (e.g. Guyana and Sri Lanka) or – in most cases – the post-communist societies in Central and Eastern Europe re-established as democracies only after 1989. With regard to citizenship the situation is less positive: almost 40% of the countries failed to guarantee full political and civil rights to their citizens in 1993. Hence the actual practice of parliamentary democracy, in terms of the concept of Polyarchy, appears quite well-spread across our universe at the *elite*-level, but this is less true at the level of the population in these countries (see also: Schmidt, 1995b: 264-292; Lane and Ersson, 1993). However, we feel that most countries included in this data-collection do perform reasonably well with regard to 'democraticness' (with the exception of systems with an interruption of democratic rights – see category III – and also South Africa before 1994, India, Sri Lanka, Macedonia and Romania).[2]

In addition to the criterion of "democraticness" we have checked a number of democratic systems in Asia, Africa and Latin-America in deciding whether or not to include them on the basis of being more or less parliamentary. Firstly, we scrutinised whether or not their system is semi-presidential (if it was not clearly presidential or parliamentary). Secondly, whether or not party competition and alternation of governments was prevalent. For these reasons we excluded Argentina (see also: Lijphart, 1992: 132), Chile and Haïti (idem, 1992: 130-131), Tanzania, Zimbabwe and Zambia (all one-party systems of governance); the Philippines, Thailand and Malaysia (all either presidentalist or low on democraticness in practice).

Thirdly, we excluded most of the Caribbean islands (the "West Indies") because they are comparatively speaking insignificant in terms of size. Instead, we sampled two of these cases to represent the rest: Jamaica and Guyana.

All in all, the countries included in this data-set have in common a constitutionally organised parliamentary polity and governments that are responsible to parliament and are regularly accountable to the population through freely contested elections. This situation has prevailed in all the countries under review from and after 1945. Thus, all our cases are also *democratic party-governments*, i.e. representatives of political parties are the crucial actors with respect to the formation, actions and termination of government in relation to parliament.

---

[2] Systems with parliamentary democracy, but being lower than 5 on Polyarchy and higher than 5 on Citizen Rights have been excluded from the data-set (except for South Africa I).

1.4. Parties, Ministries and Party Control of Government

Whatever one may think of the present position and role of parties within politics, these more or less unitary political actors are still the main agents in government formation and accountability. Even if their role may seemingly be waning in some countries, it is clear that they have fulfilled it during most of the period under review here (Bingham Powell, 1982; Castles, 1982; Schmidt, 1982; Pinkey, 1993; Schmidt, 1995b).

Political parties contest elections in order to gain access to government. In the process of government formation parties put forward nominees to participate in government. This goes for every type of government: be it majoritarian or coalition. In the first type, information on office holders may shed light on the factional representation of a party in government (see: Budge and Keman, 1990: Appendix A), and reshuffles of government between elections may tell us about changes *within* parties. Japan and the United Kingdom are examples that spring to mind (Baerwald, 1986: 132-139; Budge, 1985). Information about the composition of minority governments, in particular which parties (conditionally) support it, may be useful to the researcher in finding out to what extent a particular distribution of offices, or appointments of certain individuals help to prolong its existence (Strøm, 1984). In coalitions it goes almost without saying that information about which parties participate and which offices and/or competencies they take, is important for studying coalition theory and the related outcomes in terms of policy formation (Budge/Keman, 1990; Laver and Shepsle, 1996). Hence data on the composition of government in terms of participating parties and their representation, as well as which ministry they hold, is essential for the study of party government in parliamentary democracies. Particularly important in this respect is the difference between ministry and related competencies (i.e. policy areas).

A ministry is an organisational unit within the state of which the minister is *politically* the responsible head. In many countries ministers head ministries with more than one 'competency' or policy area (e.g. the Ministry of Social Affairs and Labour, or the Ministry of Health and Environment, etc.) or have more than one function in government (e.g. being ministerial Head and Deputy Prime Minister). It is important to distinguish between these for theoretical and empirical reasons. For instance, a researcher who is interested in the degree of party-control of a coalition government may wish to know how many offices each participating party holds (e.g. to compute the proportional representation of a party in a government for comparison with its legislative size in parliament; Paloheimo, 1984). Conversely, other researchers may be more interested in knowing which fields of public policy formation are covered by which parties (e.g. in relation to the ideological or programmatic profile of a party; Budge and Keman, 1990; Laver and Shepsle, 1994). Hence, depending on the theoretical question at hand, it makes a difference what is counted empirically. Moreover both the structure of governments and their bureaucratic organisation differ across countries: in one country there are a few ministers entrusted with many competencies, in other countries there are as many ministers as competencies. For comparative purposes it is then vital to be able to distinguish between office-holders (i.e. ministers) and the distribution of competencies (i.e. the portfolios or policy areas).

In summary: this data-collection aims at presenting information on the composition of parliamentary government, at the level of individuals (i.e. ministers) and of collective government (i.e. cabinet). In addition, information on the distribution of government seats and party affiliation is also presented (indicating policy-seeking behaviour). This type of information can be made use of in multifarious ways to study party-government in parliamentary democracies (Klingemann et al., 1994; Warwick, 1994; Laver and Shepsle, 1996; Keman, 1997).

1.5. What is a Government and how long does it last?

A topic that perpetually recurs in the literature on the functioning of governments is how to define a government, which is intrinsically linked with measuring its duration (e.g. Van Roozendaal, 1992, Warwick, 1994; Lijphart, 1999, 129-134). In particular, cross-national and intertemporal variation in duration is a much-debated issue. Whether one analyses this from the viewpoint of stability or as part of the distribution of power within a political system, it is important to have a clear picture of the number of governments and the durability of different types of government, in relation to the support they have in parliament, the ideological *tendance* of a government and the number of parties represented in that government (see: Schmidt, 1996; Keman, 1997).

Before discussing the duration of government we elaborate on the definition of 'government' as it has been used throughout this data-book: it encompasses any administration that is formed after an election and continues in the absence of:

(a) a change of Prime Minister;
(b) a change in the party composition of the Cabinet; or
(c) resignation in an inter-election period followed by re-formation of the government with the same Prime Minister and party composition.

This definition is obviously stricter than most others are, particularly those used in much of the literature on coalitions. This is particularly true in regard to formal resignation. Yet it makes sense to include this as a cut-off point, since a resignation generally changes the political situation in some significant aspects. The effect of our decision has been an increase in the total number of governments recorded. However, the differences with the results - for instance - of Von Beyme, Paloheimo and Lane et al., although they exist, are not enormously great, and are explicable by our inclusion of caretaker governments and the operation of the resignation rule.

Another respect in which we differ from some other specialist treatments concerns the date of the initial constitution of a government. Whereas there is great unanimity as to dates of termination there is less in regard to formation. The main reason lies in the different ways in which governments are brought into being in different countries and in constitutional processes: this is particularly so in a number of the continental European countries where a considerable lapse of time occurs between the ending of a government and the installation of a new government by the Head of State. Most conspicuous in this respect are Belgium, Denmark, and The Netherlands (the maximum lapse of time being almost nine months, in which there is no new government and the old one is not allowed to introduce new bills or to make politically controversial decisions). To a lesser extent these lapses of time can also be found in Finland, Italy, Norway, Sweden and Turkey. Von Beyme only gives the begin, not the ending of a government, Paloheimo follows another operational rule assuming that governments - although continuing as caretakers with clipped wings - are still constitutionally entrusted with full powers. In this book – as in the previous one (1993) – we have chosen to follow Von Beyme's operational rule, namely to take the date of investiture as the beginning of a (new) government. Hence the duration of a government is the number of days between the investiture of a government and the date of investiture of the succeeding government. Any difference in these dates has been checked by means of *Keesing's Contemporary Archives/Record of World Events.*

This discussion on the 'beginning' and 'end' of a government spills over into the question of how to measure its duration: the unit of measurement chosen is *days* rather than months (Schmidt, 1995a), years (Paloheimo, 1984), or percentage of the electoral period in office, also known as the 'survival rate' (Sanders and Herman, 1977; Lane et al., 1997). The reason is quite simple: as days are the most basic unit of measurement, this information will allow every researcher to transform the data in accordance with his or her needs. In particular the last mentioned measure (percentage of the interelectoral period) is a vulnerable one, for in some systems the electoral period is not fixed, or as a 'rule of the game' elections are anticipated whenever the government is confronted with either (the threat of) a vote of non-confidence or dissension within government. In other cases this is not so. Again, for reasons of consistency and comparability we have opted for the most simple and straightforward method of recording the data.

1.6. Ministers and the Distribution of Offices and Competencies

Most data available up to now only cover the number or percentage of offices held by parties represented in government (Spuler, 1972; Paloheimo, 1984; Lane et al., 1997 are to some extent an exception). However important these data may be in order to analyse, for example, coalition theory, or the impact of parties on policy formation, they are insufficient to dig deeper into these matters. The actual distribution of ministries-cum-portfolios is a crucial type of information needed to check the plausibility of theories in the field of national and comparative politics (see also: Budge and Keman, 1990; Laver and Schofield, 1990; Austin-Smith and Banks, 1990). For this reason we have assembled data that gives maximum information on individual ministers *in* government, i.e. the party affiliation of each minister as well as the portfolio-cum-competencies that he or she holds. Additionally, we also report the name and sex of each office holder. This will be helpful not only for national researchers, but also for comparativists, since through this information one can link these data to, for example, an existing data set on the (social) background of ministers (Blondel and Thiebault, 1991: 199-202). This latter covers all West European parliamentary democracies (N=15) between 1945-1984 at the level of individual ministers and the ministries they have held during their career. One can now link the names in one data-set to those in the other and thus relate the 'political' features of a minister to his or her 'personal' background and career-pattern (see for example: Krouwel, 1999).

This information will also be valuable to those who want to use the *Political Data Yearbook,* the annual data-issue of the *European Journal of Political Research* in a historical perspective. For in these issues the composition of cabinets in terms of members, competencies and party affiliation is provided as well as the reasons for termination, nature of reshuffles and dates for the beginning and end of governments.[3] Another comparable source is the *Political Data Handbook* edited by Jan-Erik Lane, David McKay and Ken Newton (1997). Apart from comparative information on political parties and the institutions of the state, this contains a country-by-country shortlist of the main ministries and postwar governments (parties in government, Prime Minister and number of ministers for each party). The data in this book will enable the researcher to be more specific on the division of offices within government and its composition. Last, but not least, the data on the level of ministers and ministries can be used to develop variables at a more aggregated level within governments and to study the pay-offs for parties. For instance, if one wishes to analyse the extent to which certain parties 'colonise' certain segments within governments or the separate ministries, *per se* or in relation to political or social factors, the data-collection in this book contains the necessary information (see, for example: Blondel and Thiebault, 1991: Ch. 7; Budge and Keman, 1990: Chapters 5 & 6; Laver and Shepsle, 1994, 1996; Schmidt, 1995a).

Aggregation or grouping of portfolios-cum-competencies enables the researcher to analyse, for example, the relation between specific policy areas and party control of government, as well as to see to what extent parties get

---

[3]   The *Political Data Handbook* has been published annually in European Journal of Political Research since 1992 (Volume 22/4) see for the subsequent Handbooks: volume 24/4 (1993) 26/3-4 (1994); 28/3-4 (1995); 30/3-4 (1996); 32/3-4 (1997); 34/3-4 (1998).

what they want in terms of their ideological or programmatic stance. More-over, by using the data in this manner one is able to overcome problems of comparability. By aggregating the data on the basis of competencies one can construct groups within government that have the same meaning in different countries, whereas this is often not the case on the level of individual ministers holding various competencies, or ministries that are assigned tasks which partly overlap with ministries with the same name in other countries or are different altogether (Klingemann et al., 1994; Keman, 1997).

To sum up: the data presented in this book will enable students of demo-cratic politics to analyse in more detail and depth the process of party government in parliamentary and semi-presidential systems at various levels of measurement. These data are presented in such a manner that they enable the researcher to use them for country specific purposes, on the one hand, and for cross-national and intertemporal analyses, on the other hand. In addition, the format of the data collection is such that it enables the researcher to adapt it to his or her needs, as well as to develop (new) variables in order to replicate and to advance existing research on *parties and government*.

1.7. Institutions and Parliamentary Governance

It goes almost without saying that, if one wishes to study parliamentary government, knowledge of the political institutions – i.e. the "rules of the game" – is a prerequisite. To put it differently: government actions are the result of political actions (mainly of parties and their representatives in parliament and government) that are, in turn, driven by the institutions and existing practices that typify a democratic political system. Most if not all, 'rules of the game' are based upon or derived from a nation's (written) constitution. The related laws (like e.g. electoral systems, rules regulating the actions of the executive, directives regarding central and non-central govern-ance, etc.) direct both the opportunities *and* constraints of representative government *vis-à-vis* parliament and population (and vice versa, of course). In addition, the constitutional rules, or: institutional design of the polity, strongly influence the political behaviour of parties in parliament and government and thus the scope and range of political actions. Hence, in order to analyse parliamentary government it is almost obligatory to take into account the institutional design of the political systems under review (Bingham Powell, 1982; Lijphart, 1984; Budge and Keman, 1990; Strøm, 1990; Schmidt, 1995b; Colomer, 1996; Laver and Shepsle, 1996; Keman, 1996).

To our surprise there do not exist many *comparative* overviews that specifi-cally provide this type of information in more detail. Of course, there are handbooks and almanacs (e.g. Inter-Parliamentary Union, 1986; the CIA Handbook; the Statemen's Yearbook; Maddex, 1996) but the information is almost always organised by country or, at best, confined to regions (e.g. Lane et al., 1995; Colomer, 1996; Budge et al., 1997). Given this state of affairs we shall present this type of information in the next chapter of this book. In addition we shall provide country-specific constitutional information for each case preceding the country/case-tables.

The institutional information provided in Chapter 2 is not intended to be comprehensive, but is collected with the purpose of aiding the analysis of parliamentary and semi-presidential government. The following clusters of information - representing the *institutional design* of all the countries involved in this book - have been developed in a *cross-national* fashion:

I = *Head of State*, i.e. title and status as well as the formal powers of the Head of State, in particular in relation to government and parliament.

II = *State Format*, i.e. the type of state (Federal or Unitary), but more importantly the extent to which governmental powers are centralised or not, and the extent to which sub-national government and parliament are more or less autonomous in terms of their right to 'decide' and to 'act'. In addition, information is provided with regard to the possibilities of other bodies and organised interests than those representing central government to "veto" the decisions and related actions of central government (see also: Colomer, 1996; Schmidt, 1995b).

III = *Structure of Parliament*, i.e. basic information on the parliamentary system: number of Chambers, size of the Parliament, term in office and rules concerning dissolution of parliament which is important for its relationships with government (Budge and Keman, 1990; LeDuc et al., 1996).

IV = *Electoral system*, i.e. the rules directing the mode of representation, eligibility for office, electoral threshold. In effect, information regarding the "representativeness" of the democratic system (Reeve and Ware, 1992).

V = *Executive-legislative relations*, i.e. the possible modes of interaction between parliament and government. As is clear from section 1.2 this is vital information, not only for semi-presidential systems but also for parliamentary government in general. The information we provide focuses on matters like investiture, votes of confidence, and limits to parliamentary prerogatives. We have attempted to develop summary measures that indicate the balance between the executive and legislative powers, on the one hand, with respect to Parliament, and the role of the Head of State with respect to Parliament, on the other (Lijphart, 1984, 1999).

VI = *Decision Rules in Parliament* and by means of *Referendum*, i.e. systematically recording by what type of majority decisions are made by parliament, how many members must be present to have a (legitimate) vote and how the constitution can be changed or amended. In addition, we discuss here the type of referendum that exists in the polity, who initiates it and what the outcome means for government.

VII = *Features of Government*, i.e. the internal organisation of *cabinet* Government, which is indicated by the relationship with parliament of ministers (being MP or not), the role of the Prime Minister in government and whether or not cabinet government is collectively organised. In addition we have indicated the extent to which both government and parliament are constrained in proposing bills (or not).

VIII = *Controls and Checks by Rule of Laws*, i.e. the specification of the role of the judiciary and other powers as regards reviewing the legitimacy and constitutionality of law-making. In addition, and following Lijphart (1984; 1999) we have developed a measure (Keman, 1997: Ch 1.) of constitutional flexibility.

In sum: chapter 2 provides data on the institutional design of parliamentary systems. This is explicitly done from a cross-national perspective and serves the purpose of enhancing the study of parliamentary government.

As a demonstration of what is possible and feasible with this type of data we present in chapter 3 of the book a cursory and preliminary analysis of the relationship between *Duration* of government *and Reasons for Termination*. This exercise makes full use of the data presented in chapter 2. In addition, a number of the features of party government are related to both institutional factors and features of the direction and working of the party systems in the parliamentary democracies that figure in this book.

1.8   Operationalisation: Conceptual Validity and Data Reliability

The governmental data are all collected by country, the period studied is the post-war era (1945 to 1998) and information is organised at different levels of aggregation:
1. On the level of governments:
    -party-support and the complexion of government;
    -duration and type of government;
    -reshuffles and modes of termination;
2. On the level of separate ministries:
    -political parties (affiliation);
    -competencies and portfolios;
    -individual features (name & sex)
The party-in-government-or-in-support variable as well as the portfolio variables are primarily based on *Keesing's Contemporary Archives/ Record of World Events*, but at the same time have been cross-checked with the information provided by Von Beyme, Paloheimo, Mackie & Rose (1990), and Lane et al. (1997) and country specific sources.

Both von Beyme (1985) and Paloheimo (1984) inform us on the role of parties in government, and the operational differences between them are not great. *Party in Government* are those parties that are represented in government by holding one or more offices at the level of minister. *Party in Support of Government* are those parties that are not represented at the ministerial level but which at the same time support the investiture of that government. If there was a difference of opinion we resorted to *Keesing's Contemporary Archives/ Record of World Events*. There were differences between *Keesing's* and Paloheimo (1984) and Lane et al. (1997) with regard to the number of portfolios held by each party. The reason for this is twofold: on the one hand, Paloheimo and Lane et al. only count ministers rather than competencies; on the other, it is genuinely difficult in some cases (in particular, governments of the 'Westminster model') to know who and what is part of the government and who and what is not. Hence there are problems in determining the exact number of ministers. Again, when in doubt, we resorted to Keesing's Contemporary Archives and to country-specialists. Therefore, with regard to operationalising the ministerial variables we opted for scoring both the actual ministers as well as ministries. That is to say we counted the number of portfolios (i.e. competencies) held by each party and the individuals who held a post in a government. Hence the minister, as well as his or her competencies, is considered to be the carrier of party influence in government.

It should be noted that in our conceptualisation of party *government* we focus exclusively on *cabinet* government. Cabinet Government is in our view the core of government as regards *decisionmaking* on the one hand, and with respect to the control of ministries (or: departments), on the other. Hence, we do not include so-called " junior" ministers, who belong to a certain ministry and have no separate competency regarding the policy area *per se*. As a consequence we do also not include the so-called 'front-bench' members of government. These members of the government often have the title of minister, but have no right to vote in the cabinet. This is often the case in Anglo-Saxon governments. In sum: the composition of government as presented in the country tables is directed to those members of government who had decision-making powers and/or are assigned to a specific ministry in government (see also: Blondel and Müller-Rommel, 1993; Budge and Newton et al., 1997: 240-243; Budge and Keman, 1990: 99).

Another feature of government life is their *Reason for Termination*. Insofar as data have been collected, they are rather fragmentary and often unreliable. Given the considerable cross-national variation in duration of government, it is not only relevant to know *when* a government ceased to exist, but even more, *how and why* this came about. Firstly, because it may indicate how inter- and intraparty behaviour is related to features of party-control of government. Secondly, because the reason for termination may very well affect future processes of government formation. Thirdly, it may inform us on cross-national and intertemporal variation in the nature of legislative-executive relationships in a country be it a majoritarian government, a coalition, or a minority government (Lupia and Strøm, 1995).

Apart from von Beyme (1985) and Budge and Keman (1990) we have not come across data on *Reasons for Termination of governments* in the existing literature. Following von Beyme (1985: 375-405) we developed a classification:

1 = Elections. These include any election stipulated by law or constitution as well as anticipated elections, which are not required by law;

2 = Voluntary resignation of the Prime Minister;

3 = Resignation of the Prime Minister due to health reasons.

Both these last two reasons should be considered as non-political ones, but mode 2 may well be a cover-up for factional dispute within a party or government (as for instance occurs frequently in Japan). Yet, since we cannot distinguish 'real' from 'fake' reasons, we have accepted them entirely on face value.

4 = Dissension within government. This covers those instances when either a coalition breaks up without external pressure or when there are publicised quarrels and/or movement of personnel. Often these incidents are not discussed in the literature since in many cases they have no visible consequence for a government defined in a more general way than we have defined it here.

5 = Lack of parliamentary support. This reason for termination, of course, lies at the heart of any parliamentary democracy. We have counted here every instance when parties either withdrew support from government, or there occurred a (successful) vote of no confidence (or similar parliamentary action).

6 = Intervention by the Head of State.

7 = Broadening of the coalition. This covers any termination of government to allow for a broadening or extension of the existing government coalition with the inclusion of new parties (regardless of the final result).

We collected these data from *Keesing's Contemporary Archives/Record of World Events*. In addition, we compared our data with those of Von Beyme (1985). There was little disagreement except for the fact that we have identified more governments and have found more variation in the reasons for termination. Frequently more than one reason is mentioned by von Beyme: in these cases we have followed Keesing's Contemporary Archives. In a number of cases we were not able to locate a reason for termination.

In addition to these government variables (dates of investiture and reasons of termination) we have developed two variables representing *Types of Government* and the *Ideological Tendance* in government and parliament:

Type of Government (ToG) is based on the number of parties participating and their parliamentary status. The following six types of government make up our classification (see also: Lijphart, 1984: 60f; Laver and Schofield, 1990: 97f):

1 = Single Party Government: one party takes all government seats and has a parliamentary majority.

2 = Minimal Winning Coalition: all participating parties are necessary to form a majority government.

3 = Surplus Coalition: this comprises those coalition governments, which exceed the minimal-winning criterion.[4]

4 = Single Party Minority Government: the party in government does not possess a majority in Parliament.

5 = Multi Party Minority Government: the parties in government do not possess a majority in Parliament.

---

[4]   Only those government coalitions are included which contain more parties than are strictly necessary for obtaining a majority in parliament. Parties supporting the government but not holding an office are not taken into account.

6 = Caretaker Government: the government formed is not intended to undertake any kind of serious policy-making, but is only minding the shop temporarily.

In the literature a special, if not idiosyncratic (sub-) type of government is mentioned: *Divided Government* ((Lijphart, 1999; Schmidt, 1996; Weaver and Rockman, 1993; Alesina and Rosenthal, 1995). A government is divided if and when the Head of State (in our case this is only relevant in semi-presidential regimes) or the Head of Government is confronted with a hostile majority in (one of the chambers of) parliament. Such a situation can occur due to staggered elections (e.g. the midterm elections in the USA, or the elections for the *Bundesrat* in Germany or the uneasy relation between the president and government in France during a so-called *Cohabitation*; see also: Gallagher et al., 1995: 17). If such a situation has occurred we have indicated this in the country tables.

To decide whether or not there has occurred a situation of divided government, we used the following rules: divided government is meaningful in, firstly, (semi-)presidential systems with uni- and bicameral parliaments. Secondly, in parliamentary systems with 'strong' bicameralism. Thirdly, in unicameral systems, if and when there is a difference between the party of the president and the majority party or parties in parliament, in particular if this other party (or parties) is in government. In countries in which the president is also head of government, like Botswana and South Africa, the president is, as head of government, directly accountable to parliament. This means that a situation of divided government is unlikely. Combining the above criteria, the following countries in our dataset in which there may be divided government emerge:

Estonia
Finland
France (V)
Lithuania
Poland
Russia
Slovakia
Slovenia
Turkey
USA

Especially in the countries in Central and Eastern Europe (Estonia, Lithuania, Poland, Slovakia, Slovenia), and in Russia, it is difficult to establish whether there is divided government or not. The party system is still very much in flux. And even where the party of the president and the government initially were the same, as in Slovakia, the president and the Prime Minister soon fell out. In Finland, the president's party is usually part of the governing coalition. Only during government 44 and 45 this was not the case. In France, we have divided government during governments 49, 54, 55 and 57. In Poland during government 1 and 8. In Turkey, the president, elected by the National

Assembly, usually is a representative of the majority party in parliament. There was divided government, however, during the governments 32 and 33. Lastly, in the USA, we see a situation of divided government during (parts of) the administrations of Truman (Dem), Nixon (Rep), Ford (Rep), Carter (Dem), Reagan (Rep), Bush (Rep), and Clinton (Dem).

The Ideological Complexion of Government and Parliament (CPG) is an indicator, which introduces a more qualitative aspect to government composition. It attempts to account for the relative strength of parties in government with reference to the Left-Right dimension, through a five-point scale in which the proportional shares of the Left, Centre and Right are transformed into scores (1 to 5) representing the degree of dominance of either party both in parliament and government. It is mostly used to relate the degree of party-control of a government to its policy guided actions (see: Castles, 1982; Keman, 1988; Budge and Keman, 1990; Schmidt, 1992). It is operationalised as follows:

1 = Right-wing dominance (share of seats in Government and supporting parties in Parliament larger than 66.6 per cent)

2 = Right-Centre complexion (share of seats of Right and Centre parties in Government and supporting parties between 33.3 and 66.6 per cent each)

3 = Balanced situation (share of Centre larger than 50 per cent in Government and in Parliament; or if Left and Right form a government together not dominated by one side or the other)

4 = Left-Centre complexion (share of seats of Left and Centre parties in Government and supporting parties between 33.3 and 66.6 per cent each)

5 = Left-wing dominance (share of seats in Government and supporting parties in Parliament larger than 66.6 per cent)

These scores have been collected and calculated for the period 1945-1996 on an annual basis and have then been compiled for each government (see Keman 1988: Appendix; Inglehart and Huber, 1995, Kim and Fording, 1998).

Finally, we have included the number of *Reshuffles* occurring during a government's term. A reshuffle is defined as the simultaneous movement or replacement of two or more Cabinet Ministers. The theoretical argument for counting the number of reshuffles is that parties are assumed to act in unity when there is a premium on doing so and external pressures are great - as in coalition formation and indeed during the lifetime of coalitions. Where both the premium on unity and external pressures are less, the Prime Minister, as a member of a faction, will use the powers given by the constitutional conventions to dismiss or transfer representatives of other factions in order to benefit his or her own faction (Rose and Suleiman, 1980; Budge and Keman, 1990: 208).

The composite variables that are formed on the basis of raw data in this collection have been scrutinised regarding their *validity* and *reliability*. The relationships between different variables did not indicate too high a degree of correspondence. Moreover, the correlations that are significant make perfect sense. In addition, our 'test' revealed that the classification of, for instance,

'Type of Government', 'Political and Ideological Complexion of Parliament and Government', and 'Reason for Termination' are well differentiated, i.e. they are hardly ever interrelated and hence do not overlap. This implies that the construction and measurement of these composite variables is valid and reliable. In view of our discussion in Section 1.2, we contend that – in general – the *validity* (i.e. the relationship between concept and indicator) of the data appears to be strong. This is in particular the case regarding their use in comparative analyses (Klingemann, et. al., 1994; Pennings, et al., 1999). To enhance the *reliability* of the data collected we not only cross-checked them, but also sent the country information separately to country specialists (see the Preface & Acknowledgements). In this way we were also safeguarded from errors and spelling mistakes. Although some errors will inevitably emerge, we can with some confidence claim that the data presented here are as reliable as seems feasible.

1.9. Glossary and Format of Data Set and Structure of Presentation

In the next chapters we shall present information on the institutional design of all countries involved in the datacollection. These data are organised in comparative tables and divided into five clusters (see Section 1.3). The description of the variables is reported for each cluster-table and footnotes are provided for country specific information (if needed). The sources of informa-tion are in basically the publications of the *Inter-Parliamentary Union* (1986) and *Maddex* (1998). In addition specific information was collected by using *web sites*. These sites are reported in the Appendix on *Sources* used.

In Chapters 4 - 51, information will be presented by country and by go-vernment. The basic format for chapters 4 - 49 (excluding Russia and the USA) is as follows: rows represent governments (= cases), columns present data on and within each government (= variables). Party names follow the coding of Mackie and Rose (1993), names of individuals are spelled according to the original language and sex will be indicated (by means of an asterisk=* for female Ministers). Each case/country begins with a general table of all govern-ments included and with information on the overall features of each government as well as a short outline of its institutional framework. The structure of the general tables country is as follows:[5]

Gov = Identification Number of government

Begin = Date of investiture of government

Dur = Duration of government in days

RfT = Reason for termination of government

ToG = Type of government (* denotes if and when there is a divided government)[6]

---

[5]   If required, explanatory notes will be given at the bottom of each country table.

[6]   A Parliamentary government is considered divided if the Executive is confronted with a

Py1, Py2, …. PyN = Government party(ies), seats in parliament
Seats = Total elected seats in (the Lower House of) Parliament
CPG = Political complexion of parliament and government
NoM = Number of ministers in government (only full cabinet members, no Ministers of State, Junior Ministers etc. unless stated otherwise)
Prime Minister (py) = Full name (party)
   The subsequent tables for each country/case contain information with respect to the composition of governments on the level of ministers (by name and party), ministries and related competencies. This is organised as follows:
Deputy PM = Deputy Prime Minister
Py = Party of minister(s)
Foreign Affairs = The Head of the Ministry of Foreign Affairs
Defence = the Head of the Ministry of Defence and/or ministers with related and/or subdivided competencies like Navy, Army, Air Force, Defence Production etc.
Interior = Head of the Ministry of the Interior and/or ministers with related and/or subdivided competencies such as Police, Civil Service, Local Government, Citizenship etc.
Justice = Head of the Ministry of Justice and/or ministers with related and/or subdivided competencies such as Attorney General, Solicitor-General etc.
Finance = Head of the Ministry of Finance and/or ministers with related and/or subdivided competencies like Treasury, Budget, Taxation etc.
Economic Aff. = Head of the Ministry of Economic Affairs and/or ministers with related and/or subdivided competencies like (Regional) Economic Planning or Development, Small Businesses etc.
Labour = Head of Ministry of Labour and/or Unemployment and/or minister with this particular competency
Education = Head of Ministry of Education (and Science) and/or ministers with related and/or subdivided competencies such as Technology or Technological Development
Health = self explanatory
Housing = self explanatory
Agriculture = Head of the Ministry of Agriculture (Fisheries and Forestry) and/or ministers with related and/or subdivided competencies such as Food, Marine, etc.
Industry/Trade = Head of Ministry of Industry and/or Trade and/or ministers with related and/or subdivided competencies like Foreign Trade, Commerce, State Industries (if not attributed to Public Works - see below)
Environment = self explanatory
Social Affairs = Head of Ministry of Social Affairs and/or ministers with related and/or subdivided competencies such as Youth, Family, Sport,

---

majority in parliament which is different from the parties in government or when - in a asymmetric cameral system – the majority is not in government in one of the chambers (see: Lijphart, 1989; Weaver and Rockman, 1993).

Women, Industrial Relations, Welfare, Social Security etc.

Public Works = Head of Ministry of Public Works and/or Infrastructure and/or ministers with related and/or subdivided competencies like (Public) Transport, Energy, Post, Telecommunications, Merchant Marine, Civil Aviation, National Resources, Construction (if not specifically Housing - see above), Urban Development etc.

Other = All Ministers without Portfolio, and all remaining ministries and/or competencies which could not be fitted in the above framework but who are a member but who are a member of cabinet. To name a few examples: Religion, Culture, Information, Development Co-operation and Tourism; regional competencies like Scotland, Wales, Northern Ireland (UK), Flemish and Walloon regions (Belgium), and specific territories (Australia, Canada); intriguing competencies such as Lord Privy Seal or Chancellor of the Duchy of Lancaster (UK); leaders of the government majority in both houses of parliament (Anglo-saxon countries); Aboriginal and Ethnic Affairs (Australia), etc.

Res = Reshuffles, the simultaneous movement or replacement of two or more Cabinet Ministers.

The data for the Russian Federation (chapter 50) and the United States of America (chapter 51) have been organised by presidential administration (Spuler, 1972), and include the various cabinet posts, the officals occupying these posts, and their term in office. Additionally, the composition of Congress (USA) and Duma (Russia) in terms of parties represented and the number of their seats is presented.

References

Alesina, A., H. Rosenthal (1995) *Partisan Politics, Divided Government, and the Economy*, Cambridge, Cambridge University Press

Austin-Smith, D. and J. Banks (1990) 'Stable Portfolio Allocation', *American Political Science Review*, 84: 891-906.

Baerwald, H.H. (1986) *Party Politics in Japan*, London: Allen and Unwin

Beetham, D. (ed.) (1994) *Defining and Measuring Democracies*, London: Sage.

Bingham Powell, G. Jr. (1982) *Contemporary Democracies: Participation, Stability, and Violence*, Cambridge/London: Harvard University Press.

Blondel, J. (1987) *Political Leadership. Towards a General Analysis*, London: Sage.

Blondel, J. and J.-L. Thiebault (eds.) (1991) *The Profession of Government Minister in Western Europe*, London: Macmillan

Blondel, J. and F. Müller-Rommel (1993) (eds.) *Governing together : the extent and limits of joint decision-making in Western European cabinets*, Basingstoke etc. : Macmillan; etc.

Budge, I. (1985) 'Party Factions and Government Reshuffles' *European Journal of Political Research*, 13:327-334.

Budge, I. and H. Keman (1990, 1993) *Parties and Democracy. Coalition Formation and Government Functioning in Twenty States*, Oxford: Oxford University Press.

Budge, I. (1996) *The new challenge of direct democracy*, Cambridge: Polity Press

Budge, I., K. Newton, et al. (1997) *The Politics of the New Europe: Atlantic to Urals*, London: Longman.

Castles, F.G. (ed.) (1982) *The Impact of Parties. Politics and Policies in Democratic Capitalist States*, London: Sage.

Colomer, Josep, M. (ed.) (1996) *Political Institutions in Europe*, London: Routledge.

Dahl, R.A. (1971) *Polyarchy. Participation and opposition*, New Haven/London: Yale University Press.

Duverger, M. (1992) 'A New Political System Model: Semi-Presidential Government' in: A. Lijphart (ed.) *Parliamentary versus Presidential Government*, Oxford: Oxford University Press: 142-149.

Freedom House (1995) *Freedom in the World. The Annual Survey of Political Rights and Civil Liberties, 1994-1995* (eds.: A. Karatnycky, K. Cavanaugh, J. Finn), New York: Freedom House.

Gallagher, M., P. Mair and M. Laver (1995) *Representative Government in Western Europe* (2nd edition), New York etc.: McGraw-Hill.

Hague, R., M. Harrop and S. Breslin (1998) *Comparative Government and Politics. An introduction* (4th edition), Basingstoke: MacMillan.

Held, D. (1987) *Models of Democracy*, Cambridge: Polity Press.

Huber, E., C. Ragin and J.D. Stephen (1993) 'Social Democracy, Christian Democracy, Constitutional Structure, and the Welfare State', in: *American Journal of Sociology*, 99/3: 711-749.

Huber, E. and R. Inglehart (1995) 'Expert Interpretations of Party Space and Party Locations in 42 Societies' *Party Politics*, 1/1: 73-111.

Jaggers, K and T.R.Gurr (1995) *Transitions to Democracy: Tracking the Third Wave with Polity Indicators of Democracy and Autocracy*, University of Maryland (manuscript).

Keman, H. (1988) *The Development towards Surplus Welfare. Social Democratic Politics and Policies in Advanced Capitalist Democracies (1965-1984)*, Amsterdam: CT-Press.

Keman, H. (1996) 'Konkordanzdemokratie und Korporatismus aus der Perspektive eines rationalen Institutionalismus' *Politische Vierteljahresschrift*, 37/3: 494-516.

Keman, H. (1997) *The Politics of Problem Solving in Post-war Democracies*, Basingstoke: MacMillan.

Kerr, C. (1987) 'The Swiss Party System: Steadfast and Changing' in: Daalder, H., *Party Systems in Denmark, Austria, Switzerland, the Netherlands, and Belgium*, London: Pinter Publishers: 107-192.

Kim H. and R.C. Fording (1998) 'Voter ideology in Western democracies, 1946-1989' European journal of political research, 33/1: 73-98.

Klingemann, H.-D., R.I. Hofferbert, I. Budge and T. Bergman, H. Keman, F. Pétry and K. Strøm (1994) *Parties, Policies and Democracy*, Boulder: Westview Press.

Krouwel, A. (1999) *The Catch-all Party in Western Europe 1945-1990: a Study in Arrested Development*, Ph.D. Dissertation, Amsterdam: Vrije Universiteit.

Lane, J.-E. and S. Ersson (1993) 'The political Trinity: Liberty, Equality and Fraternity', in: H. Keman (ed.) *Comparative Politics. New Directions in Theory and Method*, Amsterdam: Vu University Press, pp. 191-216.

Lane, J.-E., D. McKay and K. Newton (1997) *Political Data Handbook. OECD Countries* (2nd edition), Oxford: Oxford University Press.

Laver, M. and N. Schofield (1990) *Multiparty Government. The Politics of Coalition in Europe*, Oxford: Oxford UP.

Laver, M. and K.A. Shepsle (eds.) (1994) *Cabinet Ministers and Parliamentary Government*, Cambridge: Cambridge University Press.

Laver, M. and K.A. Shepsle (1996) *Making and Breaking Governments. Cabinets and Legislatures in Parliamentary Democracies*, Cambridge: Cambridge University Press.

LeDuc, L., R. Niemi, P. Norris (eds.) (1996) *Elections and Voting in Global Perspective*, Thousand Oaks (CA)/London: Sage.

Lijphart, A. (1984) *Democracies*. Patterns of Majoritarian and Consensus Government in 21 Countries, New Haven/London:Yale University Press.

Lijphart, A. (1991) 'Constitutional Choices for new Democracies' *Journal of Democracy*, 2/1: 72-84.

Lijphart, A. (ed.) (1992) *Parliamentary versus Presidential Government*, Oxford: Oxford University Press.

Lijphart, A. (1994) 'Democracies: Forms, Performance, and Constitutional Engineering' *European Journal of Political Research*, 25/1: 1-18.

Lijphart A. (1999) *Patterns of democracy : government forms and performance in thirty-six countries,* New Haven CT: Yale University Press.

Linz, J.J. (1990) 'The Virtues of Parliamentarianism' *Journal of Democracy* 1/1: 84-91.

Lupia, A. and K. Strøm (1995) 'Coalition Termination and the Strategic Timing of Parliamentary Elections' *The American political science review*, 89/3: 648-668.

Mackie, T. and R. Rose (1990) *The International Almanac of Electoral History* (2nd edition), London: Macmillan.

Maddex, R.L. (1998) *Constitutions of the World*, London: Routledge.

Paloheimo, H. (1984) *Governments in Democratic Capitalist States 1950-1983: A Data Handbook*. University of Turku Studies on Political Science, No. 8.

Pennings, P., H. Keman and J. Kleinnijenhuis (1999) *Doing Research in Political Science*. An introduction to comparative methods and statistics, London: Sage.

Pinkey, R. (1993) *Democracy in the Third World*, Buckingham: Open University Press.

Reeve, A. and A.Ware (1992) *Electoral Systems: a Comparative and Theoretical Introduction*, London: Routledge.

Roozendaal, P. van (1992) *Cabinets in Multi-party Democracies. The Effect of Dominant and Central Parties on Cabinet Composition and Durability*, Amsterdam: Thesis Publishers.

Rose, R. and E.N. Suleiman (eds.) (1980) *Presidents and Prime Ministers*, Washington D.C.: American Enterpirse Institute.

Sanders, D.and V. Herman (1977) 'The Stability and Survival of Governments Western Democracies' *Acta Politica* 12: 346-377.

Schmidt, M.G. (1982) 'The Role of the Parties in Shaping Macroeconomic Policy' in: F.G. Castles (ed.) *The Impact of Parties. Politics and Policies in Democratic Capitalist States*, London: Sage.

Schmidt, M.G. (1992) *Lexikon der Politik. Westliche Industriegesellschaften*, München: Beck Verlag

Schmidt, M.G. (1995a) *Wörterbuch zur Politik*, Stuttgart: Kröner Verlag.

Schmidt, M.G. (1995b) *Demokratietheorien. Eine Einführung*, Opladen: Leske+Budrich.

Schmidt, M.G. (1996) 'When parties matter: A review of the possibilities and limits of partisan influence on public policy' *European journal of political research*, 30/2: 155-184.

Schumpeter, J.A. (1950) *Capitalism, Socialism and Democracy*, New York (etc.): Harper & Brothers.

Spuler, B. (1972) *Regenten und Regierungen der Welt*, Bielefeld/Würzburg: Ploetz

Steiner, J. (1986) *European Democracies*, New York: Longman

Strøm, K. (1984) 'Minority Governments in Parliamentary Democracies'. "The Rationality of Nonwinning Cabinet Solutions" *Comparative Political Studies*, 17/2: 199-227.

Strøm, K. (1990) *Minority Government and Majority Rule*, New York: Cambridge University Press.

Van Hanen, T. (1997) *Prospects of Democracy: A Study of 172 Countries*, Londen: Routledge.

Verney, D.V. (1992) 'Parliamentary Government and Presidential Government' in: A. Lijphart (ed.) *Parliamentary versus Presidential Government*, Oxford: Oxford University Press.

Von Beyme, K. (1985) *Political Parties in Western Democracies*, Aldershot, Gower.

Warwick, P.V. (1994) *Government Survival in Parliamentary Democracies*, Cambridge: Cambridge University Press.

Weaver, R.K. and B.A. Rockman (eds.) (1993) *Do Institutions Matter? Government Capabilities in the United States and Abroad*, Washington (DC): The Brookings Institution.

Woldendorp, J.J., H. Keman and I. Budge (1993) *Handbook of Democratic Government. Party Government in 20 Democracies (1945-1990)*, Dordrecht: Kluwer Academic Publishers

Woldendorp, J.J., H. Keman and I. Budge (1993a) 'Political Data 1945-1990. Party Government in 20 Democracies' *European Journal of Political Research*, 24/1: 1-120.

Woldendorp, J.J., H. Keman and I. Budge (1998) 'Party Government in 20 democracies: an update (1990-1995)' *European Journal of Political Research*, 33/1: 125-164.

CHAPTER 2

THE INSTITUTIONAL FEATURES OF PARLIAMENTARY GOVERN-
MENT

2.1. Introduction

In the introductory chapter we have defined Parliamentary Government as
democratic if and when they are representative (by means of elections) and
subject to a constitutionally warranted rule of law. It is essential therefore to
know how and to what extent the relationships between the 'powers' in a
democratic system are "shared" as well as "divided". Second, it is important
to understand to what extent and in what ways government is capable of
deciding upon public matters and formulating public policies. This is not only
a result of power sharing and power division, but also depends on the
institutional design of the state. This is what we call the "State Format".
Apart from whether or not the Head of State is elected and what exact powers
he or she may have, the State Format can be seen as indicative of the policy
making capabilities of a parliamentary government (Weaver and Rockman,
1993). In other words: how strong is national government and how is it
organised?

Of course, this is not only a matter of the State Format *per se*, but also - or
even more so – dependent on the prerogatives of parliament. These rights
determine by and large the relationship between the *Executive* and the
Legislative: to what extent can parliament alter or amend governmental policy
formation? And, when can a government be sent away? Or, alternatively, in
what ways can government send parliament home? Finally, are there provisions – other than parliamentary elections – for calling directly on the people?
All these features influence not only the *type* of parliamentary democracy that
exists, but also direct the possible *behaviour* of governments. The same line
of reasoning applies also to the organisation of government itself (is it a
collegial body, or is there a Prime Minister with separate powers at his/her
disposal, which he/she, for instance, shares with the Head of State?), and to
the role of the Judiciary as regards upholding the Rule of Law vis-à-vis
government and parliament.

In summary: the institutional design of any democratic state is a paramount factor with respect to analysing the *Room to Manoeuvre* available to
political actors (see for this: Keman, 1997). Without knowledge of these
institutional features, or the "rules of the political game", it is difficult to
understand and to assess the *role of democratic government* within a country
or by means of comparison.

Stressing the importance of political institutions for the study of democratic government is neither an innovation, nor is it uncontested. Ever since the study of government became an academic concern the role of constitutions, related laws and specific rules has been on the research agenda (e.g.: Bryce, 1921). The innovation is that the "rules of the political game" are presently considered as constituting political practice and shaping the political behaviour of actors (parties, movements, citizens, and governments). In other words: rather than seeing the formal rules of a polity as a given framework, institutions are seen as an *explanans* of polities. Thus, institutions are not so much parameters, but also empirical variables that serve the purpose of developing *positive* theories of government (Alt and Shepsle, 1990; Shepsle, 1997; Keman, 1997; Laver, 1998). The comparative approach is well suited to develop such (middle-range) theories (Lijphart, 1984; 1992; Budge and Keman, 1990; Tsebelis, 1990; Putnam, 1993; Laver and Shepsle, 1994; Lane and Ersson, 1999). It is for this reason that we think it important to devote this chapter – before giving the basic information on the composition of governments – to the institutional framework within which these governments actually operate and which by and large defines their institutional *room to manoeuvre*.

What is contested about the impact and role of political institutions is the extent to which they directly influence the behaviour of the actors involved in terms of democratic quality (Lijphart, 1994; Weaver and Rockman, 1993; Schmidt, 1995a; Colomer, 1996; Lane and Ersson, 1999; Castles, 1998; Keman, 1999). On the one hand, it is argued, that the institutional design of democratic government is crucial for its capacity "to translate citizen preferences into public policies" (Lijphart, 1984: 3). On the other hand, it is maintained that political institutions "structure the relationship between individuals in various units of the polity" (Hall, 1986: 19). Whereas Lijphart obviously emphasises the 'chain of democratic control and command' departing from the (individual) citizen and ending with the eventual (collective) choice for a society, Hall focuses more on the organisation of democratic governance *per se* and how it works. Hence quality of democracy is considered in terms of *responsive and accountable* government by Lijphart (and others: Schmidt, 1995b; Budge, 1996; Keman, 1996), and by means of its *efficient and effective* organisation by Hall (and others: North, 1990; Weaver and Rockman, 1993). This discussion is at the heart of theories regarding the nature and working of parliamentary government: is the government capable of responsible decision making and of accountable policy implementation?

Although it is contested whether or not institutions, all other things remaining equal, are crucial for the working of democratic government, most – if not all – students of political science consider them as necessary. The comparative information presented in this chapter can be helpful in deciding these issues as well as furthering investigations into the quality of democratic governance (Budge, 1996; Keman, 1997; Lijphart, 1999).

The organisation of this chapter is as follows: in eight Tables we will describe the following institutional arrangements of parliamentary democracies comparatively: 1. Head of State, 2. State Format and Organisation, 3. Structure of Parliament, 4. Electoral System, 5. Relations between the Executive and Legislative, 6. Decision Rules in Parliament and by Referendum, 7. Features of Government, 8. Legislation – Promulgation – Validation. Each of these will be introduced through a short description of the variables in terms of their contents or meaning as well as of their comparative quality. In addition, the exact operationalisation of these concepts will be given (see: Pennings et al., 1999: Chapter 3 & 4). Each Table will be furnished with explanatory notes where these are deemed necessary. Finally, there is a short discussion of the cross-national distribution and its potential significance. These eight Tables, we believe, form a logical sequence of what constitutes the institutional design of a democratic system, however, they also can be employed separately to study the role and working of parliamentary government.

2.2. Heads of State

In parliamentary systems the Head of State is often seen as a figurehead or, more positively, as the symbol of the unity and sovereignty of the national state. To a large extent this must be true since the position and the constitutional powers of the President or Monarch *vis-à-vis* government, parliament, as well as the military and the civil service, define the differences between presidentialism and parliamentarism (Lijphart, 1992). Nevertheless, even a titular Head of State has certain symbolic powers that can very well turn into real power. One only needs to remember the role played by the Italian presidents during the transitory period of the Italian Republic in the early nineties. Recent examples are for instance the decision of the former Belgian king Baldwin to abdicate for 24 hours so that the government could sign a law on liberalising abortion; another example is formed by the Presidents of Ireland (Robinson) and Italy (Scalfaro) who - by using their formal powers in an unprecedented way - could influence government. These illustrations of the role (sometimes) played by Heads of State serve the purpose to demonstrate that comparable institutions can very well lead to different situations in practice (see for this also: Hague et al., 1993: 322-323). One can point at the role of monarchs in keeping the national polities stable (as in Belgium) or even in maintaining the democracy (Spain). In general, however, the Head of State in parliamentary systems must be seen as the political institution that safeguards the constitution, performs largely ceremonial duties and is (more or less) important in periods of transition (as during the formation of governments in the Netherlands).

In Table 2.1 we have, of course, made a distinction between constitutional monarchs, who are Head of State by *heritage* (a right enshrined in the constitution) and the *elected* President. It should be noted that the number of polities with a monarch as Head of State is quite high (14 out of 47, i.e. 28%). However, this number is to some extent misleading since it involves Governors General who represent the Queen as Head of the British Commonwealth. These high officers are appointed in consultation with the government of the member-state involved and are in office for a limited period only. They really are figureheads and only once in recent history has a General Governor used his powers to dismiss the Prime Minister (Whitlam in Australia, 1975). Geographically the concentration of monarchs is also noteworthy: with the exception of Spain and Japan all the kings and queens are found in north-western Europe.

In Table 2.1 we also distinguish between presidential Heads of State who are elected directly and indirectly. To some (most notably Duverger, 1980), a directly elected president is stronger than an indirectly elected president is. The main reason is that a directly elected president represents the (majority of the) popular will and thus has a stronger legitimate power-base. If, in addition, one takes into account the institutional possibility that a president can have a longer term than parliament and government *and* often has the power to dissolve parliament, to appoint a prime minister, or to sack a government, it seems plausible to assume that under such conditions an elected president is not merely a figurehead and the system appears to be semi-presidential. The information in the Tables 3 (Terms of Lower House), 4 (Right of Dissolution), 5 (Power of Head of State over Parliament) shows that constitutionally the president in many countries *can* avail himself of certain power-bases. Apart from France and Finland this occurs in states like Bulgaria, Estonia, Lithuania, Pakistan, Poland, Romania, South Africa and Turkey. Of these countries only the presidents in Estonia and Pakistan are elected indirectly. According to Lijphart (1984: 88), however, the president only has genuine executive powers, comparable to those in Russia and the United States in a few of these systems. As has been indicated Switzerland is an outlier here. This is not only due to its rotation mechanism whereby the Chairman of the Federal Council is elected for only one year (to perform ceremonial duties). It is also due to the fact that he or she remains active as a member of the council as a "primus inter pares". In addition, his/her term is limited to one year, whereas the cross-national average for one term is five years for elected Heads of State. Overall the distribution of presidents elected directly as opposed to those elected indirectly is 55% against 45% (see Figure 2.1.1). From Figure 2.1.2 it becomes clear that of the 47 parliamentary systems included in this table 17% are monarchies (excluding the governor-general), a small majority of the elected Heads of State are directly elected and they serve on average about five years (and in most cases cannot serve more than two consecutive terms; see for this the constitutional information that precedes the country tables in the chapters 4ff). All in all, apart from countries with a monarchy, the Head of State is an important part of the institutional design of the democratic state.

Table 2.1: Heads of State

Country	Monarchy	President	Pres.El:dir	Pres.El:ind	TermHoS
Australia	1	0	0	0	GG
Austria	0	1	1	0	6
Bangladesh	0	1	0	1	5
Belgium	1	0	0	0	Life
Botswana	0	1*	0	1	5
Bulgaria	0	1	1	0	5
Canada	1	0	0	0	GG
Czech Rep.	0	1	0	1	5
Denmark	1	0	0	0	Life
Estonia	0	1	0	1	5
Finland	0	1	1	0	6
France V	0	1	1	0	7
Germany	0	1	0	1	5
Greece	0	1	0	1	5
Guyana	0	1	0	1	5
Hungary	0	1	0	1	5
Iceland	0	1	1	0	4
India	0	1	0	1	5
Ireland	0	1	1	0	7
Israel	0	1	0	1	5
Italy	0	1	0	1	7
Jamaica	1	0	0	0	GG
Japan	1	0	0	0	Life
Latvia	0	1	0	1	3
Lithuania	0	1	1	0	5
Luxembourg	1	0	0	0	Life
Macedonia	0	1	1	0	5
Malta	0	1	0	1	5
Namibia	0	1	1	0	5
Netherlands	1	0	0	0	Life
New Zealand	1	0	0	0	GG
Norway	1	0	0	0	Life
Pakistan	0	1	0	1	5
Poland	0	1	1	0	5
Portugal	0	1	1	0	5
Romania	0	1	1	0	4
Russian Fed	0	1	1	0	4
Slovakia	0	1	0	1	5
Slovenia	0	1	1	0	5
South Africa	0	1*	0	1	5
Spain	1	0	0	0	Life
Sri Lanka	0	1	1	0	6
Sweden	1	0	0	0	Life
Switzerland	0	1*	0	1	1
Turkey	0	1	0	1	7
United Kingdom	1	0	0	0	Life
United States	0	1	1	0	4

Explanation:

Country   = Self evident (N = 47)

Monarchy = Hereditary type of Head of State (=HoS)

NB: GG indicates governor-general and is appointed by the British Government to represent the Queen (as Head of the British Commonwealth)

President = Elected Head of State

Pres.El: Dir = Directly elected by the electorate (1=Yes; 0=No)

Pres.El:Ind = Indirectly elected by a democratically elected body (1=Yes; 0=No)

Term HoS = Fixed term in office (years)

Notes:

President:

*In South Africa and Botswana the President is also leader of the Government; in Switzerland the Chairman of the Federal Council is not only member of the government but the office of chairman is yearly rotated by means of elections in the Federal Assembly. This means that in these cases the Head of State is directly accountable to Parliament.

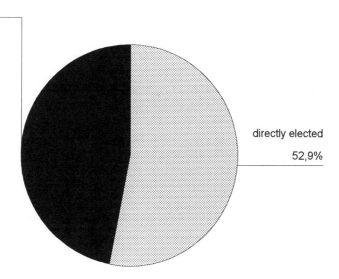

indirectly elected

47,1%

directly elected

52,9%

Figure 2.1.1 Electoral Status of Presidents

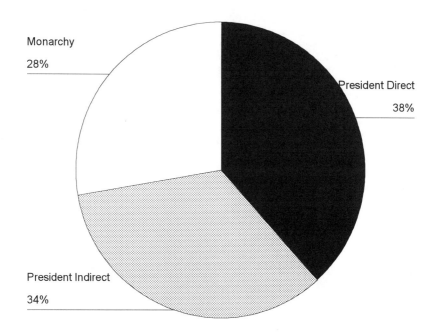

Figure 2.1.2 Types of Head of State

2.3. The State Format and Organisation

How government actually governs is to a large extent dependent on the so-called State Format (Tilly, 1975). In most constitutions the type of state is defined in terms of being either a unitary or a federal system. This distinction appears quite straightforward, but it has provoked considerable disputes among political scientists (see for example: Riker, 1975; Scharpf, 1994; Elazar, 1995; 1997; Lane & Ersson, 1997).

This debate concerns the relationship between the constitutional *type* of state (i.e. unitary versus federal (see Figure 2.2.1)) and the *organisational* features of the national state in terms of centralisation, on the one hand, and the degree of institutional autonomy of sub-national units within the state, on the other (Lijphart, 1984; Weaver & Rockman, 1993; Lane & Ersson, 1999). In Table 2.2 we have therefore not only included a distinction in terms of federal or unitary systems, but also one in terms of the institutional autonomy of other (mostly sub-national and territorial) units of government as well as of individual citizens and organised interests. In addition the degree of fiscal centralisation of the state and the extent to which non-central agencies can act

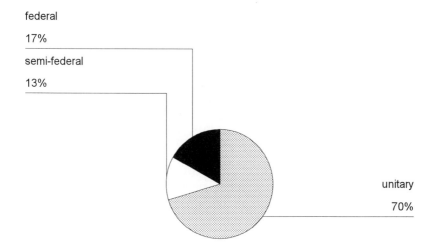

Figure 2.2.1 Distribution of Federal, Semi-Federal and Unitary States

independently have listed (see also: Lijphart, 1984; Colomer, 1996; Schmidt, 1996). Hence, in Table 2.2 we present information on the way how the state is *organised* as regards its *decision making* role, i.e. federal or not and decentralised or not in relation to the degree of institutional autonomy of respectively the "Centre" and its parts. The other variables are developed to indicate the extent to which the state format is designed to be more or less centralised in terms of *policy implementation* (on what level of governance: local or not) and revenue sharing (who has the "power of the purse": national government alone, or other, mostly sub-national, public bodies as well?).

The variable *Fiscal Governance* in Table 2.2 refers to the extent to which national government has a monopoly with respect to raising and allocating tax revenues (Lane et al., 1997 and statistical publications of OECD, IMF and World Bank).[7] This measure indicates the "power of the purse" and it goes almost without saying: no control over money, no control over policy-making (see: Castles, 1998). A low level of Fiscal Governance thus indicates the relative independence of *sub-national* governance (see Figure 2.2.2).

The variable *DeCentral* is a measure of the territorial organisation of the polity in terms of other units of governance than central government. By examining the number of non-central tiers of government in combination with rights constitutionally given to these units, scores have been attributed as follows 3: other units have specific rights; 2: sub-national units have some

---

[7]   The ratio representing *FiscalGov* is based on Central Government Revenues as a % of General Government Revenues. Given the constraints regarding the information available on non-central revenues for all cases involved we used this as a yardstick rather than a more valid one which would, however, exclude a large number of cases.

Table 2.2: StateFormat and Organisation

Country	FedvsUni	FiscalGov	DeCentral	Autonomy	Veto
Australia	1	77%	2	5	6
Austria	0.5	70	3	4	5
Bangladesh	0	77	2	3	4
Belgium	0.5	92.5	2	4	4
Botswana	0	86	2	3	2
Bulgaria	0	78	1	2	3
Canada	1	47	3	6	4
Czech Rep.	0	70	2	1	3
Denmark	0	67.5	3	4	4
Estonia	0	89	1	1	3
Finland	0	70	3	4	3
France V	0	80	2	3	5
Germany	1	53	3	6	5
Greece	0	92	1	0	3
Guyana	0	92	1	1	2
Hungary	0	91	2	2	3
Iceland	0	78.5	3	2	3
India	1	70	3	6	4
Ireland	0	97	2	1	4
Israel	0	96	1	2	1
Italy	0.5	92.5	2	3	5
Jamaica	0	63	1	2	2
Japan	0	60	3	3	5
Latvia	0	77	1	1	5
Lithuania	0	83	2	2	5
Luxembourg	0	84	1	2	2
Macedonia	0	44	2	4	5
Malta	0	NA	1	1	1
Namibia	0	97	2	2	NA
Netherlands	0	95	1	2	3
New Zealand	0	93	1	0	3
Norway	0	71.5	3	4	5
Pakistan	1	69	3	5	4
Poland	0	90	2	3	4
Portugal	0	92	1	2	4
Romania	0	90	1	0	4
Russian Fed	1	78	3	4	5
Slovakia	0	76	2	1	4
Slovenia	0	87	2	2	4
South Africa	0.5	50	3	6	6
Spain	0.5	81	2	4	6
Sri Lanka	0.5	81	3	4	3
Sweden	0	49	3	4	2
Switzerland	1	42.5	3	7	6
Turkey	0	81	1	2	4
United Kingdom	0	98	2	3	2
United States	1	54	3	7	5

Explanation:
FedvsUni = Federal: 1; Semi-Federal: 0.5; Unitary: 0 (see: Lane and Ersson, 1997)
FiscalGov = Central Government Revenues as a % of General Government
DeCentral = Degree of Autonomy for sub-national government: 3 = high; 2 = medium; 1 = low
Autonomy = Composite Index of non-central independence from Central government
Veto = Degree of Veto-points available vis-à-vis Central government
N.B: NA = Data Not Available

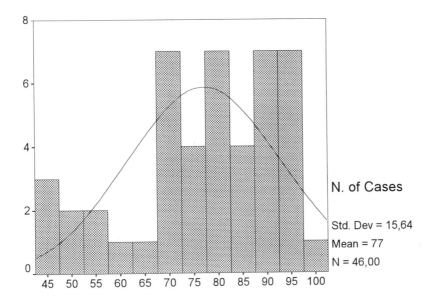

Percentages represent level of Fiscal Centralisation

Figure 2.2.2 Levels of Fiscal Governance

independent rights; 1: all other cases. The scores are based on constitutional information and related information in Maddex (1996) and Banks and Muller (1998).

The two remaining variables, *Autonomy* and *Veto*, are adapted from the ideas of Schmidt (1996); Colomer (1996); Lane & Ersson (1997); and Keman (1998), and computed by the authors.

(*Institutional*) *Autonomy* indicates the degree of local or regional discretionary powers of non-central units of governance. It is an additive index and an indicator of how *independent the non-central units of government are* as regards policy making (or: the Right-to-Act, see: Keman, 1998; Braun, 1999). The operationalisation of this variable is as follows:

• If a country has a degree of Fiscal Centralisation lower than 75% a score of 2 is obtained, if more than 75% a score of 1 and if neither is the case: 0 (see: *FiscalGov* in Table 2.2);

• If regional autonomy is formally laid down (as is the case in federalist states) then a score of 2 is assigned, if it is semi-federalist system: 1, and if neither is the case: 0;

• If the state is considered to be highly centralised (see: *DeCentral* in Table 2.2) then a score of 0 is given, if it is medium 1, and in all remaining cases: 2;

If Local Government is mentioned in the constitution in combination with independent rights and its own representative body it obtains a score of 2, if one of the conditions is met 1, all other cases: 0.

Added together the *maximum score possible is 8.*

Veto indicates the presence or absence of institutional provisions support-ing the democratic and independent rights of those who are not part of government or the civil service (see: Huber, Ragin and Stephens, 1993; Colomer, 1996; Elazar, 1997). Positive scores are awarded for the availability of political institutions to which citizens and organised interests can appeal in order to prevent the state (central or local) from acting, or to promote alternative decision-making by the people themselves (Schmidt, 1996: 172; Castles, 1998: 82-83). The following indicators compose this additive index:

• Is there a referendum and can it be organised by the "people" and is it binding? (based on Table 2.6). This gives a score of 2 if the "people" can initiate a binding referendum; if there exists only the possibility of a referen-dum then a score of 1 is given; and if there is no such option at 'all: 0.

• Is there a bicameral parliament and is it "strong"? (see: Lijphart, 1984: 104-5; 1999: 211-312) Strong Bicameralism is assigned 2, the weak version 1 and Unicameralism: 0.

• Does Government dominate Parliament or not, (i.e. can it continue despite parliamentary censure? (based on Table 2.5, the variable Parl$\rightarrow$ Gov). A score over 1.0 = 2, over 0.5 = 1 and all other cases are scored 0.

• Finally, a 'rigid' constitution is seen as a strong 'veto-point' for the executive. Hence, if this is the case a score of 2 is assigned, if neither rigid nor flexible 1 and all other cases are scored 0 (based on Table 2.8; see on this also: Lijphart, 1999: 218-223).

Added together the *maximum score possible is 8.*

These indicators can be considered as "veto-points" or as impediments from the point of view of the national government and, of course, are barriers to the central government "deciding" and to "acting" autonomy unilaterally. The higher the values of Autonomy and Veto (i.e. closer to the maximum score of 8) the less independent and autonomous national governments are (Schmidt, 1996; Keman, 1999). Hence the variables reported in Table 2.2 are important for understanding from a cross-national point of view how "strong" national government can be. To put it differently: (Institutional) Autonomy and Veto (points) represent the extent to which civil society has a distinctive part to play in politics (Cf. Putnam, 1993). This institutional context indicates then how large the actual "room to manoeuvre" is for discrete policy-making by national governments.

The results of Table 2.2 show that the constitutional type of state does provide clues about centralisation and institutional autonomy and veto-rights. This could be expected. What is striking, however, is the large cross-national variation in these features across the universe.

First of all, although only 30.2% of all the states are federal or semi-federal, only 29.2% of all states (N=47) are characterised by a genuinely high degree of fiscal centralisation (see also: Barwise and Castles, 1991). In addition, decentralisation of the polity also varies widely. Only 33% of the states do not give the powers to decide and act to lower tiers of government. There seems to be a difference between the constitutional set up and the actual institutional design of most parliamentary democracies. Many are more or less decentralised and the lower tier governments have their own financial resources. Hence, constitutional features like the devolution of decision making and fiscal decentralisation can well impede national governments. If this is accompanied by high degrees of Autonomy of local and regional government and Veto points on the part of individuals and organised interests, one may well expect that governing from the (national) centre requires a lot of manoeuvring in order to make decisions (at all) *and* to make policies work (in the end).

If we take a score of more than 3 as a cut-off point for more than less institutional Autonomy and citizen's Veto points (the actual range is between 0 and 7), then we observe that *Veto* is a much more widespread phenomenon (62% of all cases) than is the case with institutional *Autonomy* for sub-national governmental (38 %) (see Figure 2.2.3). Most parliamentary democracies can be considered as well articulated with respect to human rights and the political rights of individuals and organised interests (see also: Schmidt, 1995b: Vanhanen, 1997). However, what also appears interesting is the fact that the polities that score (relatively) high on Autonomy *and* Veto all belong to the Federal and semi-Federal systems (except Italy and Norway, but see: Putnam, 1993). Again this makes sense, since territorial power division, based on power sharing between various units of government requires a clear and unambiguous set of rules in order to guarantee democratic *and* effective government (Dahl, 1956; Elazar, 1997).

Apart from Finland and Sri Lanka, where Autonomy is above the cut-off point but Veto points are limited, the other countries with a low score on Veto can be characterised as more than less centralised states: 34% have less Veto points for its citizens and organised interests than in the other polities (note, however, that this is a *relative* measure as compared to all countries of the world; Vanhanen, 1997). Hence, in many countries (N = 16) there appears to be a relation between the absence of Autonomy and Veto points. This demonstrates that the cross-national variation as regards the State Format of parliamentary democracies is considerably larger than is often thought. The

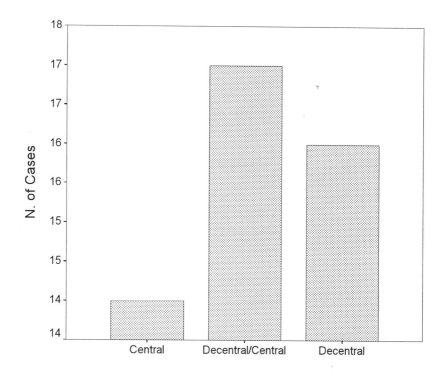

Figure 2.2.3 Distribution of Centralised and Decentralised States

main point, however, with respect to the data on parliamentary government is, that the position and role of governments ought to be taken into account when one wishes to examine the process of governance in terms of its *democratic* performance (i.e. procedural practice) and related *material* performance (i.e. policy making; Castles, 1998; Keman, 1998). We think that the variables presented in Table 2.2 can be of assistance in this respect.

2.4. The Structure of Parliament

Central to any parliamentary government is, of course, how this crucial institution of *indirect* democracy is organised. In Table 2.3 we have reported the basic features of the parliamentary structure in the 47 democracies under review here: uni- versus bicameralism, the size of the Chambers of Parliament and the term in office of the representatives (in years). The most important differences between assemblies (i.e. Parliament as a whole) are the *number* of Chambers and the *size* of these Chambers (Blondel, 1973).

53.2% Of all the countries are characterised by a *bicameral* structure of Parliament. Bicameralism as opposed to unicameralism is the traditional feature of the democracies that were founded before the Second World

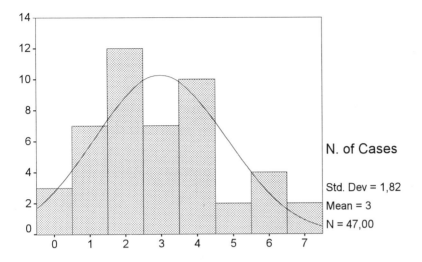

Values represent Index given in Table 2.2

Figure 2.2.4 Index of Sub-national Autonomy

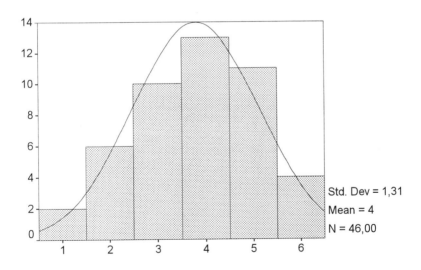

Values as given in Table 2.2

Figure 2.2.5 Index of Veto-points versus Central Government

Table 2.3 The Structure of Parliament

Country	Unicameral	Bicameral	SeatsLH	SeatsUH	TermLH	termUH
Australia	0	1	148	76	3	6
Austria	0	1	183	63*	4	5/6*
Bangladesh	1	0	330**	-	5	-
Belgium	0	1	150	71**	4	4
Botswana	0	1	47**	15****	5	-
Bulgaria	1	0	240	-	4	-
Canada	0	1	295*	104***	5	life (75)
Czech Rep.	0	1	200	81	4	6
Denmark	1	0*	179	-	4	-
Estonia	1	0	101	-	4	-
Finland	0,5	0,5	200	-	4	-
France V	0	1	577	319	5	9
Germany	0	1	672*	69*	4	4*
Greece	1	0	300	-	4	-
Guyana	1	0	65**	-	5	-
Hungary	1	0	386	-	4	-
Iceland	0.5*	0.5*	63	-	4	-
India	0	1	545**	245	5	6
Ireland	0	1	166*	60	5	5
Israel	1	0	120	-	4	-
Italy	0	1	630	323	5	5
Jamaica	0	1	60	26**	5	5
Japan	0	1	500	252	4	6
Latvia	1	0	100	-	4	-
Lithuania	1	0	141	-	4	-
Luxembourg	0,5	0,5	64	-	5	-
Macedonia	1	0	120	-	4	-
Malta	1	0	65*	-	5	5
Namibia	0	1	72**	26	5	6
Netherlands	0	1	150	75*	4	4
New Zealand	1	0*	120	-	3	-
Norway	0,5	0,5	165	-	4	4
Pakistan	0	1	237**	87	5	6
Poland	0	1	460	100	4	4
Portugal	1	0	230	-	4	-
Romania	0	1	343	143	4	4
Russian Fed	0	1	450	178*	4	4*
Slovakia	1	0	150	-	4	-
Slovenia	0	1	90**	40	4	5
South Africa	0	1	400	90	5	5
Spain	0	1	350	257	4	4
Sri Lanka	1	0	225	-	6	-
Sweden	1	0*	349	-	3	-
Switzerland	0	1	200	46*	4	4
Turkey	1	0	550	-	5	-
United Kingdom	0	1	651*	1121***	5	life
United States	0	1	435*	100	2	6

Explanation:
Unicameral = Parliament consists of one Chamber only (1 = Yes; 0 = No)
Bicameral = Parliament consists of an Upper & a Lower House (1 = Yes; 0 = No)
NB: if a parliament is known as "hybrid" a score is assigned of 0,5 in each of these columns (see: Lijphart, 1984: 91; Gallagher et al., 1995: 41)
Seats LH = Number of Seats in the Lower House (absolute Number)
Seats UH = Number of Seats in the Upper House (absolute Number)
Term LH = Maximum years of term, i.e. in office as MP
Term UH = Maximum years of term, i.e. in office as MP

Notes:
Uni/Bicameralism:
* Iceland shifted to unicameralism in 1991, New Zealand in 1950, Denmark in 1953, and Sweden in 1970 (Lijphart, 1999: 202; and note 8 below)
Seats Lower House:
* The number can vary according to change in the population either nation-wide or in the constituency.
** A limited number of seats are allocated to specific parts of the population (often to certain minorities: regional, sex, religion, language etc.) or are appointed by the Head of State to reduce disproportional representation.
Seats Upper House:
* The seats are elected by regional bodies.
** Part is assigned by means of co-optation.
*** In the House of Lords one becomes a member by virtue of either hereditary right or by appointment through the Queen.
**** The House of Chiefs consists of the chiefs of the eight principal tribes, four elected sub-chiefs, and three members selected by the other 12 (CIA-Factbook-website; see appendix on Sources).
Term Upper House:
* The term can vary due to differences between the electoral term of the electing (regional) Body and that of the Upper House.

War.[8] The main idea behind a bicameral Parliament is that it provides a system of 'checks and balances', on the one hand, and the opportunity to represent territorial (or sometimes: functional) interests, on the other. Arend Lijphart (1984: 91-104) adds to these arguments the issue whether or not the society to be represented is pluralistic in sociocultural terms. This may have been true originally. The fact that many of the "newer" democracies have a unicameral system appears now to contradict this. More important are the questions of *weak versus strong* bicameralism and the *duration* of the Parliament. "Weak" *versus* "strong" bicameralism involves the relative position of the two chambers in terms of constitutional rights. In his recently published "Patterns of Democracy", Lijphart has specified for 36 democracies the extent to which they have a 'stronger' or 'weaker' type of bicameralism (see: Lijphart, 1999: 212 and 314). Applied to our set countries this

---

[8]   Most 'new' democracies have a unicameral system, except for Jamaica and Namibia. However, in these cases the Upper House is not or only in part elected. Instead the members of these chambers are appointed by the Head of State or co-opted from other bodies. In addition, it should be mentioned that in some of the 'older' democracies, for example in New Zealand and Scandinavia, the bicameral system has been changed to a unicameral system (Hague et al., 1993).

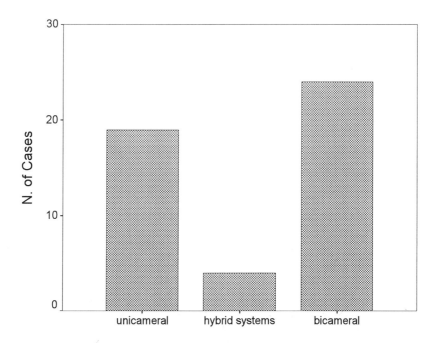

Figure 2.3.1 Unicameralism and Bicameralism

would mean that 12 systems could be characterised as "strong" (i.e. 25% of all cases in Table 2.3 or 48% of all bicameral systems).

In many countries the Second Chamber or Upper House is in this respect subordinate to the Lower House.[9] The Upper House still has some powers, but mainly a delaying effect on policy making. In the "strong" version the legislative powers are equal for both chambers. This situation can be found in many federal systems. The logic being, of course, to share power between the federal state and the territorial units. The effect of strong bicameralism on the working of government is that government can be supported by a majority in the Lower House, whereas this need not be the case in the Upper House (or: this situation arises due to elections if they are not simultaneously held; LeDuc et al., 1996: 284). If and when such a situation occurs we can speak of a "divided" parliamentary government (see also: Weaver and Rockman, 1993). Obviously this impairs the "Room to Manoeuvre" for government in terms of efficient and effective *policy-making*.

The *term of office* is often not the same for both the Houses, but – contrary to what the literature suggests (Hague et al., 1993) – in most systems under

---

[9]   In Table 2.3 we shall use the distinction between Upper and Lower House and not Second and First Chambers respectively. Note that in the Netherlands the First Chamber is referred to as the Upper House and the Second Chamber is the Lower House, i.e. the more important one.

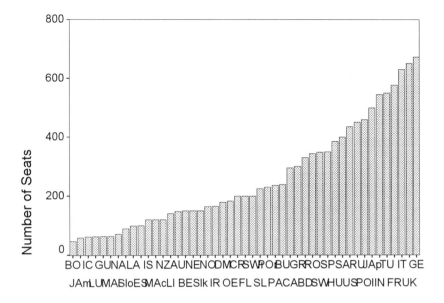

Size of Lower House in ascending order

Figure 2.3.2 Size of Lower House in Seats

review the term of office is equal, although elections are not often held simultaneously (the exception is where the Upper House is appointed for life: Canada and the United Kingdom). This difference may also affect the working and lifetime of a government; in particular if and when we speak of 'divided government'.

The cross-national distribution of unicameralism versus bicameralism is roughly 40/60% (see Figure 2.3.1). Yet, we have also indicated an anomaly: hybrid parliamentary systems (having a value of 0.5 in the Table). The four hybrid parliaments are basically unicameral but are (and can be) formally divided in two parts. According to Lijphart "it is incorrect, however, to view these two divisions as truly separate chambers of a bicameral parliament" (1984: 91).

The *size of Parliament* varies considerably with the largest Lower Houses being concentrated in Western Europe (and Germany having the largest in absolute numbers of seats) (see Figure 2.3.2). In some cases the number of seats varies according to changes in the population as a whole, or due to changes in the territorial distribution of the electorate. In general, the number of seats of the Lower House corresponds to the size of the population.[10] On average the number of seats in the systems under review is 261 in the Lower

---

[10]   Which is not the same as being represented proportionally, this depends on the electoral formula translating votes into seats; see for this: Reeve and Ware, 1992; Lijphart, 1994, and section 2.4.

House and 123 in the Upper House. If one inspects the *ranges* across the countries the large variation among the countries in Table 2.3 is demonstrated. For instance the range of the number of seats in the Lower House is 578 and for the Upper House 313 (excluding the House of Lords in the United Kingdom). The term of office is quite similar and the largest variation is with respect to the Upper Houses: in France it is 9 years, but in most cases it is between 4 and 6 years. On average the term of office is 4.1 years for the Lower House and 5.1 years for the Upper House in the countries represented in Table 2.3.

In summary: the structural features of parliament are important for the working and duration of government. In particular, the existence of a bicameral system may well affect the "Room to Manoeuvre" of government. Except for the size of parliament most other features are more or less similar cross-nationally.

2.5. Features of the Electoral System

Defining characteristics of parliamentary democracy is having elections at regular intervals. Table 2.4 provides information on the electoral systems of the 47 parliamentary democracies. Considering the vast amount of comparatively based literature on electoral systems and elections there is little need to elaborate on this at length.[11]

In Table 2.4 below two basic features are reported: First, how regularly elections must be held and who decides on whether or not to hold an election earlier. Second, which electoral formula is used to allocate parliamentary seats and what level of support is access to needed for Parliament. In addition, the minimal *Electoral Age* and the year of introduction of *Universal Suffrage* is reported.

Whether the term of Parliament is fixed or not (the latter is only the case in five countries) is significant in relation to the *duration of government* as we have operationalised this (see Chapter 1). In addition the decision to hold elections earlier – the right to *Dissolve Parliament* (i.e. Dissolution in Table 2.4) – is obviously also quite important. This decision is regulated by the constitution in most cases and – with the exception of five countries – it always involves the Head of State in co-operation (or after consultation) with government (in most cases the Prime Minister) or Parliament. The exceptions to this rule are Guyana, Israel, Macedonia, Norway, Sweden and the United States.

The maximum term of the Lower House of Parliament varies between 3 to 5 years. As regards the Upper House this is often longer or different due to the Upper House being elected by means of staggered procedures or formed

---

[11]   For instance Rae, 1967; Nohlen, 1978; Bingham Powell, 1982; Bogdanor and Butler, 1983; Lijphart, 1999:144-150; Schmidt, 1995b; LeDuc et al., 1996.

by means of appointment or election by other (often territorial) representative bodies.

The electoral formula employed, however, remains the single most important variable as regards popular representation and thus the relationship between parliamentary government and the population at large. It forms the basis for legitimate governance. The division of electoral formulas in Table 2.4 below is as follows (LeDuc et al., 1996: 54):

- Majority Systems
- Plurality Systems
- Mixed Systems
- Proportional Representation Systems

Majority Systems are characterised by the fact that the constituencies are single-member districts in which the candidate with more than 50% of the vote gets the seat in parliament. In our set of countries it characterises Australia (with the procedure of Alternative Vote), and France, where – if necessary – the absolute majority is usually obtained in a second round (see: Lijphart, 1984: 152-153).

Plurality Systems differ from the majority procedure in that the candidate supported by the largest number of votes gets elected (regardless whether or not this is in a single or a multi-member district). The common feature underlying plurality and majority electoral systems is the principle of "winner takes all" and thus the electors who not have supported the winning candidate are not represented in parliament. This can well produce a biased outcome at the national level because the votes cast for parties do not represent the distribution of seats in the national parliament. This can lead to so-called "manufactured majorities" and more often than not to one-party governments.

Mixed and Proportional systems can be considered as alternatives: in *Proportional Systems*, the seats are divided according to the relative number of votes on each (party) list of candidates across the country (regardless whether or not these are aggregated in local districts; nation-wide constituencies are only to be found in Israel and the Netherlands). The outcome is seen as more representative of the electorate as a whole and the Proportional system is clearly the system used most often (i.e. in 50% of the countries). This is particularly the case in Europe where many countries choose it after the First World War and, more recently, after the transition from a people's democracy to a liberal democracy.[12]

The *Mixed Systems*, are combinations of Plurality and Proportional systems. Basically they try to correct the disproportionality of Plurality electoral results by combining the advantages of both procedures. They occur in eight countries and in Ireland, where the electoral formula for allocating seats is the Single Transferable Vote (see for this Gallagher et al., 1995: 286-288). The

---

[12]   The final distribution of seats to parties is dependent on the electoral formula which is characterized by either the method of the highest-averages or the largest-remainder; see for details: LeDuc et al., 1996: 57-61.

variation in electoral systems, especially as regards the electoral formulas, is considerable. It is an important variable with respect to assessing the composition and working of any parliamentary government (Budge and Keman, 1990; Laver and Schofield, 1990; Warwick, 1994). First of all, the electoral system determines the degree of disproportionality and thus the democratic legitimacy of the government. Secondly, depending on the electoral formula it influences the number of parliamentary parties represented and thus the characteristics of the party system *per se* (Reeve and Ware, 1992).

These consequences of the electoral system for government are reinforced if there is an *electoral threshold*. It combines two features. On the one hand, the electoral threshold refers to a nation-wide percentage of the votes that a party (or a coalition of parties) must obtain in order to gain seats in parliament. On the other hand, it refers to rules, which compensate for not obtaining enough votes nationally by having sufficient votes within a defined territory (see: LeDuc et al., 1996: 63). At first glance, the cross-national variation seems quite large. Thus the actual formation, functioning and termination of parliamentary government should vary considerably. The *Dissolution* of Parliament, for example, demonstrates this: in 26% of all cases this decision is shared between two constitutional actors – in most cases the Head of State and the Prime Minister – who thus share the key role as regards terminating parliament and government. Only in two countries, Israel and Macedonia, does parliament alone has the right to dissolve itself. In 30% of countries the Head of State decides on his dissolution on his own (although in practice there is almost always some consultation with the political leadership). In two countries, Guyana and Sweden, it is the Prime Minister who has this prerogative. Finally in Norway and the US elections cannot be anticipated. It may be concluded that the dissolution of parliament is in most cases either shared or in the hands of the Head of State who is supposed to stand "beyond the parties and government".

The distribution of electoral systems is clearly tilted towards the Proportional System: it exists in 60% of all systems. The Mixed Systems are in the minority (17%), whereas Plurality and Majority rules direct electoral outcomes in 23% of the countries presented in Table 2.4. There are Electoral Thresholds in 40% of the parliamentary democracies. At present the electoral age for voting is 18 years in almost all countries (there are only five exceptions to this "rule") and in only five countries is voting – which is a right for every citizen - also compulsory (Bogdanov and Butler, 1983).

All in all, the electoral systems of the 47 democracies under review here have more in common than not. In particular 'proportionality' is a basic rule as is the representation eligibility for voting in terms of age.

Table 2.4 Features of the Electoral System

Country	Fixed Term	Dissolution	ElSystem	ElThreshold	ElAge/Comp	Un.Suffrage
Australia	yes=3yr	Mo+PM	Majority (AV)	0	18/C	1908*
Austria	yes=4/*	Pr(+Pa)	PR	4%	19*	1918
Bangladesh	yes=5	Pr	Plurality	0	18	1972
Belgium	yes=4	Mo(+PM)	PR	33%****	18/C	1948**
Botswana	yes=5	Pr	Plurality	0	18	1965
Bulgaria	yes=4	Pr(+Pa)**	PR	4%	18	1944
Canada	yes=5	Mo+PM	Plurality	0	18	1920*
Czech Rep.	yes=4/6	Pr	PR	5/7/11%**	18	1920
Denmark	yes=4	Mo+PM	PR	0	18	1915
Estonia	yes=4	Pr+PM	PR	0	18	1918
Finland	yes=4	Pr	PR	0	18	1906
France V	yes=5/9	Pr+PM*	Majority/Plurality	0	18	1946
Germany	yes=4	Pr	Plur+PR	5%*	18	1919
Greece	yes=4	Pr+PM	PR	0	18/C**	1952
Guyana	yes=5	PM	PR	0	18	1953
Hungary	yes=4	Pr(+Pa)	Plur+PR**	5%***	18	1953
Iceland	yes=4	PR+PM	PR	0	20	1915
India	yes=5	Pr+PM*	Plurality	0	18	1950
Ireland	no=5/7	Pr+PM	PR (STV)	0	18	1918
Israel	no (=4)	Pa	PR***	1,50%	18	1948
Italy	yes=5	Pr	Plur+PR	4%***	18	1946
Jamaica	yes=5	Mo(PM)	Plurality	0	18	1944
Japan	no=4/6	Mo+PM	Plur+PR*	0	20	1947
Latvia	yes=3	Pr***	PR(Pref)	5%	18	1918

Country	FixedTerm	Dissolution	ElSystem	ElThreshold	ElAge/Comp	Un.Suffrage
Lithuania	yes=4	Pr+PM	Plur+PR	5%****	18	1921
Luxembourg	yes=5	Mo	PR	0	18	1919
Macedonia	yes=4	Pa	Plur+PR	5%***	18	1946
Malta	yes=5	Pr	PR (STV)	0	18	1947
Namibia	yes=5/6	Pr	PR	0	18	1989
Netherlands	yes=4	Mo+Gov**	PR***	0	18	1919
New Zealand	no	(Mo+)PM	Plur+PR	5%*	18	1893
Norway	yes=4	None	PR	0	18	1913
Pakistan	yes=5/6	Pr(+PM)	Plurality	0	21	1947
Poland	yes=4/4	Pr (+Pa)	PR(Pref)	5/8%**	18	1918
Portugal	yes=4	Pr*	PR	0	18	1974
Romania	yes=4/4	Pr (+Pa)	PR	3/8%**	18	1946
Russian Fed	yes=4/*	Pr	Plur+PR*	5%***	18	1918
Slovakia	yes=4	Pr	PR	5%	18	1920
Slovenia	yes=4/5	Pr	PR	0	18***	1945
South Africa	yes=3 to 5yrs	Pr	PR	0	18	1994
Spain	yes=4	Mo(+PM)*	PR	0	18	1931
Sri Lanka	yes=6	Pr	PR(Pref)	12,50%	18	1947
Sweden	yes=3	PM	PR	4/12%	18	1921
Switzerland	yes=4	None**	PR	0	18/C**	1971
Turkey	yes=5	Pr	PR	10%	18/C	1930
United Kingdom	no (=5 max)	Mo+PM	Plurality	0	18	1928
United States	yes=2/6	None	Plurality	0	18	1920

Explanation:
Fixed Term = indicating whether or not there is a limit mentioned in the constitution: Yes/No; the number refers to the length of term between elections in years.
NB: The number after / is the maximum for the Upper House.

Dissolution = the prerogative of dissolving parliament rests with: Mo = Monarch/Head of State; Pr = President/Head of State; Pa = Parliament; PM = Prime Minister; Gov = Government. Note that in many cases it involves two or more actors who must act together (indicated by +) or by means of mutual consultation (indicated by brackets)

ElSystem = Electoral System: the formula that directs the way votes are translated into seats after the election. Majority = requires an absolute majority within a constituency; Plurality = requires a simple majority within a constituency; PR = Proportional Representation

NB: AV = Alternative Vote; STV = Single Transferable Vote within a constituency; Pref = Preferential Voting

ElThreshold = Minimum requirements for (coalition of) parties to gain access to parliament

ElAge/Comp = Minimum age (in years) required for voting and whether or not voting is compulsory (indicated by C)

Universal Suffrage = The right for each citizen - regardless other criteria - to participate in all elections by means of voting

Notes:

Fixed Term:

* The term is variable due to the electoral intervals governing the elections for the Upper House (see notes under Table 3 re. TermUH).

Dissolution:

* Dissolution of Parliament is only possible after one year.

** Dissolution is compulsory if and when a constitutional change is proposed and accepted by Parliament.

*** The decision of the President must be confirmed by means of a referendum. If negative the President must resign.

Electoral system:

* The Proportional system is not meant to be corrective, it is a dual system (see: LeDuc et al., 1996:63).

** The Mixed system is intended to correct for "manufactured" results and the proportional outcomes are directly related to the re-distribution of the seats.

*** In the Netherlands and Israel there is a nation-wide constituency.

Electoral Threshold:

* If instead of the national percentage a local seat is obtained the party gains access to Parliament.

** The higher percentages are required if a coalition of two or more parties form a list.

*** Percentage mentioned concerns the minimum of votes required for parties in order to obtain seats which are distributed according to proportionality.

**** At least 33% of the quota in at least one arrondissement.

Electoral Age & Compulsory Vote:

* Only in Presidential elections.

** Only if between 21-70 years of age (Greece); and only in some cantons (Switzerland).

*** If employed from the age of 16.

Universal Suffrage:

* Certain ethnic groups were excluded until the 1960s.

** After World War I widows of soldiers got the right to vote.

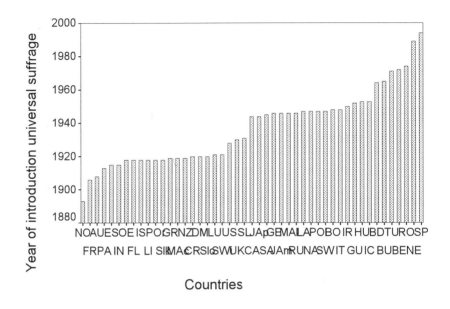

Figure 2.4.1 Year of Introduction of Universal Suffrage

What differs is the electoral threshold for parties, on the one hand, and the specific electoral formula translating votes into seats, on the other (see for more detail: Reeve and Ware, 1992; Lijphart, 1999; LeDuc et al., 1996). The introduction of Universal Suffrage – now prevalent everywhere (but see Figure 2.4.1) – also shows that the process of democratisation took quite a while in some countries (Spoormans, 1988; Therborn, 1997).

2.6. The Relations between Executive and Legislative

This relationship is a crucial one in any parliamentary democracy. Yet, at the same time variation in the relations between these two powers is bewildering and complex. This is in large part due to the fact that – in contrast to Presidentialism – these powers are fused, if not overlapping. This is a consequence of the fact that governments are formed on the basis of the parties present in parliament. Thus parties are represented at both levels. Hague et al. (1993: 323) state that governments can be considered as the 'governing committee of parliament'. The term party *government* is another expression of this view and is reflected in the various *types* of government that can be distinguished (see also: Budge and Keman, 1990; Gallagher et al., 1995: 28-30).

In the country tables, i.e. the Chapters 4 to 51, where we report on government composition in the countries under review, we have therefore indicated the *type* of government as well as the power relations between the parties in government and parties *in* parliament (= CPG). Here we focus primarily on the *formal relationships* between parliament and government. Of course, the actual *practice* of parliamentary governance is not the same as the formal *rules* reported in this table. To mention some of these disparities between the formal framework and the actual behaviour of government:

• in most parliamentary systems the formal right to introduce bills is mainly exercised by government and not parliament;

• parliamentary control is exercised more often than not through committees rather than in parliamentary sessions;

• there is a 'reactive' relationship between parliament and government rather than an 'active' directing one (Mezey, 1979).

Nevertheless the variables reported below do represent important benchmarks of the 'room to manoeuvre' of parliamentary government in relation to its principal counterparts: the Head of State and Parliament itself.

The first two variables: Votes of *Investiture* and (non) *Confidence* can be considered as prime indicators of how a government comes into existence and how it can be terminated. If a vote of Investiture is constitutionally required it imposes a barrier when there is no majority in parliament. This is the case in 38% of all the countries under review here. In a few cases the Head of State can ignore the outcome of the vote, but in practice this will hardly ever occur. Likewise, in practice, most newly formed governments will seek consent from parliament regardless whether or not a formal vote of investiture is required. In particular for a coalition government parliamentary consent is quite vital and may have an impact on the duration of a government (see Chapter 3 for this). The vote of (non-) *Confidence* is perhaps even more important for the life of a government. In most democracies (82%) government *must* resign if the majority of parliament carries such a vote. It should be understood though that this parliamentary 'weapon' is a two-edged sword: often governments bring forward a motion of confidence themselves. Hence, it is in many polities not simply a prerogative of parliament alone (Laver and Schofield, 1990). A special requirement, finally, exists in Spain and Germany (and recently in Belgium). In these countries an alternative government must be ready to take over, that is: a majority in parliament cannot vote against government, unless they provide a majority for another government.

In short, these rules – affecting both the life and death of government – demonstrate that the contrast between "strong" parliaments in presidential systems and "weak" parliaments in cabinet-dominated systems is too simplistic. Together with the powers of the Head of State the existence of these rules can make and break governments. This is an option that is not available, for instance, to Congress in the United States. In the table below we present some indicators of relationships between Head of State and Parliament and between Government and Parliament, and those relating to the 'powers' of Parliament over Government. We believe that the *interrelationship* between these three institutions is crucial for understanding the extent to which (parliamentary) government is capable of governing, and – *vice versa* – the extent to which parliament is able to influence affairs.

The first measure (*Parl* $\rightarrow$ *Gov*) concerns the powers of parliament to make or break governments. In the view of Arend Lijphart this is crucial for understanding cross-national variation in the duration of government (Lijphart, 1999: 129-134). Here we report the extent to which parliament is a necessary factor in installing a government and whether or not it can terminate it on its own.

The second measure (*HoS* $\rightarrow$ *Parl*) refers mainly to the independent powers of the Head of State and his direct influence over government in terms of its composition and executive powers. The higher the scores on this index are, the more the parliamentary system can be considered as 'semi-presidential'.

Yet, this depends to a large extent on how independent Government is from Parliament, on the one hand, and reliant on the President to govern, on the other. We have operationalised these relationships by focussing on whether government can ignore votes of (non-) confidence and/or whether or not it can dissolve parliament. This is reported below by the variable *Gov* $\rightarrow$ *Parl*.

These three measures are adequate indicators of the interrelationship between the main actors of any parliamentary system. In addition, the indicators demonstrate the relative interdependence of each actor (or "power") which can then be discussed in terms of "weaker" and "stronger" parliaments, "cabinet-dominated" versus "assembly-dominated" government, and the accountability of party government (Klingemann et al., 1994).

The final variable – *ExLegBal* – is an attempt to arrive at a composite index of the relative strength of the executive and legislative powers. As will be discussed below the *balance* between the central actors is unequally distributed in favour of government (with or without the help of the Head of State). This observation is concurrent with the mainstream ideas of many politicians and the general public: parliaments, although formally considered the ultimate power are more often than not restricted to a re-active rather than to a pro-active or directing role in parliamentary democracies. Formal votes of Investiture (42.5%) and of (non-) Confidence (83%) are quite a common requirement in most parliamentary democracies (see also Figure 2.5.1). In practice, they are exercised with restraint. As one can see from the information in the separate country tables on *Reasons for Termination* it is clear that – with the exception of a few countries – "Lack of parliamentary support" does occur but not as frequently as other Reasons for Termination. In fact, both prerogatives are genuine "worst case" scenarios and only are used if and when the existing coalition loses support, or a 'crisis' has hit government or country (Budge and Keman, 1990). In sum: these formal instruments

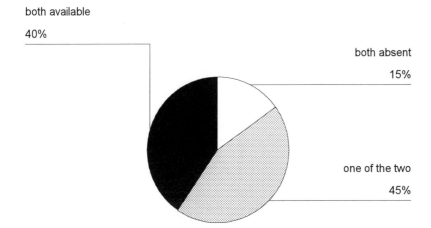

Figure 2.5.1 Vote of Investiture and (no) Confidence

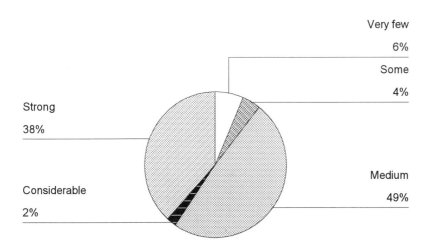

Figure 2.5.2 Diustribution of the Powers of Parliament over Government

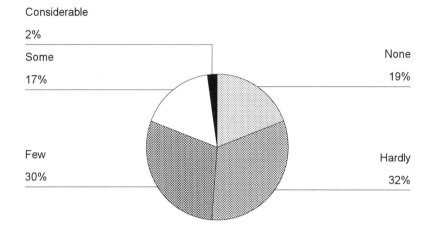

Figure 2.5.3 Distribution of the Powers of the Head of State over Parliament

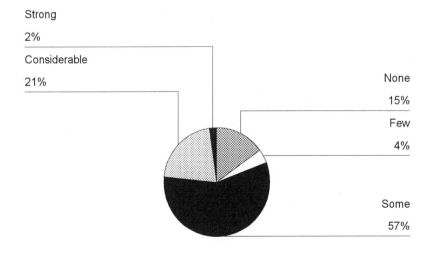

Figure 2.5.4 Distribution of the Powers of Government over Parliament

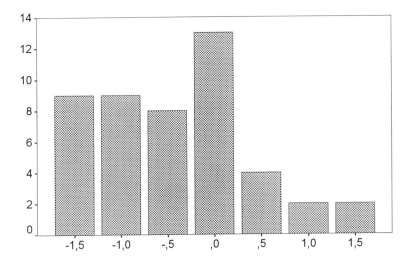

0= Balanced; -= toward Government; += toward Parliament

Figure 2.5.5 Balance between the Powers of the Executive and the Legislature

are used only when necessary, and indicate at the same time the "ultimo ratio" of parliamentary powers. This is reflected in the variable (*Parl → Gov*) (see Figure 2.5.2).

Apart from five countries: Finland, France, Guyana, New Zealand, and Switzerland, these instruments are indeed available to parliament. What is remarkable though, is the fact that the systems that use both the vote of Investiture and Confidence (Dismissal) are 'new' democracies which developed institution-ally either after the Second World War in the defeated nations (Germany, Japan, Italy), or are the successors to (Fascist) dictatorship (Spain and Portugal). In the same vein we find these features in most post-communist and post-colonial parliamentary systems (see also: Hague et al., 1993). Apparently, the 'new' democracies have felt the need to develop the countervailing powers of parliament. However, they have also felt a need to enhance the power of the Head of State over Parliament (and Government): in 41.6% of all cases the President (never the Monarch!) can dissolve parliament and interfere in the process of government formation. Only in a minority of cases are these powers extended to executive functions (see Figure 2.5.3). Apart from France and Finland, the President is in a strong position in many of the postcolonial and postcommunist democracies. In other words: the Head of State is crucial in establishing a *balance* between parliament and government.

This is to some extent visible in the power of Government *over* Parliament: in only nine cases, (17.6%) has government constitutionally limited

Table 2.5 Relations between the Executive and the Legislature

Country	Investiture	Confidence	Parl->Gov	HoS->Parl	Gov->Parl	ExLegBal
Australia	0	1	1	0,5	1	-0.5
Austria	0	1	1	0.5	1	-0.5
Bangladesh	0	1	1	1	1.5	-0.5
Belgium	0*	1	1.5	0.5	1.5	-1
Botswana	0	1	1	1.5	1	-1.5
Bulgaria	1	1	2	1.5	0	0.5
Canada	0	1	1	0.5	1	-0.5
Czech Rep.	1	1	2	1	1	0
Denmark	0	1*	1	0	1	0
Estonia	1	1	2	1.5	0	0.5
Finland	0	0*	0.5	0.5	1	-1
France V	0*	0	0.5	1	1	-1.5
Germany	1	1**	2	0.5	1	0.5
Greece	1	1*	1.5	0.5	1	0
Guyana	0	0	0	0	1	-1
Hungary	1	1	2	0.5	0	1.5
Iceland	0	1	1	1	1	-1
India	0	1	1	0.5	1	-0.5
Ireland	1	1*	2	0.5	1.5	0
Israel	1*	1	2	0	1	1
Italy	1	1	2	1	0.5	0.5
Jamaica	0	1	1	0.5	1	-0.5
Japan	0	1	1	0	1.5	-0.5
Latvia	1	1*	2	1	0	1
Lithuania	1	1	2	1.5	1.5	-1
Luxembourg	0	1	1	0	1	0
Macedonia	1	1	2	0.5	0	1.5
Malta	0	1	1	0.5	1	-0.5
Namibia	0	1*	1	1	1	-1
Netherlands	0	1	1	0.5	0.5	0
New Zealand	0	0*	0.5	0.5	1	-1
Norway	0	1	1	0	1	0
Pakistan	0	1	1	1	1.5	-2
Poland	1	1	2	1	1	0
Portugal	1	1	2	1	1	0
Romania	1	1	2	1	1	0
Russian Fed	1**	0*	1.5	1.5	0	0
Slovakia	1	1	2	1.5	0	0.5
Slovenia	1	1	2	1.5	1	-0.5
South Africa	0	1*	2	1	1	0
Spain	1	1**	2	0.5	1.5	0
Sri Lanka	0	1	1	1	1	-1
Sweden	1**	1*	2	0	2	0
Switzerland	0	0	0	0	1	*
Turkey	1	1	2	2	1	-1
Un. Kingdom	0	1	1	0.5	1.5	-1
Un. States	0	0	0	1	0	*

Explanation
Investiture = Formal vote of Investiture is required (1=Yes; 0=No).
Confidence = Government must resign if it loses the Vote of Confidence. 1 = Losing a vote of (non-)
Confidence always results in the resignation of government (or, alternatively, in the dissolution of parliament
(see Table 4)); 0 = Not required (or can be ignored by the government).
Parl→Gov = Extent to which Parliament is dominant over Government. It is a cumulative index: It is
constructed by adding up scores of:
   - Vote of Investiture is necessary condition to govern (1,0)
   - Vote of Confidence is necessary condition to continue to govern (1,0).
HoS→Parl = Extent to which the Head of State can influence the composition and (continuation) of the
existence of a Government. Hence, it indicates the independent power of the Head of State vis-à-vis
Parliament. This variable is constructed by adding up the scores of:
   - HoS is directly involved in the formation of Government (0,5)
   - HoS can dissolve Parliament (0.5)
   - HoS has also executive powers (1,0).
Gov→Parl = Extent to which Government is dominant over Parliament. It is constructed by adding up scores
of:
   - Government can ignore losing a Vote of Confidence (0.5)
   - Government (or PM) can dissolve Parliament: 1,0 (if shared with Head of State, then: 0,5)
ExLegBal = Extent to which the relationship between the Executive and Legislative powers are more/less
balanced. This variable is a composite index constructed on the basis of the foregoing three variables. A
positive score implies dominance of Parliament over the executive powers (including the Head of State); a
negative score implies dominance of Government and/or Head of State over Parliament. The closer the score is
to 0 the more balanced the relationship between Executive and a Legislative power in a parliamentary
democratic polity is assumed to be. The scores are computed by deducting (Parl->Gov) from the sum of
[(HoS->Parl) + (Gov->Parl)]. For example *Australia* has a final score of −0.5 i.e.: $(1 - [0.5 + 1] = -0.5)$, and
the Netherlands is balanced, i.e. 0 $(1 - [0.5 + 0.5] = 0)$, whereas *Finland*'s score is −1: $(0,5 - [0.5 + 1] = -1)$.

Notes:
Investiture:
* The Head of State can ignore the vote of investiture.
** Only concerns the Prime Minister
Vote of (non-) Confidence:
* Motion must be directed against the Prime Minister (but has same effect).
** Only if it concerns a "constructive" vote, i.e. it is valid if and when there is an alternative majority in
parliament supporting another government.
ExLegBal: It should be noticed that Switzerland and the USA are different from a straightforward Parliamen-
tary system of Government: the former because of its "direct" character which is embodied in the Referendum
instrument (see Table 6) and the latter because of the specific nature of the American Presidential system (see:
Lijphart, 1992: 24-26). Hence the scores in these cases do not reflect the full nature of relations between the
Executive and Legislature.

---

power vis-à-vis Parliament (a score of 0 or 0.5). Apart from Italy and The
Netherlands these nine include seven Central-East European polities. In all
other cases governments can be seen as having considerable *independent*
powers to govern and not having to rely on Parliament and/or the Head of
State to act as the executive power of the nation (see Figure 2.5.4).

The result of the complex interrelations between Parliament, Head of State
and Government is made transparent in the variable *ExLegBal*, i.e. *the
balance between the Executive and Legislature* in parliamentary democracies.
From Table 2.5 and Figure 2.5.5 it can be deducted that only 12 countries
have a balanced relationship between Parliament and Government, and even
less have a Parliament that *dominates* over Government (Bulgaria, Estonia,
and Greece). In one fifth of all cases one can conclude that parliament is

weak, whereas in 59% the relationship is more or less balanced (i.e. between +/– 0.5). Hence, we can contend that Parliament is not always 'weak' nor is it hardly ever 'strong', but – taking into account the prerogatives of the Head of State – in most cases the relation between the Executive and Legislature is of a balanced nature. Hence we may well conclude that in most parliamentary democracies the powers are relatively balanced, but also that it will depend on the specific instruments of parliament as regards decision making whether or not their power can be wielded effectively with respect to party government.

2.7. Decision Rules in Parliament and the Role of Referendums

Assemblies in parliamentary democracies have in general the ultimate say as regards policy making. In other words: they have the authority to make laws. But in practice the responsibility for proposing bills, introducing new measures or changing existing laws and regulations rests with the executive, i.e. the party government. In fact, parliamentary activities focus more on discussing governmental proposals, scrutinising legislation, investigating actions of government (and, of course, of ministers) and influencing policy making by motions of censure, amending bills and voting on motions of non-confidence. Indeed, parliament mainly decides these matters by means of voting, since the parties of government are pitted against those in opposition. In practice, however, most legislative decisions are made without much division in parliament. They have been decided in committees or by forging compromises between the party leadership of different parties before the actual voting in parliament takes place. It is only if there is a threat of stalemate or when there is a majority against government that the decision rules come into play with respect to the policymaking capacity of government.

In Table 2.6 we have listed some indicators of the voting procedures in the assemblies under review here: the *Quorum*, i.e. the requirements for having a legitimate meeting in the first place and to have a valid vote. Apart from Israel and the Scandinavian assemblies all countries have some kind of a minimal requirement which ranges from half of the total membership to a specified (smaller) portion of all members of parliament. The quorum was originally designed to ensure that – given the indirect nature of liberal democracy –representation is minimally sufficient to make decisions that affect the nation as a whole. Conversely, it can also be used to forestall or at least delay decision-making. In other words the absence of members can be used as an institutional device *against* government action. However, in practice this hardly happens and more often than not there are provisions to avoid a continued (ab-) use of this power.

Table 2.6 Decision Rules in Parliament and by Referendum

Country	Quorum	Maj.Simple	Maj.Constit	RefType	Who/B-C	N of Refs
Australia	1/3 of M	Simple V	Abs.Maj.(2)	2	G-E/B	23
Austria	1/3 of M	Absolute V	2/3 of V (2)	2	G-Pa/B*	2
Bangladesh	1/5 of M	Simple V	2/3 of V (2)	1	G/B	2
Belgium	Abs.Maj. of M	Absolute V	2/3 of V (2)	1	G/C	1
Botswana	9 Members	Simple V*	Abs.Maj.(2)	1	NA/B**	1
Bulgaria	Abs.Maj. of M	Absolute V*	2/3(3/4) of M	1	Pa-H/C	0
Canada	20LH/15UH	Simple V	Abs.Maj (2)**	1	G/C	1
Czech Rep.	1/3 of M	Absolute V*	3/5 of M	0	none	0
Denmark	Abs.Maj. of M	Simple V	Simple V*	2	Pa/B	13
Estonia	Abs.Maj. of M	Simple V*	Abs.Maj.-3/5M	1	Pa/B***	0
Finland	None	Simple V	2/3 of V*	1	G/C	1
France V	Abs.Maj. of M	Simple V	3/5 of V***	2	H-G/B	7
Germany	Abs.Maj. of M	Simple V*	2/3 of V (2)	1	NA/B**	0
Greece	¼ of M	Absolute M	Abs.Maj+3/5M	2	H/B	4
Guyana	1/3 of M.	Simple V.	2/3 0f V.	1	NA/B**	1
Hungary	Abs.Maj. of M	Simple V*	2/3 of M	1	H-Pa/B	5
Iceland	½ of M	Simple V***	Abs.Maj.(2)	1	H/B	0
India	1/10 of M	Simple V	2/3 of V (2)**	0	none	0
Ireland	20LH/15UH	Simple V	Simple V	2	H-Pa/B	18
Israel	None	Simple M	Simple V	0	none	0
Italy	Abs.Maj. of M	Simple M**	Abs. Maj.	1	E/B	33
Jamaica	16LH/8UH	Simple V.	¾ of M	1	Pa/B**	0
Japan	1/3 of M	Simple M	2/3 of V (2)	1	NA/B**	0
Latvia	Abs.Maj. of M	Absolute M*	2/3 of M	2	H-E/B	0
Lithuania	Abs.Maj. of M	Absolute M*	2/3 of M	2	Pa-E/B	0
Luxembourg	Abs.Maj. of M	Absolute V	2/3 of V	1	G/C	0
Macedonia	Abs.Maj. of M	Absolute V	2/3 of M	2	Pa-E/B	0

THE INSTITUTIONAL FEATURES OF PARLIAMENTARY GOVERNMENT

Country	Quorum	Maj.Simple	Maj.Constit	RefType	Who/B-C	N of Refs
Malta	¼ of M	Simple M	2/3 of M	0	none	0
Namibia	Abs.Maj. of M	Simple V	2/3 of M	1	Pa/B**	0
Netherlands	Abs.Maj. of M	Simple V**	2/3 of V(2)*	0	none	0
New Zealand	20 M	Simple V	Simple V	2	G/B	8
Norway	None	Simple V	2/3 of M	1	G/B	3
Pakistan	¼ of M	Simple V*	2/3 of M(2)	1	H/B	1
Poland	Abs.Maj. of M	Simple V*	2/3 of M(of LH)	1	H-Pa/B	2
Portugal	Abs.Maj. of M	Simple V	2/3 or 4/5 of M	1	H/B	0
Romania	Abs.Maj. of M	Absolute M	2/3 ofM(2) &Ref	2	H-Pa/B	1
Russian Fed	Abs.Maj. of M	Absolute M*	3/5 of M**	1	H/B	1
Slovakia	Abs.Maj. of M	Absolute V	3/5 of M	2	H-Pa-E/B	1
Slovenia	Abs.Maj. of M	Simple V	2/3 of M	1	Pa-E/B	0
South Africa	Abs.Maj. of M	Simple M*	2/3 of M*/**	1	Pa-H/B	4
Spain	Abs.Maj. of M	Simple M*	Simple M	2	G-Pa/B*	3
Sri Lanka	20 M	Simple V	2/3 of M	2	G/B	1
Sweden	None	Simple V***	Simple V	1	G/Pa-B/C	3
Switzerland	Abs.Maj. of M	Simple V	Simple V+Ref**	2	E/B	275
Turkey	1/3 of M	Simple V	3/5 of V	1	H/B	4
United Kingdom	40LH/30UH	Simple V	Simple V	1	G/C	1
United States	Abs.Maj. of M	Simple V**	2/3 of M(2)**	1	NA/B**	0

Explanation:

Quorum = Number of Members who have to be present in order to have a legitimate vote in parliament

NB: 'Abs.Maj' signifies that of all appointed members at least 50% must be present; the ratios and absolute figures are self-evident and refer always to total number of Members of Parliament; M = Members; LH = Lower House; UH = Upper House (See: Table 3, SeatsUH & SeatsLH)

Maj.Simple = Minimal required majority for decision-making in parliament

NB: 'Absolute' signifies that the vote must be carried by the majority of all members present (see: Quorum above). Simple implies the majority of all the votes cast

Maj.Constit = Parliamentary Majority required to change or to amend the Constitution

NB: see Quorum for explanation; V = of all votes cast; M = of all members present; (2) = of both Houses and/or two Readings required; Ref = Referendum required.

RefType = Right of the Electorate to cast their vote re. specified issues

NB: 0 = No referendum possible; 1 = Referendum is optional; 2 = Referendum is constitutionally required

Who/B-C = Who has the right to initiate a Referendum? What is the consequence of the outcome of a referendum? Is it consultative or is binding?

NB: Who: G = Government; H = Head of State; Pa = (minority in) Parliament: E = portion of Electorate. Outcome is: B = Binding; C = Consultative

N of Refs = Number of nation-wide Referendums held either after 1945 or since the country became an independent democratic nation.

Notes:

Maj.Simple:

* A Qualified Majority is required re. Votes of Investiture, Confidence or to appoint/elect the Head of State.

** A Qualified Majority is required if the Act of the Realm is changed and/or an act involves a change in the borders of Regions and Communities.

*** A Qualified Majority is required to defer national decision-making to an international body.

Maj.Constit:

* after the next General Elections the Vote must be carried again.

** Consent from the sub-national units is required.

*** A Simple Majority suffices if and only if accompanied by a Referendum.

Who/B-C:

* If not called for by government then the outcome is consultative.

** Constitution allows for a referendum, but has never been held.

*** In case of a defeat the issue will be decided by Parliament after the next General Election.

The second variable in Table 2.6 is therefore more important and crucial for actual decision-making: what type of majority is required to have a decisive outcome? This rule is identical for all democracies represented in Table 2.6: a *simple majority* carries the decision in their favour. There is some variation in what exactly constitutes this simple majority. First of all it may refer to *all votes* cast (not necessarily that all *Members* of Parliament *present* must have voted). The second option implies that at least *half* of the Members *present* must have voted in favour of the proposal put forward. In other cases a decision is only carried if there is an *absolute* majority available, that is half-plus-one of all *potential* members or votes. All three options are used throughout the 47 parliamentary systems considered here. The 'absolute' option appears to be more prevalent in the Central-Eastern democracies than elsewhere. Gaining a simple majority of the votes cast is, however, the most common rule for decision-making. The exceptions to this are clarified in the Notes to Table 2.6 and concern other decisions than those regarding the Constitution, which require a Qualified *Majority*, i.e. larger than a simple majority.

The principle of having a *Qualified Majority* is, of course, to have broad support for those measures and laws that are considered as vital for the system or are seen as sensitive for segments of the population. An example of this is the procedure as regards the impeachment of the Head of State, or changing the boundaries of the nation-state, or joining a supra-national body (like the EU). Other matters may involve the prerogatives of parliament or the collective rights of people (for instance as regards the use of language in Fryslân and Vlaanderen). However, in most cases rights and prerogatives, in particular individual ones, are enshrined in the constitution and therefore it is the majority required for *constitutional amendments* that is important.

We have therefore focused on the type of decision-making majority that is required to *change* or to *amend* the *constitution*. Apart from those nations that do not have a written constitution (like Great Britain, Israel, New Zealand) it is only the older Scandinavian democracies that do not require a Qualified Majority to change the constitution. Yet, at the same time the Referendum can and sometimes must play a role in this respect (we discuss this below). Almost all other democracies have some kind of Qualified Majority for constitutional amendments, which ranges from *60% to 67%* and in some cases *to 75% of the vote*. In most cases there are additional conditions that must be met like the fact that sub-national units of the state must assent to the constitutional change or that the majority must be qualified in both Chambers, or that it must be carried again (e.g. after the next general election; see: Lijphart, 1999: 217-223). All in all, it is obvious that changing or amending the constitution implies a complex and difficult type of decision-making based on a variety of rules that are more often than not "Veto Points", i.e. opportunities for any reasonably sized group to block the procedure.

Another way of influencing or counteracting governmental decision-making concerns the popular Referendum. Whatever way it is used and is shaped, it is considered by many as a (necessary) supplement to the working of representative or indirect democracy. Referendums can be seen as a means to *re*-present essential bills to the population at large, or as a means to consult the electorate or as a means to find nation-wide consent. Conversely, it can also be used as a means to give the population greater influence to initiate public policy or to prevent certain governmental measures. Most of the countries under review here do have provisions for referendums. Until recently, the Referendum was not widely or frequently used. Butler and Ranney (1994:5) report that since 1970 about 400 referendums have been held across the world. This is roughly 50% of all nation-wide referendums organised throughout history. Hence, one may conclude that it is becoming an increasingly popular instrument within representative democracy (see Figure 2.6.1).

Although the principle underlying a Referendum may be simple, the way it is used and organised is not. We have therefore indicated in Table 2.6 various applications and usage under *RefType*. First of all, there is the question of whether or not it can be used at all. This is *not* the case in five countries: the Czech Republic, India, Israel, Malta and the Netherlands. Secondly, whether or not it is required for certain issues or that its use is optional. In just over one third of all cases its use is constitutionally required. In all other cases it is thus an option, which has, however, never been used in seven countries. This variable usage and also its relative frequency (see for this the variable: *N of Refs*; see Figure 2.6.2) are closely related to the question of *who* can call a referendum and *what* the consequences are of the outcome.

This is reported in the variable *Who/B-C* in Table 2.6. We have distinguished between who is the *initiator*: Government, Parliament, Head of State, or (a part of) the population. As is clear from Table 2.6 it usually concerns a *combination* of possible initiators and the variation is large. The most frequent initiators are Parliament and the Head of State, who together account for two-thirds of all cases, whereas the Electorate and Government can initiate a referendum in one-thirds of the cases. Hence, although the referendum is a widespread phenomenon the number of institutional actors that can bring it into use is limited. As for the consequences of the Referendum the distinction made is between a *Binding* outcome (= B) and an outcome which is of a *Consultative* nature (= C). In most cases (70%) the outcome is binding. The consulting function of the referendum is less prevalent and often used as an option next to the binding one. In only five countries – Belgium, Canada, Finland, Luxembourg and the United Kingdom – a Referendum is consultative. Finally, it can be observed that, notwithstanding the increased use of referendums in many countries, in a number of countries likes Germany, Japan, Luxembourg, Portugal and the USA, this instrument of 'direct' democracy has never been used on the national level.

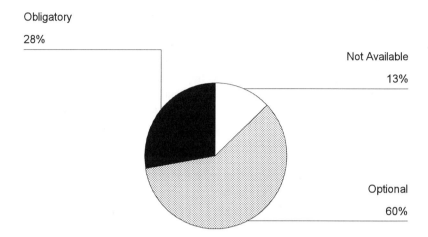

Figure 2.6.1 Types of Referendums in 47 Democracies

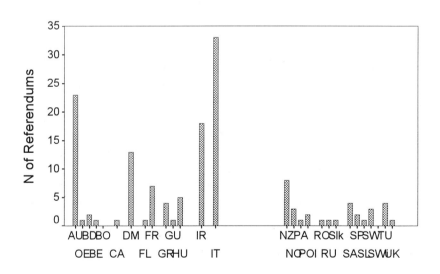

Figure 2.6.2 Number of Referendums held after 1945
(excluding Switzerland)

Looking at the two clusters of decision making rules (i.e. those *in* Parliament and those *by* the Population) one can clearly see that the rules concerning the *Quorum* and *Simple Majority* decision-making are to a large degree similar across our universe. This is not the case as regards the decision rules governing changes or amendments to the constitution. In our view this reflects to some extent the political history of a nation. The longer and more stable representative democracy has been, the more flexible the constitution appears to be and *vice versa* (we discuss this in more detail in Table 2.8).

The clusters of rules regarding Referendums are less homogeneous across the democracies under review here. Not only is the status quite variable (see *RefType*) but also – as we already noted – there is quite some cross-national variation with respect to who initiates a referendum and what the consequences are. What is most striking is that the actual use of the Referendum varies considerably across our universe of cases. Leaving aside Swiss practice, it is noticeable that systems with the *same* rules make a *very different* use of this option. In only four nations more than 10 referendums have been held nation-wide after 1945. These account for 78 plebiscites (out of a total of 136 or 57.4%, discounting the 275 Swiss referendums).

The overall conclusion of this section on decision rules is that the 'normal' practice of parliamentary decision making is more similar than dissimilar across most democracies. Yet, it appears that the special rules either by qualified majority in parliament or by means of a referendum are quite dissimilar and variable in their organisation and usage.

2.8. Features of Government

Parliamentary Government – often also called "cabinet-government" (Blondel and Müller-Rommel, 1993) – is characterised by a paradoxical relationship among ministers (in particular if they represent different parties), on the one hand, and between the ministers and Prime Minister, on the other hand. This tension is encapsulated by the fact that party government is in need of a certain degree of *collegiality* as regards policy-making as a whole and co-ordination between departments. It is among the principal assignments of the *Prime Minister* to achieve cohesion, especially in a coalition, and to direct policy. As is clear from the literature the cohesion and homogeneity of government is achieved in various ways. In Table 2.7 some of the factors which indicate this are listed.

The first variable mentioned, Minister in Parliament (or not), i.e. *MininParl* shows the extent to which office in the executive is separated from the office of being legislative actor. In 40% of the cases under review both must be held together. In 27% a minister cannot be a Member of Parliament.[13] In

---

[13] The former option has the danger that by losing the seat in parliament the government needs to be changed; the latter option may induce the appointment of professionals rather than politicians (see: Blondel/Thiebault, 1991).

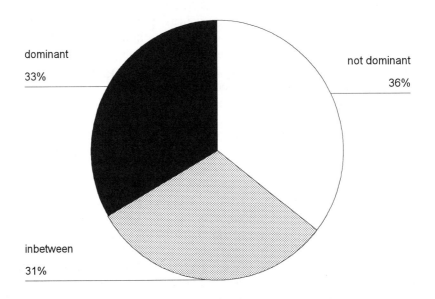

Figure 2.7.1 Dominance of Prime Minister over Cabinet

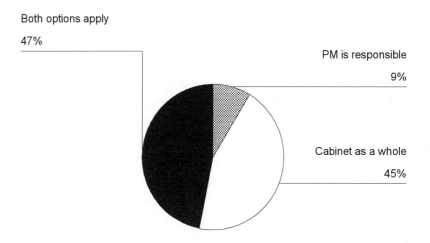

Figure 2.7.2 Distribution Collective Responsibility

the remainder of the countries it is left to the individual member of government which option to choose (see Figure 2.7.1).

The influence if not power of a Prime Minister varies considerably across the different systems. Discounting the impact of personality and type of parties in a coalition, we have attempted to characterise the influence of the *position* of the Prime Minister in party-government (Weller, 1985; Jones, 1991; King, 1994). A survey of the literature has led to the construction of the variable: *PMdominant*. It refers to whether or not the Prime Minister is clearly situated *above* ministers (having the casting vote in policy making, independent power to hire and fire ministers, and being primarily responsible for government to parliament). If the Prime Minister is clearly 'Primus-inter-Pares' (i.e. first amongst equals), meaning that ministers serve *with* the Prime Minister, rather than *under* him or her, we classify the position of the Prime Minister as *not* dominant. Any other situation has been labelled as 'in-between'. The actual categorisation presented below in Table 2.7 is, of course, quite subjective, but may nevertheless be helpful in judging how government perform in terms of duration and policy-making (Lijphart, 1999: 113-115). The cross-national distribution is more or less equal for the three categories and it appears that in majoritarian systems the Prime Minister is quite powerful (but also in many other countries like Austria, Germany, Greece, Spain and Portugal). In other cases one may well suspect that the role and position of the Prime Minister is to some extent dependent on the power of the Head of State and of Parliament (see Figure 2.7.2).

The third variable indicating the working of government is the extent to which party government shares a *collective responsibility*. The more this is a feature of a party government, in particular in coalitions, the more effectively it can make policies and make them work On the one hand, collective responsibility reinforces the cohesiveness *vis-à-vis* parliament. On the other hand, a cohesive government with a shared policy stance can cope more adequately with the potential countervailing power of a united civil service and bureaucracy. In fact – as Table 2.7 shows – only in four cases are there apparently no devices which promote co-operation by cohesion: Austria, Germany, Great Britain and the United States. The other options (which are not mutually exclusive) occur equally frequently (see Figure 2.7.2).

The final two variables in Table 2.7 list the powers of *initiative* for Government and Parliament. This right to propose bills is virtually unlimited for government. The Lower House of Parliament (if it concerns a bi-cameral system) is restricted in their right to initiate law making in many cases if it concerns proposals that have fiscal implications. On the one hand, this is the case with respect to taxation; on the other hand, the proposal may not be conducive to negative fiscal developments.

As has been stated earlier, parliamentary government is a fused system in which the powers are not straightforwardly separated as is the case in most presidential systems (Lijphart, 1992). This means *inter alia* that not only in practice, but also formally government as the executive agency is hardly

TABLE 2.7 Features of Government

Country	MininParl	Pmdominant	CollectiveDM	InitiativeG	InitiativeP
Australia	1	Yes	3	No Limitation	Except BT
Austria	2	Inbetween	1	No Limitation	Except BT*
Bangladesh	1*	Yes	3	No Limit**	Except BT
Belgium	2	Inbetween	2	No Limitation	Except FB
Botswana	1	No	2	No Limitation	Except BT
Bulgaria	0	Yes	3	No Limitation	No Limitation
Canada	2	Yes	3	No Limitation	Except BT
Czech Rep.	2	No	2	No Limitation	No Limitation
Denmark	2	Inbetween	3	No Limitation	No Limitation
Estonia	0	Inbetween	3	No Limitation	No Limit**
Finland	2	Inbetween	2	No Limitation	No Limitation
France V	0	Inbetween	2	No Limitation	Except BT & FB
Germany	2	Yes	1	No Limitation	Except BasicLaw
Greece	2	Yes	3	No Limitation	Except BT & FB
Guyana	2	No	2	No Limitation	Except BT
Hungary	2	Inbetween	3	No Limitation	No Limit**
Iceland	2	No	3	No Limitation	No Limitation
India	1	Yes	2	No Limitation	Except FB**
Ireland	1*	Yes	2	No Limitation	No Limitation
Israel	1	Yes	2	No Limit*	No Limit***
Italy	2	No	2	No Limit*	Except BT&BF*
Jamaica	1	Yes	2	No Limitation	Except BT
Japan	1**	Inbetween	2	No Limitation	No Limit****
Latvia	2	Inbetween	3	No Limitation	No Limit*/**
Lithuania	2	Yes	3	No Limitation	No Limit*/**
Luxembourg	0	No	3	No Limitation	No Limitation
Macedonia	0	Inbetween	3	No Limitation	No Limit*
Malta	1	Inbetween	2	No Limitation	Except FB
Namibia	1	No	3	No Limitation	No Limitation
Netherlands	0	No	3	No Limitation	LH only+FB
New Zealand	1	Yes	2	No Limitation	No Limitation
Norway	0	No	3	No Limitation	No Limitation
Pakistan	1	No	2	No Limitation	Except BT
Poland	2	Inbetween	3	No Limit**	No Limit**
Portugal	0	Yes	2	No Limit*	Except BT & FB
Romania	2	No	3	No Limitation	Except BT*
Russian Fed	0	Inbetween	2	No Limitation	Except FB*
Slovakia	0	Inbetween	2	No Limitation	No Limitation
Slovenia	2	Inbetween	3	No Limitation	LH only*
South Africa	2	No	3	No limit*	LH only*
Spain	2	Yes	2	No Limitation	Except FB
Sri Lanka	1	No	2	No Limitation	Except BT
Sweden	0	Inbetween	3	No Limitation	No Limitation
Switzerland	0	No	2	No Limitation	No limit*
Turkey	1(PM)	Inbetween	1	No Limitation	No Limitation
Un. Kingdom	1	Yes	3	No Limit**	Except BT
Un. States	0	No PM	1	No right of I.	No Limitation

Explanation:

MininParl = Compatibility of Offices whilst in Government

NB: 0 = not compatible with being Member of Parliament; 1 = Minister is required to be Member of Parliament; 2 = Optional, not required by law.

PMdominant = Prime Minister has special competences which go beyond other Members of Government.

CollectiveResp = Extent to which the government as a whole is directly responsible for its actions.

NB: 1 = PM and/or individual ministers are responsible; 2 = Government is collectively responsible; 3 = Both possibilities apply

InitiativeG = Right of Government to initiate law making

InitiativeP = Right of Parliament to initiate law making

Limitations are: BT = Proposals with implications for Taxation are not allowed; FB = Proposals that are not fiscally balanced are not allowed

Notes:

MininParl:

* Not more than two ministers can be Senators simultaneously

** PM and Deputy PM as well as 50% of Government must be MPs.

InitiativeG: Apart from the USA there are no limitations to governments in this respect.

* In Israel and Italy government is not allowed to reintroduce the same Bill after rejection during that Session of Parliament.

** In Bangladesh the President must assent to the introduction of fiscal bills. In the UK government is not allowed to present a Bill to the House of Lords which has fiscal consequences.

InitiativeP:

* The electorate has also the right to initiate proposals

** Unless the Head of State approves; he/she can also initiate proposals

*** Not allowed to reintroduce the same Bill after rejection during that Session of Parliament

**** If the proposal is carried by 20 MP's. In case of BT the proposal must be supported by 50 MP's.

---

constrained in proposing bills and producing measures. In fact, only in Israel, Italy, Bangladesh and the United Kingdom there are some limitations and these do not seriously jeopardise governmental efficacy. It is rather the other way around: in order to provide efficient and effective governance, so it seems, parliamentary initiatives are often limited. As Table 2.7 shows, in only 25% of all the systems are there no limitations at all. Two out of the three cases with limitations concern fiscal constraints that must be observed by parliament. As most policy-making is related to the "power of the purse" this may well imply a serious limitation of the Right of Initiative. Conversely, it may also facilitate efficient and proficient governance. Whichever, one can conclude from Table 2.7 that the Right of Initiative in parliamentary democracy is shared between the Executive and the Legislature, but the latter appears to be more limited in regard to exercise its role than the former.

2.9. Legislation – Promulgation – Validation

In any constitutional democracy the role and position of the *Judiciary* is of prime importance as regards upholding the constitutional rights of individuals *and* of society as a whole. Who is empowered to control the agents and actions emanating from the political system? In Table 2.8 we have reported three variables which reflect on the position and role of the judiciary, or related equivalent officers (like Councils of State or Head of State), particularly in regard to *constitutional review*.

The first variable reports which agency, if any, reviews law making independently of the executive and legislature (= *ExternalRev*). The second concerns the internal reviewing process, i.e. by parliament itself. The third simply reports when a law becomes binding, i.e. at what stage in the external and internal reviewing process.

The final variable *FlexiCon* in Table 2.8 concerns the extent to which the constitution is more or less "rigid" (as Lijphart calls it) or, conversely: more or less flexible. As we already put forward in section 2.6 this is an important feature of any democracy. It concerns the relationship between politics and society. Since the constitutionality of state actions, and thus of government in particular, is guaranteed by means of the so-called existing "Rule of Law" (Schmidt, 1995b; Keman, 1996). The operationalisation is an additive index. In fact it is an extended version of the one developed by Lijphart (1984: 213-214).

Even a cursory glance at Table 2.8 shows that the Internal Reviewing process is not a widely used instrument to safeguard the constitutionality of lawmaking (26%). In one-third of the cases where an Internal Review is mentioned, it is only required if a portion of parliament demands this. Half of all democracies under review here have an External Reviewing process that is conducted by the Judiciary. Apart from Russia and Switzerland all federal states require a Judicial Review. This is not surprising, since we know that, generally speaking, federal constitutional arrangements tend to be more elaborate than in many other states (Riker, 1975; Lane and Ersson, 1997). Therefore federal systems depend strongly on formal rules regulating power sharing (Elazar, 1995; Lijphart, 1999). However, in many unitary systems the Judiciary is also primarily involved in the external reviewing process. Yet, the exceptions to having an external review are more interesting (Israel, New Zealand, and the United Kingdom). Here it is Parliament and no other power that can decide upon the constitutionality of governmental action (Hague et al., 1993: 279). This can easily be understood by the fact that there is no written constitution in these polities (see Table 1 in Chapter 1). In Switzerland the final say (or: consent given) rests with the 'people' by means of a Referendum. In the Netherlands and Luxembourg the judiciary is not allowed to review the constitutionality of laws post hoc. In 60% of the cases laws become binding only after they have been reviewed, whereas in 18% of the countries the promulgation of a law per se makes it (for the time being) binding. Hence, in most instances the validation process precedes the public status of a law in the countries under review.

The final variable is seen by many as a prime indicator of how far the constitution has an independent position within the democratic organisation of a country. According to Lijphart (1999: 228-229) the underlying idea of having an independent or – in his words – "rigid" constitution is that it serves as an anti-majoritarian device. It prevents unrestricted rule. Its provisions can only be counteracted by a strong judicial review or by complicated procedures. We concur with this view. But we think that – apart from the Judicial Review process – other barriers to changing the constitution (see Table 2.6) should be taken into account. This has led us to develop the variable Flexi-Con, which combines the decision rules in regard to constitutional change and the existing reviewing processes within the polity (see also: Bogdanor, 1988). The values are reported above and show the following:

- Only 3 countries are extremely flexible (value = 1): Israel, New Zealand, and the United Kingdom. This comes as no surprise since all these countries have an unwritten constitution and see parliament as the ultimate body for reviewing purposes.
- Only 3 countries are extremely rigid: Japan, Pakistan, and Romania (having a score of 3). The common factor underlying these cases is their history of militarism and dictatorship. Yet, this is not unique to these cases within our set of countries (Greece and Turkey).
- The 6 countries with a rather flexible constitution are mostly post-communist democracies (the exception is Botswana). This observation appears to contradict the earlier one regarding the existence of an extremely rigid constitution.
- All other 36 cases can be seen as slightly tilted towards inflexibility, having a score of 2 or 2.5. However, the differences between these cases are in part artefacts of the operationalisation. Hence, these cases can be seen as belonging to one category.

All in all this composite measure of constitutional flexibility demonstrates, not surprisingly, that all parliamentary democracies have a number of requirements that contribute to the independent status of their constitution. Secondly, that the distribution of values across the countries shows that there is a high degree of convergence in this respect (see Figure 2.8.1). Finally, it means that whatever the composition of government is, whatever type of government is involved, and however large the dominance of a party may be, there are ample veto points and formal barriers to constrain governments from going astray in order to preserve the democratic quality of parliamentary government.

TABLE 2.8: Legislation-Promulgation-Validation

	ExternalRev	InternalRev	Validation	FlexiCon
Australia	Jud	No	After	2.5
Austria	Jud+Hos	No	After	2.5
Bangladesh	Jud+Hos	No	After	2.5
Belgium	Council+Hos	No	Before	2.5
Botswana	Council+Hos	Yes(UH)	After	1.5
Bulgaria	Council	No	After	1.5
Canada	Jud	No	Before+After	2.5
Czech Rep.	Council	No	After	1.5
Denmark	Jud	Yes*	Before+After	2.5
Estonia	Jud*	No	After	1.5
Finland	HoS	Yes	Before+After	2.5
France V	Council	Yes*	Before	2.5
Germany	Jud+Hos	No	Before+After	2.5
Greece	Jud	No	After	2.5
Guyana	Jud	Yes	After	2.5
Hungary	Council*	No	After	2
Iceland	Jud	No	After	2
India	Jud	No	After	2.5
Ireland	Jud+Hos	No	Before	2.5
Israel	None	No	After	1
Italy	Jud	No	After	2
Jamaica	Jud	No	After	2.5
Japan	Jud	No	After	3
Latvia	Jud	No	After	2.5
Lithuania	Council	No	After	2
Luxembourg	Council**	Yes	Before+After	2
Macedonia	Council	No	After	2.5
Malta	Jud	No	After	2
Namibia	Jud	No	After	2
Netherlands	Council**	Yes	Before	2.5
New Zealand	None	No	None	1
Norway	Jud	No	After	2.5
Pakistan	Jud+Hos	Yes*	Before+After	3
Poland	Council*	No	After	2
Portugal	Jud	No	Before+After	2.5
Romania	Council*	No	After	3
Russian Fed	Councel+Hos	No	After	2
Slovakia	Council	No	After	1.5
Slovenia	Council	No	After	1.5
South Africa	Jud	No*	After	2.5
Spain	Council+Hos	Yes	Before+After	2
Sri Lanka	Jud	No	Before	2
Sweden	Jud	No	None	2
Switzerland	None	Yes	Before	2.5
Turkey	Jud	Yes	Before+After	3
United Kingdom	None	No	None	1
United States	Jud+Hos	Yes	Before+After	3

Explanation:
ExternalRev =Review of laws in relation to the Constitution by bodies external to Government and Parliament
NB: J = by the judiciary; HoS = By Head of State; C = by special Council (of State); "+" indicates a necessary
combination
InternalRev = Review of Laws in relation to the Constitution by Parliament
Validation = Validation of laws takes place Before and (+)/or After promulgation of the law (i.e. the law
becomes binding for all citizens)
FlexiCon = Flexible Constitution
NB: The lower the score the more flexible (or less rigid) the Constitution is
Operationalisation of the additive index FlexiCon (maximum = 3.5):
Qualified Majority is required for changing/amending the Constitution = 1;
If by an Absolute Majority or Two Readings are required = .5; if else = 0
External Review by Judiciary = 1; by HoS and/or Council = .5; if not = 0
Internal Review required = .5; if not = 0
Referendum required = 1; if optional = .5; if not = 0

Notes:
ExternalRev:
* Initiated by the Head of State (or by the Speakers of Parliament).
** Concerns a formal pre-view and – if required – a judicial re-view.
InternalRev:
* If required by portion of Members of Parliament.

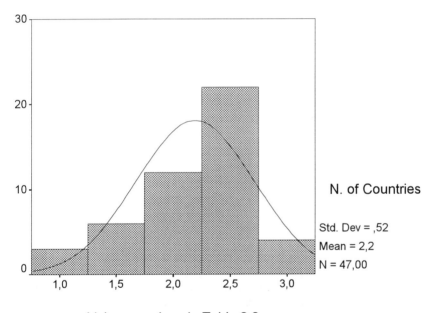

Values as given in Table 2.8

Figure 2.8.1 Index of Constitutional Flexibility

References

Alt, J.E., K.A. Shepsle (1990) *Perspectives on Positive Political Economy*, Cambridge: Cambridge University Press.

Banks, A.S., T.C. Muller (eds.) (1998) *Political Handbook of the World 1998*, Binghamton (NY): CSA Publications.

Barwise. K., F.G. Castles (1991) The "New Federalism". Fiscal Centralisation and Public Policy Outcomes. *Discussion Paper. no. 27. Canberra (ACT): The Australian National University.* Graduate program in public policy.

Bingham Powell, G. Jr. (1982) *Contemporary Democracies: Participation, Stability, and Violence*, Cambridge/London: Harvard University Press.

Blondel, J. (1973) *Comparative Legislatures*, Englewood Cliffs (NJ): Prentice Hall.

Blondel, J., J.-L. Thiebault (eds.) (1991) *The Profession of Government Minister in Western Europe*, London: Macmillan

Blondel, J., F. Müller-Rommel (eds.) (1993) *Governing Together: the Extent and Limits of Joint Decison-making in Western European Cabinets*, Basingstoke: MacMillan.

Bogdanor, V. (1988) *Constitutions in Democratic Politics*, Aldershot: Gower.

Bogdanor, V., D. Butler (eds.) (1983) *Democracy and Elections. Electoral Systems and Their Consequences*, Cambridge: Cambridge University Press.

Braun, D. (1999) 'Towards a Heuristic Framework of the Territorial Division of Power in Comparative Public Policy Research'' in: *Journal of Public Policy* (forthcoming).

Bryce (1921) *Modern Democracies*, New York (NY): MacMillan.

Budge, I. and H. Keman (1990) *Parties and Democracy. Coalition Formation and Government Functioning in Twenty States*, Oxford: Oxford University Press.

Budge, I. (1996) *The New Challenge of Direct Democracy*, Cambridge: Polity Press.

Butler, D., A. Ranney (eds.) (1994) *Referendums around the World: The Growing Use of Direct Democracy*, Washington (DC)/London: American Enterprise Institute/MacMillan.

Castles. F.G. (1998) *Comparative Public Policy.* Cheltenham: Edward Elgar.

Colomer, J.M. (ed.) (1996) *Political Institutions in Europe*, London: Routledge.

Dahl, R.A. (1956) *A Preface to Democratic Theory*, Chicago: University of Chicago Press.

Duverger, M. (1980) 'A New Political System Model: Semi-Presidential Government', in: *European Journal of Political Research,* 8/2:165-187

Elazar, D.J. (1995) 'Federalism', in: S.M. Lipset (ed.) *The Encyclopedia of Democracy.* London: Routledge. 2: 472-482.

Elazar, D.J. (1997) 'Contrasting Unitary and Federal Systems', in: *International Political Science Review*, 18/3: 237-251.

Gallagher, M., M. Laver, P. Mair (1995) *Representative Government in Western Europe*, New York etc., McGraw-Hill (2nd edition).

Hague, R., M. Harrop & S. Breslin (1993; see also 1998) *Comparative Government and Politics. An introduction*, Basingstoke: MacMillan.

Hall, P. (1986) *Governing the Economy. The Politics of State Intervention in Britain and France,* Cambridge/Oxford: Polity Press.

Huber, E., C. Ragin & J.D. Stephen (1993) 'Social Democracy, Christian Democracy, Constitutional Structure, and the Welfare State', in: *American Journal of Sociology*, 99: 711-749.

Jones, G. (ed) (1991) *West European Prime Ministers*, London: Frank Cass.

Keman, H. (1996) 'Konkordanzdemokratie und Korporatismus aus der Perspektive eines rationalen Institutionalismus', in: *Politische Vierteljahresscrift*, 37/3: 494-516.

Keman, H. (1997) *The Politics of Problem Solving in Postwar Democracies*, Basingstoke: MacMillan.

Keman, H. (1998) Federalism and Socioeconomic Performance, *Paper Joint Sessions of the ECPR* in Warwick.

Keman, H. (1999) 'Political Stability in Divided Societies: A Rational-Institutional Explanation', in: *Australian Journal of Political Science*, 34/2: 249-268

King, A. (1994) ' "Chief Executives " in Western Europe', in: I. Budge, D. McKay (eds.), *Developing Democracy: Comparative Research in Honour of J.F.P. Blondel*, London: Sage.

Klingemann, H.-D., R.I. Hofferbert, I. Budge, H. Keman, F. Petry, K. Strom, and T. Bergmann (1994) *Parties, Policies and Democracy*, Boulder: Westview Press.

Lane, J.-E., S.O. Ersson (1997) 'Is Federalism Superior?', in: A. Steunenberg, F. van Vught (eds.), *Political Institutions and Public Policy*, Dordrecht: Kluwer Academic Publishers.

Lane, J.-E., S.O. Ersson (1999) *Politics and Society in Western Europe*, London etc.: Sage

Lane, J.-E., D. McKay, K. Newton (1997) *Political Data Handbook: OECD Countries*, Oxford: Oxford University Press (2nd ed.).

Laver, M. (1998) *Private Desires, Political Action. An Invitation to the Politics of Rational Choice*, London etc: Sage.

Laver, M. and N. Schofield (1990) *Multiparty Government. The Politics of Coalition in Europe*, Oxford: Oxford University Press.

Laver, M. and K.A. Shepsle (eds.) (1994) *Cabinet Ministers and Parliamentary Government*, Cambridge: Cambridge University Press.

LeDuc, L., R. Niemi, P. Norris (eds.) (1996) *Elections and Voting in Global Perspective*, Thousand Oaks (CA)/London: Sage.

Lijphart, A. (1984) *Democracies. Patterns of Majoritarian and Consensus Government in 21 Countries*, New Haven/London:Yale University Press.

Lijphart, A. (ed.) (1992) *Parliamentary versus Presidential Government*, Oxford: Oxford University Press.

Lijphart, A. (1994) 'Democracies: Forms, Performance, and Constitutional Engineering', in: *European Journal of Political Research*, 25: 1-17.

Lijphart A. (1999) *Patterns of Democracy : Government Forms and Performance in Thirty-six Countries*, New Haven CT: Yale University Press.

Maddex, R.L. (1996) *Constitutions of the World*, London: Routledge.

Mezey, M. (1979) *Comparative Legislatures*, Durham (NC): Duke University Press.

Nohlen, D. (1978) *Wahlsysteme der Welt – Daten und Aanlysen: Ein Handbuch*, München: Piper.

North, D.C.(1990) *Institutions, Institutional Change and Economic Performance*, Cambridge, Cambridge University Press.

Pennings, P., H. Keman, J. Kleinnijenhuis (1999) *Doing Research in Political Science : an Introduction to Comparative Methods and Statistics*, London: Sage.

Putnam, R. (1993) *Making Democracy Work: Civic Traditions in Modern Italy*, Princeton (NJ): Princeton University Press.

Rae, D.W. (1967) *The Political Consequences of Electoral Laws*, New Haven: Yale University Press.

Reeve, A., A.Ware (1992) *Electoral Systems: a Comparative and Theoretical Introduction*, London: Routledge.

Riker, W.H. (1975) 'Federalism', in: F.I Greenstein, N.W. Polsby (eds.), *Handbook of Political Science, 5: Governmental Institutions and Processes*, Reading (Mass): Addison-Wesley.

Scharpf., F.W. (1994) 'Federal Arrangements and Multi-Party Systems', in: *Australian Journal of Political Science*, 30 (special issue): 27-39.

Schmidt, M.G. (1995a) *Wörterbuch zur Politik*, Stuttgart: Kröner Verlag.

Schmidt, M.G. (1995b) *Demokratietheorien. Eine Einführung*, Opladen: Leske+Budrich.

Schmidt, M.G. (1996) 'When parties matter: A review of the possibilities and limits of partisan influence on public policy' in: *European Journal of Political Research*, 30/2: 155-184.

Shepsle, K.A. (1997) 'Studying Institutions: Some Lessons from the Rational Choice Approach', in: J. Farr et al., *Political Science in History, Research Programs and Political Traditions*, Cambridge: Cambridge University Press.

Spoormans, H. (1988) *'Met uitsluiting van voorregt'. Het ontstaan van de liberale democratie in Nederland*. Amsterdam: SUA.

Therborn, G. (1977) 'Capital and Suffrage', in: *New Left Review* 103: 3-42.

Tilly, C. (ed.) (1975) *The Formation of National States in Western Europe*, Princeton (NJ): Princeton University Press.

Tsebelis, G. (1990) *Nested Games. Rational Choice in Comparative Politics*, Berkeley/Los Angeles/Oxford: University of California Press.

VanHanen, T. (1997) *Prospects of Democracy: A Study of 172 Countries*, London: Routledge.

Warwick, P.V. (1994) *Government Survival in Parliamentary Democracies*, Cambridge: Cambridge University Press.

Weaver, R., B. Rockman (eds.) (1993) *Do Institutions Matter? Government Capabilities in the United States and Abroad*, Washington (DC): The Brookings Institution.

Weller, P. (1985) *First among Equals: Prime Ministers in Westminster Systems*, Sydney: Allen and Unwin.

CHAPTER 3

THE STABILITY OF PARLIAMENTARY DEMOCRACIES: DURATION AND TERMINATION OF GOVERNMENTS

3.1. Introduction

The data that will be presented in the following chapter concerns the *composition* and *features* of government which distinguish each government from the other. These differences are *both* of a cross-national nature and inter-temporal in character. Hence, the data as presented and elaborated in terms of operationalisations and usage's in comparative politics can be employed *across* the parliamentary democracies under review, as well as to study the variation within each country (see also: Döring , 1995).

In the preceding chapter we have presented the institutional features of parliamentary democracy. The rationale being that the study of democratic government is always embedded in an institutional design, or: the 'rules of the political game', that influence the behaviour of the actors involved – i.e. the parties in government and in parliament. In other words: the data on parliamentary government that are presented in this book are obviously of importance to understand the 'life and times' of government.

In this chapter we set out to demonstrate the possibilities of *both* types of data by applying them to a widely debated topic in comparative politics: the stability of parliamentary democracies. This demonstration of the possible use does not aim to find the definitive answer to the question of stability, but rather to show the (future) users of this type of data how these can be utilised and thus to make them familiar with the potential of the data-collection (see for guidelines for this type of comparative cross-national analysis: Lane and Ersson, 1994; Peters, 1998, Pennings et al., 1999).

In sum: this chapter differs from the first two in that it reports a preliminary analysis of some of the data in the book. While the relationships examined are substantively interesting, our primary purpose is to illustrate some of the uses to which the data can be put in a pooled, cross-national framework over time.

In the literature on comparative governments stability of party government is a much-contested notion. Most of the authors use *duration* as a meaningful 'proxy' for stability (Bingham Powell, 1982; Lijphart, 1984; Laver and Schofield, 1990; Budge and Keman, 1990; Gallagher et al., 1995; Lane and Ersson, 1999). Sanders and Herman (1977) are exceptional in basing their analysis on the *rate of survival* of government, i.e. on the proportion of time spent in office in relation to the electoral calendar, as an indicator of government durability.

Various explanations have been offered as to why government durability as a *cross-national* variable also indicates their ability to govern *effectively* (Browne et al., 1984; Strom, 1985; Warwick, 1994; Van Roozendaal, 1997). The positive connection between duration (stability) and effectiveness, however, can be questioned. The period of governance need not directly be related to *effective* government in terms of material policy making. What duration may well indicate is the government's relative dominance over parliament (Lijphart, 1999; Keman, 1999). In this chapter we shall therefore analyse both *duration in government* and *reasons for termination*. Both variables can be considered as indicators of the relationship between parliament and government (see also: Budge and Keman, 1990), and have been described and operationalised in Chapter 1 (section 5 and 8). They are documented throughout the country tables that follow in this book.

In the discussion of the political and institutional factors that are used to explain variation in government duration in the literature fall into three groups:

• *Features of parliamentary cabinet government:* type of government; ideological composition of government;* parliamentary support for government.

• *Institutional features*: plurality, majority and proportional elections; executive power of the Head of State; structure of parliament, i.e. weak versus strong bi-cameralism as well as the formal relationship between the Executive and Legislative.

• *Party system features*; the number of (relevant) parties; the degree of polarisation; the existence of conflict dimensions in society.

The data in this book allow for a systematic analysis of these political and institutional actors, in particular for a cross-national analysis over time.

In section 2 we report the aggregated results on *government duration* for all the democracies included in this book (except for the presidential regimes: Russia and the USA). In addition, the relationship between duration and reasons for termination will be discussed. Furthermore, the main characteristics of party government *per se* will be presented in relation to both duration and termination of government. In section 3 we will consider the impact of *institutional* features on duration and termination. In section 4 the political features of the nations under review are the focus of this descriptive analysis.

3.2. Duration and Reasons for Termination and the Features of Party Government in Parliamentary Democracies

The distinctive features of cabinet government in parliamentary democracies are – apart from its duration and termination – the type of government, its complexion and its support in parliament. These characteristics determine the way it works and how representative it is in terms of ideology, and how far

---

* The data on the ideological composition of government used in this analysis are not wholly identical with those in the country chapters. This is mainly due to transformation and aggregation from the country level to cross-time case level averages. Yet the results are still comparable to the variation within each country.

Table 3.1 Features of Party Government

Country	Duration	Termination	Type of Government	Colour of Government	Support in Parliament	Number of Governments
Australia	660.8	1.4	1.8	2.46	58.7%	28
Austria	917.2	1.8	2.0	3.30	76.7%	20
Bangladesh	525.1	4.3	2.1	NA	66.5%	7
Belgium	510.9	3.5	2.5	2.39	63.2%	36
Botswana	1.464.4	1.0	1.0	NA	86.7%	7
Bulgaria	391.3	2.7	5.0	3.0	46.0%	3
Canada	946.6	1.8	2.1	1.0	55.2%	20
Czech Rep.	739.4	1.0	2.0	1.6	56.7%	5
Denmark	637.6	3.0	4.1	3.2	40.6%	28
Finland	404.3	3.2	3.6	2.6	52.8%	45
France	335.6	3.4	3.2	2.1	62.7%	56
Germany	660.0	2.3	2.7	1.9	55.1%	25
Greece	303.3	2.7	3.0	2.9	54.4%	52
Hungary	757.0	1.0	3.0	2.0	59.4%	2
Iceland	880.0	2.9	2.2	2.5	56.8%	21
India	1.050.0	1.9	2.1	3.1	57.6%	17
Ireland	900.1	2.8	2.8	1.5	50.9%	20
Israel	409.5	3.3	3.1	3.2	61.0%	42
Italy	330.8	3.4	3.7	1.6	53.5%	55
Jamaica	1.303.6	1.2	1.0	5.0	75.4%	10
Japan	460.8	2.2	2.1	1.2	54.4%	40
Latvia	435.0	2.5	5.0	NA	44.0%	2
Lithuania	585.0	3.5	1.0	4.0	51.8%	2
Luxembourg	1.135.8	1.9	2.1	2.3	70.8%	16
Macedonia	435.0	4.0	3.0	3.0	88.0%	1
Malta	1.582.4	1.1	1.4	2.9	51.9%	8
Netherlands	879.1	2.4	3.3	2.0	61.8%	20
New Zealand	793.8	1.7	1.1	2.5	56.0%	24
Norway	774.5	2.0	3.2	3.6	47.1%	24
Pakistan	446.3	3.6	2.4	NA	65.3%	19
Poland	251.2	4.4	3.8	2.7	47.9%	6
Portugal	586.4	3.2	2.3	2.4	52.7%	12
Romania	453.4	3.8	3.0	3.0	52.9%	5
Slovakia	180.2	4.3	2.4	2.4	53.6%	5
Slovenia	502.3	3.0	2.3	2.7	60.0%	3
South Africa	960.3	1.5	1.2	1.3	70.5%	17
Spain	982.9	1.1	3.1	3.1	49.8%	7
Sri Lanka	648.4	3.1	2.8	3.5	56.3%	21
Sweden	752.0	1.9	3.3	4.1	37.4%	24
Switzerland	365.1	1.0	2.9	1.9	80.6%	52
Turkey	465.0	3.0	2.3	2.9	65.2%	37
United Kingdom	995.4	1.4	1.2	2.5	54.5%	19
Mean	601.4	2.5	2.7	2.4	58.9%	20.6
SD	490.6	1.8	1.5	1.3	16.3%	15.9
N=	865	816	850	810	837	42

Explanation:
See for the operationalisation of reasons for termination, type of government and colour of government chapter
1, section 8. Duration is measured in days and support in parliament as the percentage of seats held by parties
supporting the government (see Chapter 4-49).
Mean=Arithmic Mean; SD= Standard Deviation. N= valid cases available
Missing cases are: Czechosolvakia, Estonia, Guyana, Russia and the USA; France and South Africa are treated
as one system.

one or more parties dominate in government. Table 3.1 shows the cross-national variation in these characteristics across the countries included in this book.

First of all it can be noticed that the overall *Duration of Government* (in days) is less than two years for the total set of countries. However, it is also obvious from the *Standard Deviation* (490.6) that the variation around this average is large. More to the point is the observation therefore that in the majority of the 865 cases a government lasts for a year (see Figure 3.1). Governments in Botswana, India, Jamaica, Luxembourg, Malta, Canada, South Africa, Spain, and the United Kingdom last above or just under 1,000 days. The governments in Bulgaria, Finland, France, Greece, Israel, Italy, Japan, Turkey, and most Central and East European countries cluster around the *Mode*, i.e. they last approximately a year (and in Switzerland, but this is

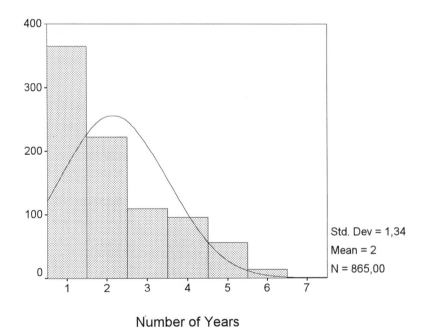

Std. Dev = 1,34
Mean = 2
N = 865,00

Number of Years

Figure 3.1 Duration of Government in Years

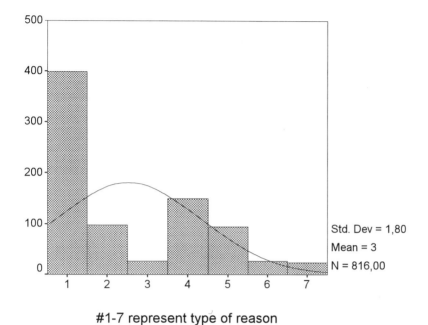

#1-7 represent type of reason

Figure 3.2 Reasons for Termination(see also Tables 3.2 and 3.3)

an artefact due to our operationalisation: see also Lijphart, 1999: 134).

In sum: the cross-national variation in Duration of Government is considerable and can therefore be considered as a meaningful subject for further analysis.

The *Reasons for Termination* (see Figure 3.2) show less variation across the 816 governments on which we collected this information. Yet, the *Mode* (1.0) shows that in the majority of the cases elections are reason for terminating the existing government, they account for 49% of the cases. Resignation of the Prime Minister accounts for 15%; conflict within government for 18% and with parliament for 12%. Altogether, these reasons for termination account for 94% of all government terminations. The remaining 6% are missing cases. This result appears as a confirmation of 'common sense' as regards the (expected) working of parliamentary systems vis-à-vis party government. For, according to our definition in chapter 1, parliamentary government is accountable to the electorate as well as to parliament (which is 76% of all reasons for termination).

Yet, it is interesting to investigate in what way these reasons for termination are related to the duration of government (Grofman and Van Roozendaal, 1994; Keman, 1997; Lijphart, 1999).

Although the correlation between Duration and Termination is relatively low (r = –.27), it is significant at the 0.01 level (N = 816), implying that it is a

Table 3.2 Average Duration by Reason for Termination

Reason for Termination	Average Duration	% of all cases
#1: elections	746.1	49%
#2: resignation of PM (voluntary)	565.2	12%
#3: resignation of PM (ill health)	667.5	3%
#4: dissension within government	451.3	18%
#5: lack of parliamentary support	410.7	12%
#6: intervention head of state	565.7	3%
#7: broadening coalition	348.6	3%
All Reasons	601.4	100%

Explanation: See for operationalisation Chapter 1

Table 3.3 Reasons for Termination and Duration of Government for less than 1 year, more than 3 years and between 1 and 3 years

	Government Duration		
Reason for Termination	< 1 year	≥ 1 year ≤ 3 years	> 3 years
* Elections	41.2%	36.9%	75.8%
* PM resigns	10.3%	22.9%	7.6%
* Conflict in Government	21.1%	18.1%	7.1%
* Conflict with Parliament	13.6%	12.1%	2.2%
* Other reasons	6.5%	7.3%	2.1%
Missing cases	7.3%	9.7%	5.2%

Explanation: Reasons #2 and #3 as well as #6 and #7 are taken together. The percentages represent the proportional frequencies for each column.

meaningful relationship. A closer inspection of this relationship discloses how the various reasons for termination are related to duration of government (Table 3.2).

Obviously (regular and anticipated) elections not only account for half of the cases but are also associated with the longest duration of government. If and when conflict arises, it apparently reduces the lifetime of a government (*Mode* = 252.0). Even if such a conflict is solved by broadening a coalition (Reason #7) then it does not really enhance duration. Hence, it is *political conflict* – either within cabinet government or between the executive and the legislature – which is important in understanding the duration of government in most parliamentary systems.

Finally, we have examined more closely at what reasons for termination account for the differences in duration, clustered in three categories: less than one year, between one and three years, and governments lasting more than three years (Table 3.3).

It is clear that elections are the most prevalent reason for termination if a government lasts longer than three years. Equally obvious is the fact that one out of three governments that lasts less than three years is terminated by political conflict (either with parliament or within the cabinet). Hence, discounting the role of the PM for the time being, it is clear that institutional

Table 3.4 Bi-variate Relations between Duration and Termination of Government and
Features of Government

	Duration of Government	Reasons for Termination
Type of Government	-.38*	.21*
Colour of Government	.14*	.01
Parliamentary Support	.08	-.15

Explanation:
See Tables 1 and 5 for operationalisations of the variables. The results are Pearson Product Moment
coefficients.
* = significant at the 0.05 level (two-tailed).

factors, on the one hand, and party political factors, on the other, by and large
determine the duration of a parliamentary government (King et al., 1990;
Browne et al., 1984). From this survey, we can conclude that duration and
termination are moderately related to each[14] other and that electoral reasons
for termination are always the most important ones, in which case governments – not surprisingly – last longer.

Let us now turn to the features that define the political complexion of the
parliamentary cabinet governments under review in this book. In Table 3.1
three features were reported: Type of Government, Complexion of Party
Government and the Parliamentary Support for Government. The bi-variate
relations between these variables and Duration of Government and Reasons
for Termination are shown in Table 3.4.

Although the results reported appear not very high, they are significant. In
particular this is the case for the Type of Government and the Colour of
Government. We interpret this result as that these features of party government are relevant for its duration and how governments end. Below in
Table 3.5 we report a breakdown of these variables. The distribution of the
Type of Government and *Colour of Party Government* across the countries is
reported below.

As can immediately be seen, the cross-national variation is large, but the
variation within each country is limited. If one, for example, inspects the
Anglo-Saxon democracies it is obvious that their majoritarian tendencies
influence the type of government which prevails: single party government is
more or less the 'rule'. Conversely, many West European countries show a
strong tendency to form coalition cabinets, often also with minority support,
particularly in Scandinavia and in Ireland (Strom, 1985). Below in Table 3.6
duration and termination have been cross-tabulated against duration, reasons
for termination, and parliamentary support.

---

[14]   On the aggregated level of national political systems the correlations between duration and
termination is significantly higher: r = -.69. The caveat is therefore that *inter*-system differences
are more visible than *intra*-system ones. See for a discusion of this Pennings et al., 1999:
chapter 2.

Table 3.5: Distribution of Types of Government and Colour of Government aggregated (in %) by country

Country	Type of Government						Colour of Government				
	1	2	3	4	5	6	1	2	3	4	5
Australia	36%	54%	7%	0%	3%	0%	61%	4%	0%	0%	35%
Austria	20	70	5	5	0	0	5	5	60	15	15
Bangladesh	72	0	0	14	0	14	Not Available				
Belgium	8	64	14	3	5.5	5.5	19	23	58	0	0
Botswana	100	0	0	0	0	0	Not Available				
Bulgaria(*)	0	0	0	50	50	0	0	0	100	0	0
Canada	65	0	0	35	0	0	100	0	0	0	0
Czech Rep. (*)	20	60	20	0	0	0	40	60	0	0	0
Denmark	0	14	0	50	36	0	36	0	11	14	39
Finland	7	14	44	9	17	9	11	27	65	5	2
France	2	12.5	68	5	9	3.5	45	20	25	0	10
Germany	4	64	16	0	0	16	64	4	8	24	0
Greece	35	16	14	8	2	25	34	18	32	16	0
Hungary	0	0	100	0	0	0	0	100	0	0	0
Iceland	0	86	5	9	0	0	19	19	52	10	0
India	65	6	6	12	5.5	5.5	0	0	88	12	0
Ireland	35	20	0	20	25	0	60	30	10	0	0
Israel	0	35	48	0	5	12	21	0	19	60	0
Italy	0	6	52	20	15	7	41	55	4	0	0
Jamaica	100	0	0	0	0	0	0	0	0	0	100
Japan	57.5	2.5	17.5	17.5	5	0	87.5	2.5	10	0	0
Latvia (*)	0	0	0	0	100	0	Not Available				

Country	Type of Government						Colour of Government				
	1	2	3	4	5	6	1	2	3	4	5
Lithuania (*)	100	0	0	0	0	0	0	0	0	100	0
Luxembourg	0	93	7	0	0	0	37.5	62.5	0	0	0
Macedonia (*)	0	0	100	0	0	0	0	0	100	0	0
Malta	87.5	0	0	12.5	0	0	12.5	37.5	0	50	0
Netherlands	0	35	45	0	0	20	50	5	45	0	0
New Zealand	96	4	0	0	0	0	54	8	0	4	34
Norway	25	12.5	0	46	5	0	29	4	0	8	59
Pakistan	47	21	11	0	5	16	Not Available				
Poland	0	33	17	0	33	17	0	67	0	33	0
Portugal	50	20	0	20	20	10	0	67	22	11	0
Romania	20	20	20	20	20	0	0	0	100	0	0
Slovakia (*)	0	80	0	20	0	0	0	60	40	0	0
Slovenia (*)	0	67	33	0	0	0	0	33	67	0	0
South Africa	87	6	7	0	0	0	88	0	12	0	0
Spain	29	0	0	71	0	0	0	43	0	57	0
Sri Lanka	33	5	24	28	10	0	0	0	57	33	10
Sweden	12.5	21	0	58	8.5	0	20.5	0	0	12.5	67
Switzerland	0	11.5	88.5	0	0	0	11.5	88.5	0	0	0
Turkey	44	26.5	6	12	6.5	6	14	6	58	22	0
United Kingdom	95	0	0	5	0	0	63	0	0	0	37

Explanation:
Countries with (*) have less than 5 cases. The figures for each country add up to 100% per case. Both variables are described in full in chapter 1, section 8. Type of Government runs from 1 (single party government) to 6 (caretaker government). Colour of Government represents the ideological tendency. It runs from 1 (rightwing dominance), through 3 (centre dominance) to 5 (leftwing dominance).

Table 3.6 Distribution of Type of Government, Colour of Government, and Parliamentary Support with Duration and Termination of Government

Type of Government	Duration	Termination	Frequency (N=850)
#1: single party majority	878.2	1.8	26.6%
#2: minimal winning	674.8	2.8	23.6%
#3: surplus coalition	460.9	2.8	24.4%
#4: single party minority	575.3	3.0	12.7%
#5: minority coalition	358.8	3.3	7.1%
#6: caretaker	114.2	1.5	5.6%
Colour of Government	Duration	Termination	Frequency (N=810)
#1: right-wing dominance	672.9	2.3	34.3%
#2: right-centre	416.3	2.5	19.6%
#3: balanced	589.0	2.9	24.7%
#4: left-centre	576.9	2.7	10.5%
#5: left-wing dominance	868.0	2.1	10.9%
Parliamentary Support	Duration	Termination	*Frequency (N=836)*
≥ 67.7%	642.6	2.1	26.2%
≥ 50.0%	681.4	2.5	51.7%
<50.0%	439.0	3.1	22.1%

Explanation:
See for overall averages and number of cases Table 3.1 and for country scores Table 3.5.
Frequency: proportional distribution of the cases by column (in %).

The relationship between type of government, duration and reasons for termination is perhaps not a strong one, but it is obvious that single party governments do indeed last longer than any other type. In addition, they are the most frequent type, albeit only marginally. This is understandable, noticing that the modal reason for termination is electoral (#1). Types 2 and 3, making up 48% of the aggregated total, are quite similar in their mix of reasons for termination, but not as regards their duration. Surplus coalitions tend to live shorter than minimal winning coalitions (on average even shorter than single party minority governments!). Caretaker governments (# 6) are indeed doing what is expected of them: they mind the shop until elections are called.

The overall average duration being 610 days, Table 3.6 demonstrates that 62.9% of all governments that are either minimal winning or single party governments last distinctively longer than multiparty coalitions (whether or not supported by a parliamentary majority). This conclusion is corroborated by the fact that the duration of government appears hardly to be enhanced if parliamentary support exceeds two-thirds of parliament.

The colour of government shows no systematic relationship with duration and termination. More interesting is the observation that the more Left-wing oriented governments (#4 and #5) form only 21.4% of the aggregated total (see also Figure 3.3). The reasons for termination appear to be equally distributed which may well point to the fact that ideological differences do not affect duration nor the termination of government in a specific way. The termination of government, however, is related to its parliamentary amount of

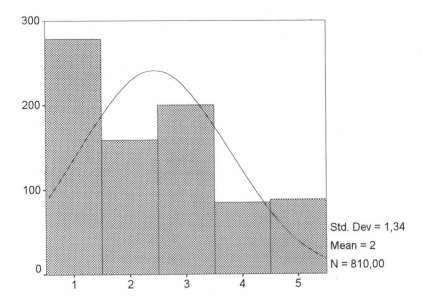

1= Rightwing; 3= Centre; 5= Leftwing Government

Figure 3.3 Colour of Party Government

support. As we already observed, it is not a matter of how much, but rather being in a majority or not. And as Table 3.6 shows, this appears also to be related to the reason for termination.

All in all it appears that the type of government is not only quite variable, but also – given its more or less structural character *within* countries – that political-institutional factors may well account for the aggregated variation. The same conclusion can be drawn with respect to the colour of party government: it varies considerably *across* the democratic types of government under review, but less so *within* the separate countries (in only five cases: Denmark, France, Greece, Malta and the Netherlands there is no specific "colour" category above the 50% mark, i.e. there is not a particular ideology dominating in the party system, see Table 3.5). Hence, the ideological complexion of government appears to be *nationally* structured. Bearing in mind that in almost all countries the 'rule of the game' is that the government has at least a simple majority in parliament (see Table 3.6) and that the composition and type of party system within nations is quite stable, we may expect that – together with the existing institutional features - party system features will determine the formation and continuation of government (Pridham, 1986; Budge and Keman, 1990; Gallagher et al., 1995).

3.3. Explanations of Government Stability: the Impact of Institutions

The 'stability' of party government in parliamentary democracies is influenced by the institutional context (Warwick, 1994; Lijphart, 1999). In this section we shall make use of three variables that represent the institutional context of parliamentary democracy:

Electoral systems: it is expected that majoritarian devices will promote one-party governments. In addition, "mixed" electoral systems will be conducive to minimal winning coalitions, since these systems tend to produce central and dominant parties (see: Bingham Powell, 1982; Grofman and Van Roozendaal, 1994). From these arguments it follows that there should be a relationship between electoral systems and type of government, as well as with duration and termination.

Head of State: in Chapter 2 we have emphasised the constitutional powers of the Head of State, for example with regard to the right to dissolve parliament. Another prerogative is the extent to which he/she is involved in the formation of cabinet government and the appointment of the Prime Minister and cabinet ministers (see also: King et al., 1990; Warwick, 1994). Hence, it can be assumed that the relative powers of the Head of State in a country can have an impact on both the duration and termination of government.

Powers of Parliament: the extent to which parliament has the power of investiture and the right of formal dismissal can be considered as an important feature in both duration and termination of government. Whether or not this feature has a negative or positive impact on both duration and termination of government is not clear (see: Bingham Powell, 1982, Browne et al., 1984; Warwick, 1994).

Structure of Parliament: another feature of Parliament is whether it is bicameral or not, and, if it is bicameral, whether the other chamber is "strong" or not (Lijphart, 1999: 205-212). The "stronger" each of the two chambers is, the more vulnerable government will be. In addition, since the Upper House in many countries is elected in a staggered way and often not simultaneously with the Lower House, it can occur that a situation of "divided government" arises (see also: Weaver and Rockman, 1993; Schmidt, 1996). Hence, it may be expected that, if and when parliamentary powers of investiture and dismissal are available, or there is a situation of strong bicameralism (see Figure 3.4), both the duration and termination of government will obviously be affected.

In Table 3.7 we compare the *means* of, respectively, the duration of government and the reason for termination with various features of the institutional design of 42 parliamentary democracies. Most of these features have been presented an reported in Chapter 2, in particular in Section 6, Table 2.5.

Table 3.7 shows that there is a bi-variate pattern between institutions and the duration and termination of government. This is particularly and significantly the case with reasons for termination. The relationships found are positively related to the powers of the Head of State and Parliament. This

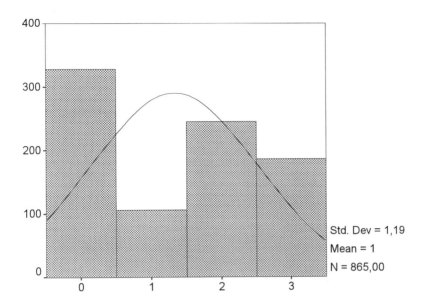

Unicameral; 1=Hybrid; 2=Weak and 3=Strong Bicameralism

Figure 3.4 Weak versus Strong Bicameralism

indicates that (relative) powerful actors, not belonging to government, do influence its life and thus possibly also its course. Hence, it appears justified to say the government in parliamentary democracies is and can be checked by countervailing powers (see also: Bingham Powell, 1982). Apparently this does not determine the duration of government directly. One suspects that the various institutions together will be more influential than separately. The results of Table 3.7 nevertheless do allow for some interesting observations.

Parliamentarism is a good example: the bi-variate relationship between duration and the strength of parliamentary powers is -.18 (significant at the 0.01 level). The comparison by category demonstrates that it appears more difficult for the weaker type of parliament to terminate government. The divide is clearly between 'strong' parliaments and the other two types of parliamentarism: governments in the latter case last almost twice as long as governments that face a 'strong' parliament. Yet, surprisingly enough, this difference is not observed as regards the reasons for termination. All reasons appear to be in use in all parliaments.

This is much less the case with respect to the cross-national difference in powers of the Head of State. Although the stronger the *direct influence of the Head of State* is, the longer government appears to be able to stay in power. However, there is no difference with countries with a 'weak' Head of State.

Table 3.7 Political Institutions and Duration and Termination of Government

Institutions	Duration (average)	Termination (average)	% of Total
Electoral Systems:	r = .10*	r = -.08*	N = 865/816
Majoritarian	712.5	2.28	23.8%
Mixed	697.2	2.28	11.4
Proportional	546.4	2.66	64.8
Heads of State:	r = -.08	r = .29*	
Strong	643.9	3.00	7.8%
Medium	485.0	3.30	25.4
Weak	642.8	2.24	66.8
Bi-cameralism:	r = -.03	r = -.18*	
Strong	739.1	1.95	21.5%
Weak	542.0	2.68	28.3
Hybrid	692.8	1.78	13.3
Unicameral	580.1	2.85	36.9
Parliamentarism	r = -.10*	r = .12*	
Strong	388.4	3.06	29.7%
Medium	678.6	2.28	55.6
Weak	707.3	2.98	14.7

Explanation:
See Chapter 2, Table 5 for definitions and values by country. Bi-variate relations are Pearson Product Moment coefficients (* = significant at the 0.01 level).

As soon as his (or her) direct influence is medium institutionalised, this relationship fades. Yet, as regards the reasons for termination, it is obvious that the weaker the Head of State is, the more government ends by means of elections.

The impact of *bicameralism* seems to be that unicameral and weak systems show a shorter duration of government than the other two categories. In fact, "strong" and "hybrid" bicameralism appears to produce more enduring governments. The opposite picture emerges as regards reasons for termination: in strong and hybrid parliaments elections dominate. Yet, it could be suggested that here, more often than not, other mechanisms (like federal institutions or a strong Head of State) weaken this effect on duration (see also: Lijphart, 1999: 214-215).

As regards the *electoral systems*, proportional representation, often seen as conductive to multi-partyism, is clearly different from the mixed and majoritarian systems: in PR-systems the duration of governments is considerably lower, almost half a year difference on average. The electoral system differences do not much influence reasons for termination. This is not surprising since elections *follow* – more often than not – the termination of a government or they are constitutionally determined *beforehand* (Fig. 3.5).

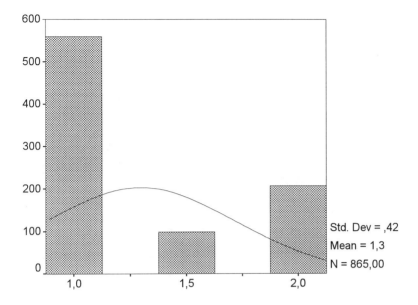

1= PR-system; 1,5= Mixed System; 2= Plurality System

Figure 3.5 Distribution of Electoral Systems

Generally speaking, it can be put forward that the *separate* institutions of parliamentary democracy do make a difference, but these differences also make clear that the cross-national pattern is neither clear-cut, nor straightforward. We would suggest that it is the design – i.e. the composition of the various institutions as a whole – that will matter with respect to duration and termination of parliamentary government. Hence, the comparative analysis should be extended towards the national level. Having said this, the conclusion is that both duration and termination of government seem related to the institutional features of parliamentary democracy. It is also clear that parliament does matter, as does the head of state. The influence of the latter is often underrated in the literature. Yet, the conclusion must be there is no direct universal pattern for the countries under review here.

3.4. The Impact of Party System Features on Government Stability

In contrast to the institutional and constitutional features of parliamentary democracy, much attention has been paid to a wide array of factors related to the party system with respect to the composition and functioning of party government (Bingham Powell, 1982; Browne, et al., 1984; Strom, 1985; Mair and Smith, 1989; Budge and Keman, 1990; Warwick, 1994; Gallagher, et al.,

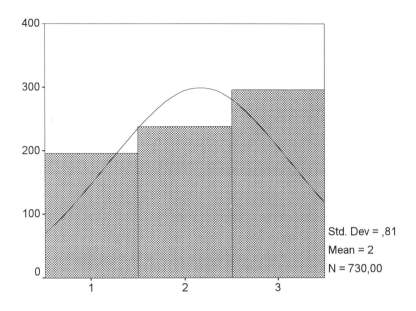

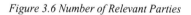

= Low fragmentation; 2 = Medium; 3= High fragmentation

Figure 3.6 Number of Relevant Parties

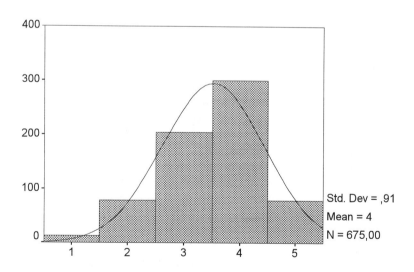

1 = Low degree and 5 = High Degree of Polarisation

Figure 3.7 Degree of Polarisation of the Party Systems

1995; Keman, 1997; Pennings and Lane, 1998; Lijphart, 1999). The interactions between parties and the organisation of party systems have been a focal point of research on the making and breaking of government. In this section we shall focus on the following variables: the number (of relevant) parties in parliament, the degree of polarisation in terms of Left and Right, as well as the existence of conflicting issues permeating party differences.

Parliamentary government is often characterised as a 'fused' system. This implies that parties in government are considered to be related directly to their behavioural features as competing parties in parliament. Hence, the way party systems are organised, and thus parties interact, is important for the viability of party government (see also: Sartori, 1976; von Beyme, 1985; Laver and Schofield, 1990; Keman, 1997). From this it follows that the degree of polarisation within a party system may well influence the duration of government. Likewise, the extent to which deep seated conflicts, based on societal cleavages (language, religion, ethnicity and socio-economic disparities), are politically organised and permeate the party system, will influence the reasons for termination that prevail in a political system. Finally, if and when a party system is characterised by many relevant parties (i.e. *Regierungsfähig* as well as having blackmail potential), then it can be expected that this feature can make a difference to the duration and termination of party government in a parliamentary democracy.

Following the mainstream arguments in this respect, we shall examine whether or not the degree of *polarisation* (in terms of Left and Right; see: Klingemann et al., 1994; Huber and Inglehart, 1995), on the one hand, and the number of (relevant) *parties* in parliament (Budge and Keman, 1990), on the other, have actually an effect on the functioning of government. In addition, we include a variable which can be used as a proxy for political cleavages: *issues* that are of a structural nature in society (see for this: Lijphart, 1999: 87-89, Table 5.3). All three variables can be seen as indicators of executive dominance in the parliamentary democracies under review. It goes almost without saying that the higher the level of polarisation, and the number of relevant issues and parties is, the more volatile, if not vulnerable, the life of government will be. The extent to which this is the case is investigated in Table 3.8.

Even at first glance it is obvious that a fragmented party system does not enhance the duration of party government. However, although this is expected, this does not go directly together with a proliferation of many political issues in society. Only when many issues are relevant then the life of party government is shortened, as the bi-variate relationship indicates.

For the degree of polarisation, the comparative differences are insignificant.

All in all, one can draw the conclusion that indeed high levels of fragmentation and the occurrence of issues have an impact on the duration of government. However, their absence does not necessarily produce a longer duration. Based on our observations, the bi-variate relations between the

Table 3.8 Political Features and the Duration and Termination of Government

Party System Features	Duration (average)	Termination (average)	% of Cases
Fragmentation:	r = -.28*	r = .19*	N = 865
Low Number of Parties	760.9	1.85	27%
Medium Number	638.9	2.60	32.5
High Number	488.4	2.76	40.5
Polarisation:	r = -.15*	r = .14*	
Low degree	355.1	3.67	1.8%
Moderate	713.4	2.44	12.2
Medium	583.6	2.20	30.8
High	626.1	2.51	43.9
Very high	482.0	2.95	11.2
Issue Dimensions	r = -.30*	r = .17*	
Few (<1.5)	676.2	2.14	29.7%
Some (< 2.5)	813.6	2.45	27.8
Many (> 2.5)	596.4	2.95	42.5

Explanation:

Fragmentation is taken from Lijphart (1999: 312) and transformed into four categories.

Polarisation is taken from Castles and Mair (1984), and Huber and Inglehart (1995); the original data have been transformed into five categories (the original scales run from 1-10).

Issue Dimensions are taken from Lijphart (1999: 80-81) and transformed into three categories.

Missing cases for Polarisation = 190; for Fragmentation = 135; for Issue Dimensions = 60.

features of party systems and the reasons for termination are quite weak. To put it differently, it appears – with the exception of low degrees of fragmentation - that the reasons for termination are dependent on the specific situation at hand which apparently drives the behaviour of the participants involved. This would suggest that the effects of party systems on party government is more rather than less mediated by both the type and colour of the existing government, as well as by the particular set of institutions present (see also: Pridham, 1986; Grofman and Van Roozendaal, 1994; Laver and Shepsle, 1996; Budge, 1996). If this is a correct and tenable conclusion, then it seems that the direction and working of a party system is not only a phenomenon driven by national characteristics, but also only indirectly relevant for the duration and termination of government.

3.5. Conclusions

Above we have demonstrated how the data collection, which is presented in the subsequent chapters can be analysed in relation to a number of political and institutional variables. These variables have been taken either from the preceding Chapter 2 or adapted from other existing data sets (like: LeDuc et al., 1996; Lijphart, 1999). We hope that this chapter has shown the usefulness

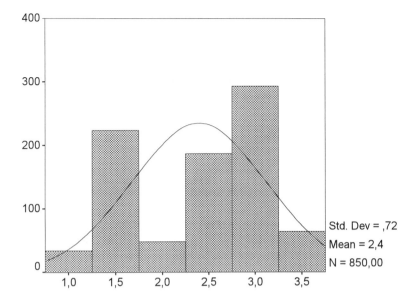

Numbers represent the level of Conflict Dimensions

Figure 3.8 Conflict Dimensions in Party Systems

of these data on party government. Other applications are, of course, perfectly feasible and – so we hope – will be undertaken to further the study of parliamentary democracy.

Another point made in this chapter is that, in our view, the study of *party government* should always be located *within the context of parliamentary democracy*. Overall it is very important to recognise the embeddedness of parties, governments and other political actors in the political institutions of liberal democracy, and the (structured) interaction between those political actors.

The empirical evidence presented here of the relations between institutions and actors in over 40 parliamentary democracies demonstrates not only that all these features can be considered together, but also that there is considerable room for improving our knowledge as regards the *functioning and working of party government* (Budge and Keman, 1990). On the one hand, we can observe that the cross-nationally patterned variations affirm existing ideas emanating from the mainstream literature on parties, governments, and democracy. On the other hand, it is equally obvious that a number of logically, and also intuitively, expected relations do not always occur.

This is no wonder: some of the indicators are either too crude or too static to be able to grasp the finesses of political behaviour and the related impact of institutions (see for useful discussions: Tsebelis, 1990; Scharpf, 1994; Laver and Shepsle, 1996; Keman, 1997, 1999; Lijphart, 1999). In addition, not all types of institutionalised behaviour can and will be understood from a sheer comparative perspective alone. This caveat does however not discount the *comparative approach*, but simply emphasises the obvious fact that *political systems* must also be analysed in their own right. Putting them in a cross-national perspective, we believe, will only bring the *specifica differentia* of national political systems more strongly to the fore.

References

Bingham Powell, G. Jr. (1982) *Contemporary Democracies: Participation, Stability, and Violence*, Cambridge/London: Harvard University Press.

Browne, E.C., J.P. Frendreis, and D.W. Gleiber (1984) 'An "Events" Approach to the Problem of Cabinet Stability', in: *Comparative Political Studies*, 17, 2: 167-197.

Budge, I., H. Keman (1990) *Parties and Democracy. Coalition Formation and Government Functioning in Twenty States*, Oxford: Oxford University Press.

Budge, I. (1996) *The New Challenge of Direct Democracy*, Cambridge: Polity Press.

Castles, F., P. Mair (1984) 'Left-Right Political Scales: Some Expert Judgements', in: *European Journal of Political Research*, 12: 73-88.

Döring, H. (ed.) (1995) *Parliaments and Majority Rule in Western Europe*, Frankfurt/New York: Campus Verlag/St. Martin's Press.

Duverger, M. (1980) 'A New Political System Model: Semi-Presidential Government', in: *European Journal of Political Research,* 8/2:165-187

Gallagher, M., M. Laver, P. Mair (1995) *Representative Government in Western Europe*, New York etc., McGraw-Hill (2nd edition).

Grofman, B., P. van Roozendaal (1994) 'Toward a Theoretical Explanation of Premature Cabinet Termination with Application to Post-War Cabinets in the Netherlands', in: *European Journal of Political Research*, 26: 155-170.

Huber, E., R. Inglehart (1995) 'Expert Interpretations of Party Space and Party Locations in 42 Societies' *Party Politics*, 1/1: 73-111.

Keman, H. (1997) *The Politics of Problem Solving in Postwar Democracies*, Basingstoke: MacMillan.

Keman, H. (1998) *Federalism and Socioeconomic Performance, Paper Joint Sessions of the ECPR* in Warwick.

Keman, H. (1999) 'Political Stability in Divided Societies: A Rational-Institutional Explanation', in: *Australian Journal of Political Science*, 34/2: 249-268

King, G., J.E. Alt, N.E. Burns, and M. Laver (1990) 'A Unified Model of Cabinet Dissolution in Parliamentary Democracies', in: *American Journal of Political Science*, 34, 3: 846-871.

Klingemann, H.-D., R.I. Hofferbert, I. Budge, H. Keman, F. Petry, K. Strom, and T. Bergmann (1994) *Parties, Policies and Democracy*, Boulder: Westview Press.

Lane, J.-E. and S.O. Ersson (1994) *Comparative Politics: An Introduction and New Approach*, Cambridge, Polity Press.

Lane, J.-E., S.O. Ersson (1999) *Politics and Society in Western Europe*, London etc.: Sage.

Laver, M. N. Schofield (1990) *Multiparty Government. The Politics of Coalition in Europe*, Oxford: Oxford University Press.

Laver, M., K.A. Shepsle (1996) *Making and Breaking Governments: Cabinets and Legislatures in Parliamentary Democracies,* Cambridge: Cambridge University Press.

LeDuc, L., R. Niemi, P. Norris (eds.) (1996) *Elections and Voting in Global Perspective*, Thousand Oaks (CA)/London: Sage.

Lijphart, A. (1984) *Democracies. Patterns of Majoritarian and Consensus Government in 21 Countries*, New Haven/London:Yale University Press.

Lijphart A. (1999) *Patterns of democracy : government forms and performance in thirty-six countries*, New Haven CT: Yale University Press.

Mair, P., G. Smith (1989) *Understanding Party System Change in Western Europe*, London, Frank Cass.

Pennings, P., J.-E. Lane (eds.)(1998) *Comparing Party System Change*, London, Routledge.

Peters, G.B. (1998) *Comparative Politics: Theory and Methods*, London/New York, MacMillan/New York University Press.

Pennings, P., H. Keman, J. Kleinnijenhuis (1999) *Doing research in political science : an introduction to comparative methods and statistics*, London: Sage.

Pridham, G. (ed) (1986) *Coalitional behaviour in Theory and Practice: An Inductive Model for Western Europe*, Cambridge, Cambridge University Press.

Sanders, D., V. Herman (1977) 'The Survival and Stability of Governments in Western Democracies', in: *Acta Politica*, 3: 346-377.

Sartori, G. (1976) *Parties and Party Systems: A Framework for Analysis*, Cambridge, Cambridge University Press.

Scharpf., F.W. (1997) *Games real actors play: actor-centered institutionalism in policy research*, Boulder (CO), Westview Press.

Schmidt, M.G. (1996) 'When parties matter: A review of the possibilities and limits of partisan influence on public policy' in: *European journal of political research*, 30/2: 155-184.

Strøm, K. (1985) 'Party Goals and Government Performance in Parliamentary Democracies', in: *American Political Science Review*, 79: 738-754.

Taagepera, R., M.A. Shugart (1989) *Seats and Votes: The Effects and determinants of Electoral Systems*, New Haven, Yale University Press.

Tsebelis, G. (1990) *Nested Games. Rational Choice in Comparative Politics*, Berkeley/Los Angeles/Oxford: University of California Press.

Van Roozendaal, P. (1997) 'Government Survival in Western Multi-party Democracies: The Effect of Credible Exit Threats via Dominance', in: *European Journal of Political Research*, 32, 1: 71-92.

Von Beyme, K. (1985) *Political Parties in Western Democracies*, Aldershot, Gower.

Warwick, P.V. (1994) *Government Survival in Parliamentary Democracies*, Cambridge: Cambridge University Press.

Weaver, R., B. Rockman (eds.) (1993) *Do Institutions Matter? Government Capabilities in the United States and Abroad*, Washington (DC): The Brookings Institution.

COMPOSITION-DURATION-PERSONNEL OF PARTY GOVERNMENT BY COUNTRY (1945-1998)

4. AUSTRALIA

The ceremonial Head of State is the British Monarch, represented by a Governor-General.

The State is decentralised and Federal.

Parliament is bicameral with an elected Upper House of 76 and a Lower House of 147 members. The latter is more powerful than the Upper House in that its support is crucial for the Government. However, the Upper House is unusually powerful with a wide range of co-equal powers.

Majority voting (Alternative Voting) in single-member constituencies of approximately 60-70,000 electors elects members of the Lower House for a flexible three-year term. Members of the Upper House are elected for a six-year term.

Parliament has a quorum of one-third of all members. Votes are carried by a majority of all votes cast. Constitutional amendments need a majority of all members in both Houses and require popular consent by a binding referendum. A referendum may also be called on other issues, by the government and a portion of the electorate. The outcome is binding.

The political executive is the Prime Minister and the Cabinet. No vote of investiture is required, nor a vote of confidence likely, so long as the Government maintains a relative majority in the Lower House. Government is both collectively and individually responsible to parliament. The Prime Minister and ministers are leaders and members of parliament for the majority party or party alliance in the Lower House. The Prime Minister has a dominant position in government.

There is a Supreme Court for constitutional review of legislation.

AUSTRALIA 1945–1998

Gov	Begin	Dur	Rft	Tog	Py1	Py2	Seats	CPG	Nom	Prime Minister (Py)
1	13.07.45	475	1	1	ALP 49		74	4	19	Chifley, J.B. (ALP)
2	31.10.46	1145	1	1	ALP 43		74	4	19	Chifley, J.B. (ALP)
3	19.12.49	508	1	2	LIB 55	CNT 19	122	2	19	Menzies, R.G. (LIB)
4	11.05.51	1155	1	2	LIB 52	CNT 17	121	2	20	Menzies, R.G. (LIB)
5	09.07.54	551	1	2	LIB 47	CNT 17	121	2	20	Menzies, R.G. (LIB)
6	11.01.56	1063	1	2	LIB 57	CNT 18	122	2	12	Menzies, R.G. (LIB)
7	09.12.58	1110	1	2	LIB 58	CNT 19	122	2	12	Menzies, R.G. (LIB)
8	23.12.61	724	1	2	LIB 45	CNT 17	122	2	12	Menzies, R.G. (LIB)
9	17.12.63	771	2	2	LIB 52	CNT 20	122	2	12	Menzies, R.G. (LIB)
10	26.01.66	322	1	2	LIB 52	CNT 20	122	2	12	Holt, H.E. (LIB)
11	14.12.66	369	3	2	LIB 61	CNT 21	124	2	12	Holt, H.E. (LIB)
12	18.12.67	23	2	2	LIB 61	CNT 21	124	2	11	McEwen, J. (CNT)
13	10.01.68	49	x	2	LIB 61	CNT 21	124	2	12	Gorton, J.G. (LIB)
14	28.02.68	622	1	2	LIB 61	CNT 21	124	2	12	Gorton, J.G. (LIB)
15	11.11.69	495	2	2	LIB 46	CNT 20	125	2	13	Gorton, J.G. (LIB)
16	21.03.71	639	1	2	LIB 46	CNT 20	125	2	13	McMahon, W. (LIB)
17	19.12.72	540	1	1	ALP 67		125	4	27	Whitlam, E.G. (ALP)
18	12.06.74	518	6	1	ALP 66		127	4	27	Whitlam, E.G. (ALP)
19	12.11.75	36	1	5	LIB 40	CNT 22	127	2	15	Fraser, J.M. (LIB)
20	18.12.75	732	1	3	LIB 68	CNT 23	127	1	12	Fraser, J.M. (LIB)
21	20.12.77	1048	1	3	LIB 67	CNT 19	125	1	14	Fraser, J.M. (LIB)
22	02.11.80	859	1	2	LIB 54	CNT 20	125	2	14	Fraser, J.M. (LIB)
23	11.03.83	643	1	1	ALP 75		125	4	13	Hawke, R.J.L. (ALP)
24	13.12.84	951	1	1	ALP 82		148	4	17	Hawke, R.J.L. (ALP)
25	22.07.87	986	1	1	ALP 86		148	4	16	Hawke, R.J.L. (ALP)

AUSTRALIA 1945–1998

Gov	Begin	Dur	RfT	ToG	Py1	Py2	Seats	CPG	NoM	Prime Minister (py)
26	03.04.90	633	2	1	ALP 78		148	4	16	Hawke, R.J.L. (ALP)
27	27.12.91	453	1	1	ALP 77		148	4	18	Keating, P.J. (ALP)
28	24.03.93	1081	1	1	ALP 80		148	4	20	Keating, P.J. (ALP)
29	11.03.96			3	LIB 76	NP 18	148	2	15	Howard, J. (LIB)

-Gov 13: Following his election to the Federal House of Representatives in the by-election at Higgins, the PM, Gorton, announced that he would form a new government.

Gov	Deputy PM	Py	Foreign Affairs	Py	Defence	Py	Interior	Py	Justice	Py
1			Evatt, H.V.	ALP	Forde, F.M.	ALP	Johnson, H.V.	ALP	Evatt, H.V.	ALP
					Beasley, J.A.	ALP	Collings, J.S.	ALP		
					Makin, N.J.O.	ALP				
					Drakeford, A.S.	ALP				
2			Evatt, H.V.	ALP	Riordan, W.J.F.	ALP	Johnson, H.V.	ALP	Evatt, H.V.	ALP
					Chambers, C.	ALP	Scully, W.J.	ALP		
					Armstrong, J.I.	ALP				
					Drakeford, A.S.	ALP				
					Dedman, J.J.	ALP				
3			Spender, P.C.	LIB	Francis, J.	LIB	McBride, P.A.M.	LIB	Spicer, J.A.	LIB
					Harrison, E.J.	LIB	*Lyons, E.	LIB		
					White, T.D.	LIB				
4	Fadden, A.W.	CNT	Casey, R.G.	LIB	McBride, P.A.M.	LIB	Kent Hughes, W.S.	LIB	Spicer, J.A.	LIB
					McMahon, W.	LIB	Harrison, E.J.	LIB		
					Francis, J.	LIB				
					Harrison, E.J.	LIB				

AUSTRALIA 1945–1998

Gov	Deputy PM	Py	Foreign Affairs	Py	Defence	Py	Interior	Py	Justice	Py
5	Fadden, A.W.	CNT	Casey, R.G.	LIB	McBride, P.A.M. Francis, J. Townley, A.G. Harrison, E.J.	LIB LIB LIB LIB	Kent Hughes, W.S. Harrison, E.J.	LIB LIB	Spicer, J.A.	LIB
6	Fadden, A.W.	CNT	Casey, R.G.	LIB	McBride, P.A.M. O'Sullivan, N. Townley, A.G. Harrison, E.J.	LIB LIB LIB LIB	Harrison, E.J.	LIB	Spicer, J.A.	LIB
7	McEwen, J.	CNT	Casey, R.G.	LIB	Townley, A.G.	LIB	Spooner, W.H.	LIB	Barwick, G.	LIB
8	McEwen, J.	CNT	Barwick, G.	LIB	Townley, A.G.	LIB	Spooner, W.H.	LIB	Barwick, G.	LIB
9	McEwen, J.	CNT	Barwick, G.	LIB	Hasluck, P.M.C.	LIB	Spooner, W.H.	LIB		
10	McEwen, J.	CNT	Hasluck, P.M.C.	LIB	Fairhall, A.	LIB	Hulme, A.S.	LIB		
11	McEwen, J.	CNT	Hasluck, P.M.C.	LIB	Fairhall, A.	LIB	Anthony, J.D.	CNT		
12			Hasluck, P.M.C.	LIB	Fairhall, A.	LIB				
13	McEwen, J.	CNT	Hasluck, P.M.C.	LIB	Fairhall, A.	LIB				
14	McEwen, J.	CNT	Hasluck, P.M.C.	LIB	Fairhall, A.	LIB	Hulme, A.S.	LIB		
15	McEwen, J.	CNT	McMahon, W.	LIB	Fraser, J.M.	LIB	Nixon, P.J.	CNT		
16	Anthony, J.D.	CNT	Bury, L.H.E.	LIB	Gorton, J.G.	LIB	Hulme, A.S.	LIB	Bowen, N.H.	LIB
17	Barnard, L.H.	ALP	Whitlam, E.G. Morrison, W.L.	ALP ALP	Barnard, L.H.	ALP			Murphy, L.K.	ALP
18	Cairns, J.F.	ALP	Willesee, D.	ALP	Barnard, L.H.	ALP			Murphy, L.K.	ALP
19	Anthony, J.D.	CNT	Peacock, A.S.	LIB	Killen, D.J.	LIB	Greenwood, I. Drake-Brockman, T.	LIB CNT	Greenwood, I.	LIB
20	Anthony, J.D.	CNT	Peacock, A.S.	LIB	Killen, D.J.	LIB	Withers, R.G.	LIB		
21	Anthony, J.D.	CNT	Peacock, A.S.	LIB	Killen, D.J.	LIB	Withers, R.G.	LIB		
22	Anthony, J.D.	CNT	Street, A.A.	LIB	Killen, J.D.	LIB			Durack, P.	LIB
23	Bowen, L	ALP	Hayden, W.	ALP	Scholes, G.	ALP			Evans, G.	ALP
24	Bowen, L	ALP	Hayden, W.	ALP	Beazley, K.E.	ALP			Bowen, L.	ALP

AUSTRALIA 1945–1998

Gov	Deputy PM	Py	Foreign Affairs	Py	Defence	Py	Interior	Py	Justice	Py
25	Bowen, L.	ALP	Hayden, W.	ALP	Beazley, K.E.	ALP	Young, M. West, S.	ALP ALP		
26	Keating, P.	ALP	Evans, G.	ALP	Ray, R.	ALP	Hand, G. Bolkus, N. Howe, B.	ALP ALP ALP	Duffy, M.	ALP
27			Evans, G.		Ray, R.	ALP	Hand, G. Bolkus, N.	ALP ALP	Duffy, M.	ALP
28	Howe, B.	ALP	Evans, G.	ALP	Ray, R.	ALP	Howe, B. Bolkus, N. McMullen, B.	ALP ALP ALP	Kerr, D. Lavarch, M.	ALP ALP
29	Fischer, T.	NP	Downer, A.	LIB	McLachlan, I	LIB				

Gov	Finance	Py	EconomicAff.	Py	Labour	Py	Education	Py	Health	Py
1	Chifley, J.B.	ALP			Holloway, E.J.	ALP			Fraser, J.M.	ALP
2	Chifley, J.B.	ALP			Holloway, E.J.	ALP			McKenna, N.E.	ALP
3	Fadden, A.W.	CNT			Holt, H.E.	LIB			Page, E.	CNT
4	Fadden, A.W.	CNT			Holt, H.E.	LIB			Page, E.	CNT
5	Fadden, A.W.	CNT			Holt, H.E.	LIB			Page, E.	CNT
6	Fadden, A.W.	CNT			Holt, H.E.	LIB				
7	Holt, H.E.	LIB			McMahon, W.	LIB	Casey, R.G.	LIB		
8	Holt, H.E.	LIB			McMahon, W.	LIB				
9	Holt, H.E.	LIB			McMahon, W.	LIB			Wade, H.W.	CNT
10	McMahon, W.	LIB			Bury, L.H.E.	LIB	Gorton, J.G.	LIB		
11	McMahon, W.	LIB			Bury, L.H.E.	LIB	Gorton, J.G.	LIB		
12	McMahon, W.	LIB			Bury, L.H.E.	LIB	Gorton, J.G.	LIB		

AUSTRALIA 1945–1998

Gov	Finance	Py	EconomicAff.	Py	Labour	Py	Education	Py	Health	Py
13	McMahon, W.	LIB			Bury, L.H.E.	LIB	Fraser, J.M.	LIB		
14	McMahon, W.	LIB			Bury, L.H.E.	LIB	Fraser, J.M.	LIB		
15	Bury, L.H.E.	LIB			Snedden, B.M.	LIB	Bowen, N.H.	LIB		
16	Snedden, B.M.	LIB			Lynch, P.R.	LIB	Fairbairn, D.	LIB		
17	Crean, F.	ALP			Cameron, C.R.	ALP	Beazley, K.E. / Morrison, W.L.	ALP / ALP	Everingham, D.N.	ALP
18	Crean, F.	ALP			Cameron, C.R.	ALP	Beazley, K.E. / Morrison, W.L.	ALP / ALP	Everingham, D.N.	ALP
19	Lynch, P.R.	LIB			Street, A.A.	LIB	*Guilfoyle, M.G.C. / Cotton, R.C.	LIB / LIB	Chipp, D.	LIB
20	Lynch, P.R.	LIB			Street, A.A.	LIB	Garrick, J.L.	LIB		
21	Robinson, E. / Howard, J.	LIB / LIB			Street, A.A.	LIB	Garrick, J.L.	LIB		
22	Howard, J. / *Guilfoyle, M.G.C.	LIB / LIB			Viner, I.	LIB				
23	Keating, P.	ALP			Willis, R.	ALP	*Ryan, S.	ALP		
24	Keating, P. / Walsh, P.	ALP / ALP			Willis, R.	ALP	*Ryan, S.	ALP		
25	Keating, P. / Walsh, P.	ALP / ALP			Dawkins, J.	ALP	Dawkins, J.	ALP	Blewett, N.	ALP
26	Keating, P. / Willis, R.	ALP / ALP			Dawkins, J.	ALP	Dawkins, J.	ALP	Howe, B. / Blewett, N.	ALP / ALP
27	Dawkins, J. / Willis, R.	ALP / ALP			Beazley, K.	ALP	Button, J. / Beazley, K.	ALP / ALP	Howe, B.	ALP
28	Dawkins, J. / Willis, R.	ALP / ALP			Beazley, K.	ALP	Beazley, K. / Griffiths, A.	ALP / ALP	Richardson, G.	ALP
29	Costello, P. / Fahey, J.	LIB / LIB			Reith, P. / *Vanstone, A.	LIB / LIB	Moore, J. / *Vanstone, A.	LIB / LIB	Wooldridge, M.	LIB / LIB

AUSTRALIA 1945–1998

Gov	Housing	Py	Agriculture	Py	Industry/Trade	Py	Environment	Py
1	Lazzarini, H.P.	ALP	Scully, W.J.	ALP	Ashley, W.P.	ALP		
					Scully, W.J.	ALP		
					Keane, R.V.	ALP		
2	Lemmon, N.	ALP	Pollard, R.T.	ALP	Courtice, B.	ALP		
					Ashley, W.P.	ALP		
					Pollard, R.T.	ALP		
3	Casey, R.G.	LIB	McEwen, J.	CNT	McEwen, J.	CNT		
					O'Sullivan, L.	LIB		
					Casey, R.G.	LIB		
4	Kent Hughes, W.S.	LIB	McEwen, J.	CNT	McEwen, J.	CNT		
					O'Sullivan, N.	LIB		
					Beale, H.O.	LIB		
5	Kent Hughes, W.S.	LIB	McLeay, G.	LIB	McEwen, J.	CNT		
					McLeay, G.	LIB		
					O'Sullivan, N.	LIB		
					Beale, H.O.	LIB		
6					McEwen, J.	CNT		
7					McEwen, J.	CNT		
8			Adermann, C.F.	CNT	McEwen, J.	CNT		
9			Adermann, C.F.	CNT	McEwen, J.	CNT		
					Henty, N.H.D.	LIB		
					Fairhall, A.	LIB		
10			Adermann, C.F.	CNT	McEwen, J.	CNT		
					Henty, N.H.D.	LIB		
11			Adermann, C.F.	CNT	McEwen, J.	CNT		
					Henty, N.H.D.	LIB		

AUSTRALIA 1945–1998

Gov	Housing	Py	Agriculture	Py	Industry/Trade	Py	Environment	Py
12			Anthony, J.D.	CNT	McEwen, J.	CNT		
					Henty, N.H.D.	LIB		
13			Anthony, J.D.	CNT	McEwen, J.	CNT		
					Anderson, K.M.	LIB		
14			Anthony, J.D.	CNT	McEwen, J.	CNT		
					Anderson, K.M.	LIB		
					Sinclair, I.M.	CNT		
15			Anthony, J.D.	CNT	McEwen, J.	CNT		
					Anderson, K.M.	LIB		
					Sinclair, I.M.	CNT		
16			Sinclair, I.M.	CNT	Anthony, J.D.	CNT		
					Anderson, K.M.	LIB		
17	Johnson, L.R.	ALP	Wreidt, K.S.	ALP	Murphy, L.K.	ALP	Cass, M.H.	ALP
					Cairns, J.F.	ALP		
					Connor, R.F.X.	ALP		
18	Johnson, L.R.	ALP	Wreidt, K.S.	ALP	Murphy, L.K.	ALP	Cass, M.H.	ALP
					Cairns, J.F.	ALP		
					Connor, R.F.X.	ALP		
					Enderby, K.E.	ALP		
19	Carrick, J.L.	LIB	Sinclair, I.M.	CNT	Anthony, J.D.	CNT	Peacock, A.S.	LIB
					Greenwood, I.	LIB		
					Cotton, R.C.	LIB		
20	Greenwood, I.J.	LIB	Sinclair, I.M.	CNT	Anthony, J.D.	CNT	Greenwood, I.J.	LIB
					Cotton, R.C.	LIB		
21			Sinclair, I.M.	CNT	Anthony, J.D.	CNT		
					Lynch, P.R.	LIB		
22			Nixon, P.J.	CNT	Anthony, J.D.	CNT		
					Lynch, P.R.	LIB		

AUSTRALIA 1945–1998

Gov	Housing	Py	Agriculture	Py	Industry/Trade	Py	Environment	Py
23					Bowen, L.	ALP		
					Button, J.	ALP		
					Walsh, P.	ALP		
24	West, S.	ALP	Kerin, J.	ALP	Button, J.	ALP		
					Evans, G.	ALP		
					Dawkins, J.	ALP		
25			Kerin, J.	ALP	Button, J.	ALP	Brown, J.	ALP
26			Kerin, J.	ALP	Evans, G.	ALP	*Kelly, R.	ALP
27	Howe, B.	ALP	Button, J.	ALP	*Kelly, R.	ALP		
			Evans, G.	ALP				
28	Howe, B.	ALP	Crean, S.	ALP	Cook, P.	ALP	*Kelly, R.	ALP
					Griffiths, A.	ALP		
29					Fischer, T.	LIB	Hill, R.	LIB
					Anderson, J.	LIB		
					Moore, J.	LIB		

Gov	SOCIAL AFFAIRS (PY)	PUBLIC WORKS (PY)	OTHER (PY)	RES
1	Holloway, E.J. (ALP)	Drakeford, A.S. (ALP)	Ward, E.J. (ALP)	2
	Frost, C.W. (ALP)	Calwell, A.A. (ALP)		
	Calwell, A.A. (ALP)	Lazzarini, H.P. (ALP)		
	Fraser, J.M. (ALP)	Dedman, J.J. (ALP)		
		Ward, E.J. (ALP)		
		Cameron, D. (ALP)		

AUSTRALIA 1945–1998

Gov	Social Affairs (py)	Public Works (py)	Other (py)	Res
2	Holloway, E.J. (ALP) Barnard, H.C. (ALP) McKenna, N.E. (ALP) Calwell, A.A. (ALP)	Drakeford, A.S. (ALP) Dedman, J.J. (ALP) Cameron, D. (ALP) Calwell, A.A. (ALP) Lemmon, N. (ALP) Ward, E.J. (ALP)	Ward, E.J. (ALP)	0
3	Holt, H.E. (LIB) Cooper, W.J. (CNT) Spooner, W.H. (LIB)	Harrison, E.J. (LIB) White, T.D. (LIB) Anthony, H.L. (CNT) McLeay, G. (LIB) Beale, O.H. (LIB) Casey, R.G. (LIB)	Spender, P.C. (LIB)	3
4	Holt, H.E. (LIB) Cooper, W.J. (CNT) Townley, A.G. (LIB)	Kent Hughes, W.S. (LIB) McLeay, G. (LIB) Anthony, H.L. (CNT) Spooner, W.H. (LIB)	Hasluck, P.M.C. (LIB)	1
5	Holt, H.E. (LIB) Cooper, W.J. (CNT) McMahon, W. (LIB)	Townley, A.G. (LIB) Kent Hughes, W.S. (LIB) Anthony, H.L. (CNT) Spooner, W.H. (LIB) McLeay, G. (LIB)	Harrison, E.J. (LIB) Hasluck, P.M.C. (LIB)	0
6	Holt, H.E. (LIB)	Townley, A.G. (LIB) Spooner, W.H. (LIB)	O'Sullivan, N. (LIB) Hasluck, P.M.C. (LIB)	4
7	McMahon, W. (LIB) Downer, A.R. (LIB)	Spooner, W.H. (LIB) Paltridge, S.D. (LIB) Davidson, C.W. (LIB)	Spooner, W.H. (LIB) Hasluck, P.M.C. (LIB)	1
8	McMahon, W. (LIB) Downer, A.R. (LIB)	Spooner, W.H. (LIB) Paltridge, S.D. (LIB) Davidson, C.W. (LIB)	Hasluck, P.M.C. (LIB)	0

AUSTRALIA 1945–1998

Gov	Social Affairs (py)	Public Works (py)	Other (py)	Res
9	McMahon, W. (LIB)	Spooner, W.H. (LIB) Paltridge, S.D. (LIB)		3
10	Bury, L.H.E. (LIB)	Hulme, A.S. (LIB) Fairbairn, D. (LIB) Gorton, J.G. (LIB)	Fairbairn, D. (LIB) Henty, N.H.D. (LIB) Barnes, C.E. (CNT)	0
11	Bury, L.H.E. (LIB)	Hulme, A.S. (LIB) Fairbairn, D. (LIB)	Gorton, J.G. (LIB) Henty, N.H.D. (LIB)	1
12	Bury, L.H.E. (LIB) Sinclair, I.M. (CNT)	Hulme, A.S. (LIB) Fairbairn, D. (LIB)	Gorton, J.G. (LIB)	0
13	Bury, L.H.E. (LIB)	Sinclair, I.M. (CNT) Hulme, A.S. (LIB) Fairbairn, D. (LIB)		0
14	Bury, L.H.E. (LIB)	Sinclair, I.M. (CNT) Hulme, A.S. (LIB) Fairbairn, D. (LIB)	Anderson, K. (LIB)	0
15	Snedden, B.M. (LIB)	Hulme, A.S. (LIB) Sinclair, I.M. (CNT) Swartz, R.W.C. (LIB)	Snedden, B.M. (LIB) Anderson, K.M. (LIB)	2
16	Lynch, P.R. (LIB)	Swartz, R.W.C. (LIB) Hulme, A.S. (LIB) Nixon, P.J. (CNT)	Swartz, R.W.C. (LIB) Anderson, K.M. (LIB)	1
17	Hayden, W.G. (ALP) Grassby, A.J. (ALP) Bishop, R. (ALP)	Cavanagh, J.L. (ALP) Patterson, R.A. (ALP) McClelland, D. (ALP) Daly, F.M. (ALP) Uren, T. (ALP) Jones, C.K. (ALP) Bowen, L.F. (ALP) Connor, R.F.X. (ALP)	Murphy, L.K. (ALP) Daly, F.M. (ALP) Willesee, D. (ALP) Bryant, G.M. (ALP) Stewart, F.E. (ALP) Enderby, K.E. (ALP)	2

AUSTRALIA 1945–1998

Gov	Social Affairs (py)	Public Works (py)	Other (py)	Res
18	Cameron, C.R. (ALP) Hayden, W.G. (ALP) Wheeldon, J. (ALP)	Patterson, R.A. (ALP) McClelland, D. (ALP) Uren, T. (ALP) Bowen, L.F. (ALP) Bishop, R. (ALP) Jones, C.K. (ALP) Daly, F.M. (ALP) Connor, R.F.X. (ALP)	Willesee, D. (ALP) Murphy, L.K. (ALP) Patterson, R.A. (ALP) Daly, F.M. (ALP) Cavanagh, J.L. (ALP) Bryant, G.M. (ALP) Stewart, F.E. (ALP)	5
19	Street, A.A. (LIB) Chipp, D. (LIB) Cotton, R.C. (LIB)	Anthony, J.D. (CNT) Carrick, J.L. (LIB) Nixon, P.J. (CNT) Withers, R.G. (LIB)	Sinclair, I.M. (CNT) Withers, R.G. (LIB) Drake-Brockman, T. (CNT)	0
20	Street, A.A. (LIB)	Nixon, P.J. (CNT)	Garrick, J.L. (LIB) Greenwood, I.J. (LIB)	2
21	Street, A.A. (LIB) *Guilfoyle, M.G.C. (LIB)	Nixon, P.J. (CNT)	Viner, I. (LIB)	4
22	Viner, I. (LIB) Peacock, A.S. (LIB) Chaney, F. (LIB)	Sinclair, I.M. (CNT) Garrick, J. (LIB)	Sinclair, I.M. (CNT) Garrick, J. (LIB)	3
23	Willis, R. (ALP) West, S. (ALP) Grimes, D. (ALP) *Ryan, S. (ALP)	Walsh, P. (ALP)	West, S. (ALP) Young, M. (ALP)	3
24	Willis, R. (ALP) Hurford, C. (ALP) Howe, B. (ALP)	Grimes, D. (ALP) Evans, G. (ALP)	Hurford, C. (ALP) Button, J. (ALP) Young, M. (ALP)	1
25	Young, M. (ALP) Willis, R. (ALP) Howe, B. (ALP)	Evans, G. (ALP) Kerin, J. (ALP) Blewett, N. (ALP)	Young, M. (ALP) Button, J. (ALP) Brown, J. (ALP)	2

AUSTRALIA 1945–1998

Gov	Social Affairs (py)	Public Works (py)	Other (py)	Res
26	Richardson, G. (ALP) Hand, G. (ALP) Cook, P. (ALP)	Blewett, N. (ALP) Kerin, J. (ALP)	Button, J. (ALP) Hand, G. (ALP) *Kelly, R. (ALP)	4
27	Blewett, N. (ALP) *Kelly, R. (ALP) Cook, P. (ALP)	Howe, B. (ALP) Richardson, G. (ALP) Griffiths, A. (ALP) Collins, B. (ALP) Crean, S. (ALP)	Howe, B. (ALP) Hand, G. (ALP) *Kelly, R. (ALP) Griffiths, A. (ALP)	1
28	Faulkner, J. (ALP) *Kelly, R. (ALP) Brereton, L. (ALP)	Howe, B. (ALP) Crean, S. (ALP) Collins, B. (ALP)	*Kelly, R. (ALP) Bolkus, N. (ALP) Griffiths, A. (ALP) Lee, M. (ALP)	3
29	*Newman, J. (LIB) Wooldridge, M. (LIB) *Vanstone, A. (LIB)	Anderson, J. (LIB) Alston, R. (LIB) Sharp, J. (LIB)	Hill, R. (LIB) Alston, R. (LIB) *Newman, J. (LIB) Moore, J. (LIB) Sharp, J. (LIB)	

5. AUSTRIA

The Head of State is a President directly elected for six years, with a maximum of two terms.

Austria is a quasi-federal state. Although the states (Länder) share powers with the federal government their competencies are limited if not obsolete. Most areas of policymaking are centralised, as is the case with fiscal authority.

Parliament is bicameral with an Upper House (Bundesrat) of 63 seats, elected by the parliaments of the states for a period of five to six years. The Lower House (Nationalrat) of 183 seats is directly elected by proportional representation (Hare) for a fixed term of four years in multi-member constituencies of variable size, as they cannot cut through Länder boundaries. The smallest constituency, Burgenland (207,000 electors) has 3 seats. The threshold for the Lower House is 4%, and a party must have gained at least one seat in one of the constituencies. The Nationalrat has substantially more powers than the Bundesrat.

Parliament has a quorum of one-third of all members. Votes are carried by an absolute majority of all members present. Constitutional amendments need a two-thirds majority of all members in both Houses. For certain issues a referendum is constitutionally required. Both government and parliament may call a referendum. The outcome is binding

The Chancellor (Prime Minister) is appointed by the President and he forms the government. The President is not part of the government. No vote of investiture is needed, but in practice governments must rely on a majority in parliament. During its lifetime the government can face a vote of no confidence. Losing a vote of confidence always results in resignation of the government. Government is collectively responsible to parliament. Individual ministers may also be members of parliament. The Chancellor has a dominant position in government.

The Constitutional Court reviews cases concerning the constitution and federal laws. The Head of State may also request a constitutional review of lawmaking.

AUSTRIA 1945–1998

Gov	Begin	Dur	Rft	Tog	Py1	Py2	Py3	Seats	CPG	Nom	Prime Minister (Py)
1	18.12.45	1420	1	3	ÖVP 85	SPÖ 76	KPÖ 4	165	4	13	Figl, L. (ÖVP)
2	07.11.49	1242	4	2	ÖVP 77	SPÖ 67		165	4	11	Figl, L. (ÖVP)
4	23.06.56	1117	1	2	ÖVP 82	SPÖ 74		165	4	12	Raab, J. (ÖVP)
3	02.04.53	1178	4	2	ÖVP 74	SPÖ 73		165	4	11	Raab, J. (ÖVP)
5	15.07.59	476	3	2	ÖVP 79	SPÖ 78		165	4	12	Raab, J. (ÖVP)
6	04.11.60	159	1	2	ÖVP 79	SPÖ 78		165	4	12	Raab, J. (ÖVP)
7	12.04.61	711	2	2	ÖVP 79	SPÖ 78		165	4	12	Gorbach, A. (ÖVP)
8	24.03.63	376	4	2	ÖVP 81	SPÖ 76		165	4	12	Gorbach, A. (ÖVP)
9	03.04.64	568	1	2	ÖVP 81	SPÖ 76		165	4	12	Klaus, J. (ÖVP)
10	23.10.65	178	1	2	ÖVP 81	SPÖ 76		165	4	12	Klaus, J. (ÖVP)
11	19.04.66	1464	1	1	ÖVP 85			165	3	13	Klaus, J. (ÖVP)
12	22.04.70	548	1	4	SPÖ 81			165	4	13	Kreisky, B. (SPÖ)
13	22.10.71	1468	1	1	SPÖ 93			183	4	14	Kreisky, B. (SPÖ)
14	29.10.75	1289	1	1	SPÖ 93			183	4	14	Kreisky, B. (SPÖ)
15	10.05.79	1475	1	1	SPÖ 95			183	4	14	Kreisky, B. (SPÖ)
16	24.05.83	1119	2	2	SPÖ 90	FPÖ 11		183	4	15	Sinowatz, F. (SPÖ)
17	16.06.86	219	1	2	SPÖ 90	FPÖ 12		183	4	16	Vranitzky, F. (SPÖ)
18	21.01.87	1425	1	2	SPÖ 80	ÖVP 77		183	4	15	Vranitzky, F. (SPÖ)
19	17.12.90	1444	1	2	SPÖ 80	ÖVP 60		183	4	15	Vranitzky, F. (SPÖ)
20	30.11.94	468	4	2	SPÖ 65	ÖVP 52		183	4	16	Vranitzky, F. (SPÖ)
21	12.03.96			2	SPÖ 71	ÖVP 40		183	4	14	Vranitzky, F. (SPÖ)

-Gov 1: KPÖ-minister Altmann, K. stepped down from government on November 19, 1947.

AUSTRIA 1945–1998

Gov	Deputy PM	Py	Foreign Affairs	Py	Defence	Py	Interior	Py	Justice	Py
1	Schärf, A.	SPÖ	Figl, L.	ÖVP			Helmer, O.	SPÖ	Gerö, J.	NONA
2	Schärf, A.	SPÖ	Gruber, K.	ÖVP			Helmer, O.	SPÖ	Tschadek, O.	SPÖ
3	Schärf, A.	SPÖ	Gruber, K.	ÖVP			Helmer, O.	SPÖ	Gerö, J.	NONA
4	Schärf, A.	SPÖ	Figl, L.	ÖVP	Graf, F.	ÖVP	Helmer, O.	SPÖ	Tschadek, O.	SPÖ
5	Pittermann, B.	SPÖ	Kreisky, B.	SPÖ	Graf, F.	ÖVP	Afritsch, J.	SPÖ	Tschadek, O.	SPÖ
6	Pittermann, B.	SPÖ	Kreisky, B.	SPÖ	Graf, F.	ÖVP	Afritsch, J.	SPÖ	Broda, C.	SPÖ
7	Pittermann, B.	SPÖ	Kreisky, B.	SPÖ	Schleinzer, K.	ÖVP	Afritsch, J.	SPÖ	Broda, C.	SPÖ
8	Pittermann, B.	SPÖ	Kreisky, B.	SPÖ	Schleinzer, K.	ÖVP	Olah, F.	SPÖ	Broda, C.	SPÖ
9	Pittermann, B.	SPÖ	Kreisky, B.	SPÖ	Prader, G.	ÖVP	Olah, F.	SPÖ	Broda, C.	SPÖ
10	Pittermann, B.	SPÖ	Kreisky, B.	SPÖ	Prader, G.	ÖVP	Czettel, H.	SPÖ	Broda, C.	SPÖ
11	Bock, F.J.	ÖVP	Toncik-Sorinj, L.	ÖVP	Prader, G.	ÖVP	Hetzenauer, F.	ÖVP	Klecatsky, H.	ÖVP
12	Häuser, R.	SPÖ	Kirchschläger, R.	SPÖ	Freihsler, J.	SPÖ	Rösch, O.	SPÖ	Broda, C.	SPÖ
13	Häuser, R.	SPÖ	Kirchschläger, R.	SPÖ	Lütgendorf, K.	SPÖ	Rösch, O.	SPÖ	Broda, C.	SPÖ
14	Häuser, R.	SPÖ	Bielka-Karltreu, E.	SPÖ	Lütgendorf, K.	SPÖ	Rösch, O.	SPÖ	Broda, C.	SPÖ
15	Androsch, H.	SPÖ	Pahr, W.	SPÖ	Lanc, E.	SPÖ	Lausecker, K.	SPÖ	Broda, C.	SPÖ
16	Steger, N.	FPÖ	Lanc, E.	SPÖ	Frischenschlager, F.	FPÖ	Blecha, K.	SPÖ	Ofner, H.	FPÖ
17	Steger, N.	FPÖ	Jankowitsch, P.	SPÖ	Krünes, H.	FPÖ	Blecha, K.	SPÖ	Ofner, H.	FPÖ
18	Mock, A.	ÖVP	Mock, A.	ÖVP	Lichal, R.	ÖVP	Blecha, K.	SPÖ	Foregger, E.	NONA
19	Riegler, J.	ÖVP	Mock, A.	ÖVP	Fasslabend, W.	ÖVP	Löschnak, F. / Riegler, J.	SPÖ / ÖVP	Michalek, N.	NONA
20	Busek, E.	ÖVP	Mock, A.	ÖVP	Fasslabend, W.	ÖVP	Löschnak, F.	SPÖ	Michalek, M.	NONA
21	Schüssel, W.	ÖVP	Schüssel, W.	ÖVP	Fasslabend, W.	ÖVP	Einem, C.	SPÖ	Michalek, N.	NONA

AUSTRIA 1945–1998

Gov	Finance	Py	Economic Aff.	Py	Labour	Py	Education	Py	Health	Py
1	Zimmermann, G.	NONA					Hurdes, F.	ÖVP		
2	Margaretha, E.	ÖVP					Hurdes, F.	ÖVP		
3	Kamitz, R.	ÖVP					Kolb, E.	ÖVP		
4	Kamitz, R.	ÖVP					Drimmel, H.	ÖVP		
5	Kamitz, R.	ÖVP					Drimmel, H.	ÖVP		
6	Heilingsetzer, E.	ÖVP					Drimmel, H.	ÖVP		
7	Klaus, J.	ÖVP					Drimmel, H.	ÖVP		
8	Korinek, F.	ÖVP					Drimmel, H.	ÖVP		
9	Schmitz, W.	ÖVP					Pıffl-Percevic, T.	ÖVP		
10	Schmitz, W.	ÖVP	Bock, F.	ÖVP			Pıffl-Percevic, T.	ÖVP		
11	Schmitz, W.	ÖVP					Pıffl-Percevik, T.; Kotzina, V.	ÖVP; ÖVP		
12	Androsch, H.	SPÖ					Gratz, L.; Firnberg, H.	SPÖ; SPÖ		
13	Androsch, H.	SPÖ					Sinowatz, A.; Firnberg, H.	SPÖ; SPÖ	*Leodolter, I.	SPÖ
14	Androsch, H.	SPÖ					Sinowatz, A.; Firnberg, H.	SPÖ; SPÖ	*Leodolter, I.	SPÖ
15	Androsch, H.	SPÖ					Sinowatz, A.; Firnberg, H.	SPÖ; SPÖ	*Leodolter, I.	SPÖ
16	Salcher, H.	SPÖ					Zilk, H.; Fischer, H.; Sekanina, K.	SPÖ; SPÖ; SPÖ	Steyrer, K.	SPÖ
17	Lacina, F.	SPÖ					Moritz, H.; Fischer, H.	SPÖ; SPÖ	Kreuzer, F.	SPÖ
18	Lacina, F.	SPÖ	Graf, R.	ÖVP	Dallinger, A.	SPÖ	*Hawlicek, H.; Tuppy, H.	SPÖ; ÖVP		

AUSTRIA 1945–1998

Gov	Finance	Py	EconomicAff.	Py	Labour	Py	Education	Py	Health	Py
19	Lacina, F.	SPÖ	Schüssel, W. / Streicher, R.	ÖVP / ÖVP	Hesoun, J.	SPÖ	Scholten, R. / Busek, E.	SPÖ / ÖVP	Ettl, H.	SPÖ
20	Lacina, F.	SPÖ	Schüssel, W. / Klima, V.	ÖVP / SPÖ	Hesoun, J.	SPÖ	Busek, E. / Scholten, R.	ÖVP / SPÖ	*Krammer, C.	SPÖ
21	Klima, V.	SPÖ	Farnleitner, J.	ÖVP	Hums, F.	SPÖ	Scholten, R. / *Gehrer, E.	SPÖ / ÖVP	*Krammer, C.	SPÖ

Gov	Housing	Py	Agriculture	Py	Industry/Trade	Py	Environment	Py
1			Kraus, J.	ÖVP	Fleischacker, E.	ÖVP		
2			Kraus, J.	ÖVP	Waldbrunner, E. / Kolb, E.	SPÖ / ÖVP		
3			Thoma, F.	ÖVP	Waldbrunner, E. / Böck-Greissau, J.	SPÖ / ÖVP		
4			Thoma, F.	ÖVP	Illig, U.	ÖVP		
5			Hartmann, E.	ÖVP	Bock, F.J. / Pittermann, B.	ÖVP / SPÖ		
6			Hartmann, E.	ÖVP	Bock, F.J. / Pittermann, B.	ÖVP / SPÖ		
7			Hartmann, E.	ÖVP	Bock, F.J. / Pittermann, B.	ÖVP / SPÖ		
8			Hartmann, E.	ÖVP	Bock, F.J. / Pittermann, B.	ÖVP / SPÖ		
9			Schleinzer, K.	ÖVP	Bock, F.J.	ÖVP		
10			Schleinzer, K.	ÖVP		ÖVP		

AUSTRIA 1945–1998

Gov	Housing	Py	Agriculture	Py	Industry/Trade	Py	Environment	Py
11	Kotzina, V.	ÖVP	Schleinzer, K.	ÖVP	Bock, F.J.	ÖVP		
12			Öllinger, H.	SPÖ	Staribacher, J.	SPÖ		
13			Weihs, O.	SPÖ	Staribacher, J.	SPÖ	*Leodolter, I.	SPÖ
14			Weihs, O.	SPÖ	Staribacher, J.	SPÖ	*Leodolter, I.	SPÖ
15			Haiden, G.	SPÖ	Staribacher, J.	SPÖ	*Leodolter, I.	SPÖ
16			Haiden, G.	SPÖ	Steger, N.	FPÖ	Steyrer, K.	SPÖ
17			Schmidt, E.	SPÖ	Steger, N.	FPÖ	Kreuzer, F.	SPÖ
18			Riegler, J.	ÖVP	Streicher, R.	SPÖ	*Flemming, M.	ÖVP
19			Fischler, F.	ÖVP			*Flemming, M.	ÖVP
20			Molterer, W.	ÖVP			*Rauch-Kallat, M.	ÖVP
21			Molterer, W.	ÖVP			Bartenstein, M.	ÖVP

Gov	Social Affairs (py)	Public Works (py)	Other (py)	Res
1	Maisel, H.K. (SPÖ) Frenzel, H. (SPÖ)	Krauland, P. (ÖVP) Uebeleis, V. (SPÖ) Altmann, K. (KPÖ)		0
2	Maisel, H.K. (SPÖ)	Waldbrunner, E. (SPÖ) Kolb, E. (ÖVP)		1
3	Maisel, H.K. (SPÖ)	Waldbrunner, E. (SPÖ) Böck-Greissau, J. (ÖVP)		0
4	Proksch, H.A. (SPÖ)	Waldbrunner, K. (SPÖ) Illig, U. (ÖVP)		0
5	Proksch, H.A. (SPÖ)	Waldbrunner, K. (SPÖ)		0
6	Proksch, H.A. (SPÖ)	Waldbrunner, K. (SPÖ)		0

AUSTRIA 1945–1998

Gov	Social Affairs (py)	Public Works (py)	Other (py)	Res
7	Proksch, H.A. (SPÖ)	Waldbrunner, K. (SPÖ) Bock, F.J. (ÖVP)		0
8	Proksch, H.A. (SPÖ)	Probst, O. (SPÖ) Bock, F.J. (ÖVP)		0
9	Proksch, H.A. (SPÖ)	Probst, O. (SPÖ) Bock, F.J. (ÖVP)		0
10	Proksch, H.A. (SPÖ)	Probst, O. (SPÖ)		0
11	Rehor, G. (ÖVP)	Weiss, L. (ÖVP)		1
12	Häuser, R. (SPÖ)	Moser, J. (SPÖ) Frühbauer, E. (SPÖ)		0
13	Häuser, R. (SPÖ)	Moser, J. (SPÖ) Frühbauer, E. (SPÖ)		0
14	Häuser, R. (SPÖ)	Moser, J. (SPÖ) Lanc, E. (SPÖ)		2
15	Weissenberg, G. (SPÖ)	Rösch, O. (SPÖ) Moser, J. (SPÖ)		2
16	Dallinger, A. (SPÖ) *Karl, E. (SPÖ)	Sekanina, K. (SPÖ) Lausecker, K. (SPÖ) Steger, N. (FPÖ)		2
17	Dallinger, A. (SPÖ) *Fröhlich-Sandner, G. (SPÖ)	Übleis, H. (SPÖ) Streicher, R. (SPÖ) Steger, N. (FPÖ)	Löschnak, F. (SPÖ)	0
18	Dallinger, A. (SPÖ) *Flemming, M. (ÖVP)	Streicher, R. (SPÖ)	Löschnak, F. (SPÖ) Neisser, H. (ÖVP)	2
19	*Dohnal, J. (SPÖ) Hesoun, J. (SPÖ) Ettl, H. (SPÖ) *Flemming, M. (ÖVP)	Streicher, R. (ÖVP)	Scholten, R. (SPÖ)	2

AUSTRIA 1945–1998

Gov	Social Affairs (py)	Public Works (py)	Other (py)	Res
20	*Dohnal, J. (SPÖ) Hesoun, J. (SPÖ) *Krammer, C. (SPÖ) *Moser, S. (ÖVP)	Klima, V. (SPÖ)	Busek, E. (ÖVP) Scholten, R. (SPÖ)	2
21	Hums, F. (SPÖ) *Krammer, C. (SPÖ) *Konrad, H. (SPÖ)		*Gehrer, E. (ÖVP)	

6. BANGLADESH

The Head of State is a President elected indirectly.

The State is centralised and unitary.

Parliament is unicameral, with a House of 330 members elected for a five-year flexible term by plurality voting in constituencies of around 150,000 electors. Parliament has a quorum of one-fifth of all members. Votes are carried by a majority of all votes cast. Constitutional amendments require a two-thirds majority of all votes cast. A referendum is optional and may be called by the government. The outcome is binding.

The Prime Minister and Cabinet form the government. No vote of investiture is required, and a vote of no confidence is unlikely, as long as the government maintains a relative majority in parliament. The government will fall whenever it ceases to control a relative legislative majority. The government is both collectively and individually responsible to parliament. The Prime Minister and other government ministers are leaders and members of parliament for the party or electoral alliance with the majority of seats in Parliament. The Prime Minister has a dominant position in government.

There is a Supreme Court for constitutional review.

BANGLADESH 1973-1998

Gov	Begin	Dur	RfT	ToG	Py1	Py2	Py3	Seats	CPG	NoM	Prime Minister (py)
1	16.03.73	680	x	1	AL 293			300		21	Rahman, M. (AL)
2	15.04.79	957	x	1	BJD 207			300		31	Rahman, S.A. (BJD)
3	27.11.81	77	6	1	BJD 207			300		24	Rahman, S.A. (BJD)
4	12.02.82	40	x	1	BJD 207			300		12	Rahman, S.A. (BJD)
5	20.03.91	183	x	4	BJD 139 (+25)	[Jamaat-i-Islami 18]		300 (+30)		12	*Zia, K. (BJD)
6	19.09.91	1678	6	1	BJD 144 (+25)			300 (+30)		22	*Zia, K. (BJD)
7	03.04.96	61	1	6				300 (+30)		11	Rahman, M.H. (NONA)
8	23.06.96			3	AL 146	JD 32	JSD-Rab 1	300 (+30)		14	*Wajed, H. (AL)

- Insufficient information to classify governments on CPG-scale.
- [] Denotes party supporting the government without participating in it.
- Independence from Pakistan 26 March 1971.
- First general elections after independance 7 March 1973.
- Gov 1: Reason for termination is constitutional change to presidential system on 25 January 1975.
- Gov 2: Presidential system changed to a semi-presidential system. Parliament is a sovereign body with powers to impeach the president and approve the budget. The president and vice-president are part of the cabinet. The president is head of state and head of government. The prime minister chairs the cabinet meetings. Reason for Termination is assassination of the president during an attempted military coup on 30 May 1981.
- Gov 4: Reason for Termination is military coup on 24 March 1982.
- Gov 5: First government after free general elections on 27 February 1991. Parliament consisted of 300 elected seats, plus 30 seats reserved for women. Those seats were distributed among the elected parties proportionaly to the number of seats won in the election. BJD had 25 women seats. Reason for Termination is restauration of full parliamentary government by referendum.
- Gov 6: After by-elections on 11 September 1991 BJD had 144 elected seats plus 25 women seats.
- Gov 7: Care-taker government of non-aligned personalities to organise new elections after the elections of 25 February 1996 were widely challenged. New elections were held on 12 June 1996.
- Gov 8: Distribution of seats reserved for women unknown.

BANGLADESH 1973-1998

Gov	Deputy PM	Py	Foreign Affairs	Py	Defence	Py	Interior	Py	Justice	Py
1			Hossain, K.	AL	Rahman, D.	AL	Ukil, A.M.	AL	Dhar, M.	AL
							+Rahman, M.	AL		
2	Badruddoza Chowdhury, A.Q.M.	BJD	Huq, M.S.	BJD	++Rahman, Z.	BJD	Chowdhury, A.H.	BJD	+++Sattar, A.	BJD
	Ahmed, M.	BJD					Rahman, A.S.M.M.	BJD		
3	Ahmed, J.	BJD	Huq, M.S.	BJD	+++Sattar, A.	BJD	Matin, M.A.	BJD	Khan, T.H.	BJD
							Chowdhury, A.H.	BJD		
4			Huq, M.S.	BJD	+++Sattar, A.	BJD	Rahman, S.A.	BJD	Rahman, S.A.	BJD
							Matin, M.A.	BJD		
5			Rahman, A.S.M.M.	BJD			*Zia, K.	BJD	Hafiz, M.G.	BJD
							Talukder, A.S.	BJD		
6			Rahman, A.S.M.M.	BJD	*Zia, K.	BJD	*Zia, K.	BJD	Hafiz, M.G.	BJD
							Talukder, A.S.	BJD		
							Chowdhury, A.M.	BJD		
7			Rahman, M.H.	NONA			Rahman, M.H.	NONA	Ahmed, S.I.	NONA
							Ahmed, S.I.	NONA		
8			Azad, A.S.	AL	*Wajed, H.	AL	Rahman, M.Z.	AL		
							Uttam, R.I.B.	AL		

-Gov 1: +Rahman, M. not the PM.

-Gov 2: ++Rahman, Z. also president; +++ Sattar, A. also vice-president.

-Gov 3, 4: +++Sattar, A. also president.

BANGLADESH 1973-1998

Gov	Finance	Py	Economic Aff.	Py	Labour	Py	Education	Py	Health	Py
1	Ahmet, T.	AL	Rahman, M.	AL	Chowdhury, A.Z.A.	AL	Ali, M.Y.	AL	Chowdhury, M.	AL
2	Huda, M.N.	BJD	Majtab, F.	BJD	Bari, S.A.	BJD	+Rahman, Z.; Rahman, S.A.	BJD; BJD	Badruddoza Chowdhury, A.Q.M.	BJD
3	Rahman, M.S.	BJD	++Sattar, A.	BJD	Ahmed, R.	BJD	Rahman, S.A.	BJD	Biswar, A.R.	BJD
4	Mahtab, F.	BJD	++Sattar, A.	BJD	Hamid, K.A.	BJD	++Sattar, A.; Khan, T.H.	BJD; BJD	Hamid, K.A.	BJD
5	Rahman, S.	BJD	Rahman, S.; Ali, K.	BJD; BJD			Chowdhury, B.	BJD	Chowdhury, K.	BJD
6	Rahman, S.	BJD	Anwar, M.K.; Khan, Z.	BJD; BJD	Bhuiyan, A.M.	BJD	Sirkar, S.	BJD	Chowdhury, K.	BJD
7	Mahmud, W.	NONA	Chowdhury, S.B.; Mahmud, W.	NONA; NONA	*Chowdhury, N.	NONA	Yumus, M.; Haq, S.	NONA; NONA	Khan, A.R.	NONA
8	Kibria, S.A.M.	AL	*Wajed, H.; Ahmed, T.	AL; AL	*Wajed, H.	AL	Sadeque, A.S.H.K.	AL	*Wajed, H.; Yousuf, S.	AL; AL

- Gov 2: +Rahman, Z. also president.
- Gov 3, 4: ++Sattar, A. also president.

Gov	Housing	Py	Agriculture	Py	Industry/Trade	Py	Environment	Py
1	Hussain, M.S.	AL	Samad, M.A.; Serniabat, A.R.	AL; AL	Islam, S.N.; Kamaruzzaman, A.H.M.	AL; AL		AL; AL
2			Islam, N.; Rahman, K.M.O.	BJD; BJD	Rahman, M.S.; Ahmed, J.; Biswas, A.R.; Ali, M.			BJD; BJD; BJD; BJD

BANGLADESH 1973-1998

Gov	Housing	Py	Agriculture	Py	Industry/Trade	Py	Environment	Py
3			Mahtab, F	BJD	Ahmed, J.	BJD		
					Rahman, A.S.M.M.	BJD		
					Ali, Y.	BJD		
4			Choudhury, A.H.	BJD	+Huda, M.N.	BJD		
					Ali, Y.	BJD		
5			Haq, M.	BJD	Khan, S.I.	BJD		
6			Haq, M.	BJD	Khan, S.I.	BJD	Al-Noman, A.	BJD
			Islam, M.S.	BJD				
			Shah, H.	BJD				
			Al-Noman, A.	BJD				
7	Elaki, S.M.	NONA	Yumus, M.	NONA	Chowdhury, S.B.	NONA	Yumus, M.	NONA
			Chowdhury, S.B.	NONA				
			Nasiruddin, A.Z.M.	NONA				
8			*Wajed, H.	AL	*Wajed, H.	AL	*Wajed, H.	AL
			*Choudry, M.	AL	Ahmed, T.	AL		

- Gov 4: +Huda, M.N. also vice-president.

BANGLADESH 1973-1998

Gov	Social Affairs (py)	Public Works (py)	Other (py)	Res
1	Chowdhury, A.Z.A. (AL)	Ali, M. (AL)	Rahman, M. (AL)	2
		Ahmed, K.M. (AL)	Ahmet, T. (AL)	
		Aziz, A. (AL)	Ahmed, K.M. (AL)	
		Majumder, P.B. (AL)	Ali, M.Y. (AL)	
		Hussain, M.S. (AL)	+Rahman, M. (AL)	
		Osmani, M.A.G. (AL)	Hussain, M.S. (AL)	
		ChowdhuryM. (AL)	Choudhury, M.M.R. (AL)	
			Serniabat, A.R. (AL)	
			Chowdhury, M. (AL)	
			Dhar, M. (AL)	
2	Chowdhury, S.H. (BJD)	Ahmed, M. (BJD)	++Rahman, Z. (BJD)	3
	Bari, S.A. (BJD)	Huq, N. (BJD)	+++Sattar, A. (BJD)	
	*Rahman, A. (BJD)	Akim, A. (BJD)	Huda, M.N. (BJD)	
	Hamid, K.A. (BJD)	Khan, H. (BJD)	Khan, A.M. (BJD)	
		Hussain, A. (BJD)	Huq, M.M. (BJD)	
		Matin, M.A. (BJD)	Chowdhury, A.H. (BJD)	
		Islam, M. (BJD)	Chowdhury, S.H. (BJD)	
			Matin, M.A. (BJD)	
			Huq, M.A. (BJD)	

BANGLADESH 1973-1998

Gov	Social Affairs (py)	Public Works (py)	Other (py)	Res
3	Chowdhury, S.H. (BJD) Qasim, A. (BJD)	Huq, M.M. (BJD) Chowdhury, S.H. (BJD) Hasnat, A. (BJD) Alim, A. (BJD) Haque, K.A. (BJD) Islam, A.K.M.M. (BJD) Siddiqui, L.K. (BJD)	Chowdhury, S.H. (BJD) Sarkar, E.A. (BJD) Khan, T.H. (BJD) Hasnat, A. (BJD) Khan, A.M. (BJD) Rahman, A. (BJD) Islam, A.K.M.M. (BJD) Chowdhury, A.H. (BJD) Siddiqui, L.K. (BJD)	0
4	Hamid, K.A. (BJD)	+++Sattar, A. (BJD) Choudhury, S.N. (BJD) Islam, A.K.M.M. (BJD) Khan, T.H. (BJD)	+++Sattar, A. (BJD) Rahman, S.A. (BJD) Islam, A.K.M.M. (BJD) Khan, T.H. (BJD)	0
5		*Zia, K. (BJD) Haq, M. (BJD) Ahmed, O. (BJD) Anwar, M.K. (BJD)	Talukder, A.S. (BJD)	0

BANGLADESH 1973-1998

Gov	Social Affairs (py)	Public Works (py)	Other (py)	Res
6	Islam, T. (BJD)	Haq, M. (BJD) Ahmed, O. (BJD) Ali, K. (BJD) Huda, N. (BJD) Hossain, K.M. (BJD) Mian, R.I. (BJD)	*Zia, K. (BJD) Talukder, A.S. (BJD)	2
7	Haq, S. (NONA) *Chowdhury, N. (NONA)	Rahman, M.H. (NONA) Elaki, S.M. (NONA) Chowdhury, J.R. (NONA)	Rahman, M.H. (NONA) Ahmed, S.I. (NONA) Haq, S. (NONA) Nasiruddin, A.Z.M. (NONA) Khan, A.R. (NONA) Elaki, S.M. (NONA)	0
8		*Wajed, H. (AL) Razzak, A. (AL) Khan, N. (AL) Nasim, M. (AL) Manju, A.H. (JD) Rab, A.S.M.A. (JSD-Rab)	*Wajed, H. (AL) Rahman, M.Z. (AL) *Choudhry, M. (AL)	1

- Gov 1: +Rahman, M. not the PM.
- Gov 2: ++Rahman, Z. also president; +++Sattar, A. also vice-president.
- Gov 4: ++++Sattar, A. also president.

7. BELGIUM

Belgium is a constitutional Monarchy. The constitution was substantially revised between 1970 and 1993. The King is Head of State with by and large only ceremonial duties.

The constitutional revision has dramatically changed the state format from a unitary in the direction of a federal system, as a result of linguistic divisions. The Federal Government is restricted to the powers that are expressly attributed to it. All other matters are given to the geographic regions (2) and/or communities (3). However, the state, including the fiscal authority, is still centralised, albeit in transition.

Parliament is bicameral: the linguistic communities (including the bi-lingual capital, Brussels), elect the Upper House (Senate) of 182 seats for a term of four years. The Lower House of Deputies of 212 seat is directly elected on the basis of proportional representation (Hare) for a fixed term of four years in twenty-one multi-member constituencies which vary in size of the number of electors. However, the quota of deputies elected from each constituency is recalculated for each election so as to equalise the number of votes required to elect a deputy across the constituencies. Parties need to collect at least 33% of the quota in at least one of the constituencies.

The Senate is considered to be a chamber of deliberation, whereas the House of Deputies has full legislative powers.

Parliament has a quorum of at least 50 per cent of all members. Votes are carried by a majority of all members present. Some issues require a majority of all members. Amendments to the constitution are subject to approval by a two-thirds majority of votes cast in both Houses after elections are held. The government can initiate a consultative referendum.

Government is parliamentary. A vote of investiture is formally required but can be ignored by King and Cabinet. The government may also face a vote of no confidence. Losing a vote of confidence always results in resignation of the government. Its members must be taken equally from the two regions, or states (Flanders and Wallonia). Government is collectively responsible to parliament. Individual ministers may also be members of parliament. The Prime Minister has no dominant position in government.

Constitutional review of legislation is limited and is exercised by the Court of Cassation and the Court of Arbitration.

BELGIUM 1945–1998

Gov	Begin	Dur	RfT	ToG	Py1	Py2	Py3	Py4	Py5	Py6	Seats	CPG	NoM	Prime Minister (py)
1	11.02.45	171	4	3	CVP 73	BSP 64	LP 33	KPB 9			181	4	18	Acker, A. van (BSP)
2	01.08.45	222	1	2	BSP 64	LP 33	KPB 10	DU 13	ICAT 6		181	3	18	Acker, A. van (BSP)
3	11.03.46	21	5	5	BSP 69	LP 17					202	4	17	Spaak, P.H. (BSP)
4	01.04.46	123	5	2	BSP 69	LP 17	KPB 23				202	4	19	Acker, A. van (BSP)
5	02.08.46	237	4	2	BSP 69	LP 17	KPB 23				202	4	19	Huysmans, C. (BSP)
6	27.03.47	610	5	2	BSP 69	CVP 92					202	4	19	Spaak, P.H. (BSP)
7	26.11.48	264	1	2	BSP 69	CVP 92					202	4	17	Spaak, P.H. (BSP)
8	17.08.49	317	4	2	CVP 105	LP 29					212	2	17	Eyskens, G. (CVP)
9	30.06.50	49	5	1	CVP 108						212	3	15	Duvieusart, J. (CVP)
10	18.08.50	515	4	1	CVP 108						212	3	16	Pholien, J. (CVP)
11	15.01.52	828	1	1	CVP 108	LP 25					212	3	16	Houtte, J. van (CVP)
12	22.04.54	1526	1	2	BSP 86	LP 25					212	4	16	Acker, A. van (BSP)
13	26.06.58	134	5	4	CVP 104						212	3	16	Eyskens, G. (CVP)
14	07.11.58	665	4	2	CVP 104	LP 21					212	2	21	Eyskens, G. (CVP)
15	02.09.60	235	1	2	CVP 104	LP 21					212	2	20	Eyskens, G. (CVP)
16	25.04.61	1555	1	2	CVP 96	BSP 84					212	4	20	Lefevre, T. (CVP)
17	28.07.65	235	4	2	CVP 77	BSP 64					212	4	20	Harmel, P. (CVP)
18	20.03.66	821	6	2	CVP 77	LP 48					212	2	19	Vandenboeynants, P. (CVP)
19	18.06.68	1312	4	2	CVP 69	BSP 59					212	4	27	Eyskens, G. (CVP)
20	21.01.72	371	4	2	CVP 47	PSC 20	BSP 61				212	4	19	Eyskens, G. (CVP)
21	26.01.73	454	5	3	BSP 61	CVP 47	PSC 20	PVV 20			212	4	22	Leburton, E. (BSP)
22	25.04.74	48	7	5	CVP 50	PSC 22	PVV 21	PLP 22			212	2	19	Tindemans, L. (CVP)
23	12.06.74	911	4	2	CVP 50	PSC 22	PVV 21	PLP 12	RW 13		212	3	21	Tindemans, L. (CVP)
24	09.12.76	176	5	2	CVP 50	PSC 22	PVV 21	PRLW 12	RW 13		212	3	25	Tindemans, L. (CVP)
25	03.06.77	504	4	3	CVP 56	PSC 24	BSP 62	FDF 10 20	VU 20		212	3	23	Tindemans, L. (CVP)
26	20.10.78	165	1	6	CVP 56	PSC 24	BSP 62	FDF 10	VU 20		212	3	22	Vandenboeynants, P. (PSC)

BELGIUM 1945–1998

Gov	Begin	Dur ·	RfT	ToG	Py1	Py2	Py3	Py4	Py5	Py6	Seats	CPG	NoM	Prime Minister (py)
27	03.04.79	295	4	3	CVP 57	PSC 25	BSP 26	PSB 32	FDF 11		212	4	25	Martens, W. (CVP)
28	23.01.80	116	5	2	CVP 57	PSC 25	BSP 26	PSB 32			212	4	24	Martens, W. (CVP)
29	18.05.80	157	4	3	CVP 57	PSC 25	BSP 26	PSB 32	PVV 22	PRL 14	212	3	27	Martens, W. (CVP)
30	22.10.80	166	4	2	CVP 57	PSC 25	BSP 26	PSB 32			212	4	25	Eyskens, G. (CVP)
31	06.04.81	255	4	2	CVP 57	PSC 25	BSP 26	PSB 32			212	4	25	Eyskens, G. (CVP)
32	17.12.81	1442	4	2	CVP 43	PSC 18	PVV 21	PRL 22			212	2	16	Martens, W. (CVP)
33	28.11.85	691	4	2	CVP 49	PSC 20	PVV 22	PRL 22			212	2	15	Martens, W. (CVP)
34	20.10.87	234	1	6	CVP 49	PSC 20	PVV 22	PRL 22			212	2	16	Martens, W. (CVP)
35	09.06.88	1373	1	2	CVP 43	PSC 19	PSB 40	BSP 32	VU 16		212	4	18	Martens, W. (CVP)
36	13.03.92	1194	1	2	CVP 39	PSC 18	PSB 35	BSP 27			212	4	15	Dehaene, J.-L. (CVP)
37	23.06.95			2	CVP 29	PSC 12	PSB 21	BSP 20			150	4	15	Dehaene, J.-L. (CVP)

- Gov 37·: First federal government under new constitution.

Gov	Deputy PM	Py	Foreign Affairs	Py	Defence	Py	Interior	Py	Justice	Py
1			Spaak, P.-H.	BSP	Mundeleer, L.	BSP	Glabbeke, A. van	LP	Warnaffe, Ch. du	CVP
2			Spaak, P.-H.	BSP	Mundeleer, L.	BSP	Glabbeke, A. van	LP	Gregoire, M.	DU
3	Acker, A. van	BSP	Spaak, P.-H.	BSP	Defraiteur, R.	NONA	Merlot, J.	BSP	Rolin, H.	BSP
4	Devèze, A.	LP	Spaak, P.-H.	BSP	Defraiteur, R.	NONA	Buisseret, A.	LP	Glabbecke, A. van	LP
5			Spaak, P.-H.	BSP	Defraiteur, R.	NONA	Buisseret, A.	LP	Lilar, A.	LP
6			Spaak, P.-H.	BSP	Defraiteur, R.	NONA	Vermeylen, P.	BSP	Struye, P.	CVP
7	Eyskens, G.	CVP	Spaak, P.-H.	BSP	Defraiteur, R.	NONA	Vermeylen, P. / Merlot, J.	BSP / BSP	Melen, H.M. de	CVP
8	Devèze, A.	LP	Zeeland, P. van		Devèze, A.	CVP	Vleeschauwer, A. de	LP	Lilar, A.	LP
9		CVP	Zeeland, P. van		Melen, H.M. de	CVP	Vleeschauwer, A. de	CVP	Wiart, H.C. de	CVP
10			Zeeland, P. van	CVP	Greef, E. de	CVP	Brasseur, M.	NONA	Moyersoen, L.	CVP

BELGIUM 1945–1998

Gov	Deputy PM	Py	Foreign Affairs	Py	Defence	Py	Interior	Py	Justice	Py
11			Zeeland, P. van	CVP	Greef, E. de	NONA	Moyersoen, L.	CVP	Pholien, J.	CVP
12			Spaak, P.-H.	BSP	Spinoy, A.	BSP	Vermeylen, P.	BSP	Lilar, A.	LP
13			Wigny, P.	CVP	Gilson, A.	CVP	Heger, Ch.	CVP	Harmel, P.	CVP
14	Lilar, A.	LP	Wigny, P.	CVP	Gilson, A.	CVP	Lefebvre, R.	LP	Merchiers, L.	LP
15	Lefebvre, R.	LP	Wigny, P.	CVP	Gilson, A.	CVP	Vreven, R. Harmel, P. Lefebvre, R	LP CVP LP	Lilar, A.	LP
16	Spaak, P.-H.	BSP	Spaak, P.-H.	BSP	Seghers, P.	BSP	Gilson, A.	CVP	Vermeylen, P.	BSP
17	Spinoy, A. Segers, P.-W. Leburton, E.	BSP CVP BSP	Spaak, P.-H.	BSP	Moyersoen, L.	BSP	Vranckx, A. Harmel, P.	BSP CVP	Wigny, P.	CVP
18	Clerq, W. de	PVV	Harmel, P.	CVP	Poswick, Ch.	CVP	Vanderpoorten, H.	PVV	Wigny, P.	CVP
19	Merlot, J.-J.	BSP	Harmel, P.	CVP	Segers, P.W.	CVP	Harmegnies, L. Pêtre, R.	BSP CVP	Vranckx, A.	BSP
20	Cools, A.	BSP	Harmel, P.	CVP	Vandenboeynants, P.	PSC	Eislande, R. van	CVP	Vranckx, A.	BSP
21	Tindemans, L. Clercq, W. de	CVP PVV	Eislande, R. van	CVP	Vandenboeynants, P.	CVP	Close, E. Hanotte, L.	BSP PVV	Vanderpoorten, H.	PVV
22			Eislande, R. van	CVP	Vandenboeynants, P.	CVP	Hanin, Ch.	PSC	Vanderpoorten, H.	PVV
23			Eislande, R. van	CVP	Vandenboeynants, P.	CVP	Michel, J. Perin, F. Vandekerckhove, R.	PSC RW CVP	Vanderpoorten, H.	PVV
24			Eislande, R. van	CVP	Vandenboeynants, P.	CVP	Michel, J. Toussaint, M. Vandekerckhove, R.	PSC PRLW CVP	Vanderpoorten, H.	PVV
25	Vandenboeynants, P. Hurez, L.	PSC BSP	Simonet, H.	BSP	Vandenboeynants, P.	PSC	Boel, H.	PSC	Eislande, R. van	CVP
26	Eislande R. van Hurez, L.	CVP BSP	Simonet, H.	BSP	Vandenboeynants, P.	PSC	Boel, H.	PSC	Eislande, R. van	CVP

BELGIUM 1945–1998

Gov	Deputy PM	Py	Foreign Affairs	Py	Defence	Py	Interior	Py	Justice	Py
27	Vandenboeynants Spitaels, G. Claes, W.	PSC BSP BSP	Simonet, H.	BSP	Vandenboeynants, P.	PSC	Gramme, G. Calewaert, W.	PSC BSP	Eislande, R. van	CVP
28	Desmarets, J. Spitaels, G. Claes, W.	PSC BSP BSP	Simonet, H.	BSP	Desmarets, J.	PSC	Gramme, G. Calewaert, W.	PSC BSP	Eislande, R. van	CVP
29	Vanderpoorten, H. Spitaels, G.	PVV BSP	Nothomb, C.F.	PSC	Poswick, Ch.	PRL	Vanderpoorten, H. Moureaux, P.	PVV PSB	Vanderpoorten, H.	PVV
30	Spitaels, G. Claes, W. Desmarets, J.	BSP BSP PSC	Nothomb, C.F.	PSC	Swaelen, F.	CVP	Mathot, G. Moureaux, P. Chabert, J.	BSP PSB CVP	Moureaux, P.	PSB
31	Mathot, G. Claes, W. Desmarets, J.	BSP BSP PSC	Nothomb, C.F.	PSC	Swaelen, F.	CVP	Mathot, G. Moureaux, P. Chabert, J.	BSP PSB CVP	Moureaux, P.	PSB
32	Nothomb, C. F. Gol, J. Clerq, W. de	PSC PRL PVV	Tindemans, L.	PSC	Vreven, F.	PVV	Nothomb, C. F. Gol, J. Dehaene, J.-L.	PSC PRL CVP	Moureaux, P.	PRL
33	Nothomb, C.F. Gol, J. Verhofstadt, G. Maystadt, P.	PSC PRL PVV PSC	Tindemans, L.	PSC	Donnéa, F.-X. de	PRL	Nothomb, C.F. Gol, J. Dehaene, J.-L.	PSC PRL CVP	Gol, J.	PRL
34	Nothomb, C.F. Gol, J. Verhofstadt, G. Maystadt, P.	PSC PRL PVV PSC	Tindemans, L.	PSC	Donnéa, F.-X. de	PRL	Gol, J. Dehaene, J.-L. Michel, J.	PRL CVP PSC	Gol, J.	PRL
35	Moureaux, P. Claes, W. Dehaene, J-L. Wathelet, M.	PSB BSP CVP PSC	Tindemans, L.	CVP	Coëme, G.	PSB	Moureaux, P. Dehaene, J-L. Tobback, L.	PSB CVP BSP	Wathelet, M.	PSC

BELGIUM 1945–1998

Gov	Deputy PM	Py	Foreign Affairs	Py	Defence	Py	Interior	Py	Justice	Py
	Schiltz, H.	VU								
36	Coëme, G. Claes, W. Wathelet, M.	PSB BSP PSC	Claes, W.	CVP	Delcroix, L.	BSP	Tobback, L.	CVP	Wathelet, M.	PSC
37	Van Rompuy, H. Di Rupo, E. Wathelet, M. Vande Lanotte, J.	CVP PS PSC SP	Derijke, E.	SP	Wathelet, M.	PSC	Vande Lanotte, J.	SP	De Clerck, S.	CVP

Gov	Finance	Py	Economic Aff.	Py	Labour	Py	Education	Py	Health	Py
1	Eyskens, G.	CVP	Smael, A. de	NONA	Troclet, L.-E.	BSP	Buisseret, A.	LP	Marteaux, A.	KPB
2	Voghel, F. de	NONA	Smael, A. de	NONA	Troclet, L.-E.	BS	Buisseret, A.	LP	Marteaux, A.	KPB
3	Voghel, F. de	NONA	Troclet, L.-E.	NONA	Acker, A. van	BSP	Collard, L.	BSP	Beneden, van	NONA
4	Voghel, F. de Merlot, J.	NONA BSP	Devèze, A.	NONA	Troclet, L.-E.	LP	Vos, H.	BSP	Marteaux, A.	KPB
5	Vauthier, J. Merlot, J.	NONA BSP	Liebaert, H.	NONA	Troclet, L.-E.	LP	Vos, H.	BSP	Marteaux, A.	KPB
6	Eyskens, G. Merlot, J.	CVP BSP	Groote, P. de	NONA	Troclet, L.-E.	BSP	Huysmans, C.	BSP	Verbist, A.	CVP
7	Eyskens, G.	CVP	Groote, P. de	CVP	Troclet, L.-E.	BSP	Huysmans, C.	BSP	Straeten-Waillet, X-F.	CVP
8	Liebaert, H.	LP	Duvieusart, J.	LP	Behogne, O.	CVP	Mundeleer, L.	LP	Glabbeke, A. van	LP
9	Houtte, J. van	CVP	Eyskens, G.	CVP	Behogne, O.	CVP	Harmel, P.	CVP	Taeye, A. de	CVP
10	Houtte, J. van	CVP	Coppé, A.	CVP	Daele, G. van den	CVP	Harmel, P.	CVP	Taeye, A. de	CVP
11	Janssen, A.-E.	CVP	Duvieusart, J.	CVP	Daele, G. van den	CVP	Harmel, P.	CVP	Taeye, A. de	CVP
12	Liebaert, H.	LP	Rey, J.	LP	Troclet, L.-E.	BSP	Collard, L.	BSP	Leburton, E.	BSP

134

BELGIUM 1945–1998

Gov	Finance	Py	Economic Aff.	Py	Labour	Py	Education	Py	Health	Py
13	Houtte, J. van	CVP	Scheyven, R.	CVP	Servais, L.	CVP	Hemelryck, M. van	CVP	Houben, R.	CVP
14	Houtte, J. van	CVP	Vanderschueren, J.	LP	Behogne, O.	CVP	Moureaux, Ch.	LP	Meyers, P.	CVP
15	Houtte, J. van	CVP	Vanderschueren, J. Dequae, A.	LP CVP	Urbain, Y.	CVP	Moureaux, Ch.	LP	Meyers, P.	CVP
16	Dequae, A.	CVP	Lefevre, T. Spinoy, A.	CVP BSP	Servais, L.	CVP	Larock, V.	BSP	Custers, J.	CVP
17	Eyskens, G.	CVP	Spinoy, A. Pierson, M.-A.	BSP BSP	Servais, L.	CVP	Dehousse, F.	BSP	Bertrand, A.	CVP
18	Clercq, W. de Henrion, R.	PVV PVV	Offelen, J. van	PVV	Servais, L.	CVP	Grootjans Vandenboeynants, P.	PVV CVP	Hulpiau, R.	CVP
19	Snoy et d'Oppuers, J. Cools, A.	CVP BSP	Merlot, J.-J.	BSP	Major, L.	BSP	Vermeylen, P. Dubois, A. Leferre, T.	BSP BSP CVP	Namèche, L.	BSP
20	Cools, A. Vlerick, A.	BSP CVP	Simonet, H.	BSP	Major, L.	BSP	Hurez, L. Claes, W.	BSP BSP	Servais, L.	PSC
21	Tindemans, L. Clercq, W. de	CVP PVV	Claes, W.	BSP	Glinne, E.	BSP	Calewaert, W. Toussaint, M. Hanin, Ch.	BSP PVV PSC	Jaeger, J. de	CVP
22	Clercq, W de	PVV	Oleffe, A.	PSC	Califice, A.	PSC	Croo, H. de Humblet, A.	PVV PSC	Jaeger, J. de	CVP
23	Clercq, W. de	PVV	Oleffe, A.	PSC	Califice, A.	PSC	Croo, H. de Humblet, A.	PVV PSC	Jaeger, J. de	CVP
24	Clercq, W. de Geens, G.	PVV CVP	Herman, F. Bertrand, P.	PSC RW	Califice, A.	PSC	Croo, H. de Humblet, A. Geens, G.	PVV PSC CVP	Jaeger, J. de	CVP
25	Geens, G.	CVP	Claes, W.	BSP	Spitaels, G.	BSP	Ramaekers, J. Michel, J. Vandekerckhove, H.	BSP PSC VU	Dhoore, L.	CVP

BELGIUM 1945–1998

Gov	Finance	Py	Economic Aff.	Py	Labour	Py	Education	Py	Health	Py
26	Geens, G.	CVP	Claes, W.	BSP	Spitaels, G.	BSP	Ramaekers, J. / Michel, J. / Vandekerckhove, H.	BSP / PSC / VU	Dhoore, L.	CVP
27	Spitaels, G. / Geens, G.	BSP / CVP	Claes, W.	BSP	Wulf, R.	BSP	Ramaekers, J. / Hoyaux, J. / Outers, L.	BSP / PSB / FDF	Dhoore, L.	CVP
28	Spitaels, G.	BSP	Claes, W.	BSP	Wulf, R. de	BSP	Ramaekers, J. / Hoyaux, J. / Gramme, G.	PSB / PSB / PSC	Dhoore, L.	CVP
29	Henrion, R. / Geens, G.	PRL / CVP	Claes, W.	BSP	Wulf, R. de	BSP	Desmarets, J. / Calewaert, W. / Mathot, G.	PSC / BSP / PSB	Califice, A.	PSC
30	Mathot, G. / Eyskens, M.	BSP / CVP	Claes, W.	BSP	Wulf, R. de	BSP	Calewaert, W. / Busquin, F. / Maystadt, P.	BSP / PSB / PSC	Dhoore, L.	CVP
31	Mathot, G. / Vandeputte, R.	BSP / CVP	Claes, W.	BSP	Wulf, R. de	BSP	Calewaert, W. / Busquin / Maystadt, P.	BSP / PSB / PSC	Dhoore, L.	CVP
32	Clerq, W. de / Maystadt. P.	PVV / PSC	Eyskens, M.	CVP	Hansenne, M.	PSC	Coens, D. / Tromont. M. / Maystadt, P.	CVP / PRL / PSC		
33	Verhofstadt, G. / Eyskens, M.	PVV / CVP	Maystadt, P.	PSC	Hansenne, M.	PSC	Damseaux, A. / Coens, D. / Verhofstadt, G.	PRL / CVP / PVV		
34	Verhofstadt, G. / Eyskens, M.	PVV / CVP	Maystadt, P.	PSC	Hansenne, M.	PSC	Damseaux, A. / Coens, D. / Verhofstadt, G.	PRL / CVP / PVV		

BELGIUM 1945–1998

Gov	Finance	Py	Economic Aff.	Py	Labour	Py	Education	Py	Health	Py
35	Maystadt, P.	PSC	Claes, W. Wathelet, M. Schiltz, H.	BSP PSC VU	Hansenne, M.	PSC	Ylieff, Y. Claes, W. Schiltz, H.	PSB BSP VU		
36	Maystadt, P. *Offeciers-Van De Wiele, M.	PSC CVP	Wathelet, M. Bourgeois, A.	PSC CVP	*Smet, M.	CVP	Dehousse, J-M.	PSB	*Onkelinx, L.	PSB
37	Van Rompuy, H. Maystadt, P.	CVP PSC	Di Rupo, E. Pinxten, K.	PS CVP	*Smet, M.	CVP	Ylieff, Y.	PS	Colla, M.	SP

Gov	Housing	Py	Agriculture	Py	Industry/Trade	Py	Environment	Py
1			Delvaux, L.	CVP	Kronacker, P.	LP		
2			Lefèvre, R.	LP	Kronacker, P.	LP		
3			Wauters, A.	NONA	Kronacker, P. Smaele, A. de	NONA LP		
4	Terfve, J.	KPB	Levebvre, R.	LP	Kronacker, P.	LP		
5			Lefebvre, R.	LP	Kronacker, P.	LP		
6			Orban, M.	CVP	Duvieusart, J. Fernig, G.M. de Straeten-Waillet, X-F.	CVP NONA CVP		
7			Orban, M.	CVP	Duvieusart, J. Fernig, G.M. de	CVP NONA		
8			Orban, M.	CVP	Zeeland, P. van	CVP		
9			Orban, M.	CVP				
10			Héger, Ch.	CVP	Meurice, J.	CVP		
11			Héger, Ch.	CVP	Meurice, J.	CVP		
12			Lefèvre, R.	LP	Larock, V.	BSP		

BELGIUM 1945–1998

Gov	Housing	Py	Agriculture	Py	Industry/Trade	Py	Environment	Py
13			Vleeschauwer, A. de	CVP	Dequae, A.	CVP		CVP
14			Vleeschauwer, A. de	CVP	Offelen, J. van	LP		LP
15			Vleeschauwer, A. de	CVP	Offelen, J. van	LP		LP
16			Héger, Ch.	CVP	Brasseur, M.	CVP		CVP
17	*Riemaecker-L. M. de	CVP	Héger, Ch.	CVP		CVP		
18	*Riemaecker-L. M. de	CVP	Héger, Ch.	CVP	Winter, A. de	PVV		
19	Breyne, G.	CVP	Héger, Ch.	CVP	Fayat, H.	BSP		
20			Tindemans, L.	CVP				
21			Lavens, A.	CVP				
22		PLP	Lavens, A.	CVP	Toussaint, M.	PLP	Jaeger, J. de	CVP
23		CVP	Lavens, A.	CVP	Toussaint, M.	PLP		
24	Califice, A. / Aal, H.-F. van	PSC / PSC	Lavens, A.	CVP	Knoops, E.	PRLW		
25			Humblet, A.	PSC	Bruyne, H. de	VU	Dhoore, L.	CVP
26			Humblet, A.	PSC	Bruyne, H. de	VU	Dhoore, L.	CVP
27			Lavens, A.	CVP	Outers, L.	FDF	Dhoore, L.	CVP
28			Lavens, A.	CVP	Urbain, R.	PSB	Dhoore, L.	CVP
29			Lavens, A.	CVP	Urbain, R.	PSB	Califice, A.	PSC
30			Lavens, A.	CVP	Urbain, R.	PSB	Maystadt, P.	PSC
31			Lavens, A.	CVP	Urbain, R.	PSB	Maystadt, P.	PSC
32					Gol, J. / Clerq, W. de	PRL / PVV		
33					Croo, H. de	PVV		
34					Croo, H. de	PVV		
35					Urbain, R.	PSB		
36			Bourgeois, A.	CVP	Urbain, R.	PSB	*Onkelinx, L.	PSB
37			Pinxten, K.	CVP	Maystadt, P.	PSC		

BELGIUM 1945–1998

Gov	Social Affairs (py)	Public Works (py)	Other (py)	Res
1	Troclet, L.-E. (BSP) Pauwels, H. (CVP) Lalmand, E. (KPB)	Ronguaux, E. (BS Vos, H. (BSP) Ronse, E. (CVP)	Bruyn, E. de (CVP)	0
2	Troclet, L.-E. (BSP) Branden Reeth, A. vd (ICAT) Lalmand, E. (KPB)	Ronguaux, E. (BSP) Vos, H. (BSP) Basyn, J. (DU	Godding, R. (LP)	0
3	Fernig, M. de (NONA) Vermeylen, P. (BSP)	Vos, H. (BSP) Rongvaux, E. (BSP) Vermeylen, P. (BSP)	Craeybeeck, M (BSP)	0
4	Troclet, L.-E. (BSP) Lalmand, E. (KPB)	Smaele, A. de (NONA) Rongvaux, E. (BSP) Borremans, J. (KP)B Acker, A. van (BSP)	Godding, R. (LP)	0
5	Troclet, L.-E. (BSP) Lalmand, E. (KPB)	Terfve, J. (KPB) Rongvaux, E. (BSP) Borremans, J. (KP)B Groote, P. de (NONA)	Godding, R. (LP)	0
6	Troclet, L.-E. (BSP)	Man, R. de (CVP) Acker, A. van (BSP) Behogne, D. (CVP) Delattre, A. (BSP)	Wigny, P. (CVP)	0
7	Merlot, J.	Man, R. de (CVP) Acker, A. van (BSP) Behogne, O. (CVP)	Wigny, P. (CVP)	0
8	Behogne, O. (CVP)	Rey, J. (LP) Segers, P. (CVP) Buisseret, A. (LP)	Wigny, P. (CVP) Wiart, H.C. de (CVP) Dierckx (LP)	0

BELGIUM 1945–1998

Gov	Social Affairs (py)	Public Works (py)	Other (py)	Res
9	Behogne, O. (CVP)	Coppé, A. (CVP) Dequae, A. (CVP) Segers, P. (CVP)	Wigny, P. (CVP)	0
10	Daele, G. van den (CVP)	Behogne, O. (CVP) Segers, P. (CVP) Boodt, A.F. de (CVP)	Dequae, A. (CVP)	0
11	Daele, G. van den (CVP)	Coppé, A. (CVP) Segers, P. (CVP) Behogne, O. (CVP)	Dequae, A. (CVP)	0
12	Bossaert, O. (LP)	Anseele, E. (BSP) Glabbeke, A. van (LP)	Buisseret, A. (LP)	1
13	Vandenboeynants, P. (CVP)	Segers, P. (CVP) Meyers, P. (CVP)	P)étillon, L. (CVP)	0
14	Servais, L. (CVP) Vandenboeynants, P. (CVP)	Seghers, P. (CVP) Audenhovem, O. van (LP)	Hemelryck, C. van (CVP) Scheyven, R. (CVP)Meersch, W. van der (CVP) Harmel, P. (CVP)	0
15	Servais, L. (CVP) Vandenboeynants, P. (CVP)	Seghers, P. (CVP) Audenhoven, O. van (LP)	Aspremont-Lynden, H. d' (CVP)	0
16	Leburton, E. (BSP) Declerck, A.-M. (CVP) Custers, J. (CVP)	Merlot, J. (BSP) Bertrand, A. (CVP) Busiaux, M. (BSP)	Spaak, P.-H. (BSP)	0
17	Segers, P.-W. (CVP) Brouhon, H. (BSP) Alcantara, A. d' (CVP) *Riemaecker-L., M. de (CVP)	Jaeger, J. de (CVP) Anseele, E. (BSP) Urbain, Y. (CVP) Leburton, E. (BSP)		0
18	Paepe, P. de (CVP) Alcantara, A. d' (CVP) *Riemaecker-L., M.L. de (CVP)	Jaeger, J. de (CVP) Bertrand, A. (CVP)	Wigny, P. (CVP) Elslande R. van (CVP)	0

BELGIUM 1945–1998

Gov	Social Affairs (py)	Public Works (py)	Other (py)	Res
19	P)aepe, P. (CVP) Hanin, Ch. (CVP) Breyne, G. (CVP)	Jaeger, J. de (CVP) Bertrand, A. (CVP) Anseele, E. (BSP)	Scheyven, R. (CVP) P)arisis, A. (CVP) Mechelen, F. van (CVP) Tindemans, L. (CVP) Terwagne, F. (BSP)	2
20	Namèche, L. (BSP) Tindemans, L. (CVP)	Jaeger, J. de (CVP) Delmotte, F. (BSP) Anseele, E. (BSP)	Hanin, Ch. (PSC) Mechelen, F. van (CVP)	0
21	Acker, F. van (BSP) Hanotte, L. (PVV) Jaeger, J. de (CVP)	Califice, A. (PSC) Anseele, E. (BSP)Falize, P. (BSP)	Falize, P. (BSP) Chabert, J. (CVP) Grafé, J.-P. (PSC) Cudell, G. (BSP)	0
22	P)aepe, P. de (CVP) Olivier, L. (P)LP) Jaeger, J. de (CVP)	Defraigne, J. (P)LP) Chabert, J. (CVP)	Elslande, R. van (CVP) Vandenboeynants, P. (PSC) Califice, A. (PSC) *Backer-V.O., R. de (CVP) Grafé, J.-P. (PSC)	0
23	P)aepe, P. de (CVP) Olivier, L. (P)LP) Jaeger, J. de (CVP)	Defraigne, J. (P)LP) Chabert, J. (CVP)	Elslande, R. van (CVP) Vandenboeynants (PSC) Califice, A. (PSC) *Backer-V.O., R. de (CVP) Grafé, J.-P. (PSC)	1
24	Dhoore, L. (CVP) Moreau, R. (RW Hanotte, L. (PRL)W Jaeger, J. de (CVP)	Olivier, L. (PRL)W Kempinaire, A. (PVV) Chabert, J. (CVP)	Elslande, R. van (CVP) Vandenboeynants (PSC) Califice, A. (PSC) *Backer-V.O., R. de (CVP) Aal, H.-F. van (PSC)	0

BELGIUM 1945–1998

Gov	Social Affairs (py)	Public Works (py)	Other (py)	Res
25	Califice, A. (PSC) Wijninckx, J. (BSP) Humblet, A. (PSC)	Mathot, G. (BSP) Chabert, J. (CVP) Defosset, L. (FDF Hurez, L. (BSP)	Mathot, G. (BSP) Defosset, L. (FDF Outers, L. (FDF Dehousse, J.-M. (BSP) *Backer-V.O., R. de (CVP)	0
26	Califice, A. (PSC) Wijninckx, J. (BSP) Humblet, A. (PSC)	Mathot, G. (PSB) Chabert, J. (CVP) Defosset, L. (FDF Hurez, L. (BSP)	Mathot, G. (BSP) Defosset, L. (FDF Outers, L. (FDF Dehousse, J.-M. (BSP) *Backer-V.O., R. de (CVP)	0
27	Califice, A. (PSC) Lavens, A. (CVP)	Mathot, G. (BSP) Chabert, J. (CVP) Calewaert, W. (BSP) Urbain, R. (PSB)	Eyskens, M. (CVP) *Backer-V.O., R. de (CVP) Hansenne, M.(PSC) Galle, M. (BSP) Dehousse, J.-M. (BSP) Defosset, L. (FDF	0
28	Califice, A. (PSC) Lavens, A. (CVP)	Mathot, G. (PSB) Chabert, J. (CVP) Calewaert, W. (BSP) Baudson, A. (PSB)	Eyskens, M. (CVP) *Backer-V.O., R. de (CVP) Hansenne, M. (PSC) Galle, M. (BSP) Dehousse, J.-M. (BSP) Goor, C. (PSC)	0
29	Dhoore, L. (CVP) Deroo, H. (PVV) Lavens, A. (CVP)	Spitaels, G. (PSB) Chabert, J. (CVP) Deworme, E. (PSB) Decroo, H. de (PVV)	Eyskens, M. (CVP) Galle, M. (BSP) *Backer-V.O., R. de (CVP) Kempinaire, A. (PVV) Hansenne, M. (PSC) Dehousse, J.-M. (PSB) Goor, C. (PSC)	0

BELGIUM 1945–1998

Gov	Social Affairs (py)	Public Works (py)	Other (py)	Res
30	Desmarets, J. (PSC) Dhoore, L. (CVP) Mainil, P. (PSC)	Chabert, J. (CVP) Maystadt, P. (PSC) Féaux, V. (PSB) Willockx, F. (BSP) Spitaels, G. (BSP) Desmarets, J. (PSC)	Coens, D. (CVP) Galle, M (BSP) Geens, G. (CVP) Hansenne, M. (PSC) Dehousse, J.-M. (PSB) Degroeve, A. (PSB)	0
31	Desmarets, J. (PSC) Dhoore, L. (CVP) Mainil, P. (PSC)	Chabert, J. (CVP) Maystadt, P. (PSC) Féaux, V. (PSB) Willockx, F. (BSP)	Coens, D. (CVP) Galle, M (BSP) Geens, G. (CVP) Hansenne, M. (PSC) Dehousse, J.-M. (PSB) Degroeve, A. (PSB)	0
32	Dehaene, J.-L. (CVP) Demuyter, A. (PRL)	Olivier, L. (PRL) Croo, H. de (PVV)	Demuyter, A. (PRL)	1
33	Dehaene, J.-L. (CVP) Buchmann, J. (PVV)	Croo, H. de (PVV) Olivier, L. (PRL) Nothomb, C.F. (PSC)	Donnéa, F.-X. de (PRL)	1
34	Dehaene, J.-L. (CVP) Buchmann, J. (PVV)	Croo, H. de (PVV) Olivier, L. (PRL) Nothomb, C.F. (PSC)	Donnéa, F.-X. de (PRL)	0
35	Busquin, F. (PSB) VandenBrande. L. (CVP)	Willockx, F. (BSP) Tobback, L. (BSP) Geens, A. (CVP) Biest, A. van der (PSB) Dehaene, J.-L. (CVP)		1
36	Moureaux, P. (PSB) Willockx, F. (BSP) *Smet, M. (CVP) *Onkelinx, L. (PSB)	Coëme, G. (PSB)	Moureaux, P. (PSB) Urbain, R. (PSB) Tobback, L. (BSP)	4

BELGIUM 1945–1998

Gov	Social Affairs (py)	Public Works (py)	Other (py)	Res
37	*De Galan, M. (PS) Colla, M. (SP)	Di Rupo, E. (PS) Daerden, M. (PS)	*Smet, M. (CVP) Flahaut, A. (PS)	

8. BOTSWANA

The Head of State and of Government is the President, who is elected for a five-year term by an absolute majority of the 40 members of the National Assembly (Lower House of Parliament).

The State is fairly centralised and unitary.

Parliament is bicameral. The Upper House consists of 15 Chiefs who only review constitutional and chieftainly matters. The 40 members of the National Assembly are elected for a fixed term of five years by the single member simple plurality (first past the post) system in constituencies of about 15,000 electors.

The quorum for the National Assembly is 9 members, plus the president of the Assembly. Votes are carried by a simple majority of those present and voting. The only issue requiring a qualified majority is the election of the Head of State, which requires an absolute majority of all members. There is no provision for a referendum.

The President nominates the cabinet. The President chairs the cabinet. No vote of investiture is required. The government may face a vote of no confidence. Losing a vote of confidence always results in resignation of the government. The government is collectively responsible to parliament. Individual ministers are members of parliament. The President has a dominant position in government.

The Upper House reviews constitutional matters.

BOTSWANA 1966-1998

Gov	Begin	Dur	RfT	ToG	Py1	Seats	CPG	NoM	Prime Minister (py)
1	30.09.66	1119	1	1	BDP 28	31		8	Khama, S. (BDP)
2	23.10.69	1833	1	1	BDP 24	31		8	Khama, S. (BDP)
3	30.10.74	1817	1	1	BDP 27	32		10	Khama, S. (BDP)
4	21.10.79	271	x	1	BDP 29	32		12	Khama, S. (BDP)
5	18.07.80	1519	1	1	BDP 29	32		12	Masire, Q.K.J. (BDP)
6	14.09.84	1855	1	1	BDP 28	34 (+4)		13	Masire, Q.K.J. (BDP)
7	13.10.89	1837	1	1	BDP 31	34 (+6)		11	Masire, Q.K.J. (BDP)
8	24.10.94		1		BDP 26 (+4)	40 (+6)		12	Masire, Q.K.J. (BDP)

- Insufficient information to classify governments on CPG-scale.
- Date of Independence 30 September 1966. When Botswana became independent the British parliamentary system which had been in use was changed. The prime minister became president elected by an absolute majority of the National Assembly.
- Gov 4: Reason for Termination is death of president Khama.
- Gov 6: The National Assembly consists of 34 elected seats plus 4 seats elected by the assembly.
- Gov 7: The National Assembly consists of 34 elected seats plus 4 seats elected by the assembly and 2 seats occupied ex officio.
- Gov 8: The National Assembly consists of 40 elected seats plus 4 seats nominated by the president and 2 seats occupied ex officio.

Gov	Deputy PM	Py	Foreign Affairs	Py	Defence	Py	Interior	Py	Justice	Py
1	Masire, Q.K.J.	BDP	Nwako, M.P.K.	BDP		BDP	Dambe, A.M. Tsheko, T.	BDP BDP		
2	Masire, Q.K.J.	BDP					Nwako, M.P.K. Kgabo, E.M.K.	BDP BDP		
3	Masire, Q.K.J.	BDP					Kgari, B.K. Magekgenene, L.	BDP BDP		
4	Masire, Q.K.J.	BDP	Mogwe, A.M.	BDP		BDP	*Disele, K.L. Seretse, L.M.	BDP BDP		

BOTSWANA 1966-1998

Gov	Deputy PM	Py	Foreign Affairs	Py	Defence	Py	Interior	Py	Justice	Py
5	Seretse, L.M.	BDP	Mogwe, A.M.	BDP		BDP	Seretse, L.M. *Disele, K.L.	BDP BDP		
6	Seretse, L.M.	BDP	*Chiepe, G.K.T.	BDP		BDP	Seretse, L.M. Kgabo, E. Mothibamele, J.L.	BDP BDP BDP		
7	Mmusi, P.S.	BDP	*Chiepe, G.K.T.	BDP	Masire, Q.K.J.	BDP	Mmusi, P.S. Balopi, P. Merafhe, M.	BDP BDP BDP		
8	Mogae, F.	BDP	Merafhe, M.	BDP	Masire, Q.K.J.	BDP	Kedikilwe, P. Balopi, P. Temane, B.K.	BDP BDP BDP		

Gov	Finance	Py	Economic Aff.	Py	Labour	Py	Education	Py	Health	Py
1	Masire, Q.K.J.	BDP	Haskins, J.G.	BDP	Thema, B.C.	BDP	Thema, B.C.	BDP	Nwako, M.P.K.	BDP
2	Haskins, J.G.	BDP	Masire, Q.K.J.	BDP	Nwako, M.P.K.	BDP	Morake, K.P.	BDP	Nwako, M.P.K.	BDP
3	Masire, Q.K.J.	BDP	Masire, Q.K.J.	BDP			Morake, K.P.	BDP	Magekgenene, L.	BDP
4	Masire, Q.K.J.	BDP	Masire, Q.K.J.	BDP			Morake, K.P.	BDP	Magekgenene, L.	BDP
5	Mmusi, P.S.	BDP	Mmusi, P.S.	BDP			Morake, K.P.	BDP	Magekgenene, L.	BDP
6	Mmusi, P.S.	BDP	Mmusi, P.S.	BDP			Morake, K.P.	BDP	Morake, K.P.	BDP
7	Mogae, F.	BDP	Mogae, F. Kedikilwe, P.	BDP BDP	Balopi, P.	BDP	Molomo, R.	BDP		
8	Mogae, F.	BDP	Mogae, F. Kgoroba, G.	BDP BDP	Temane, B.K.	BDP	*Chiepe, G.K.T.	BDP	Butale, C.	BDP

BOTSWANA 1966-1998

Gov	Housing	Py	Agriculture	Py	Industry/Trade	Py	Environment	Py
1			Nwako, M.P.K.	BDP	Haskins, J.G.	BDP		
2			Tsheko, T.	BDP	Segogo, M.K.	BDP		
3			Masisi, E.S.	BDP	*Chiepe, G.K.T.	BDP		
4			Meswele, W.	BDP	Nwako, M.P.K.	BDP		
5			Meswele, W.	BDP	Nwako, M.P.K.	BDP		
6			Meswele, W.	BDP	Nwako, M.P.K.	BDP		
7					Kedikilwe, P.	BDP		
8	Balopi, P.	BDP	Blackbeard, R.	BDP	Kgoroba, G.	BDP		

Gov	Social Affairs (py)	Public Works (py)	Other (py)	Res
1	Thema, B.C. (BDP)	Haskins, J.G. (BDP) Tseobebe, N.M. (BDP)		0
2		Segokgo, M.K. (BDP)	Kgabo, E.M.K. (BDP)	0
3		Segokgo, M.K. (BDP) Haskins, J.G. (BDP)	Segokgo, M.K. (BDP) Magekgenene, L. (BDP)	0
4		Kwelagobe, D.K. (BDP) Mmusi, P.S. (BDP) *Chiepe, G.K.T. (BDP)	Seretse, L.M. (BDP)	0
5		Blackbeard, C. (BDP) Kwelagobe, D.K. (BDP) *Chiepe, G.K.T. (BDP)	Seretse, L.M. (BDP)	1

BOTSWANA 1966-1998

Gov	Social Affairs (py)	Public Works (py)	Other (py)	Res
6		Mogwe, A.M. (BDP)	Mothibamele, J.L. (BDP)	2
		Blackbeard, C. (BDP)	Seretse, L.M. (BDP)	
		Kwelagobe, D.K. (BDP)		
7		Mogwe, A.M. (BDP)	Mmusi, P.S. (BDP)	1
		Butale, C. (BDP)	Merafhe, M. (BDP)	
8		Kwelagobe, D.K. (BDP)	Kidikilwe, P. (BDP)	
		Magang, D. (BDP)	Balopi, P. (BDP)	

9. BULGARIA

The new constitution dates from 1991. The Head of State, the President, is directly elected for a five-year term.

Bulgaria is a unitary state with strong centralisation.

Parliament is unicameral. The National Assembly of 240 seats is directly elected for a four-year term by proportional representation (d'Hondt - with a 4% threshold) in constituencies varying in size from approximately 600,000 tot 1,200,000 electors.

Parliament has a quorum of at least 50 per cent of all members. Votes are carried by a majority of all members present. Some issues need an absolute or two-thirds majority of all members. Constitutional amendments require a three-quarter majority of all members. A referendum is optional and may be called by the Head of State and by parliament. The outcome is binding.

Government is parliamentary and a vote of investiture is required. During its lifetime the government can also face a vote of no confidence. Losing either vote always results in resignation of the government. Government is both collectively and individually responsible to parliament. Being a minister is not compatible with being a Member of Parliament. The Prime Minister has a dominant position in government.

Both Parliament and President are the dominant actors within this new democracy.

There is a Supreme Court for constitutional review of lawmaking. The court also supervises the public administrative bodies.

BULGARIA 1991-1998

Gov	Begin	Dur	RfT	ToG	Py1	Seats	CPG	NoM	Prime Minister (py)
1	08.11.91	418	5	4	SDS 110	240	3	14	Dimitrov, F. (SDS)
2	30.12.92	647	2	x		240	3	14	Berov, L. (NONA)
3	08.10.94	109	1	6		240	3	8	*Indzhova, R. (SDS)
4	25.01.95	748	4	1	BSP 125	240	4	18	Videnov, Z. (BSP)
5	12.02.97	98	1	6		240	4	17	Sofiyanski, S. (SDS)
6	21.05.97		1	1	SDS 137	240	3	17	Kostov, I. (SDS)

- Gov 1: SDS = Union of Democratic Forces.
- Gov 2: Type of Government is government of 'experts' of 'non-party figures'.
- Gov 3: Type of Government is caretaker government. Party affiliation of individual ministers unknown, unless stated.
- Gov 4: BSP includes AS-BZNS and Ecoglasnost Political Club (EPC). Government also includes a number of 'independent technocrats'.
- Gov 5: Type of Government is caretaker. Party affiliation individual ministers unknown, most ministers probably SDS. No BSP ministers.
- Gov 6: SDS (United Democratic Forces) includes SDS proper, Democratic Party, BZNS (Bulgarian Agrarian People's Party) and Social Democratic Party.

Gov	Deputy PM	Py	Foreign Affairs	Py	Defence	Py	Interior	Py	Justice	Py
1	Ganev, S.	SDS	Ganev, S.	SDS	Ludznev, D.	SDS	Sokolov, Y.	SDS		
	Vasilev, N.	SDS								
2	Karabashev, V.	NONA	Berov, L.	NONA	Aleksandrov, V.	NONA	Mikhaylov, V.	NONA	Vulchev, M.	NONA
	Neev, N.	NONA								
	Matinchev, E.	NONA								
3	Trifonov, I.		Stancioff, I.		Noev, B.		Chervenkov, C.		Teodor, C.	
	*Vucheva, K.									
	Vasilev, N.	SDS								

BULGARIA 1991-1998

Gov	Deputy PM	Py	Foreign Affairs	Py	Defence	Py	Interior	Py	Justice	Py
4	Gechev, R. Konakchiev, D. Tsochev, K. Svetoslav, S.	BSP BSP NONA BSP/AS-BZNS	Pirinski, G.	BSP	Pavlov, D.	NONA	Nachev, L.	BSP	Chervenyakov, M.	BSP
5	Bozhkov, A. Anvhev, K.		Stalev, S.		Ananiev, G.		Bonev, B.		Anvhev, K.	
6	Bozhkov, A. Kakurdzhiev, E. Metodiev, E.	SDS SDS SDS	*Mikhaylova, N.	SDS	Ananiev, G.	SDS	Bonev, B. Tegarinski, M.	SDS SDS	Gotsev, V.	SDS

Gov	Finance	Py	Economic Aff.	Py	Labour	Py	Education	Py	Health	Py
1	Kostov, I.	SDS			Danov, M.	SDS	Vasilev, N.	SDS	+Vasilev, N.	SDS
2	Aleksandrov, S.	NONA			Matinchev, E.	NONA	Todorov, M.	NONA	Gogulov, D.	NONA
3										
4	Kostov, D.	NONA	Gechev, R. Tsochev, K.	BSP NONA	Aralski, M.	NONA	Dimitrov, I.	NONA	*Vitkova, M.	BSP
5	Gavrinsky, S.				Neykov, I.		Lalov, I.		Takov, E.	
6	Radev, M.	SDS			Neykov, I.	SDS	Metodiev, V.	SDS	Boyadzhiev, P.	SDS

- Gov 1: +Vasilev, N. not Vasilev, N. (DPM, Education)

BULGARIA 1991-1998

Gov	Housing	Py	Agriculture	Py	Industry/Trade	Py	Environment	Py
1	Karadimov, N.	SDS	Dimitrov, S.	SDS	Pushkarov, I.	SDS	Vasilev, V.	SDS
2			Tanev, G.	NONA	Karabashev, V.	NONA	Bosevski, V.	NONA
					Bikov, R.	NONA		
3								
4			Chichibaba, V.	BSP/AS-BZNS	Tsochev, K.	NONA	Georgiev, G.	BSP-EPC
					Vuchev, K.	NONA		
5			Khristov, R.		Bozhkov, A.		Filipov, I.	
					Khristov, R.			
					*Bobeva, D.			
6			Vurbanov, V.	SDS	Bozhkov, A.	SDS	*Maneva, E.	SDS
					Vasilev, V.	SDS		

Gov	Social Affairs (py)	Public Works (py)	Other (py)	Res
1	Danov, M. (SDS)	Aleksandrov, A. (SDS) Pushkarov, I. (SDS) Karadimov, N. (SDS)	*Konstantinova, E. (SDS) Karadimov, N. (SDS)	1
2	Matinchev, E. (NONA)	Neev, N. (NONA) Totev, K. (NONA)	Totev, K. (NONA) Todorov, M. (NONA)	1
3				
4	Aralski, M. (NONA)	Konakchiev, D. (BSP) Stamenov, S. (NONA)	Konakchiev, D. (BSP) Kostov, G. (NONA)	2

BULGARIA 1991-1998

Gov	Social Affairs (py)	Public Works (py)	Other (py)	Res
5	Neykov, I.	Karadimov, N. Stoilov, G. Kraus, W.	Karadimov, N. Tabakov, E.	0
6	Neykov, I. (SDS)	Kraus, W. SDS *Maneva, E. (SDS)	Kakurdzhiev, E. (SDS) Gotsev, V. (SDS) Vasilev, V. (SDS) *Moskova, E. (SDS)	

10. CANADA

The British Monarch is ceremonial Head of State and is represented by a Governor-General. The Governor-General has mainly formal powers.

Canada is a Federation where the constituent Provinces have more effective power than in most.

Parliament is bicameral. The Upper House (Senate) with 104 members is appointed and only exerts occasional blocking powers. Effective authority rests with the Lower House (House of Commons), elected for a five-year term. Elections for the 295 members take place in single member constituencies (ridings, average size 60,000) by plurality voting (no minimum vote). The House of Commons has a quorum of twenty members, the Senate of fifteen members. Votes are carried by a majority of all votes cast. Constitutional amendments require a three-fifth majority of all votes cast. A referendum is optional and may be called by the government. The outcome is binding.

The Cabinet with senior Government Ministers is the effective executive. The government is almost always single party but quite often this is not in a majority in the House of Commons but only in a plurality. It often gets external support from a minority party. There is no vote of investiture. And a vote of no confidence is unlikely as long as the government commands a relative majority in parliament. Losing a vote of confidence always results in resignation of the government. The government is both collectively and individually responsible to parliament. Ministers have to be a member of one of the Houses of parliament. The Prime Minister has a dominant position in government.

There is a Supreme Court for review of constitutional matters, particularly with regard to the division of power between the Federation and the Provinces.

CANADA 1945–1998

Gov	Begin	Dur	RfT	ToG	Py1	Seats	CPG	NoM	Prime Minister (py)
1	30.08.45	1174	2	1	LIB 125	245	3	20	Mackenzie, W.L. (LIB)
2	16.11.48	222	1	1	LIB 125	245	3	20	St. Laurent, L. (LIB)
3	26.06.49	1506	1	1	LIB 193	262	3	22	St. Laurent, L. (LIB)
4	10.08.53	1420	1	1	LIB 171	264	3	21	St. Laurent, L. (LIB)
5	21.06.57	283	1	4	CON 112	264	2	21	Diefenbaker, J.G. (CON)
6	31.03.58	1592	1	1	CON 208	265	1	21	Diefenbaker, J.G. (CON)
7	09.08.62	256	5	4	CON 116	265	2	20	Diefenbaker, J.G. (CON)
8	22.04.63	971	1	4	LIB 129	265	3	24	Pearson, L.B. (LIB)
9	18.12.65	855	2	4	LIB 131	265	3	23	Pearson, L.B. (LIB)
10	21.04.68	76	1	4	LIB 131	265	3	25	Trudeau, P.E. (LIB)
11	07.07.68	1604	1	1	LIB 155	264	3	28	Trudeau, P.E. (LIB)
12	27.11.72	619	5	4	LIB 109	264	3	27	Trudeau, P.E. (LIB)
13	08.08.74	1761	1	1	LIB 141	264	3	28	Trudeau, P.E. (LIB)
14	04.06.79	273	5	4	CON 136	282	3	11	Clark, J. (CON)
15	03.03.80	1214	2	1	LIB 147	282	3	27	Trudeau, P.E. (LIB)
16	30.06.83	445	1	1	LIB 147	282	3	25	Turner, J.N. (LIB)
17	17.09.84	1541	1	1	CON 211	281	1	30	Mulroney, B. (CON)
18	07.12.88	1672	2	1	CON 170	295	2	22	Mulroney, B. (CON)
19	25.06.93	132	1	1	CON 156	295	2	25	*Campbell, K. (CON)
20	04.11.93	1315	1	1	LIB 177	295	3	23	Chrétien, J.-C. (LIB)
21	11.06.97		1	1	LIB 155	301	3	28	Chrétien, J.-C. (LIB)

CANADA 1945–1998

Gov	Deputy PM	Py	Foreign Affairs	Py	Defence	Py	Interior	Py	Justice	Py
1			Mackenzie, W.L.	LIB	Abbot, D. Gibson, C.	LIB LIB		LIB LIB	St. Laurent, L. Jean, J.	LIB LIB
2	Robertson, N.	LIB	Pearson, L.B.	LIB	Claxton, B.	LIB		LIB	Garson, S. Jean, J.	LIB LIB
3	Robertson, N.	LIB	Pearson, L.B.	LIB	Claxton, B.	LIB		LIB	Garson S. Lapointe, H	LIB LIB
4	Robertson, N.	LIB	Pearson, L.B.	LIB	Claxton, B. Howe, C.D.	LIB LIB	Harris, W.	LIB	Garson, S. Campney, R.	LIB LIB
5			Smith, S.E.	CON	Pearkes, G. Green, H.	CON CON	Fulton, D.	CON	Fulton, D. Balcer, L.	CON CON
6			Smith, S.E.	CON	Pearkes, G. Green, H.	CON CON	Fulton, D.	CON	Fulton, D. Balcer, L.	CON CON
7			Green, H.	CON	Harkness, D. O'Hurley, R.	CON CON	Bell, R.A.	CON	Fleming, D.	CON
8			Martin, P.J.J.	LIB	Hellyer, P.T. Drury, C.M.	LIB LIB	Lamontagne, M. Favreau, G.	LIB LIB	Chevrier, L. MacNaught, J.W.	LIB LIB
9			Martin, P.J.J.	LIB	Hellyer, P.T. Drury, C.M.	LIB LIB	Favreau, G.	LIB	Cardin, L. Pennell, L.	LIB LIB
10			Sharp, M.	LIB	Cadieux, L. Drury, C.M.	LIB LIB			Turner, J.N. Trudeau, P.	
11			Sharp, M.	LIB	Cadieux, L. Jamieson, D.	LIB LIB	MacDonald, D.S.	LIB	MacIlraith, G. Turner, J.N.	LIB
12			Sharp, M.	LIB	Richardson, J.	LIB	MacEachen, A.J.	LIB	Lang, O. Allmand, W.	LIB LIB
13			MacEachen, A.J.	LIB	Richardson, J.	LIB	Faulkner, J. Sharp, M.	LIB	Lang, O. Allmand, W.	LIB LIB

CANADA 1945–1998

Gov	Deputy PM	Py	Foreign Affairs	Py	Defence	Py	Interior	Py	Justice	Py
14			*MacDonald, F.	CON			Baker, W.	CON	Flynn, J.	CON
							Jarvis, W.	CON		CON
15	MacEachen, A.J.	LIB	MacGuigan, M.	LIB	Lamontagne, G.	LIB	Pinard, Y.	LIB	Chrétien, J.-C.	LIB
									Kaplan, R.	LIB
16	Chrétien, J.	LIB	Chrétien, J.	LIB	Blais, J.-J.	LIB	Ouellet, A.	LIB	Johnston, D.	LIB
									Kaplan, R.	LIB
17	Nielsen, E.	CON	Clark, J.	CON	Coates, R.	CON	Nielsen, E.	CON	MacKay, E.	CON
			McLean, W.	CON					Crosbie, J.	CON
18	Mazankowski, D.	CON	Clark, J.	CON	McKnight, W.	CON	Mazankowski, D.	CON	Lewis, J.	CON
							McDougall, B.	CON		
							Weiner, G.	CON		
19	Charest, J.	CON	Beatty, P.	CON	Siddon, T.	CON	Dick, P.	CON	Lewis, D.	CON
							Lewis, D.	CON	Blais, P.	CON
							Valcourt, B.	CON		
							Weiner, G.	CON		
20	*Copps, S.	LIB	Ouellet, A.	LIB	Collenette, D.	LIB	Marchi, S.	LIB	Rock, A.	LIB
									Gray, H.	LIB
21	Gray, H.	LIB	Axworthy, L.	LIB	Eggleton, A.	LIB	Dion, S.	LIB	*McLellan, A.	LIB
							Robillard, L.	LIB	Scott, A.	LIB

Gov	Finance	Py	Economic Aff.	Py	Labour	Py	Education	Py	Health	Py
1	McCann, J.	LIB			Mitchell, H.	LIB		LIB	Claxton, B.	LIB
	Isley, J.	LIB								
	Martin, P.J.J.	LIB								

CANADA 1945–1998

Gov	Finance	Py	Economic Aff.	Py	Labour	Py	Education	Py	Health	Py
2	Abbot, D. McCann, J.	LIB LIB			Mitchell, H.	LIB			Martin, P.J.J.	LIB
3	Abbot, D. McCann, J.	LIB LIB			Mitchell, H.	LIB			Martin, P.J.J.	LIB
4	Abbot, D. McCann, J.	LIB LIB			Gregg, M.	LIB			Martin, P.J.J.	LIB
5	Fleming, D. Nowlan, G.	CON CON			Starr, M.	CON			Monteigh, W.	CON
6	Fleming, D. Nowlan, G.	CON CON			Starr, M.	CON			Monteigh, W.	CON
7	Nowlan, G. Flemming, J.H.	CON CON			Starr, M.	CON			Monteigh, W.	CON
8	Gordon, W.L. Garland, J.R.	LIB LIB			MacEachen, A.J.	LIB			*La Marsh, J.	LIB
9	Sharp, M. Benson, E.J.	LIB LIB			Benson, E.J. Marchand, J.	LIB LIB			MacEachen, A.J.	LIB
10	Benson, E.J. Chrétien, J.	LIB LIB			Marchand, J. Pépin, J.-L.	LIB LIB			MacEachen, A.J.	LIB
11	Drury, C.M. Benson, E.J. Côté, J.-P.	LIB LIB LIB			MacEachen, A.J. MacKasey, B.S.	LIB LIB			Munro, J.C.	LIB
12	Turner, J.N. Drury, C.M. Stanbury, R.	LIB LIB LIB	Jamieson, D.	LIB	Munro, J.C. Andras, R.	LIB LIB			Lalonde, M.	LIB
13	Turner, J.N. Chrétien, J. Basford, R.	LIB LIB LIB	Jamieson, D.	LIB	Munro, J.C. Andras, R.	LIB LIB			Lalonde, M.	LIB

CANADA 1945–1998

Gov	Finance	Py	Economic Aff.	Py	Labour	Py	Education	Py	Health	Py
14	Baker, W.	CON	Cotret, R.R. de	CON			Hnatyshyn, R.	CON		CON
	Crosbie, J.	CON								
	Stevens, S.	CON								
15	MacEachen, A.J.	LIB	Lapointe, C.	LIB	Axworthy, L.L.	LIB	Roberts, J.	LIB	*Bégin, M.	LIB
	Rompkey, W.	LIB	De Bane, P.	LIB						
	Johnston, D.	LIB								
16	Lalonde, M.	LIB	Smith, D.	LIB	Ouellet, A.	LIB	Lumley, E.	LIB	*Bégin, M.	LIB
	MacLaren, R.	LIB	Ouellet, A.	LIB	Roberts, J.	LIB				
	Gray, H.	LIB								
17	Cotret, R. de	CON	Stevens, S.	CON	*MacDonald, F.	CON	Siddon, T.	CON	Epp, J.	CON
	Beatty, P.	CON			McKnight, W.	CON				
	Wilson, M.	CON								
18	Cotret, R. de	CON							Beatty, P.	CON
	Jelinek, O.	CON								
	Wilson, M.	CON								
19	Loiselle, G.	CON	Nicholson, R.	CON	Valcourt, B.	CON	Charest, J.	CON	*Collins, M.	CON
	Edwards, J.	CON	Schneider, L.	CON			Nicholson, R.	CON		
	Turner, G.	CON								
20	Martin, P.	LIB	Axworthy, L.	LIB	Axworthy, L.	LIB	*Fairbairn, J.	LIB	*Marleau, D.	LIB
	Eggleton, A.	LIB								
21	Martin, P.	LIB			MacAuly, L.	LIB			Rock, A.	LIB
	Dhaliwal, H.	LIB			Pettigrew, P.	LIB				

CANADA 1945–1998

Gov	Housing	Py	Agriculture	Py	Industry/Trade	Py	Environment	Py
1			Gardiner, J.	LIB	Mackinnon, J.	LIB		
			Bridges, H.	LIB	Glen, J.	LIB		
2			Gardiner, J.	LIB	MacKinnon, J.	LIB		
			Mayhew, R.	LIB	Howe, C.D.	LIB		
3			Gardiner, J.	LIB	Howe, C.D.	LIB		
			Mayhew, R.	LIB	Gibson, C.	LIB		
4			Gardiner, J.	LIB	Howe, C.D.	LIB		
			Sinclair, J.	LIB	Prudham, G.	LIB		
					Winters, R.	LIB		
5			Maclean, A.	CON	Churchill, G.	CON		
			Harkness, D.	CON	Comtois, P.	CON		
					Hamilton, A.	CON		
6			Maclean, A.	CON	Churchill, G.	CON		
			Harkness, D.	CON	Comtois, P.	CON		
					Hamilton, A.	CON		
7			Maclean, J.	CON	Dinsdale, W.	CON		
			Hamilton, A.	CON	Martineau, P.	CON		
			Maclean, J.	CON	Hees, G.	CON		
			Nowlan, G.	CON				
			Flemming, J.H.	CON				
8			Robichaud, H.	LIB	Sharp, M.	LIB		
			Nicholson, J.R.	LIB	Benidickson, W.M.	LIB		
			Hays, H.	LIB	Laing, A.	LIB		
9			Robichaud, H.	LIB	Pépin, J.-L.	LIB		
			Greene, J.J.	LIB	Drury, C.M.	LIB		
					Winters, R.	LIB		

CANADA 1945–1998

Gov	Housing	Py	Agriculture	Py	Industry/Trade	Py	Environment	Py
10			Robichaud, H. Sauvé, M. Greene, J.J.	LIB LIB LIB	Drury, C.M. Pépin, J.-L Turner, J.N.	LIB LIB LIB		
11			Marchand, J. Davis, J. Olson, H.A.	LIB LIB LIB	Pépin, J.-L. Greene, J.J. Basford, R.	LIB LIB LIB		
12			Lang, O. Whelan, E.F.	LIB LIB	Gray, H. MacDonald, D. Gillespie, A.	LIB LIB LIB	Davis, J.	LIB
13			Whelan, E.F. LeBlanc, R. Lang, O.	LIB LIB LIB	Gillespie, A. MacDonald, D.	LIB LIB	Sauvé, J.	LIB
14					Hnatyshyn, R. Cotret, R.R. de	CON CON		
15			Whelan, E.F. Leblanc, R.	LIB LIB	Gray, H. Lalonde, M. Ouellet, A. De Bane, P.	LIB LIB LIB LIB	Roberts, J.	LIB
16			Axworthy, L.L. Breau, H. Ferguson, R.	LIB LIB LIB	Lumley, E. Regan, G. Fox, F.	LIB LIB LIB	Caccia, C.	LIB
17			Fraser, J. Wise, J.	CON CON	Cote, M. *Carney, P. Kelleher, J.	CON CON CON	*Blais-Grenier, S.	CON
18			Mazankowski, D. Sidon, T. Wise, J.	CON CON CON	Valcourt, B. Epp, J. Crosby, J.	CON CON CON	Bouchard, B.	CON

CANADA 1945–1998

Gov	Housing	Py	Agriculture	Py	Industry/Trade	Py	Environment	Py
19			Mayer, C.	CON	Charest, J.	CON	Vincent, P.	CON
			*Sparrow, B.	CON	Hockin, T.	CON		
			Reid, R.	CON				
20			Goodale, R.	LIB	MacLaren, R.	LIB	*Copps, S.	LIB
			Tobin, B.	LIB	Manley, J.	LIB		
21			Anderson, D.	LIB	Marchi, S.	LIB	*Stewart, C.	LIB
			Vanchief, L.	LIB	Manley, J.	LIB		

Gov	Social Affairs (py)	Public Works (py)	Other (py)	Res
1	Mackenzie, I. (LIB)	Martin, P.J.J. (LIB)	Robertson, W. (LIB)	2
		Howe, C.D. (LIB)		
		Fournier, A. (LIB)		
		Chevrier, L. (LIB)		
		Bertrand, E. (LIB)		
2	Gregg, M. (LIB)	Howe, C.D. (LIB)	Robertson, W. (LIB)	0
		Fournier, A. (LIB)	Bradley, G. (LIB)	
		Chevrier, L. (LIB)		
		Bertrand, E. (LIB)		
3	Gregg, M. (LIB)	Fournier, A. (LIB)	Robertson, W. (LIB)	3
		Chevrier, L. (LIB)	Bradley, G. (LIB)	
		Rinfret, E. (LIB)	MacKinnon, J. (LIB)	
			Winters, R. (LIB)	

CANADA 1945–1998

Gov	Social Affairs (py)	Public Works (py)	Other (py)	Res
4	Lapointe, H. (LIB)	Harris, W. (LIB) Chevrier, L. (LIB) Rinfret, T. (LIB) Lesage, J. (LIB)	Robertson, W. (LIB)	1
5	Brooks, A. (CON) Monteigh, W. (CON)	Green, H. (CON) Hees, G. (CON) Hamilton, W. (CON) Hamilton, A. (CON)	MacDonnell, J.M. (CON) Browne, W. (CON) Fairclough, E. (CON)	0
6	Brooks, A. (CON) Monteigh, W. (CON)	Green, H. (CON) Hees, G. (CON) Hamilton, W. (CON) Hamilton, A. (CON)	MacDonnell, J.M. (CON) Browne, W. (CON) Fairclough, E. (CON)	1
7	Churchill, G. (CON) Monteigh, W. (CON)	Fulton, D. (CON) *Fairclough, E. (CON) Balcer, L. (CON) Dinsdale, W. (CON)	McClutcheon, M. (CON)	0
8	Teillet, R. (LIB) *La Marsh, J. (LIB)	Denis, A. (LIB) McIlraith, G.J. (LIB) Deschalets, J.-P. (LIB) Laing, A. (LIB)	MacDonald, W.R. (LIB) Tremblay, R. (LIB)	2
9	Teillet, R. (LIB) MacEachen, A.J. (LIB)	Pickersgill, J.W. (LIB) McIlraith, G.J. (LIB) Laing, A. (LIB) Côté, J.-P. (LIB) Pépin, J.-L. (LIB)	Turner, J.N. (LIB) Connolly, J.J. (LIB)	3

CANADA 1945–1998

Gov	Social Affairs (py)	Public Works (py)	Other (py)	Res
10	Turner, J.N. (LIB) MacEachen, A.J. (LIB) Teillet, R. (LIB)	Pépin, J.-L. (LIB) Hellyer, P.T. (LIB) MacIlraith, G.J. (LIB) Laing, A. (LIB) Côté, J.-P. (LIB) Sauvé, M. (LIB)	Laing, A. (LIB) Martin, P.J.J. (LIB) Granger, C. (LIB) MacKasey, B.S. (LIB) MacDonald, D.S. (LIB) Munro, J.C. (LIB) Pelletier, G. (LIB) Davis, J. (LIB)	0
11	Dubé, J.-E. (LIB) Basford; R. (LIB) Munro, J.C. (LIB)	Hellyer, P.T. (LIB) Laing, A. (LIB) Kierans, E. (LIB) Greene, J.J. (LIB) Chrétien, J. (LIB) Marchand, J. (LIB)	Martin, P.J.J. (LIB) Andras, R. (LIB) Richardson, J. (LIB) Lang, O. (LIB)	4
12	Gray, H. (LIB) MacDonald, D.J. (LIB) Lalonde, M. (LIB)	MacDonald, D. (LIB) Dubé, J.-E. (LIB) Basford, R. (LIB) Marchand, J. (LIB) Pelletier, G. (LIB) Goyer, J.-P. (LIB) Ouellet, A. (LIB) Chrétien, J. (LIB)	Chrétien, J. (LIB) Martin, P.J.J. (LIB)	0

CANADA 1945–1998

Gov	Social Affairs (py)	Public Works (py)	Other (py)	Res
13	MacDonald, D.J. (LIB) Lalonde, M. (LIB) Ouellet, A. (LIB)	Drury, C.M. (LIB) Marchand, J. (LIB) MacDonald, D. (LIB) Pelletier, G. (LIB) Goyer, J.-P. (LIB) MacKasey, B.S. (LIB) Danson, B. (LIB) Buchanan, J. (LIB)	Buchanan, J. (LIB) Perrault, R. (LIB)	6
14		Lasalle, R. (CON) MacDonald, D. (CON) Hnatyshyn, R. (CON)	Flynn, J. (CON)	0
15	MacDonald, D.J. (LIB) *Erola, J. (LIB) *Bégin, M. (LIB) Ouellet, A. (LIB) Chrétien, J. (LIB)	Ouellet, A. (LIB) Pépin, J.-L. (LIB) Munro, J.C. (LIB) Lalonde, M. (LIB) Blais, J.-J. (LIB) Fox, F. (LIB) Cosgrove, P. (LIB)	Perrault, R. (LIB)	5
16	*Bégin, M. (LIB) Campbell, B. (LIB) Lapierre, J. (LIB)	Lumley, E. (LIB) Regan, G. (LIB) Lapointe, C. (LIB) Axworthy, L.L. (LIB) Frith, D. (LIB)	Smith, D. (LIB) Frith, D. (LIB) MacEachen, A.J. (LIB) Collenette, D. (LIB)	0
17	Epp, J. (CON) Hees, G. (CON) Cote, M. (CON)	LaSalle, R. (CON) Mazankowski, D. (CON) Crombie, D. (CON) André, H. (CON) *Carney, P. (CON)	Crombie, D. (CON) Roblin, D. (CON) Hnatyshyn, R. (CON)	4

CANADA 1945–1998

Masse, M. (CON)

Gov	Social Affairs (py)	Public Works (py)	Other (py)	Res
18	Weiner, G. (CON) Beatty, P. (CON) Merrithew, G. (CON) Valcourt, B. (CON)	Masse, M. (CON) Mackay, E. (CON) Cadieux, P. (CON) Dick, P. (CON) Epp, J. (CON)	Cadieux, P. (CON)	3
19	Charest, J. (CON) *Collins, M. (CON) McCreath, P. (CON)	Dick, P. (CON) Corbeil, J. (CON) *Sparrow, B. (CON)	Mayer, C. (CON) *Landry, M. (CON) Weiner, G. (CON) Lewis, D. (CON) *Browes, P. (CON) Reid, R. (CON)	0
20	Collenette, D. (LIB)	Martin, P. (LIB) Massé, M. (LIB) Young, D. (LIB) *McLellan, A. (LIB) Irwin, R. (LIB) Dingwall, D. (LIB) Eggleton, A. (LIB)	*Fairbairn, J. (LIB) Gray, H. (LIB) Dupuy, M. (LIB) Dingwall, D. (LIB) Irwin, R. (LIB) Anderson, D. (LIB) Massé, M. (LIB)	4
21	Mifflin, F. (LIB)	Collenette, D. (LIB) Goodale, R. (LIB) Gagliano, A. (LIB)	*Copps, S. (LIB) *Marleau, D. (LIB) *Stewart, J. (LIB) Boudria, D. (LIB) Graham, A. (LIB)	

11. CZECH AND SLOVAK FEDERATIVE REPUBLIC 1990-1992

Gov	Begin	Dur	RfT	ToG	Py1	Py2	Py3	Seats	CPG	NoM	Prime Minister (py)
1	27.06.90	737	1	3	Civic Forum/PAV 170	KDS-ČSL 40		300	1	16	Čalva, M. (PAV)
2	03.07.92	182	x	2	ODS-KDS 85	HZDS 57	KDU-ČSL 13	300	2	10	Straski, J. (ODS-KDS)

- Gov 1: Oversized coalition because a 3/5 majority was needed to amend the constitution.
- Gov 2: Reason for Termination is demise of Czech and Slovak Federative Republic on 31 December 1992 after Slovakia declared independence on 17 July 1992.

Gov	Deputy PM	Py	Foreign Affairs	Py	Defence	Py	Interior	Py	Justice	Py
1	Vales, V.	NONA	Dienstbier, J.	Civic F.	Vacek, M.	NONA	Langos, J.	PAV		
	Rychetský, P.	NONA								
	Miklosko, J.	KDS-ČSL								
	Dienstbier, J.	Civic F.								
2	Filkus, R.	HZDS	Moravčik, J.	HZDS	Andrejcak, I.	NONA	Cermak, P.	ODS-KDS		
	Cic, M.	HZDS								
	Macek, M.	ODS-KDS								
	Baudýs, A.	KDU-ČSL								

Gov	Finance	Py	Economic Aff.	Py	Labour	Py	Education	Py	Health	Py
1	Klaus, V.	Civic F.	Vales, V.	NONA	Miller, P.	Civic F.				
			Dlouhý, V.	Civic F.						
			Hoffmann, P.	NONA						
2	Klak, J.	ODS-KDS	Filkus, R.	HZDS	Macek, M.	ODS-KDS				
			Cic, M.	HZDS						
			Kubecka, J.	HZDS						

169

CZECH AND SLOVAK FEDERATIVE REPUBLIC 1990-1992

Gov	Housing	Py	Agriculture	Py	Industry/Trade	Py	Environment	Py
1					Stracar, S.	PAV		
2					Strasky, J.	ODS-KDS	Macek, M.	ODS-KDS

Gov	Social Affairs (py)	Public Works (py)	Other (py)	Res
1	Miller, P. (Civic F.)	Nezval, J. (NONA) Petrík, T. (NONA)	Miklosko, J. (KDU-ČSL) Vavrousek, J. (NONA) *Kořínková, K. (NONA)	1
2	Macek, M. (ODS-KDS)	Baudýs, A. (KDU-ČSL)		0

12. CZECH REPUBLIC

The republic was constitutionally founded in 1993. The Head of State has largely ceremonial functions and is indirectly elected by both Houses of parliament for a five-year term.

The Czech Republic is now a unitary and centralised state.

Parliament is weakly bicameral. The Senate of 81 seats and the Chamber of Deputies of 200 seats are elected by proportional representation (d'Hondt - with an electoral threshold of 5, 7, or 11%, depending on the number of parties forming an alliance) in constituencies varying between approximately 500,000 to 1,000,000 electors.

Parliament has a quorum of one-third of all members. Votes are carried by a majority of all members present. Some issues require a qualified majority ranging from an absolute to a three-fifth majority of all members. Constitutional amendments require a majority of three-fifth of all members in both Houses.

Government rests on parliamentary support. The Cabinet is the supreme organ of executive power A vote of investiture is required before it takes office. Government can also face a vote of no confidence. Losing either vote always results in resignation of the government.

Government is collectively responsible to parliament. Individual ministers may be members of parliament. The Prime Minister has no dominant position in government.

There is a Constitutional Court for review of lawmaking.

CZECH REPUBLIC 1992-1998

Gov	Begin	Dur	RfT	ToG	Py1	Py2	Py3	Seats	CPG	NoM	Prime Minister (py)
1	03.07.92	182	x	2	ODS-KDS 66+10	KDU-ČSL 15	ODA 14	200	2	17	Klaus, V. (ODS-KDS)
2	01.01.93	1281	1	2	ODS-KDS 66+10	KDU-ČSL 15	ODA 14	200	2	19	Klaus, V. (ODS-KDS)
3	05.07.96			5	ODS 68	KDU-ČSL 18	ODA 13	200	2	16	Klaus, V. (ODS)

- Gov 1: Reason for Termination is the demise of the Czech and Slovak Federative Republic (Czechoslovakia) on 31 December 1992.

Gov	Deputy PM	Py	Foreign Affairs	Py	Defence	Py	Interior	Py	Justice	Py
1	Kočárník, I. Kalvoda, J. Lux, J.	ODS ODA KDU-ČSL	Zielenic, J.	ODS			Ruml, J.	ODS-KDS	Kalvoda, J. Novák, J.	ODA ODS
2	Kočárník, I. Lux, J. Kalvoda, J.	ODS KDU-ČSL ODA	Zielenic, J.	ODS	Baudýs, A.	KDU-ČSL	Ruml, J.	ODS-KDS	Novák, J.	ODS
3			Zielenic, J.	ODS	Vyborny, M.	KDU-ČSL	Ruml, J.	ODS	Kalvoda, J.	ODA

Gov	Finance	Py	Economic Aff.	Py	Labour	Py	Education	Py	Health	Py
1	Kočárník, I.	ODS	Dyba, K. Skalický, J Beclehrádek, S.	ODS ODA KDU-ČSL	Vodička, J.	ODS	Pitcha, P.	ODS-KDS	Lom, P.	ODS
2	Kočárník, I.	ODS	Dyba, K. Skalický, J. Beclehrádek, S.	ODS ODA KDU-ČSL	Vodička, J.	ODS	Pitcha, P.	ODS-KDS	Lom, P.	ODS
3	Kočárník, I.	ODS			Vodička, J.	ODS	Pilip, I.	ODS	Strasky, J.	ODS

CZECH REPUBLIC 1992-1998

Gov	Housing	Py	Agriculture	Py	Industry/Trade	Py	Environment	Py
1			Lux, J.	KDU-ČSL	Dlouhý, V.	ODA	Benda, F.	ODS-KDS
2			Lux, J.	KDU-ČSL	Dlouhý, V.	ODA	Benda, F.	ODS-KDS
3	Schneider, J.	KDU-ČSL	Lux, J.	KDU-ČSI	Dlouhý, V.	ODA	Skalický, J.	ODA

Gov	Social Affairs (py)	Public Works (py)	Other (py)	Res
1	Pitcha, P. (ODS-KDS) Vodička, J. (ODS)		Dlouhý, V. (ODA) Kabát, J.(KDU-ČSL) Necmec, I. (ODS)	0
2	Vodička, J. (ODS)	Strasky, J. (ODS-KDS)	Dlouhý, V. (ODA) Kabát, J.(KDU-ČSL) Necmec, I. (ODS)	1
3	Vodička, J. (ODS)	Riman, M. (ODS)	Talir, J. (KDU-ČSL) Schneider, J. (KDU-ČSL) Bratinka, P. (ODA)	1

13. DENMARK

The constitutional revision of 1953 basically reinstalled the 1849 version.

The country is a hereditary Kingdom with parliamentary government.

Denmark is a unitary and centralised state, although the discretionary powers given to communities are considerable. The Faröer Islands and Greenland are both autonomous regions.

Parliament (Folketing) has been unicameral since 1953. Its 179 members are elected by proportional representation (St. Lagüe) for a fixed term of four years in multi-member constituencies of variable size. The number of deputies is proportional to the size of the constituency, thus preserving strict proportionality.

Parliament has a quorum of at least 50 per cent of all members. Votes are carried by a majority of votes cast. For some issues a qualified majority of three-quarters of votes cast is required. Constitutional amendments require a majority of all votes cast, but have to be approved by referendum. For other issues also, a referendum is constitutionally required. A referendum is initiated by parliament. The outcome is binding.

Governments need no vote of investiture, yet may face a vote of no confidence directed at the Prime Minister only. In turn the Prime Minister, acting together with the Head of State, can dissolve the Folketing. Losing a vote of confidence always results in the resignation of the government (and possibly new elections).

Government is collectively and individually responsible to parliament. Individual ministers may also be members of parliament. The Prime Minister has a rather prominent role in government.

Constitutional review of lawmaking in view of the constitution is limited and exercised by the Supreme Court on request only.

DENMARK 1945–1998

Gov	Begin	Dur	RfT	ToG	Py1	Py2	Py3	Py4	Py5	Seats	CPG	NoM	Prime Minister (py)
1	08.11.45	735	5	4	LIB 38	[RAD 11]				148	2	14	Kristensen, K. (LIB)
2	13.11.47	1037	5	4	SD 57	[RAD 10]				148	4	16	Hedtoft, H. (SD)
3	15.09.50	42	5	4	SD 59					149	4	14	Hedtoft, H. (SD)
4	27.10.50	921	1	5	CON 27	LIB 32				149	2	13	Eriksen, E. (LIB)
5	05.05.53	148	1	5	CON 26	LIB 33				149	2	13	Eriksen, E. (LIB)
6	30.09.53	489	3	4	SD 74					175	4	14	Hedtoft, H. (SD)
7	01.02.55	847	1	4	SD 74	[RAD 14]				175	4	13	Hansen, H.C. (SD)
8	28.05.57	998	3	2	SD 70	RAD 14	JP 9			175	4	16	Hansen, H.C. (SD)
9	21.02.60	271	1	2	SD 70	RAD 14	JP 9			175	4	15	Kampmann, V. (SD)
10	18.11.60	655	3	5	SD 76	RAD 11				175	4	17	Kampmann, V. (SD)
11	04.09.62	753	1	5	SD 76	RAD 11				175	4	17	Krag, J.O. (SD)
12	26.09.64	793	1	4	SD 76	[RAD 10]	[SPP 10]			175	4	17	Krag, J.O. (SD)
13	28.11.66	430	5	4	SD 69	[SPP 20]				175	4	19	Krag, J.O. (SD)
14	01.02.68	1348	1	2	RAD 27	LIB 34	CON 37			175	2	17	Baunsgaard, H.T.I. (RAD)
15	11.10.71	360	2	4	SD 70					175	4	18	Krag, J.O. (SD)
16	05.10.72	440	1	4	SD 70					175	4	18	Jørgensen, A. (SD)
17	19.12.73	421	1	4	LIB 22					175	2	12	Hartling, P. (LIB)
18	13.02.75	743	5	4	SD 53	[RAD 13]	[SPP 9]	[COM 7]	[LSP 4]	175	4	15	Jørgensen, A. (SD)
19	25.02.77	551	7	4	SD 65	LIB 21				175	4	17	Jørgensen, A. (SD)
20	30.08.78	422	4	5	SD 65	LIB 21				175	4	20	Jørgensen, A. (SD)
21	26.10.79	797	5	4	SD 68					175	4	17	Jørgensen, A. (SD)
22	31.12.81	253	4	4	SD 59					175	4	20	Jørgensen, A. (SD)
23	10.09.82	498	5	5	CON 26	LIB 21	CDM 15	CPP 4		175	2	21	Schlüter, P. (CON)
24	21.01.84	1328	1	5	CON 42	LIB 23	CDM 8	CPP 5		175	2	21	Schlüter, P. (CON)
25	10.09.87	267	5	5	CON 38	LIB 19	CDM 9	CPP 4		175	2	23	Schlüter, P. (CON)
26	03.06.88	927	5	5	CON 35	LIB 22	RAD 10			175	2	21	Schlüter, P. (CON)

DENMARK 1945–1998

Gov	Begin	Dur	RfT	ToG	Py1	Py2	Py3	Py4	Py5	Seats	CPG	NoM	Prime Minister (py)
27	18.12.89	770	2	5	CON 30	LIB 29	CDM 8	CPP 4		179	2	19	Schlüter, P. (CON)
28	25.01.93	609	1	2	SD 71	RAD 7	CDM 8			179	4	24	Rasmussen, N. (SD)
29	26.09.94			5	SD 62	RAD 8	CDM 5			179	4	20	Rasmussen, N. (SD)

[] Denotes parties supporting government without participating in it.

Gov	Deputy PM	Py	Foreign Affairs	Py	Defence	Py	Interior	Py	Justice	Py
1			Rasmussen, G.	NONA	Petersen, H.	LIB	Kjaer, E.	LIB	Elmquist, A.	LIB
2			Rasmussen, G.	NONA	Hansen, R.	SD	Andersen, A.	SD	Busch-Jensen, N.	SD
3			Rasmussen, G.	NONA	Hansen, R.	SD	Smörum, J.	SD	Steincke, K.K.	SD
4			Kraft, O.B.	CON	Petersen, H.	LIB	Möller, A.	CON	*Pedersen, H.	LIB
5			Kraft, O.B.	CON	Petersen, H.	LIB	Möller, A.	CON	*Pedersen, H.	LIB
6			Hansen, H.C.	SD	Hansen, R.	SD	Kjaerböl, J.	SD	Haekkerup, H.	SD
7			Hansen, H.C.	SD	Hansen, R.	SD	Kjaerböl, J.	SD	Haekkerup, H.	SD
8			Hansen, H.C.	SD	Hansen, P.	SD	Olesen, S.	JP	Haekkerup, H.	SD
9			Krag, J.O.	SD	Hansen, P.	SD	Olesen, S.	JP	Haekkerup, H.	SD
10			Krag, J.O.	SD	Hansen, P.	SD	Knudsen, H.R.	SD	Haekkerup, H.	SD
11			Haekkerup, P.	SD	Hansen, P.	SD	Jensen, L.P.	SD	Haekkerup, H.	SD
12			Haekkerup, P.	SD	Gram, V.	SD	Haekkerup, H.	SD	Nielsen, K.A.	SD
13			Krag, J.O.	SD	Gram, V.	SD	Haekkerup, H.	SD	Nielsen, K.A.	SD
14			Hartling, P.	LIB	Ninn-Hansen, E.	CON	Sörensen, P.	CON	Thestrup, K.	CON
15			Andersen, K.B.	SD	Olesen, K.	SD	Jensen, E.	SD	Nielsen, K.A.	SD
16			Andersen, K.B.	SD	Olesen, K.	SD	Jensen, E.	SD	Nielsen, K.A.	SD
17			Guldberg, O.	LIB	Brøndum, E.	LIB	Sörensen, J.	LIB	*Lind, N.	LIB

DENMARK 1945–1998

Gov	Deputy PM	Py	Foreign Affairs	Py	Defence	Py	Interior	Py	Justice	Py
18			Andersen, K.B.	SD	Møller, O.	SD	Jensen, E.	SD	Møller, O.	SD
19			Andersen, K.B.	SD	Møller, O.	SD	Jensen, E.	SD	Møller, O.	SD
20			Christophersen, H.	LIB	Søgaard, P.	LIB	Enggaard, K.	LIB	*Lind, N.	LIB
21			Olesen, K.	SD	Søgaard, P.	SD	Rasmussen, H.	SD	Rasmussen, H.	SD
22			Olesen, K.	SD	Søgaard, P.	SD	Rasmussen, H.	SD	Espersen, O.	SD
23	Christophersen, H.	LIB	Ellemann-Jensen, U.	LIB	Engell, H.	LIB	*Holberg, B.	CON	Ninn-Hansen, E.	CON
24	Christophersen, H.	LIB	Ellemann-Jensen, U.	LIB	Engell, H.	LIB	*Holberg, B.	CON	Ninn-Hansen, E.	CON
25			Elleman-Jensen, U.	LIB	Collet, B.J.	LIB	Pedersen, T.	CON	Ninn-Hansen, E.	CON
26			Elleman-Jensen, U.	LIB	Enggaard, K.	LIB	Pedersen, T.	LIB	Ninn-Hansen, E.	CON
27			Elleman-Jensen, U.	LIB	Enggaard, K.	LIB	Pedersen, T.	LIB	Engell, H.	CON
28			Petersen, N.H.	RAD	Haekkerup, H.	SD	*Weiss, B.	SD	*Gjellerup, P.	SD
29			Petersen, N.H.	RAD	Haekkerup, H.	RAD	*Weiss, B.	SD	Westh, B.	SD

Gov	Finance	Py	Economic Aff.	Py	Labour	Py	Education	Py	Health	Py
1	Kristensen, T.	LIB			Larsen, S.P.	LIB	Hartling, M.R.	LIB		
2	Hansen, H.C.	SD			Sörensen, M.	SD	Frisch, H.	SD		
3	Kampmann, V.	SD			Kjaerböl, J.	SD	Bomholt, J.	SD		
4	Kristensen, T.	LIB			Sörensen, P.	CON	Hvidberg, F.	CON		
5	Kristensen, T.	LIB			Sörensen, P.	CON	Hvidberg, F.	CON		
6	Kampmann, V.	SD			Ström, J.	SD	Bomholt, J.	SD		
7	Kampmann, V.	SD	Krag, J.O.	SD	Krag, J.O.	SD	Bomholt, J.	SD		
8	Kampmann, V.	SD	Dahlgaard, B.; Krag, J.O.	RAD; SD	Bundvad, K.	SD	Jörgensen, J.	RAD		

DENMARK 1945–1998

Gov	Finance	Py	Economic Aff.	Py	Labour	Py	Education	Py	Health	Py
9	Kampmann, V.	SD	Dahlgaard, B. / Krag, J.O.	RAD / SD	Bundvad, K.	SD	Jörgensen, J.	RAD		
10	Philip, K.	RAD	Dahlgaard, B.	RAD	Bundvad, K.	SD	Jörgensen, J.	RAD		
11	Knudsen, H.R.	SD	Philip, K.	RAD	Bundvad, K.	SD	Petersen, K.H.	RAD		
12	Hansen, P.	SD			Dinesen, E.	SD	Andersen, K.B.	SD		
13	Grünbaum, H.	SD	Nørgaard, I.	SD	Dinesen, E.	SD	Andersen, K.B.	SD		
14	Möller, P.	CON	Andersen, P.N.	LIB	Dahlgaard, L.	RAD	Larsen, H.	RAD		
15	Grünbaum, H. / Haekkerup, P.	SD / SD	Haekkerup, P. / Nørgaard, I.	SD / SD	Dinesen, E.	SD	Heinesen, K.	SD		
16	Grünbaum, H. / Haekkerup, P.	SD / SD	Haekkerup, P. / Nørgaard, I.	SD / SD	Dinesen, E.	SD	Heinesen, K.	SD		
17	Andersen, A.	LIB	Andersen, P.N.	LIB	Philipsen, J.	LIB	*Nielsen, T.	LIB		
18	Heinesen, K. / Jakobsen, S.	SD / SD	Haekkerup, P. / Nørgaard, I.	SD / SD	Dinesen, E.	SD	*Bjerregaard, R.	SD		
19	Heinesen, K. / Kampmann, J.	SD / SD	Haekkerup, P.	SD	Jensen, E.	SD	*Bjerregaard, R.	SD		
20	Heinesen, K. / Andersen, A.	SD / LIB	Andersen, A.	LIB	Auken, S.	SD	*Bjerregaard, R.	SD		
21	Jakobsen, S. / Hjortnaes, K.	SD / SD	Nørgaard, I.	SD	Auken, S.	SD	*Bennedsen, D.	SD		
22	Heinesen, K. / Lykketoft, M.	SD / SD	Nørgaard, I.	SD	Auken, S.	SD	*Bennedsen, D.	SD		
23	Christophersen, H. / Foighel, I.	LIB / CON	Andersen, A.	LIB	*Möller, G.F.	CON	Haarder, B.	LIB		
24	Christophersen, H. / Foighel, I.	LIB / CON	Andersen, A.	LIB	*Möller, G.F.	CON	Haarder, B.	LIB		
25	Simonsen, P. / Rasmussen, A.F.	CON / LIB	Jacobsen, E. / Enngaard, K.	CON / LIB	Dyremose, H.	CON	Haarder, B.	LIB	*Laustsen, A.	CON

DENMARK 1945–1998

Gov	Finance	Py	Economic Aff.	Py	Labour	Py	Education	Py	Health	Py
26	Simonsen, P. Rasmussen, A.F.	CON LIB	Petersen, N.H.	RAD	Dyremose, H.	CON	Haarder, B. Schlüter, P.	LIB CON	*Kock-Petersen, E.	CON
27	Dyremose, H.	CON	Rasmussen, A.F.	LIB	Kirkegaard, K.E.	CON	Haarder, B.	LIB	*Larsen, E.	LIB
28	Stavad, O. Lykketoft, M.	SD SD	*Jelved, M.	RAD	*Andersen, J.	SD	Jensen, O.V. Bergstein, S.	RAD CD	Lund, T.	SD
29	Lykketoft, M. Stavad, O.	SD SD	*Jelved, M.	RAD	*Andersen, J.	SD	Jensen, F. Jensen, O.V.	SD RAD	*Herloev Andersen, Y.	CD

Gov	Housing	Py	Agriculture	Py	Industry/Trade	Py	Environment	Py
1			Eriksen, E.	LIB	Villemôs, J. Kristensen, A.	LIB LIB		
2			Bording, K. Christiansen, C.	SD SD	Krag, J.O.	SD		
3	Kjaerböl, J.	SD	Petersen, C. Christiansen, C.	SD SD	Hansen, H.C.	SD		
4	Möller, A.	CON	Hauch, H. Rée, K.	LIB LIB	Weikop, O.	CON		
5	Möller, A.	CON	Sönderup, J. Rée, K.	LIB LIB	Rytter, A.	CON		
6	Kjaerböl, J.	SD	Smôrum, J. Christiansen, C.	SD SD	*Groes, L.	SD		
7	Kjaerböl, J.	SD	Smôrum, J. Christiansen, C.	SD SD	Krag, J.O. *Groes, L.	SD SD		

DENMARK 1945–1998

Gov	Housing	Py	Agriculture	Py	Industry/Trade	Py	Environment	Py
8	Bundvad, K.	SD	Skytte, K. / Pedersen, O.	RAD / JP	Philip, K.	RAD		
9	Bundvad, K.	SD	Skytte, K. / Pedersen, O.	RAD / JP	Philip, K.	RAD		
10	Jensen, C.P.	SD	Skytte, K. / Normann, A.C.	RAD / RAD	Jensen, L.P.	SD		
11	Jensen, C.P.	SD	Skytte, K. / Normann, A.C.	RAD / RAD	Baunsgaard, H.T.I.	RAD		
12	Andresen, K.	SD	Thomsen, C. / Larsen-Bjerre, H.	SD / SD	Jensen, L.P.	SD		
13	Andresen, K.	SD	Thomsen, C. / Knudsen, J.R.	SD / SD	Dahlgaard, T.	SD		
14	Hastrup, A.	CON	Larsen, P. / Normann, A.C.	LIB / RAD	Thomsen, K.	CON		
15	Nielsen, H.	SD	Frederiksen, I. / Thomsen, C.	SD / SD	Jensen, E.	SD		
16	Nielsen, H.	SD	Frederiksen, I. / Thomsen, C.	SD / SD	Jensen, E.	SD		
17	Philipsen, J.	LIB	Kofoed, N.A.	LIB	Andersen, P.N.	LIB	Hansen, H.	LIB
18	Nielsen, H.	SD	Dalgaser, P.	SD	Jensen, E.	SD	Nielsen, H.	SD
19	Hove, O.	SD	Dalgaser, P. / Jakobsen, S.	SD / SD	Nørgaard, I.	SD	Matthiasen, N.	SD
20	Olsen, E.	SD	Kofoed, N.A. / Jakobsen, S.	LIB / SD	Christiansen, A.	LIB	Nørgaard, I.	SD
21	Olsen, E.	SD	Dalgaser, P.	SD	Jensen, E.	SD	Nørgaard, I.	SD
22	Olsen, E.	SD	Westh, B. / Hjortnaes, K.	SD / SD	Jensen, E.	SD	Holst, E.	SD

DENMARK 1945–1998

Gov	Housing	Py	Agriculture	Py	Industry/Trade	Py	Environment	Py
23	Bollmann, N.	CDM	Kofoed, N.A. Grove, H.	LIB CON	Stetter, I.	CON	Christensen, C.	CPP
24	Bollmann, N.	CDM	Kofoed, N.A. Grove, H.	LIB CON	Stetter, I.	CON	Christensen, C.	CPP
25	Kofod-Svendsen, F.	CPP	Toernaes, L. Gammelgaard, L.P.	LIB CON	Wilhjelm, N.	CON	Christensen, C.	CDM
26	*Laustsen, A.	CON	Toernaes, L. Gammelgaard, L.P.	LIB CON	Wilhjelm, N.	CON	*Dybkjaer, L.	RAD
27	Hovmand, S.E.	LIB	Toernaes, L. Kirk, K.	LIB CON	*Lundholt, A.B.	CON	Moeller, P.S.	CON
28	Kofod Svensen, F.	CPP	Westh, B.	SD	Troejborg, J. *Jakobsen, M.	SD CD	Auken, S.	SD
29	Simonsen, O.L.	SD	Dam Christensen, H.	SD	*Jakobsen, M.	CD	Auken, S.	SD

Gov	Social Affairs (py)	Public Works (py)	Other (py)	Res
1	Larsen, S.P. (LIB)	Eigaard, N. (LIB)	Hermansen, C. (LIB) Federspiel, P. (LIB)	1
2	Ström, J. (SD)	Petersen, C. (SD)	Buhl, W. (SD) Nielsen, F. (SD) *Jensen, F. (SD)	0
3	Ström, J. (SD)	Nielsen, F. (SD)	*Koch, B. (SD)	0
4	Sörensen, P. (CON)	Larsen, V. (CON)	Sönderup, J. (LIB)	0
5	Sörensen, P. (CON)	Larsen, V. (CON)	Hermansen, C. (LIB)	0

DENMARK 1945–1998

Gov	Social Affairs (py)	Public Works (py)	Other (py)	Res
6	Ström, J. (SD)	Petersen, C. (SD)	Krag, J.O. (SD) *Koch, B. (SD)	1
7	Ström, J. (SD)	Petersen, C. (SD)	*Koch, B. (SD)	1
8	Bomholt, J. (SD)	Lindberg, K. (SD)	Lindberg, K. (SD) Dahlgaard, B. (RAD) *Koch, B. (SD) Starcke, V. (JP)	1
9	Bomholt, J. (SD)	Lindberg, K. (SD)	Lindberg, K. (SD) Dahlgaard, B. (RAD) *Koch, B. (SD) Starcke, V. (JP)	1
10	Bomholt, J. (SD)	Lindberg, K. (SD)	*Koch, B. (SD) Gam, M. (NONA)	1
11	Bundvad, K. (SD)	Lindberg, K. (SD)	*Koch, B. (SD) Bomholt, J. (SD) Gam, M. (NONA)	2
12	Bundvad, K. (SD)	Lindberg, K. (SD)	*Koch, B. (SD) Sölvöj, H. (SD) Jensen, C.P. (SD)	0
13	Bundvad, K. (SD) *Larsen-Ledet, C. (SD)	Horn, S. (SD)	Dahlgaard, T. (SD) Möller, O. (SD) Sölvöj, H. (SD) Jensen, C.P. (SD) *Koch, B. (SD)	2
14	*Lind, N. (LIB)	Hastrup, A. (CON) Guldberg, O. (LIB)	Normann, A.C. (RAD) Thomsen, K. (CON) Pedersen, A.F. (LIB) Petersen, K.H. (RAD)	1

DENMARK 1945–1998

Gov	Social Affairs (py)	Public Works (py)	Other (py)	Res
15	*Gredal, E. (SD)	Kampmann, J. (SD)	Nørgaard, I. (SD) Matthiasen, N. (SD) Hertling, K. (NONA) *Bennedsen, D. (SD)	0
16	*Gredal, E. (SD)	Kampmann, J. (SD)	Nørgaard, I. (SD) Matthiasen, N. (SD) Hertling, K. (NONA) *Bennedsen, D. (SD)	1
17	Sørensen, J. (LIB)	Damsgaard, K. (LIB)	*Lind, N. (LIB) Damsgaard, K. (LIB) Hansen, H. (LIB)	0
18	*Gredal, E. (SD)	Matthiasen, N. (SD)	Nørgaard, I. (SD) Matthiasen, N. (SD) Hansen, J.P. (SD)	1
19	*Gredal, E. (SD)	Olesen, K. (SD)	Matthiasen, N. (SD) *Oestergaard, L. (SD) Hansen, J.P. (SD)	1
20	Jensen, E. (SD)	Hansen, I. (LIB)	Jensen, E. (SD) Matthiasen, N. (SD) *Oestergaard, L. (SD) Hansen, J.P. (SD) Haekkerup, P. (SD)	0
21	*Bjerregaard, R. (SD)	Knudsen, J.R. (SD) Nielson, P. (SD)	Matthiasen, N. (SD) *Oestergaard, L. (SD) Hansen, J.P. (SD)	2
22	Hansen, B. (SD)	Hansen, J.K. (SD) Nielson, P. (SD)	*Oestergaard, L. (SD) *Larsen, T.L. (SD)	0

DENMARK 1945–1998

Gov	Social Affairs (py)	Public Works (py)	Other (py)	Res
23	Simonsen, P. (CON)	Melchior, A. (CDM) Enggaard, K. (LIB)	Christensen, C. (CPP) *Kock-Petersen, E. (LIB) *Jacobsen, M. (CDM) Hoeyem, T. (CDM)	0
24	Simonsen, P. (CON)	Melchior, A. (CDM) Enggaard, K. (LIB)	Christensen, C. (CPP) *Kock-Petersen, E. (LIB) *Jacobsen, M. (CDM) Hoeyem, T. (CDM)	2
25	*Stilling-Jacobsen, M. (CDM)	Christensen, F.N. (CDM) Hovmand, S.E. (LIB)	Gammelgaard, L.P. (CON) Wilhjelm, N. (CON) *Madsen, M. (LIB) Clausen, H.P. (CON)	0
26	Olsen, A. (RAD)	Bilgrav-Nielsen, J. (RAD) Clausen, H.P. (CON)	Jensen, O.V. (RAD) Rechenorff, T. (CON)	1
27	*Andersen, E.W. (LIB)	Ikast, K. (CON)	Pedersen, T. (LIB) *Rostboell, G. (CON) Rechendorff, T. (CON)	0
28	*Jespersen, K. (SD)	Sjursen, J. (CPP) Mortensen, H. (SD) Melchior, A. (CD)	Melchior, A. (CD) *Degn, H. (SD) *Hilden, J. (SD) Andersen, A.O. (CD)	1
29	*Jespersen, K. (SD)	Simonsen, O.L. (SD) Troejborg, J. (SD) Auken, S. (SD)	*Jelved, M. (RAD) Nielson, P. (SD) *Weiss, B. (SD) *Hilden, J. (SD)	

14. ESTONIA

The Head of State is an indirectly elected President, who serves for a five-year term, with a two term maximum.

Estonia is a unitary state, but local government has discretionary rights and certain fiscal powers.

Parliament (Riigoku) is unicameral. Its 101 members are elected by proportional representation (d'Hondt) for a fixed term of four years in constituencies of variable size. The number of deputies is adjusted to the number of electors in each constituency.

Parliament has a quorum of at least 50 per cent of all members. Votes are carried by a majority of all votes cast. For some issues a qualified majority is required, ranging from a majority to a two-thirds majority of all members. Amending the constitution is a complicated matter. It can be done in three ways. Firstly, through a binding referendum. A proposal for a referendum requires a three-fifth majority of all members of parliament. Secondly, through two ballot rounds, requiring a majority of all members of parliament in the first round, and a three-fifth majority of all members in the second round. Thirdly, with a three-fifth majority of all members, a proposal becomes 'a matter of urgency', after which a two-thirds majority of all members is required to carry the vote.

A referendum is optional and may be called by parliament (see above). The outcome is binding. If the proposal does not fetch a majority in the referendum, the President will call early elections for parliament.

The President nominates the Prime Minister, who, with his or her ministers, needs a vote of investiture in parliament to form the government. During its lifetime, a government can also face a vote of no confidence. Losing a vote of confidence always results in resignation of the government. Government is both collectively and individually responsible to parliament. Being a minister is not compatible with being a Member of Parliament. The Prime Minister has a rather prominent position in government.

The Chancellor, aided by the National Court, supervises the legality of governmental and presidential actions, adjudicates on the constitutionality of laws, and regulates the bureaucracy and local government.

ESTONIA 1992 – 1998

Gov	Begin	Dur	RfT	ToG	Py1	Py2	Py3	Seats	CPG	NoM	PM(py)
1	21.10.92	682	5	2	Isamaa 29	Moderates 12	ERSP 10	101	2	9	Laar, M. (Isamaa)
2	03.11.94	165	1	6				101	3	16	Tarand, A. (NONA)
3	17.04.95	102	4	2	KMU 41	K 16		101	2	14	Vähi, T. (KMU-K)
4	03.11.95	396	4	2	KMU 41	R 19		101	2	15	Vähi, T. (KMU-K)
5	02.12.96	102	2	4	KMU 41			101	2	15	Vähi, T. (KMU-K)
6	14.03.97			5	KMU-K ?			101	2	14	Siiman, M. (KMU-K)

- Date of independence: 20 August 1991.
- Date of first free post independence general elections: 20 September 1992.
- Gov 1-6: Ongoing proces of partyformation (splitting, merging, renaming, factionalising, etcetera).
- Gov 1: There is an official coalition agreement between Isamaa, Moderates, and ERSP (Estonian National Independence Party); however, the initial government apparently consists of Isamaa ministers only.
- Gov 3: KMU is election coalition between Coalition Party (K) and Rural Union Bloc (MU); K is Centre Party.
- Gov 4: R is Estonian Reform Party.
- Gov 6: Type of Government is minority coalition between KMU-K (seats unknown) and 'three smaller pensioners and farmers parties' (names and seats unknown); the latter were apparently not represented in government, all ministers were KMU-K members.

Gov	Deputy PM	Py	Foreign Affairs	Py	Defence	Py	Interior	Py	Justice	Py
1			Velliste, T.	Isamaa	Rebas, H.	Isamaa	*Parek, L.	Isamaa	Kaama, K.	Isamaa
2			Luik, J.		Tupp. E.		Kaama, K.		Adams, J.	
3			Sinijärv, R.	KMU-?	Öövel, A.	KMU-K	Savisaar, E.	K	Varul, P.	KMU-K
4	Kallas, S.	R	Kallas, S.	R	Öövel, A.	KMU-K	Rask, M.	R	Varul, P.	KMU-K
5			Ilves, T.H.	KMU-K	Öövel, A.	KMU-K	Sinijärv, R.	KMU-K	Varul, P.	KMU-K
6			Ilves, T.H.	KMU-K	Öövel, A.	KMU-K	Sinijärv, R.	KMU-K	Varul, P.	KMU-K

ESTONIA 1992 – 1998

Gov	Finance	Py	Economic Affairs	Py	Labour	Py	Education	Py	Health	Py
1	Uurike, M.	Isamaa	Saarmann, A.	Isamaa						
2	Lipstock, A.		Jurgensen, T.				Olesk, P.			
3	Opmann, M.	KMU-K	Tonisson, L.	K			Kreitzburg, P.	K		
4	Opmann, M.	KMU-K	Lipstock, A.	R			Aavisko, J.	R		
5	Opmann, M.	KMU-MU	Leimann, J.	KMU-K	Aro, T.	KMU-K	Loik, R.	KMU-?		
6	Opmann, M.	KMU-K	Leimann, J.	KMU-K			Klassen, M.	KMU-K		

Gov	Housing	Py	Agriculture	Py	Industry/Trade	Py	Environment	Py
1								
2			Tamm, A.				Hanson, V.	
3			Mändmets, I.	KMU-MU			Reiljan, V.	KMU-MU
4			Mändmets, I.	KMU-MU			Reiljan, V.	KMU-MU
5			Mändmets, I.	KMU-MU			Reiljan, V.	KMU-MU
6			Varik, A.	KMU-K			Reiljan, V.	KMU-K

Gov	Social Affairs (py)	Public Works (py)	Other (py)	Res
1	Lauristin, M. (ISamaa)		Luik, J. (Isamaa)	2
2	Viliosius, T.	Meister, A.	Luik, J. / Olesk, P. / *Hanni, L. / Niitenberg, A. / Nestor, E. / Kaevats, U.	0

ESTONIA 1992 – 1998

Gov	Social Affairs (py)	Public Works (py)	Other (py)	Res
3	Oviir, S.(K	Kallo, K. (K)	Kreitzburg, P. (K) Allik, J. (KMU-K) Lippmaa, E. (KMU-K)	0
4	Vilosius, T. (R)	Kukk, K. (R)	Lippmaa, E. (KMU-K) Kubri, T. (KMU-MU) Allik, J. (KMU-K)	1
5	Aro, T. (KMU-K)	Vare, R. (KMU-K)	Allik, J. (KMU-K) *Veidemann, A. (KMU-K) Kubri, T. (KMU-MU)	0
6	Aro, T. (KMU-K)	Vare, R. (KMU-K)	Allik, J. (KMU-K) *Veidemann, A.(KMU-K)	

15. FINLAND

The constitution has vested discretionary power in the Head of State. Since 1991 the president has been elected directly for a six-year term. He or she shares executive powers with the Council of State (Government). The Prime Minister is Chairman of the Council of State and deputy to the President.

Finland is a unitary state with decentralised features. The Aaland Islands have a devolved government.

Parliament (Eduskunta) is unicameral. Its 200 members are elected by proportional representation (d'Hondt) for a fixed term of four years in multi-member constituencies of variable size. The number of deputies is strictly proportional to the size of the electorate.

Since 1992 the Eduskunta has lost influence due to the fact that the earlier requirement to find two-third majorities for decision making has been reduced to simple majority voting, without quorum. For some issues, like constitutional amendments, a two-thirds majority of votes cast is required. The Head of State has a legislative veto. A referendum is optional, and may be called by the government. The outcome is not binding.

Government does not need a vote of investiture and can not face a vote of no confidence. It is collectively responsible to parliament. Individual ministers may also be members of parliament. The Prime Minister has a rather prominent position in government

There is no constitutional review of lawmaking, but both the Chancellor of Justice and the Supreme Court independently supervise the compatibility of laws in view of the constitution.

FINLAND 1945–1998

Gov	Begin	Dur	RfT	ToG	Py1	Py2	Py3	Py4	Py5	Seats	CPG	NoM	Prime Minister (py)
1	17.04.45	342	2	3	KESK 49	SDP 50	[RKP15]	FPP 9	SKDL 49	200	4	12	Paasikivi, (NONA)
2	25.03.46	857	1	3	KESK 49	SDP 50	RKP 15	SKDL 49		200	4	12	Pekkala, M. (SKDL)
3	29.07.48	596	2	4	SDP 54					200	4	13	Fagerholm, K. (SDP)
4	17.03.50	306	7	5	KESK 56	RKP 14	FPP 5	[KOK 32]		200	2	10	Kekkonen, U. (KESK)
5	17.01.51	63	4	3	KESK 56	SDP 54	RKP 14	FPP 5		200	4	11	Kekkonen, U. (KESK)
6	21.03.51	183	1	6	KESK 56	RKP 14	FPP 5			200	3	7	Kekkonen, U. (KESK)
7	20.09.51	658	2	3	KESK 51	SDP 53	RKP 15	FPP 10		200	4	11	Kekkonen, U. (KESK)
8	09.07.53	130	5	5	KESK 51	RKP 15				200	3	11	Kekkonen, U. (KESK)
9	16.11.53	170	6	6	KOK 28	RKP 15	FPP 10			200	2	11	Tuomioja, S. (FPP)
10	05.05.54	169	4	3	KESK 53	SDP 54	RKP 13			200	4	11	Törngren, R. (RKP)
11	20.10.54	500	2	2	KESK 53	SDP 54				200	4	10	Kekkonen, U. (KESK)
12	03.03.56	450	4	3	KESK 53	SDP 54	RKP 13	FPP 13		200	4	11	Fagerholm, K. (SDP)
13	27.05.57	36	4	5	KESK 53	RKP 13	FPP 13			200	3	11	Sukselainen, V.J. (KESK)
14	02.07.57	62	7	5	KESK 53	FPP 13				200	3	11	Sukselainen, V.J. (KESK)
15	02.09.57	88	5	5	KESK 53	SKOG 6	FPP 13			200	4	11	Sukselainen, V.J. (KESK)
16	29.11.57	148	5	x	[KESK 53]	[SKOG 6]	[FPP 13]			200	-	11	Fieandt, R. von (NONA)
17	26.04.58	125	1	x	KESK 48		SDP 48			200	4	12	Kuuskoski, R. (KESK)
18	29.08.58	137	4	3	KESK 48	KOK 29	[SDP48]	RKP 14	FPP 8	200	3	11	Fagerholm, K. (SDP)
19	13.01.59	913	2	4	KESK 48	[RKP 14]		[KOK 29]		200	3	11	Sukselainen, V.J. (KESK)
20	14.07.61	273	6	4	KESK 53					200	3	11	Miettunen, M. (KESK)
21	13.04.62	557	4	2	KESK 53	KOK 32	RKP 14	FPP 13		200	2	11	Karjalainen, A. (KESK)
22	22.10.63	57	4	2	KESK 53	KOK 32	RKP 14	FPP 13		200	2	10	Karjalainen, A. (KESK)
23	18.12.63	269	x	6						200	-	12	Lehto, R.R. (NONA)
24	12.09.64	622	1	2	KESK 53	KOK 32	RKP 14	FPP 13		200	2	11	Virolainen, J. (KESK)
25	27.05.66	665	2	3	KESK 49	SDP 55	SKDL41	TPSL 7		200	4	11	Paasio, R. (SDP)

FINLAND 1945–1998

Gov	Begin	Dur	RfT	ToG	Py1	Py2	Py3	Py4	Py5	Seats	CPG	NoM	Prime Minister (py)
26	22.03.68	783	1	3	KESK 49	SDP 55	RKP 12	SKDL 41	TPSL 7	200	4	12	Koivisto, M. (SDP)
27	14.05.70	62	6	x	[KESK37]	[SDP 51]	[KOK37]	[RKP 12]	[FPP 8]	200	3	12	Aura, T. (FPP)
28	15.07.70	254	4	3	KESK 37	SDP 51	RKP 12	FPP 8	SKDL 36	200	4	13	Karjalainen, A. (KESK)
29	26.03.71	217	4	3	KESK 37	SDP 51	RKP 12	FPP 8		200	4	14	Karjalainen, A. (KESK)
30	29.10.71	117	1	6	KESK 37	KOK 37	SDP 51	FPP 8		200	3	13	Aura, T. (FPP)
31	23.02.72	194	2	4	SDP 55					200	4	14	Paasio, R. (SDP)
32	04.09.72	1012	4	2	[KESK35]	[SDP 55]	[RKP 10]	[FPP 7]		200	4	16	Sorsa, K. (SDP)
33	13.06.75	170	1	x	KESK 35	KOK 34	SDP 55	RKP 10	FPP 7	200	3	17	Liinamaa, K. (SDP)
34	30.11.75	304	4	3	KESK 39	SDP 54	RKP 10	FPP 9	SKDL 40	200	4	18	Miettunen, M. (KESK)
35	29.09.76	228	6	5	KESK 39	RKP 10	FPP 9			200	3	16	Miettunen, M. (KESK)
36	15.05.77	291	4	3	KESK 39	SDP 54	RKP 10	FPP 9	SKDL 40	200	4	15	Sorsa, K. (SDP)
37	02.03.78	449	1	3	KESK 39	SDP 54	FPP 9	SKDL 40		200	4	14	Sorsa, K. (SDP)
38	25.05.79	1007	2	3	KESK 36	SDP 52	RKP 10	SKDL 35		200	4	17	Koivisto, M. (SDP)
39	25.02.82	308	4	3	KESK 36	SDP 52	RKP 10	SKDL 35		200	4	17	Sorsa, K. (SDP)
40	30.12.82	128	1	5	KESK 36	SDP 52	RKP 10			200	4	17	Sorsa, K. (SDP)
41	07.05.83	1454	1	3	KESK 38	SDP 57	RKP 11	FRP 17		200	4	17	Sorsa, K. (SDP)
42	30.04.87	1216	4	3	SDP 56	KOK 53	RKP 13	FRP 9		200	4	18	Holkeri, H. (KOK)
43	28.08.90	214	1	3	SDP 56	KOK 53	RKP 13			200	4	17	Holkeri, H. (KOK)
44	26.04.91	1115	4	3**	KESK 55	KOK 40	RKP 12	SKL 8		200	3	17	Aho, E. (KESK)
45	20.06.94	296	1	2**	KESK 55	KOK 40	RKP 12			200	3	16	Aho, E. (KESK)
46	13.04.95			3	SDP 63	KOK 39	VL 22	RKP 12	Greens 9	200	3	18	Lipponen, P. (SDP)

** divided government
- [] Party supporting the government without participating in it.
- Gov 15, 17: SKOG is left-wing 'SKOG-group' within SDP.
- Gov 16: 'Business Cabinet'.
- Gov 17: Non-party government, ministers did not officially represent their respective parties KESK (5); SKOG (2); FPP (1); NONA (1).
- Gov 23: Reason for Termination, Mr Virolainen, Parliamentary leader of KESK, succeeded 11.09.64 to replace the Non-party government by a government supported by a Parliamentary majority.

FINLAND 1945–1998

- Gov 27: Government of `experts'. Ministers `associated with': SDP (3); KESK (3); KOK (1); RKP (1); NONA (3).
- Gov 33: Non-political temporary government which included members of the previous coalition, plus a conservative and 5 non-party ministers.

Gov	Deputy PM	Py	Foreign Affairs	Py	Defence	Py	Interior	Py	Justice	Py
1			Enckell, C.	NONA	Pekkala, M.	SKDL	Leino, Y.	SKDL	Kekkonen, U.	KESK
2	Kallinen, Y.	SDP	Enckell, C.	NONA	Pekkala, M.	SKDL	Leino, Y.	SKDL	Pekkala, E.	SKDL
3			Enckell, C.	NONA	Skog, E.	SDP	Simonen, A.	SDP	Suontausta, T.	SDP
4			Gartz, Å.	RKP	Tiitu, K.	KESK	Kekkonen, U.	KESK	Kannisto, H.	FPP
5			Gartz, Å.	RKP	Skog, E.	SDP	Sukselainen, V.J.	KESK	Aura, T.	FPP
6			Gartz, Å.	RKP			Sukselainen, V.J.	KESK	Aura, T.	FPP
7			Tuomioja, S.	FPP	Skog, E.	SDP	Sukselainen, V.J.	KESK	Högström, S.	RKP
8			Törngren, R.	RKP	Kleemola, K.	KESK	Sukselainen, V.J.	KESK	Högström, S.	RKP
9			Törngren, R.	RKP	Hetemäki, P.	KOK	Kannisto, H.	FPP	Kuuskoski, R.	NONA
10			Kekkonen, U.	KESK	Skog, E.	SDP	Leskinen, V.	SDP	Puhakka, Y.	NONA
11			Virolainen, J.	KESK	Skog, E.	SDP	Leskinen, V.	SDP	Simonen, A.	SDP
12			Törngren, R.	RKP	Skog, E.	SDP	Väyrynen, V.	SDP	Helminen, A.H.	NONA
13			Virolainen, J.	KESK	Pakkanen, A.	KESK	Kytta, H.	FPP	Helminen, A.H.	NONA
14			Virolainen, J.	KESK	Pakkanen, A.	KESK	Kytta, H.	FPP	Helminen, A.H.	NONA
15			Virolainen, J.	KESK	Malinen, P.	FPP	Aura, T.	NONA	Söderhjelm, J.O.	NONA
16			Hynninen, P.J.	NONA	Lehmus, K.	NONA	Kiukas, U.	NONA	Kaira, K.	NONA
17			Hynninen, P.J.	NONA	Björkenheim, L.	NONA	Kyttä, H.	NONA	Söderhjelm, J.O.	NONA
18	Virolainen, J.	KESK	Virolainen, J.	KESK	Wiherheimo, T.	KOK	Pakkanen, A.	KESK	Högström, S.	RKP
19	Törngren, R.	+RKP	Törngren, R.	+RKP	Häppölä, L.	KESK	Palovesi, E.	KESK	Hannikainen, A.	KESK
20			Karjalainen, A.	KESK	Björkenheim, L.	NONA	Luukka, E.	NONA	Lehtosalo, P.	KESK
21			Merikoski, V.	FPP	Pentti, A.	KESK	Erkkilä, E.	KESK	Söderhjelm, J.O.	RKP
22			Merikoski, V.	FPP	Pentti, A.	KESK	Erkkilä, E.	KESK	Söderhjelm, J.O.	RKP

FINLAND 1945–1998

Gov	Deputy PM	Py	Foreign Affairs	Py	Defence	Py	Interior	Py	Justice	Py
23			Hallama, J.	NONA	Leinonen, K.	NONA	Hannus, A.	NONA	Merimaa, O.	NONA
24			Karjalainen, A.	KESK	Pentti, A.	KESK	Ryhtä, N.	KESK	Söderhjelm, J.O.	RKP
25			Karjalainen, A.	KESK	Suorttanen, S.	KESK	Viitanen, M.	SDP	Simonen, A.	TPSL
26	Virolainen, J.	KESK	Karjalainen, A.	KESK	Suorttanen, S.	KESK	Väyrynen, A.	SDP	Simonen, A.	TPSL
27			Leskinen, V.	SDP	Pentti, A.	KESK	Hiltunen, T.	KESK	Liinamaa, K.	SDP
28	Helle, V.	SDP	Leskinen, V.	SDP	Gestrin, K.	RKP	Jämsen, A.	KESK	Tuominen, E.	SKDL
29	Helle, V.	SDP	Leskinen, V.	SDP	Gestrin, K.	RKP	Jämsen, A. / Laaksonen, M.	KESK / SDP	Laaksonen, M.	SDP
30	Hetemäki, P.	KOK	Mattila, O.J.	KESK+	Pentti, A.	KESK	Tuominen, H.	NONA	Lang, K.-J.	NONA
31			Sorsa, K.	SDP	Hostila, S.	SDP	Viitanen, M.	SDP	Paavola, P.	SDP
32			Karjalainen, A.	KESK	Gestrin, K.	RKP	Tuominen, H.	NONA	Louekoski, M.	SDP
33			Mattila, O.J.	KESK	Huurtamo, E.	KOK	Koski, H. / Strömmer, A.	SDP / KESK	*Anttila, I.	FPP / KESK
34	Sorsa, K.	SDP	Sorsa, K.	SDP	Melin, I.	RKP	Tiilikainen, P. / Hänninen, O.	SDP / SKDL	Gestrin, K.	RKP
35	Karjalainen, A.	KESK	Korhonen, K.	KESK	Westerlund, S.	FPP	Uusitalo, E.	KESK	Gestrin, K.	RKP
36	Virolainen, J.	KESK	Väyrynen, P.	KESK	Tähkämaa, T.	KESK	Uusitalo, E.	KESK	Salo, T.	FPP
37	Virolainen, J.	KESK	Väyrynen, P.	KESK	Tähkämaa, T.	KESK	Uusitalo, E.	KESK	Nikola, P.	FPP
38	Uusitalo, E.	KESK	Väyrynen, P.	KESK	Aikäs, L.	KESK	Uusitalo, E. / Koikkalainen, J.	KESK / SDP	Taxell, C.	RKP
39	Pekkala, A.	KESK	Stenbäck, P.	RKP	Saukkonen, J.	KESK	Ahde, M. / Jokela, M.	SDP / KESK	Taxell, C.	RKP
40	Pekkala, A.	KESK	Stenbäck, P.	RKP	Saukkonen, J.	KESK	Ahde, M. / Jokela, M.	SDP / KESK	Taxell, C.	RKP
41	Väyrynen, P.	KESK	Väyrynen, P.	KESK	Pihlajamäki, V.	KESK	Luttinen, M. / Ahde, M.	SDP / SDP	Taxell, C.	RKP
42	Sorsa, K.	SDP	Sorsa, K.	SDP	Norrback, O.	RKP	Rantanen, J.	SDP	Louekoski, M.	SDP

FINLAND 1945-1998

Gov	Deputy PM	Py	Foreign Affairs	Py	Defence	Py	Interior	Py	Justice	Py
43			Paasio, P.	SDP	*Rehn, E.	RKP	Rantanen, J.	SDP	*Halonen, T.	SDP
44			Väyrynen, P.	KESK	*Rehn, E.	RKP	Pekkarinen, M.	KESK	*Pokka, H.	KESK
45	Kanerva, I.	KOK	Haavisto, H.	KESK	*Rehn, E.	RKP	Pekkarinen, M.	KESK	*Jätteenmäki, A.	KESK
46			*Halonen, T. / Norrback, O.	SDP / RKP	*Taina, A.	KOK	Enestam, J.-E. / Backman, J.	RKP / SDP	Niinistoe, S.	KOK

- Gov 19: +RKP = as a private individual not representing RKP.
- Gov 30: KESK+ = 'associated with' KESK.

Gov	Finance	Py	Economic Aff.	Py	Labour	Py	Education	Py	Health	Py
1	Tuomija, S.	FPP					Helo, J.	SKDL		
2	Törngren, R.	RKP					Kilpi, E.	SDP		
3	Hiltunen, O.	SDP					Oittinen, R.	SDP		
4	Sukselainen, V.J.	KESK					Heljas, L.	KESK		
5			Hiltunen, O.	SDP			Heljas, L.	KESK		
6							Heljas, L.	KESK		
7	Rantala, V.	SDP					Oittinen, R.	SDP		
8	Niukkanen, J.	KESK					Virolainen, J.	KESK		
9	Junnila, T.	KOK					Salminen, A.	KOK		
10	Sukselainen, V.J.	KESK					Virolainen, J.	KESK		
11	Tervo, P.	SDP					*Saalasti, K.	KESK		
12	Simonen, A.	SDP					Virolainen, J.	KESK		
13	Meinander, N.	RKP					*Saalasti, K.	KESK		
14	Miettunen, M.	KESK					*Saalasti, K.	KESK		
15			Miettunen, M.	KESK			*Saalasti, K.	KESK		

FINLAND 1945–1998

Gov	Finance	Py	Economic Aff.	Py	Labour	Py	Education	Py	Health	Py
16	Hietanen, L.	NONA					Oittinen, R.	NONA		
17	Nurmela, I.O.	NONA					Vilkuna, K.	NONA		
18	Hetemäki, P.	KOK					Kajatsalo, K.	FPP		
19	Sarjala, W.	KESK					Hosia, H.	KESK		
20	Sarjala, W.	KESK					Hosia, H.	KESK		
21	Karttunen, O.	KOK					Hosia, A.	FPP		
22	Karttunen, O.	KOK					Hosia, A.	FPP		
23	Rekola, E.	NONA					Oittinen, R.	NONA		
24	Kaitila, E.	FPP					Saukkonen, J.	KOK		
25	Koivisto, M.	SDP					Oittinen, R.	SDP		
26	Raunio, E.	SDP					Virolainen, J.	KESK		
27	Hetemäki, P.	KOK			Timonen, E.	KESK	Numminen, J.	NONA		
28	Tallgren, C.O.	RKP			Helle, V.	SDP	Itälä, J.	FPP+		
29	Tallgren, C.O.	RKP			Helle, V.	SDP	Itälä, J.	FPP+		
30	Hetemäki, P.	KOK			Liinamaa, K.	SDP	Lauerkoski, M.	SDP	*Lahtinen, A.	SDP
31	Koivisto, M.	SDP			Helle, V.	SDP	Sundqvist, U.	SDP	Kaipainen, O.	SDP
32	Virolainen, J.	KESK			Nevalainen, V.	SDP	Sundqvist, U.	SDP	*Karkinen, S.	SDP
	Niskanen, E.	SDP					*Väänänen, M.	KESK	Pekkarinen, P.	KESK
33	Tuominen, H.	NONA	Ahtiala, P.	NONA	Paananen, I.	SDP	Posti, L.	NONA	*Lahtinen, A.	SDP
	Varjas, T.	SDP							Teir, G.	RKP
34	Paavela, P.	SDP	Karpola, R.	KESK	Aitio, P.	SKDL	Väyrynen, P.	KESK	*Toivanen, I.	FPP
	Luukka, V.	NONA					Kivistö, K.	SKDL	*Työläjärvi, P.	SDP
35	Rekola, E.	NONA	Karjalainen, A.	KESK	Väyrynen, P.	KESK	*Väänänen, M.	KESK		
	Loikkanen, J.	KESK								
36	Paavela, P.	SDP			Aalto, A.	SKDL	Gestrin, K.	RKP	*Työläjärvi, P.	SDP
	Rekola, E.	NONA					Kivistö, K.	SKDL	Martikainen, O.	KESK

FINLAND 1945–1998

Gov	Finance	Py	Economic Aff.	Py	Labour	Py	Education	Py	Health	Py
37	Paavela, P.	SDP			Aalto, A.	SKDL	Itälä, J.	FPP		
	Rekola, E.	NONA					Kivistö, K.	SKDL		
38	Pekkala, A.	KESK			Aalto, A.	SKDL	Stenbäck, P.	RKP	*Luja-Penttilä, S.	SDP
	*Työläjärvi, P.	SDP					Kivistö, K.	SKDL	*Eskelinen, K.-H.	KESK
39	Forsman, M.	SDP			Kajamoja, J.	SKDL	Kivistö, K.	SKDL	Söderman, J.	SDP
	Pekkala, A.	KESK					*Suonio, K.	SDP	*Väänänen, M.	KESK
40	Pekkala, A.	KESK			Helle, V.	SDP	*Suonio, K.	SDP	Taipale, V.	SDP
	Laine, J.	SDP					Salo, A.	SDP	*Väänänen, M.	KESK
41	Pekkala, A.	KESK			Leppänen, U.	FRP	*Suonio, K.	SDP	*Kuuskoski-Vikatmaa, E.	KESK
	Laine, J.	SDP					Björkstrand, G.	RKP	Taipale, V.	SDP
	Vennamo, P.	FRP								
42	Liikanen, E.	SDP			Puhakka, M.	SDP	Taxell, C.	RKP	*Pesola, H.	KOK
	*Puolanne, U.	KOK					*Piipari, A.-L.	SDP	*Halonen, T.	SDP
43	Louekoski, M.	SDP			Puhakka, M.	SDP	Norrback, O.	RKP	Miettinen, M.	KOK
	*Puolanne, U.	KOK					*Kasurinen A.-L.	SDP	*Hämäläinen, T.	SDP
44	Viinanen, I.	KOK			Kanerva, I.	KOK	*Uosukainen, R.	KOK	*Kuuskoski, E.	KESK
45	Viinanen, I.	KOK			Kanerva, I.	KOK	Heinonen, O.-P.	KOK	Huuhtanen, J.	KESK
							*Isohookana-Asunma, T.	KESK		
46	Viinanen, I.	KOK			*Jaakonsaari, L.	SDP	Heinonen, O.-P.	KOK	*Huttu, T.	VL
	*Alho, A.	SDP								

- Gov 28 & 29: FPP+ = associated with FPP.

Gov	Housing	Py	Agriculture	Py	Industry/Trade	Py	Environment	Py
1			Jutila, K.T.	KESK	Gartz, Å.	KESK		
2			Vesterinen, V.	KESK	Takki, U.	SDP		
					Vilhula, T.	KESK		

FINLAND 1945–1998

Gov	Housing	Py	Agriculture	Py	Industry/Trade	Py	Environment	Py
3			Lepistö, L.	SDP	Takki, U.	SDP		
					Toivonen, O.	SDP		
4			Vilhula, T.	KESK	Tuomioja, S.	FPP		
5			Miettunen, M.	KESK	Tervo, P.	SDP		
6			Miettunen, M.	KESK				
7			Miettunen, M.	KESK	Tervo, P.	SDP		
8			Miettunen, M.	KESK	Aura, T.	NONA		
9			Jutila, K.	NONA	Aura, T.	NONA		
10			Kalliokoski, V.	KESK	Tervo, P.	SDP		
11			Kalliokoski, V.	KESK	Simonen, A.	SDP		
12			Miettunen, M.	KESK	Kleemola, K.	KESK		
13			Miettunen, M.	KESK	Kaitila, E.	FPP		
14			Eskola, K.	KESK	Kaitila, E.	FPP		
15			Eskola, K.	KESK	Kaitila, E.	FPP		
16			Pertula, H.	NONA	Kivekäs, L.	NONA		
17			Lehtosalo, P.	NONA	Kivekäs, L.	NONA		
18			Miettunen, M.	KESK	Hiltunen, O.	SDP		
19			Jaakkola, E.	KESK	Karjalainen, A.	NONA		
20			Virolainen, J.	KESK	Hustich, I.	NONA		
21			Virolainen, J.	KESK	Wiherheimo, T.A.	KOK		
22			Virolainen, J.	KESK	Wiherheimo, T.A.	KOK		
23			Suomela, S.	NONA	Mattila, O.	NONA		
24			Jussila, M.	KESK	Wiherheimo, T.A.	KOK		
25			Kaasalainen, N.	KESK	Salonen, O.	SDP		
26			Miettunen, M.	KESK	Teir, G.	RKP		
27			Westermarck, N.	NONA	Mattila, O.	KESK		

FINLAND 1945–1998

Gov	Housing	Py	Agriculture	Py	Industry/Trade	Py	Environment	Py
28			Kaasalainen, N.	KESK	Berner, A. Mattila, O.	FPP KESK		
29			Kaasalainen, N.	KESK	Berner, A. Mattila, O. Salonen, O	FPP KESK+ SDP		
30			Suomela, S.	NONA	Korhonen, G. Rossi, R.	NONA NONA		
31			Happonen, L.	SDP	Lindblom, S. Linnamo, J.	SDP SDP		
32			Haukipuro, E.	KESK	Teir, G. Linnamo, J.	RKP SDP		
33			Ihamuotila, V.	KESK	Rytkönen, A. Uitto, J.	NONA NONA		
34	Hänninen, O.	SKDL	Linna, H.	KESK	Rantala, E. Lehto, S.	SDP NONA		
35			Virolainen, J.	KESK	Berner, A. Aminoff, C.-G.	FPP RKP		
36			Virolainen, J.	KESK	Rantala, E.	SDP		
37			Virolainen, J.	KESK	Rantala, E.	SDP		
38			Tähkämaa, T.	KESK	Sundqvist, U. Rekola, E.	SDP NONA	Koikkalainen, J.	SDP
39			Tähkämaa, T.	KESK	Ollila, E. Rekola, E.	KESK NONA		
40			Tähkämaa, T.	KESK	Ollila, E. Berner, A.	KESK FPP		
41			Yläjärvi, T.	KESK	Lindblom, S. Laine, J.	SDP SDP	Ahde, M.	SDP

FINLAND 1945–1998

Gov	Housing	Py	Agriculture	Py	Industry/Trade	Py	Environment	Py
42			Pohjala, T.T.	KOK	Suominen, I. Salolainen, P.	KOK KOK	Bärlund, K.	SDP
43			Pohjola, T.T.	KOK	Suominen, I. Salolainen, P.	KOK KOK	Bärlund, K.	SDP
44	*Rusanen, P.	KOK	Pura, M.	KESK	Salolainen, P. Juhantalo, K.	KOK KESK	*Pietikäinen, S.	KOK
45	*Rusanen, P.	KOK	Pesälä, M.	KESK	Kääriäinen, S. Salolainen, P.	KESK KOK	*Pietikäinen, S.	KOK
46			Hemilae, K.	IND	Kalliomäki, A.	SDP	Haavisto, P.	Greens

- Gov 29: KESK+ =associated with KESK.

Gov	Social Affairs (py)	Public Works (py)	Other (py)	Res
1	Kilpi, E. (SDP)	Vuori, E.A. (SDP)	Hillilä, K. (KESK)	2
2	Janhunen, O.M. (SKDL)	Kaijalainen, L. (KESK)	Kallinen, Y. (SDP) *Kuusinen, H. (SKDL)	2
3	Liljeström, V. (SDP)	Peltonen, O. (SDP)	Aaltonen, A. (SDP)	0
4	Törngren, R. (RKP)	Miettunen, M. (KESK)		0
5	Vesterinen, V. (KESK)	Peltonen, O. (SDP)		0
6	Vesterinen, V. (KESK)			0
7	Törngren, R. (RKP)	Peltonen, O. (SDP)		0
8	Hietanen, L. (NONA)	Makinen, E. (NONA)		0
9	Kaitila, E. (FPP)	Serlachius, E. (NONA)		0
10	*Leivo-Larsson, T. (SDP)	Miettunen, M. (KESK)		0
11	Peltonen, O. (SDP)	Miettunen, M. (KESK)		0

FINLAND 1945–1998

Gov	Social Affairs (py)	Public Works (py)	Other (py)	Res
12	Saari, E. (FPP)	Palovesi, E. (KESK)		0
13	*Karvikko, I. (FPP)	Eskola, K. (KESK)		0
14	*Karvikko, I. (FPP)	Sarjala, V. (KESK)		0
15	*Malkamäki, A. (SKOG)	Sarjala, V. (KESK)		0
16	Varis, H. (NONA)	Sumu, A. (NONA)		0
17	Liljeström, V. (SKOG)	Kastari, P. (KESK)	*Leivo-Larsson, T. (SKOG)	0
18	Leskinen, V. (SDP)	Eskola, K. (KESK)		0
19	*Simonen, V. (KESK)	Kleemola, K. (KESK)		1
20	*Simonen, V. (KESK)	Kleemola, K. (KESK)		0
21	Saarinen, O. (NONA+)	Savela, V. (KESK)		0
22		Savela, V. (KESK)		0
23	Ojala, O. (NONA)	Niskala, M. (NONA)	Nuorvala, A. (NONA)	0
24	Tenhiälä, J. (FPP)	Teir, G. (RKP)		0
25	Koivunen, M. (SKDL)	Suonpää, L. (SKDL)		0
26	*Tiekso, A.-L. (SKDL)	Aitio, P. (SKDL)	Linnamo, J. (SDP)	0
27	Korhonen, G. (NONA)	Niskala, M. (NONA)		0
28	*Tiekso, A.-L. (SKDL)	Saarto, V. (SKDL)		2
29	Kuusi, P. (SDP)	Haapasola, K. (SDP)		0
30	*Lahtinen, A. (SDP)	Timonen, E. (KESK)		0
31	Kaipainen, O. (SDP)	Nevalainen, V. (SDP)	Louekoski, M. (SDP)	0
32	*Karkinen, S. (SDP) Pekkarinen, P. (KESK)	Tarjanne, P. (FPP)		0
33	Ahtiala, P. (NONA) *Lahtinen, A. (SDP) Teir, G. (RKP)	Timonen, E. (KESK)		0

FINLAND 1945–1998

Gov	Social Affairs (py)	Public Works (py)	Other (py)	Res
34	*Toivanen, I. (FPP) *Työläjärvi, P. (SDP)	Hjerppe, K. (SKDL)		0
35	*Toivanen, I. (FPP) *Kangas, O. (KESK)	Granvik, R. (RKP)	Karjalainen, A. (KESK)	0
36	*Työläjärvi, P. (SDP) Martikainen, O. (KESK)	Saarto, V. (SKDL)		0
37	*Työläjärvi, P. (SDP) Martikainen, O. (KESK)	Saarto, V. (SKDL)		0
38	*Luja-Penttilä, S. (SDP) *Eskelinen, K.-H. (KESK)	Saarto, V. (SKDL)		0
39	Söderman, J. (SDP) *Väänänen, M. (KESK)	Wahlström, J. (SKDL)		2
40	Taipale, V. (SDP) *Väänänen, M. (KESK)	Brelin, R. (SDP)	Salo, A. (SDP)	0
41	*Kuuskoski-Vikatmaa, E. (KESK) Taipale, V. (SDP)	Puhakka, M. (SDP)		1
42	*Pesola, H. (KOK) *Halonen, T. (SDP)	Vennamo, P. (FRP)	Taxell, C. (RKP) *Piipari, A.-L. (SDP) Kanerva, I. (KOK)	1
43	Miettinen, M. (KOK) *Hämäläinen, T. (SDP)	Kanerva, I. (KOK)		0
44	*Kuuskoski, E. (KESK)	Norrback, O. (RKP)	*Isohookana-Asunmaa, T. (KESK) Kankaanniemi, T. (SKL)	0
45	Huuhtanen, J. (KESK)	Norrback, O. (RKP)		
46	*Moenkäre, S. (SDP) *Huttu, T. (VL)	*Linnainmaa, T. (KOK)	Andersson, C. (VL)	1

- Gov 21: NONA+; but representing the Socialist Confederation of Finnish Trade Unions (SAK).

16.1. FRANCE 4th Republic 1945–1959

Gov	Begin	Dur	RiT	ToG	Py1	Py2	Py3	Py4	Py5	Seats	CPG	NoM	Prime Minister (py)
1	23.11.45	67	2	3	MRP 141	PSF 134	PCF 148	RSP 35		522	4	22	De Gaulle, C. (NONA)
2	29.01.46	140	1	3	MRP 141	PSF 134	PCF 148			522	4	20	Gouin, F. (PSF)
3	19.06.46	146	1	3	MRP 160	PSF 115	PCF 146			522	4	22	Bidault, G. (MRP)
4	12.12.46	36	1	6	PSF 115					544	4	17	Blum, L. (PSF)
5	17.01.47	111	4	3	PSF 90	MRP 158	RSP 55	PCF 166		544	4	26	Ramadier, P. (PSF)
6	08.05.47	167	7	2	PSF 90	MRP 158	RSP 55			544	4	25	Ramadier, P. (PSF)
7	23.10.47	30	4	3	PSF 90	MRP 158	RSP 55	IND 70		544	4	13	Ramadier, P. (PSF)
8	22.11.47	248	4	3	PSF 90	MRP 158	RSP 55	GAUL 5		544	4	12	Schuman, R. (MRP)
9	24.07.48	43	4	3	PSF 90	MRP 158	RSP 55	IND 70		544	3	19	Marie, A. (RSP)
10	05.09.48	8	4	3	PSF 90	MRP 158	RSP 55	IND 70		544	3	15	Schuman, R. (MRP)
11	13.09.48	410	4	3	PSF 90	MRP 158	RSP 55	IND 70	GAUL 5	544	3	15	Queuille, H. (RSP)
12	28.10.49	102	4	3	PSF 90	MRP 158	RSP 55	IND 70	GAUL 5	544	3	18	Bidault, G. (MRP)
13	07.02.50	145	5	3	MRP 158	RSP 55	IND 70	GAUL 5		544	2	17	Bidault, G. (MRP)
14	02.07.50	10	5	3	MRP 158	RSP 55	IND 70	GAUL 5		544	2	21	Queuille, H. (RSP)
15	12.07.50	241	5	3	RSP 55	MRP 158	PSF 90	IND 70	GAUL 5	544	3	22	Pleven, R. (GAUL)
16	10.03.51	154	1	3	RSP 77	PSF 94	MRP 82	IND 87	GAUL107	544	3	22	Queuille, H. (RSP)
17	11.08.51	162	5	3	RSP 77	MRP 82	IND 87	GAUL 107		544	2	24	Pleven, R. (GAUL)
18	20.01.52	48	4	3	RSP 77	MRP 82	IND 87	GAUL 107		544	2	26	Faure, E. (RSP)
19	08.03.52	305	4	3	RSP 77	MRP 82	IND 87	GAUL 107		544	2	17	Pinay, A. (IND)
20	07.01.53	170	5	3	RSP 77	MRP 82	IND 87	GAUL 107		544	2	23	Mayer, R. (RSP)
21	26.06.53	356	5	3	RSP 77	MRP 82	IND 87	GAUL 107		544	2	22	Laniel, J. (IND)
22	19.06.54	249	5	3	RSP 77	MRP 82	IND 87	GAUL 107		544	2	16	Mendès-France, P. (RSP)
23	23.02.55	340	1	3	RSP 77	MRP 82	IND 87			544	2	19	Faure, E. (RSP)
24	31.01.56	497	4	5	PSF 88	RSP 73	GAUL 16			544	4	13	Mollet, G. (PSF)
25	11.06.57	148	4	5	PSF 88	RSP 73	GAUL 16			544	4	14	Bourgès-Maunoury, M. (RSP)

FRANCE 4th Republic 1945–1959

Gov	Begin	Dur	RfT	ToG	Py1	Py2	Py3	Py4	Py5	Seats	CPG	NoM	Prime Minister (py)
26	06.11.57	189	1	3	RSP 73	PSF 88	GAUL 16	MRP 71	IND 95	544	3	17	Gaillard, F. (RSP)
27	14.05.58	23	4	3	MRP 57	RSP 23	IND 133	GAUL 198	IND 133	544	2	17	Pflimlin, P. (MRP)
28	01.06.58	221	1	3	GAUL 198	MRP 57	PSF 44	RSP 23	IND 133	544	2	24	De Gaulle, C. (GAUL)

- Gov 1-7: RSP includes UDSR.
- Gov 8 ff: GAUL includes UDSR, ARS, URAS, RDA, PAY.
- Gov 21: GAUL includes ARS and URAS.
- Gov 26, 27, 28: GAUL includes RDA.

Gov	Deputy PM	Py	Foreign Affairs	Py	Defence	Py	Interior	Py	Justice	Py
1			Bidault, G.	MRP	De Gaulle, C. / Tillon, C. / Michelet, E.	NONA / PCF / MRP	Tixier, A.	PSF	Teitgen, P.-H.	MRP
2	Thorez, M. / Gay, F.	PCF / MRP	Bidault, G.	MRP	Tillon, C. / Michelet, E.	PCF / MRP	Le Troquer, A.	PSF	Teitgen, P.-H.	MRP
3	Gouin, F. / Thorez, M.	PSF / PCF	Bidault, G.	MRP	Tillon, C. / Michelet, E.	PCF / MRP	Depreux, E.	PSF	Teitgen, P.-H.	MRP
4					Le Troquer, A.	PSF	Depreux, E.	PSF	Ramadier, P.	PSF
5	Teitgen, P.-H. / Thorez, M.	MRP / PCF	Bidault, G.	MRP	Billoux, F. / Coste-Floret, P. / Jacquinot, L.	PCF / MRP / IND	Depreux, E.	PSF	Marie, A.	RSP
6	Teitgen, P.-H.	MRP	Bidault, G.	MRP	Delbos, Y. / Coste-Floret, P. / Jacquinot, L.	RSP / MRP / IND	Depreux, E.	PSF	Marie, A.	RSP
7			Bidault, G.	MRP	Teitgen, P.-H.	MRP	Depreux, E.	PSF	Marie, A.	RSP
8			Bidault, G.	MRP	Teitgen, P.-H.	MRP	Moch, J.	PSF	Marie, A.	RSP

FRANCE 4th Republic 1945–1959

Gov	Deputy PM	Py	Foreign Affairs	Py	Defence	Py	Interior	Py	Justice	Py
9	Blum, L. Teitgen, P.-H.	PSF MRP	Schuman, R.	MRP	Mayer, R.	RSP	Moch, J.	PSF	Lecourt, R.	MRP
10	Marie, A.	RSP	Schuman, R.	MRP	Mayer, R.	RSP	Moch, J.	PSF	Lecourt, R.	MRP
11	Marie, A.	RSP	Schuman, R.	MRP	Ramadier, P. Colin, A.	RSP IND	Moch, J.	PSF	Marie, A.	RSP
12	Queuille, H. Moch, J.	RSP PSF	Schuman, R.	MRP	Pleven, R.	UDSR	Moch, J.	PSF	Marie, A.	RSP
13	Queuille, H.	RSP	Schuman, R.	MRP	Pleven, R.	UDSR	Queuille, H.	RSP	Mayer, R.	RSP
14	Bidault, G.	MRP	Schuman, R. Reynaud, P.	MRP IND	Pleven, R.	UDSR	Giacobbi, P.	RSP	Mayer, R.	RSP
15			Schuman, R.	MRP	Moch, J.	PSF	Queuille, H.	RSP	Mayer, R.	RSP
16	Mollet, G. Pleven, R. Bidault, G.	PSF UDSR MRP	Schuman, R.	MRP	Moch, J.	PSF	Queuille, H.	RSP	Mayer, R.	RSP
17	Mayer, R. Bidault, G.	RSP MRP	Schuman, R.	MRP	Bidault, G. Bourgès-Maunoury, M.	MRP RSP	Brune, C.	RSP	Faure, E.	RSP
18	Queuille, H. Bidault, G.	RSP MRP	Schuman, R.	MRP	Bidault, G. Bourgès-Maunoury, M.	MRP RSP	Brune, C.	RSP	Martinaud-Déplat, L.	RSP
19	Queuille, H.	RSP	Schuman, R.	MRP	Pleven, R.	UDSR	Brune, C.	RSP	Martinaud-Déplat, L.	RSP
20	Queuille, H.	RSP	Bidault, G.	MRP	Pleven, R.	RSP	Brune, C.	RSP	Martinaud-Déplat, L.	RSP
21	Reynaud, P. Queuille, H. Teitgen, P.-H.	IND RSP MRP	Bidault, G.	MRP	Pleven, R.	RSP	Martinaud-Déplat, L. Barrachin, E.	RSP ARS	Ribeyre, P.	PAY
22			Mendès-France, P.	RSP	Koenig, P.	GAUL	Mitterand, F.	UDSR	Hugues, E.	RSP
23			Pinay, A.	IND	Koenig, J. Antier, P.	GAUL PAY	Bourges-Maunoury, M.	RSP	Schuman, R.	MRP
24			Pineau, C.	PSF	Bourgès-Maunoury, M.	RSP	Jules, G.	RSP	Mitterand, F.	UDSR
25			Pineau, C.	PSF	Morice, A.	RSP	Jules, G.	RSP	Corniglion-Molinier	RGR

FRANCE 4th Republic 1945–1959

Gov	Deputy PM	Py	Foreign Affairs	Py	Defence	Py	Interior	Py	Justice	Py
26			Pineau, C.	PSF	Chaban-Delmas, M.	GAUL	Bourgès-Maunoury, M.	RSP	Lecourt, R.	MRP
27			Pleven, R.	RSP	Chevigné de, P.	MRP	Faure, M.	RSP	Lecourt, R.	MRP
28			Couve de Murville, M.	NONA	De Gaulle, C.	GAUL	Pelletier, E.	NONA	Debré, M.	GAUL
					Guilaumat, P.	NONA				

Gov	Finance	Py	Economic Aff.	Py	Labour	Py	Education	Py	Health	Py
1	Pleven, R.	UDSR			Croizat, A.	PCF	Giacobbi, P.	PCF	Prigent, R.	MRP
2	Philip, A.	PSF	Philip, A.	PSF	Croizat, A.	PCF	Naegelen, E.	PCF	Prigent, R.	MRP
3	Schuman, R.	MRP			Croizat, A.	PCF	Naegelen, M.	PCF	Arthaud, R.	PCF
4	Philip, A.	PSF	Philip, A.	PSF	Mayer, D.	PSF	Naegelen, E.	PSF	Segelle, P.	PSF
			Gouin, F.	PSF						
5	Schuman, R.	MRP	Philip, A.	PSF	Croizat, A.	PSF	Naegelen, M	PSF	Marrane, A.	PCF
6	Schuman, R.	MRP	Philip, A.	PSF	Mayer, D.	PSF	Naegelen, M.	PSF	Prigent, R.	MRP
7	Schuman, R.	MRP	Moch, J.	PSF	Mayer, D.	PSF	Naegelen, M.	PSF		
8	Mayer, R.	RSP	Mayer, R.	RSP	Mayer, D.	PSF	Naegelen, M.	PSF	*Poinso-Chapui, G.	MRP
9	Reynaud, P.	IND	Reynaud, P.	IND	Mayer, D.	PSF	Delbos, Y.	PSF	Schneiter, P.	RSP
10	Pineau, C.	PSF	Pineau, C.	PSF	Mayer, D.	PSF	Révillon, T.	PSF	Schneiter, P.	RSP
11	Queuille, H.	RSP	Queuille, H.	RSP	Mayer, D.	PSF	Delbos, Y.	PSF	Schneiter, P.	RSP
12	Petsche, M.	NONA	Petsche, M.	NONA	Segelle, P.	NONA	Delbos, Y.	MRP	Schneiter, P.	RSP
13	Petsche, M.	NONA	Petsche, M.	NONA	Bacon, P.	NONA	Delbos, Y.	MRP	Schneiter, P.	RSP
14	Petsche, M.	NONA	Petsche, M.	NONA	Bacon, P.	NONA	Morice, A.	MRP	Schneiter, P.	RSP
15	Petsche, M.	NONA	Petsche, M.	NONA	Bacon, P.	NONA	Lapie, P-O.	MRP	Schneiter, P.	PSF
16	Petsche, M.	NONA	Petsche, M.	NONA	Bacon, P.	NONA	Lapie, P-O.	MRP	Schneiter, P.	PSF
17	Mayer, R.	RSP	Mayer, R.	RSP	Bacon, P.	RSP	Marie, A.	MRP	Ribeyre, P.	PAY
	Courant, P.	IND								

FRANCE 4th Republic 1945–1959

Gov	Finance	Py	Economic Aff.	Py	Labour	Py	Education	Py	Health	Py
18	Faure, E. / Courant, P.	RSP / IND	Buron, R.	MRP	Bacon, P.	MRP	Marie, A.	RSP	Ribeyre, P.	PAY
19	Pinay, A.	IND	Pinay, A.	IND	Garet, P.	IND	Marie, A.	RSP	Ribeyre, P.	PAY
20	Bourgès-Maunoury, M. / Moreau, J.	RSP / IND	Buron, R.	MRP	Bacon, P.	MRP	Marie, A.	RSP	Boutemy, A.	IND
21	Faure, E.	RSP	Faure, E.	RSP	Bacon, P.	MRP	Marie, A.	RSP	Coste-Floret, P.	MRP
22	Faure, E.	RSP			Claudius-Pétit, E.	UDSR	Berthoin, J.	RGR	Aujoulat, L.	IND
23	Pflimlin, P.	MRP	Pflimlin, P.	MRP	Bacon, P.	MRP	Berthoin, J.	RSP	Lafay, B.	RSP
24	Lacoste, R.	PSF	Lacoste, R.	PSF			Billeres, R.	RSP		
25	Gaillard, F.	RSP	Gaillard, F.	RSP			Billeres, R.	RSP		
26	Pflimlin, P.	MRP	Pflimlin, P.	MRP	Bacon, P.	MRP	Billeres, R.	RSP	Houphouet-Boigny, F.	RDA
27	Faure, M.	RSP	Faure, M.	RSP	Bacon, P.	MRP	Bordenave, J.	RSP		
28	Pinay, A.	IND			Bacon, P.	MRP	Berthoin, J.	RSP	Chenot, B.	NONA

Gov	Housing	Py	Agriculture	Py	Industry/Trade	Py	Environment	Py
1	Dautry, R.	NONA	Tanguy-Prigent, P.	PSF	Billoux, F. / Paul, M.	PCF / PCF		
2	Billoux, F.	PCF	Tanguy-Prigent, P. / Longchambon,	PSF / NONA	Paul, M.	PCF		
3	Billoux, F.	PCF	Tanguy-Prigent, P. / Farge,	PSF / NONA	Menthon, F. de / Paul, M.	MRP / PCF		
4			Tanguy-Prigent, P.	PSF	Lacoste, R. / Moch, J.	PSF / PSF		

FRANCE 4th Republic 1945–1959

Gov	Housing	Py	Agriculture	Py	Industry/Trade	Py	Environment	Py
5	Tillon, C.	PCF	Tanguy-Prigent, P.	PSF	Lacoste, R. / Letourneau, J.	PSF / MRP		
6	Letourneau, J.	MRP	Tanguy-Prigent, P.	PSF	Letourneau, J. / Lacoste, R.	MRP / PSF		
7			Roclore, M.	IND	Lacoste, R.	PSF		
8	Coty, R.	NONA	Pflimlin, P.	MRP	Lacoste, R.	PSF		
9			Pflimlin, P.	MRP	Lacoste, R.	PSF		
10			Pflimlin, P.	MRP	Lacoste, R.	PSF		
11			Pflimlin, P.	MRP	Lacoste, R.	PSF		
12			Pflimlin, P.	MRP	Lacoste, R.	PSF		
13			Valay, G.	MRP	Louvel, J.-M.	MRP		
14	Claudius-Petit, E.	UDSR	Pflimlin, P.	MRP	Louvel, J.-M.	MRP		
15			Pflimlin, P.	MRP	Louvel, J.-M. / Deferre, G.	MRP / PSF		
16	Claudius-Petit, E.	UDSR	Pflimlin, P.	MRP	Louvel, J.-M. / Deferre, G.	MRP / PSF		
17	Claudius-Petit, E.	RSP	Antier, P.	PAY	Morice, A. / Louvel, J.-M. / Pflimlin, P.	RSP / MRP / MRP		
18			Laurens, C.	PAY	Morice, A. / Bonnefous, E.	RSP / UDSR		
19			Laurens, C.	PAY	Louvel, J.-M.	MRP		
20	Courant, P.	IND	Laurens, C.	PAY	Louvel, J.-M. / Ribeyre, P.	MRP / PAY		
21	Lemaire, M.	URAS	Houdet, R.	IND	Louvel, J.-M.	MRP		
22	Lemaire, M.	GAUL	Houdet, R.	IND	Bourges-Maunoury, M.	RSP		

FRANCE 4th Republic 1945–1959

Gov	Housing	Py	Agriculture	Py	Industry/Trade	Py	Environment	Py
23	Duchet, R.	IND	Sourbet, J.		Morice, A.	RSP		
24								
25								
26			Boscary-Monsservin, M.	IND	Bonnefous, E. / Ribeyre, P.	UDSR / IND		
27	Garet, P.	IND	Boscary-Monsservin, M.	IND	Ribeyre, P.	IND		
28	Sudreau, P.	NONA	Houdet, R.	IND	Ramonet, E.	RSP		

Gov	Social Affairs (py)	Public Works (py)	Other (py)	Res
1	Croizat, A. (PCF)	Moch, J. (PSF) / Thomas, E. (PSF)	Teitgen, P.-H. (MRP) / Matreaux, A. (NONA) / Soustelle, J. (UDSR) / Thorez, M. (PCF) / Vincent-Auriol, (PSF) / Gay, F. (MRP) / Jacquinot, L. (NONA)	0
2	Croizat, A. (PCF) / Casanova, L. (PCF)	Moch, J. (PSF) / Letourneau, J.(MRP)	Thorez, M. (PCF) / Gay, F. (MRP) / Moutet, M. (PSF)	0
3	Croizat, A. (PCF) / Casanova, L. (PCF)	Moch, J. (PSF) / Letourneau, J.(MRP)	Gay, F. (MRP) / Varenne, P. (PSF) / Prigent, R. (MRP)	0

FRANCE 4th Republic 1945–1959

Gov	Social Affairs (py)	Public Works (py)	Other (py)	Res
4	Mayer, D. (PSF) Segelle, P. (PSF) Lejeune, M. (PSF)	Moch, J. (PSF) Thomas, E. (PSF)	Moutet, M. (PSF) Mottet, G. (PSF) Augustin, L. (PSF)	0
5	Croizat, A. (PCF) Mitterand, F. (UDSR) Bourdan, P. (UDSR)	Moch, J. (PSF) Maroselli, A. (RSP)	Marrane, (PCF) Moutet, M. (PSF) Delbos, Y. (RSP) Roclore, M. (IND) Gouin, F. (PSF)	0
6	Mayer, D. (PSF) Mitterand, F. (RSP) Bourdan, P. (RSP)	Moch, J. (PSF) Maroselli, A. (RSP) Thomas, E. (PSF)	Prigent, R. (MRP) Moutet, M. (PSF) Bechard, P. (PSF) Roclore, M. (IND) Gouin, F. (PSF)	0
7	Mayer, D. (PSF)	Moch, J. (PSF)	Bechard, P. (PSF) Delbos, Y. (RSP)	0
8	Mayer, D. (PSF) Mitterand, F. (UDSR)	Pineau, C. (PSF)	Coste-Floret, P. (MRP)	0
9	Mayer, D. (PSF) Maroselli, A. (RSP)	Pineau, C. (PSF) Coty, R. (IND)	Schneiter, P. (MRP) Coste-Floret, P. (MRP) Ramadier, P. (PSF) Queuille, H. (RSP)	0
10	Mayer, D. (PSF) Catoire, J. (MRP)	Queuille, H. (RSP) Coty, R. (IND)	Coste-Floret, P. (MRP)	0
11	Mayer, D. (PSF) Betolaud, R. (IND)	Pineau, C. (PSF) Claudius-Pétit, E. (UDSR)	Schneiter, P. (MRP) Coste-Floret, P. (MRP)	0

FRANCE 4th Republic 1945–1959

Gov	Social Affairs (py)	Public Works (py)	Other (py)	Res
12	Segelle, P. (PSF) Jacquinot, L. (IND)	Pineau, C. (PSF) Claudius-Pétit, E. (UDSR) Thomas, E. (PSF)	Letourneau, J. (MRP) Teitgen, P.-H. (MRP)	0
13	Jacquinot, L. (IND)	Chastellain, J. (IND) Claudius-Pétit, E. (UDSR) Brune, M. (RGR)	Letourneau, J. (MRP) Teitgen, P.-H. (MRP)	0
14	Bacon, P. (MRP) Jacquinot, L. (IND)	Claudius-Pétit, E.(UDSR) Bourgès-Maunoury, (RSP) Brune, C. (RSP) Tinguy du Pouet, de (MRP)	Schneiter, P. (MRP) Coste-Floret, P. (MRP) Letourneau, J. (MRP)	0
15	Bacon, P. (MRP) Jacquinot, L. (IND)	Pinay, A. (IND) Claudius-Pétit, E.(UDSR) Brune, C. (RSP)	Mitterand, F. (RSP) Letourneau, J. (MRP) Mollet, G. (PSF) Gazier, A. (PSF) Giacobbi, P. (RSP)	0
16	Bacon, P. (MRP) Jacquinot, L. (IND)	Pinay, A. (IND) Brune, C.(RSP)	Mitterand, F. (UDSR) Letourneau, J. (MRP) Gazier, A. (PSF)	0
17	Bacon, P. (MRP) Temple, E. (IND)	Pinay, A. (IND) Laniel, J. (IND)	Louvel, J.-M. (MRP) Jacquinot, L. (IND) Queuille, H. (RSP) Petsche, M. (IND) Letourneau, J. (MRP) Buron, R. (MRP)	2

FRANCE 4th Republic 1945–1959

Gov	Social Affairs (py)	Public Works (py)	Other (py)	Res
18	Bacon, P. (MRP) Temple, E. (IND)	Pinay, A. (IND) Claudius-Pétit, E. (UDSR) Duchet, R. (RSP) Louvel, J.-M. (MRP)	Ribeyre, P. (PAY) Letourneau, J. (MRP) Pflimlin, P. (MRP) Jacquinot, L. (IND) Coste-Floret, P. (RSP) Mitterand, F. (UDSR) Laniel, J. (IND)	0
19	Garet, P. (IND) Temple, E. (IND)	Morice, A. (RSP) Claudius-Pétit, E. (UDSR) Duchet, R. (IND)	Ribeyre, P. (PAY) Pflimlin, P. (MRP) Letourneau, J. (MRP)	0
20	Bacon, P. (MRP) Bergasse, H. (ARS)	Morice, A. (RSP) Duchet, R. (IND)	Jacquinot, L. (IND) Bonnefous, E. (UDSR) Coste-Floret, P. (MRP) Letourneau, J. (MRP)	1
21	Bacon, P. (MRP) Mutter, A. (PAY)	Chastellain, J. (IND) Ferri, P. (URAS)	Mitterand, F. (RSP) Jacquinot, L. (IND) Corniglion-Molinier, (URAS)	0
22	Claudius-Pétit, E. (UDSR) Temple, E. (IND)	Chaban-Delmas, J. (GAUL)	Chambre, G. La (IND) Buron, R. (MRP) Fouchet, C. (GAUL)	2
23	Bacon, P. (MRP) Triboulet, R. (GAUL)	Corniglion-Molinier, (GAUL) Bonnefous, E. (RSP)	Palewski, G. (GAUL) Teitgen, P.-H. (MRP) July, P. (GAUL)	1
24	Gazier, A. (PSF) Tanguy-Prigent, F. (PSF) Billeres, R. (RSP)		Mitterand, F. (UDSR) Deferre, G. (PSF) Catroux, G. (NONA) Houphouet-Boigny, F. (UDSR) Mendes-France, P. (RSP)	0

FRANCE 4th Republic 1945–1959

Gov	Social Affairs (py)	Public Works (py)	Other (py)	Res
25	Gazier, A. (PSF) Dublin, A. (RSP)	Bonnefous, E. (UDSR)	Jacquet, G. (PSF) Lacoste, R. (PSF) Lejeune, M. (PSF) Houphouet-Boigny, F. (UDSR)	0
26	Quinson, A. (RGR)	Garet, P. (IND) Bonnefous, E. (UDSR)	Jacquet, G. (PSF) Lejeune, M. (PSF) Lacoste, R. (PSF)	0
27	Bacon, P. (MRP) Badie, V. (RSP)	Maroselli, A. (RSP) Bonnefous, E. (UDSR)	Mutter, A. (IND) Corniglion-Molinier, (RGR) Colin, A. (MRP) Houphouet-Boigny, F. (RDA)	0
28	Michelet, E. (GAUL)	Buron, R. (MRP) Thomas, E. (PSF)	Cornut-Gentille, B. (NONA) Lejeune, M. (PSF) Soustelle, J. (GAUL) Malraux, A. (NONA) Boulloche, A. (NONA) Mollet, G. (PSF) Pflimlin, P. (MRP) Houphouet-Boingny, F. (RDA) Jacquinot, J. (IND)	0

16.2. FRANCE V

The Vth Republic dates from 4 October 1958 and is semi-presidential. The President is Head of State, and has since 1962 been directly elected for a seven year term. He or she holds considerable power: appoints and dismisses officials, including the Prime Minister; communicates independently with parliament; and can call national referendums.

France is a unitary state with strong centralisation, although in the 1980s some power was devolved to economic regions.

Parliament is bicameral, consisting of the Upper House (Senate) and the Lower House (National Assembly). The Senate of 319 seats is elected indirectly for a nine-year term by regional bodies. The National Assembly of 577 seats is elected directly for a five-year term by constituency-based plurality voting (absolute majority with double ballot) in constituencies of variable size with an average of 60,000 electors.

Parliament has a quorum of at least 50 per cent of all members. Votes are carried by a majority of all votes cast. Some issues require a qualified majority of all members present. Constitutional amendments may be proposed by the President, the Prime Minister and by members of parliament and must pass both Houses with a majority of three-fifth of votes cast. A referendum is optional, and is called by the Head of State. The outcome is binding.

Relations between the executive and legislative bodies are complex, in particular if there is a situation of "cohabitation", where the presidency is controlled by one party and parliament by another. Parliament is weak vis-à-vis government and President, as its controlling instruments are limited by the constitution: government can act by decree in all matters where it is not explicitly forbidden.

Governments do not need a vote of investiture and can survive a vote of no confidence. Nevertheless, they are normally expected to command a majority in parliament. Government is collectively responsible to parliament. Individual ministers can not be Member of Parliament at the same time. The Prime Minister has a rather prominent position in government.

The Constitutional Council (external to the administration) and the Council of State (internal to the administration) review laws and administrative decrees for their constitutionality.

FRANCE 5th Republic 1959–1998

Gov	Begin	Dur	RfT	ToG	Py1	Py2	Py3	Py4	Py5	Seats	CPG	NoM	Prime Minister (py)
29	08.01.59	1193	1	3	GAUL198	RSP 23	MRP 57	IND 133		465	2	21	Debré, M. (UNR)
30	15.04.62	31	5	3	UNR 198	MRP 57	IND 133			465	2	22	Pompidou, G. (NONA)
31	16.05.62	204	7	3	UNR 198	IND 133				465	2	20	Pompidou, G. (NONA)
32	06.12.62	1130	1	3	UNR 230	IND 18				465	2	22	Pompidou, G. (NONA)
33	09.01.66	454	2	3	UNR 230	IND 18				465	2	18	Pompidou, G. (NONA)
34	08.04.67	419	6	2	UNR 191	VREP 41				470	2	22	Pompidou, G. (VREP)
35	31.05.68	42	1	5	VREP 41					470	2	22	Pompidou, G. (VREP)
36	12.07.68	345	2	3	UDR 282	IND 64				470	1	19	Couve de Murville, M. (UDR)
37	22.06.69	1111	6	3	UDR 282	PDM 26	IND 64			470	1	19	Chaban-Delmas, M. (UDR)
38	07.07.72	272	1	3	UDR 282	PDM 26	IND 64			470	1	20	Messmer, P. (UDR)
39	05.04.73	330	7	2	UDR 178	CDP 21	IND 54			473	2	22	Messmer, P. (UDR)
40	01.03.74	88	1	2	UDR 178	CDP 21	IND 54			473	2	16	Messmer, P. (UDR)
41	28.05.74	812	6	3	UDR 178	CDP 21	IND 54	REF 30	MRG 11	473	2	16	Chirac, J. (UDR)
42	17.08.76	225	4	3	UDR 178	CDS 21	IND 54	MRG 11		473	2	18	Barre, R. (CDS)
43	30.03.77	370	1	3	RPR 178	CDS 21	IND 54	MRG 11		473	2	15	Barre, R. (CDS)
44	04.04.78	1144	1	3	UDF 124	RPR 142				474	2	20	Barre, R. (UDF)
45	22.05.81	32	1	6	PSF 268					474	4	31	Mauroy, P. (PSF)
46	23.06.81	637	6	3	PSF 268	PCF 43				474	5	36	Mauroy, P. (PSF)
47	22.03.83	487	6	3	PSF 268	PCF 43				474	5	23	Mauroy, P. (PSF)
48	23.07.84	604	1	1	PSF 268					474	4	23	Fabius, L. (PSF)
49	20.03.86	784	1	5**	RPR 146	UDF 128				556	2	25	Chirac, J. (RPR)
50	13.05.88	45	6	5	PSF 210	UDF 53				556	4	19	Rocard, M. (PSF)
51	28.06.88	1052	6	4	PSF 269					577	4	22	Rocard, M. (PSF)
52	15.05.91	322	6	4	PSF 269					577	4	20	*Cresson, E. (PSF)
53	02.04.92	362	1	4	PSF 269					577	4	20	Bérégovoy, P. (PSF)

FRANCE 5th Republic 1959–1998

Gov	Begin	Dur	RfT	ToG	Py1	Py2	Py3	Py4	Py5	Seats	CPG	NoM	Prime Minister (py)
54	30.03.93	779	2	2**	RPR 247	UDF 205				577	2	24	Balladur, E. (RPR)
55	18.05.95	182	2	2**	RPR 257	UDF 213				577	2	27	Juppé, A. (RPR)
56	08.11.95	573	1	2	RPR 257	UDF 213				577	2	17	Juppé, A. (RPR)
57	03.06.97			2**	PSF 241	PCF 38	RSP 12	Greens 7		577	4	14	Jospin, L. (PSF)

** = divided government

- Gov 29: GAUL includes RDA and UNR.
- Gov 31: UNR includes UDT.
- Gov 32, 33, 34: UNR includes UDT.
- Gov 34, 35: VREP includes IND.
- Gov 44: UDF = APP-UDF + UDF-CDS + UDF-PR.
- Gov 45, 46, 47, 50, 51: PSF includes MRG.
- Gov 48: PSF includes PSU and MRG.
- Gov 49: UDF includes UDF-RP and UDF-CDS.
- Gov 50: UDF = UDF-PR.
- Gov 51: UDF = UDF-PR and UDF-CDS; Individuals from UDF-CDS and UDF-RAD participated in the government.
- Gov 52: Individuals from France Unie and Ecology Generation participated in the Government.
- Gov 54-56: UDF = UDF-PR, UDF-PPDF, UDF-RAD and UDF-CDS.

Gov	Deputy PM	Py	Foreign Affairs	Py	Defence	Py	Interior	Py	Justice	Py
29			Couve de Murville, M.	NONA	Guillaumat, P.	NONA	Berthoin, J.	RSP	Michelet, E.	UNR
30			Couve de Murville, M.	NONA	Messmer, P.	NONA	Frey, R.	UNR	Foyer, J.	UNR
31			Couve de Murville, M.	NONA	Messmer, P.	NONA	Frey, R.	UNR	Foyer, J.	UNR
32			Couve de Murville, M.	NONA	Messmer, P.	NONA	Frey, R.	UNR	Foyer, J.	UNR
33			Couve de Murville, M.	NONA	Messmer, P.	NONA	Frey, R. / Joxe, L.	UNR / UNR	Foyer, J.	UNR
34			Couve de Murville, M.	NONA	Messmer, P.	NONA	Fouchet, C.	UNR	Joxe, L.	VREP

FRANCE 5th Republic 1959–1998

Gov	Deputy PM	Py	Foreign Affairs	Py	Defence	Py	Interior	Py	Justice	Py
35			Debré, M.	VREP	Messmer, P.	NONA	Marcellin, R.	IND	Capitant, R.	VREP
36			Debré, M.	VREP	Messmer, P.	NONA	Marcellin, R.	IND	Capitant, R.	VREP
37			Schumann, M.	UDR	Debré, M.	UDR	Marcellin, R.	IND	Pleven, R.	PDM
38			Schumann, M.	UDR	Debré, M.	UDR	Marcellin, R.	IND	Pleven, R.	PDM
39			Jobert, M.	NONA	Galley, R.	UDR	Marcellin, R. Peyrefitte, A.	IND UDR	Taittinger, J.	UDR
40			Jobert, M.	NONA	Galley, R.	UDR	Chirac, J.	UDR	Taittinger, J.	UDR
41			Sauvagnargues, J.	NONA	Soufflet, J.	UDR	Poniatowski, M. Servan-Schreiber, J.-J.	IND MRG	Lecanuet, J.	CDP
42			Guiringaud, L. de	NONA	Bourges, Y.	UDR	Poniatowski, M.	IND	Guichard, O.	UDR
43			Guiringaud, L. de	NONA	Bourges, Y.	RPR	Bonnet, C.	IND	Peyrefitte, A.	RPR
44			Guiringaud, L. de	NONA	Bourges, Y.	RPR	Bonnet, C.	UDF	Peyrefitte, A.	RPR
45			Cheysson, C.	PSF	Hernu, C.	PSF	Deferre, G.	PSF	Faure, M.	MRG
46			Cheysson, C.	PSF	Hernu, C.	PSF	Deferre, G. Le Pors, A.	PSF PCF	Badinter, R.	PSF
47			Cheysson, C.	PSF	Hernu, C.	PSF	Deferre, G.	PSF	Badinter, R.	PSF
48			Cheysson, C.	PSF	Hernu, C.	PSF	Deferre, G. Joxe, P. Dumas, R.	PSF PSF PSF	Badinter, R.	PSF
49			Raimond, J.-B.	NONA	Giraud, A.	NONA	Pasqua, C. Chavannes, G. Pandraud, R. Charette, H. de	RPR UDF RPR UDF	Chalandon, A.	RPR
50			Dumas, R.	PSF	Chevènement, J.-P.	PSF	Joxe, P. Durafour, M.	PSF UDF	Arpaillange, P.	PSF
51			Dumas, R.	PSF	Chevènement, J.-P.	PSF	Joxe, P. Durafour, M.	PSF UDF	Arpaillange, P.	PSF

FRANCE 5th Republic 1959–1998

Gov	Deputy PM	Py	Foreign Affairs	Py	Defence	Py	Interior	Py	Justice	Py
52			Dumas, R.	PSF	Joxe, P.	PSF	Soisson, J.-P. Delebarre, M. Marchand, P.	France Unie PSF PSF	Nallet, H.	PSF
53			Dumas, R.	PSF	Joxe, P.	PSF	Quilès, P. Delebarre, M. Tapie, B.	PSF PSF NONA	Vanzelle, M.	PSF
54			Juppé, A.	RPR	Léotard, F.	UDF-PR	Pasqua, C. *Veil, S. Rossinot, A.	RPR NONA UDF-RAD	Méhaignerie, P.	UDF-CDS
55			Charette, H. de	UDF-PR	Millon, C.	UDF-PR	Debré, J.-L. Goasguen, C. Puech, J.	RPR UDF-CDS UDF-PR	Tourbon, J.	RPR
56			Charette, H. de	UDF-PPDF	Millon, C.	UDF-RAD	Debré, J.-L. Gaudin, J.-C. Perben, D.	RPR UDF-PR RPR	Tourbon, J.	RPR
57			Védrine, H.	PSF	Richard, A.	PSF	Chevènement, J.-P. Zuccarelli, E.	MDC RSP	*Guigou, E.	PSF

Gov	Finance	Py	Economic Aff.	Py	Labour	Py	Education	Py	Health	Py
29	Pinay, A.	IND	Pinay, A.	IND	Bacon, P.	MRP	Boulloche, A.	NONA	Chenot, B.	NONA
30	Giscard d'Estaing, V.	IND	Giscard d'Estaing, V. Palewski, G.	IND UNR	Bacon, P.	MRP	Sudreau, P. Palewski, G.	NONA UNR	Fontanet, J.	NONA
31	Giscard d'Estaing, V.	IND	Giscard d'Estaing, V. Palewski, G.	IND UNR	Grandval, G.	UDT	Sudreau, P. Palewski, G.	NONA UNR	Marcellin, R.	IND
32	Giscard d'Estaing, V.	IND	Giscard d'Estaing, V. Palewski, G.	IND UNR	Grandval, G.	UDT	Fouchet, M. Palewski, G.	NONA UNR	Marcellin, R.	IND

FRANCE 5th Republic 1959–1998

Gov	Finance	Py	Economic Aff.	Py	Labour	Py	Education	Py	Health	Py
33	Debré, M.	UNR	Debré, M.	UNR			Fouchet, C. Peyrefitte, A.	IND UNR		
34	Debré, M.	UNR	Debré, M.	UNR			Peyrefitte, A.	UNR		
35	Couve de Murville, M.	NON A	Couve de Murville, M.	NONA			Ortoli, F. Malene, C. de la	NONA VREP		
36	Ortoli, F.	UDR	Ortoli, F.	UDR			Faure, E. Galley, R.	UDR NONA		
37	Giscard d'Estaing, V.	IND	Giscard d'Estaing, V.	IND	Fontanet, J.	PDM	Guichard, O.	UDR	Boulin, R.	UDR
38	Giscard d'Estaing, V.	IND	Giscard d'Estaing, V.	IND			Fontanet, J.	CDP	Foyer, J.	UDR
39	Giscard d'Estaing, V.	IND	Giscard d'Estaing, V.	IND	Gorse, G.	UDR	Fontanet, J.	CDP	Poniatowski, M.	IND
40	Giscard d'Estaing, V.	IND	Giscard d'Estaing, V.	IND	Gorse, G.	UDR	Fontanet, J.	CDP	Poniatowski, M.	IND
41	Fourcade, J.-P.	IND	Fourcade, J.-P.	IND	Durafour, M.	REF	Haby, R.	NONA	*Veil, S.	NONA
42	Barre, R. Durafour, M.	CDS MRG	Barre, R. Durafour, M.	CDS MRG	Beullac, C.	NONA	Haby, R.	NONA	*Veil, S.	NONA
43	Barre, R. Boulin, R.	CDS RPR	Barre, R. Boulin, R.	CDS RPR	Beullac, C.	NONA	Haby, R.	NONA	*Veil, S.	NONA
44	Papon, M.	RPR	Monory, R.	UDF	Boulin, R.	RPR	Beullac, C. *Saunier-Seité, A.	UDF	*Veil, S.	NONA
45	Delors, J. Fabius, L.	PSF PSF	Delors, J.	PSF	Auroux, J.	PSF	Savery, A.	PSF	Hervé, E.	PSF
46	Delors, J. Fabius, L.	PSF PSF	Delors, J.	PSF	Auroux, J.	PSF	Savery, A. Rigout, M.	PSF PCF	Ralite, J.	PCF
47	Delors, J.	PSF	Delors, J.	PSF			Savery, A. Rigout, M.	PSF PCF		

FRANCE 5th Republic 1959–1998

Gov	Finance	Py	Economic Aff.	Py	Labour	Py	Education	Py	Health	Py
48	Bérégovoy, P.	PSF	Bérégovoy, P.	PSF	Delebarre, M.	PSF	Delebarre, M. Chevènement, J.-P.	PSF PSF		
49	Juppé, A.	RPR	Balladur, E.	RPR	Séguin, P.	RPR	Monoroy, R. Devaquet, A.	UDF RPR	*Barzach, M.	RPR
50	Bérégovoy, P.	PSF	Bérégovoy, P.	PSF	Delebarre, M.	PSF	Jospin, L.	PSF		
51	Bérégovoy, P.	PSF	Bérégovoy, P.	PSF	Soisson, J.-P.	UDF-PR	Jospin, L. Soisson, J.-P. Curien, H.	PSF UDF-PR PSF	Evin, C.	PSF
52	Bérégovoy, P.	PSF	Bérégovoy, P.	PSF	*Aubry, M.	NONA	Jospin, L. *Aubry, M. Quilès, P. Curien, H.	PSF NONA PSF PSF		
53	Sapin, M.	PSF			*Aubry, M.	NONA	Lang, J. *Aubry, M. Curien, H.	PSF NONA PSF	Kouchner, B.	NONA
54	Sarkozy, N.	RPR	Alphandéry, E. Madelin, A.	UDF-CDS UDF-PR	Giraud, M.	RPR	Bayrou, F. Giraud, M. Fillon, F.	UDF-CDS RPR RPR	*Veil, S.	NONA
55	Madelin, A.	UDF-PR	Madelin, A. Arthuis, J. Raffarin, J.-P.	UDF-PR UDF-CDS UDF-PR	Barrot, J.	UDF-CDS	Bayrou, F.	UDF-CDS	*Hubert, E.	RPR
56	Arthuis, J.	UDF-CDS	Arthuis, J. Raffarin, J.-P.	UDF-CDS UDF-PPDF	Barrot, J.	UDF-CDS	Bayrou, F.	UDF-CDS		
57	Strauss-Kahn, D.	PSF	Strauss-Kahn, D.	PSF	*Aubry, M.	PSF	Allegre, C.	PSF		

FRANCE 5th Republic 1959–1998

Gov	Housing	Py	Agriculture	Py	Industry/Trade	Py	Environment	Py
29	Sudreau, P.	NONA	Houdet, R.	IND	Jeanneney, J.-M.	NONA		
30			Pisani, E.	GD	Maurice-Bokanowski, M.	UNR		
31			Pisani, E.	GD	Maurice-Bokanowski, M.	UNR		
32	Maziol, J.	UNR	Pisani, E.	GD	Maurice-Bokanowski, M.	UNR		
33			Faure, E.	GD	Peyrefitte, A. Faure, E.	UNR GD		
34	Pisani, E.	VREP	Faure, E.	VREP	Guichard, O.	UNR		
35	Galley, R.	NONA	Faure, E.	VREP	Chalandon, A. Malene, C. de la	VREP VREP		
36	Chalandon, A.	UDR	Boulin, R.	UDR	Bettencourt, A. Galley, R.	IND NONA		
37	Chalandon, A.	UDR	Duhamel, J.	PDM	Ortoli, F.	UDR		
38	Guichard, O.	UDR	Chirac, J.	UDR	Charbonnel, J. Bourges, Y.	UDR UDR	Poujade, R.	UDR
39	Guichard, O.	UDR	Chirac, J.	UDR	Charbonnel, J. Royer J.	UDR NONA	Poujade, R.	UDR
40			Marcellin, R.	IND	Guena, Y. Guichard, O.	UDR UDR	Peyrefitte, A.	UDR
41			Bonnet, C.	IND	d'Ornano, M. Ansquer, V.	IND UDR		
42			Bonnet, C.	IND	d'Ornano, M. Brousse, P. Rossi, A.	IND MRGAD MRG		
43	Mehaignerie, P.	CDS			Monory, R. Rossi, A.	CDS MRG	d'Ornano, M.	IND
44	Mehaignerie, P.	UDF			Giraud, A. Deniau, J.F. Barrot, J.	NONA UDF UDF	d'Ornano, M.	UDF

FRANCE 5th Republic 1959–1998

Gov	Housing	Py	Agriculture	Py	Industry/Trade	Py	Environment	Py
45	Quilliot, R.	PSF	*Cresson, E.	PSF	Joxe, P. Jobert, M. Delelis, A.	PSF PSF PSF	Crepeau, M. Le Pensec, L.	MRG PSF
46	Quilliot, R.	PSF	*Cresson, E.	PSF	Dreyfus, P. Jobert, M. Delelis, A.	PSF PSF PSF	Crepeau, M. Le Pensec, L.	MRG PSF
47	Quilliot, R.	PSF	Rocard, M.	PSF	Fabius, L. *Cresson, E. Crépeau, M.	PSF PSF MRG		
48	Quilès, P.	PSF	Rocard, M.	PSF	*Cresson, E. Crépeau, M. Curien, H.	PSF MRG PSF	*Bouchardeau, H.	PSU
49			Guillaume, F.	NONA	Méhaignerie, P. Madelin, A. Noir, M. Cabana, C.	UDF UDF RPR RPR	Carignon, A.	RPR
50	Faure, M.	MRG	Nallet, H.	PSF	Faroux, R.	PSF		
51	Faure, M.	MRG	Nallet, H.	PSF	Faroux, R. Rausch, J.-M.	PSF UDF		
52	Quilès, P.	PSF	Mermaz, L.	PSF			Lalonde, B.	Ecology Generation
53	Bianco, J.-L.	NONA	Mermaz, L.	PSF	Strauss-Kahn, D.	PSF	*Royal, S.	PSF
54	Charette, H. de	UDF-PR	Puech, J.	UDF-PR	Longuet, G.	UDF-PR	Barnier, M.	RPR
55	Périssol, P.-A.	RPR	Vasseur, P.	UDF-PR	Galland, Y.	UDF-RAD	*Lepage, C.	former Ecology Generation
56	Pons, B.	RPR	Vasseur, P.	UDF-PR	Borotra, F.	RPR	*Lepage, C.	NONA
57	Gayssot, J.-C.	PCF	Le Pensec, L.	PSF	Strauss-Kahn, D.	PSF	*Voynet, D.	Greens

FRANCE 5th Republic 1959–1998

Gov	Social Affairs (py)	Public Works (py)	Other (py)	Res
29	Triboulet, R. (MRP)	Buron, R. (MRP) Cornut-Gentille, B. (UNR)	Frey, R. (GAUL) Soustelle, J. (UNR) Jacquinot, F. (IND) Houphouet-Boigny, F. (RDA) Lecourt, R, (MRP) Malraux, A. (NONA)	5
30	Triboulet, R. (UNR)	Maziol, J. (UNR) Buron, R. (MRP) Schumann, M. (MRP) Marette, J. (UNR)	Malraux, A. (NONA) Pflimlin, P. (MRP) Jacquinot, L. (IND) Joxe, L. (NONA) Dusseaulx, R. (UNR)	0
31	Triboulet, R. (UNR)	Pompidou, G. (NONA) Maziol, J. (UNR) Dusseaulx, R. (UNR) Marette, J. (UNR)	Gorse, G. (UNR) Malraux, A. (NONA) Joxe, L. (NONA) Jacquinot, L. (IND)	0
32	Sainteney, J. (UDT)	Jacquet, M. (UNR) Marette, J. (UNR)	Triboulet, R. (UNR) Peyerefitte, A. (UNR) Missoffe, F. (UNR) Malraux, A. (NONA) Jacquinot, L. (UNR) Joxe, L. (NONA)	0
33	Jeanneney, J.-M. (NONA) Misoffe, F. (UNR) Sanguinetti, A. (UNR)	Pisani, E. (GD) Marette, J. (UNR)	Malraux, A. (NONA) Bilotte, P. (UNR)	0

FRANCE 5th Republic 1959–1998

Gov	Social Affairs (py)	Public Works (py)	Other (py)	Res
34	Jeanneney, J.-M. (NONA) Duvillard, H. (UNR) Missoffe, F. (UNR)	Pisani, E. (VREP) Guena, Y. (UNR) Chamant, J. (IND)	Gorse, G. (VREP) Malraux, A. (NONA) Michelet, E. (UNR) Bilotte, P. (UNR) Schumann, M. (VREP) Frey, R. (UNR) Marcellin, R. (IND)	0
35	Schumann, M. (VREP) Nungesser, R. (VREP) Duvillard, H. (VREP)	Galley, R. (NONA) Chamant, J. (IND) Bettencourt, A. (IND) Boulin, R. (VREP)	Guena, Y. (VREP) Le Theule, J. (VREP) Malraux, A. (NONA) Michelet, E. (VREP) Rey, H. (VREP)	0
36	Schumann, M. (UDR) Duvillard, H. (UDR)	Chalandon, A. (UDR) Chamant, J. (IND) Guena, Y. (UDR) Guichard, O. (UDR)	Malraux, A. (NONA) Frey, R. (UDR) Jeanneney, J.-M. (UDR)	1
37	Fontanet, J. (PDM) Boulin, R. (UDR) Duvillard, H. (UDR)	Chalandon, A. (UDR) Mondon, R. (IND) Galley, R. (UDR) Bettencourt, A. (IND)	Michelet, E. (UDR) Frey, R. (UDR) Rey, H. (UDR)	1
38	Faure, E. (UDR) Bord, A. (UDR)	Guichard, O. (UDR) Galley, R. (UDR) Germain, H. (UDR)	Duhamel, J. (PDM) Boulin, R. (UDR) Bettencourt, A. (IND)	0
39	Gorse, G. (UDR) Poniatowski, M. (IND) Bord, A. (UDR)	Guichard, O. (UDR) Guena, Y. (UDR) Germain, H. (UDR)	Malaud, P. (IND) Comiti, J. (UDR) Stasi, B. (CDP) Druon, M. (NONA)	1

FRANCE 5th Republic 1959–1998

Gov	Social Affairs (py)	Public Works (py)	Other (py)	Res
40	Gorse, G. (UDR) Poniatowski, M. (IND)	Guichard, O. (UDR) Royer, J. (NONA)	Peyrefitte, A. (UDR) Lecat, J.-P. (UDR) Germain, H. (UDR)	0
41	Jarrot, A. (UDR)	Galley, R. (UDR)	Abelin, P. (CDP)	1
42	Ansquer, V. (UDR)	Lecanuet, J. (CDS) Fourcade, J.-P. (IND) d'Ornano, M. (IND)	Galley, R. (UDR) Boulin, R. (UDR)	0
43	*Veil, S. (NONA)	Fourcade, J.-P. (IND)	d'Ornano, M. (IND) Galley, R. (RPR)	0
44	*Veil, S. (NONA) Soisson, J.-P. (UDF) d'Ornano, M. (UDF)	Le Theule, J. (RPR) Lecat, J.-P. (RPR)	Galley, R. (RPR)	4
45	*Questiaux, N. (PSF) *Avice, E. (PSF) Laurain, J. (PSF) *Roudy, Y. (PSF) Henry, A. (PSF)	Rocard, M. (PSF) Chevènement, J.-P. (PSF) Mermaz, L. (PSF) Fillioud, G. (PSF) Mexandeau, L. (PSF)	Chandernagor, A. (PSF) Cot, J.-P. (PSF) Lang, J. (PSF) Labarrère, A. (PSF)	0
46	*Questiaux, N. (PSF) *Avice, E. (PSF) Laurain, J. (PSF) *Roudy, Y. (PSF) *Lalumière, C. (PSF) Le Garrec, J. (PSF)	Rocard, M. (PSF) Fiterman, C. (PCF) Chevènement, J.-P. (PSF) Fillioud, G. (PSF) Hervé, E. (PSF) Mexandeau, L. (PSF)	Chandernagor, A. (PSF) Cot, J.P. (PSF) Henry, A. (PSF) Lang, J. (PSF) Labarrère, A. (PSF)	1
47	Bérégovoy, P. (PSF) *Avice, E. (PSF) *Roudy, (PSF) Ralite, J. (PCF)	Quilliot, R. (PSF) Fiterman, C. (PCF) Mexandeau, L. (PSF) Fabius, L. (PSF)	*Avice, E. (PSF) *Cresson, E. (PSF) Lang, J. (PSF) Labarrère, A. (PSF) Chandernagor, A. (PSF) Nucci, C. (PSF)	0

FRANCE 5th Republic 1959–1998

Gov	Social Affairs (py)	Public Works (py)	Other (py)	Res
48	Delebarre, M. (PSF) *Dufoix, (PSF) *Roudy, (PSF) Calmat, A. (PSF) Quilès, P. (PSF)	Mexandeau, L. (PSF)	*Cresson, E. (PSF) Lang, J. (PSF) Labarrère, A. (PSF) Nucci, C. (PSF)	3
49	Séguin, P. (RPR)	Charette, H. de (UDF) Douffiagues, J. (UDF) Léotard, F. (UDF) Méhaignerie, P. (UDF) Madelin, A. (UDF)	Léotard, F. (UDF) Madelin, A. (UDF) Pons, B. (RPR) Aurillac, M. (RPR) Rossinot, A. (UDF)	2
50	Delebarre, M. (PSF) Jospin, L. (PSF)	Faure, M. (MRG) Mermaz, L. (PSF) Quilès, P. (PSF) Faroux, R. (PSF) Lang, J. (PSF)	*Cresson, E. (PSF) Pelletier, J. (UDF) Lang, J. (PSF) Poperen, J. (PSF) Le Pensec, L. (PSF)	0
51	Jospin, L. (PSF) Evin, C. (PSF)	Faure, M. (MRG) Faroux, R. (PSF) Delebarre, M. (PSF) Quilès, P. (PSF) Lang, J. (PSF)	Lang, J. (PSF) Le Pensec, L. (PSF) Poperen, J. (PSF) *Cresson, E. (PSF) Pelletier, J. (UDF) Evin, C. (PSF) Delebarre, M. (PSF)	2
52	Bianco, J.-L. (NONA) *Bredin, F. (PSF)	Lang, J. (PSF) Quilès, P. (PSF)	Delebarre, M. (PSF) Lang, J. (PSF) *Avice, E. (PSF) Le Pensec, L. (PSF) Poperen, J. (PSF) Quilès, P. (PSF)	0

FRANCE 5th Republic 1959–1998

Gov	Social Affairs (py)	Public Works (py)	Other (py)	Res
53	Teulade, R. (NONA) *Bredin, F. (PSF)	Bianco, J.-L. (NONA) Zuccarelli, E. (MRG)	Lang, J. (PSF) Kouchner, B. (NONA) Le Pensec, L. (PSF)	0
54	*Veil, S. (NONA) *Alliot-Marie, M. (RPR) Mestre, P. (UDF)	Longuet, G. (UDF-PR) Bosson, B. (UDF-CDS) Carignon, A. (RPR)	*Veil, S. (NONA) Bosson, B. (UDF-CDS) Sarkozy, N. (RPR) Roussin, M. (RPR) Perben, D. (RPR) Carignon, A. (RPR) Tourbon, J. (RPR)	0
55	Barrot, J. (UDF-CDS) Raoult, E. (RPR) *Codaccioni, C. (RPR) Drut, G. (RPR) Pasquini, P. (RPR)	Pons, B. (RPR) Fillon, F. (RPR)	Pons, B. (RPR) Romani, R. (RPR) Douste-Blazy, P. (UDF-CDS) Peretti, J.-J. de (RPR) *Panafieu, F. de (RPR)	0
56	Barrot, J. (UDF-CDS)	Pons, B. (RPR) Borotra, F. (RPR)	Pons, B. (RPR) Romani, R. (RPR) Douste-Blazy, P. (UDF-CDS)	1
57	*Aubry, M. (PSF) *Buffet, M.-G. (PCF)	Gayssot, J.-C. (PCF) *Trautmann, C. (PSF)	*Guigou, E. (PSF) *Trautmann, C. (PSF) *Voynet, D. (Greens)	

17. GERMANY

In October 1990 East and West Germany were (re-) united as the Federal Republic of Germany under the constitution of 1949.

The President, with mainly ceremonial duties, is indirectly elected for a five year term by a federal convention selected from the Bundesrat (all members) and the Bundestag (a matching equal number).

Germany is a Federal State with limited decentralisation. The tasks and policy competencies of the "Länder" (States) are circumscribed and can not run counter to the general interest or federal government. Hence, although the Länder possess a high degree of co-governance and share decision-making powers with the Federal State, genuine decentralisation on the local level is quite limited.

The mechanism of power sharing is expressed at the federal level by symmetrical bicameralism. This can well induce situations of 'divided government' since delegates of the Länder governments form the Bundesrat (Upper House) of 68 seats. The Bundestag (Lower House) is elected for a fixed term of four years by a mixed electoral system: proportional representation (d'Hondt) for half of the members and plurality voting in constituencies for the other half. For the PR-vote, the Länder are the constituencies. Plurality voting takes place in single-member constituencies of varying size. On average they comprise 180,000 electors. The overall party balance is adjusted to fit the results of the PR vote. There is a national threshold of 5% of the vote, but if a party obtains a seat in a constituency, it gains access to parliament.

Parliament has a quorum of 50 per cent of all members. Votes are carried by a majority of votes cast. Some issues require a qualified majority of all members present. Constitutional amendments require a two-thirds majority of all votes cast in both Houses. A referendum is constitutionally required with regard to Länder boundary changes or Länder amalgamations. For other issues it is optional and is called by the government. The outcome is binding.

The pivot of government is the Federal Chancellor (Prime Minister), who is appointed by the President and can only be removed by means of a "constructive vote of no confidence": by putting forward an alternative candidate who must be supported by a majority of all members in the Bundestag. Other ministers are deputies to the Chancellor and appointed formally by the President. Ministers are individually responsible to parliament and may also be members of parliament. The Chancellor has a dominant position in government. Although the Chancellor is powerful, the legislature is a strong countervailing power – in particular under circumstances of divided government.

The Constitutional Court (Bundesverfassungsgericht), whose members are elected by parliament, has a wide jurisdiction. The Court decides on the constitutionality of lawmaking, and can be considered as an additional countervailing power.

GERMANY 1945–1998

Gov	Begin	Dur	RfT	ToG	Py1	Py2	Py3	Py4	Seats	CPG	NoM	Prime Minister (py)
1	15.09.49	1485	1	2	CDU 139	FDP 52	DP 17		410	2	14	Adenauer, K. (CDU)
2	09.10.53	652	4	3	CDU 243	FDP 48	DP 15	GBHE 27	509	3	16	Adenauer, K. (CDU)
3	23.07.55	242	4	3	CDU 243	FDP 48	DP 15		509	3	16	Adenauer, K. (CDU)
4	21.03.56	580	1	3	CDU 243	FDP 48	DP 15		509	3	18	Adenauer, K. (CDU)
5	22.10.57	983	4	3	CDU 270	DP 17			519	3	17	Adenauer, K. (CDU)
6	01.07.60	501	1	1	CDU 270				519	3	18	Adenauer, K. (CDU)
7	14.11.61	370	4	2	CDU 242	FDP 67			521	3	21	Adenauer, K. (CDU)
8	19.11.62	25	4	6	CDU 242				521	3	16	Adenauer, K. (CDU)
9	14.12.62	306	2	2	CDU 242	FDP 67			521	3	21	Adenauer, K. (CDU)
10	16.10.63	741	1	2	CDU 242	FDP 67			521	3	20	Erhard, L. (CDU)
11	26.10.65	367	4	2	CDU 245	FDP 49			518	3	21	Erhard, L. (CDU)
12	28.10.66	34	2	6	CDU 245				518	3	18	Erhard, L. (CDU)
13	01.12.66	1056	1	2	CDU 245	SPD 202			518	4	20	Kiesinger, K. (CDU)
14	22.10.69	938	5	2	SPD 224	FDP 30			518	4	16	Brandt, W. (SPD)
15	17.05.72	212	1	2	SPD 223	FDP 26			518	4	16	Brandt, W. (SPD)
16	15.12.72	517	2	2	SPD 230	FDP 41			518	4	18	Brandt, W. (SPD)
17	16.05.74	944	1	2	SPD 230	FDP 41			518	4	16	Schmidt, H. (SPD)
18	15.12.76	1420	1	2	SPD 214	FDP 39			518	4	16	Schmidt, H. (SPD)
19	04.11.80	682	4	2	SPD 218	FDP 53			519	4	16	Schmidt, H. (SPD)
20	17.09.82	17	5	6	SPD 218				519	4	13	Schmidt, H. (SPD)
21	04.10.82	177	1	6	CDU 226	FDP 53			519	3	17	Kohl, H. (CDU)
22	30.03.83	1442	1	2	CDU 244	FDP 34			520	3	17	Kohl, H. (CDU)
23	11.03.87	1303	x	2	CDU 223	FDP 46			519	3	19	Kohl, H. (CDU)
24	04.10.90	105	1	2	CDU 305	FDP 59			663	3	19	Kohl, H. (CDU)
25	17.01.91	1400	1	2	CDU 319	FDP 79			663	3	25	Kohl, H. (CDU)
26	17.11.94			2	CDU 294	FDP 47			672	3	19	Kohl, H. (CDU)

GERMANY 1945–1998

- CDU includes CDU proper plus CSU.
- Gov 4: split in FDP; FVP (16 seats in parliament) continues to participate in government.
- Gov 6: split in DP; 9 of the 15 MP's join the CDU.
- Gov 23: Reason for Termination is re-unification of Germany and subsequent increase in number of MP's from 519 to 663, and the inclusion of 5 ministers from the new eastern Länder in the Federal government.

Gov	Deputy PM	Py	Foreign Affairs	Py	Defence	Py	Interior	Py	Justice	Py
1	Blücher, F.	FDP	Adenauer, K. / Blücher, F.	CDU / FDP			Heinemann, G.	CDU	Dehler, T.	FDP
2	Blücher, F.	FDP	Adenauer, K. / Blücher, F.	CDU / FDP	Blank, T.	CDU	Schröder, G.	CDU	Neumayer, F.	FDP
3	Blücher, F.	FDP	Brentano di Tremezzo, H. von / Blücher, F.	CDU / FDP	Blank, T.	CDU	Schröder, G.	CDU	Neumayer, F.	FDP
4	Blücher, F.	FDP	Brentano di Tremezzo, H. von / Blücher, F.	CDU / FDP	Blank, T.	CDU	Schröder, G.	CDU	Neumayer, F.	FDP
5	Erhard, L.	CDU	Brentano di Tremezzo, H. von	CDU	Strauss, F.-J.	CSU	Schröder, G.	CDU	Schäffer, F.	CSU
6	Erhard, L.	CDU	Brentano di Tremezzo, H. von	CDU	Strauss, F.-J.	CSU	Schröder, G.	CDU	Schäffer, F.	CSU
7	Erhard, L.	CDU	Schröder, G.	CDU	Strauss, F.-J.	CSU	Höcherl, H.	CSU	Stammberger, W.	FDP
8	Erhard, L.	CDU	Schröder, G.	CDU	Strauss, F.-J.	CSU	Höcherl, H.	CSU		
9	Erhard, L.	CDU	Schröder, G.	CDU	Strauss, F.-J.	CSU	Höcherl, H.	CSU	Stammberger, W.	FDP
10	Mende, E.	FDP	Schröder, G.	CDU	Hassel, K.-U. von	CDU	Lücke, P.	CDU	Bucher, W.	FDP
11	Mende, E.	FDP	Schröder, G.	CDU	Hassel, K.-U. von	CDU	Lücke, P.	CDU	Jaeger, R.	CSU
12			Schröder, G.	CDU	Hassel, K.-U. von	CDU	Lücke, P.	CDU	Jaeger, R.	CSU
13	Brandt, W.	SPD	Brandt, W.	SPD	Schröder, G.	CDU	Lücke, P.	CDU	Heinemann, G.	SPD
14	Scheel, W.	FDP	Scheel, W.	FDP	Schmidt, H.	SPD	Genscher, H.-D.	FDP	Jahn, G.	SPD
15	Scheel, W.	FDP	Scheel, W.	FDP	Schmidt, H.	SPD	Genscher, H.-D.	FDP	Jahn, G.	SPD
16	Scheel, W.	FDP	Scheel, W.	FDP	Leber, G.	SPD	Genscher, H.-D.	FDP	Jahn, G.	SPD

GERMANY 1945–1998

Gov	Deputy PM	Py	Foreign Affairs	Py	Defence	Py	Interior	Py	Justice	Py
17	Genscher, H.-D.	FDP	Genscher, H.-D.	FDP	Leber, G.	SPD	Maihofer W.	FDP	Vogel, H.J.	SPD
18	Genscher, H.-D.	FDP	Genscher, H.-D.	FDP	Leber, G.	SPD	Maihofer W.	FDP	Vogel, H.J.	SPD
19	Genscher, H.-D.	FDP	Genscher, H.-D.	FDP	Apel, H.	SPD	Baum, G.R.	FDP	Vogel, H.J.	SPD
20					Apel, H.	SPD			Vogel, H.J.	SPD
21	Genscher, H.-D.	FDP	Genscher, H.-D.	FDP	Wörner, M.	CDU	Zimmermann, F.	CDU	Engelhard, H.A.	FDP
22	Genscher, H.-D.	FDP	Genscher, H.-D.	FDP	Wörner, M.	CDU	Zimmermann, F.	CDU	Engelhard, H.A.	FDP
23	Genscher, H.-D.	FDP	Genscher, H.-D.	FDP	Wörner, M.	CDU	Zimmermann, F.	CDU	Engelhard, H.A.	FDP
24	Genscher, H.-D.	FDP	Genscher, H.-D.	FDP	Stoltenberg, G.	FDP	Schäuble, W.	CDU	Engelhard, H.A.	FDP
25	Genscher, H.-D.	FDP	Genscher, H.-D.	FDP	Stoltenberg, G.	FDP	Schäuble, W.	CDU	Kinkel, K.	FDP
26	Kinkel, K.	FDP	Kinkel, K.	FDP	Rühe, V.	FDP	Kanther, M.	CDU	*Leutheusser-Schnarrenberger, S.	FDP

Gov	Finance	Py	Economic Aff.	Py	Labour	Py	Education	Py	Health	Py
1	Schäffer, F.	CDU	Erhard, L.	CDU	Storch, A.	CDU		CDU		
2	Schäffer, F.	CDU	Erhard, L.	CDU	Storch, A.	CDU		CDU		
3	Schäffer, F.	CDU	Erhard, L.	CDU	Storch, A.	CDU		CDU		
4	Schäffer, F.	CDU	Erhard, L.	CDU	Storch, A.	CDU		CDU		
5	Etzel, F. / Lindrath, H.	CDU / CDU	Erhard, L.	CDU	Blank, T.	CDU		CDU		
6	Etzel, F. / Lindrath, H.	CDU / CDU	Erhard, L.	CDU	Blank, T.	CDU		CDU		
7	Starke, H. / Lenz, H.	FDP / FDP	Erhard, L.	CDU	Blank, T.	CDU		CDU	*Schwarzhaupt, E.	CDU
8			Erhard, L.	CDU	Blank, T.	CDU		CDU	*Schwarzhaupt, E.	CDU

GERMANY 1945–1998

Gov	Finance	Py	Economic Aff.	Py	Labour	Py	Education	Py	Health	Py
9	Starke, H. Lenz, H.	FDP FDP	Erhard, L.	CDU	Blank, T.	CDU		CDU	*Schwarzhaupt, E.	CDU
10	Dahlgrün, R. Dollinger, W.	FDP CSU	Schmücker, K.	CDU	Blank, T.	CDU	Lenz, H.	FDP	*Schwarzhaupt, E.	CDU
11	Dahlgrün, R. Dollinger, W.	FDP CSU	Schmücker, K.	CDU	Katzer, H.	CDU	Stoltenberg, G.	CDU	*Schwarzhaupt, E.	CDU
12	Dollinger, W. Schmücker, K.	CSU CDU	Schmücker, K.	CDU	Katzer, H.	CDU	Stoltenberg, G.	CDU	*Schwarzhaupt, E.	CDU
13	Strauss, F.-J. Schmücker, K.	CSU CDU	Schiller, K.	SPD	Katzer, H.	CDU	Stoltenberg, G.	CDU	*Strobel, K.	SPD
14	Möller, A.	SPD	Schiller, K.	SPD	Ahrendt, W.	SPD	Leussink, H.	NONA	*Strobel, K.	SPD
15	Möller, A. Schiller, K.	SPD SPD			Ahrendt, W.	SPD	Dohnanyi, K. von	SPD	*Strobel, K.	SPD
16	Schmidt, H.	SPD	Friederichs, H.	SPD	Ahrendt, W.	FDP	Dohnanyi, K. von Ehmke, H.	SPD SPD	*Focke, K.	SPD
17	Apel, H.	SPD	Friederichs, H.	SPD	Ahrendt, W.	FDP	Rohde, H. Matthöfer, H.	SPD SPD	*Focke, K.	SPD
18	Apel, H.	SPD	Friederichs, H.	SPD	Ehrenberg, H.	FDP	Rohde, H. Matthöfer, H.	SPD SPD	*Huber, A.	SPD
19	Matthöfer, H.	SPD	Lambsdorff, O.	SPD	Ehrenberg, H.	FDP	Schmude, J. Bülow, A. von	SPD SPD	*Huber, A.	SPD
20	Matthöfer, H.	SPD			Ehrenberg, H.	SPD	Schmude, J. Bülow, A. von Matthöfer, H.	SPD SPD SPD	*Huber, A.	SPD
21	Stoltenberg, G.	CDU	Lambsdorff, O.	FDP	Blüm, N.	CDU	*Wilms, D. Riesenhuber, H.	CDU CDU	Geissler, H.	CSU
22	Stoltenberg, G.	CDU	Lambsdorff, O.	FDP	Blüm, N.	CDU	*Wilms, D. Riesenhuber, H.	CDU CDU	Geissler, H.	CSU

GERMANY 1945–1998

Gov	Finance	Py	Economic Aff.	Py	Labour	Py	Education	Py	Health	Py
23	Stoltenberg, G.	CDU	Bangemann, M.	FDP	Blüm, N.	CDU	Mölleman, J. / Riesenhuber, H.	FDP / CDU	*Süssmuth, R.	CDU
24	Waigel, T.	CSU	Haussmann, H.	FDP	Blüm, N.	CDU	Riesenhuber, H. / Mölleman, J.W.	CDU / FDP	*Lehr, U.M.	CDU
25	Waigel, T.	CSU	Mölleman, J.W.	FDP	Blüm, N.	CDU	Riesenhuber, H. / Ortleb, R.	CDU / FDP	*Hasselfeldt, G.	CDU
26	Waigel, T.	CSU	Rexrodt, G.	FDP	Blüm, N.	CDU	Rüttgers, J.	CDU	Seehofer, H.	CSU

Gov	Housing	Py	Agriculture	Py	Industry/Trade	Py	Environment	Py
1	Wildermuth, E.	FDP	Niklas, W.	CDU				
2	Preusker, V.E.	FDP	Lübke, H.	CDU				
3	Preusker, V.E.	FDP	Lübke, H.	CDU				
4	Preusker, V.E.	FDP	Lübke, H.	CDU				
5	Lücke, P.	CDU	Lübke, H.	CDU				
6	Lücke, P.	CDU	Lübke, H.	CDU				
7	Lücke, P.	CDU	Schwarz, W.	CDU				
8	Lücke, P.	CDU	Schwarz, W.	CDU				
9	Lücke, P.	CDU	Schwarz, W.	CDU				
10	Lücke, P.	CDU	Schwarz, W.	CDU				
11	Bucher, E.	FDP	Höcherl, H.	CDU				
12	Heck, B.	CDU	Höcherl, H.	CDU				
13	Lauritzen, L.	SPD	Höcherl, H.	CDU				
14	Lauritzen, L.	SPD	Ertl, J.	FDP				
15	Lauritzen, L.	SPD	Ertl, J.	FDP				
16	Vogel, H.J.	SPD	Ertl, J.	FDP				

GERMANY 1945–1998

Gov	Housing	Py	Agriculture	Py	Industry/Trade	Py	Environment	Py
17	Ravens, K.	SPD	Ertl, J.	FDP				
18	Ravens, K.	SPD	Ertl, J.	FDP				
19	Haack, V.	SPD	Ertl, J.	FDP				
20	Haack, V.	SPD						
21	Schneider, O.	CDU	Ertl, J.	FDP	Dollinger, W.	CSU		
22	Schneider, O.	CDU	Kiechle, I.	CSU				
23	Schneider, O.	CDU	Kiechle, I.	CSU			Töpfer, K.	CDU
24	*Hasselfeldt, G.	CSU	Kiechle, I.	CSU			Töpfer, K.	CDU
25	*Adam-Schwätzer, I.	FDP	Kiechle, I.	CSU			Töpfer, K.	CDU
26	Töpfer, K.	CDU	Borchert, J.	CSU			*Merkel, A.	CDU

Gov	Social Affairs (py)	Public Works (py)	Other (py)	Res
1		Seebohm, H.-C. (DP) Schuberth, L. (CSU)	Blücher, F. (FDP) Kaiser, J. (CDU) Lukascherk H. (CDU) Hellwege, H. (DP)	0
2		Seebohm, H.-C. (DP) Balke, S. (CSU)	Blücher, F.(FDP) Würmeling, F.-J. (CDU) Oberländer, T. (CDU) Kaiser, J. (CDU) Hellwege, H. (DP)	0
3		Seebohm, H.-C. (DP) Balke, S. (CSU)	Blücher, F.(FDP) Würmeling, F.-J. (CDU) Oberländer, T. (CDU) Kaiser, J. (CDU)	0

GERMANY 1945–1998

Gov	Social Affairs (py)	Public Works (py)	Other (py)	Res
4		Seebohm, H.-C. (DP) Balke, S. (CSU)	Blücher, F. (FDP) Würmeling, F.-J. (CDU) Oberländer, T. (CDU) Kaiser, J. (CDU) Merkatz, H.J. von (DP) Strauss, F.-J. (CSU)	1
5	Blank, T. (CDU)	Seebohm, H.-C. (DP) Stücklen, R. (CSU)	Balke, S. (CSU) Lemmer, E. (CDU) Oberländer, T. (CDU) Merkatz, H.J. von (DP)	0
6	Blank, T. (CDU)	Seebohm, H.-C. (CDU) Stücklen, R. (CSU)	Würmeling, F.-J. (CDU) Balke, S. (CSU) Lemmer, E. (CDU) Oberländer, T. (CDU) Merkatz, H.J. von (CDU)	0
7	Blank, T. (CDU)	Seebohm, H.-C. (CDU) Stücklen, R. (CSU)	Würmeling, F.-J. (CDU) Balke, S. (CSU) Scheel, W. (FDP) Krone, H. (CDU) Mischnik, W. (FDP) Lemmer, E. (CDU) Merkatz, H.J. von (CDU)	0
8	Blank, T. (CDU)	Seebohm, H.-C. (CDU) Stücklen, R. (CSU)	Würmeling, F.-J. (CDU) Balke, S. (CSU) Krone, H. (CDU) Lemmer, E. (CDU) Merkatz, H.J. von (CDU)	0

GERMANY 1945–1998

Gov	Social Affairs (py)	Public Works (py)	Other (py)	Res
9	Blank, T. (CDU)	Seebohm, H.-C. (CDU) Stücklen, R. (CSU)	Würmeling, F.-J. (CDU) Balke, S. (CSU) Krone, H. (CDU) Lemmer, E. (CDU) Merkatz, H.J. von (CDU) Mischnik, W. (FDP) Scheel, W. (FDP)	0
10		Seebohm, H.-C. (CDU) Stücklen, R. (CSU)	Heck, B. (CDU) Krüger, H. (CDU) Scheel, W. (FDP) Niederalt, A. (CSU)	0
11		Seebohm, H.-C. (CDU) Stücklen, R. (CSU)	Westrick, L. (CDU) Scheel, W. (FDP) Niederalt, A. (CSU) Gradl, J.B. (CDU) Krone, H. (CDU)	0
12		Seebohm, H.-C. (CDU) Stücklen, R. (CSU)	Dollinger, W. (CSU) Heck, B. (CDU) Westrick, L. (CDU) Niederalt, A. (CSU) Gradl, J.B. (CDU) Krone, H. (CDU)	0
13		Leber, G. (SPD) Dollinger, W. (CSU)	Heck, B. (CDU) Hassel, K.-U. von (CDU) Wehner, H. (SPD) Schmid, C. (SPD) Wischnewski, H.-J. (SPD)	1

GERMANY 1945–1998

Gov	Social Affairs (py)	Public Works (py)	Other (py)	Res
14		Leber, G. (SPD)	Franke, E. (SPD) Eppler, E. (SPD) Ehmke, H. (SPD)	0
15		Leber, G. (SPD)	Franke, E. (SPD) Eppler, E. (SPD) Ehmke, H. (SPD)	1
16	Arendt, W. (SPD)	Lauritzen, L. (SPD)	Franke, E. (SPD) Eppler, E. (SPD) Bahr, E. (SPD) Maihofer, W. (FDP)	0
17	Arendt, W. (SPD)	Gscheidle, K. (SPD)	Franke, E. (SPD) Eppler, E. (SPD)	0
18		Gscheidle, K. (SPD)	Franke, E. (SPD) *Schlei, M. (SPD)	1
19	Ehrenberg, H. (SPD)	Gscheidle, K. (SPD)	*Huber, A. (SPD) Franke, E. (SPD) Offergeld, R. (SPD)	1
20	Ehrenberg, H. (SPD)	Gscheidle, K. (SPD)	*Huber, A. (SPD) Franke, E. (SPD) Offergeld, R. (SPD)	1
21		Schwarz-Schilling, C. (CDU)	Geissler, H. (CSU) Warnke, J. (CSU) Barzel, R. (CDU)	0
22	Blüm, N. (CDU)	Dollinger, W. (CSU) Schwarz-Schilling, C. (CDU)	Warnke, J. (CSU) Windelen, H. (CDU)	0
23	Blüm, N. (CDU)	Warnke, J. (CSU) Schwarz-Schilling, C. (CDU)	Klein, H. (CSU) *Wilms, D. (CDU) Schäuble, W. (CDU)	1

GERMANY 1945–1998

Gov	Social Affairs (py)	Public Works (py)	Other (py)	Res
24	Blüm, N. (CDU) *Lehr, U.M. (CDU)	Zimmermann, F. (CSU) Schwarz-Schilling, C. (CDU)	*Wilms, D. (CDU) Warnke, J. (CSU) Seiters, R. (CDU) Klein, , (CSU) Mazière, L. de (CDU) *Bergmann-Pohl, S. (CDU) Krause, G. (CDU) Ortleb, R. (FDP) Walther, H.-J. (CSU)	0
25	Blüm, N. (CDU) *Merkel, A. (CDU) *Rönsch, H. (CDU)	Krause, G. (CDU) Schwarz-Schilling, C. (CDU)	Seiters, R. (CDU) Spranger, C.-D. (CSU)	4
26	Blüm, N. (CDU) *Nolte, C. (CDU)	Bötsch, W. (CDU) Wissmann, M. (CDU)	Spranger, C.-D. (CSU) Bohl, F. (CDU)	

18. GREECE

Although considered by many as the cradle of democracy, the Greek constitution is relatively new (1975).

The Head of State, the President, has largely ceremonial functions, and is indirectly elected by the legislature for a five-year term.

Greece is a unitary state with a strongly centralised polity.

Parliament is unicameral; its 300 members are elected by (reinforced) proportional representation (Hagenbach) in 13 constituencies of variable size with representation proportional to the size of the electorate. In particular the leading party gets an additional bonus of seats to secure majority government.

Parliament has a quorum of one-quarter of all members. Votes are carried by a majority of all members present. Constitutional amendments need an absolute majority of all members, plus a three-fifths majority of all members present. A referendum is optional and may be called by the Head of State. The outcome is binding.

The Prime Minister, formally appointed by the President, must be the parliamentary leader of the largest party. The government depends on a vote of confidence, which serves as a vote of investiture. Governments can also face a vote of no confidence during their lifetime. Losing either vote always results in resignation of the government. Government is both collectively and individually responsible to parliament. Individual ministers may also be members of parliament. The Prime Minister has a dominant position in government.

The Constitutional Court is responsible for constitutional review after validation of laws.

GREECE 1946-1998

Gov	Begin	Dur	RtT	ToG	Py1	Py2	Py3	Py4	Py5	Py6	Py7	Seats	CPG	NoM	Prime Minister (py)
0	04.04.46	14	1	x	POP 206	NPU 68	LIB 48					354	1	10	Poulitsas, P. (NONA)
1	18.04.46	200	x	1	POP 206	LIB-Nat	LIB-Ref					354	1	17	Tsaldaris, C. (POP)
2	04.11.46	84	4	1	POP 206	LIB-Nat	LIB-Ref					354	1	21	Tsaldaris, C. (POP)
3	27.01.47	214	4	3	POP 206	NPU 68	LIB-Nat	LIB-Ref	LIB-Ven	Soc Dem	NP	354	1	14	Maximos, D. (POP)
4	29.08.47	10	7	1	POP 206							354	1	11	Tsaldaris, C. (POP)
5	08.09.47	437	4	3	POP 206	LIB-Sof	[LIB-Ven]	[Soc Dem]				354	1	23	Sofoulis, T. (LIB-Sof)
6	18.11.48	63	2	2	POP 124	LIB-Sof 25	[RP 20]	[NP 11]				354	1	22	Sofoulis, T. (LIB-Sof)
7	20.01.49	162	x	3	POP 124	LIB-Sof 25	LIB-Ven 54	New Party	NU 9	[SOC DEM]		354	1	29	Sofoulis, T. (LIB-Sof)
8	01.07.49	189	4	3	POP 124	LIB-Sof 25	LIB-Ven 54	NU 9				354	1	24	Diomidis, A. (LIB-?)
9	06.01.50	76	1	6								354	-	17	Theotokis, J. (POP)
10	23.03.50	23	2	5	LIB 56	NUP 7						250	2	9	Venizelos, S. (LIB)
11	15.04.50	128	4	2	EPEK 45	LIB 53	SOC Dem 35					250	4	16	Plastiras, N. (EPEK)
12	21.08.50	7	7	4	LIB 56							250	1	7	Venizelos, S. (LIB)
13	28.08.50	16	5	3	LIB 56	Soc Dem 35	NP 7	[EPEK 45]	[NUP 7]			250	3	17	Venizelos, S. (LIB)
14	13.09.50	51	4	3	LIB 56	POP 62	Soc Dem 35	NP 7				250	3	22	Venizelos, S. (LIB)
15	03.11.50	90	x	2	LIB 56	Soc Dem 35	[POP 62]					250	3	18	Venizelos, S. (LIB)
16	01.02.51	152	4	2	LIB 56	Soc Dem 35	[EPEK 45]					250	3	11	Venizelos, S. (LIB)
17	03.07.51	27	2	2	LIB 56	[EPEK 45]	[POP 35]					250	-	6	Venizelos, S. (LIB)
18	30.07.51	90	1	6								250	-	7	Venizelos, S. (LIB)
19	28.10.51	348	2	2	EPEK 74	LIB 57						258	3	17	Plastiras, N. (EPEK)
20	10.10.52	44	1	6								258	-	15	Kioussopoulos, D. (NONA)
21	23.11.52	1047	x	1	GRAL 247							300	1	19	Papagos, A. (GRAL)
22	06.10.55	97	1	1	GRAL 247							300	1	16	Karamanlis, C. (GRAL)
23	11.01.56	49	1	6	GRAL 247							300	1	19	Karamanlis, C. (GRAL)
24	29.02.56	796	4	1	ERE 165							300	2	18	Karamanlis, C. (ERE)
25	05.05.58	12	1	6								300	-	12	Georgakopoulos, C. (NONA)
26	17.05.58	1223	1	1	ERE 173							300	2	16	Karamanlis, C. (ERE)
27	21.09.61	44	1	6								300	-	18	Dovas, C. (NONA)

GREECE 1946-1998

Gov	Begin	Dur	RfT	ToG	Py1	Py2	Py3	Py4	Py5	Py6	Py7	Seats	CPG	NoM	Prime Minister (py)
28	04.11.61	592	2	1	ERE 176							300	2	18	Karamanlis, C. (ERE)
29	19.06.63	101	2	6								300	-	17	Pipinelis, P. (NONA)
30	28.09.63	41	1	6								300	-	16	Mavromihalis, S. (NONA)
31	08.11.63	53	5	4	CU 138							300	3	21	Papandreou, G. (CU)
32	31.12.63	50	1	6								300	-	17	Paraskevopoulos, J. (NONA)
33	19.02.64	513	6	1	CU 171							300	3	21	Papandreou, G. (CU)
34	16.07.65	35	5	1	CU 171							300	3	16	Athanassiades-Novas, G. (CU)
35	20.08.65	28	5	4	Diss-CU 36							300	3	12	Tsirimokos, E. (Diss-CU)
36	17.09.65	461	4	2	Diss-CU 45	ERE 99	PP 8					300	2	25	Stefanopoulos, S. (Diss-CU)
37	22.12.66	102	2	6								300	-	17	Paraskevopoulos, J. (NONA)
38	03.04.67	18	x	6	ERE 99							300	-	16	Kanellopoulos, P. (ERE)
39	26.07.74	119	1	x								--	3	19	Karamanlis, C. (ERE)
40	22.11.74	1102	1	1	ND 220							300	1	20	Karamanlis, C. (ND)
41	28.11.77	893	2	1	ND 171							300	2	22	Karamanlis, C. (ND)
42	09.05.80	530	1	1	ND 171							300	2	24	Rallis, G. (ND)
43	21.10.81	1323	1	1	PASOK 172							300	4	21	Papandreou, A. (PASOK)
44	05.06.85	51	x	1	PASOK 172							300	4	15	Papandreou, A. (PASOK)
45	26.07.85	1437	1	1	PASOK 172							300	4	25	Papandreou, A. (PASOK)
46	02.07.89	102	x	2	ND 145	SYN 28						300	2	23	Tzannetakis, T. (ND)
47	12.10.89	41	1	6								300	-	21	Grivas, I. (NONA)
48	22.11.89	83	4	3	ND 148	PASOK 128	SYN 21					300	3	21	Zolotas, Z. (NONA)
49	13.02.90	57	1	6								300	-	21	Zolotas, Z. (NONA)
50	11.04.90	1281	4	4	ND 150							300	2	21	Mitsotakis, C. (ND)
51	13.10.93	831	3	1	PASOK 170							300	4	19	Papandreou, A. (PASOK)
52	22.01.96	246	1	1	PASOK 170							300	4	20	Simitis, C. (PASOK)
53	24.09.96			1	PASOK 162							300	4	20	Simitis, C. (PASOK)

GREECE 1946-1998

- [] Denotes parties supporting the government without participating in it.
- Governments 9, 18, 20, 23, 25, 27, 29, 30, 32, 37, 38, 47 and 49 were all non-political caretaker governments to organise elections. Government 39 and 48 main task was also to organise elections.
- Roughly between mid-1946 and end-1949 a civil war was waged in Greece. Most of the country was subject to martial law. Between December 1949 and February 1950 martial law was gradually lifted. This period covers governments 0-10.
- Gov 0: Type of Goverment interim government just after the elections of 31 March 1946.
- Gov 1, 2: A few National Liberals and Reformist Liberals participated in the government. Number of Seats in Parliament unknown.
- Gov 3: Number of Seats in Parliament for various Liberal f(r)actions, Social Democrats and National Party unknown. Continuously new party groups were formed, factions defected from the mother party or were driven out by others, etcetera.
- Gov 5: Number of Seats in Parliament for various Liberal f(r)actions and Social Democrats unknown.
- Gov 7: Number of Seats in Parliament for New Party and Social Democrats unknown. Reason for Termination is death of PM. The five party leaders Sofoulis, T. (LIB-Sof); Tsaldaris, C. (POP); Kanellopoulos, P. (NU); Venizelos, S. (LIB-Ven) and Markezinis, S. (NP) formed an inner cabinet.
- Gov 15: Reason for Termination was to give the PM the possibility to reduce the number of ministries.
- Gov 17: Main task of government was to reform the electoral system to create larger parties through elections.
- Gov 21: Reason for Termination is death of PM.
- Gov 24: General elections of 19 February 1956 were the fist elections in wich women had the vote.
- Gov 34: Reason for Termination is failing to receive a vote of confidence in Parliament. The CU split: 146 deputies followed Papandreou; 25 dissidents voted for the government with ERE (107).
- Gov 35, 36: Diss-CU is dissident (anti-Papandreou) faction of CU.
- Gov 38: Reason for Termination is military coup on 21 April 1967.
- Gov 39: Type of government is first civilian 'transitional' or 'national' government to restore parliamentary democracy. Main task is to organise elections.
- Gov 44: Reason for Termination is that government fulfilled its main task: restructuring of ministries.
- Gov 46: Government's main item is to initiate proceedings against Papandreou, A. of PASOK. Reason for Termination unclear. Government stepped down to make room for a caretaker cabinet to organise new elections.

GREECE 1946-1998

Gov	Deputy PM	Py	Foreign Affairs	Py	Defence	Py	Interior	Py	Justice	Py
0			Tsaldaris, C.		Mavromihalis, P.	POP	Theotokis, J.	POP	Tsaldaris, C.	POP
1			Tsaldaris, C.	POP	Mavromihalis, P.	POP	Theotokis, J. Theotokis, S.	POP POP	Hadjipanos, P.	POP POP
2	Gonatas, S.	LIB-Nat	Tsaldaris, C.	POP	Dragoumis, F. Londos, D. Protopapadakis, A.	POP POP POP	Kyrozis, J. Kalkanis, C.	POP POP	Hadjipanos, P.	POP
3	Tsaldaris, C. Venizelos, S.	POP LIB-Ven	Tsaldaris, C.	POP	Stratos, G. Kanellopoulos, P.	POP NPU	Papandreou, G. Kanellopoulos, P.	Soc-Dem NPU	Alexandris, A.	LIB-Ref
4			Tsaldaris, C. Mavromihalis, P.	POP POP	Stratos, G.	POP	Papathanassis, A.	POP	Papadimos, A.	POP
5	Tsaldaris, C.	POP	Tsaldaris, C.	POP	Stratos, G. Sakellariou, A. Digas, D.	POP POP LIB-Sof	Rendis, C. Mavromihalis, P.	LIB-Sof POP	Ladas, C.	LIB-Sof
6	Tsaldaris, C.	POP	Tsaldaris, C.	POP	Rendis, C. Mavromihalis, P. Protopapadakis, A.	LIB-Sof POP POP	Dendidakis, P. Hadjipanos, P.	LIB-Sof POP	Melas, G.	LIB-Sof
7	Diomides, A.	LIB-?	Tsaldaris, C.	POP	Kanellopoulos, P. Protopapadakis, A.	NU POP	Rendis, C. Zaïmis, F.	LIB-Sof LIB-Sof	Melas, G.	LIB-Sof
8	Tsaldaris, C. Venizelos, S. Kanellopoulos, P.	POP LIB-Ven NU	Tsaldaris, C.	POP	Kanellopoulos, P. Vasiliadis, G. Protopapadakis, A.	NU ? POP	Zaïmis, F. Rendis, C.	LIB-Sof LIB-Sof	Melas, G.	LIB-Sof
9			Pipinellis, P.	NONA	Ipitis, J.	NONA	Lianopoulos, N. Bouropoulos, A.	NONA NONA	Papaeliou, E.	NONA
10	Kanellopoulos, P.	NUP	Venizelos, S.	LIB	Kanellopoulos, P.	NUP	Katsotas, P.	LIB	Kassimatis, G.	LIB
11	Papandreou, G.	Soc Dem	Plastiras, N.	EPEK	Manouilides, F.	Soc Dem	Papandreou, G. Garoufalias, P.	Soc Dem Soc Dem	Tsatsos, T.	Soc Dem

GREECE 1946-1998

Gov	Deputy PM	Py	Foreign Affairs	Py	Defence	Py	Interior	Py	Justice	Py
12			Venizelos, S.	LIB	Venizelos, S.	LIB	Kasimatis, G.	LIB	Bakopoulos, N.	LIB
13	Papandreou, G. Zervas, N.	Soc Dem NP	Venizelos, S.	LIB	Rendis, C.	LIB	Modis, G. Theologitis, A.	LIB Soc Dem	Lagakos, E.	Soc Dem
14	Tsaldaris, C. Papandreou, G.	POP Soc Dem	Venizelos, S.	LIB	Karamanlis, C. Kazanas, G.	POP POP	Gianopoulos, D. Theologitis, A.	POP Soc Dem	Lagakos, E.	Soc Dem
15	Papandreou, G.	Soc Dem	Venizelos, S.	LIB	Vgenopoulos, A.	?	Theologitis, A. Bakopoulos, N.	Soc Dem LIB	Lagakos, E.	Soc Dem
16	Papandreou, G.	Soc Dem	Venizelos, S.	LIB		LIB	Bakopoulos, N.	LIB	Lagakos, E.	Soc Dem
17			Venizelos, S.	LIB		LIB	Bakopoulos, N.	LIN		
18	Tsouderos, E.	LIB	Politis, J.	NONA	Spiliotopoulos, P.	NONA	Kioussopoulos, D.	NONA	Bouropoulos, A.	NONA
19	Venizelos, S.	LIB	Venizelos, S.	LIB	Sakellariou, A.	LIB	Rendis, C.	EPEK	Papaspyrou, D.	EPEK
20			Dragoumis, F.	NONA	Pitsikas, J.	NONA	Kioussopoulos, D.	NONA	Maridakis, G.	NONA
21			Stefanopoulos, S.	GRAL	Kanellopoulos, P.	GRAL	Lycourezos, P.	GRAL	Babakos, D.	GRAL
22			Theotokis, S.	GRAL	Karamanlis, C.	GRAL	Triandafilis, I.	GRAL	Adamopoulos, C.	GRAL
23			Theotokis, S.	GRAL	Karamanlis, C.	GRAL	Triandafilis, I. Lianopoulos, N.	GRAL NONA	Adamopoulos, C. Bouropoulos, A.	GRAL NONA
24	Apostolides, A.	ERE	Theotokis, S.	ERE	Protopapadakis, A.	ERE	Makris, D.	ERE	Papakonstandinou, C.	ERE
25			Pesmatzoglou, M.	NONA			Georgakopoulos, C.	NONA	Dimitrakakis, C.	NONA
26			Averof-Tossitzas, E.	ERE	Karamantis, C.	ERE	Makris, D.	ERE	Kallias, C.	ERE
27	Paraskevopoulos, I.	NONA	Pesmatzoglou, M.	NONA	Potamianos, C.	NONA	Dovas, C. Lianopoulos, S.	NONA NONA	Tsiridanis, A.	NONA
28	Kanellopoulos, P.	ERE	Averof-Tossitzas, E.	ERE	Protopapadakis, A.	ERE	Rallis, G.	ERE	Papakonstandinou, C.	ERE
29					Dragoumis, F.	NONA	Panagiotopoulos, C.	NONA	Pagoulatos, H.	NONA
30			Economou-Gouras, P.	NONA	Papanikolopoulos, D.	NONA	Mavromihalis, S.	NONA	Sgouritsas, C.	NONA
31	Venizelos, S. Stefanopoulos, S.	CU CU	Venizelos, S.	CU	Papanikolopoulos, D.	NONA	Kostopoulos, S.	CU	Papaspyrou, D.	CU

GREECE 1946-1998

Gov	Deputy PM	Py	Foreign Affairs	Py	Defence	Py	Interior	Py	Justice	Py
32			Ksanthopoulos-Palamas, C.	NONA	Papanikolopoulos, D.	NONA	Paraskevopoulos, J. Papaioannou, C.	NONA NONA	Siondis, I.	NONA
33	Stefanopoulos, S.	CU	Kostopoulos, S.	CU	Garoufalias, P.	CU	Toumbas, I.	CU	Polyhronides, P.	CU
34			Melas, G.	CU	Kostopoulos, S.	CU	Toumbas, I.	CU	Papasyrou, D.	CU
35			Tsirimokos, E.	Diss-CU	Kostopoulos, S.	Diss-CU	Alamanis, S. Zaimis, F.	Diss-CU Diss-CU	Papaspyrou, D.	Diss-CU
36	Athanassiadis-Novas, G. Tsirimokos, E.	Diss-CU Diss-CU	Tsirimokos, E.	Diss-CU	Kostopoulos, S.	Diss-CU	Zaimis, F. Apostolakos, C.	Diss-CU Diss-CU	Papaspyrou, D.	Diss-CU
37			Economou-Gouras, P.	NONA	Paraskevopoulos, J.	NONA	Tzanetis, S. Stratos, C.	NONA NONA	Maniatis, J.	NONA
38			Kanellopoulos, P.	ERE	Papaligouras, P.	ERE	Theotokis, S. Rallis, G.	ERE ERE	Tsatsos, C.	ERE
39	Mavros, G.	CU	Mavros, G.	CU	Averof-Tossitzas, E.	ERE	Gikas, S. Stratos, C.	ERE NONA	Papakonstandinou, C.	ERE
40			Bitsios, D.	ND	Averof-Tossitzas, E.	ND	Stefanopoulos, C. Gikas, S.	ND ND	Stefanakis, C.	ND
41	Papakonstandinou, C.	ND	Papaligouras, P. Kondogeorgis, G.	ND ND	Averof-Tossitzas, E.	ND	Stratos, C. Balkos, A.	ND ND	Stamatis, G.	ND
42	Papakonstandinou, C.	ND	Mitsokatis, C. Kondogeorgis, G.	ND ND	Averof-Tossitzas, E.	ND	Stratos, C. Davakis, D.	ND ND	Stamatis, G.	ND
43			Haralambopoulos, J.	PASOK	Papandreou, A.	PASOK	Gennimatas, G. Skoularikis, I.	PASOK PASOK	Alexandris, E.	PASOK
44			Haralambopoulos, J.	PASOK	Papandreou, A.	PASOK	Tsouras, A. Koutsogiorgas, A.	PASOK PASOK	Papaioannou, M.	PASOK

GREECE 1946-1998

Gov	Deputy PM	Py	Foreign Affairs	Py	Defence	Py	Interior	Py	Justice	Py
45	Haralambopoulos, J.	PASOK	Papoulias, C. Pagalos, T.	PASOK PASOK	Papandreou, A.	PASOK	Koutsogiorgas, A. Tsouras, A.	PASOK PASOK	Magakis, G.-A.	PASOK
46			Tzannetakis, T. Papoulias, G.	ND ND	Varvitsiotis, J. Vassiliadis, I.	ND ND	Konstandopoulos, N. Kefalogiannis, E.	SYN ND	Kouvelis, F.	SYN
47			Papoulias, G.	ND	Degiannis, T.	NONA	Skouris, B. Manikas, D.	NONA NONA	Stamatis, C.	PASOK
48			Samaras, A,		Tzannetakis, T.	ND	Katrivanos, T. Manikas, D.	SYN NONA	Stamatis, C.	PASOK
49			Samaras, A.		Degiannis, T.	NONA	Katrivanos, T. Manikas, D.	SYN NONA	Stamatis, J.	ND
50	Tzannetakis, T. Kanellopoulis, A.	ND ND	Samaras, A.		Varvitziotis, I.	ND	Kouvelas, S. Vassiliadis, J.	ND ND	Kanellopoulos, A.	ND
51			Papoulias, C.	PASOK	Arsenis, G.	PASOK	Tsohatzopoulos, A. Papathemelis, S.	PASOK PASOK	Kouvelakis, G.	PASOK
52			Pagalos, T.	PASOK	Arsenis, G.	PASOK	Tsohatzopoulos, A. Gitonas, C.	PASOK PASOK	Venizelos, E.	PASOK
53			Pagalos, T.		Tsohatzopoulos, A.	PASOK	Papadopoulos, A. Romeos, G.	PASOK PASOK	Giannopoulos, E.	PASOK

- Gov 5: Tsaldaris, C. (POP); Ladas, C. (LIB-Sof); Stratos, G. (POP); Rendis, C. (LIB-Sof) formed an inner cabinet chaired by Tsaldaris to coördinate policy before submission to full cabinet.

GREECE 1946-1998

Gov	Finance	Py	Economic Aff.	Py	Labour	Py	Education	Py	Health	Py
0	Stefanopoulos, S.	POP	Alexandris, A.	LIB-Ref	Stefanopoulos, S.	POP	Tsaldaris, C.	POP	Tsaldaris, C.	POP
1	Helmis, D.	POP	Stefanopoulos, S. Alexandris, A.	POP LIB-Ref	Stratos, A.	POP	Papadimos, A.	POP	Kalatzakos, A.	POP
2	Helmis, D.	POP	Stefanopoulos, S. Mihalakopoulos, A.	POP LIB-Ref	Karamanlis, C.	POP	Papadimos, A.	POP	Kakaras, A.	POP
3	Tsaldaris, C.	POP	Tsaldaris, C. Stefanopoulos, S. Kostopoulos, S.	POP POP LIB-Ven	Karamanlis, C.	POP	Papadimos, A.	POP	Gonatas, S.	LIB-Nat
4			Helmis, D.	POP	Protopapadakis, A.	POP	Papadimos, A.	POP	Kotzianos, M.	POP
5	Helmis, D.	POP	Vervoutis, G. Stefanopoulos, S.	LIB-Sof POP	Protopapadakis, A.	POP	Papadimos, A.	POP	Orfanidis, A.	LIB-Sof
6	Helmis, D.	POP	Stefanopoulos, S.	POP	Bakopoulos, G.	POP	Vourdoubas, D.	POP	Georgiladakis, E.	LIB-Sof
7			Stefanopoulos, S. Helmis, D. Kapsalis, A.	POP POP ?	Gonis, E.	?	Tsatsos, C.	?	Rodopoulos, C.	POP
8			Stefanopoulos, S. Helmis, D. Mavros, G.	POP POP ?	Loulakakis, E.	?	Tsatsos, C.	?	Rodopoulos, C.	POP
9	Mantzavinos, G.	NONA	Stefanopoulos, S. Papakyriakopoulos, J.	POP NONA	Zeppos, D.	NONA	Economou, G.	NONA	Voilas, V.	NONA
10	Zaïmis, F.	LIB	Zaïmis, F. Kassimatis, G.	LIB LIB	Malamidas, E.	LIB	Athanassiades-Novas, G.	LIB	Glavanis, J.	LIB
11	Kartalis, G.	EPEK	Tsouderos, E. Melas, I.	EPEK EPEK	Michael, I.	EPEK	Athanassiades-Novas, G.	LIB	Glavanis, J.	LIB
12			Zaïmis, F. Averof-Tossitzas, E.	LIB LIB	Kasimatis, G.	LIB	Bakopoulos, N.	LIB	Zaïmis, F.	LIB

GREECE 1946-1998

Gov	Finance	Py	Economic Aff.	Py	Labour	Py	Education	Py	Health	Py
13			Averof-Tossitzas, E. / Kostopoulos, S.	LIB / LIB					Kostopoulos, A.	Soc Dem
14	Kostopoulos, S.	LIB	Averof-Tossitzas, E. / Stefanopoulos, S.	LIB / POP	Mandas, L.	POP	Bakopoulos, N.	LIB	Kostopoulos, A.	Soc Dem
15	Kostopoulos, S. / Giannopoulos, J.	LIB / Soc Dem	Papandreou, G. / Kostopoulos, S. / Averof-Tossitzas, E.	Soc Dem / LIB / LIB	Lagakos, E.	Soc Dem	Bakopoulos, N.	LIB	Kostopoulos, A.	Soc Dem
16	Kostopoulos, S.	LIB	Papandreou, G.	Soc Dem	Bakatselos, G.	LIB	Papandreou, G.	Soc Dem		
17	Kostopoulos, S.	LIB		LIB	Bakatselos, G.	LIB				
18			Tsouderos, E.	LIB		LIB				
19	Evelpidis, C.	EPEK	Kartalis, G. / Papapolitis, S.	EPEK / EPEK			Mihael, J.	EPEK		EPEK
20	Mertikopoulos, T.	NONA	Zolotas, Z.	NONA	Paraskevopoulos, J.	NONA	Fragistas, C.	NONA		
21	Papagiannis, C.	GRAL	Markezinis, S. / Kapsalis, A.	GRAL / GRAL	Gonis, E.	GRAL	Theotokis, S.	GRAL	Adamopoulos, C.	GRAL
22	Apostolides, A.	GRAL	Apostolides, A. / Paparigopoulos, V.	GRAL / GRAL	Polyzogopoulos, S.	GRAL	Gerokostopoulos, A.	GRAL		
23	Apostolides, A.	GRAL	Apostolides, A. / Paparigopoulos, V.	GRAL / GRAL	Polyzogopoulos, S.	GRAL	Gerokostopoulos, A.	GRAL		
24	Thiveos, C.	ERE	Helmis, D.	ERE	Bournias, L.	ERE	Levandis, P.	ERE		
25	Mertikopoulos, T.	NONA		NONA	Kapodistrias, J.	NONA	Lianopoulos, N.	NONA		
26	Papakonstandinou, C.	ERE	Protopapadakis, A. / Dertilis, L.	ERE / ERE	Dimitzatos, A.	ERE	Vogiatzis, G.	ERE		
27	Mertikopoulos, T.	NONA	Ariotis, C.	NONA	Kapodistrias, J.	NONA	Stratos, C.	NONA		
28	Theotokis, S.	ERE	Papaligouras, P. / Pipenelis, P.	ERE / ERE	Hrisantopoulos, C.	ERE	Kassimatis, G.	ERE		

GREECE 1946-1998

Gov	Finance	Py	Economic Aff.	Py	Labour	Py	Education	Py	Health	Py
29	Sofronopoulos, G.	NONA	Ariotis, C.	NONA	Rokas, C.	NONA	Stratos, C.	NONA		NONA
30	Gazis, N.	NONA	Paraskevopoulos, J.	NONA	Kyriakopoulos, V.	NONA	Siondis, J.	NONA		NONA
31	Mitsotakis, C.	CU	Stefanopoulos, S. Mavros, G. Papapolitis, S.	CU CU CU	Bakatselos, G.	CU	Papandreou, G.	CU		CU
32	Ndais, A.	NONA	Paraskevopoulos, J.	NONA	Stambelos, C.	NONA	Kourmoulis, G.	NONA		NONA
33	Mitsotakis, C.	CU	Mavros, G. Melas, G.	CU CU	Bakatselos, G.	CU	Papandreou, G.	CU		CU
34	Alamanis, S.	CU	Mitsotakis, C. Vernikos, A.	CU CU	Bakatselos, G.	CU	Athanassiades-No Vas, G.	CU	Diamandopoulos, J.	CU
35	Alamanis, S.	Diss-CU	Kostopoulos, S.	Diss-CU	Galinos, M.	Diss-CU	Savopoulos, E.	Diss-CU	Galinos, M.	Diss-CU
36	Melas, G.	Diss-CU	Mitsotakies, C. Kothris, E.	Diss-CU Diss-CU	Bakatselos, G.	Diss-CU	Alemanis, S.	Diss-CU	Manoussis, S.	Diss-CU
37	Steriotis, P.	NONA	Paraskevopoulos, J. Tselos, E.	NONA NONA	Stabelos, C.	NONA	Theodorakopoulos, J.	NONA	Hrysikos, J.	NONA
38	Papakonstandinou, C.	ERE	Pipinelis, P.	ERE	Stamatis, G.	ERE	Kassimatis, G.	ERE	Theotokis, S.	ERE
39	Pezmatzoglou, J.	NONA	Zolotas, Z. Kanellopoulos, A.	NONA CU	Laskaris, C.	NONA	Tsatsos, C. Louros, N.	NONA		ERE NONA
40	Devletoglou, E.	ND	Papaligouras, P. Boutos, J.	ND ND	Laskaris, C.	ND	Trypanis, K. Zeppos, P.	ND		ND ND
41	Boutos, J.	ND	Panagiotopoulos, G. Rallis, G.	ND ND	Laskaris, C.	ND	Varvitsiotis, J. Plytas, G.	ND		ND ND
42	Evert, M.	ND	Boutos, J. Dimas, S.	ND	Laskaris, C.	ND	Taliadouros, A. Adrianopoulos, A.	ND		ND ND

GREECE 1946-1998

Gov	Finance	Py	Economic Aff.	Py	Labour	Py	Education	Py	Health	Py
43	Dzettakis, E.	PASOK	Lazaris, A. Akritidis, N.	PASOK PASOK	Kaklamanis, A.	PASOK	Verivakis, E. *Merkouri, M.	PASOK		PASOK PASOK
44	Arsenis, G.	PASOK	Arsenis, G.	PASOK	Tsohatzopoulis, A.	PASOK	Kaklamanis, A. *Merkouri, M.	PASOK PASOK	Gennimatas, G.	PASOK
45	Tsovalas, D. Athanassopoulos, N.	PASOK PASOK	Simitis, C. Akritidis, N.	PASOK PASOK	Giannopoulos, E.	PASOK	Kaklamanis, A. Verivakis, E.	PASOK PASOK	Gennimatas, G.	PASOK
46	Samaras, A.	ND	Souflias, G. Hatzigakis, S. adrianopoulos, A.	ND ND ND	Papamargaris, T.	ND	Kondogiannopoulos, V. *Psarouda-Benaki, A. Papakonstandinou, M.	ND ND ND	Evert, M.	ND
47	Agapitos, G.	ND	Kondogeorgis, G.	ND	Koukiadis, I.	NONA	Despotopoulos, C. Sakelaridis, P.	NONA NONA		
48	Souflias, G.	ND	Gennimatas, G. Varvitsiotis, J.	PASOK ND	Kaklamanis, A.	PASOK	Simitis, C. Peponis, A.	PASOK PASOK	Merikas, G.	NONA
49	Agapitos, G.	ND	Kondogeorgis, G. Gamaletos, T.	ND NONA	Koukiadis, I.	NONA	Despotopoulos, K. Sakelaridis, P.	NONA NONA	Merikas, G.	NONA
50	Paleokrassas, J.	ND	Souflias, G. Ksiarhas, A.	ND ND	Kalatzakos, A.	ND	Kondogiannopoulos, V. Dimas, S.	ND ND	*Giannakou-Koutsikou, M.	ND
51	Gennimatas, G.	PASOK	Gennimatas, G. Simitis, C.	PASOK PASOK	Giannopoulos, E.	PASOK	Fatouros, D. Simitis, C.	PASOK PASOK	Kremastinos, D.	PASOK
52	Papadopoulos, A.	PASOK	Papandoniou, J. *Papandreou, V.	PASOK PASOK	Giannopoulos, E.	PASOK	Papandreou, G. *Papandreou, V.	PASOK PASOK	Peponis, A.	PASOK
53	Papandoniou, J.	PASOK	Papandoniou, J. *Papandreou, V.	PASOK PASOK	Papioannou, M.	PASOK	Arsenis, G.	PASOK PASOK	Gitonas, C.	PASOK

GREECE 1946-1998

Gov	Housing	Py	Agriculture	Py	Industry/Trade	Py	Environment	Py
0	Gonatas, S.	LIB-Nat	Theotokis, J.	POP				
			Stefanopoulos, S.	POP				
1			Papathanassis, A.	POP				
2			Kantzias, P.	POP				
			Papathanassis, A.	POP				
3			Tsaldaris, C.	POP				
4	Stratos, G.	POP	Papathanassis, A.	POP				
			Sakellariou, A.	POP				
5			Zaïmis, F.	LIB-Sof				
			Papathanassis, A.	POP				
6			Gondikas, D.	LIB-Sof				
			Goulopoulos, C.	POP				
7			Goulopoulos, C.	POP				
8			Goulopoulos, C.	POP				
9			Papakyriakopoulos, J.	NONA				
			Mavromatis, J.	NONA				
10			Gondikas, D.	LIB				
11			Hatzigiannis, D.	Soc Dem				
			Manetas, C.	EPEK				
12			Averof-Tossitzas, E.	LIB				
13			Lambropoulos, A.	Soc Dem				
14			Lambropoulos, A.	Soc Dem				
15			Lambropoulos, A.	Soc Dem				
16			Lambropoulos, A.	Soc Dem	Giavanis, J.	LIB		
					Makas, L.	Soc Dem		
17					Giavanis, J.	LIB		

GREECE 1946-1998

Gov	Housing	Py	Agriculture	Py	Industry/Trade	Py	Environment	Py
18								
19			Alamanis, S.	EPEK	Papapolitis, S.	EPEK		
					Athanassiades-Novas, G.	LIB		
20			Hatzidakis, A.	NONA	Paraskevopoulos, J.	NONA		
21			Apostolidis, A.	GRAL	Protopapadakis, A.	GRAL		
22			Papakonstandinou, C.	GRAL	Vasilikos, V.	GRAL		
23			Papakonstandinou, C.	GRAL	Vasilikos, V.	GRAL		
24			Averof-Tossitzas, E.	ERE	Papaligouras, P.	ERE		
25			Fragistas, C.	NONA	Steriopoulos, S.	NONA		
26			Adamopoulos, C.	ERE	Martis, N.	ERE		
27			Hristodoulou, N.	NONA	Triandafilis, A.	NONA		
					Farmakidis, N.	NONA		
28			Adamopoulos, C.	ERE	Zissakis, Z.	ERE		
29			Talellis, D.	NONA	Mavrikis, P.	NONA		
					Drossopoulos, G.	NONA		
30			Xanthakis, I.	NONA	Triandafilis, A.	NONA		
					Dendias, M.	NONA		
31			Baltatzis, A.	CU	Zigdis, J.	CU		
32			Xanthakis, I.	NONA	Steriotis, P.	NONA		
					Zervas, L.	NONA		
33			Baltatzis, A.	CU	Zigdis, J.	CU		
34			Vasmatzidis, C.	CU	Loulakakis, E.	CU		
35			Stefanopoulos, G.	Diss-CU	Savopoulos, E.	Diss-CU		
					Papadimitriou, D.	Diss-CU		
36			Vasmatzidis, C.	Diss-CU				
37			Hristodoulou, N.	NONA	Tsigridis, N.	NONA		

GREECE 1946-1998

Gov	Housing	Py	Agriculture	Py	Industry/Trade	Py	Environment	Py
38	Averof-Tossitzas, E.	ERE			Iordanoglou, I.	ERE		
					Theodossiadis, A.	ERE		
39			Papaspyrou, D.	CU	Protopapas, H.	CU		
40			Iordanoglou, H.	ND	Konofagos, C.	ND		
41			Taliadouros, A.	ND	Evert, M.	ND		
42			Kanellopoulos, A.	ND	Manos, S.	ND	Plytas, G.	ND
43			Simitis, C.	PASOK	Peponis, A.	PASOK	Tritsis, A.	PASOK
44			Simitis, C.	PASOK	Akritidis, N.	PASOK	Kouloumbis, E.	PASOK
45			Pottakis, J.	PASOK	Verivakis, E.	PASOK	Kouloumbis, E.	PASOK
			Moraitis, G.	PASOK				
46			Dimas, S.	ND	Papakonstandinou, M.	ND	Kouvelas, S.	ND
47			Liapis, J.	ND	Sakelaridis, P.	NONA	Liaskas, K.	NONA
					Gamaletsos, T.	NONA		
48			Dimas, S.	ND	Peponis, A.	PASOK	Liaskas, K.	NONA
49			Liapis, J.	ND	Sakelaridis, P.	NONA	Liaskas, K.	NONA
50			Papakonstandinou, M.	ND	Dimas, S.	ND	Manos, S.	ND
51			Moraitis, G.	PASOK	Simitis, C.	PASOK	Laliotis, C.	PASOK
52			Tzoumakas, S.	PASOK	*Papandreou, V.	PASOK	Laliotis, C.	PASOK
53			Tzoumakas, S.	PASOK	*Papandreou, V.	PASOK	Laliotis, C.	PASOK

GREECE 1946-1998

Gov	Social Affairs (py)	Public Works (py)	Other (py)	Res
0	Stefanopoulos, S. (POP)	Tsaldaris, C. (POP) Theotokis, C. (POP) Gonatas, S. (LIB-Nat)	Venizelos, S. (POP) Papandreou, G. (POP) Kanellopoulos, P. (NPU)	0
1	Lazanas, G. (POP)	Gonatas, S. (LIB-Nat) Abraam, N. (LIB-Nat) Papadimitriou, D. (LIB-Nat) Perottis, A. (LIB-Nat)		0
2	Kotzianos, M. (POP)	Gonatas, S. (LIB-Nat) Abraam, N. (LIB-Nat) Papadimitriou, D. (POP) Perottis, A. (LIB-Nat)	Hadjipanos, P. (POP) Rodopoulos, C. (POP) Alexandris, A. (LIB-Ref)	0
3		Venizelos, S. (LIB-Ven) Alexandris, A. (LIB-Ref) Gonatas, S. (LIB-Nat)	Tsaldaris, C. (POP) Venizelos, S. (LIB-Ven) Zervas, N. (NP)	1
4	Kotzianos, M. (POP)	Mavromihalis, P. (POP) Stratos, G. (POP) Hadjipanos, P. (POP) Protopapadakis, A. (POP) Sakellariou, A. (POP)	Rodopoulos, C. (POP)	0
5	Kotzianos, M. (POP)	Digas, D. (LIB-Sof) Iassonides, L. (LIB-Sof) Hadjipanos, P. (POP) Londos, D. (POP) Kizamis, T. (LIB-Sof) Birakis, A. (LIB-Sof)	Rodopoulos, C. (POP)	1

GREECE 1946-1998

Gov	Social Affairs (py)	Public Works (py)	Other (py)	Res
6	Karamanlis, C. (POP)	Malamidas, E. (LIB-Sof) Chrysostomou, G. (LIB-Sof) Mavrogordatos, M. (LIB-Sof) Londos, D. (POP)	Eilanos, M. (POP)	0
7	Karamanlis, C. (POP)	Venizelos, S. (LIB-Ven) Vasiliadis, G. (?) Nikolhaïdis, S. (?) Hadjipanos, P. (POP) Papadogiannis, E. (POP) Vourdoubas, D. (POP) Averof-Tossitzas, E. (?) Marinakis, E. (?)	Venizelos, S. (LIB-Ven) Markezinis, S. (NP) Diomides, A. (?) Tsatsos, C. (?) Korozos, K. (?) Eilanos, M. (POP) Stefanopoulos, V. (?) Loulakis, E. (?)	1
8	Karamanlis, C. (POP)	Nikolaïdis, S. (?) Hadjipanos, P. (POP) Papadogiannis, E. (?) Vourdoubas, D. (POP) Averof-Tossitzas, E. (?)	Venizelos, S. (LIB-Ven) Tsatsos, C. (?) Mavros, G. (?) Eilanos, M. (POP) Korozos, K. (?)	0
9	Voilas, V. (NONA)	Stilianides, S. (NONA) Koroneos, G. (NONA) Kamilos, P. (NONA)	Steriopoulos, S. (NONA)	0
10	Glavanis, J. (LIB)	Malamidas, E. (LIB) Athanassiades-Novas, G. (LIB)	Kassimatis, G. (LIB)	3
11	Glavanis, J. (LIB)	Havinis, T. (LIB) Glavanis, J. (LIB) Psarros, H. (LIB) Kostopoulos, S. (LIB)	Kassimatis, G. (LIB)	0

GREECE 1946-1998

Gov	Social Affairs (py)	Public Works (py)	Other (py)	Res
12	Zaïmis, F. (LIB)	Bakopoulos, N. (LIB) Zaïmis, F. (LIB) Averof-Tossitzas, E. (LIB) Kassimatis, G. (LIB) Kostopoulos, S. (LIB)	Bakopoulos, N. (LIB) Kostopoulos, S. (LIB) Iasonidis, L. (LIB)	0
13		Averof-Tossitzas, E. (LIB) Eksarhos, N. (Soc Dem) Kizanis, T. (?) Giannopoulis, J. (Soc Dem)	Papandreou, G. (Soc Dem) Lambrianides, L. (?) Malamidas, E. (LIB) Vgenopoulos, A. (?)	0
14	Zaïmis, F. (LIB)	Zaïmis, F. (LIB) Zervas, N. (NP) Kantzias, P. (POP) Eksarhos, N. (SOC DEM)	Rodopoulos, P. (POP) Kothris, E. (LIB) Iassonides, L. (LIB)	0
15	Zaïmis, F. (LIB)	Zervas, N. (NP) Eksarhos, N. (Soc Dem) Zaïmis, F. (LIB) Giannopoulos, J. (Soc Dem) Kothris, E. (LIB) Averof-Tossitzas, E. (LIB)	Bakopoulos, N. (LIB) Iassonides, L. (LIB) Vgenopoulos, A. (?) Giannopoulos, J. (Soc Dem) Kothris, E. (LIB) Choutas, S. (?) Alexandris, K. (?)	1
16		Giannopoulos, J. (Soc Dem) Malamidas, E. (LIB)	Papandreou, G. (Soc Dem)	0
17				0
18		Malamidas, E. (LIB)	Steriopoulos, S. (NONA)	0

GREECE 1946-1998

Gov	Social Affairs (py)	Public Works (py)	Other (py)	Res
19	Zaimis, F. (LIB)	Bourdaras, G. (EPEK) Havinis, T. (LIB) Krasadakis, N. (LIB)	Varvoutis, G. (LIB) Spais, L. (EPEK)	1
20	Pezmatzoglou, M. (NONA)	Koroneos, G. (NONA) Tsafos, D. (NONA) Harbouris, G. (NONA)	Stassinopoulos, M. (NONA) Fragistas, C. (NONA) Steriopoulos, S. (NONA)	0
21	Adamopoulos, C. (GRAL)	Karamanlis, C. (GRAL) Levandis, P. (GRAL) Psaros, H. (GRAL)	Tsouderos, E. (GRAL) Sifneos, P. (GRAL) Stratos, A. (GRAL)	2
22	Levandis, P. (Gral)	Eftaksias, L. (GRAL) Voyatzis, I. (GRAL)	Rallis, G. (GRAL) Exmidaris, G. (GRAL) Babakos, D. (GRAL)	0
23	Levandis, P. (Gral)	Eftaksias, L. (GRAL) Voyatzis, I. (GRAL)	Rallis, G. (GRAL) Exmidaris, G. (GRAL) Babakos, D. (GRAL) Fragistas, H. (NONA)	0
24	*Tsaldaris, L. (ERE)	Rallis, G. (ERE) Kotiadis, S. (ERE)	Paparigopoulos, V. (ERE) Kassimatis, G. (ERE) Tsatos, C. (ERE)	3
25	Malaspinas, S. (NONA)	Pipas, D. (NONA) Tsafos, D. (NONA)	Spiliotopoulos, P. (NONA)	0
26	Stratos, A. (ERE)	Gikas, S. (ERE) Adrianopoulis, G. (ERE)	Tsatsos, C. (ERE) Theologitis, A. (ERE)	0
27	Haramis, J. (NONA)	Tsafos, D. (NONA) Pipas, D. (NONA)	Stratos, C. (NONA) Gazsis, N. (NONA) Pitsikas, T. (NONA)	0

GREECE 1946-1998

Gov	Social Affairs (py)	Public Works (py)	Other (py)	Res
28	Stratos, A. (ERE)	Gikas, S. (ERE) Kotiadis, S. (ERE)	Makris, D. (ERE) Manendis, D. (ERE)	1
29	Kyriakou, J. (NONA)	Markakis, G. (NONA) Potamianos, A. (NONA) Stratigis, E. (NONA)	Stratos, C. (NONA) Papaflessas, G. (NONA) Fragistas, H. (NONA)	0
30	Svarounis-Trikorfos, N. (NONA)	Ntais, A. (NONA) Hatzidakis, A. (NONA)	Tsimbidaros, P. (NONA) Fragistas, H. (NONA)	0
31	Houtas, S. (CU)	Bakopoulos, N. (CU) Alamanis, S. (CU) Polyhronides, P. (CU)	Athanassiades-Novas, G. (CU) Eksarhos, N. (CU) Giannopoulos, J. (CU) Toumbas, I. (CU) Katsotas, P. (CU)	0
32	Manos, A. (NONA)	Pipas, D. (NONA) Stratos, N. (NONA) Spanidis, A. (NONA)	Zakinthinos, D. (NONA) Kavazarakis, N. (NONA)	0
33	Katsotas, P. (CU)	Houtas, S. (CU) Alamanis, S. (CU) Biris, S. (CU)	Papandreou, A. (CU) Taliadouris, C. (CU) Stefanidis, M. (CU) Arvanitakis, E. (CU) Vardinogiannis, P. (CU)	3
34	Apostolakos, C. (CU)	Mitsotakis, C. (CU) Kostis, D. (CU) Roussopoulos, A. (CU)	Avramidis, C. (CU)	1
35	Manolopoulos, T. (Diss-CU)	Toumbas, I. (Diss-CU) Stefanopoulos, G. (Diss-CU) Droulias, A. (Diss-CU)	Tsiri Mokos, E. (Diss-CU) Droulias, A. (Diss-CU)	0

GREECE 1946-1998

Gov	Social Affairs (py)	Public Works (py)	Other (py)	Res
36	Galinos, M. (Diss-CU)	Toumbas, I. (Diss-CU) Giannopoulos, A. (Diss-CU) Glavanis, J. (Diss-CU) Mavridoglou, I. (Diss-CU)	Toumbas, I. (Diss-CU) Alamanis, S. (Diss-CU) Manopoulos, T. (Diss-CU) Karatheodoros, A. (PP) Vourdoubas, D. (ERE) Diamandopoulos, J. (Diss-CU) Pagoutsos, A. (Diss-CU) Salvopoulos, E. (Diss-CU)	3
37	Hrysikos, J. (NONA)	Pipas, D. (NONA) Stassinopoulos, E. (NONA) Kostiris, A. (NONA)	Hristou, P. (NONA) Karmiris, N. (NONA)	0
38	Rallis, G. (ERE)	Rodopoulos, C. (ERE) Frondistis, A. (ERE) Kefalogiannis, E. (ERE)	Kassimatis, G. (ERE) Vourdoubas, D. (ERE)	0
39	Kokkebis, A. (CU)	Magakis, G.-A. (NONA) Milonas, G. (CU) Mineos, J. (NONA)	Rallis, G. (ERE) Tsatsos, C. (ERE)	0
40	Derdemezis, V. (ND)	Stratos, C. (ND) Vogiatzis, G. (ND) Papadogonas, A. (ND)	Rallis, G. (ND) Trypanis, K. (ND) Zeppos, P. (ND) Martis, N. (ND)	4
41	Doksiadis, S. (ND)	Evert, M (ND) Zardinidis, N. (ND) Papadogonas, A. (ND) Kefalogiannis, E. (ND)	Stefanopoulos, K. (ND) Varvitsiotis, J. (ND) Plytas, G. (ND) Martis, N. (ND)	1

258

GREECE 1946-1998

Gov	Social Affairs (py)	Public Works (py)	Other (py)	Res
42	Doksiadis, S. (ND)	Manos, S. (ND) Tzannetakis, T. (ND) Panagiotopoulos, G. (ND) Fikioris, J. (ND)	Paleokrassas, J. (ND) Stefanopoulos, K. (ND) Taliadouros, A. (ND) Adrianopoulos, A. (ND) Plytas, G. (ND) Martis, N. (ND)	3
43	Avgerinos, P. (PASOK)	Peponis, A. (PASOK) Tsohatzopoulos, A. (PASOK) Giannopoulos, E. (PASOK) Giotas, E. (PASOK)	Koutsogiorgas, A. (PASOK) *Merkouri, M. (PASOK) Tritsis, A. (PASOK) Intzes, V. (PASOK Koulombis, E. (PASOK)	6
44	Gennimatas, G. (PASOK)	Kouloumbis, E. (PASOK) Arsenis, G. (PASOK) Verivakis, E. (PASOK)	Papandreou, A. (PASOK) Tsohatzopoulos, A. (PASOK) Koulombis, E. (PASOK) Kaklamanis, A. (PASOK) Lazaris, A. (PASOK) *Merkouri, M. (PASOK)	0
45	Gennimatas, G. (PASOK)	Kouloumbis, E. (PASOK) Verivakis, E. (PASOK) Papadimitriou, G. (PASOK) Aleksandris, E. (PASOK)	Tsohatzopoulos, A. (PASOK) Kaklamanis, A. (PASOK) *Merkouri, M. (PASOK) Papadopoulos, J. (PASOK) Styriou, K. (PASOK)	10

GREECE 1946-1998

Gov	Social Affairs (py)	Public Works (py)	Other (py)	Res
46	Evert, M. (ND)	Kouvelas, S. (ND) Papakonstandinou, M. (ND) Gelestathis, N. (ND) Pavlidis, A. (ND)	Tzannetakis, T. (ND) Kanellopoulos, A. (ND) Kefalogiannis, E. (ND) Hadjinikolaou, P. (ND) Mylonas, G. (ND)	0
47	Merikas, G. (NONA)	Liaskas, C. (NONA) Sakelaridis, P. (NONA) Moutsopoulos, G. (NONA) Pappas, N. (NONA)	Themelis, N. (NONA) Kondogeorgis, G. (ND) Mylonas, G. (ND) Deligiannis, I. (NONA) Foussas, A. (NONA) Liaskas, C. (NONA)	0
48	Merikas, G. (NONA)	Peponis, A. (PASOK) Tsohatzopoulos, A. (PASOK) Pappas, N. (NONA)	Themelis, N. (NONA) Tzannetakis, T. (ND) Kouvelas, S. (ND) Deligiannas, I. (NONA) Foussas, A. (NONA)	0
49	Merikas, G. (NONA)	Liaskas, K. (NONA) Sakellaridis, P. (NONA) Moutsopoulos, G. (NONA) Pappas, N. (NONA)	Themelis, N. (NONA) Kondogeorgis, G. (ND) Despotopoulos, K. (NONA) Mylonas, G. (ND) Deligiannis, I. (NONA) Foussas, A. (NONA) Liaskas, K. (NONA)	0

GREECE 1946-1998

Gov	Social Affairs (py)	Public Works (py)	Other (py)	Res
50	*Giannakou-Koutsikou, M. (ND)	Mitsotakis, C. (ND) Dimas, S. (ND) Gelestanis, N. (ND) Manos, S. (ND)	Tzannetakis, T. (ND) Evert, M. (ND) Souflias, G. (ND) Kondogiannopoulos, V. (ND) Manos, S. (ND) Tzitzikostas, G. (ND) Missailides, G. (ND) Theodorakis, M. (ND)	7
51	Kremastinos, D. (PASOK)	Karsifaras, G. (PASOK) Laliotis, C. (PASOK) Simitis, C. (PASOK) Haralambopoulos, J. (PASOK)	Peponis, A. (PASOK) Fatouros, D. (PASOK) *Merkouri, M. (PASOK) Triaridis, C. (PASOK) Skandalidis, C. (PASOK)	2
52	Giannopoulos, E. (PASOK) Peponis, A. (PASOK)	Styriou, K. (PASOK) Laliotis, C. (PASOK) *Papandreou, V. (PASOK) Kastanidis, H. (PASOK)	Papandreou, G. (PASOK) Benos, S. (PASOK) Petsalnikos, F. (PASOK) Kotsakas, A. (PASOK) Laliotis, C. (PASOK) *Papandreou, V. (PASOK) Reppas, D. (PASOK)	0

GREECE 1946-1998

Gov	Social Affairs (py)	Public Works (py)	Other (py)	Res
53	Papaioannou, M. (PASOK) Gitonas, C. (PASOK)	*Papandreou, V. (PASOK) Laliotis, C. (PASOK) Soumakis, S. (PASOK) Kastanidis, C. (PASOK)	Papadopoulos, A. (PASOK) Laliotis, C. (PASOK) Arsenis, G. (PASOK) Venizelos, E. (PASOK) Petsalnikos, F. (PASOK) *Papazoe, E. (PASOK) Reppas, D. (PASOK) Pashalidis, G. (PASOK)	

19. GUYANA

The Head of State, the President, is directly elected for a five-year term.

The State is centralised and unitary.

Parliament is unicameral. Of its 65 members, 53 are elected by proportional representation (Hare), and 12 are regional representatives. There is a flexible term between elections - the maximum is five years.

Parliament has a quorum of one-third of members. Votes are carried by a simple majority of members present. Constitutional amendments require a two-thirds majority of members present. If a constitutional amendment does not get enough support in the assembly a referendum must be called by the government. The result is binding. Referendums are only held on constitutional matters.

The President is the most powerful part of the executive. Parliament has no direct power over him or her. The President appoints the Cabinet. No vote of investiture is required. There is also no vote of any confidence. The government is collectively responsible to parliament. The Vice-President is the Prime Minister and must be a Member of Parliament. Other members of the government may also be members of parliament. The Prime Minister has no dominant position in government.

There is a Supreme Court for constitutional review of legislation.

GUYANA 1964-1998

Gov	Begin	Dur	RfT	ToG	Py1	Py2	Seats	CPG	NoM	Prime Minister (py)
1	14.12.64	1829	1	2	PNC 22	UF 7	53		13	Burnham, L.F.S. (PNC)
2	17.12.69	1312	1	1	PNC 30		53			Burnham, L.F.S. (PNC)
3	21.07.73	2720	1	1	PNC 37		53		9	Burnham, L.F.S. (PNC)
4	31.12.80	1679	x	1	PNC 41		53		15	Reid, P.A. (PNC)
5	06.08.85	175	1	1	PNC 41		53		16	Green, H. (PNC)
6	28.01.86	2446	1	1	PNC 42		53		11	Green, H. (PNC)
7	09.10.92	1609	x	1	PPP-Civic 28		53		13	Hinds, S. (PPP-Civic)
8	06.03.97			1	PPP-Civic 28		53			*Jagan, J. (PPP-Civic)

- Insufficient information to classify governments on CPG-scale.
- Party differences mainly ethnic.
- Date of independence 26 May 1966.
- Gov 2: Composition and Starting date (second half of December 1969) unknown.
- 22 February 1970 Guyana becomes a republic. President elected by National Assembly.
- 6 October 1980 (from government 4) an executive presidency is established. The president is Head of State and Head of Government. One of the vice-presidents is also prime minister.
- Gov 4: Reason for Termination is death of president Burnham. President Hoyte, H.D. (PNC) takes over.
- Gov 7: Reason for Termination is death of president Jagan. President Hinds, S. (PPP-Civic) takes over.
- Gov 8: Composition unknown.

Gov	Deputy PM	Py	Foreign Affairs	Py	Defence	Py	Interior	Py	Justice	Py
1	Reid, P.A.	PNC					Reid, P.A.	PNC	Burnham, L.F.S.	PNC
	Bissember, N.J.	PNC					Cheeks, R.R.	UF		
2										
3	Reid, P.A.	PNC	Ramphal, S.S.	PNC	Burnham, L.F.S.	PNC	Burnham, L.F.S.	PNC	Ramphal, S.S.	PNC
							Clarke, O.E.	PNC		
4			Jackson, R.E.	PNC	Burman, L.F.S.	PNC	Moore, S.	PNC	Shahabuddeen, M.	PNC

GUYANA 1964-1998

Gov	Deputy PM	Py	Foreign Affairs	Py	Defence	Py	Interior	Py	Justice	Py
5	Shahabuddeen, M.	PNC					Hoyte, H.D.	PNC	Shahbuddeen, M.	PNC
	*Burnham, V.	PNC								
6	Shahabuddeen, M.	PNC	Jackson, R.E.	PNC			Hoyte, H.D.	PNC	Shahbuddeen, M.	PNC
	Chandisingh, R.	PNC								
	*Burnham, V.	PNC								
7			Jagan, C.	PPP-Civic			Mohamed, F.	PPP-Civic	de Santos, B.	PPP-Civic
8										

Gov	Finance	Py	Economic Aff.	Py	Labour	Py	Education	Py	Health	Py
1	d'Aguiar, P.S.	UF			Merriman, C.A.	PNC	*Gaskin, W.		Bissember, N.J.	PNC
2										
3	Hope, F.E.	PNC	Reid, P.A.	PNC			*Field-Ridley, S.	PNC		
			King, K.	PNC						
4	Hoyte, H.D.	PNC	Hoyte, H.D.	PNC			Chandisingh, R.	PNC		
			Corbin, R.H.O.	PNC			Thomas, J.R.	PNC		
5										
6	Greenidge, C.	PNC	Chandisingh, R.	PNC			*Burnham, V.	PNC		
			Haslyn Parris, W.	PNC						
7					Jeffrey, H.	PPP-Civic	Bisnauth, D.	PPP-Civic		
					*Chandarpal, I.	PPP-Civic				
8										

GUYANA 1964-1998

Gov	Housing	Py	Agriculture	Py	Industry/Trade	Py	Environment	Py
1	Bissember, N.J.	PNC	John, L.	PNC	Kendall, W.O.R.	PNC		PNC
			Jordan, R.J.	PNC				
2								
3	Narina, S.	PNC	Reid, P.A.	PNC				
4			Tyndall, J.A.	PNC	Hope, F.E.	PNC		
5								
6			Corbin, R.H.O.	PNC	Murray, W.	PNC		
7			Persaud, R.D.	PPP-Civic				
8			Collymore, C.	PPP-Civic				

Gov	Social Affairs (py)	Public Works (py)	Other (py)	Res
1	*Gaskin, W. (PNC)	Coreid, E.F. (PNC)	Mahraj, D. (PNC)	2
	Merriman, C.A. (PNC)	Kasim, R. (PNC)		
		Jordan, R.J. (PNC)		
2				2
3		*Field-Ridley, S. (PNC)		2
4	Green, H. (PNC)	Burnham, L.F.S. (PNC)	Burnham, L.F.S. (PNC)	
		Reid, P.A. (PNC)	Reid, P.A. (PNC)	
		Naraine, S.S. (PNC)	Hoyte, H.D. (PNC)	
		Jack, H.O. (PNC)	Green, H. (PNC)	
			Naraine, S.S. (PNC)	
			Ramsaroop, B. (PNC)	
			Hope, F.E. (PNC)	
			Clarke, O.E. (PNC)	

GUYANA 1964-1998

Gov	Social Affairs (py)	Public Works (py)	Other (py)	Res
5		*Harewood-Benn, Y. (PNC)	Hoyte, H.D. (PNC) Green, H. (PNC) Shahabuddeen, M. (PNC) *Burnham, V. (PNC)	0
6	*Burnham, V. (PNC)	Prashad, S. (PNC)	Hoyte, H.D. (PNC) Green, H. (PNC) Shahabuddeen, M. (PNC) Chandisingh, R. (PNC) *Burnham, V. (PNC)	6
7	*Chandarpal, I. (PPP-Civic)	Harripersaud, N. (PPP-Civic)	Hinds, S. (PPP-Civic) Rohee, C. (PPP-Civic) Nagamootoo, M. (PPP-Civic) Luncheon, R. (PPP-Civic) Harripersaud, N. (PPP-Civic)	1
8			*Jagan, J. (PPP-CIVIC)	

20. HUNGARY

The Hungarian constitution dates from 1989.

The Head of State, the President, is indirectly elected for a four-year term by a two-thirds majority of all members of the legislature. He or she exercises extensive appointing powers. Legislation needs his or her assent.

Hungary is a unitary and centralised state.

Parliament is unicameral. The National Assembly of 386 seats is elected for a fixed term of four years by a complex mixed electoral system of proportional representation (d'Hondt) and plurality voting, with a threshold of 5%. The 25 regions for PR-voting considerably vary in size and are rather disproportionate in terms of the number of members returned. Plurality voting takes place in 176 single-member constituencies, which also considerably vary in size. On average they comprise of 45,000 electors.

Parliament has a quorum of at least 50 per cent of all members. Votes are carried by a two-thirds majority of all members present. Some issues require a qualified majority ranging from a majority of those voting to a two-thirds majority of all members. Constitutional amendments require a majority of two-thirds of all members. A referendum is optional, and may be called by the Head of State and parliament. The outcome is binding.

The Prime Minister, although appointed by the President, needs to be sure of the confidence of Parliament beforehand. Governments undergo a vote of investiture after presenting their programme to parliament. They can also face a vote of no confidence. Losing either vote always results in resignation of the government. Government is both collectively and individually responsible to parliament. The office of Member of Parliament is incompatible with that of minister. The Prime Minister has a rather prominent position in government.

The Constitutional Court has the final word regarding the constitutionality of laws and a judgement can be requested by anyone.

HUNGARY 1990-1998

Gov	Begin	Dur	RfT	ToG	Py1	Py2	Py3	Seats	CPG	NoM	Prime Minister (py)
1	23.05.90	1308	x	3	MDF 165	FKGP 44	KDNP 21	386	2	17	Antall, J. (MDF)
2	21.12.93	206	1	3	MDF 165	FKGP 44	KDNP 21	386	2	18	Boross, P. (MDF)
3	15.07.94			3	MSZP 209	SZDSZ 70		386	5	14	Horn, G. (MSZP)

- Gov 1: Reason for termination is death of PM.

Gov	Deputy PM	Py	Foreign Affairs	Py	Defence	Py	Interior	Py	Justice	Py
1			Jeszensky, G.	MDF	Für, L.	MDF	Horváth, B.	MDF	Balsai, I.	MDF
2			Jeszensky, G.	MDF	Für, L.	MDF	Kónya, I.	MDF	Balsai, I.	MDF
3	Kuncze, G.	SZDSZ	Kovács, L.	MSZP	Keleti, G.	MSZP	Kuncze, G.	SZDSZ	Vastagh, P.	MSZP

Gov	Finance	Py	Economic Aff.	Py	Labour	Py	Education	Py	Health	Py
1	Rabár, F.	NONA	Kádár, B.	NONA	Györiványi, S.	NONA	Andrásfalvy, B.	FKGP		MDF
2	Szabó, I.	MDF	Kádár, B.	NONA	Kiss, G.	NONA	Mádl, F.	FKGP		NONA
3	Békesi, L.	MSZP		MSZP	*Kósa Kovács, M.	MSZP	Fodor, G.	MSZP		SZDSZ

Gov	Housing	Py	Agriculture	Py	Industry/Trade	Py	Environment	Py
1		FKGP	Nagy, F.J.	FKGP	Bod, P.Á.	MDF	Keresztes, S.	MDF
2		FKGP	Szabó, J.	FKGP	Latorcai, J.M.	KDNP	Gyurkó, J.	MDF
3		MSZP	Lakos, L.	MSZP	Pál, L.	MSZP	Baja, F.	MSZP

HUNGARY 1990-1998

Gov	Social Affairs (py)	Public Works (py)	Other (py)	Res
1	Surján, L. (KDNP)	Siklóós, C. (MDF)	Andrásfalvy, B. (MDF) Horváth, B. (MDF) Gerbovits, J. (FKGP) Kiss, G. (FKGP) Mádl, F. (NONA)	3
2	Surján, L. (KDNP)	Schamschula, G. (MDF)	Füzessy, T. (KDNP) Szabó, T. (MDF) Nagy, J.F. (FKGP) Pungor, E. (NONA)	0
3	Kovács, P. (MSZP)	Lotz, K. (SZDSZ)	Katona, B. (MSZP)	3

21. ICELAND

The Head of state, The President, is directly elected for a four-year term. The President has largely ceremonial duties.

It is a unitary state with some autonomy at the community level.

Parliament is unicameral albeit of a 'hybrid' kind: after election it divides itself into two working bodies. Its 84 members are elected by proportional representation (d'Hondt) for a fixed term of four years in constituencies, which are very variable in size. They range from 40,000 electors in Reykjavik to 15,000 elsewhere. However, representation is adjusted to the number of electors

Parliament also regulates the judicial system, but without affecting it's independent working. It has a quorum of at least 50 per cent of all members. Votes are carried by a majority of votes cast. Some issues require a qualified majority of two-thirds of all members present. Constitutional amendments need a majority of all members in both sections of parliament. Referendums are optional and may be called by the Head of State. The outcome is binding.

The Council of State rules the country. The President and the government form the Council of State. Government does not need a vote of investiture, but must be able to rely on the confidence of a majority in parliament. During its lifetime the government can face a vote of no confidence. Losing a vote of confidence always results in resignation of the government. Government is both collectively and individually responsible to parliament. Individual ministers may also be members of parliament. The Prime Minister has a rather prominent position in government.

The Supreme Court reviews the constitutionality of both laws and procedures of implementation.

ICELAND 1945–1998

Gov	Begin	Dur	RfT	ToG	Py1	Py2	Py3	Py4	Py5	Seats	CPG	NoM	Prime Minister (py)
1	21.10.44	866	4	2	IP 20	USP/PA 10	SDP 9			60	3	5	Thors, O. (IP)
2	04.02.47	1036	1	2	IP 19	SDP 7	PP 13			60	3	6	Stefansson, S.J. (SDP)
3	07.12.49	96	5	2	IP 19	PP 17	SDP 7			60	2	6	Steinthorsson, S. (PP)
4	13.03.50	1279	1	2	PP 17	IP 19				60	2	6	Steinthorsson, S. (PP)
5	13.09.53	1047	4	2	PP 16	IP 21				60	2	6	Thors, O. (IP)
6	25.07.56	882	4	2	PP 17	SDP 8	USP/PA 8			60	4	6	Jonasson, H. (PP)
7	23.12.58	332	4	4	SDP 8					60	4	4	Jonsson, E. (SDP)
8	20.11.59	1455	3	2	IP 24	SDP 8				60	2	6	Thors, O. (IP)
9	14.11.63	1306	1	2	IP 24	SDP 8				60	3	7	Benediktsson, B. (IP)
10	12.06.67	1125	3	2	IP 23	SDP 9				60	3	7	Benediktsson, B. (IP)
11	10.07.70	339	1	2	IP 23	SDP 9				60	3	7	Hafstein, J. (IP)
12	14.06.71	1172	4	2	PP 17	USP/PA 10	ULL 5			60	4	7	Johannesson, O. (PP)
13	29.08.74	1463	1	2	IP 25	PP 17				60	2	8	Hallgrimsson, G. (IP)
14	31.08.78	410	4	2	PP 12	SDP 14	USP/PA 14			60	4	9	Johannesson, O. (PP)
15	15.10.79	116	1	4	SDP 14					60	4	6	Gröndal, B. (SDP)
16	08.02.80	1202	5	3	PP 17	IP 21	USP/PA 11			60	3	10	Thoroddsen, G. (IP)
17	26.05.83	1504	1	2	PP 14	IP 23				60	2	10	Hermannsson, S. (PP)
18	08.07.87	448	5	2	PP 13	IP 18	SDP 10			63	3	11	Palsson, T. (IP)
19	28.09.88	366	7	2	PP 13	USP/PA 8	SDP 10	[REP 1]		63	4	9	Hermannsson, S. (PP)
20	28.09.89	579	1	2	PP 13	USP/PA 8	SDP 10	CP 10	[REP1]	63	4	11	Hermannsson, S. (PP)
21	30.04.91	1454	1	2	IP 26	SDP 10				63	2	10	Oddsson, D. (IP)
22	23.04.95			2	IP 25	SDP 15				63	2	10	Oddsson, D. (IP)

- [] Denotes party supporting the government without participating in it.

ICELAND 1945–1998

Gov	Deputy PM	Py	Foreign Affairs	Py	Defence	Py	Interior	Py	Justice	Py
1									Jonsson, F.	SDP
2			Benediktsson, B.	IP					Benediktsson, B.	IP
3			Benediktsson, B.	IP					Benediktsson, B.	IP
4			Benediktsson, B.	IP					Benediktsson, B.	IP
5			Gudmundsson, K.	PP	Gudmundsson, K.	PP			Benediktsson, B.	IP
6			Gudmundsson, G.	SDP					Jonasson, H.	PP
7			Gudmundsson, G.	SDP					Skarphedinson, F.	SDP
8			Gudmundsson, G.	SDP					Benediktsson, J.	IP
9			Gudmundsson, G.	SDP					Hafstein, J.	IP
10			Gudmundsson, G.	SDP					Hafstein, J.	IP
11			Jonsson, E.	SDP					*Auduns, A.	SDP
12			Agustsson, E.	PP					Johannesson, O.	PP
13			Agustsson, E.	PP					Johannesson, O.	PP
14			Gröndal, B.	SDP					Hermansson, S.	PP
15			Gröndal, B.	SDP					Gylfason, V.	SDP
16			Johannesson, O.	PP					Thordarsen, F.	IP
17			Halgrimsson, G.	IP					Helgason, J.	PP
18			Hermannsson, S.	PP					Sigurdsson, J.	SDP
19			Hannibalsson, J.L.	SDP					Asgrimsson, H.	PP
20			Hannibalsson, J.L.	SDP					Gudbartsson, O.	CP
21			Hannibalsson, J.L.	SDP					Pálsson, T.	IP
22			Asgrimsson, H.	PP					Pálsson, T.	IP

ICELAND 1945–1998

Gov	Finance	Py	Economic Aff.	Py	Labour	Py	Education	Py	Health	Py
1	Magnusson, P.	IP					Jakobson, A.	USP/PA		
2	Josefsson, J.	IP					Johnsson, E.	FP		
3	Jonsson, E.	PP					Olafsson, B.	IP	Steinthorsson, S.	PP
4	Jonsson, E.	PP					Olafsson, B.	IP	Steinthorsson, S.	PP
5	Jonsson, E.	PP					Benediktsson, B.	IP		
6	Jonsson, E.	PP					Gislason, G.	SDP	Vladimarsson, H.	USP/PA
7	Gudmundsson, G.	SDP					Gislason, G.	SDP		
	Gislason, G.	SDP								
8	Thoroddsen, G.	IP								
9	Thoroddsen, G.	IP					Gislason, G.	SDP		
10	Thoroddsen, G.	IP					Gislason, G.	SDP		
11	Jonsson, M.	IP								
12	Sigurdsson, H.	PP			Kjartansson, M.	USP/PA	Olafsson, M.T.	ULL	Kjartansson, M.	USP/PA
13	Matthiesen, M.	IP					Hjalmarsson, V.	PP	Bjarnason, M.	IP
14	Arnasson, T.	PP					Arnalds, R.	USP/PA	Magnusson, M.	SDP
15	Björgvinsson, S.	SDP					Gylfason, V.	SDP	Magnusson, M.	SDP
16	Arnalds, R.	USP/PA							Gestasson, S.	USP/PA
17	Gudmundsson, A.	IP					*Helgadottir, R.	IP	Bjarnason, M.	IP
18	Hannibalsson, J.	SDP					Gunnarsson, B.	IP	Bjarnason, G.	IP
19	Grimsson, U.	USP/PA					Gestsson, S.	USP/PA	Bjarnason, G.	PP
20	Grimsson, U.	USP/PA	Hermannsson, S.	PP			Gestsson, S.	USP/PA	Bjarnason, G.	PP
21	Sophusson, F.	IP					Einarsson, O.G.	IP	Björgvinsson, S.	SDP
22	Sophusson, F.	IP					Bjarnason, B.	IP	*Palmadottir, I.	PP

ICELAND 1945–1998

Gov	Housing	Py	Agriculture	Py	Industry/Trade	Py	Environment	Py
1			Magnusson, P. Jonsson, F.	IP SDP	Magnusson, P.	IP		
2			Josefsson, J. Asgeirsson, B.	IP FP	Johnsson, E.	SDP		
3			Jonasson, H.	PP	Olafsson, B. Thors, O.	IP IP		
4			Jonasson, H.	PP	Olafsson, B. Thors, O.	IP IP		
5			Thors, O. Steinthorsson, S.	IP PP	Jonsson, I.	IP		
6			Jonsson, E. Josefsson, L.	PP USP/PA	Gislason, G. Josefsson, L.	SDP USP/PA		
7			Jonsson, E. Skarphedinson, F.	SDP SDP	Gislason, G.	SDP		
8			Benediktsson, J. Gislason, G. Jonsson, I.	IP SDP IP	Benediktsson, J.	IP		
9			Hafstein, J. Jonsson, E. Jonsson, I.	IP SDP IP	Hafstein, J. Gislason, G.	IP SDP		
10			Hafstein, J. Jonsson, E. Jonsson, I.	IP SDP IP	Hafstein, J. Gislason, G.	IP SDP		
11			Thorsteisson, E. Jonsson, I.	SDP IP	Gislason, G.	SDP		
12			Sigurdsson, H. Josefsson, L.	PP USP/PA	Kjartansson, M.	USP/PA		
13			Sigurdsson, H. Bjarnason, M.	PP IP	Johannesson, O. Thoroddsen, G.	PP IP		

ICELAND 1945–1998

Gov	Housing	Py	Agriculture	Py	Industry/Trade	Py	Environment	Py
14			Hermansson, S.	PP	Guttormsson, H.	USP/PA		
			Johannesson, K.	SDP	Gestsson, S.	USP/PA		
15			Johanesson, K.	SDP				
			Sigurjonsson, B.	SDP				
16			Hermannsson, S.	PP	Arnason, T.	PP		
			Jonsson, P.	IP	Guttormsson, H.	USP/PA		
17			Helgason, J.	PP	Hermansson, S.	IP		
			Asgrimsson, H.	PP	Mathiesen, M.	IP		
18			Helgason, J.	PP	Sigurdsson, J.	SDP		
			Asgrimsson, H.	PP	Sophusson, F.	IP		
19			Asgrimsson, H.	PP	Hannibalsson, J.	SDP		
			Sigfusson, S.	USP/PA	Sigurthsson, J.	SDP		
20			Asgrimsson, H.	PP	Hannibalsson, J.	SDP	Solnes, J.	CP
			Sigfusson, S.	USP/PA	Sigurthsson, J.	SDP		
21			Pálsson, T.	IP	Sigurthsson, J.	SDP	Gudnason, E.	SDP
			Blöndal, H.	IP				
22			Pálsson, T.	IP	Ingolfsson, F.	PP	Bjarnason, G.	PP
			Bjarnason, G.	PP				

Gov	Social Affairs (py)	Public Works (py)	Other (py)	Res
1	Jonsson, F. (SDP)	Jonsson, E. (SDP)		0
2	Stefansson, S.J. (SDP)	Johnsson, E. (SDP)		0
		Johnsson, E. (PP)		
3	Steinthorsson, S. (PP)	Olafsson, B. (IP)		0
		Jonasson, H. (PP)		

ICELAND 1945–1998

Gov	Social Affairs (py)	Public Works (py)	Other (py)	Res
4	Steinthorsson, S. (PP)	Olafsson, B. (IP) Jonasson, H. (PP)		0
5	Steinthorsson, S. (PP)			0
6	Vladimarsson, H. (USP/PA)			0
7		Jonsson, E. (SDP)		0
8	Gislason, G. (SDP)	Jonsson, I. (IP)		0
9	Jonsson, E. (SDP)	Jonsson, I. (IP)	Hafstein, J. (IP)	0
10	Jonsson, E. (SDP)	Jonsson, I. (IP)	Hafstein, J. (IP)	0
11			*Auduns, A. (SDP) Gislason, G. (SDP)	0
12	Vladimarsson, H. (ULL)	Vladimarsson, H. (ULL)		0
13	Thoroddsen, G. (IP) Bjarnason, M. (IP)	Thoroddsen, G. (IP) Sigurdsson, H. (PP)		0
14		Arnalds, R. (USP/PA)	Hermansson, S. (PP) Arnalds, R. (USP/PA)	0
15	Magnusson, M. (SDP)	Magnusson, M. (SDP)	Gylfason, V. (SDP)	0
16	Gestasson, S. (USP/PA)	Hermannsson, S. (PP)	Gislason, I. (PP)	0
17	Bjarnason, M. (IP) Stefansson, A. (PP)	Bjarnason, M. (IP) Hermansson, S. (IP)	Helgason, J. (PP)	1
18	Bjarnason, G. (PP) *Sigurdardottir, J. (SDP)	Mathiesen, M. (IP)	Sigurdsson, J. (SDP) Gunnarsson, B. (IP)	0
19	*Sigurdardottir, J. (SDP) Bjarnason, G. (PP)	Sigfusson, S. (USP/PA)	Asgrimsson, H. (PP) Gestsson, S. (USP/PA) Sigurthsson, J. (SDP)	0
20	*Sigurdardottir, J. (SDP) Bjarnason, G. (PP)	Sigfusson, S. (USP/PA)	Gudbartsson, O. (CP) Gestsson, S. (USP/PA) Solnes, J. (CP)	0
21	*Sigurthardottir, J. (SDP)	Blöndal, H. (IP)	Oddsson, D. (IP) Pálsson, T. (IP)	2

ICELAND 1945–1998

Gov	Social Affairs (py)	Public Works (py)	Other (py)	Res
22	Petursson, P. (PP)	Blöndal, H. (IP)	Oddsson, D. (IP)	
			Pálsson, T. (IP)	

22. INDIA

The Head of State is a President, indirectly elected for a five-year term. His or her functions are largely ceremonial.

The State is Federal and decentralised.

Parliament is bicameral. The Upper House has 245 members and sits for six years. The dominant Lower House (Lok Sabha) of 545 members is elected for a five-year term by plurality voting in constituencies of around 750,000 each.

Parliament has a quorum of one-tenth of all members. Votes are carried by a majority of all votes cast. Some issues require a qualified majority of two-thirds of all members present. Constitutional amendments require a two-thirds majority of all votes cast in both Houses. There is no referendum.

The President nominally appoints the government, but the executive power lies in the hands of the Prime Minister and the Cabinet. There is no vote of investiture, but governments need to retain the support of a (relative) majority of the Lower House to survive. During its lifetime a government can face a vote of no confidence. Losing that vote always results in resignation of the government. The government is collectively responsible to parliament. The Prime Minister and other ministers are the leaders of the majority party or coalition in the Lower House. Ministers are required to be members of parliament. The Prime Minister has a dominant position in government.

There is a Supreme Court for constitutional review of legislation.

INDIA 1947-1998

Gov	Begin	Dur	RfT	ToG	Py1	Py2	Py3	Py4	Py5	Seats	CPG	NoM	Prime Minister (py)
1	15.08.47	1644	1	3	Congress 202	Sikh 4	Indian Christian 2	Parsee ?	Hindu Mhas 1	223	3	14	Nehru, J. (Congress)
2	14.05.52	1889	1	1	Congress 362					497	3	15	Nehru, J. (Congress)
3	17.04.57	1817	1	1	Congress 371					494	3	13	Nehru, J. (Congress)
4	08.04.62	793	x	1	Congress 361					494	3	17	Nehru, J. (Congress)
5	09.06.64	594	x	1	Congress 361					494	3	16	Shastri, L.B. (Congress)
6	24.01.66	413	1	1	Congress 361					494	3	16	*Gandhi, I. (Congress)
7	13.03.67	1466	1	1	Congress 282					520	3	19	*Gandhi, I. (Congress)
8	18.03.71	2201	1	1	Congress 350					518	3	13	*Gandhi, I. (Congress)
9	27.03.77	853	4	1	Janata 302+					544	3	20	Desai, M.R. (Janata)
10	28.07.79	170	1	6	Janata-S	Congress-O 16				544	3	19	Singh, C. (Janata-S)
11	14.01.80	1753	x	1	Congress-I 351					542	3	15	*Gandhi, I. (Congress-I)
12	01.11.84	60	1	1	Congress-I 351					542	3	14	Gandhi, R. (Congress-I)
13	31.12.84	1797	1	1	Congress-I 403					544	3	15	Gandhi, R. (Congress-I)
14	02.12.89	343	4	2	NF 144	BJ 88	LF 51			545	3	18	Singh, V.P. (NF-JD)
15	10.11.90	223	1	2/4	JD-S 61	[Congress-I 220+]				545	3	15	Shekhar, C. (JD-S)
16	21.06.91	1807	1	4	Congress-I 226					545	3	16	Rao, P.V.N. (Congress-I)
17	01.06.96	27	7	5	UF 167					545	4	13	Deve Gowda, H.D. (UF-JD)
18	28.06.96			5	UF 179					545	4	18	Deve Gowda, H.D. (UF-JD)

- Independence date 15 August 1947.
- Gov 1: On 25 July 1946 elections were held for the Constituent Assembly for the whole subcontinent, including Pakistan. The Congress Party obtained 202 of the 295 elected seats. After partition, the Constituent Assembly minus the Moslem League representatives, functions as parliament for India. Total seats 223.
- First elections for the Lok Sabha (House of the People) after independence were held from 25 October 1951 - 21 February 1952.
- Gov 4, 5: Reason for Termination is death of PM.
- Gov 7: Allthough elections are the Reason for Termination, the need to organise elections arose from grave difficulties within the Congress Party wich split in November 1969, causing the government to lose it's majority in parliament.
- Gov 8: To quell the opposition against the government inside and outside parliament major changes were made to India's 1949 constitution on 11 November 1976:
  > Organisations engaging in 'anti-national activities' might be banned;
  > President must act in accordance with advise from the Cabinet;

INDIA 1947-1998

> Lok Sabha from 5-year term to 6-year term;

> President should decide whether a person was disqualified from becoming/being MP because of corrupt practices;

> Only Supreme Court might rule that a 'central' law was unconstitutional; two-thirds majority required;

> Central government can send troops to maintain order in a state without consent of state government;

> President might declare State of Emergency in only a part of India;

> President's rule may remain in force in a state for a year without parliament being required to renew it;

> No amendment to constitution might be called into question in any court;

> For two years after an amendment coming into force President may amend constitution by order; India was renamed from 'a sovereign democratic republic' to 'a sovereign socialist secular democratic republic'.

- Gov 9: Janata Party was a merger of Janata Party proper (271), with Congres for Democracy (28), Revolutionary Socialist Party (3), Jan Sangh (?) and Bharatiya Lok Dal (?). In total 302+ seats in parliament. The new government announced that all constitutional changes made in 1975/1976 would be repealed. A bill to that effect was adopted by parliament in December 1977.

- Gov 10: The Janata Party had split into Janata Party proper and Janata Party Secular. Number of seats unknown. Congress-O had obtained 16 seats during the previous elections. Because the government could not aquire a majority in parliament, parliament was dissolved and the government remained in a caretaker capacity until the elections in January 1980.

- Gov 11: Reason for Termination is assasination of PM.

- Gov 14: National Front consisted of Janata Dal (141), Telugu Desam (2) and Congress-S (1). Left-Front consisted of CPI-M (32), CPI (12) and smaller parties (7).

- Gov 15: Janata Dal-S is Shekar faction of Janata Dal.

- Gov 17: United Front parties include Janata Dal (43), CPI-M (33), Tamil Maanila Congress (20), Samajwadi Party (17), Dravida Munnetra Kazagham (17), Telugu Desam Party-Naidu (16), Revolutionary Socialist Party (5), Asam Gana Parishad (5), Indian National Congress-Tiwari (4), Forward Bloc (3), Madhya Pradesh Vikas Party (2), Karnataka Congress Party (1) and Maharastrawadi Gomantak Party (1).

- Gov 18: United Front parties include same parties as during government 17, plus CPI (12).

INDIA 1947-1998

Gov	Deputy PM	Py	Foreign Affairs	Py	Defence	Py	Interior	Py	Justice	Py
1			Nehru, J.	Congress	Singh, S.B.	Sikh	Patel, S.V.	Congress	Ambedkar, R.	Congress
2			Nehru, J.	Congress	Gopolaswami Ayyangar, N.	Congress	Katju, K.N.	Congress	Biswas, C.C.	Congress
3			Nehru, J.	Congress	Krishna Menon, V.K.	Congress	Pant, G.B.	Congress		
4			Nehru, J.	Congress	Krishna Menon, V.K.	Congress	Shastri, L.B.	Congress	Sen, A.K.	Congress
5			Shastri, L.B.	Congress	Chavan, Y.B.	Congress	Nanda, G.L.	Congress		
							Sen, A.K.	Congress		
6			Singh, S.S.	Congress	Chavan, Y.B.	Congress	Nanda, G.L.	Congress	Pathak, G.S.	Congress
7	Desai, M.R.	Congress	Chagla, C.C.	Congress	Singh, S.S.	Congress	Chavan, Y.B.	Congress	Govinda Menon, P.	Congress
8			Singh, S.S.	Congress	Ram, J.	Congress	*Gandhi, I.	Congress	Gokhale, H.R.	Congress
9			Vajpayee, A.B.	Janata-JS	Ram, J.	Janata-CFD	Singh, C.	Janata-BLD	Bhushan, S.	Janata
10	Chavan, Y.B.	Congress-O	Mishra, S.N.	Janata-S	Subramaniam, C.	Congress-O	Chavan, Y.B.	Congress-O	Kacker, S.N.	Janata-S
11			Rao, P.V.N.	Congress-I	*Gandhi, I.	Congress-I	Singh, Z.	Congress-I	Shankar, P.S.	Congress-I
12			Gandhi, R.	Congress-I	Chavan, S.B.	Congress-I	Rao, P.V.N.	Congress-I	Kanshal, J.	Congress-I
13			Gandhi, R.	Congress-I	Rao, P.V.N.	Congress-I	Chavan, S.B.	Congress-I	Sen, A.	Congress-I
14	Lal, D.	NF-JD	Gujral, I.K.		Singh, V.P.	NF-JD	Sayeed Mufti, M.		Goswami, D.	LF-AGP
							Singh, V.P.	NF-JD		
15	Lal, D.	JD-S	Shukla, V.C.	JD-S	Shekhar, C.	JD-S	Shekhar, C.	JD-S	Swamy, S.	JD-S
16			Solanki, M.	Congress-I	Pawar, S.	Congress-I	Rao, P.V.N.	Congress-I		
							Chavan, S.B.	Congress-I		
							Reddy, K.V.B.	Congress-I		
17			Gujral, I.K.	UF-JD	Singh Yadav, M.	UF-SP	Deve Gowda, H.D.	UF-JD	Chidambaram, P.	UF-IMC
18			Gujral, I.K.	UF-JD	Singh Yadav, M.	UF-SP	Gupta, I.	UF-CPI		

INDIA 1947-1998

Gov	Finance	Py	Economic Aff.	Py	Labour	Py	Education	Py	Health	Py
1	Shanmukham Chetty, R.K.	Congress	Bhabha, C.H.	Parsee	Ram, J.	Congress	Nehru, J. / Azad, M.	Congress / Congress	*Kaur, R.A.	Congress
2	Deshmukh, C.	Congress	Nanda, G.L. / Krishnamachari, T.T.	Congress / Congress	Giri, V.V.	Congress	Azad, A.K.	Congress	*Kaur, R.A.	Congress
3	Krishnamachari, T.T.	Congress	Desai, M.R. / Nanda, G.L.	Congress / Congress	Nanda, G.L.	Congress	Azad, A.K.	Congress		
4	Desai, M.R.	Congress	Nanda, G.L. / Reddy, K.C.	Congress / Congress	Nanda, G.L.	Congress	Shrimali, K.L. / Kabir, H.	Congress / Congress		
5	Krishnamachari, T.T.	Congress			Sanjivayya, D.	Congress	Chagla, M.C.	Congress		
6	Chaudhuri, S.	Congress	Mehta, A. / Shah, M.	Congress / Congress	Ram, J.	Congress	Chagla, M.C.	Congress		
7	Desai, M.R.	Congress	Singh, D. / Mehta, A.	Congress / Congress	Hathi, J.	Congress	Sen, T.	Congress		
8	Chavan, Y.B.	Congress	*Gandhi, I.	Congress			Ray, s.S.	Congress	Shah, K.K.	Congress
9	Patel, H.M.	Janata-BLD	Dharia, M.	Janata-CFD	Varma, P.	Janata	Chunder, P.C.	Janata	Narain, N.	Janata-BLD
10	Bahuguna, H.N.	Janata-S	Desai, H.	Congress-O	Rahman, F.	Janata-S	Singh, K.	Congress-O	Ray, R.	Janata-S
11	Venkataraman, R.	Congress-I	Mukherjee, P.K.	Congress-I	Patnaik, J.B.	Congress-I	Shankaranand, B.	Congress-I	Shankaranand, B.	Congress-I
12	Mukherjee, P.K.	Congress-I	Mukherjee, P.K. / Rao, P.V.N.	Congress-I / Congress-I	Patil, V.	Congress-I	Gandhi, R.	Congress-I	Shankaranand, B.	Congress-I
13	Singh, V.P.	Congress-I	Gandhi, R. / Rao, P.V.N.	Congress-I / Congress-I			Gandhi, R. / Pant, K.C.	Congress-I / Congress-I	*Kidwai, M.	Congress-I
14	Dandavate, M.	NF-JD	Nehru, A.K.		Paswan, R.V.		Singh, V.P.	NF-JD	Routray, N.	

INDIA 1947-1998

Gov	Finance	Py	Economic Aff.	Py	Labour	Py	Education	Py	Health	Py
15	Sinha, Y.	JD-S	Swamy, S.	JD-S	Pande, R.	JD-S			Shakul-Ul-Rehman	JD-S
16	Singh, M.	Congress-I					Rao, P.V.N.	Congress-I	Fotedar, M.L.	Congress-I
17	Chidambaram, P.	UF-TMC			Bommai, S.R. Arunachalam, M. Singh Ramoowakia, B. Naidu, Y.	UF-JD UF-TMC IND UF-TPD-N	Deve Gowda, H.D.	UF-JD		
18	Chidambaram, P.	UF-TMC			Deve Gowda, H.D. Bommai, S.R. Arunachalam, M. Naidu, Y.	UF-JD UF-JD UF-TMC UF-TPD-N				

Gov	Housing	Py	Agriculture	Py	Industry/Trade	Py	Environment	Py
1			Prasad, R.	Congress	Mookerjee, S.P.	Hindu Mhas		
2	Singh, S.S.	Congress	Kidway, R.A.	Congress	Krishnamachari, T.T. Reddy, K.C.	Congress Congress		
3	Reddy, K.C.	Congress	Jain, A.P.	Congress	Desai, M.R.	Congress		
4			Patil, S.K.	Congress	Reddy, K.C. Subramaniam, C.	Congress Congress		
5			Subramaniam, C.	Congress	Singh, S.S.	Congress		
6			Subramaniam, C.	Congress	Sanjivayya, D.	Congress		
7			Ram, J.	Congress	Ahmed, F.A.	Congress		

INDIA 1947-1998

Gov	Housing	Py	Agriculture	Py	Industry/Trade	Py	Environment	Py
8			Ahmed, F.A.	Congress	Chaudhury, M.H.	Congress		
9	Bakht, S.	Janata	Singh Badal, P.	Janata	Verma, B.	Janata-JS		
10	Kinkar, R.	Janata-S	Prakash, B.	Janata-S	Reddy, K.B.	Congress-O		
11	Sethi, P.C.	Congress-I	Singh, R.B.	Congress-I	Venkataraman, R.	Congress-I		
					Sharma, A.P.	Congress-I		
12	Singh, B.	Congress-I	Singh, R.B.	Congress-I	Reddy, V.B.	Congress-I		
13	Gafoor, A.	Congress-I	Gandhi, R.	Congress-I	Gandhi, R.	Congress-I	Gandhi, R.	Congress-I
			Singh, B.	Congress-I				
14			Singh, V.P.	NF-JD	Singh, A.	NF-JD	Singh, V.P.	NF-JD
			Lal, D.	NF-JD	Yadav, S.			
15			Lal, D.	JD-S	Singh, H.D.N.	JD-S		
16			Jakhar, B.	Congress-I	Rao, P.V.N.	Congress-I		
17			Deve Gowda, H.D.	UF-JD	Chidambaram, P.	UF-TMC		
			Prasad Yadav, D.	UF-JD	Maran, M.	UF-DMK		
					Prasad Yadav, D.	UF-JD		
18			Mishra, C.	UF-CPI	Chidambaram, P.	UF-TMC		
			Prasad Yadav, D.	UF-JD	Maran, M.	UF-DMK		
					Prasad Yadav, D.	UF-JD		

Gov	Social Affairs (py)	Public Works (py)	Other (py)	Res
1		Patel, S.V. (Congress)	Patel, S.V. (Congress)	6
		Matthai, J. (Indian Christ.)		
		Kidwai, R.A. (Congress)		
		Gadgil, N.V. (Congress)		

INDIA 1947-1998

Gov	Social Affairs (py)	Public Works (py)	Other (py)	Res
2		Azad, A.K. (Congress) Ram, J. (Congress) Shastri, L.B. (Congress) Singh, S.S. (Congress)	Nanda, G.L. (Congress) Biswas, C.C. (Congress)	7
3		Nehru, J. (Congress) Ram, J. (Congress) Shastri, L.B. (Congress) Singh, S.S. (Congress) Reddy, K.C. (Congress) Patil, S.K. (Congress)	Jain, A.P. (Congress)	4
4		Ram, J. (Congress) Singh, S.S. (Congress) Ibrahim, H.M. (Congress) Malaviya, K.D. (Congress) Reddy, B.G. (Congress)	Patil, S.K. (Congress) Kabir, H. (Congress) Sinha, S.N. (Congress)	4
5		Shastri, L.B. (Congress) *Gandhi, I (Congress) Patil, S.K. (Congress) Sen, A.K. (Congress) Reddy, S. (Congress) Kabir, H. (Congress) Sinha, S.N. (Congress) Dasappa, H.C. (Congress)	Subramaniam, C. (Congress) Sinha, S.N. (Congress) Tyagi, M. (Congress)	2

INDIA 1947-1998

Gov	Social Affairs (py)	Public Works (py)	Other (py)	Res
6		*Gandhi, I. (Congress) Patil, S.K. (Congress) Sinha, S.N. (Congress) Reddy, S. (Congress) Ahmed, F.A. (Congress)	Subramaniam, C. (Congress) Sinha, S.N. (Congress) Reddy, S. (Congress) Ram, J. (Congress)	1
7	Mehta, A. (Congress)	*Gandhi, I. (Congress) Singh, K. (Congress) Mehta, A. (Congress) Poonacha, C.M. (Congress) Singh, R.S. (Congress) Rao, V.K.R.V. (Congress) Reddy, M.C. (Congress) Shah, K.K. (Congress)	Hathi, J. (Congress) Ram, J. (Congress) Singh, K. (Congress) Singh, R.S. (Congress) Sinha, S.N. (Congress)	4
8	Ray, S.S. (Congress) Shah, K.K. (Congress)	*Gandhi, I. (Congress) Hanumanthaiya, K. (Congress) Singh, K. (Congress) Bahadur, R. (Congress) Chaudhury, M.H. (Congress) Kumaramangalam, S.M. (Congress)	Ahmed, F.A. (Congress) Singh, K. (Congress) Bahadur, R. (Congress) Ray, S.S. (Congress)	10

INDIA 1947-1998

Gov	Social Affairs (py)	Public Works (py)	Other (py)	Res
9	Chunder, P.C. (Janata)	Advani, L.K. (Janata)	Bakht, S. (Janata)	3
	Narain, N. (Janata-BLD)	Singh Badal, P. (Janata)	Bhushan, S. (Janata)	
		Bakht, S. (Janata)	Chunder, P.C. (Janata)	
		Dandavate, M. (Janata)	Dharia, M. (Janata-CFD)	
		Dharia, M. (Janata-CFD)	Kaushik, P. (Janata-RSP)	
		Kaushik, P. (Janata-RSP)	Patel, H.M. (Janata-BLD)	
		Patnaik, B. (Janata-BLD)	Varma, P. (Janata)	
		Ramachandran, P. (Janata)		
		Bahuguna, H.N. (Janata-CFD)		
		Fernandes, G. (Janata-RSP)		
10	Ray, R. (Janata-S)	Pai, T.A. (Congress-O)	Kinkar, R. (Janata-S)	1
		Patnaik, B. (IND)	Zulfiqarullah, ? (Janata-S)	
		Kaushik, P. (Janata-S)	Qureshi, M.S. (Congress-O)	
		Desai, H. (Congress-0)	Kacker, S.N. (Janata-S)	
		Prakash, B. (Janata-S)		
		Kinkar, R. (Janata-S)		
		Zulfiqarullah, ? (Janata-S)		
		Pant, K.C. (Congress-O)		
		Qureshi, M.S. (Congress-O)		

INDIA 1947-1998

Gov	Social Affairs (py)	Public Works (py)	Other (py)	Res
11	Shankaranand, b. (Congress-I)	Ghani Khan Choudhury, A.B.A. (Congress-I) Tripathi, K. (Congress-I) Sathe, V. (Congress-I) Sharma, A.P. (Congress-I) Sethi, P.C. (Congress-I) Patnaik, J.B. (Congress-I) Singh, B.N. (Congress-I) Mukherjee, P.K. (Congress-I)	Patnaik, J.B. (Congress-I) Singh, B.N. (Congress-I)	9
12	Patil, V. (Congress-I) Shankaranand, B. (Congress-I) Singh, B. (Congress-I)	Ghani Khan Choudhury, A.B.A. (Congress-I) Patil, V. (Congress-I) Sathe, V. (Congress-I) Shankar, P.S. (Congress-I) Singh, B. (Congress-I)	Gandhi, R. (Congress-I) Kanshal, J. (Congress-I) Singh, B. (Congress-I) Singh, R.B. (Congress-I) *Kidwai, M. (Congress-I)	0
13	Gandhi, R. (Congress-I) *Kidwai, M. (Congress-I)	Gandhi, R. (Congress-I) Shankaranand, B. (Congress-I) Lal, B. (Congress-I) Singh, R.B. (Congress-I) Sathe, V. (Congress-I) Patil, V. (Congress-I)	Gandhi, R. (Congress-I) Singh, B. (Congress-I) Bhagat, H.K.L. (Congress-I) Singh, R.B. (Congress-I)	11
14	Singh, V.P. (NF-JD) Paswan, R.V. () Routray, N. ()	Fernandes, G. (NF-JD) Khan, A.M. () Gurupadasami, M.S. () Upendra, P. (TF-JD) Unnikrishnan, K.P. (NF-Congress-S) Goswami, D. (LF-AGP) Mirdha, N.R. (NF-JD)	Singh, V.P. (NF-JD) Nehru, A.K. () Maran, M. (LF-DMK) Mirdha, N.R. (NF-JD)	1

INDIA 1947-1998

Gov	Social Affairs (py)	Public Works (py)	Other (py)	Res
15	Shakul-Ur-Rehman, ? (JD-S)	Shekhar, C. (JD-S) Malaviya, S.P. (JD-S) Mishra, J. (JD-S) Kalvi, K.S. (JD-S) Koyadia, M. (JD-S) Sen, A.K. (JD-S) Singh, R.B. (JD-S)	Lal, D. (JD-S) Malaviya, S.P. (JD-S) Saran, D.R. (JD-S) Singh, R.B. (JD-S)	1
16	Singh, A. (Congress-I) Fotedar, M.L. (Congress-I) Kesri, S. (Congress-I)	Rao, P.V.N. (Congress-I) Sharief, C.K.J. (Congress-I) Scindia, M.R. (Congress-I) Shankaranand, B. (Congress-I) Shukla, V.C. (Congress-I)	Rao, P.V.N. (Congress-I) Azad, G.N. (Congress-I)*Kaul, S. (Congress-I) Reddy, K.V.B. (Congress-I) Scindia, M.R. (Congress-I)	6
17	Prasad Yadav, D. (UF-JD) Singh Ramoowalia, B. (IND)	Vilas Paswan, R. (UF-JD) Bommai, S.R. (UF-JD) Ibrahim, C.M. (UF-JD) Venkataraman, T.G. (UF-DMK)	Deve Gowda, H.D. (UF-JD) Gujral, I.K. (UF-JD) Vilas Paswan, R. (UF-JD) Arunachalam, M. (UF-TMC) Ibrahim, C.M. (UF-JD) Naidu, Y. (UF-TDP-N)	0
18	Deve Gowda, H.D. (UF-JD) Prasad Yadav, D. (UF-JD) Singh Ramoowalia, B. (IND)	Deve Gowda, H.D. (UF-JD) Vilas Paswan, R. (UF-JD) Ibrahim, C.M. (UF-JD) Venkataraman, T.G. (UF-DMK) Prasad Baisha, B. (UF-AGP)	Deve Gowda, H.D. (UF-JD) Naidu, Y. (UF-TDP-N) Kumar Jena, S. (UF-JD) Mishra, J. (UF-SP)	1

23. IRELAND

The Head of State, the President, is directly elected for a seven-year term. He or she has mainly formal and symbolic political functions.

The State is highly centralised both legislatively and administratively, with local government closely supervised by the central administration.

Parliament is bicameral. The indirectly elected and partly nominated Senate (Seanad) with 60 seats sits for a flexible five year term and has little power compared to the Lower House of Representatives (Dail). The Dail has 166 members, elected for a flexible five-year term by proportional representation (Single Transferable Vote) within relatively small three to four member constituencies (on average 60,000 electors).

Parliament has a quorum of twenty members (Dail) or 15 members (Seanad). Votes, also on constitutional amendments, are carried by a majority of all votes cast. The Head of State and parliament may call a referendum. The outcome is binding.

The political executive is the Cabinet presided over by the Prime Minister. The Cabinet is coterminous with the government except for some minor posts. The Government does not include the President. There is no formal vote of investiture, but the emergence of frequent coalition governments have led to the initial debate on their programme being regarded more or less as such. The government can also face a vote of no confidence during its lifetime. Losing a vote of confidence always results in resignation of the government. The government is collectively responsible to the Dail. Members have to come from either the Dail or Seanad. The Prime Minister has a rather prominent position in government, but that position has been curtailed by the growing frequency of coalitions which requires inter-party negotiation in Cabinet.

There is limited constitutional review by the Supreme Court on matters referred to it by the Government.

291

IRELAND 1945–1998

Gov	Begin	Dur	RfT	ToG	Py1	Py2	Py3	Py4	Seats	CpG	NoM	Prime Minister (py)
1	18.02.48	1211	5	5	FG 31	LAB 14	CNT 7	CNP 10	147	2	14	Costello, J.A. (FG)
2	13.06.51	1085	5	4	FF 69				147	3	12	Valera, E. de (FF)
3	02.06.54	1022	5	2	FG 50	LAB 19	CNT 5		147	2	14	Costello, J.A. (FG)
4	20.03.57	825	2	1	FF 78				147	3	12	Valera, E. de (FF)
5	23.06.59	841	1	1	FF 78				147	3	14	Lemass, S. (FF)
6	11.10.61	1268	1	4	FF 70				144	3	15	Lemass, S. (FF)
7	01.04.65	588	3	1	FF 72				144	3	15	Lemass, S. (FF)
8	10.11.66	965	1	1	FF 72				144	3	15	Lynch, J.A. (FF)
9	02.07.69	1351	1	1	FF 75				144	3	15	Lynch, J.A. (FF)
10	14.03.73	1574	1	2	FG 54	LAB 19			144	2	15	Cosgrave, L. (FG)
11	05.07.77	889	2	1	FF 84				148	3	15	Lynch, J.A. (FF)
12	11.12.79	567	1	1	FF 84				148	3	15	Haughey, C.J. (FF)
13	30.06.81	252	5	5	FG 65	LAB 15			166	2	15	Fitzgerald, G.M.D. (FG)
14	09.03.82	280	5	4	FF 81				166	3	15	Haughey, C.J. (FF)
15	14.12.82	1547	4	2	FG 70	LAB 16			166	2	15	Fitzgerald, G.M.D. (FG)
16	10.03.87	855	1	4	FF 81				166	3	15	Haughey, C.J. (FF)
17	12.07.89	944	2	5	FF 77	PD 6			166	2	15	Haughey, C.J. (FF)
18	11.02.92	327	4	5	FF 77	PD 6			166	2	15	Reynolds, A. (FF)
19	12.01.93	702	4	2	FF 68	LAB 33			166	4	15	Reynolds, A. (FF)
20	15.12.94	922	1	5	FG 45	LAB 33	SDL 4		166	3	15	Bruton, J. (FG)
21	26.06.97			5	FF 77	PD 4			166	3	15	Ahern, B. (FF)

- As of Gov 10, the number of Ministers is fixed on 15; the Attorney-General is not a member of government.

IRELAND 1945–1998

Gov	Deputy PM	Py	Foreign Affairs	Py	Defence	Py	Interior	Py	Justice	Py
1	Norton, W.	LAB	Macbride, S.	CNP	O'Higgins, T.F.	FG	Murphy, J.	LAB	MacEoin, S. / Lavery, C.	FG / FG
2	Lemass, S.	FF	Aiken, F.J.F.	FF	Traynor, O.	FF	Smith, P.	FF	Boland, G.	FF
3	Norton, W.	LAB	Cosgrave, L.	FG	MacEoin, S.	FG	O'Donnel, P.	FG	Everett, J. / MacGilligan, P.	LAB / FG
4	Lemass, S.	FF	Aiken, F.J.F.	FF	Boland, K.	FF	Smith, P.	FF	Traynor, O. / O'Caoimh, A.	FF / FF
5	MacEntee, J.F.	FF	Aiken, F.J.F.	FF	Boland, K.	FF	Blaney, N.T.	FF	Traynor, O. / O'Caoimh, A.	FF / FF
6	MacEntee, J.F.	FF	Aiken, F.J.F.	FF	Bartley, G.	FF	Blaney, N.T.	FF	Haughey, C.J. / O'Caoimh, A.	FF / FF
7	Aiken, F.J.F.	FF	Aiken, F.J.F.	FF	Hilliard, M.	FF	Blaney, N.T.	FF	Lenihan, B.J.B. / Condon, C.	FF / FF
8	Aiken, F.J.F.	FF	Aiken, F.J.F.	FF	Hilliard, M.	FF	Boland, K.	FF	Lenihan, B.J.B. / Condon, C.	FF / FF
9	Childers, E.H.	FF	Hillary, P.J.	FF	Gibbons, J.J.	FF	Boland, K.	FF	O'Morain, M.	FF
10	Corish, B.	LAB	Fitzgerald, G.M.D.	FG	Donegan, P.S.	FG	Tully, J.	LAB	Cooney, P.M.	FG
11	Colley, G.	FF	O'Kennedy, M.	FF	Malloy, R.	FF	Barrett, S.	FF	Collins, G.	FF
12	Colley, G.	FF	Lenihan, B.J.B.	FF	Faulkner, P.	FF	Colley, G.	FF	Collins, G.	FF
13	O'Leary, M.	LAB	Dooge, J.	FG	Tully, J.P.	LAB	Barry, P.	FG	Mitchell, J.	FG
14	Macsharry, R.	FF	Collins, G.	FF	Power, P.	FF	Burke, R.	FF	Doherty, S.	FF
15	Spring, D.	LAB	Barry, P.	FG	Cooney, J.P.	FG	Spring, D.	LAB	Noonan, M.	FG
16	Lenihan, B.J.B.	FF	Lenihan, B.J.B.	FF	Noonan, M.J.	FF	Flynn, P.	FF	Collins, G.	FF
17	Lenihan, B.J.B.	FF	Collins, W.G.	FF	Lenihan, B.J.B.	FF	Flynn, P.	FF	Burke, R.	FF
18	Wilson, J.	FF	Andrews, D.	FF	Wilson, J. / Woods, M.	FF / FF	Smith, M.	FF	Flynn, P.	FF

IRELAND 1945–1998

Gov	Deputy PM	Py	Foreign Affairs	Py	Defence	Py	Interior	Py	Justice	Py
19	Spring, D.	LAB	Spring, D.	LAB	Andrews, D.	FF	Smith, M.	FF	*Geoghegan-Quinn, M. / Taylor, M.	FF / LAB
20	Spring, D.	LAB	Spring, D.	LAB	Coveney, H.	FG	Howlin, B.	LAB	*Owen, N.	FG
21	*Harney, M.	PD	Burke, R.	FF	Andrews, D.	FF	Dempsey, N.	FF	O'Donoghue, J.	FF

Gov	Finance	Py	Economic Aff.	Py	Labour	Py	Education	Py	Health	Py
1	MacGilligan, P.	FG					Mulcahy, R.	FG	Browne, N.C.	CNP
2	MacEntee, J.F.	FF					Moylan, S.	FF	Ryan, J.	FF
3	Sweetman, G.	FG					Mulcahy, R.	FG	O'Higgins, T.F.	FG
4	Ryan, J.	FF					Lynch, J.A.	FF	MacEntee, J.F.	FF
5	Ryan, J.	FF					Hillary, P.J.	FF	MacEntee, J.F.	FF
6	Ryan, J.	FF					Hillary, P.J.	FF	MacEntee, J.F.	FF
7	Lynch, J.A.	FF					Colley, G.J.	FF	O'Malley, D.B.	FF
8	Haughey, C.J.	FF			Hillary, P.J.	FF	O'Malley, D.B.	FF	Flanagan, S.M.	FF
9	Haughey, C.J.	FF			Brennan, J.	FF	Faulkner, P.	FF	Childers, E.H.	FF
10	Ryan, R.	FG			O'Leary, M.	LAB	Burke, R.	FG	Corish, B.	LAB
11	Colley, G.	FF	O'Donoghue, M.	FF	Fitzgerald, G.	FF	Wilson, J.	FF	Haughey, C.J.	FF
12	O'Kennedy, M.	FF			Fitzgerald, G.	FF	Wilson, J.	FF	Woods, M.	FF
13	Bruton, J.	FG			Kavanagh, L.	LAB	Boland, J.	FG	*Desmond, E.	LAB
14	Macsharry, R.	FF			Fitzgerald, E.	FF	O'Donoghue, M.	FF	Woods, M.	FF
15	Dukes, A.	FG			Kavanagh, L.	LAB	Hussey, G.	FG	Desmond, B.	LAB
16	MacSharry, R.	FF			Ahern, B.	FF	*O'Rourke, M.	FF	O'Hanlon, R.	FF
17	Reynolds, A.	FF			Ahern, B.	FF	*O'Rourke, M.	FF	O'Hanlon, R.	FF
18	Ahern, B.	FF			Cowan, B.	FF	Brennan, S.	FF	O'Connell, J.	FF
19	Ahern, B.	FF	Quinn, R.	LAB			*Bhreathnach, N.	LAB	Howlin, B.	LAB

IRELAND 1945–1998

Gov	Finance	Py	Economic Aff.	Py	Labour	Py	Education	Py	Health	Py
20	Quinn, R.	LAB			Bruton, R.	FG	*Bhreathnach, N.	LAB	Noonan, M.	FG
21	McCreevy, C.	FF			*Harney, M.	PD	Martin, M.	FF	Cowan, B.	FF

Gov	Housing	Py	Economic Aff.	Py	Agriculture	Py	Labour	Py	Industry/Trade	Py	Education	Py	Environment	Py
1	Murphy, J.	LAB			Dillon, J.	NONA			Morissey, D.	FG				
2	Smith, P.	FF			Walsh, T.	FF			Lemass, S.	FF				
3	O'Donnel, P.	FG			Dillon, J.	FG			Norton, W.	LAB				
4	Smith, P.	FF			Aiken, F.	FF			Lemass, S.	FF				
5	Blaney, N.T.	FF			Smith, P.	FF			Lynch, J.A.	FF				
6	Blaney, N.T.	FF			Smith, P.	FF			Lynch, J.A.	FF				
7	Blaney, N.T.	FF			Haughey, C.J.	FF			Hillary, P.J.	FF				
8	Boland, K.	FF			Blaney, N.T.	FF			Colley, G.T.	FF				
9	Boland, K.	FF			Blaney, N.T.	FF			Colley, G.J.	FF				
10	Tully, J.	LAB			Clinton, C.C.	FG			Keating, J.	LAB				
11	Barrett, S.	FF			Gibbons, J. / Lenihan, B.J.B.	FF		FF / FF						
12	Colley, G.	FF			MacSharry, R. / Power, P.	FF			O'Malley, D.	FF			Barret, S. / Colley, G.	FF / FF
13	Barry, P.	FG			Dukes, A. / Fitzpatrick, T.	FG			Kelly, J.	FG / FG			Barry, P.	FG
14	Burke, R.	FF			Lenihan, B.J.B.	FF			Reynolds, A. / O'Malley, D.	FF			Burke, R.	FF
15	Spring, D.	LAB			Deasy, A.	FG			Bruton, J. / Cluskey, F.	FG / LAB			Spring, D.	LAB

IRELAND 1945–1998

Gov	Housing	Py	Agriculture	Py	Industry/Trade	Py	Environment	Py
16	Flynn, P.	FF	O'Kennedy, M. / Daly, B.	FF / FF	Reynolds, A.	FF	Flynn, P.	FF
17	Flynn, P.	FF	O'Kennedy, M. / Wilson, J.P.	FF / FF	O'Malley, D.J.O.	PD	Flynn, P.	FF
18	Smith, M.	FF	Walsh, J.	FF	O'Malley, D.J.O.	PD	Smith, M.	FF
19	Smith, M.	FF	Walsh, J.	FF	McCreevy, C.	FF	Smith, M.	FF
20	Howlin, B.	LAB	Yates, I.	FG	Bruton, R.	FG	Howlin, B.	LAB
21	Dempsey, N.	FF	Walsh, J.	FF	*Harney, M.	PD	Dempsey, N.	FF

Gov	Social Affairs (py)	Public Works (py)	Other (py)	Res
1	Norton, W. (LAB)	Everett, J. (LAB)	Blowick, J. (CNT)	1
2	Ryan, J. (FF)	Childers, E.H. (FF)		0
3	Corish, B. (LAB)	Keyes, M. (LAB)	Mulcahy, R. (FG) / Blowick, J. (CNT)	0
4	Smith, P. (FF)	Blaney, N.T. (FF)	Lynch, J.A. (FF) / Childers, E.H. (FF)	0
5	MacEntee, J.F. (FF)	Childers, E.H. (FF) / Hilliard, M.F. (FF)	Childers, E.H. (FF) / O'Moráin, M. (FF)	1
6	Boland, K. (FF)	Childers, E.H. (FF) / Hilliard, M.F. (FF)	O'Moráin, M. (FF)	1
7	Boland, K. (FF)	Childers, E.H. (FF) / Brennan, J. (FF)	O'Moráin, M. (FF)	1
8	Brennan, J. (FF)	Childers, E.H. (FF)	O'Moráin, M. (FF)	1
9	Boland, K. (FF)	Lenihan, B.J.B. (FF) / Lalor, P.J. (FF)	Colley, G.J. (FF) / Flanagan, S.M. (FF) / O'Kennedy, M. (FF)	2

IRELAND 1945–1998

Gov	Social Affairs (py)	Public Works (py)	Other (py)	Res
10	Corish, B. (LAB)	Barry, P. (FG) O'Brien, C.C. (LAB)	Fitzpatrick, T. (FG) O'Donnell, T.G. (FG)	0
11	Haughey, C.J. (FF)	Faulkner, P. (FF)	Gallagher, D. (FF)	
12			Colley, G. (FF) Reynolds, A. (FF) *Groghegan-Quinn, M.G. (FF)	0
13	*Desmond, E. (LAB)	Cooney, P. (FG)	O'Leary, M. (LAB) O'Toole, P. (FG)	1
14	Woods, M. (FF)	Wilson, J.C. (FF)	Fitzgerald, E. (FF) Reynolds, A. (FF) O'Malley, D. (FF) Flynn, P. (FF) Daly, B. (FF)	1
15	Desmond, B. (LAB)	Mitchell, J. (FG)	Bruton, J. (FG) Cluskey, F. (LAB) Boland, J. (FG) Barrett, S. (FG) O'Toole, P. (FG)	2
16	Woods, M. (FF)	Burke, R. (FF) Wilson, J.P. (FF)	Haughey, C.J. (FF) MacSharry, R. (FF) Burke, R. (FF) Wilson, J.P. (FF)	1
17	Woods, M. (FF)	Molloy, R. (PD) Brennan, S. (FF)	Haughey, C.J. (FF) Molloy, R. (PD) Brennan, S. (FF)	0
18	McCreevy, C. (FF)	*Geoghegan-Quinn, M. (FF) Molloy, R. (PD)	Wilson, J. (FF)	0

IRELAND 1945–1998

Gov	Social Affairs (py)	Public Works (py)	Other (py)	Res
19	Woods, M. (FF) Taylor, M. (LAB)	Cowan, B. (FF)	Higgins, M.D. (LAB) McCreevy, C. (FF)	0
20	Taylor, M. (LAB) De Rossa, P. (LAB)	Lowry, M. (FG)	Kenny, E. (FG) Higgins, M.D. (LAB) 0	
21	Cowan, B. (FF) Ahern, D. (FF) McDaid, J. (FF)	*O'Rourke, M. (FF) Woods, M. (FF)	Andrews, D. (FF) McDaid, J. (FF) De Valera, S. (FF)	

24. ISRAEL

Israel is one of the few countries in the world not to have a written constitution. This is not to say that parts of it are not written down, however - for instance, in the Transition Law of 1948, or in the Basic Law of Government which introduced changes in the system of appointing the Prime Minister in 1992.

The Head of State is a largely ceremonial President indirectly elected for a five-year term.

The state is extremely centralised and unitary.

Parliament (Knesset) is unicameral. Its 120 members are elected by proportional representation on party lists (d'Hondt – with a threshold of 1.5%). The whole country is the constituency.

There is no quorum for parliament. Votes are carried by a majority of all votes cast. For some issues a qualified majority of all members is required. For constitutional amendments a majority of all votes cast suffices. There is no referendum.

Since 1996, in accordance with the constitutional revision of 1992, the Prime Minister has been elected directly. This means that the person who forms the government may not be the leader of the largest party in the Knesset. He or she forms a government from members of the Knesset.

There is a formal vote of investiture. If unable to form a government, defeated on the vote of investiture, or if the government breaks up or loses a vote of confidence, the government resigns. The Prime Minister can then dissolve the Knesset to call fresh elections, but has also to subject him- or herself simultaneously to re-election as Prime Minister. The government is collectively responsible to parliament. Although ministers are chosen from the Knesset, being a minister is not compatible with being a Member of Parliament. Because Israeli governments are precarious multi-party coalitions, the Prime minister is in a weak position vis-à-vis both parliament and government. Consequently, he or she has no dominant position in government.

The Supreme Court reviews legislation.

ISRAEL 1948–1998

G o v	Begin	Dur	R f T	T o G	Py1	Py2	Py3	Py4	Py5	Py6	Py7	Py8	Py9	Seats	C P G	N o M	Prime Minister (py)
0	14.05.48	300	1	x												13	Ben-Gurion, D.
1	10.03.49	599	4	3	MPAI 46	URF 16	PROG 5	SEPH 5						120	3	12	Ben-Gurion, D. (MPAI)
2	30.10.50	126	5	3	MPAI 46	URF 16	PROG 5	SEPH 5						120	3	13	Ben-Gurion, D. (MPAI)
3	05.03.51	216	1	6	MPAI 46	URF 16	PROG 5	SEPH 5						120	3	13	Ben-Gurion, D. (MPAI)
4	07.10.51	443	7	2	MPAI 50	URF 15								120	4	13	Ben-Gurion, D. (MPAI)
5	23.12.52	380	3	3	MPAI 50	GZ 23	HMIZ 8	PROG 4	MIZR 2					120	3	16	Ben-Gurion, D. (MPAI)
6	07.01.54	538	4	3	MPAI 50	GZ 23	HMIZ 8	PROG 4	MIZR 2					120	3	15	Sharett, M. (MPAI)
7	29.06.55	126	1	6	MPAI 50	HMIZ 8	PROG 4	MIZR 2						120	4	12	Sharett, M. (MPAI)
8	02.11.55	796	2	3	MPAI 45	NRP 11	AA 10	MPAM 9	PROG 5					120	4	16	Ben-Gurion, D. (MPAI)
9	06.01.58	176	4	3	MPAI 45	NRP 11	AA 10	MPAM 9	PROG 5					120	4	16	Ben-Gurion, D. (MPAI)
10	01.07.58	385	2	3	MPAI 45	AA 10	MPAM 9	PROG 5						120	4	13	Ben-Gurion, D. (MPAI)
11	21.07.59	148	1	6	MPAI 45	AA 10	MPAM 9	PROG 5						120	4	13	Ben-Gurion, D. (MPAI)
12	16.12.59	413	2	3	MPAI 52	NRP 12	MPAM 9	AA 7	PROG 6					120	4	16	Ben-Gurion, D. (MPAI)

ISRAEL 1948–1998

Gov	Begin	Dur	RfT	ToG	Py1	Py2	Py3	Py4	Py5	Py6	Py7	Py8	Py9	Seats	CPG	NoM	Prime Minister (py)
13	31.01.61	275	1	6	MPAI 52	NRP 12	MPAM 9	AA 7	PROG 6					120	4	16	Ben-Gurion, D. (MPAI)
14	02.11.61	599	2	2	MPAI 46	NRP 12	AA 8							120	4	16	Ben-Gurion, D. (MPAI)
15	24.06.63	547	2	2	MPAI 46	NRP 12	AA 8							120	4	15	Eshkol, L. (MPAI)
16	22.12.64	383	1	2	MPAI 46	NRP 12	AA 8	[PAIS 2]						120	4	17	Eshkol, L. (MPAI)
17	10.01.66	507	7	3	ALNM 49	NRP 11	MPAM 8	ILIB 5	[PAIS 2]					120	4	18	Eshkol, L. (MPAI)
18	01.06.67	655	3	3	ALNM 49	HRUT 26	NRP 11	RAFI 10	MPAM 8	ILIB 5	[PAIS 2]			120	4	20	Eshkol, L. (MPAI)
19	17.03.69	273	1	3	ALNM 49	HRUT 26	NRP 11	RAFI 10	MPAM 8	ILIB 5	[PAIS 2]			120	4	21	*Meir, G. (MPAI)
20	15.12.69	232	4	3	ALNM 60	GHAL 26	NRP 12	ILIB 4						120	3	24	*Meir, G. (MPAI)
21	04.08.70	1310	1	3	ALNM 60	NRP 12	ILIB 4	[GHAL 26]						120	4	18	*Meir, G. (MPAI)
22	06.03.74	89	2	3	LAB 54	NRP 10	ILIB 4							120	4	22	*Meir, G. (MPAI)
23	03.06.74	148	4	2	LAB 54	ILIB 4	CRIT 3							120	4	19	Rabin, I. (MPAI)
24	29.10.74	784	4	3	LAB 54	NRP 10	ILIB 4							120	4	21	Rabin, I. (MPAI)
25	21.12.76	180	1	6	LAB 54	ILIB 4								120	4	18	Rabin, I. (MPAI)

ISRAEL 1948–1998

Gov	Begin	Dur	RfT	ToG	Py1	Py2	Py3	Py4	Py5	Py6	Py7	Py8	Py9	Seats	CPG	NOM	Prime Minister (py)
26	19.06.77	126	7	2	LIK 45	NRP 12	[AIS 4]	[PAIS 1]						120	2	13	Begin, M. (LIK)
27	24.10.77	1381	4	3	LIK 45	NRP 12	DASH 11	[AIS 4]	[PAIS 1]					120	2	17	Begin, M. (LIK)
28	05.08.81	717	7	2	LIK 48	NRP 6	TAMI 3	[AIS 4]	[THYA 3]					120	2	18	Begin, M. (LIK)
29	23.07.83	79	2	2	LIK 48	NRP 6	TAMI 3	[AIS 4]	[THYA 3]					120	2	18	Begin, M. (LIK)
30	10.10.83	339	3	2	LIK 48	NRP 6	TAMI 3	THYA 3	[AIS 4]					120	2	20	Shamir, I. (LIK)
31	13.09.84	767	1	3	LAB 44	LIK 41	NRP 4	SHAS 4	SNUI 3	MSHA 2	OMET 1	[AIS 2]	[YHAD 3]	120	3	17	Peres, S. (LAB)
32	20.10.86	794	2	3	LAB 44	LIK 41	NRP 4	SHAS 4	SNUI 3	MSHA 2	OMET 1	[AIS 2]	[YHAD 3]	120	3	17	Shamir, I. (LIK)
33	22.12.88	536	4	3	LIK 40	LAB 39	[SHAS 6]	[NRP 5]						120	3	12	Shamir, I. (LIK)
34	11.06.90	158	7	2	LIK 40	SHAS 6	NRP 5	THYA 3	TZOM 2	[IND 3]	[DHAT 2]	[MDET 2]		120	2	19	Shamir, I. (LIK)
35	16.11.90	79	7	2	LIK 40	SHAS 6	NRP 5	THYA 3	TZOM 2	[IND 3]	[DHAT 2]			120	2	19	Shamir, I. (LIK)
36	03.02.91	330	4	3	LIK 40	SHAS 6	NRP 5	THYA 3	AIS 4	[IND 3]	[DHAT 2]			120	2	20	Shamir, I. (LIK)
37	30.12.91	23	4	2	LIK 40	SHAS 6	NRP 5	THYA 3	AIS4	[IND 3]	[DHAT 2]			120	2	19	Shamir, I. (LIK)

ISRAEL 1948–1998

Gov	Begin	Dur	RfT	ToG	Py1	Py2	Py3	Py4	Py5	Py6	Py7	Py8	Py9	Seats	CPG	NOM	Prime Minister (py)
38	22.01.92	175	1	5	LIK 40	SHAS 6	NRP 5							120	2	17	Shamir, I. (LIK)
39	13.07.92	429	5	2	LAB 44	MRET 12	SHAS 6	[HDASH 3]	[ADP 2]					120	4	17	Rabin, I. (LAB)
40	15.09.93	466	7	2	LAB 44	MRET 12	SHAS 6	[HDASH 3]	[ADP 2]					120	4	16	Rabin, I. (LAB)
41	25.12.94	327	x	2	LAB 44	MRET 12	HDASH 3	[ADP 2]						120	4	21	Rabin, I. (LAB)
42	22.11.95	146	1	5	LAB 44	MRET 12	YI'UD 2	HDASH 3	[ADP 2]					120	4	20	Peres, S. (LAB)
43	18.06.96		3	3	LIK 32	SHAS 10	NRP 9	YB 7	UTJ 4	TW 4	[MOLDET 2]			120	2	18	Netanyahu, B. (LIK)

- [] Denotes party supporting the government without participating in it.
- Gov 0: provisional government.
- Gov 8: NRP is election co-operation of HMIZ & MIZR.
- Gov 20: Alignment=election coöperation of MAPAI, Ahdut Avoda(AA), MAPAM and RAFI; GAHAL=election co-operation of Herut and Liberals.
- Gov 22: Labour is election co-operation of MAPAI and MAPAM.
- Gov 26: LIKUD includes Shlomzion.
- Gov 27: DASH has 15 seats in Knesset, but a dissident faction decided not to co-operate in this government.
- Gov 33: Labour did not include MAPAM.
- Gov 39: Reason for Termination is withdrawl of SHAS from coalition.
- Gov 41: Reason for Termination is assasination of PM Rabin.
- Gov 42: YI'UD is breakaway faction of TZOMET.
- Gov 43: First government under new constitution with a directly elected PM. Likud includes GESHER and TZOMET.

ISRAEL 1948–1998

Gov	Deputy PM	Py	Foreign Affairs	Py	Defence	Py	Interior	Py	Justice	Py
0			Shertok, M.		Ben-Gurion, D.		Grünbaum, I. / Shitreet, B.		Rosenblüth, F.	PROG
1			Sharett, M.	MPAI	Ben-Gurion, D.	MPAI	Shapiro, M.H. / Shitreet, B.	URF / SEPH	Rosenblüth, F.	PROG
2			Sharett, M.	MPAI	Ben-Gurion, D.	MPAI	Shapiro, M.H. / Shitreet, B.	URF / SEPH	Rosen, P.	PROG
3			Sharett, M.	MPAI	Ben-Gurion, D.	MPAI	Shapiro, M.H. / Shitreet, B.	URF / SEPH	Rosen, P.	PROG
4			Sharett, M.	MPAI	Ben-Gurion, D.	MPAI	Shapiro, M.H. / Shitreet, B.	URF / MPAI	Joseph, D.	MPAI
5			Sharett, M.	MPAI	Ben-Gurion, D.	MPAI	Rokach, I. / Shitreet, B.	GZ / MPAI	Rosen, P.	PROG
6			Sharett, M.	MPAI	Lavon, P.	MPAI	Rokach, I. / Shitreet, B.	GZ / MPAI	Rosen, P.	PROG
7			Sharett, M.	MPAI	Ben-Gurion, D.	MPAI	Shapiro, M.H. / Shitreet, B.	HMIZ / MPAI	Rosen, P.	PROG
8			Sharett, M.	MPAI	Ben-Gurion, D.	MPAI	Ben-Yehuda, I. / Shitreet, B.	AA / MPAI	Rosen, P.	PROG
9			Sharett, M.	MPAI	Ben-Gurion, D.	MPAI	Ben-Yehuda, I. / Shitreet, B.	AA / MPAI	Rosen, P.	PROG
10			*Meyerson, G.	MPAI	Ben-Gurion, D.	MPAI	Ben-Yehuda, I. / Shitreet, B.	AA / MPAI	Rosen, P.	PROG
11			*Meyerson, G.	MPAI	Ben-Gurion, D.	MPAI	Ben-Yehuda, I. / Shitreet, B.	AA / MPAI	Rosen, P.	PROG
12			*Meir, G.	MPAI	Ben-Gurion, D.	MPAI	Shapiro, M.H. / Shitreet, B.	NRP / MPAI	Rosen, P.	PROG
13			*Meir, G.	MPAI	Ben-Gurion, D.	MPAI	Shapiro, M.H. / Shitreet, B.	NRP / MPAI	Rosen, P.	PROG

ISRAEL 1948–1998

Gov	Deputy PM	Py	Foreign Affairs	Py	Defence	Py	Interior	Py	Justice	Py
14			*Meir, G.	MPAI	Ben-Gurion, D.	MPAI	Shapiro, M.H. Shitreet, B.	NRP MPAI	Joseph, D.	MPAI
15	Eban, A.	MPAI	*Meir, G.	MPAI	Eshkol, L.	MPAI	Shapiro, M.H. Shitreet, B.	NRP MPAI	Joseph, D.	MPAI
16	Eban, A.	MPAI	*Meir, G.	MPAI	Eshkol, L.	MPAI	Shapiro, M.H. Shitreet, B.	NRP MPAI	Joseph, D.	MPAI
17			Eban, A.	MPAI	Eshkol, L.	MPAI	Shapiro, M.H. Shitreet, B.	NRP MPAI	Shapiro, Y.S.	MPAI
18			Eban, A.	MPAI	Dayan, M.	MPAI	Shapiro, M.H. Shitreet, B.	NRP MPAI	Shapiro, Y.S.	MPAI
19	Allon, Y.	AA	Eban, A.	MPAI	Dayan, M.	RAFI	Shapiro, M.H. Shitreet, B.	NRP MPAI	Shapiro, Y.S.	MPAI
20	Allon, Y.	AA	Eban, A.	MPAI	Dayan, M.	RAFI	Shapiro, M.H. Hillel, S.	NRP MPAI	Shapiro, Y.S.	MPAI
21	Allon, Y.	AA	Eban, A.	MPAI	Dayan, M.	RAFI	Shapiro, M.H. Hillel, S.	NRP MPAI	Shapiro, Y.S.	MPAI
22	Allon, Y.	AA	Eban, A.	MPAI	Dayan, M.	RAFI	Burg, J. Hillel, S.	NRP MPAI	Zadok, H.	MPAI
23	Allon, Y.	MPAI	Allon, Y.	MPAI	Peres, S.	MPAI	Hillel, S.	MPAI	Zadok, H.	MPAI
24	Allon, Y.	MPAI	Allon, Y.	MPAI	Peres, S.	MPAI	Burg, J. Hillel, S.	NRP MPAI	Zadok, H.	MPAI
25	Allon, Y.	MPAI	Allon, Y.	MPAI	Peres, S.	MPAI	Hillel, S.	MPAI	Zadok, H.	MPAI
26			Dayan, M.	IND	Weizmann, E.	LIK	Burg, J.	NRP		
27	Yadin, Y.	DASH	Dayan, M.	IND	Weizmann, E.	LIK	Burg, J.	NRP	Tamir, S.	DASH
28	Ehrlich, S. Levi, D.	LIK LIK	Shamir, I.	LIK	Sharon, A.	LIK	Burg, J.	NRP	Nissim, M.	LIK
29	Ehrlich, S. Levi, D.	LIK LIK	Shamir, I.	LIK	Sharon, A.	LIK	Burg, J.	NRP	Nissim, M.	LIK

ISRAEL 1948–1998

Gov	Deputy PM	Py	Foreign Affairs	Py	Defence	Py	Interior	Py	Justice	Py
30	Levi, D.	LIK	Shamir, I.	LIK	Arens, M.	LIK	Burg, J.	NRP	Nissim, M.	LIK
31	Shamir, I. / Navon, I. / Levi, D.	LIK / LAB / LIK	Shamir, I.	LIK	Rabin, I.	LAB	Bar-Lev, H.	LAB		
32	Peres, S. / Navon, I. / Levi, D.	LAB / LAB / LIK	Peres, S.	LAB	Rabin, I.	LAB	Bar-Lev, H.	LAB		
33	Peres, S. / Navon, I. / Levi, D.	LAB / LAB / LIK	Arens, M.	LIK	Rabin, I.	LAB	Bar-Lev, H.	LAB		
34	Levi, D. / Nissim, M.	LIK / LIK	Levi, D.	LIK	Arens, M.	LIK	Milo, R. / Der'i, A.	LIK / SHAS	Meridor, D.	LIK
35	Levi, D. / Nissim, M.	LIK / LIK	Levi, D.	LIK	Arens, M.	LIK	Milo, R. / Der'i, A.	LIK / SHAS	Meridor, D.	LIK
36	Levi, D. / Nissim, M.	LIK / LIK	Levi, D.	LIK	Arens, M.	LIK	Milo, R. / Der'i, A.	LIK / SHAS	Meridor, D.	LIK
37	Levi, D. / Nissim, M.	LIK / LIK	Levi, D.	LIK	Arens, M.	LIK	Milo, R. / Der'i, A.	LIK / SHAS	Meridor, D.	LIK
38	Levi, D. / Nissim, M.	LIK / LIK	Levi, D.	LIK	Arens, M.	LIK	Milo, R. / Der'i, A.	LIK / SHAS	Meridor, D.	LIK
39			Peres, S.	LAB	Rabin, I.	LAB	Der'i, A. / Shahal, M.	SHAS / LAB	Libai, D.	LAB
40			Peres, S.	LAB	Rabin, I.	LAB	Shahal, M.	LAB	Libai, D.	LAB
41	Peres, S.	LAB	Peres, S.	LAB	Rabin, I.	LAB	Baram, U. / Shahal, M.	LAB / LAB	Libai, D.	LAB
42			Baraq, E.	LAB	Peres, S.	LAB	Ramon, H. / Shahal, M.	LAB / LAB	Libai, D.	LAB

ISRAEL 1948–1998

Gov	Deputy PM	Py	Foreign Affairs	Py	Defence	Py	Interior	Py	Justice	Py
43	Levi, D.	LIK-GESH	Levi, D.	Gesher	Mordechai, Y.	LIK	Suissa, E.	SHAS	Ne'eman, Y.	IND
	Eitan, R.	LIK-TZOM					Kahalani, A.	TW		
	Hammer, Z.	NRP								
	Katzav, M.	LIK								

- Gov 1: Sharett, M., formerly Shertok, M.
- Gov 12: *Meir, G., formerly *Meyerson, G.

Gov	Finance	Py	Economic Aff.	Py	Labour	Py	Education	Py	Health	Py
0	Kaplan, E.				Bentov, M.					
1	Kaplan, E.	MPAI			*Meyerson, G.		Shazar, Z.	MPAI		
2	Kaplan, E.	MPAI			*Meyerson, G.		Remez, D.	MPAI	Shapiro, M.H.	URF
3	Kaplan, E.	MPAI			*Meyerson, G.		Remez, D.	MPAI	Shapiro, M.H.	URF
4	Kaplan, E.	MPAI			*Meyerson, G.		Dinaburg, B.	MPAI	Burg, J.	URF
5	Eshkol, L.	MPAI			*Meyerson, G.		Dinur, B.	MPAI	Saphir, J.	GZ
6	Eshkol, L.	MPAI			*Meyerson, G.		Dinur, B.	MPAI	Serlin, J.	GZ
7	Eshkol, L.	MPAI			*Meyerson, G.		Dinur, B.	MPAI	Joseph, D.	MPAI
8	Eshkol, L.	MPAI			*Meyerson, G.		Aranne, Z.	MPAI	Barzilai, I.	MPAM
9	Eshkol, L.	MPAI			*Meyerson, G.		Aranne, Z.	MPAI	Barzilai, I.	MPAM
10	Eshkol, L.	MPAI			Namil, M.		Aranne, Z.	MPAI	Barzilai, I.	MPAM
11	Eshkol, L.	MPAI			Namil, M.		Aranne, Z.	MPAI	Barzilai, I.	MPAM
12	Eshkol, L.	MPAI			Josephtahl, G.		Aranne, Z.	MPAI	Barzilai, I.	MPAM
13	Eshkol, L.	MPAI			Josephtahl, G.		Aranne, Z.	MPAI	Barzilai, I.	MPAM
14	Eshkol, L.	MPAI			Allon, Y.	AA	Eban, A.	MPAI	Shapiro, M.H.	NRP
15	Saphir, P.	MPAI			Allon, Y.	AA	Aranne, Z.	MPAI	Shapiro, M.H.	NRP

ISRAEL 1948–1998

Gov	Finance	Py	Economic Aff.	Py	Labour	Py	Education	Py	Health	Py
16	Saphir, P.	MPAI			Allon, Y.	AA	Aranne, Z.	MPAI	Shapiro, M.H.	NRP
17	Sapir, P.	MPAI			Allon, Y.	AA	Aranne, Z.	MPAI	Barzilai, I.	MPAM
18	Sapir, P.	MPAI			Allon, Y.	AA	Aranne, Z.	MPAI	Barzilai, I.	MPAM
19	Shareff, Z.	MPAI			Almogi, J.	RAFI	Aranne, Z.	MPAI	Barzilai, I.	MPAM
20	Sapir, P.	MPAI			Almogi, J.	RAFI	Allon, Y.	AA		
21	Sapir, P.	MPAI			Almogi, J.	RAFI	Allon, Y.	AA		
22	Sapir, P.	MPAI			Rabin, I.	MPAI	Allon, Y.	MPAI	Shemtov, V.	MPAM
23	Rabinowitz, Y.	MPAI			Baram, M.	MPAI	Yadlin, A.	MPAI	Shemtov, V.	MPAM
24	Rabinowitz, Y.	MPAI			Baram, M.	MPAI	Yadlin, A.	MPAI	Shemtov, V.	MPAM
25	Rabinowitz, Y.	MPAI			Baram, M.	MPAI	Yadlin, A.	MPAI	Shemtov, V.	MPAM
26	Ehrlich, S.	LIK					Hammer, Z.	NRP	Shostak, E.	LIK
27	Ehrlich, S.	LIK			Katz, I.	DASH	Hammer, Z.	NRP	Shostak, E.	LIK
28	Aridor, Y.	LIK	Meridor, D.	LIK	Abu-Hatzeira, A.	TAMI	Hammer, Z.	NRP	Shostak, E.	LIK
29	Aridor, Y.	LIK	Meridor, D.	LIK	Abu-Hatzeira, A.	TAMI	Hammer, Z.	NRP	Shostak, E.	LIK
30	Aridor, Y.	LIK	Meridor, D.	LIK	Uzan, A.	TAMI	Hammer, Z. Ne'eman, Y.	NRP THYA	Shostak, E.	LIK
31							Navon, I.	LAB		
32							Navon, I.	LAB		
33	Peres, S.	LAB	Moda'i, I.	LIK	Shamir, I.	LIK	Navon, I. Weizmann, E.	LAB LAB		
34	Moda'i, I.	LIK	Magen, D.	LIK	Shamir, I.	LIK	Hammer, Z. Ne'eman, Y.	NRP THYA	Olmert, E.	LIK
35	Moda'i, I.	LIK	Magen, D.	LIK	Shamir, I.	LIK	Hammer, Z. Ne'eman, Y.	NRP THYA	Olmert, E.	LIK
36	Moda'i, I.	LIK	Magen, D.	LIK	Shamir, I.	LIK	Hammer, Z. Ne'eman, Y.	NRP THYA	Olmert, E.	LIK
37	Moda'i, I.	LIK	Magen, D.	LIK	Shamir, I.	LIK	Hammer, Z. Ne'eman, Y.	NRP THYA	Olmert, E.	LIK

ISRAEL 1948-1998

Gov	Finance	Py	Economic Aff.	Py	Labour	Py	Education	Py	Health	Py
38	Moda'i, I.	LIK	Magen, D.	LIK	Shamir, I.		Hammer, Z.	NRP	Olmert, E.	LIK
39	Shochat, A.	LAB	Shitrit, S.	LAB	Rabin, I.		*Aloni, S.	MRET	Ramon, H.	LAB
40	Shochat, A.	LAB	Shitrit, S.	LAB	Rabin, I.		*Aloni, S.	MRET	Ramon, H.	LAB
41	Shochat, A.	LAB	Shitrit, S.	LAB	*Namir, O.		*Aloni, S.	MRET	Sneh, E.	LAB
42	Shochat, A.	LAB			*Namir, O.		Rubinstein, A.	MRET	Sneh, E.	LAB
43	Meridor, D.	LIK			Ishai, E.	SHAS	Hammer, Z. Begin, B.	NRP LIK	Hanegbi, T.	LIK

- Gov 5: Dinur, B., formerly Dinaburg, B.
- Gov 17: Sapir, P., formerly Saphir, P.

Gov	Housing	Py	Agriculture	Py	Industry/Trade	Py	Environment	Py
0			Zisling, A.		Bernstein, F.	MPAI		
1								
2			Lubianiker, P.	MPAI	Joseph, D.	MPAI		
3			Lubianiker, P.	MPAI	Geri, J.	NONA		
4			Eshkol, L.	MPAI	Geri, J.	NONA		
5			Naphtali, P.	MPAI	Joseph, D.	MPAI		
6			Naphtali, P.	MPAI	Bernstein, P.	GZ		
7			Naphtali, P.	MPAI	Bernstein, P.	GZ		
8			Looz, K.	MPAI	Napthali, P.	MPAI		
9			Looz, K.	MPAI	Saphir, P.	MPAI		
10			Looz, K.	MPAI	Saphir, P.	MPAI		
11			Looz, K.	MPAI	Saphir, P.	MPAI		

ISRAEL 1948-1998

Gov	Housing	Py	Agriculture	Py	Industry/Trade	Py	Environment	Py
12			Dayan, M.	MPAI	Saphir, P.	MPAI		
13			Dayan, M.	MPAI	Saphir, P.	MPAI		
14	Josephtal, G.	MPAI	Dayan, M.	MPAI	Saphir, P.	MPAI		
15	Almogi, J.	MPAI	Dayan, M.	MPAI	Saphir, P.	MPAI		
16	Almogi, J.	MPAI	Dayan, M.	MPAI	Saphir, P.	MPAI		
17	Bentov, M.	MPAM	Gvati, H.	MPAI	Zadok, H.	MPAI		
18	Bentov, M.	MPAM	Gvati, H.	MPAI	Zadok, H.	MPAI		
19	Bentov, M.	MPAM	Gvati, H.	MPAI	Zadok, H.	MPAI		
20	Shareff, Z.	MPAI	Gvati, H.	MPAI	Shareff, Z.	MPAI		
21	Shareff, Z.	MPAI	Gvati, H.	MPAI	Sapir, Y.	LIB		
22	Rabinowitz, Y.	MPAI	Gvati, H.	MPAI	Bar-Lev, H.	MPAI		
23	Ofer, A.	MPAI	Uzan, A.	MPAI	Bar-Lev, H.	MPAI		
24	Ofer, A.	MPAI	Uzan, A.	MPAI	Bar-Lev, H.	MPAI		
25	Ofer, A.	MPAI	Uzan, A.	MPAI	Bar-Lev, H.	MPAI		
26			Sharon, A.	LIK	Horrowitz, Y.	LIK		
27			Sharon, A.	LIK	Horrowitz, Y.	LIK	Patt, G.	LIK
28	Levi, D.	LIK	Ehrlich, S.	LIK	Patt, G.	LIK		
29	Levi, D.	LIK	Ehrlich, S.	LIK	Patt, G.	LIK		
30	Levi, D.	LIK	Grupper, P.	TAMI	Patt, G.	LIK		
31	Levi, D.	LIK			Sharon, A.	LIK		
32	Levi, D.	LIK			Sharon, A.	LIK		
33	Levi, D.	LIK			Sharon, A.	LIK		
34	Sharon, A.	LIK	Eitan, R.	TZOM	Nissim, M.	LIK	Shamir, I.	LIK
35	Sharon, A.	LIK	Eitan, R.	TZOM	Nissim, M.	LIK	Shamir, I.	LIK
36	Sharon, A.	LIK	Eitan, R.	TZOM	Nissim, M.	LIK	Shamir, I.	LIK
37	Sharon, A.	LIK			Nissim, M.	LIK	Shamir, I.	LIK

ISRAEL 1948–1998

Gov	Housing	Py	Agriculture	Py	Industry/Trade	Py	Environment	Py
38	Sharon, A.	LIK			Nissim, M.	LIK	Shamir, I.	LIK
39	Ben Eliezer, B.	LAB	Tzur, Y.	LAB	Harish ,M.	LAB	*Namir, O.	LAB
40	Ben Eliezer, B.	LAB	Tzur, Y.	LAB	Harish ,M.	LAB	*Namir, O.	LAB
41	Ben Eliezer, B.	LAB	Tzur, Y.	LAB	Harish ,M.	LAB	Sarid, Y.	MRET
42	Ben Eliezer, B.	LAB	Tzur, Y.	LAB	Harish ,M.	LAB	Sarid, Y.	MRET
43	Sharon, A.	LIK	Eitan, R.	LIK-TZOM	Sharansky, N.	YB	Eitan, R.	LIK-TZOM

Gov	Social Affairs (py)	Public Works (py)	Other (py)	Res
0		Bentov, M. Remez, D.	Shapiro, M.H. Fishman, J. Levine, I.M.	0
1	*Meyerson, G. (MPAI) Levine, I.M. (URP)	Remez, D. (MPAI)	Fishman, J. (URP) Shapiro, M.H. (URP)	0
2	*Meyerson, G. (MPAI) Levine, I.M. (URP)	Joseph, D. (MPAI)	Maimon, J. (URP) Shapiro, M.H. (URP)	0
3	*Meyerson, G. (MPAI) Levine, I.M. (URP)	Joseph, D. (MPAI)	Maimon, J. (URP) Shapiro, M.H. (URP)	0
4	Levine, I.M. (URP)	Pinchas, D. (URP)	Eshkol, L. (MPAI) Naphtali, P. (MPAI) Shapiro, M.H. (URP)	1

ISRAEL 1948–1998

Gov	Social Affairs (py)	Public Works (py)	Other (py)	Res
5	Shapiro, M.H. (HMIZ)	Serlin, J. (GZ) Burg, J. (MIZR)	Joseph, D. (MPAI) Lavon, P. (MPAI) Shapiro, M.H. (HMIZ)	1
6	Shapiro, M.H. (HMIZ)	Serlin, J. (GZ) Burg, J. (MIZR)	Aranne, Z. (MPAI) Joseph, D. (MPAI) Dinur, B. (MPAI) Shapiro, M.H. (HMIZ)	0
7	Shapiro, M.H. (HMIZ)	Aranne, Z. (MPAI) Burg, J. (MIZR)	Joseph, D. (MPAI) Shapiro, M.H. (HMIZ)	0
8	Shapiro, M.H. (NRP)	Carmel, M. (AA) Burg, J. (NRP)	Naphtali, P. (MPAI) Bentov, M. (MPAM) Shapiro, M.H. (NRP)	1
9	Shapiro, M.H. (NRP)	Carmel, M. (AA) Burg, J. (NRP)	Naphtali, P. (MPAI) Bentov, M. (MPAM) Shapiro, M.H. (NRP)	0
10	Ben-Gurion, D. (MPAI)	Carmel, M. (AA) Ben-Gurion, D. (MPAI)	Bentov, M. (MPAM)	0
11	Ben-Gurion, D. (MPAI)	Carmel, M. (AA) Ben-Gurion, D. (MPAI)	Bentov, M. (MPAM)	0
12	Burg, J. (NRP)	Ben-Aharon, Y. (AA)	Toledano, J.M. (NONA) Eban, A. (MPAI) Bentov, M. (MPAM)	0
13	Burg, J. (NRP)	Ben-Aharon, Y. (AA)	Toledano, J.M. (NONA) Eban, A. (MPAI) Bentov, M. (MPAM)	0
14	Burg, J. (NRP)	Ben-Aharon, Y. (AA) Sasson, E. (MPAI)	Josephtal, G. (MPAI) Wahrhaftig, Z. (NRP) Almogi, J. (MPAI)	0

ISRAEL 1948–1998

Gov	Social Affairs (py)	Public Works (py)	Other (py)	Res
15	Burg, J. (NRP)	Ben-Yehuda, I. (AA) / Sasson, E. (MPAI)	Wahrhaftig, Z. (NRP)	0
16	Burg, J. (NRP)	Ben-Yehuda, I. (AA) / Sasson, E. (MPAI)	Aranne, Z. (MPAI) / Almogi, J. (MPAI) / Wahrhaftig, Z. (NRP) / Govrin, A. (MPAI)	0
17	Burg, J. (NRP)	Sasson, E. (MPAI) / Carmel, M. (MPAI)	Aranne, Z. (MPAI) / Wahrhaftig, Z. (NRP) / Galili, I. (AA) / Kol, M. (ILIB)	1
18	Burg, J. (NRP)	Sasson, E. (MPAI) / Carmel, M. (MPAI)	Aranne, Z. (MPAI) / Wahrhaftig, Z. (NRP) / Galili, I. (AA) / Kol, M. (ILIB) / Begin, M. (HRUT)	2
19	Burg, J. (NRP)	Sasson, E. (MPAI) / Carmel, M. (MPAI)	Aranne, Z. (MPAI) / Wahrhaftig, Z. (NRP) / Galili, I. (AA) / Kol, M. (ILIB) / Begin, M. (HRUT) / Allon, Y. (AA)	0
20	Burg, J. (NRP)	Weizmann, E. (HRUT) / Rimalt, E. (LIB)	Wahrhaftig, Z. (NRP) / Kol, M. (ILIB) / Galili, I. (AA) / Peres, S. (RAFI) / Begin, M. (HRUT) / Doltzin, L. (LIB) / Shemtov, V. (MPAM) / Barzilai, I. (MPAM) / Landau, H. (HRUT)	0

ISRAEL 1948–1998

Gov	Social Affairs (py)	Public Works (py)	Other (py)	Res
21	Burg, J. (NRP)		Wahrhaftig, Z. (NRP) Kol, M. (ILIB) Galili, I. (AA) Peres, S. (RAFI) Shemtov, V. (MPAM) Barzilai, I. (MPAM)	0
22	Hazani, M. (NRP)	Yariv, A. (MPAI) Uzan, A. (MPAI)	Bar-Lev, H. (MPAI) Raphael, I. (NRP) Peres, S. (MPAI) Kol, M. (ILIB) Galili, I. (MPAI) Hausner, G. (ILIB) Rosen, S. (MPAM)	0
23		Yaakobi, G. (MPAI)	Yariv, A. (MPAI) Kol, M. (ILIB) Galili, I. (MPAI) Hausner, G. (ILIB) *Aloni, S. (CRIT) Rosen, S. (MPAM) Rabin, I. (MPAI)	0
24	Hazani, M. (NRP)	Yaakobi, G. (MPAI)	Raphael, I. (NRP) Yariv, A. (MPAI) Kol, M. (ILIB) Galili, I. (MPAI) Hausner, G. (ILIB) Rosen, S. (MPAM) Rabin, I. (MPAI)	1

ISRAEL 1948–1998

Gov	Social Affairs (py)	Public Works (py)	Other (py)	Res
25	Baram, M. (MPAI)	Yaakobi, G. (MPAI)	Yariv, A. (MPAI) Kol, M. (ILIB) Galili, I. (MPAI) Hausner, G. (ILIB) Rosen, S. (MPAM) Rabin, I. (MPAI)	0
26		Patt, G. (LIK) Moda'i, I. (LIK)	Hammer, Z. (NRP) Horrowitz, Y. (LIK) Abu-Hatzeira, A. (NRP) Levi, D. (LIK)	0
27	Katz, I. (DASH)	Patt, G. (LIK) Moda'i, I. (LIK) Amit, M. (DASH)	Hammer, Z. (NRP) Horrowitz, Y. (LIK) Abu-Hatzeira, A. (NRP) Levi, D. (LIK)	0
28	Abu-Hatzeira, A. (TAMI)	Zipori, M. (LIK) Corfu, H. (LIK) Berman, I. (LIK) Levi, D. (LIK)	Burg, J. (NRP) Abu-Hatzeira, A. (TAMI) Hammer, Z. (NRP) Sharir, A. (LIK) Moda'i, I. (LIK)	0
29	Abu-Hatzeira, A. (TAMI)	Zipori, M. (LIK) Corfu, H. (LIK) Berman, I. (LIK) Levi, D. (LIK)	Burg, J. (NRP) Abu-Hatzeira, A. (TAMI) Hammer, Z. (NRP) Sharir, A. (LIK) Moda'i, I. (LIK)	0

ISRAEL 1948–1998

Gov	Social Affairs (py)	Public Works (py)	Other (py)	Res
30	Uzan, A. (TAMI)	Moda'i, I. (LIK) Zipori, M. (LIK) Corfu, H. (LIK) Levi, D. (LIK)	Burg, J. (NRP) Uzan, A. (TAMI) Hammer, Z. (NRP) Sharir, A. (LIK) Ben-Porat, M. (IND) Doron, S. (LIK) Sharon, A. (LIK)	0
31		Levi, D. (LIK)	Weizmann, E. (LAB) Arens, M. (LIK) Sharir, A. (LIK) Burg, J. (NRP) Hurwitz, Y. (OMET) Peretz, I. (SHAS) Patt, G. (LIK) Tsur, G. (LAB) Shahal, G. (LAB) Shapiro, M.H. (MSHA)	0
32		Levi, D. (LIK)	Weizmann, E. (LAB) Arens, M. (LIK) Sharir, A. (LIK) Burg, J. (NRP) Hurwitz, Y. (OMET) Peretz, I. (SHAS) Patt, G. (LIK) Tsur, G. (LAB) Shahal, G. (LAB) Shapiro, M.H. (MSHA)	0
33	Shamir, I. (LIK)	Levi, D. (LIK) Shahal, M. (LAB)	Navon, I. (LAB) Nissim, M. (LIK)	2

ISRAEL 1948–1998

Gov	Social Affairs (py)	Public Works (py)	Other (py)	Res
34	Shamir, I. (LIK)	Ne'eman, Y. (THYA) Sharon, A. (LIK) Katsav, M. (LIK) Pinhasi, R. (LIK)	Hammer, Z. (NRP) Shaki, A. (NRP) Patt, G. (LIK) Peretz, I. (SHAS)	0
35	Shamir, I. (LIK)	Pinhasi, R. (LIK) Katsav, M. (LIK) Sharon, A. (LIK) Ne'eman, Y. (THYA)	Hammer, Z. (NRP) Patt, G. (LIK) Peretz, I. (SHAS)	0
36	Shamir, I. (LIK)	Ne'eman, Y. (THYA) Sharon, A. (LIK) Katsav, M. (LIK) Pinhasi, R. (LIK)	Hammer, Z. (NRP) Patt, G. (LIK) Peretz, I. (SHAS) Ze'evi, R. (MDET)	0
37	Shamir, I. (LIK)	Ne'eman, Y. (THYA) Sharon, A. (LIK) Katsav, M. (LIK) Pinhasi, R. (LIK)	Hammer, Z. (NRP) Patt, G. (LIK) Peretz, I. (SHAS) Ze'evi, R. (MDET)	0
38	Shamir, I. (LIK)	Sharon, A. (LIK) Katsav, M. (LIK) Pinhasi, R. (LIK)	Hammer, Z. (NRP) Shaki, A. (NRP) Patt, G. (LIK) Peretz, I. (SHAS)	0
39	Rabin, I. (LAB) Shitrit, S. (LAB)	Shahal, M. (LAB) Kessar, Y. (LAB) Rubinstein, A. (MRET)	Rabin, I. (LAB) Tzaban, Y. (MRET) Baram, U. (LAB)	1
40	Rabin, I. (LAB) Shitrit, S. (LAB)	*Aloni, S. (MRET) Kessar, Y. (LAB)	Rabin, I. (LAB) Tzaban, Y. (MERETZ) Baram, U. (LAB) Rubinstein, A. (MRET)	1
41	*Namir, O. (LAB)	*Aloni, S. (MRET) Segev, G. (YI'UD) Kessar, Y. (LAB)	Baram, U. (LAB) Tzaban, Y. (MRET) Rubinstein, A. (MRET)	2

ISRAEL 1948–1998

Gov	Social Affairs (py)	Public Works (py)	Other (py)	Res
42	*Namir, O. (LAB)	*Aloni, S. (MRET)	*Aloni, S. (MRET)	0
	Rubinstein, A. (MRET)	Ben Eliezer, B. (LAB)	Beilin, Y. (LAB)	
		Kessar, Y. (LAB)	Baram, U. (LAB)	
		Segev, G. (YI'UD)	Amital, Y. (IND)	
			Tzaban, Y. (MRET)	
			Tzur, Y. (LAB)	
			Rubinstein, A. (MRET)	
			Shitrit, S. (LAB)	
43	Ishai, E. (SHAS)	Sharon, A. (LIK)	Netanyahu, B. (LIK)	
		Levi, I. (NRP)	Hammer, Z. (NRP)	
		*Livnat, L. (LIK)	Katzav, M. (LIK)	
			Sharon, A. (LIK)	
			Edelstein, Y. (YB)	

25. ITALY

The Head of State, the President, is indirectly elected for a seven-year term. Although his or her duties are largely ceremonial, in periods of political instability the President can play a decisive role, albeit always constrained by parliament.

The constitution of 1948 states that Italy is a unitary state. However, since 1970 twenty regions have gained considerable regulatory powers, in addition to the special rights attributed to some territories in the North (Alto Adige) and the South (Sicily).

Parliament is bicameral. The Senate (Upper House) of 323 seats and the Camera dei Deputati (Lower House) of 630 seats are both elected for a fixed five year term. Since 1994 the electoral system has been a mix of proportional representation (LR-Hare) and constituency-based plurality voting. The regions for PR-voting vary markedly in size, although representation is proportional to the electorate. Plurality voting takes place in single-member constituencies of approximately 90,000 electors. There is a threshold of 4%.

Parliament has a quorum of at least 50 per cent of all members. Votes are carried by a majority of all votes cast. Some issues require a qualified majority ranging from an absolute majority of members to a two-thirds majority of all members present. Constitutional amendments require an absolute majority of all members. Referendums are optional and may be called by a portion of the electorate. The outcome is effectively binding. To improve the stability and durability of government the secret ballot in parliament has been eliminated.

Government faces both a vote of investiture and of no confidence. Losing either always results in resignation of the government. The President appoints the Prime Minister and other ministers. But the other ministers are put forward by the Prime Minister. The government is collectively responsible to parliament. Individual ministers may be also be members of parliament. The Prime Minister has no dominant position in government.

The Constitutional Court appointed equally by the judiciary, the President, and the legislature, reviews the constitutionality of laws, acts and procedures. The Court also judges conflicts between the state and sub-national bodies, and civilians.

ITALY 1945–1998

Gov	Begin	Dur	RfT	ToG	Py1	Py2	Py3	Py4	Py5	Seats	CPG	NoM	Prime Minister (py)
1	12.07.46	206	4	3	DC 207	PSIU 115	PRI 25	PCI 104	PLI 41	556	4	19	Gasperi, A. de (DC)
2	03.02.47	117	4	3	DC 207	PCI 104	PSI 115			556	4	15	Gasperi, A. de (DC)
3	31.05.47	198	2	5	DC 207	NDU 41				556	2	17	Gasperi, A. de (DC)
4	15.12.47	160	1	3	DC 207	PRI 25	PLI 41	PSDI 115		556	3	20	Gasperi, A. de (DC)
5	23.05.48	614	4	3	DC 305	PRI 9	PLI 19	PSDI 33		574	3	20	Gasperi, A. de (DC)
6	27.01.50	545	4	3	DC 305	PSDI 33	PRI 9			574	3	19	Gasperi, A. de (DC)
7	26.07.51	722	1	3	DC 305	PRI 9				574	3	16	Gasperi, A. de (DC)
8	17.07.53	31	5	4	DC 263					574	3	17	Gasperi, A. de (DC)
9	17.08.53	155	5	6	DC 263					590	3	17	Pella, G. (DC)
10	19.01.54	23	4	5	DC 263					590	3	19	Fanfani, A. (DC)
11	11.02.54	510	4	5	DC 263	PSDI 19	PLI 13			590	2	21	Scelba, M. (DC)
12	06.07.55	684	4	5	DC 263	PSDI 19	PLI 13			590	2	21	Segni, A. (DC)
13	20.05.57	407	1	4	DC 263					590	3	20	Zoli, A. (DC)
14	10.07.58	221	4	5	DC 273	PSDI 22				596	3	20	Fanfani, A. (DC)
15	16.02.59	403	5	4	DC 273					596	3	21	Segni, A. (DC)
16	25.03.60	123	5	4	DC 273					596	3	22	Tambroni, F. (DC)
17	26.07.60	575	2	4	DC 273					596	3	24	Fanfani, A. (DC)
18	21.02.62	485	1	5	DC 273	PSDI 22	PRI 6			596	3	24	Fanfani, A. (DC)
19	21.06.63	167	2	6	DC 260					630	3	23	Leone, G. (DC)
20	05.12.63	230	5	3	DC 260	PSI 87	PSDI 33	PRI 6		630	3	26	Moro, A. (DC)
21	22.07.64	581	5	3	DC 260	PSI 87	PSDI 33	PRI 6		630	3	26	Moro, A. (DC)
22	23.02.66	853	1	3	DC 260	PSI 87	PSDI 33	PRI 6		630	3	26	Moro, A. (DC)
23	25.06.68	170	2	4	DC 266					630	3	23	Leone, G. (DC)
24	12.12.68	236	4	3	DC 266	PSI 91	PRI 9			630	4	27	Rumor, M. (DC)
25	05.08.69	234	2	4	DC 266					630	3	24	Rumor, M. (DC)
26	27.03.70	132	4	3	DC 266	PSI+PSU 91	PRI 9			630	4	27	Rumor, M. (DC)

ITALY 1945–1998

Gov	Begin	Dur	RfT	ToG	Py1	Py2	Py3	Py4	Py5	Seats	CPG	NoM	Prime Minister (py)
27	06.08.70	205	4	3	DC 266	PSI+PSU 91	PRI 9			630	4	28	Colombo, E. (DC)
28	27.02.71	356	4	3	DC 266	PSI+PSU 91				630	4	27	Colombo, E. (DC)
29	18.02.72	129	1	4	DC 266					630	3	25	Andreotti, G. (DC)
30	26.06.72	439	5	2	DC 267	PSDI 29	PLI 21			630	2	26	Andreotti, G. (DC)
31	08.09.73	187	4	3	DC 267	PSI 61	PSDI 29	PRI 14		630	3	29	Rumor, M. (DC)
32	14.03.74	254	4	2	DC 267	PSI 61	PSDI 29			630	3	26	Rumor, M. (DC)
33	23.11.74	446	5	5	DC 267	PRI 14				630	3	25	Moro, A. (DC)
34	13.02.76	167	1	6	DC 267					630	3	22	Moro, A. (DC)
35	29.07.76	592	5	4	DC 263					630	3	22	Andreotti, G. (DC)
36	13.03.78	373	5	4	DC 263					630	3	21	Andreotti, G. (DC)
37	21.03.79	137	1	6	DC 263	PSDI 15	PRI 14			630	3	21	Andreotti, G. (DC)
38	05.08.79	243	5	5	DC 261	PSDI 21	PLI 9			630	2	25	Cossiga, F. (DC)
39	04.04.80	198	5	3	DC 261	PSI 62	PRI 15			630	4	28	Cossiga, F. (DC)
40	19.10.80	252	5	3	DC 261	PSI 62	PSDI 21	PRI 15		630	4	27	Forlani, A. (DC)
41	28.06.81	421	4	3	DC 261	PSI 62	PSDI 21	PRI 15	PLI 9	630	3	28	Spadolini, G. (PRI)
42	23.08.82	110	4	3	DC 261	PSI 62	PSDI 21	PRI 15	PLI 9	630	3	28	Spadolini, G. (PRI)
43	11.12.82	236	1	3	DC 261	PSI 62	PSDI 21	PLI 9		630	3	28	Fanfani, A. (DC)
44	04.08.83	1094	5	3	DC 225	PSI 73	PSDI 23	PLI 16	PRI 29	630	3	30	Craxi, B. (PSI)
45	02.08.86	259	1	3	DC 225	PSI 73	PSDI 23	PLI 16	PRI 29	630	4	30	Craxi, B. (PSI)
46	18.04.87	102	1	4	DC 225					630	3	25	Fanfani, A. (DC)
47	29.07.87	259	4	3	DC 234	PSI 94	PRI 21	PSDI 17	PLI 11	630	4	30	Goria, G. (DC)
48	13.04.88	466	5	3	DC 234	PSI 94	PRI 21	PSDI 17	PLI 11	630	4	30	De Mita, C. (DC)
49	23.07.89	631	4	3	DC 234	PSI 94	PRI 21	PSDI 17	PLI 11	630	4	32	Andreotti, G. (DC)
50	15.04.91	440	2	3	DC 234	PSI 94	PSDI 17	PLI 11		630	4	30	Andreotti, G. (DC)
51	28.06.92	305	x	3	DC 206	PSI 92	PSDI 16	PLI 17		630	4	25	Amati, G. (PSI)
52	29.04.93	8	4	3	DC 206	PSI 92	PDS 107	LVERDE 16		630	4	26	Ciampi, C.A. (NONA)
53	07.05.93	368	1	3	DC 206	PSI 92	PLI 17	PRI 27		630	4	26	Ciampi, C.A. (NONA)

ITALY 1945–1998

Gov	Begin	Dur	RfT	ToG	Py1	Py2	Py3	Py4	Py5	Seats	CPG	NoM	Prime Minister (py)
54	11.05.94	251	4	2	Freedom Alliance (366)					630	1	26	Berlusconi, S. (Forza)
55	17.01.95	484	6	x						630	x	21	Dini, L. (NONA)
56	18.05.96			5	Olive Tree 284					630	4	21	Prodi, R. (OT-PPI)

- Gov 51: Reason for Termination is desintegration of existing party system.
- Gov 54: Allliance consisted of Forza Italia (30), National Alliance (23), Lega Nord (N).
- Gov 55: Government of non-aligned ministers to get the 1996 budget through parliament. Reason for Terminiation: government succeeded in getting 1996 budget through parliament. The government remained in office in a caretaker capacity until the elections of May 1996.
- Gov 56: Olive Tree is election cooperation of PDS, PPI/Prodi List, Greens and others. Centre-Left combination.

Gov	Deputy PM	Py	Foreign Affairs	Py	Defence	Py	Interior	Py	Justice	Py
1			Gasperi, A. de	DC	Facchinetti, C. Micheli, G. Cingolani, M.	PRI DC DC	Gasperi, A. de	DC	Gullo, F.	PCI
2			Sforza, C.	IND	Gasparotto, L.	IND	Scelba, M	DC	Gullo, F.	PCI
3	Einaudi, L.	IND	Sforza, C.	IND	Cingolani, M.	DC	Scelba, M.	DC	Grassi, G.	NDU
4	Pacciardi, R. Einaudi, L. Saragat, G.	PRI PLI PSDI	Sforza, C.	IND	Fachinetti, C.	PRI	Scelba, M.	DC	Grassi, G.	PLI
5	Porzio, G. Piccioni, A. Saragat, G.	IND DC PSDI	Sforza, C.	IND	Pacciardi, R.	PRI	Scelba, M.	DC	Grassi, G.	PLI

ITALY 1945–1998

Gov	Deputy PM	Py	Foreign Affairs	Py	Defence	Py	Interior	Py	Justice	Py
6			Sforza, C.	PRI	Pacciardi, R.	PRI	Scelba, M.	DC	Piccioni, A.	DC
7	Piccioni, A.	DC	Gasperi, A. de	DC	Pacciardi, R.	PRI	Scelba, M.	DC	Zoli, A.	DC
8	Piccioni, A.	DC	Gasperi, A. de	DC	Pisanelli, G.	DC	Fanfani, A.	DC	Gonella, G.	DC
9			Pella, G.	DC	Taviani, P.E.	DC	Fanfani, A.	DC	Azara, A.	DC
10			Piccioni, A.	DC	Taviani, P.E.	DC	Andreotti, G.	DC	De Pietro, M.	DC
									Zoli, A.	DC
11	Saragat, G.	PSDI	Piccioni, A.	DC	Taviani, P.E.	DC	Scelba, M.	DC	Pietro, M. de	DC
12	Saragat, G.	PSDI	Martino, G.	PLI	Taviani, P.E.	DC	Tambroni, F.	DC	Moro, A	DC
13	Pella, G.	DC	Pella, G.	DC	Taviani, P.E.	DC	Tambroni, F.	DC	Gonella, G.	DC
14	Segni, A.	DC	Fanfani, A.	DC	Segni, A.	DC	Tambroni, F.	DC	Gonella, G.	DC
15			Pella, G.	DC	Andreotti, G.	DC	Segni, A.	DC	Gonella, G.	DC
16			Segni, A.	DC	Andreotti, G.	DC	Spataro, G.	DC	Gonella, G.	DC
17	Piccioni, A.	DC	Segni, A.	DC	Andreotti, G.	DC	Scelba, M.	DC	Gonella, G.	DC
18	Piccioni, A.	DC	Segni, A.	DC	Andreotti, G.	DC	Taviani, P.E.	DC	Bosco, G.	DC
19	Piccioni, A.	DC	Piccioni, A.	DC	Andreotti, G.	DC	Rumor, M.	DC	Bosco, G.	DC
20	Nenni, P.	PSI	Saragat, G.	PSDI	Andreotti, G.	DC	Taviani, P.E.	DC	Reale, O.	PRI
21	Nenni, P.	PSI	Saragat, G.	PSDI	Andreotti, G.	DC	Taviani, P.E.	DC	Reale, O.	PRI
22	Nenni, P.	PSI	Fanfani, A.	DC	Tremelloni, R.	PSDI	Taviani, P.E.	DC	Reale, O.	PRI
23			Medici, G.	DC	Gui, L.	DC	Restivo, F.	DC	Gonella, G.	DC
24	Martino, F. De	PSI	Nenni, P.	PSI	Gui, L.	DC	Restivo, F.	DC	Gava, S.	DC
25			Moro, A.	DC	Gui, L.	DC	Restivo, F.	DC	Gava, S.	DC
26	Martino, F. De	PSI	Moro, A.	DC	Tanassi, M.	PSU	Restivo, F.	DC	Reale, O.	PRI
27	Martino, F. De	PSI	Moro, A.	DC	Tanassi, M.	PSU	Restivo, F.	DC	Reale, O.	PRI
28	Martino, F. De	PSI	Moro, A.	DC	Tanassi, M.	PSU	Restivo, F.	DC	Colombo, E.	DC
29			Moro, A.	DC	Restivo, F.	DC	Rumor, R.	DC	Gonella, G.	DC
30			Medici, G.	DC	Tanassi, M.	PSDI	Rumor, R.	DC	Gonella, G.	DC
31			Moro, A.	DC	Tanassi, M.	PSDI	Taviani, P.E.	DC	Zagari, M.	PSI

ITALY 1945–1998

Gov	Deputy PM	Py	Foreign Affairs	Py	Defence	Py	Interior	Py	Justice	Py
32			Moro, A.	DC	Andreotti, G.	DC	Taviani, P.E.	DC	Zagari, M.	PSI
33	Malfa, U. La	PRI	Rumor, M.	DC	Forlani, A.	DC	Gui, L.	DC	Reale, O.	PRI
34			Rumor, M.	DC	Forlani, A.	DC	Cossiga, F.	DC	Bonifacio, F.P.	DC
35			Forlani, A.	DC	Lattanzio, V.	DC	Cossiga, F.	DC	Bonifacio, F.P.	DC
36			Forlani, A.	DC	Ruffini, A.	DC	Cossiga, F.	DC	Bonifacio, F.P.	DC
37	Malfa, U. La	PRI	Forlani, A.	DC	Ruffini, A.	DC	Rognoni, V.	DC	Morlino, T.	DC
38			Malfatti, F.	DC	Ruffini, A.	DC	Rognoni, V.	DC	Morlino, T.	DC
39			Colombo, E.	DC	Lagorio, L.	PSI	Rognoni, V. / Giannini, M.S.	DC / PSI	Morlino, T.	DC
40			Colombo, E.	DC	Lagorio, L.	PSI	Rognoni, V. / Darida, C.	DC / DC	Sarti, A.	DC
41			Colombo, E.	DC	Lagorio, L.	PSI	Rognoni, V. / Schietroma, D.	DC / PSDI	Darida, C.	DC
42			Colombo, E.	DC	Lagorio, L.	PSI	Rognoni, V. / Schietroma, D.	DC / PSDI	Darida, C.	DC
43			Colombo, E.	DC	Lagorio, L.	PSI	Rognoni, V. / Schietroma, D.	DC / PSDI	Darida, C.	DC
44	Forlani, A.	DC	Andreotti, G.	DC	Spadolini, G.	PRI	Scalfaro, O.L. / Gaspari, R.	DC / DC	Martinazzoli, M.	DC
45	Forlani, A.	DC	Andreotti, G.	DC	Spadolini, G.	PRI	Scalfaro, O.L. / Gaspari, R.	DC / DC	Rognoni, V.	DC
46			Andreotti, G.	DC	Gaspari, R.	DC	Scalfaro, O.L. / Paladin, L.	DC / NONA	Rognoni, V.	DC
47	Amato, G.	PSI	Andreotti, G.	DC	Zazone, V.	PLI	Fanfani, A. / Santuz, G.	DC / DC	Vassali, G.	PSI
48	De Michelis, G.	PSI	Andreotti, G.	DC	Zazone, V.	PLI	Gava, A. / Pomicino, P.	DC / DC	Vassali, G.	PSI

ITALY 1945–1998

Gov	Deputy PM	Py	Foreign Affairs	Py	Defence	Py	Interior	Py	Justice	Py
49	Martelli, C.	PSI	De Michelis, G.	PSI	Martinazzoli, M.	DC	Gava, A. / Gaspari, R.	DC / DC	Vassali, G.	PSI
50	Martelli, C.	PSI	De Michelis, G.	PSI	Rognoni, V.	DC	Scotti, V. / Martinazzoli, M. / Conte, C. / Gaspari, R. / *Boniver, M.	DC / DC / PSI / DC / PSI	Martelli, C.	PSI
51			Scotti, V.	DC	Ando, S.	PSI	Mancino, N. / Conte, C.	DC / PSI	Martelli, C.	PSI
52			Andreatta, B.	DC	Fabbri, F.	PSI	Mancino, N. / Cassese, S. / Elia, L.	DC / NONA / DC	Conso, G.	NONA
53			Andreatta, B.	DC	Fabbri, F.	PSI	Mancino, N. / Elia, L. / Cassese, S.	DC / DC / NONA	Conso, G.	NONA
54	Tatarella, G. / Maroni, R.	AN / LN	Martino, A.	FI	Previti, C.	FI	Maroni, R. / Urbani, G. / Speroni, F.E.	LN / FI / LN	Biondi, A.	FI
55			*Agnelli, S.		Corcione, D.		Brancaccio, A. / Frattini, F. / Motzo G.		Manusco, F.	
56	Veroni, W.	OT-PDS	Dini, L.	OT-IND	Andreatta, B.	OT	Napolitano, G. / Bassanini, F.	OT-PDS / OT	Flick, G.M.	OT-IND

ITALY 1945–1998

Gov	Finance	Py	Economic Aff.	Py	Labour	Py	Education	Py	Health	Py
1	Scoccimarro, M.	PCI			D'Aragona, L.	PSIU	Gonella, G.	DC		
	Corbino, E.	PLI								
2	Campilli, P.	DC			Romita, G.	PSI	Gonella, G.	DC		
3	Einaudi, L.	IND			Fanfani, A.	DC	Gonella, G.	DC		
	Pella, G.	DC								
	Vecchio, G. del	IND								
4	Einaudi, L.	PLI			Fanfani, A.	DC	Gonella, G.	DC		
	Pella, G.	DC								
	Vecchio, G. del	IND								
5	Vanoni, E.	DC			Fanfani, A.	DC	Gonella, G.	DC		
	Pella, G.	DC								
6	Vanoni, E.	DC			Marazza, A.	DC	Gonella, G.	DC		
	Pella, G.	DC								
7	Vanoni, E.	DC			Rubinacci, L.	DC	Segni, A.	DC		
8	Vanoni, E.	DC			Rubinacci, L	DC	Bettiol, G.	DC		
	Pella, G.	DC								
9	Pella, G.	DC			Rubinacci, L.	DC	Segni, A.	DC		
	Vanoni, E.	DC								
	Gava, S.	DC								
10	Vanoni, E.	DC			Gui, L.	DC	Tosato, E.	DC		
	Gava, S.	DC								
11	Tremelloni, R.	PSDI			Vigorelli, E.	PSDI	Martino, G.	PLI		
	Vanoni, E.	DC								
	Gava, S.	DC								
12	Andreotti, G.	DC			Vigorelli, E.	PSDI	Rossi, P.	PSDI		
	Gava, S.	DC								
	Vanoni, E.	DC								

ITALY 1945–1998

Gov	Finance	Py	Economic Aff.	Py	Labour	Py	Education	Py	Health	Py
13	Zoli, A. Andreotti, G. Medici, G.	DC DC DC			Gui, L.	DC	Moro, A.	DC		DC
14	Preti, L. Medici, G. Andreotti, G.	PSDI DC DC			Vigorelli, E.	PSDI	Moro, A.	DC		
15	Taviani, E. Tambroni, F.	DC DC			Zaccagnini, B.	DC	Medici, G.	DC	Giardina, C.	DC
16	Tambroni, F. Trabucchi, G. Taviani, P.	DC DC DC			Zaccagnini, B.	DC	Medici, G.	DC	Giardina, C.	DC
17	Pella, G. Taviani, P. Trabucchi, G.	DC DC DC			Sullo, F.	DC	Bosco, G.	DC	Giardina, C.	DC
18	Trabucchi, G. Malfa, U. La Tremelloni, R.	DC PRI PSDI			Bertinelli, V.	PSDI	Gui, L.	DC	Jervolino, A.R.	DC
19	Martinelli, M. Medici, G. Colombo, E.	DC DC DC			Fave, U. delle	DC	Gui, L.	DC	Jervolino, A.R.	DC
20	Tremelloni, R. Giolitti, A. Colombo, E.	PSDI PSI DC			Bosco, G.	DC	Gui, L.	DC	Mancini, G.	PSI
21	Tremelloni, R. Colombo, E. Pieraccini, G.	PSDI DC PSI					Gui, L.	DC	Mariotti, PSI	
22	Preti, L. Pieraccini, G. Colombo, E.	PSDI PSI DC			Bosco, G.	DC	Gui, L.	DC	Mariotti, L.	PSI

326

ITALY 1945–1998

Gov	Finance	Py	Economic Aff.	Py	Labour	Py	Education	Py	Health	Py
23	Ferrari-Aggradi, M. Colombo, E.	DC DC	Colombo, E.	DC	Bosco, G.	DC	Scaglia, G.B.	DC	Lanzini, E.	DC
24	Reale, O. Preti, L. Colombo, E.	PRI PSI DC			Brodolini, G.	PSI	Sullo, F.	DC	Ripamonti, C.	DC
25	Caron, G. Bosco, G. Colombo, E.	DC DC DC			Donat-Cattin, C.	DC	Ferrari-Aggradi, M.	DC	Ripamonti, C.	DC
26	Preti, L. Giolitti, A. Colombo, E.	PSU PSI DC	Giolitti, A.	PSI	Donat-Cattin, C.	DC	Misasi, R.	DC	Mariotti, L.	PSI
27	Preti, L. Giolitti, A. Ferrari-Aggradi, M.	PSU PSI DC	Giolitti, A.	PSI	Donat-Cattin, C.	DC	Misasi, R.	DC	Mariotti, L.	PSI
28	Preti, L. Giolitti, A. Ferrari-Aggradi, M.	PSU PSI DC	Giolitti, A.	PSI	Donat-Cattin, C.	DC	Misasi, R.	DC	Mariotti, L.	PSI
29	Taviani, P.E. Pella, G. Colombo, E.	DC DC DC	Taviani, P.E.	DC	Donat-Cattin, C.	DC	Misasi, R.	DC	Valsecchi, A.	DC
30	Valsecchi, A. Taviani, P.E. Malagodi, G.	DC DC PLI	Taviani, P.E.	DC	Coppo, D.	DC	Scalfaro, O.L.	DC	Gasperi, R.	DC
31	Colombo, E. Giolitti, A. Malfa, U. La	DC PSI PRI			Bertoldi, L.	PSI	Malfatti, F.M.	DC	Gui, L.	DC

ITALY 1945–1998

Gov	Finance	Py	Economic Aff.	Py	Labour	Py	Education	Py	Health	Py
32	Tanassi, M. Giolitti, A. Colombo, E.	PSDI PSI DC	Giolitti, A.	PSI	Bertoldi, L.	PSI	Malfatti, F.M.	DC	Colombo, V.	DC
33	Visentini, B. Colombo, E.	PRI DC	Andreotti, G.	DC	Toros, M.	DC	Malfatti, F.M. Pedini, M.	DC DC	Gullotti, A.	DC
34	Stammati, G. Andreotti, G. Colombo, E.	DC DC DC	Andreotti, G.	DC	Toros, M.	DC	Malfatti, F.M.	DC	Dal Falco, L.	DC
35	Pandolfi, F.M. Stammati, G. Morlino, T.	DC DC DC	Morlino, T.	DC	*Anselmi, T.	DC	Malfatti, F.M.	DC	Dal Falco, L.	DC
36	Malfatti, F.M. Morlino, T.	DC DC	Pandolfi, F.M.	DC	Scotti, V.	DC	Pedini, M.	DC	*Anselmi, T.	DC
37	Malfa, U. La Malfatti, F.M. Pandolfi, F.M.	PRI DC DC			Scotti, V.	DC	Spadolini, G.	PRI	*Anselmi, T.	DC
38	Reviglio, M. Pandolfi, F.M. Andreatta, B.	NONA DC DC			Scotti, V.	DC	Valitutti, S. Scaglia, V.	PLI DC	Altissimo, R.	PLI
39	Reviglio, M. Malfa, G. La Pandolfi, F.M.	PSI PRI DC			Foschi, F.	DC	Sarti, A. Balzamo, V.	DC PSI	Aniasi, A.	PSI
40	Reviglio, F. Andreatta, B. Malfa, G. La	PSI DC PRI			Foschi, F.	DC	Bodrato, G. Romita, P.L.	DC PSDI	Aniasi, A.	PSI
41	Formica, S. Andreatta, B. Malfa, G. La	PSI DC PRI	Malfa, G. La	PRI	Giesi, M. De	PSDI	Bodrato, G. Tesini, G.	DC DC	Altissimo, R.	PLI

328

ITALY 1945–1998

Gov	Finance	Py	Economic Aff.	Py	Labour	Py	Education	Py	Health	Py
42	Formica, S. Andreatta, B. Malfa, G. La	PSI DC PRI	Malfa, G. La	PRI	Giesi, M. De	PSDI	Bodrato, G. Tesini, G.	DC DC	Altissimo, R.	PLI
43	Forte, F. Bodrato, G. Goria, G.	PSI DC DC			Scotti, V.	DC	Falcucci, F. Romita, P.L.	DC PSDI	Altissimo, R.	PLI
44	Visentini, B. Longo, P. Goria, G.	PRI PSDI DC			Michelis, G. De	PSI	Falcucci, F. Granelli, L.	DC DC	Degan, C.	DC
45	Visentini, B. Romita, P.L. Goria, G.	PRI PSDI DC			Michelis, G. De	PSI	Falcucci, F. Granelli, L.	DC DC	Donat-Cattin, C.	DC
46	Guarino, G. Goria, G.	NONA DC			Gorrieri, E.	NONA	Granelli, L. Falcucci, F.	DC DC	Donat-Cattin, C.	DC
47	Gava, A. Colombo, E.	DC DC	Colombo, E.	DC	Formica, S.	PSI	Galloni, G. Ruberti, A.	DC PSI	Donat-Cattin, C.	DC
48	Amato, G. Fanfani, A. Colombo, E.	PSI DC DC	Fanfani, A.	DC	Formica, S.	PSI	Galloni, G. Ruberti, A.	DC PSI	Donat-Cattin, C.	DC
49	Carli, G. Pomicino, P. Formica, S.	DC DC PSI			Donat-Cattin, C.	DC	Mattarella, S. Ruberti, A.	DC PSI	De Lorenzo, F.	PLI
50	Carli, G. Pomicino, P.C. Formica, S.R.	DC DC PSI			Marini, F.	DC	Misasi, R. Ruberti, A.	DC PSI	De Lorenzo, F.	PLI
51	Goria, G. Barrucci, P. Reviglio, F.	DC NONA PSI	Reviglio, F.	PSI	Christofori, N.	DC	Fontana, A. *Jervolino, R.R.	DC DC	De Lorenzo, F.	PLI

ITALY 1945–1998

Gov	Finance	Py	Economic Aff.	Py	Labour	Py	Education	Py	Health	Py
52	Spaventa, L. Visco, V. Barrucci, P.	NONA PDS DC	Spaventa, L.	NONA	Giugni, G.	PSI	*Jervolino, R.R. Berlinguer, L.	DC PDS	*Caravaglia, M.P.	DC
53	Spaventa, L. Visco, V. Barrucci, P. Gallo, F.	NONA PDS DC NONA	Spaventa, L.	NONA	Giugni, G.	PSI	*Jervolino, R.R. Colombo, U.	DC NONA	*Caravaglia, M.P.	DC
54	Dini, L. Pagliarini, G. Tremonti, G.	IND LN IND	Mastella, C.	CCD	D'Onofrio, F. Podesta, S.	UDC LN	Costa, R.	UDC		
55	Dini, L. Fantozzi, A. Masera, R.				Treu, T.		Lombardi, G. Salvini, G.		Guzzanti, E.	
56	Ciampi, C.A. Visco, V.	OT-IND OT-PDS			Treu, T.	OT	Berlinguer, L.	OT	*Bindy, R.	OT

Gov	Housing	Py	Agriculture	Py	Industry/Trade	Py	Environment	Py
1			Segni, A.	DC	Morandi, R. Campilli, P.	PSIU DC		
2			Segni, A.	DC	Morandi, R. Vanoni, E.	PSI DC		
3			Segni, A.	DC	Togni, G. Merzagora, C.	DC IND		
4			Segni, A.	DC	Tremelloni, R. Merzagora, C.	PSDI IND		
5			Segni, A.	DC	Lombardo, M. Merzagora, C.	PSDI IND		

ITALY 1945–1998

Gov	Housing	Py	Agriculture	Py	Industry/Trade	Py	Environment	Py
6			Segni, A.	DC	Togni, G. Lombardo, M.	DC PSDI		
7			Fanfani, A.	DC	Campilli, P. Malfa, U. La Cappa, P.	DC PRI DC		
8			Salomone, R.	DC	Gava, S. Taviani, P.E.	DC DC		
9			Salomone, R.	DC	Malvestiti, P. Turroni, B.	DC DC		
10			Medici, G.	DC	Aldisio, S. dell'Amore, G.	DC IND		
11			Medici, G.	DC	Villabruna, B. Martinelli, M.	PLI DC		
12			Colombo, E.	DC	Cortese, G. Mattarella, B.	PLI DC		
13			Colombo, E.	DC	Gava, S. Bo, G. Carli, L.	DC DC NONA		
14			Ferrari-Aggradi, M.	DC	Bo, G. Starnuti, E. Colombo, E.	DC PSDI DC		
15			Rumor, M.	DC	Colombo, E. Bo, R. Del Ferrari-Aggradi, M.	DC DC DC		
16			Rumor, M.	DC	Colombo, E. Martinelli, M. Ferrari-Aggradi, M.	DC DC DC		

ITALY 1945–1998

Gov	Housing	Py	Agriculture	Py	Industry/Trade	Py	Environment	Py
17			Rumor, M.	DC	Colombo, E.	DC		
					Martinelli, M.	DC		
					Bo, G.	DC		
18			Rumor, M.	DC	Colombo, E.	DC		
					Preti, L.	PSDI		
					Bo, G.	DC		
19			Mattarella, B.	DC	Trabucchi, G.	DC		
					Bo, G.	DC		
20			Ferrari-Aggradi, M.	DC	Medici, G.	DC		
					Mattarella, B.	DC		
					Bo, G.	DC		
21			Ferrari-Aggradi, M.	DC	Medici, G.	DC		
					Mattarella, B.	DC		
					Bo, G.	DC		
22			Restivo, F.	DC	Andreotti, G.	DC		
					Tolloy, G.	PSI		
					Bo, G.	DC		
23			Sedati, G.	DC	Andreotti, G.	DC		
					Russo, C.	DC		
					Bo, G.	DC		
24			Valsecchi, A.	DC	Tanassi, M.	PSI		
					Colombo, V.	DC		
					Forlani, A.	DC		
25			Sedati, G.	DC	Magri, D.	DC		
					Misasi, R.	DC		
					Malfatti, F.M.	DC		

ITALY 1945–1998

Gov	Housing	Py	Agriculture	Py	Industry/Trade	Py	Environment	Py
26			Natali, L.	DC	Gava, S. / Zagari, M. / Piccoli, F.	DC / PSI / DC		
27			Natali, L.	DC	Gava, S. / Zagari, M. / Piccoli, F.	DC / PSI / DC		
28			Natali, L.	DC	Gava, S. / Zagari, M. / Piccoli, F.	DC / PSI / DC		
29			Natali, L.	DC	Ripamonti, C. / Piccoli, F.	DC / DC		
30			Natali, L.	DC	Ferri, M. / Matteotti, M. / Ferrari-Aggradi, M.	PSDI / PSDI / DC		
31			Ferrari-Aggradi, M.	DC	Mita, C. De / Matteotti, G. / Gulotti, A.	DC / PSDI / DC		
32			Bisaglia, A.	DC	Mita, C. De / Matteotti, G. / Gulotti, A.	DC / PSDI / DC		
33			Marcora, G.	DC	Donat-Cattin, C. / De Mita, C. / Bisaglia, A.	DC / DC / DC	Spadolini, G.	PRI
34			Marcora, G.	DC	Donat-Cattin, C. / De Mita, C. / Bisaglia, A.	DC / DC / DC	Pedini, M.	DC
35			Marcora, G.	DC	Donat-Cattin, C. / Ossola, R. / Bisaglia, A.	DC / NONA / DC		

ITALY 1945–1998

Gov	Housing	Py	Agriculture	Py	Industry/Trade	Py	Environment	Py
36			Marcora, G.	DC	Donat-Cattin, C. Ossola, R. Bisaglia, A.	DC NONA DC	Antoniozzi, D.	DC
37			Marcora, G.	DC	Nicolazzi, F. Stammati, G. Bisaglia, A.	PSDI DC DC		
38			Marcora, G.	DC	Bisaglia, A. Stammati, G. Lombardini, S.	DC DC DC	Ariosto, E.	PSDI
39			Marcora, G.	DC	Bisaglia, A. Manca, E. Michelis, G. De	DC PSI PSI	Biasini, O.	PRI
40			Bartolomei, G.	DC	Bisaglia, A. Manca, E. Michelis, G. De	DC PSI PSI	Biasini, O.	PRI
41			Bartolomei, G.	DC	Marcora, G. Capria, N. Michelis, G. Di	DC PSI PSI	Scotti, V.	DC
42			Bartolomei, G.	DC	Marcora, G. Capria, N. Michelis, G. Di	DC PSI PSI	Scotti, V.	DC
43			Mannino, C.	DC	Pandolfi, F.M. Capria, N. Michelis, G. Di	DC PSI PSI	Vernola, N.	DC
44			Pandolfi, F.M.	DC	Altissimo, R. Capria, N. Darida, C.	PLI PSI DC	Biondi, A.	PLI

ITALY 1945–1998

Gov	Housing	Py	Agriculture	Py	Industry/Trade	Py	Environment	Py
45			Pandolfi, F.M.	DC	Zazone, V. Formica, S. Degan, C. Darida, C.	PLI PSI DC DC	Lorenzo, F. De	PLI
46			Pandolfi, F.M.	DC	Tavaglini, G. Piga, F. Sarcinelli, M. Degan, C. Darida, C.	NONA NONA NONA DC DC	Pavan, M.	NONA
47			Pandolfi, F.M.	DC	Battaglia, A. Granelli, L. Ruggiero, R. Prandini, G.	PRI DC PSI DC	Ruffolo, G.	PSI
48			Mannino, C.	DC	Santuz, G. Battaglia, A. Ruggiero, R. Prandini, G. Fracanzani, C.	DC PRI PSI DC DC	Ruffolo, G.	PSI
49			Mannino, C.	DC	Battaglia, A. Ruggiero, R. Vizzini, C. Fracanzani, C.	PRI PSI PSDI DC	Ruffolo, G.	PSI
50			Goria, G.	DC	Andreotti, G. Bodrato, G. Lattanzio, V.	DC DC DC	Ruffolo, G.	PSI
51			Fontana, A.	DC	Vitalone, C. Guarino, G.	DC NONA	Ripa de Meana, C.	PSI
52			Diana, A.	DC	Savona, P. Baratta, P.	PRI PSI	Rutelli, F.	Greens

ITALY 1945–1998

Gov	Housing	Py	Agriculture	Py	Industry/Trade	Py	Environment	Py
53	Diana, A.	DC			Savona, P. / Baratta, P.	PRI / PSI	Spini, V.	PSI
54			*Poli Bortoni, A.	AN	Bernini, G. / Gnutti, V.	FI / LN	Matteoli, A.	AN
55	Lucchetti, W.				Clo', A.		Baratta, P.	
56	Pinto, M.	OT			Bersani, P. / Fantozzi, A.	OT / OT	Ranchi, E.	OT / OT-Greens

Gov	Social Affairs (py)	Public Works (py)	Other (py)	Res
1	Sereni, E. (PCI)	Aldisio, S. (DC) / Scelba, M. (DC) / Romita, G. (PSIU)	Ferrari, G. (PCI) / Macrelli, C. (PRI) / Nenni, P. (PSIU)	0
2		Sereni, E. (PCI) / Aldisio, S. (DC) / Ferrari, G. (PCI) / Cacciatore, L. (PSI)		0
3	Fanfani, A. (DC)	Tupini, U. (DC) / Corbellini, G. (IND) / Cappa, P. (DC) / Merlin, U. (DC)		0
4	Fanfani, A. (DC)	Tupini, U. (DC) / Corbellini, G. (IND) / d'Arragona, L. (PSDI) / Cappa, P. (DC)	Togni, G. (DC)	0

ITALY 1945–1998

Gov	Social Affairs (py)	Public Works (py)	Other (py)	Res
5	Fanfani, A. (DC)	Tupini, U. (DC) Corbellini, G. (DC) Jervolino, A.R. (DC)	Giovannini, A. (PLI) Tremelloni, R. (PSDI)	0
6		Aldisio, S. (DC) D'Aragona, L. (PSDI) Simonini, A. (PSDI) Spataro, G. (DC)	Gasperi, A. de (DC) Campilli, P. (DC) Malfa, U. La (PRI) Petrilli, R. (DC)	0
7	Rubinacci, L. (DC)	Malvestiti, P. (DC) Aldisio, S. (DC) Spataro, G. (DC) Sforza, C. (PRI)	0	
8	Rubinacci, L. (DC)	Spataro, G. (DC) Togni, G. (DC) Merlin, U. (DC) Mattarella, B. (DC)	Campilli, P. (DC)	0
9		Mattarella, B. (DC) Panetti, M. (DC) Tambroni, F. (DC) Merlin, U. (DC)	Campilli, P. (DC) Scoca, S. (DC)	0
10	Gui, L. (DC)	Merlin, U. (DC) Tambroni, F. (DC) Mattarella, B. (DC) Cassiani, G. (DC)	Tupini, U. (DC) Campilli, P. (DC)	0
11	Vigorelli, E. (PSDI)	Romita, G. (PSDI) Tambroni, F. (DC) Cassiani, G. (DC) Mattarella, B. (DC)	Saragat, G. (PSDI) Ponti, G. (DC) Tupini, U. (DC) Campilli, P. (DC) Caro, R. de (PLI)	1

ITALY 1945–1998

Gov	Social Affairs (py)	Public Works (py)	Other (py)	Res
12	Vigorelli, E. (PSDI)	Romita, G. (PSDI) Angellini, A. (DC) Cassiani, G. (DC) Braschi, G. (DC)	Caro, R. de (PLI) Campilli, P. (DC) Gonella, G. (DC)	1
13		Angelini, A. (DC) Matarella, B. (DC) Cassiani, G. (DC) Togni, G. (DC)	Zotta, M. (DC) Campilli, P. (DC) Bo, R. Del (DC)	0
14	Vigorelli, E. (PSDI)	Togni, G. (DC) Angelini, A. (DC) Simonini, A. (DC) Spataro, G. (DC)	Pastore, G. (DC) Giardina, C. (DC) Bo, R. Del (DC)	0
15		Togni, G. (DC) Angelini, A. (DC) Spataro, G. (DC) Jervolino, A.R. (DC)	Tupini, U. (DC) Pastore, G. (DC) Bettiol, G. (DC) Bo, G. (DC)	0
16	Zaccagnini, B. (DC)	Togni, G. (DC) Sullo, F. (DC) Maxia, A. (DC) Jervolino, A.R. (DC)	Angelini, A. (DC) Tupini, U. (DC) Pastore, G. (DC) Bo, G. (DC)	0
17	Sullo, F. (DC)	Zaccagnini, B. (DC) Spataro, G. (DC) Spallino, L. (DC) Jervolino, A.R. (DC)	Folchi, A. (DC) Pastore, G. (DC) Pisanelli, C. (DC) Tessitori, T. (DC)	0
18	Bertinelli, V. (PSDI)	Mattarella, B. (DC) Macrelli, C. (PRI) Spallino, L. (DC) Sullo, F. (DC)	Folchi, A. (DC) Codacci-Pisanelli, G. (DC) Medici, G. (DC) Pastore, G. (DC)	0

ITALY 1945–1998

Gov	Social Affairs (py)	Public Works (py)	Other (py)	Res
19	Fave, U. delle (DC)	Sullo, F. (DC) Dominedo, F. (DC) Corbellini, G. (DC) Togni, G. (DC) Russo, C. (DC)	Folchi, A. (DC) Codacci-Pisanelli, G. (DC) Pastore, G. (DC) Lucifredi, R. (DC)	0
20	Bosco, G. (DC)	Jervolino, A.R. (DC) Spagnolli, G. (DC) Russo, C. (DC) Pieraccini, G. (PSI)	Corona, A. (PSI) Pastore, G. (DC) Piccioni, A. (DC) Fave, U. delle (DC) Preti, L. (PSDI) Arnaudi, C. (PSI)	0
21		Mancini, G. (PSI) Jervolino, A.R. (DC) Spagnolli, G. (DC) Russo, C. (DC)	Corona, A. (PSI) Pastore, G. (DC) Piccioni, A. (DC) Fave, U. delle (DC) Preti, L. (PSDI) Arnaudi, C. (PSI) Scaglia, G-B. (DC)	0
22	Bosco, G. (DC)	Scalfaro, O.L. (DC) Natali, L. (DC) Spagnolli, G. (DC) Mancini, G. (PSI)	Corona, A. (PSI) Pastore, G. (DC) Piccioni, A. (DC) Scaglia, G-B. (DC) Rubinacci, L. (DC) Bertinelli, V. (PSDI)	0
23	Bosco, G. (DC)	Natali, L. (DC) Scalfaro, O.L. (DC) Luca, A. De (DC) Spagnolli, (DC)	Magri, D. (DC) Piccioni, A. (DC) Tessitori, T. (DC) Mazza, C. (DC) Caiati, I.G. (DC)	0

ITALY 1945-1998

Gov	Social Affairs (py)	Public Works (py)	Other (py)	Res
24	Brodolini, G. (PSI)	Mariotti, L. (PSI) Lupis, G. (PSI) Ferrari-Aggradi, M. (DC) Mancini, G. (PSI)	Natali, L. (DC) Taviani, P.E. (DC) Bosco, G. (DC) Gatto, E. (DC) Lauricelli, S. (PSI) Russo, C. (DC) Mazza, C. (DC)	0
25	Donat-Cattin, C. (DC)	Natali, L. (DC) Valsecchi, A. (DC) Gaspari, R. (DC) Colombo, V. (DC)	Magri, D. (DC) Scaglia, G.-B. (DC) Taviani, P.E. (DC) Bo, G. (DC) Russo, C. (DC) Gatto, E. (DC) Forlani, A. (DC)	0
26	Donat-Cattin, C. (DC)	Viglianesi, I. (PSI) Mannironi, S. (DC) Malfatti, F.M. (DC) Lauricella, S. (PSI)	Lupis, G. (PSU) Taviani, P.E. (DC) Gaspari, R. (DC) Ripamonti, C. (DC) Ferrari-Aggradi, M. (DC) Bosco, G. (DC) Gatto, E. (DC)	0
27	Donat-Cattin, C. (DC)	Viglianesi, I. (PSI) Mannironi, S. (DC) Malfatti, F.M. (DC) Lauricella, S. (PSI)	Matteotti, M. (PSU) Taviani, P.E. (DC) Gaspari, R. (DC) Ripamonti, C. (DC) Bosco, G. (DC) Gatto, E. (DC) Lupis, G. (PSU) Russo, C. (DC)	0

ITALY 1945–1998

Gov	Social Affairs (py)	Public Works (py)	Other (py)	Res
28	Donat-Cattin, C. (DC)	Viglianesi, I. (PSI) Attaguile, G. (DC) Malfatti, F.M. (DC) Lauricella, S. (PSI)	Matteotti, M. (PSU) Taviani, P.E. (DC) Gaspari, R. (DC) Ripamonti, C. (DC) Bosco, G. (DC) Gatto, E. (DC) Lupis, G. (PSU) Russo, C. (DC)	0
29	Donat-Cattin, C. (DC)	Ferrari-Aggradi, M. (DC) Scalfaro, O.L. (DC) Gava, S. (DC) Cassiani, G. (DC) Bosco, G. (DC)	Scaglia, B. (DC) Gatto, E. (DC) Russo, C. (DC) Caiati, G. (DC) Gaspari, R. (DC) Sullo, F. (DC)	0
30	Coppo, D. (DC)	Bozzi, A. (PLI) Lupis, G. (PSDI) Gioia, G. (DC) Gulotti, A. (DC)	Confalonieri, V. (PLI) Gava, S. (DC) Sullo, F. (DC) Caiati, I.G. (DC) Romita, O. (PSDI) Bergamasco, G. (PLI) Colombo, E. (DC)	0

ITALY 1945–1998

Gov	Social Affairs (py)	Public Works (py)	Other (py)	Res
31	Bertoldi, L. (PSI)	Preti, L. (PSDI) Pieraccini, G. (PSI) Togni, G. (DC) Lauricella, S. (PSI)	Mita, C. De (DC) Corona, A. (PSI) Signorello, N. (DC) Ripamonti, C. (DC) Lupis, G. (PSDI) Donat-Cattin, C. (DC) Gioia, G. (DC) Coppo, D. (DC) Toros, M. (DC) Gava, S. (DC) Bucalossi, P. (PRI)	0
32	Bertoldi, L. (PSI)	Preti, L. (PSDI) Coppo, D. (DC) Togni, G. (DC) Lauricella, S. (PSI)	Ripamonti, C. (DC) Gui, L. (DC) Pieraccini, G. (PSI) Mancini, G. (PSI) Lupis, G. (PSDI) Gioia, G. (DC) Toros, M. (DC)	0
33		Bucalossi, P. (PRI) Martinelli, M. (DC) Orlando, G. (DC) Gioia, G. (DC)	Andreotti, G. (DC) Sarti, A. (DC) Morlino, T. (DC) Cossiga, F. (DC)	0
34		Gullotti, A. (DC) Martinelli, M. (DC) Orlando, G. (DC) Gioia, G. (DC)	Pedini, M. (DC) Morlino, T. (DC) Sarti, A. (DC)	0

ITALY 1945–1998

Gov	Social Affairs (py)	Public Works (py)	Other (py)	Res
35		Gullotti, A. (DC) Ruffini, A. (DC) Colombo, V. (DC) Fabbri, F. (DC)	Antoniozzi, D. (DC) Pedini, M. (DC) Mita, L.G. de (DC)	0
36	Scotti, V. (DC)	Stammati, G. (DC) Gullotti, A. (DC) Colombo, V. (DC)	Antoniozzi, D. (DC) Pastorino, G. (DC) Mita, L.G. de (DC)	0
37	Scotti, V. (DC)	Preti, L. (PSDI) Campagna, F. (PRI) Colombo, V. (DC)	Antoniozzi, D. (DC) Di Giesi, M. (PSDI) Ariosto, E. (PSDI)	0
38	Scotti, V. (DC)	Preti, L. (PSDI) Nicolazzi, F. (PSDI) Evangelisti, F. (DC) Colombo, V. (DC)	Ariosto, E. (PSDI) Di Giesi, M. (PSDI) D'Arezzo, B. (DC) Sarti, A. (DC) Giannini, M.S. (NONA)	0
39		Formica, S. (PSI) Compagna, F. (PRI) Signorello, N. (DC) Darida, C. (DC)	Biasini, O. (PRI) D'Arezzo, B. (DC) Gasperi, R. (DC) Andreatta, B. (DC) Capria, N. (PSI) Scotti, V. (DC) Russo, V. (DC)	0
40		Formica, S. (PSI) Nicolazzi, F. (PSDI) Di Giesi, M. (PSDI) Compagna, F. (PRI)	Biasini, O. (PRI) Mazzotta, R. (DC) Scotti, V. (DC) Capria, N. (PSI) Gava, A. (DC) Signorello, N. (DC)	0

ITALY 1945–1998

Gov	Social Affairs (py)	Public Works (py)	Other (py)	Res
41		Balzamo, V. (PSI) Nicolazzi, F. (PSDI) Gaspari, R. (DC) Mannino, C. (DC)	Scotti, V. (DC) Aniasi, A. (PSI) Abis, G. (DC) Signorile, C. (PSI) Radi, L. (DC) Signorello, N. (DC) Zamberletti, G. (DC)	0
42		Balzamo, V. (PSI) Nicolazzi, F. (PSDI) Gaspari, R. (DC) Mannino, C. (DC)	Scotti, V. (DC) Aniasi, A. (PSI) Abis, G. (DC) Signorile, C. (PSI) Radi, L. (DC) Signorello, N. (DC) Zamberletti, G. (DC)	0
43	Scotti, V. (DC)	Nicolazzi, F. (PSDI) Casalinuovo, M. (PSDI) Gasperi, R. (DC) Di Giesi, M. (PSDI)	Vernola, N. (DC) Signorelli, C. (PSI) Abis, G. (DC) Biondi, A. (PLI) Fabbri, F. (PSI) Fortuna, L. (PSI) Signorello, N. (DC)	0
44		Signorile, C. (PSI) Nicolazzi, F. (PSDI) Gava, A. (DC) Carta, G. (DC)	Romita, P.L. (PSDI) Mammi, O. (PRI) Scotti, V. (DC) Forte, F. (PSI) Vito, S. De (DC) Lagorio, L. (PSI) Gullotti, A. (DC)	0

ITALY 1945–1998

Gov	Social Affairs (py)	Public Works (py)	Other (py)	Res
45		Signorile, C. (PSI) Nicolazzi, F. (PSDI) Gava, A. (DC)	Capria, N. (PSI) Mammi, O. (PRI) Vito, S. De (DC) Gullotti, A. (DC) Vizzini, C. (PSDI) Zamberletti, G. (DC) Fabbri, F. (PSI)	0
46		Gava, A. (DC)	Andreotti, G. (DC) Paladin, L. (NONA) Di Lazzaro, M. (NONA) Gullotti, A. (DC) Gifuni, G. (NONA) Zamberletti, G. (DC) Vito, S. De (DC)	0
47		De Rose, E. (PSDI) Mannino, C. (DC) Mammi, O. (PRI)	Vizzini, C. (PSDI) Carraro, F. (PSI) La Pergola, A. (PSDI) Mattarella, S. (DC) Tognoli, C. (PSI) *Jervolino, R.R. (DC) Gunella, A. (PRI) Gaspari, R. (DC)	0
48		Ferri, E. (PSDI) Mammi, O. (PRI)	Carraro, F. (PSI) Parrino, V. (PSDI) Gaspari, R. (DC) Lattanzio, V. (DC) Mattarella, S. (DC) La Pergola, A. (PSDI) *Jervolino, R.R. (DC)	0

ITALY 1945–1998

Gov	Social Affairs (py)	Public Works (py)	Other (py)	Res
49		Prandini, G. (DC) Bernini, C. (DC) Mammi, O. (PRI)	Carraro, F. (PSI) Facchiano, F. (PSDI) Misasi, R. (DC) Lattanzio, V. (DC) Sterpa, E. (PLI) Maccanico, A. (PRI) Romita, P.L. (PSDI) Conte, C. (PSI) *Jervolino, R.R. (DC)	1
50	*Jervolino, R.R. (DC)	Prandini, G. (DC) Bernini, C. (DC) Vizzini, C. (PSDI) Facchiano, F. (PSDI)	Andreotti, G. (DC) Tognoli, C. (PSI) Ruffolo, G. (PSI) Mannino, C. (DC) *Capria, N. (PSI) Sterpa, E. (PLI) Romita, P. (PSDI)	0
51	Bompiani, A. (DC)	Merloni, F. (DC) Tesini, G. (NONA) Pagani, M. (PSDI)	Reviglio, F. (PSI) *Boniver, M. (PSI) Ronchey, A. (NONA) Facchinano, F. (PSDI) Costa, R. (PLI)	1
52	*Contri, F. (PSI)	Pagani, M. (PSDI) Merloni, F. (DC) Costa, R. (PLI)	Maccanico, A. (PRI) Ronchey, A. (NONA) Barbera, A. (PDS) Spini, V. (PSI) Savona, P. (PRI)	0

ITALY 1945–1998

Gov	Social Affairs (py)	Public Works (py)	Other (py)	Res
53	*Contri, F. (PSI)	Pagani, M. (PSDI) Merloni, F. (DC) Costa, R. (PLI)	Maccanico, A. (PRI) Ronchey, A. (NONA) Paladini, L. (NONA) Savona, P. (PRI) Barile, P. (NONA)	0
54	Guidi, A. (FI)	Tatarella, G. (AN) Radice, R. (FI) Fiori, P. (AN)	Comino, D. (LN) Fisichella, D. (AN) Ferrara, G. (FI) Berlinguer, S. (IND)	0
55	Ossicini, A.	Caravale, G. Baratta, P. Gambino, A.	Paolucci, A.	2
56	Treu, T. (OT) *Turco, L. (OT) *Finocchiaro, A. (OT)	Di Pietro, A. (OT-IND) Burlando, C. (OT) Maccanico, A. (OT)	Bersani, P. (OT)	

26. JAMAICA

The ceremonial Head of State is the British Monarch, represented by a Governor-General.

The State is unitary and very centralised.

Parliament is bicameral. The 21 members of the Senate are nominated for a flexible term of five years, thirteen by the Prime Minister, and eight by the Leader of the Opposition. The predominant Lower House with 60 members is elected for a flexible term of maximum five years by plurality voting (first past the post) in constituencies of between 20,000 and 25,000 electors.

Parliament has a quorum of 16 members for the Lower House and 8 members for the Upper House. Normal votes are carried by a simple majority of votes cast. Any legislation involving Human Rights has to have a two-thirds majority of members of both Houses. This is also required on constitutional matters, along with a referendum on those matters. The outcome is binding

The executive is a Cabinet government. The Governor-General acting on behalf of the Monarch formally appoints the government. No vote of investiture is necessary to confirm the government. During its lifetime the government can face a vote of no confidence. Losing a vote of confidence always results in resignation of the government. The government is collectively responsible to parliament and consists of the leaders of the majority party in the Lower House. They are all members of parliament. The Prime Minister has a dominant position in government.

The Supreme Court constitutionally reviews legislation, with the Judicial Committee of the British Privy Council acting as the final court of appeal.

JAMAICA 1962-1998

Gov	Begin	Dur	RfT	ToG	Py1	Seats	CPG	NoM	Prime Minister (py)
1	11.04.62	1778	1	1	JLP 26	45	4	14	Bustamante, A. (JLP)
2	22.02.67	48	x	1	JLP 33	53	4	12	Sangster, D.B. (JLP)
3	11.04.67	1787	1	1	JLP 33	53	4	13	Shearer, H.L. (JLP)
4	02.03.72	1754	1	1	PNP 37	53	5	17	Manley, M.N. (PNP)
5	20.12.76	1418	1	1	PNP 47	60	5	19	Manley, M.N. (PNP)
6	07.11.80	1134	1	1	JLP 51	60	5	15	Seaga, E.P.G. (JLP)
7	16.12.83	1886	1	1	JLP 60	60	5	15	Seaga, E.P.G. (JLP)
8	13.02.89	1139	3	1	PNP 45	60	5	19	Manley, M.N. (PNP)
9	28.03.92	374	1	1	PNP 46	60	5	14	Paterson, P.J. (PNP)
10	06.04.93	1718	1	1	PNP 52	60	5	17	Paterson, P.J. (PNP)
11	19.12.97			1	PNP 50	60	5	17	Paterson, P.J. (PNP)

- Date of Independence 6 August 1962.
- Gov 2: Reason for Termination is death of PM.
- Gov 7: The elections of 15 December 1983 were boycotted by the opposition party PNP. Consequently all 60 seats were taken by the JLP.

Gov	Deputy PM	Py	Foreign Affairs	Py	Defence	Py	Interior	Py	Justice	Py
1							McNeill, R.A.		Grant, V.B.	JLP
2			Shearer, H.L.	JLP	Sangster, D.B.	JLP	Lynch, L.A.		Grant, V.B.	JLP
3			Shearer, H.L.	JLP	Shearer, H.L.		McNeill, R.A. Lynch, L.A.	JLP JLP	Grant, V.B.	JLP
4	Coore, D.H.	PNP	Manley, M.N.	PNP	Manley, M.N.		*Leon, R.	PNP	Silvera, N.	PNP
5	Coore, D.H.	PNP	Thompson, D.	PNP	Manley, M.N.		Munn, K.A. *Leon, R.	PNP PNP	Rattray, C.	PNP
6	Shearer, H.L.	JLP	Shearer, H.L.	JLP		JLP	Spaulding, W. Charles, P.	JLP JLP	Spaulding, W.	JLP

JAMAICA 1962-1998

Gov	Deputy PM	Py	Foreign Affairs	Py	Defence	Py	Interior	Py	Justice	Py
7	Shearer, H.L.	JLP	Shearer, H.L.	JLP			Spaulding, W. / Ross, A.	JLP / JLP	Spaulding, W.	JLP
8	Patterson, P.J.	PNP	Coore, D.H.	PNP	Manley, M.N.	PNP	Mullings, S. / Knight, K.D. / Brown, R.	PNP / PNP / PNP	Rattray, C.	PNP
9			Coore, D.H.		Patterson, P.J.	PNP	Knight, K.D. / Robertson, P. / Leakey, D.	PNP / PNP / PNP	Knight, K.D.	PNP
10	Mullings, S.	PNP	Robertson, P.	PNP	Patterson, P.J.	PNP	Knight, K.D. / Douglas, I. / Junor, J.	PNP / PNP / PNP	Coore, D. / Knight, K.D.	PNP / PNP
11	Mullings, S.	PNP	Mullings, S.	PNP	Patterson, P.J.	PNP	Knight, K.D. / Bertram, A.T.	PNP / PNP	Knight, K.D.	PNP

Gov	Finance	Py	Economic Aff.	Py	Labour	Py	Education	Py	Health	Py
1	Sangster, D.B.	JLP	Seaga, E.P.G.	JLP	Newland, L.G.	JLP	Allen, E.L.	JLP	Eldermire, H.W.	JLP
2	Seaga, E.P.G.	JLP	Seaga, E.P.G.	JLP	Newland, L.G.	JLP	Allen, E.L.	JLP	Eldermire, H.W.	JLP
3	Seaga, E.P.G.	JLP	Seaga, E.P.G.	JLP	Newland, L.G.	JLP	Allen, E.L.	JLP	Eldermire, H.W.	JLP
4	Coore, D.H.	PNP			Peart, E.G.	PNP	Glasspole, F.	PNP	McNeill, K.A.	PNP
5	Coore, D.H.	PNP			Peart, E.G.	PNP	Cooke, H.F.	PNP	McNeill, K.A.	PNP
6	Seaga, E.P.G.	JLP	Seaga, E.P.G.	JLP	Smith, J.A.G.	JLP	*Gilmour, M.	JLP	Baugh, K.	JLP
7	Seaga, E.P.G.	JLP	Seaga, E.P.G.	JLP	Smith, J.A.G.	JLP	*Gilmour, M.	JLP	Baugh, K.	JLP
8	Mullings, S.	PNP	Patterson, P.J.	PNP	*Simpson, P.	PNP	Dunkley, C.	PNP	Douglas, E.	JLP

JAMAICA 1962-1998

Gov	Finance	Py	Economic Aff.	Py	Labour	Py	Education	Py	Health	Py
9	Small, H.	PNP	Patterson, P.J. / Small, H.	PNP / PNP	*Simpson, P.	PNP	Whiteman, B.	PNP	Douglas, E.	PNP
10	Small, H.	PNP			*Simpson, P.	PNP	Whiteman, B.	PNP	Leakey, D.	PNP
11	Davies, O.	PNP	Davies, O.	PNP	*Simpson, P.	PNP	Whiteman, B. / Paulwell, P.	PNP / PNP	Junor, J.	PNP

Gov	Housing	Py	Agriculture	Py	Industry/Trade	Py	Environment	Py
1	Tavares, D.C.	JLP	Gyles, J.P.	JLP	Lightbourne, R.	JLP		
2	Tavares, D.C.	JLP	Gyles, J.P.	JLP		JLP		
3	Tavares, D.C.	JLP	Gyles, J.P.	JLP	Lightbourne, R.	JLP		
4	Spaulding, A.	PNP	Munn, K.A.	PNP	Patterson, P.J. / Isaacs, W.	PNP / PNP	McNeill, K.A.	PNP
5	Spaulding, A.	PNP	Belinfanti, A.K.	PNP	Patterson, P.J. / Blake, V.	PNP / PNP	McNeill, K.A.	PNP
6			Broderick, P.	JLP	Shearer, H.L. / Vaz, D.	JLP / JLP		
7			Broderick, P.	JLP	Vaz, D.	JLP		
8			Clarke, H.	PNP	Coore, D.H. / Clarke, C.	PNP / PNP		
9	Mullings, S.	PNP			Coore, D.H. / Dunkley, C.	PNP / PNP	Junor, J.	PNP

JAMAICA 1962-1998

Gov	Housing	Py	Agriculture	Py	Industry/Trade	Py	Environment	Py
10		PNP	Mullings, S.	PNP	Robertson, P. Dunkley, C.	PNP PNP	Douglas, E.	PNP
11	Douglas, E.	PNP	Clarke, R.	PNP	Mullings, S. Robertson, P. Paulwell, P.	PNP PNP PNP	Douglas, E.	PNP

Gov	Social Affairs (py)	Public Works (py)	Other (py)	Res
1	Newland, L.G. (JLP) Seaga, E.P.G. (JLP) Douglas, A. (JLP)	Lewis, N.C. (JLP)	Sangster, D.B. (JLP) McNeill, R.A. (JLP) Shearer, H.L. (JLP)	0
2	Seaga, E.P.G. (JLP) Newland, L.G. (JLP)	Lewis, N.C.	Tavares, D.C. (JLP) McNeill, R.A. (JLP)	0
3	Newland, L.G. (JLP) Douglas, A. (JLP)	Lewis, N.C. (JLP)	McNeill, R.A. (JLP)	0
4	Cooke, H.F. (PNP) Manley, D. (PNP)	Bell, E.C. (PNP) Isaacs, A. (PNP) Jones, W.V. (PNP)	Patterson, P.J. (PNP) Silvera, N. (PNP) Thompson, D. (PNP)	0
5	Manley, D. (PNP) Jones, W.V. (PNP)	Coore, D.H. (PNP) Bell, E.C. (PNP) Clarke, H. (PNP) Pagon, S. (PNP)	Patterson, P.J. (PNP) Isaacs, W. (PNP) Munn, K.A. (PNP)	7

JAMAICA 1962-1998

Gov	Social Affairs (py)	Public Works (py)	Other (py)	Res
6	Lewis, N.C. (JLP) Anderson, E. (JLP)	Seaga, E.P.G. (JLP) Golding, B. (JLP) Smith, J.A.G. (JLP) Ross, A. (JLP)	Irvine, R. (JLP) Abrahams, A. (JLP)	0
7	Lewis, N.C. (JLP) Anderson, E. (JLP)	Seaga, E.P.G. (JLP) Golding, B. (JLP) Smith, J.A.G. (JLP) Charles, P. (JLP)	Abrahams, A. (JLP) Irvine, R. (JLP)	2
8	*Simpson, P. (PNP) Manley, D. (PNP)	Ramtallie, O.D. (PNP) Pickersgill, R. (PNP) Small, H. (PNP)	Manley, M.N. (PNP) Coore, D.H. (PNP) Robertson, P. (PNP) Manley, D. (PNP) McNeill, K.A. (PNP) Pringle, F. (PNP)	4
9	*Simpson, P. (PNP) Leakey, D. (PNP)	Ramtallie, O.D. (PNP) Pickersgill, R. (PNP) Dunkley, C. (PNP)	Patterson, P.J. (PNP) Whiteman, B. (PNP) Robertson, P. (PNP) Leakley, D. (PNP) Junor, J. (PNP)	0
10	*Simpson, P. (PNP) Junor, J. (PNP)	Ramtallie, O.D. (PNP) Clarke, H. (PNP) Pickersgill, R. (PNP)	Mullings, S. (PNP) Phillips, P. (PNP) Dunkley, C. (PNP) Whiteman, B. (PNP) Junor, J. (PNP) Davies, O. (PNP)	3

JAMAICA 1962-1998

Gov	Social Affairs (py)	Public Works (py)	Other (py)	Res
11	*Simpson, P. (PNP) Bertram, A.T. (PNP)	Pickersgill, R. (PNP) Philips, P. (PNP) Bythe, K. (PNP)	Tullock, F. (PNP) Wilson, M.H. (PNP) *Simpson, P. (PNP) Phillips, P. (PNP) Whiteman, B. (PNP)	

27. JAPAN

In 1946 the Imperial Constitution was completely revised and the empire transformed into a constitutional monarchy based upon democratic principles. The Emperor's duties as Head of State became purely ceremonial.

Japan is a unitary state, although some discretionary powers are delegated to local and regional government. This is counterbalanced by a so-called "supremacy clause" favouring the national executive.

Parliament is bicameral, with the Lower House (Shugiin) being much the most powerful, having control over the budget and the final word in the selection of the Prime Minister in case of disagreement. The Shugiin of 500 seats is elected for a fixed term of four years by a mixed system of proportional representation (D'Hondt) for 200 (party)seats in eleven regions and plurality voting in single-member constituencies for 300 (member)seats. The Senate of 252 seats is elected for a fixed term of six years. Half of the members stand for election every three years.

Parliament has a quorum of one-third of all members. Votes are carried by a majority of votes cast. Some issues require a qualified majority of two-thirds of all votes cast. Constitutional amendments require a two-thirds majority of all votes cast in both Houses, plus a positive referendum. The outcome is binding.

The government does not need a vote of investiture but can face a vote of no confidence. Losing a vote of confidence always results in resignation of the government. The government is collectively responsible to parliament. The individual ministers are usually members of parliament. The Prime minister has a dominant role in government and always is the parliamentary leader of the majority party or parties in the Shugiin.

The Supreme Court has the power to interpret the constitution and of judicial review. Its working is influenced by the practices of the US judicial system. The Emperor on nomination by the Cabinet appoints the Chief Justice. All Supreme Court judges (the Chief Justice and fourteen associates) are subject to confirming elections in the first national election following their initial appointment, and after ten years of service.

JAPAN 1945–1998

Gov	Begin	Dur	RfT	ToG	Py1	Py2	Py3	Py4	Py5	Py6	Py7	Seats	CPG	NoM	Prime Minister (py)
1	22.05.46	373	1	2	LP 141	PP 94						466	2	14	Yoshida, S. (LP)
2	30.05.47	284	4	3	SP 143	PP 121	CP 31					466	3	16	Katayama, T. (SP)
3	09.03.48	224	x	3	SP 143	PP 121	CP 31					466	3	11	Ashida, H. (PP)
4	19.10.48	120	1	4	LP 131							466	2	15	Yoshida, S. (LP)
5	16.02.49	497	x	3	LP 264	PP 69						466	2	16	Yoshida, S. (LP)
6	28.06.50	854	5	1	LP 264							466	2	15	Yoshida, S. (LP)
7	29.10.52	204	5	1	LP 240							466	2	11	Yoshida, S. (LP)
8	21.05.53	567	5	4	YL 199							466	2	18	Yoshida, S. (YL)
9	09.12.54	100	1	4	DP 111	[YL 199]	[SP 138]					466	2	17	Hatoyama, I. (DP)
10	19.03.55	248	x	4	DP 185	[YL 112]						466	2	18	Hatoyama, I. (DP)
11	22.11.55	397	3	1	LDP 297							466	2	18	Hatoyama, I. (LDP)
12	23.12.56	64	3	1	LDP 297							466	2	17	Ishibashi, T. (LDP)
13	25.02.57	472	1	1	LDP 297							466	2	17	Kishi, N. (LDP)
14	12.06.58	768	2	1	LDP 287							467	2	18	Kishi, N. (LDP)
15	19.07.60	142	1	1	LDP 287							467	2	13	Ikeda, H. (LDP)
16	08.12.60	1096	1	1	LDP 296							467	2	17	Ikeda, H. (LDP)
17	09.12.63	336	3	1	LDP 283							467	2	18	Ikeda, H. (LDP)
18	09.11.64	830	1	1	LDP 283							467	2	18	Sato, E. (LDP)
19	17.02.67	1062	1	1	LDP 277							486	2	19	Sato, E. (LDP)
20	14.01.70	905	2	1	LDP 288							486	2	15	Sato, E. (LDP)
21	07.07.72	168	1	1	LDP 288							486	2	18	Tanaka, K. (LDP)
22	22.12.72	717	2	1	LDP 271							491	2	20	Tanaka, K. (LDP)
23	09.12.74	746	2	1	LDP 271							491	2	21	Miki, T. (LDP)
24	24.12.76	714	2	4	LDP 249							511	2	21	Fukuda, T. (LDP)
25	08.12.78	335	1	4	LDP 249							511	2	21	Ohira, M. (LDP)
26	08.11.79	252	5	4	LDP 248							511	2	20	Ohira, M. (LDP)

JAPAN 1945-1998

Gov	Begin	Dur	RfT	ToG	Py1	Py2	Py3	Py4	Py5	Py6	Py7	Seats	CPG	NoM	Prime Minister (py)
27	17.07.80	862	2	1	LDP 284							511	2	22	Suzuki, Z. (LDP)
28	26.11.82	395	1	1	LDP 284							511	2	18	Nakasone, Y. (LDP)
29	26.12.83	311	x	3	LDP 258	NLC 8						511	2	22	Nakasone, Y. (LDP)
30	01.11.84	628	1	3	LDP 258	NLC 8						511	2	22	Nakasone, Y. (LDP)
31	22.07.86	472	2	1	LDP 310							512	2	21	Nakasone, Y. (LDP)
32	06.11.87	575	2	1	LDP 310							512	2	20	Takeshita, N. (LDP)
33	03.06.89	67	2	1	LDP 310							512	2	21	Uno, S. (LDP)
34	09.08.89	203	1	1	LDP 310							512	2	21	Kaifu, T. (LDP)
35	28.02.90	615	3	1	LDP 275							512	2	21	Kaifu, T. (LDP)
36	05.11.91	643	5	1	LDP 275							512	2	21	Miyzawa, K.(LDP)
37	09.08.93	262	2	5	SHIN 55	JNP 35	SDP 7	KOME 51	DSP 15	SAKI 13	SHAM 4	511	3	22	Hosokawa, M. (JNP)
38	28.04.94	63	2	5	KAIS 130	KOME 2	SAKI 13					511	2	21	Hrata, T. (KAIS)
39	30.06.94	560	2	3	LDP 206	SDPJ74	SAKI 15					511	3	21	Murayama, T. (SDPJ)
40	11.01.96	301	1	3	LDP 200	SDPJ73	SAKI 21					511	3	21	Hashimoto, R. (LDP)
41	07.11.96			3	LDP 293	[SDPJ 15]	[SAKI 2]					500	2	21	Hashimoto, R.(LDP)

- Gov 3: Reason for Termination is financial scandal involving members and supporters of government.
- Gov 5: Reason for Termination is reconstruction of government representing the proportion of seats of the parties in both Houses.
- Gov 10: Reason for Termination was reconstruction of government following the merger of DP plus Liberals into LDP. DP (Democratic Party) dit not exist as a separate party during government 9. It was a combination of Progressive Party and Hatoyama Liberals. As DP proper they contested the 1955 elections.
- Gov 29: Reason for Termination was re-election Nakasone as chairman LDP and hence PM.
- Gov 37: KOME = KOMEITO, SAKI = SAKIGAKE, SHAM = SHAMINREN.
- Gov 38: KAIS = KAISHIN. KAISHIN is election co-operation of JNP (37), Shinseito (62), DSP (19), Liberal Party (7), Kai Kaku (4), Independents (1).
- Gov 41: First elections under new electoral system. Two votes, one for 300 single constituency seats and one for 200 seats under PR.

JAPAN 1945–1998

Gov	Deputy PM	Py	Foreign Affairs	Py	Defence	Py	Interior	Py	Justice	Py
1			Yoshida, S.	LP			Omura, S.	NONA	Kimura, T.	NONA
2			Ashida, H.	PP			Kimura, K.	PP	Suzuki, Y.	SP
3			Ashida, H.	PP					Suzuki, Y.	SP
4			Yoshida, S.	LP					Yoshida, S.	LP
5	Hayashi, J.	LP	Yoshida, S.	LP			Kimura, S.	PP	Ueda, S.	NONA
6	Hayashi, J.	LP	Yoshida, S.	LP			Okano, K.	LP	Ohashi, T.	LP
7			Okazaki, K.	LP			Honda, I.	LP	Inukai, T.	LP
8	Ogata, T.	YL	Okazaki, K.	YL					Inukai, T.	YL
9	Shigemitsu, M.	DP	Shigemitsu, M.	DP	Omura, S.	DP	Nishida, T.; Oasa, T.	DP; DP	Hanamura, S.	DP
10	Shigemitsu, M.	DP	Shigemitsu, M.	DP	Sugihara, A.	DP	Kawashima, S.; Oasa, T.; Okubo, T.	DP; DP; DP	Hanamura, S.	DP
11	Shigemitsu, M.	LDP	Shigemitsu, M.	LDP	Funada, N.	LDP	Ota, M.; Oasa, T.	LDP; DP	Makino, R.	LDP
12			Kishi, N.	LDP	Ishibashi, T.	LDP	Tanaka, I.	LDP	Nakamura, U.	LDP
13			Kishi, N.	LDP	Kodaki, A.	LDP	Tanaka, I.	LDP	Nakamura, U.	LDP
14			Fujiyama, A.	LDP	Sato, G.	LDP	Aoki, M.	LDP	Aichi, K.	LDP
15			Kosaka, Z.	LDP			Yamasaki, I.	LDP	Kojima, T.	LDP
16			Kosaka, Z.	LDP	Mishimura, N.	LDP	Yasui, K.	LDP	Ueki, K.	LDP
17			Ohira, M.	LDP	Fukuda, T.	LDP	Hayakawa, T.; Yamamura, S.	LDP; LDP	Kaya, O.	LDP
18			Shiina, E.	LDP	Koisumi, J.	LDP	Yoshitake, E.	LDP	Takahashi, H.	LDP
19			Miki, T.	LDP	Masuda, K.	LDP	Fujieda, S.	LDP	Tanaka, I.	LDP
20			Aichi, K.	LDP	Nakasone, Y.	LDP	Akita, D.; Araki, M.	LDP; LDP	Kobayashi, T.	LDP

JAPAN 1945–1998

Gov	Deputy PM	Py	Foreign Affairs	Py	Defence	Py	Interior	Py	Justice	Py
21			Ohira, M.	LDP	Masuhara, K.	LDP	Fukuda, H. / Kimura, T. / Hamano, S.	LDP / LDP / LDP	Kori, Y.	LDP
22	Miki, T.	LDP	Ohira, M.	LDP	Masuhara, K.	LDP	Esaki, M. / Fukuda, T.	LDP / LDP	Tanaka, I.	LDP
23	Fukuda, T.	LDP	Miyazawa, K.	LDP	Sakata, M.	LDP	Fukuda, H. / Matzusawa, Y.	LDP / LDP	Inaba, O.	LDP
24			Hatoyama, I.	LDP	Mihara, A.	LDP	Ogawa, H. / Nishimura, E.	LDP / LDP	Fukuda, H.	LDP
25			Sonoda, S.	LDP	Yamashita, G.	LDP	Shibuya, N. / Kanai, M.	LDP / LDP	Furui, Y.	LDP
26			Okita, S.	LDP	Kubota, E.	LDP	Gotoda, M. / Uno, S.	LDP / LDP	Kuraishi, T.	LDP
27			Ito, M.	LDP	Omura, J.	LDP	Ishiba, J. / Nakasone, Y.	LDP / LDP	Okuno, S.	LDP
28			Abe, S.	LDP	Tanikawa, K.	LDP	Yamamoto, S. / Saito, J.	LDP / LDP	Hatano, A.	LDP
29			Abe, S.	LDP	Kurihara, Y.	LDP	Tagawa, S. / Gotoda, M.	NLC / LDP	Sumi, J.	LDP
30			Abe, S.	LDP	Kato, K.	LDP	Furuya, T.	LDP	Shimasaki, H.	LDP
31	Kanemaru, S.	LDP	Kuranari, T.	LDP	Kurihara, Y.	LDP	Hanashi, N.	LDP	Endo, K.	LDP
32	Miyazawa, K.	LDP	Uno, S.	LDP	Kawara, T.	LDP	Kajiyama, S.	LDP	Hayashida, Y.	LDP
33	Murayama, T.	LDP	Mitsuzuka, H.	LDP	Yamasaki, T.	LDP	Sakano, S.	LDP	Tanikawa, K.	LDP
34			Nakayama, T.	LDP	Matsumo, J.	LDP	Watanabe, K.	LDP	Goto, M.	LDP
35			Nakayama, T.	LDP	Ishikawa, Y.	LDP	Okuda, K. / Shiozaki, J.	LDP / LDP	Hasegawa, S.	LDP
36	Watanabe, M.	LDP	Watanabe, M.	LDP	Miyashita, S.	LDP	Shiokawa, M. / Iwasaki, J.	LDP / LDP	Tawara, T.	LDP

JAPAN 1945–1998

Gov	Deputy PM	Py	Foreign Affairs	Py	Defence	Py	Interior	Py	Justice	Py
37	Hata, T.	SHIN	Hata, T.	SHIN	Nakanishi, K.	SHIN	Sato, K. Ohde, T.	SDPJ NONA	Mikazuki, A.	NONA
38			Kakizawa, K.	LP	Kanda, A.	DSP	Ishi, H. Ishida, K.	SHIN KOM	Nagano, S.	SHIN
39	Kono, Y.	LDP	Kono, Y.	LDP	Tamazawa, T.	LDP	Nonaka, H. Yamaguchi, T.	SDPJ LDP SDPJ	Maeda, I.	LDP
40	Kubo, W.	SDPJ	Ikeda, Y.	LDP	Usui, H.	LDP	Kurata, H. Nakanishi, S.	LDP SDPJ	*Nagao, R.	IND
41			Ikeda, Y.	LDP	Kyuma, F.	LDP	Shirakawa, K. Muto, K.	LDP LDP	Matsuura, I.	LDP

Gov	Finance	Py	Economic Aff.	Py	Labour	Py	Education	Py	Health	Py
1	Ishibashi, T.	LP					Tanaka, K.	NONA	Kawai, Y.	NONA
2	Yano, Y.	PP					Morito, T.	SP	Hitotsumatsu, S.	PP
3	Kitamura, T.	PP	Kurusu, T.	PP	Kato, K.	PP	Morito, T.	SP		
4	Izumiyama, S.	LP	Nogata, K.	LP	Masuda, K.	NONA	Shimojo, Y.	LP	Hayashi, J.	LP
5	Ikeda, H.	LP	Aoki, T.	LP	Suzuki, M.	LP	Takase, S.	LP	Hayashi, J.	LP
6	Ikeda, H.	LP	Sudo, H.	LP	Hori, S.	LP	Amano, T.	LP	Kurokawa, T.	LP
7	Mukai, T.	LP			Tatsuka, K.		Okano, K.	LP	Yamagata, K.	LP
8	Ogasawara, S.	YL			Kosaka, Z.	YL	Odate, S.	YL	Yamagata, K.	LP
9	Ichimada, H.	DP	Takasaki, T.	DP	Chiba, S.	DP	Ando, M.	DP	Tsurumi, Y.	DP
10	Ichimada, H.	DP	Takasaki, T.	DP	Nishida, T.	DP	Matsumura, K.	DP	Matsumura, K.	DP
11	Ichimada, H.	LDP	Takasaki, T.	LDP	Kuraishi, T.	LDP	Kiyose, I.	LDP	Kobayashi, E.	LDP

JAPAN 1945–1998

Gov	Finance	Py	Economic Aff.	Py	Labour	Py	Education	Py	Health	Py
12	Ikeda, H.	LDP	Uda, K.	LDP	Matsuura, S.	LDP	Nadao, H.	LDP		LDP
13	Ikeda, H.	LDP	Uda, K.	LDP	Matsuura, S.	LDP	Nadao, H.	LDP	Kanda, H.	LDP
14	Sato, E.	LDP	Miki, T.	LDP	Kuraishi, T.	LDP	Nadao, H.	LDP	Hashimoto, R.	LDP
15	Mizuta, M.	LDP			Ishida, H.	LDP	Araki, M.	LDP		LDP
16	Mizuta, M.	LDP	Sakomizu, H.	LDP	Ishida, H.	LDP	Araki, M.	LDP	Furui, Y.	LDP
17	Tanaka, K.	LDP	Miyazawa, K.	LDP	Ohashi, T.	LDP	Nadao, H.	LDP	Kobayashi, T.	LDP
18	Tanaka, K.	LDP	Takahashi, M.	LDP	Ishida, H.	LDP	Aichi, K.	LDP	Kanda, H.	LDP
19	Mizuta, M.	LDP	Miyazawa, K.	LDP	Hayakawa, T.	LDP	Kennoki, T.	LDP	Bo, H.	LDP
20	Fukuda, T.	LDP	Sato, I.	LDP	Nohara, M.	LDP	Sakata, M.	LDP	Uchida, T.	LDP
21	Ueki, K.	LDP	Arita, K.	LDP	Tamura, H.	LDP	Inaba, O. / Nakasone, Y.	LDP	Shiomi, S.	LDP / LDP
22	Aichi, K.	LDP	Kosaka, Z.	LDP	Kato, T.	LDP	Okuno, S. / Maeda, K.	LDP	Saito, K.	LDP / LDP
23	Ohira, M.	LDP	Fukuda, T.	LDP	Hasegawa, T.	LDP	Nagai, M. / Sasaki, Y.	LDP	Tanaka, M.	LDP / LDP
24	Bo, H.	LDP	Kuranari, T.	LDP	Ishida, H.	LDP	Kaifu, T. / Uno, S.	LDP	Watanabe, M.	LDP / LDP
25	Kaneko, I.	LDP	Kosaka, T.	LDP	Kurihara, Y.	LDP	Naito, Y. / Kaneko, I.	LDP	Hashimoto, R.	LDP / LDP
26	Takeshita, N.	LDP	Shoji, K.	LDP	Fujinami, T.	LDP	Ohira, M. / Osada, Y.	LDP	Noro, K.	LDP / LDP
27	Watanabe, M.	LDP	Komoto, Y.	LDP	Fujio, M.	LDP	Tanaka, T. / Nakayawa, I.	LDP	Saito, H.	LDP / LDP
28	Takeshita, N.	LDP	Shiozaki, J.	LDP	Ono, A.	LDP	Setoyama, M.	LDP	Hayashi, Y.	LDP
29	Takeshita, N.	LDP	Komoto, T.	LDP	Sakamoto, M.	LDP	Mori, Y. / Isurugi, M.	LDP	Watanabe, K.	LDP / LDP

JAPAN 1945–1998

Gov	Finance	Py	Economic Aff.	Py	Labour	Py	Education	Py	Health	Py
30	Takeshita, N.	LDP	Kaneko, I.	LDP	Yamaguchi, T.	NLC	Matsunaga, H. Takenchi, R.	LDP LDP	Masuoka, H.	LDP
31	Miyazawa, K.	LDP	Kondo, T.	LDP	Hirai, T.	LDP	Fujio, M. Mitsubayashi, Y.	LDP LDP	Saito, J.	LDP
32	Miyazawa, K.	LDP	Nakao, E.	LDP	Nakamura, T.	LDP	Nakajima, G. Ito, S.	LDP LDP	Fujimoto, T.	LDP
33	Murayama, T.	LDP	Ochi, M.	LDP	Horiuchi, M.	LDP	Nishioka, T. Nakamura, K.	LDP LDP	Koizumi, J.	LDP
34	Hashimoto, R.	LDP	*Takahara, S.	LDP	Fukushima,	LDP	Iibashi, K. Saito, E.	LDP LDP	Toida, S.	LDP
35	Hashimoto, R.	LDP	Aizawa, H.	LDP	Tsukahara, S.	LDP	Hori, K. Oshima, T.	LDP LDP	Tsushima, Y.	LDP
36	Hata, T.	LDP	Noda, T.	LDP	Kondo, T.	LDP	Hatoyama, K. Tanigawa, K.	LDP LDP	Yamashita, T.	LDP
37	Fuji, H.	SHIN	*Kubota, M.	SHIN	Sakaguchi, C.	SDPJ	*Akamatsu, R. Eda, S.	NONA	Ouchi, K.	DSP
38	Fuji, H.	SHIN	Terasawa, Y.	SHIN	Hatoyama, K.	JNP	*Akamatsu, R. Omi, M.	IND KOM	Ouchi, K.	DSP
39	Takemura, M.	SAKI	Komura, M.	LDP	Hamamoto, M.	SDPJ	Yosano, K. Tanaka, M.	LDP LDP	Ide, S.	SAK
40	Kubo, W.	SDPJ	Tanaka, S.	SAKI	Nagai, T.	SDPJ	Okuda, M. Nakagawa, H.	LDP LDP	Kan, N.	SAKI
41	Mitsuzaka, H.	LDP	Aso, T.	LDP	Okano, Y.	LDP	Kosugi, T. Chikaoka, R.	LDP LDP		

JAPAN 1945–1998

Gov	Housing	Py	Agriculture	Py	Industry/Trade	Py	Environment	Py
1			Wada, H.	NONA	Hoshijima, J.	LP		
2			Hirano, R.	SP	Mizutani, C.	SP		
3			Nagae, K.	SP	Mizutani, C.	SP		
4			Sudo, H.	LP	Oya, S.	LP		
5			Oya, S.	LP	Inagaki, H.	PP		
6			Hirokawa, K.	LP	Yokoo, S.	LP		
7			Ogasawara, S.	LP	Ikeda, H.	LP		
8			Ochida, S.	YL	Okano, K.	YL		
9			Kono, I.	DP	Ishibashi, T.	DP		
10			Kono, I.	DP	Ishibashi, T.	DP		
11			Kono, I.	DP	Ishibashi, T.	DP		
12			Ide, I.	LDP	Mizuta, M.	LDP		
13			Ide, I.	LDP	Mizuta, M.	LDP		
14			Miura, K.	LDP	Takasaki, T.	LDP		
15			Nanjo, T.	LDP	Ishii, M.	LDP		
16			Suto, H.	LDP	Shiina, E.	LDP		
17			Akagi, M.	LDP	Fukuda, H.	LDP		
18			Akagi, M.	LDP	Sakurauchi, Y.	LDP		
19			Kuraishi, T.	LDP	Kanno, W.	LDP		
20			Kuraishi, T.	LDP	Miyazawa, K.	LDP		
21			Adachi, T.	LDP	Nakasone, Y.	LDP	Koyama, O.	LDP
22			Sakurauchi, Y.	LDP	Nakasone, Y.	LDP	Miki, T.	LDP
23			Abe, S.	LDP	Komoto, T.	LDP	Ozawa, T.	LDP
24			Suzuki, Z.	LDP	Tanaka, T.	LDP	Ishihara, S.	LDP
25			Watanabe, M.	LDP	Esaki, M.	LDP	Kemura, S.	LDP
26			Muto, K.	LDP	Sasaki, Y.	LDP	Tsuchiya, Y.	LDP
27			Kameoka, T.	LDP	Tanaka, R.	LDP	Kujiraoke, H.	LDP

JAPAN 1945–1998

Gov	Housing	Py	Agriculture	Py	Industry/Trade	Py	Environment	Py
28			Kaneko, I.	LDP	Yamanaka, S.	LDP		
29			Yamamura, S.	LDP	Okonogi, H.	LDP	Ueda, M.	LDP
30			Sato, Mo.	LDP	Murata, K.	LDP	*Ishimoto, S.	LDP
31			Kato, M.	LDP	Tamura, H.	LDP	Inamura, T.	LDP
32			Sato, T.	LDP	Tamura, H.	LDP	Horiuchi, M.	LDP
33			Horinouchi, H.	LDP	Kajiyama, S.	LDP	Yamazaki, T.	LDP
34			Kano, M.	LDP	Matsunaga,	LDP	*Moriyama, M.	LDP
35			Yamamoto, T.	LDP	Muto, K.	LDP	Ishimatsu, K.	LDP
36			Tanabu, M.	LDP	Watanabe, K.	LDP	Nakamura, S.	LDP
37			Hata, E.	SHIN	Kumagai, H.	SHIN	*Hironaka, W.	KOM
38			Kato, M.	SHIN	Hata, E.	SHIN	Hamayotsu, T.	KOM
39			Okawara, T.	LDP	Hashimoto, R.	LDP	Sakurai, S.	LDP
40			Ohara, I.	LDP	Tsukahara, S.	LDP	Iwatare, S.	SDPJ
41			Fujimoto, T.	LDP	Sato, S.	LDP	Ishii, M.	LDP

Gov	Social Affairs (py)	Public Works (py)	Other (py)	Res
1	Kawai, Y. (NONA)	Hiratsuka, T. (LP)	Shidehara, K. (PP) Saito, T. (PP) Uehara, E. (LP) Ishimatsu, S. (PP) Hitotsumatsu, S. (PP)	1
2	Hitotsumatsu, S. (PP)	Tomabechi, G. (PP) Miki, T. (CP)	Wada, H. (NONA) Saito, T. (PP) Nishie, S. (SP) Hayashi, H. (PP)	0

JAPAN 1945–1998

Gov	Social Affairs (py)	Public Works (py)	Other (py)	Res
3	Takeda, G. (PP)	Okada, S. (CP) Tomiyoshi, E. (SP)		0
4	Hayashi, J. (LP)	Mautani, S. (LP) Okawa, S. (LP) Furihata, T. (LP)	Satake, H. (SRP) Ueda, S. (NONA) Iwamotu, N. (LP) Inouye, T. (LP)	0
5	Hayashi, J. (LP)	Masutani, S. (LP) Ozawa, S. (LP)	Masuda, K. (LP) Yamaguchi, K.(LP) Higai, S. (LP) Honda, I. (LP)	0
6	Kurokawa, T. (LP)	Masuda, K. (LP) Yamasaki, T. (LP) Tamura, B. (LP)	Okazaki, K. (LP)	2
7	Yamagata, K. (LP)	Sato, E. (LP) Ishii, M. (LP) Takase, S. (LP)	Hayashida, K. (LP) Onogi, H. (LP) Ogata, T. (LP) Kimura, T. (LP)	0
8	Yamagata, K. (YL)	Tatsuka, K. (YL) Ishii, M. (YL)	Kimura, T. (YL) Onogi, H. (YL) Ono, B. (YL) Ando, M. (YL) Fukunaga, K. (YL)	1
9	Tsurumi, Y. (DP)	Takeyama, Y. (DP) Miki, T. (DP) Takechi, Y. (DP)	Miyoshi, H. (DP)	0
10	Kawasaki, H. (DP)	Takeyama, Y. (DP) Miki, T. (DP) Matsuda, T. (DP)	Miyoshi, H. (DP)	0

JAPAN 1945–1998

Gov	Social Affairs (py)	Public Works (py)	Other (py)	Res
11	Kobayashi, E. (LDP)	Baba, M. (LDP) Yoshino, S. (LDP) Murakami, I. (LDP)	Shoriki, M. (LDP) Nemoto, R. (LDP)	0
12	Kanda, H. (LDP)	Nanjo, T. (LDP) Miyazawa, T. (LDP) Hirai, T. (LDP)	Okubo, T. (LDP) Ishida, H. (LDP) Kawamura, M. (LDP)	0
13	Kanda, H. (LDP)	Nanjo, T. (LDP) Miyazawa, T. (LDP) Hirai, T. (LDP)	Akaji, M. (LDP)	1
14	Hashimoto, R. (LDP)	Endo, S. (LDP) Nagano, M. (LDP) Terao, Y. (LDP)	Yamaguchi, K. (LDP) Ikeda, H. (LDP)	3
15	*Nakayama, M. (LDP)	Hashimoto, T. (LDP) Minami, Y. (LDP) Suzuki, Z. (LDP)		0
16	Furui, Y. (LDP)	Nakamura, U. (LDP) Kogure, B. (LDP) Kogane, Y. (LDP)	Ozawa, S. (LDP) Ikeda, N. (LDP)	3
17	Kobayashi, T. (LDP)	Kono, I. (LDP) Ayabe, K. (LDP) Koike, S. (LDP)	Kurogana, Y. (LDP) Sato, E. (LDP)	1
18	Kanda, H. (LDP)	Koyama, O. (LDP) Matsuura, S. (LDP) Tokuyasu, J. (LDP)	Masuhara, K. (LDP) Hashimoto, T. (LDP) Kono, I. (LDP)	3
19	Bo, H. (LDP)	Nishimura, E. (LDP) Ohashi, T. (LDP) Kobayashi, T. (LDP)	Matsudaira, I. (LDP) Nikaido, S. (LDP) Isukahara, T. (LDP) Fukunaga, K. (LDP)	2

JAPAN 1945–1998

Gov	Social Affairs (py)	Public Works (py)	Other (py)	Res
20	Uchida, T. (LDP)	Nemoto, R. (LDP) Hashimoto, T. (LDP) Ide, I. (LDP)	Hori, S.	1
21	Shiomi, S. (LDP)	Kimura, T. (LDP) Sasaki, H. (LDP) Miike, M. (LDP)	Nishida, S. (LDP) Araki, M. (LDP)	0
22	Saito, K. (LDP)	Kanemaru, S. (LDP) Shintani, T. (LDP) Kuno, C. (LDP)	Esaki, M. (LDP) Nikaido, S. (LDP) Tsubokawa, S. (LDP)	3
23	Tanaka, M. (LDP)	Kariya, T. (LDP) Kimura, M. (LDP) Murakami, I. (LDP)	Fukuda, H. (LDP) Ide, I. (LDP) Ueki, M. (LDP) Kanemaru, S. (LDP)	1
24	Watanabe, M. (LDP)	Hasegawa, S. (LDP) Tamura, H. (LDP) Komiyama, J. (LDP)	Ogana, H. (LDP) Sonoda, S. (LDP) Fujita, M. (LDP) Tazawa, K. (LDP)	1
25	Hashimoto, R. (LDP)	Tokai, M. (LDP) Moriyama, K. (LDP) Shirahama, N. (LDP)	Shibuya, N. (LDP) Tanaka, R. (LDP) Mihara, A. (LDP) Nakano, S. (LDP)	0
26	Noro, K. (LDP)	Watanabe, E. (LDP) Chisaki, U. (LDP) Onishi, M. (LDP)	Ito, M. (LDP) Obuchi, K. (LDP) Sonoda, S. (LDP)	0
27	Saito, H. (LDP)	Saito, S. (LDP) Shiokawa, M. (LDP) Yamanouchi, I. (LDP)	Miyazawa, K. (LDP) Hara, K. (LDP)	2

JAPAN 1945–1998

Gov	Social Affairs (py)	Public Works (py)	Other (py)	Res
28	Hayashi, Y. (LDP)	Utsumi, H. (LDP) Hasegawa, T. (LDP) Higaki, T. (LDP)	Gotoda, M. (LDP) Kato, K. (LDP) Saito, J. (LDP)	0
29	Watanabe, K. (LDP)	Mizuno, K. (LDP) Osoda, K. (LDP) Okuda, K. (LDP)	Fujinama, T. (LDP) Inamura, S. (LDP) Nakanishi, I. (LDP) Mogushi, T. (LDP)	0
30	Masuoka, H. (LDP)	Sato, Me. (LDP) Kibe, Y. (LDP) Yamashita, T. (LDP)	Fujinama, T. (LDP) Gotoda, M. (LDP) Kawamoto, K. (LDP) Komoto, T. (LDP) Mogushi, T. (LDP)	2
31	Saito, J. (LDP)	Hashimoto, R. (LDP) Karasawa, (LDP) Amano, K. (LDP)	Kanemaru, S. (LDP) Gotoda, M. (LDP) Tamaki, K. (LDP) Watanuki, T. (LDP)	0
32	Fujimoto, T. (LDP)	Ishihara, S. (LDP) Nakayama, M. (LDP) Ochi, I. (LDP)	Obuchi, K. (LDP) Takatori, O. (LDP) Kasuya, S. (LDP) Okuno, S. (LDP)	1
33	Koizumi, J. (LDP)	Yamamura, S. (LDP) Muraoka, K. (LDP) Noda, T. (LDP)	Shiokawa, M. (LDP) Ikeda, Y. (LDP) Inone, K. (LDP) Nonaka, E. (LDP)	0
34	Toida, S. (LDP)	Eto, T. (LDP) Oishi, S. (LDP) Harada, S. (LDP)	Yamashita, T. (LDP) Mizuno, K. (LDP) Abe, F. (LDP)	0
35	Tsushima, Y. (LDP)	Ono, A. (LDP) Fukaya, T. (LDP) Watanuki, T. (LDP)	Sakamoto, M. (LDP) Funada, S. (LDP) Sato, M. (LDP)	2

JAPAN 1945–1998

Gov	Social Affairs (py)	Public Works (py)	Other (py)	Res
36	Yamashita, T. (LDP)	Okuda, K. (LDP) Watanabe, H. (LDP) Yamasaki, T. (LDP)	Kato, K. (LDP) Ie, T. (LDP) Toya, Y. (LDP)	2
37	Ouchi, K. (DSP)	Ito, S. (SDPJ) Kanzaki, T. (KOM) Igarashi, K. (SDPJ)	Yamahana, S. (SDPJ) Takemura, M. (SAKI) Ishida, K. (KOM) Uehara, K. (SDPJ)	0
38	Ouchi, K. (DSP)	Futami, N. (KOM) Hikasa, K. (KOM) Morimoto, K. (KOM)	Kumagai, H. (SHIN) Sato, M. (SHIN) Sato, M. (SHIN)	0
39	Ide, S. (SAKI)	Kamei, S. (LDP) Oide, S. (SDPJ) Nosaka, K. (SDPJ)	Igarashi, K. (SDPJ) Ozato, S. (LDP) Osawa, K. (LDP)	1
40	Kan, N. (SAKI)	Kamei, Y. (LDP) Hino, I. (SDPJ) Nakao, E. (LDP)	Kajiyama, S. (LDP) Okabe, S. (LDP) Suzuki, K. (SDPJ)	0
41	Koizumi, J. (LDP)	Koga, M. (LDP) Horinouchi, H. (LDP) Kamei, S. (LDP)	Kajiyama, S. (LDP) Inagaki, J. (LDP) Ito, K. (LDP)	

28. LATVIA

The Saeima (parliament) indirectly elects the Head of State, the President, for a three-year term. He or she has the right to convene government meetings. He or she has also the right to dissolve parliament and the right of legislative initiative.

Latvia is a unitary and centralised state.

Parliament is unicameral. Its 100 members are elected for a fixed period of three years by proportional representation (St. Lagüe) with a five-percent threshold. The electoral unit is the whole country.

Parliament has a quorum of at least 50 per cent of all members. Votes are carried by a majority of all members present. Some issues require a qualified majority, ranging from an absolute majority to a majority of three-quarters of all members. Constitutional amendments require a majority of two-thirds of all members present (quorum) and always require popular consent by referendum. The outcome is binding. On other issues, a referendum can be held on the initiative of the President, the government or parliament. The outcome here is binding as well.

The President appoints the Prime Minister and the other members of government, but they must have the confidence of parliament by a vote of investiture. Parliament may also table votes of no confidence during the lifetime of a government. Losing either vote always results in resignation of the government. Government is both collectively and individually responsible to parliament. Individual ministers may also be members of parliament. The Prime Minister has a rather prominent position in government.

There is no judicial review. The President is entrusted with safeguarding the constitution and the conformity of public measures to the constitution.

LATVIA 1993-1998

Gov	Begin	Dur	RtT	ToG	Py1	Py2	Py3	Py4	Py5	Py6	Seats	CPG	NoM	Prime Minister (py)
1	03.08.93	408	4	5	LC 36	LZS 12		LNNK-ZP 8			100	3	14	Birkavs, V. (LC)
2	15.09.94	462	1	5	LC 36	TPA 4	[SLAT 9]				100	3	14	Gailis, M. (LC)
3	21.12.95		3		DPS 18	LC 17	TB 14	LNNK-ZP 8	LZS-LKDS-LLDP 8	LV 8	100	2	16	Skele, A. (NONA)

- [] Denotes party supporting the government without participating in it.
- Gov 2: TPA is breakaway faction of SLAT (9).

Gov	Deputy PM	Py	Foreign Affairs	Py	Defence	Py	Interior	Py	Justice	Py
1	Gailis, M.	LC	Andrejevs, G.	LC	Pavloskis, V.	LC	Gailis, M.	LC	Levits, E.	LC
	Kehris, O.	LC					Kristovskis, G.	LC		
	Levits, E.	LC								
2	Birkavs, V.	LC	Birkavs, V.	LC	Trapans, J.A.	NONA	*Teranda, V.A.	LC	Apsitis, R.	LC
	Piebalgs, A.	LC					Kristovskis, G.	LC		
	Vaivads, J.	LC								
3	Cevers, Z.	DPS	Birkavs, V.	LC	Krastins, A.	LC	Turlais, D.	DPS	Rasnacs, D.	TB
	Krastins, A.	LNNK-ZP								
	Grinblats, M.	TB								
	Kauls, A.	LV								
	Gailis, M.	LC								

LATVIA 1993-1998

Gov	Finance	Py	Economic Aff.	Py	Labour	Py	Education	Py	Health	Py
1	Osis, U.	LC	Kehris, O.	LC			Vaivads, J.	LC		
2	Piebalgs, A.	LC	Zvanitajs, J.	NONA			Vaivads, J.	LC		
3	Kreituss, A.G.	DPS	Krasts, G.	TB			Grinblats, M.	TB		

Gov	Housing	Py	Agriculture	Py	Industry/Trade	Py	Environment	Py
1			Kinna, J.	LZS			Lukins, G.	LC
2			Udris, A.	NONA			Iesalnieks, J.	TPA
3			Kauls, A.	LV			Gailis, M.	LC

Gov	Social Affairs (py)	Public Works (py)	Other (py)	Res
1	Ritenis, J. (LZS)	Gutmanis, A. (LC)	Viavads, J. (LC) / Lukins, G. (LC) / Inkens, E. (LC)	1
2	Berzins, A. (LC)	Gutmanis, A. (LC)	Iesalnieks, J. (TPA) / Dripe, J. (NONA)	1
3	Makarovs, V. (TB)	Kristopans, V. (LC)	Sparitis, O. (LZS) / Kirsteins, A. (LNNK-ZP) / Jurkans, E. (DPS)	3

29. LITHUANIA

The Head of State, the President, is directly elected for a five-year term. The President has an extensive role in foreign policy. Otherwise, his or her role in the executive is limited to appointing officials, signing decrees and laws and representing the country.

Lithuania is a unitary and centralised state.

Parliament (Seimas) is unicameral. Its 141 members are elected for a fixed term of four years by a mixed system of plurality voting and proportional representation (d'Hondt) with a five- percent threshold. Constituencies vary in size and are slightly skewed to the south-east region in terms of the relationship of deputies to electorate.

Parliament has a quorum of at least 50 per cent of all members. Votes are carried by a majority of all members present. Some issues require a qualified majority, ranging from a majority to a four-fifth majority of all members. Constitutional amendments require a two-thirds majority of all members. Constitutional amendments always require popular consent by means of a referendum. The outcome is binding. On other issues, parliament and a portion of the electorate may call a referendum. The outcome here is also binding.

The government is formed by the Prime Minister and must have the confidence of parliament, both by means of a vote of investiture, or, during its lifetime, by a vote of confidence. Losing either vote always results in resignation of the government. The government is both collectively and individually responsible to parliament. Individual ministers may also be members of parliament. The Prime Minister has a dominant position in government.

The Constitutional Court reviews the constitutionality of all laws, decrees and other measures. The Court can act either on its own initiative or on the request of the executive, the legislature or private citizens.

LITHUANIA 1992-1998

Gov	Begin	Dur	RfT	ToG	Py1	Py2	Py3	Seats	CPG	NoM	Prime Minister (py)
1	10.12.92	96	1	1	DLP 73			141	4	9	Lubys, B. (DLP)
2	16.03.93	1074	6	1	DLP 73			141	4	17	Slezevicius, A. (DLP)
3	23.02.96	278	1	1	DLP 73			141	4	18	Stankevicius, L.M. (DLP)
4	27.11.96			3	TS-LK 70	LKDP 16	LCS 13	141	3	18	Vagnorius, G. (TS-LK)

- Gov 1: Reason for Termination is the election of A. Brazauskas as President.

Gov	Deputy PM	Py	Foreign Affairs	Py	Defence	Py	Interior	Py	Justice	Py
1			Gylys, P.	DLP	Butkevicius, A.	DLP	Vaitiekunas, R.	DLP	Prapriestis, J.	DLP
2			Gylys, P.	DLP	Butkevicius, A.	DLP	Vaitiekunas, R.	DLP	Prapriestis, J.	DLP
3			Gylys, P.	DLP	Linkevicius, L.	DLP	Papovas, P. bulovas, V.	DLP DLP	Prapriestis, J.	DLP
4	Lazdinis, I.	LCS	Saudargas, A.	LKDP	Stankevicius, C.	LKDP	Skrebys, K. Ziemelis, V.	TS-LK TS-LK	Pakalniskis, V.	TS-LK

Gov	Finance	Py	Economic Aff.	Py	Labour	Py	Education	Py	Health	Py
1	Grikelis, E.	DLP	Veselka, J.	DLP		DLP				
2	Grikelis, E.	DLP	Veselka, J.	DLP		DLP	Trinkunas, D.	DLP	Briedikis, J.	DLP
3	Krizinauskas, A.	DLP			Mikaila, M.	DLP	Domarkas, V.	DLP	Vinkus, A.	DLP
4	Matilauskas, R.	TS-LK	Babilius, V.	LCI+	*Degutiene, I.	TS-LK	Zinkevicius, Z.	LKDP	Galdikas, J.	TS-LK

- Gov 4: LCI+ = Vice-President of the Lithuanian Confederation of Industrialists (LCI). Appointed by TS-LK.

LITHUANIA 1992-1998

Gov	Housing	Py	Agriculture	Py	Industry/Trade	Py	Environment	Py
1			Karazija, R.	DLP	Sinevicius, A.	DLP		
2			Kovalcikas, G.	DLP	Sinevicius, A.	DLP		
			Karazija, R.	DLP				
3			Vasiliauskas, A.	DLP	Klimasauskas, K.-J.	DLP	Bradauskas, B.	DLP
			Einoris, V.	DLP				
4			Knasys, V.	TS-LK				

Gov	Social Affairs (py)	Public Works (py)	Other (py)	Res
1				0
2	Medaiskis, T. (DLP)	Stasiyukinas, A.V. (DLP) Zindelis, G. (DLP) Vapsys, A. (DLP) Birziskis, J. (BLP)	Trinkunas, D. (DLP)	2
3	Mikaila, M. (DLP)	Abraitis, V.B. (DLP) Baranauskiene, A. (DLP) Birziskis, J. (DLP)	Nekrosius, J. (DLP)	0
4	*Degutiene, I. (TS-LK)	Caplikas, A. (LCS) Zvaliauskas, A. (TS-LK)	*Andrikiene, L. (TS-LK) Saltenis, S. (TS-LK) Caplikas, A. (LCS) Skrebys, K. (TS-LK)	

30. LUXEMBOURG

The Head of State is a hereditary Grand Duke with largely ceremonial powers.

The state is highly centralised and unitary.

Parliament is unicameral. Its 60 members are elected by proportional representation (Hagenbach) within four territorial constituencies (North, South, East & West), unequal in size, with the South being most heavily populated.

Parliament has a quorum of at least 50 per cent of all members. Votes are carried by a majority of all members present. Constitutional amendments require a two-thirds majority of all votes cast. A referendum is optional. The outcome is not binding.

The Prime Minister, generally leader of the largest party, nominates the Cabinet from members of parliament and faces a vote of investiture in parliament. There may be votes of confidence at various stages in the government's life. Losing either vote always results in resignation of the government. The government is both collectively and individually responsible to parliament. Being a minister is not compatible with being a Member of Parliament. The Prime Minister has no dominant position in government

The Constitutional Council reviews legislation.

Turnout

%
Women

1999   16.67   87%

LUXEMBOURG 1945-1998

(Handwritten notes in margin: "Left" with values .28, .40, .46, .40, .40, .44, .49, .55, .46, .45, .45, .45)

(Handwritten: CSP = CD ; SPP = Left)

Gov	Begin	Dur	RfT	ToG	Py1	Py2	Py3	Py4	Seats	CPG	NoM	Prime Minister (py)
1	20.11.45	466	x	3	CSP 25	SDP 11	DP 9	CP 5	51	3	8	Dupong, P. (CSP)
2	01.03.47	501	1	2	CSP 25	DP 9			51	2	7	Dupong, P. (CSP)
3	14.07.48	1084	1	2	CSP 22	DP 9			52	2	7	Dupong, P. (CSP)
4	03.07.51	910	3	2	CSP 21	SDP 18			52	3	6	Dupong, P. (CSP)
5	29.12.53	182	1	2	CSP 21	SDP 18			52	3	6	Bech, J. (CSP)
6	29.06.54	1369	2	2	CSP 26	SDP 17			52	3	8	Bech, J. (CSP)
7	29.03.58	333	4	2	CSP 26	SDP 17			52	3	8	Frieden, P. (CSP)
8	25.02.59	1970	1	2	CSP 21	DP 11			52	2	7	Werner, P. (CSP)
9	18.07.64	900	5	2	CSP 22	SDP 21			56	3	8	Werner, P. (CSP)
10	04.01.67	758	4	2	CSP 22	SDP 21			56	3	8	Werner, P. (CSP)
11	31.01.69	1961	1	2	CSP 21	DP 11			56	2	7	Werner, P. (CSP)
12	15.06.74	1856	1	2	DP 14	SDP 17			59	4	8	Thorn, G. (DP)
13	15.07.79	1832	1	2	CSP 24	DP 15			59	2	9	Werner, P. (CSP)
14	20.07.84	1818	1	2	CSP 25	SDP 21			64	3	9	Santer, J. (CSP)
15	14.07.89	1823	1	2	CSP 22	SDP 18			60	3	10	Santer, J. (CSP)
16	13.07.94	409	2	2	CSP 21	SDP 17			60	3	10	Santer, J. (CSP)
17	26.01.95			2	CSP 21	SDP 17			60	3	10	Juncker, J.C. (CSP)

- Gov 1: Reason for Termination unknown.

(Handwritten: 1959)

(Handwritten: SDP 13 (not in cabinet))

Gov	Deputy PM	Py	Foreign Affairs	Py	Defence	Py	Interior
1			Bech, J.	CSP	Dupong, P.	CSP	Schaus, E.
2			Bech, J.	CSP	Schaus, L.	CSP	Schaus, E.
3			Bech, J.	CSP	Dupong, P.	CSP	Schaus, E.
4			Bech, J.	CSP			Frieden, P.

LUXEMBOURG 1945–1998

Gov	Deputy PM	Py	Foreign Affairs	Py	Defence	Py	Interior	Py	Justice	Py
5			Bech, J.	CSP			Frieden, P.	CSP	Bodson, V.	SDP
6			Bech, J.	CSP	Werner, P.	CSP	Frieden, P.	CSP	Bodson, V.	SDP
7			Bech, J.	CSP	Werner, P.	CSP	Frieden, P.	CSP	Bodson, V.	SDP
8			Schaus, E.	DP	Schaus, E.	DP	Grégoire, P.	DP	Elvinger, P.	DP
9	Cravatte, H.	SDP	Werner, P.	CSP	Fischbach, M.	CSP	Cravatte, H.	SDP	Werner, P.	CSP
10	Cravatte, H.	SDP	Grégoire, P.	CSP	Grégoire, P.	CSP	Cravatte, H.	SDP	Dupong, J.	CSP
11	Schaus, E.	DP	Thorn, G.	DP			Schaus, E. / Thorn, G.	DP / DP	Schaus, E.	DP
12	Vouel, R.	SDP	Thorn, G.	SDP	Krieps, E.	DP	Krieps, E. / Wohlfahrt, J.	DP / SDP	Krieps, R.	SDP
13	Thorn, G.	DP	Thorn, G.	DP	Krieps, E.	DP	Wolter, J. / Konen, R.	DP / DP	Thorn, G.	DP
14	Poos, J.	SDP	Poos, J.	SDP	Fischbach, M.	CSP	Spautz, J. / Fischbach, M.	CSP / CSP	Krieps, R.	SDP
15	Poos, J.	SDP	Poos, J.	SDP			Spautz, J. / Fischbach, M.	CSP / CSP	Fischbach, M.	CSP
16	Poos, J.	SDP	Poos, J.	SDP	Bodry, A.	SDP	Boden, F. / Spautz, J.	CSP / CSP	Fischbach, M.	CSP
17	Poos, J.	SDP	Poos, J.	SDP	Bodry, A.	SDP	Wolter, M.	CSP	Fischbach, M.	CSP

Gov	Finance	Py	Economic Aff.	Py	Labour	Py	Education	Py	Health	Py
1	Dupong, P.	CSP	Konsbruck, G.	CSP	Krier, P.	SDP	Margue, N.	CSP	Marx, C.	CP
2	Dupong, P.	CSP	Schaus, L.	CSP	Dupong, P.	CSP	Margue, N.	CSP	Osch, A.	DP
3	Dupong, P.	CSP	Hentgen,	CSP	Dupong, P.	CSP	Frieden, P.	CSP	Osch, A.	DP

LUXEMBOURG 1945–1998

Gov	Finance	Py	Economic Aff.	Py	Labour	Py	Education	Py	Health	Py
4	Dupong, P.	CSP	Rasquin, M.	SDP	Biever, N.	SDP	Frieden, P.	CSP	Frieden, P.	CSP
5	Werner, P.	CSP	Rasquin, M.	SDP	Biever, N.	SDP	Frieden, P.	CSP	Frieden, P.	CSP
6	Werner, P.	CSP	Rasquin, M.	SDP	Biever, N.	SDP	Frieden, P.	CSP	Colling, E.	CSP
7	Werner, P.	CSP	Wilwertz, P.	SDP	Biever, N.	SDP	Frieden, P.	CSP	Colling, E.	CSP
8	Werner, P.	CSP	Elvinger, P.	DP	Colling, E.	CSP	Schaus, E.	CSP	Colling, E.	CSP
9	Werner, P. / Wehenkel, A.	CSP / SDP	Wehenkel, A.	SDP	Biever N.	SDP	Grégoire, P.	CSP	Biever N.	SDP
10	Werner, P. / Wehenkel, A.	CSP / SDP	Wehenkel, A.	SDP	Krier, A.	SDP	Dupong, J.	CSP	Krier, A.	SDP
11	Werner, P.	CSP	Mart, M.	DP	Dupong, J.	CSP	Dupong, J.	CSP	*Frieden-Kinnen, M.	CSP
12	Vouel, R.	SDP	Mart, M.	DP	Berg, B.	SDP	Krieps, R.	SDP	Krieps, E.	DP
13	Santer, J.	DP	Thorn, G.	DP	Santer, J.	DP	Boden, F.	DP	Krieps, E.	DP
14	Juncker, J-C. / Santer, J.	CSP / CSP	Poos, J.	SDP	Juncker, J-C.	CSP	Boden, F.	CSP	Berg, G.	SDP
15	Juncker, J-C. / Santer, J.	CSP / CSP	Goebbels, R.	SDP	Juncker, J-C.	CSP	Fischbach, M.	CSP	Lahure, J.	SDP
16	Juncker, J.-C. / Santer, J.	CSP / CSP	Goebbels, R.	SDP	Juncker, J.-C.	CSP	Fischbach, M.	CSP	Lahure, J.	SDP
17	Fischbach, M. / Juncker, J.-C.	CSP / CSP	Boden, F. / Goebbels, R.	CSP / SDP	Juncker, J.-C.	CSP	*Hennicot-Schoepges, E.	CSP	Lahure, J.	SDP

LUXEMBOURG 1945–1998

Gov	Housing	Py	Agriculture	Py	Industry/Trade	Py	Environment	Py
1			Bech, J. Margue, N.	CSP CSP	Krier, P.	SDP		
2			Bech, J. Margue, N.	CSP CSP	Bech, J.	CSP		
3			Hentgen,	CSP				
4			Dupong, P.	CSP				
5			Bech, J.	CSP				
6			Colling, E.	CSP				
7			Colling, E.	CSP	Bech, J.	CSP		
8			Schaus, L.	CSP	Schaus, E.	DP		
9			Colling, E.	CSP	Biever, N.	SDP		
10			Buchler, J.-P.	CSP	Krier, A.	SDP		
11			Buchler, J.-P.	CSP				
12			Hamilius, J.	DP			Krieps, E.	DP
13			Ney, C.	CSP	Werner, P. Thorn, G. Konen, R.	CSP DP DP	Bartel, J.	DP
14			Fischbach, M.	CSP	Poos, J.	SDP	Krieps, R.	SDP
15			Steichen, R.	CSP	Poos, J.	SDP	Bodry, A.	SDP
16	Boden, F. Spautz, J.	CSP CSP	*Jacobs, M.-J.	CSP	Poos, J.	SDP	Lahure, J.	SDP
17	Boden, F.	CSP	Boden, F.	CSP	Poos, J.	SDP	Lahure, J.	SDP

LUXEMBOURG 1945–1998

Gov	Social Affairs (py)	Public Works (py)	Other (py)	Res
1	Krier, P. (SDP) Marx, C. (CP)	Bodson, V. (SDP) Krier, P. (SDP)		0
2	Dupong, P. (CSP) Osch, A. (DP)	Osch, A. (DP) Schaffner, R. (DP)	Dupong, P. (CSP)	0
3	Osch, A. (DP)	Schaffner, R. (DP)		0
4		Bodson, V. (SDP) Rasquin, M. (SDP)		0
5		Bodson, V. (SDP) Rasquin, M. (SDP)		0
6	Frieden, P. (CSP) Biever, N. (SDP)	Bodson, V. (SDP)	Bodson, V. (SDP) Rasquin, M. (SDP) Wilwertz, P. (SDP)	0
7	Biever, N. (SDP)	Bodson, V. (SDP)	Cravatte, H. (SDP)	0
8	Colling, E. (CSP)	Grégoire, P. (CSP) Schaffner, R. (DP)	Schaffner, R. (DP)	0
9	Fischbach, M. (CSP) Biever, N. (SDP) Colling, E. (CSP)	Wehenkel, A. (SDP) Grégoire, P. (CSP) Bousser, A. (SDP)	Cravatte, H. (SDP) Grégoire, P. (CSP)	0
10	Dupong, J. (CSP) Krier, A. (SDP) Buchler, J-P. (CSP)	Wehenkel, A. (SDP) Bousser, A. (SDP)	Cravatte, H. (SDP) Grégoire, P. (CSP)	0
11	Mart, M. (DP) Dupong, J. (CSP) *Frieden-Kinnen, M. (CSP)	Mart, M. (DP) Buchler, J.-P. (CSP)	Thorn, G. (DP) *Frieden-Kinnen, M. (CSP)	1
12	Berg, B. (SDP) Mart, M. (DP)	Vouel, R. (SDP) Hamilius, J. (DP) Mart, M. (DP)	Thorn, G. (DP) Krieps, R. (SDP) Mart, M. (DP)	1

LUXEMBOURG 1945–1998

Gov	Social Affairs (py)	Public Works (py)	Other (py)	Res
13	Thorn, G. (DP) Wolter, J. (DP) Santer, J. (DP)	Bartel, J. (DP)	Werner, P. (CSP) Boden, F. (DP) Krieps, E. (DP)	1
14	Spautz, J. (CSP) Berg, G. (SDP)	Santer, J. (CSP) Schlechter, M. (SDP)	Santer, J. (CSP) Boden, F. (CSP) Fischbach, M. (CSP) Krieps, R. (SDP)	0
15	Poos, J. (SDP) Spautz, J. (CSP) Boden, F. (CSP) Lahure, J. (SDP)	Goebbels, R. (SDP) Bodry, A. (SDP)	Santer, J. (CSP) Poos, J. (SDP) Spautz, J. (CSP) Boden, F. (CSP) Lahure, J. (SDP) Bodry, A. (SDP)	0
16	Boden, F. (CSP) Bodry, A. (SDP) *Delvaux-Stehres, M. (SDP)	Goebbels, R. (SDP) *Delvaux-Stehres, M. (SDP)	Santer, J. (CSP) Poos, J. (SDP) Boden, F. (CSP) *Jacobs, M.-J. (CSP) Bodry, A. (SDP)	0
17	*Jacobs, M.-J. (CSP) Bodry, A. (SDP) *Delvaux-Stehres, M. (SDP)	Goebbels, R. (SDP) *Delvaux-Stehres, M. (SDP)	Juncker, J.-C. (CSP) Boden, F. (CSP) Fischbach, M. (CSP) *Jacobs, M.-J. (CSP) *Hennicot-Schoepges, E. (CSP) Poos, J. (SDP) Bodry, A. (SDP)	

31. MACEDONIA

The Head of State, the President, is directly elected for a five-year term. His or her role is by and large ceremonial. But (s)he has an important role as a political arbitrator between the (ethnically based) parties and guarantor of constitutional legality.

The State is unitary but decentralised.

Parliament is unicameral. Its 140 members are elected for a fixed term of four years by a mixed system of plurality voting and proportional representation (d'Hondt) with a five-percent threshold. Plurality voting takes place in 85 single-member constituencies, which are roughly equal in size (around 15,000 electors on average). For the PR-vote there is one nation-wide constituency. Parliament has the right to dissolve itself.

Parliament has a quorum of at least 50 per cent of its members. Votes are carried by a majority of all members present, which has to be no less than one-third of all members. For some issues a qualified majority is required, ranging from an absolute majority to a two-thirds majority of all members. Constitutional amendments require a two-thirds majority of all members and always require popular consent by a binding referendum. For other issues, parliament and citizens may also call for a referendum. The outcome here is also binding. Lastly, apart from members of parliament and the government, (a group of at least 10.000) citizens also has the right to initiate legislation.

Governments must survive a vote of investiture and can face to a vote of no confidence at any time during their lifetime. Losing either vote always results in resignation of the government. Government is both collectively and individually responsible to parliament. Being a minister is not compatible with being a Member of Parliament. The Prime Minister has no dominant position in government.

The Constitutional Court adjudicates the constitutionality of laws and other public regulations, as well as conflicts between central and local government.

MACEDONIA 1994-1998

Gov	Begin	Dur	RfT	ToG	Py1	Py2	Py3	Py4	Seats	CPG	NoM	Prime Minister (py)
1	28.11.94	452	4	3	SDSM 58	LP 29	PDP 10	SPM 8	120	3	20	Crvenkovski, B. (SDSM)
2	23.02.96			3	SDSM 58	PDP 10	SPM 8	SDSM	120	4	20	Crvenkovski, B. (SDSM)

Gov	Deputy PM	Py	Foreign Affairs	Py	Defence	Py	Interior	Py	Justice	Py
1	Miljovski, J. Zuta, B. Trpeski, L.	SDSM PDP SPM	Crvenkovski, S.	LP	Handziski, B.	SDSM	Frckovski, L.	SDSM	Popovski, V.	SDSM
2			Frckovski, L.	SDSM	Handziski, B.	SDSM	Cokrevski, T.	SDSM	Popovski, V.	SDSM

Gov	Finance	Py	Economic Aff.	Py	Labour	Py	Education	Py	Health	Py
1	Miljovski, J.	SDSM	Ivanov, R. Zuta, B.	LP PDP			*Simoska, E. *Todorova, S.	NONA SDSM	Filipche, I.	SPM
2	Fiti, T.	SDSM	Zuta, B. Bedzeti, A.	PDP PDP	Ziberi, N.	PDP	*Todorova, S. Selmani, A.	SDSM PDP	Filipche, I.	SPM

Gov	Housing	Py	Agriculture	Py	Industry/Trade	Py	Environment	Py
1			Angelov, I.	LP			Shundovsky, J.	SDSM
2			Parakeov, N.	SDSM			Shundovsky, J.	SDSM

MACEDONIA 1994-1998

Gov	Social Affairs (py)	Public Works (py)	Other (py)	Res
1	Sabriju, I. (PDP)	Shundovsky, J. (SDSM)	*Simoska, E. (NONA)	0
		Buzlevski, D. (SDSM)	Aliu, E. (PDP)	
			Shundovsky, J. (SDSM)	
			Angelov, I. (LP)	
			Trpeski, L. (SPM)	
			Hailii, M. (PDP)	
			Ismail, G. (SDSM)	
			Stefkov, S. (LP)	
2	Ziberi, N. (PDP)	Shundovsky, J. (SDSM)	Shundovsky, J. (SDSM)	
		Buzlevski, D. (SDSM)	*Todorova, S. (SDSM)	
			Unkovski, S. (SDSM)	
			Naumovski, V. (SPM)	
			Hajdari, D. (PDP)	

32. MALTA

The largely ceremonial Head of State is a President elected indirectly for a five-year term.

The State is highly centralised and unitary.

Parliament is unicameral, elected for a five year but flexible term. The 65 members are elected by proportional representation (Single Transferable Vote) in mullet-member constituencies of around 25,000 electors. Parliament has a quorum of one-quarter of all members. Votes are carried by a majority of all votes cast. Constitutional amendments require a two-thirds majority of all members present. There is no referendum.

The government, the main political executive, consists of the Prime Minister and Cabinet ministers, who are leaders of the majority party and members of parliament. No vote of investiture is required to form the government, as the constitution states (in effect) that the party with a popular majority must form the government. The government must have a relative majority in Parliament. During its lifetime the government can face a vote of no confidence. Losing a vote of confidence always results in the resignation of the government. The government is collectively responsible to parliament. The ministers are members of parliament. The Prime Minister has a rather prominent position in government.

There is a Supreme Court for constitutional review of legislation.

MALTA 1962-1998

Gov	Begin	Dur	RfT	ToG	Py1	Seats	CPG	NoM	Prime Minister (py)
0	03.03.62	1490	1	4	NP 25	50	2	8	Borg Olivier, G. (NP)
1	01.04.66	1907	1	1	NP 28	50	1	8	Borg Olivier, G. (NP)
2	21.06.71	1920	1	1	LAB 28	55	4	9	Mintoff, D. (LAB)
3	22.09.76	1913	1	1	LAB 34	65	4	12	Mintoff, D. (LAB)
4	18.12.81	1101	2	1	LAB 34	65	4	14	Mintoff, D. (LAB)
5	23.12.84	872	1	1	LAB 34	65	4	12	Mifsud Bonnici, C. (LAB)
6	14.05.87	1750	1	1	NP 35	69	2	10	Fenech Adami, E. (NP)
7	27.02.92	1706	1	1	NP 35	69	2	13	Fenech Adami, E. (NP)
8	29.10.96		1	1	LAB 35	69	4	15	Sant, A. (LAB)

- Date of Independence 21 September 1964.
- 13 December 1974 the British Monarch was replaced as Head of State by an elected president.

Gov	Deputy PM	Py	Foreign Affairs	Py	Defence	Py	Interior	Py	Justice	Py
0			Borg Olivier, G.	NP		NP	Cachia Zammit, A.	NP	Caruana Demajo, T.	NP
1			Borg Olivier, G.	NP		NP			Caruana Damajo, T.	NP
2			Mintoff, D.	LAB		LAB			Buttigieg, A.	LAB
3			Mintoff, D.	LAB		LAB	Mintoff, D.	LAB	Buttigieg, A.	LAB
4	Cassar, J. / Abela, W.	LAB / LAB	Sciberras Trigona, A.	LAB		LAB	Sant, L.	LAB	Cassar, J.	LAB
5	Cassar, J. / Abela, W.	LAB / LAB	Sciberras Trigona, A.	LAB		LAB	Mifsud Bonnici, C.	LAB	Cassar, J.	LAB
6	De Marco, G.	NP	Tabone, V.	NP		NP	De Marco, G.	NP	De Marco, G.	NP
7	De Marco, G.	NP	De Marco, G.	NP		NP	Galea, L.	NP	Fenech, J.	NP
8	Vella, G.	LAB	Vella, G.	LAB	Sant, A.	LAB	Sant, A. / Mangion, C.	LAB	Mangion, C.	LAB / LAB

MALTA 1962-1998

Gov	Finance	Py	Economic Aff.	Py	Labour	Py	Education	Py	Health	Py
0	Borg Olivier, G.	NP	Borg Olivier, G.	NP	Spiteri, J.	NP	Paris, A.	NP	Borg Olivier, P.	NP
1	Felice, G.	NP			Tabone, G.		Borg Olivier, P.	NP	Cachia Zammit, A.	NP
2	Abela, J.	LAB	Hyzler, A.	LAB	Cassar, J.	LAB	*Barbara, A.	LAB	Piscopo, D.	LAB
3	Abela, J.	LAB	Abela, W.	LAB	*Barbara, A.	LAB	Cassar, J.	LAB	Moran, V.	LAB
4	Spiteri, L.	LAB	Abela, W.	LAB	Cremona, D.	LAB	Muscat, P.	LAB	Moran, V.	LAB
5	Abela, W.	LAB	Spiteri, L.	LAB	Micallef, F.	LAB	Mifsud Bonnici, C.	LAB	Moran, V.	LAB
6	Bonello Du Puis, G.	NP					Mifsud Bonnici, U.			NP
7	Dalli, J.	NP	Bonello Du Puis, G.	NP	Mifsud Bonnici, U.	NP	Mifsud Bonnici, U.	NP		
8	Spiteri, L.	LAB	Spiteri, L.	LAB	Mifsud Bonnici, U.	LAB	Bartolo, E.		Farrugia, M.	LAB

Gov	Housing	Py	Agriculture	Py	Industry/Trade	Py	Environment	Py
0			Caruana, C.	NP	Felice, G.	NP		NP
1	Caruana Demajo, T.	NP	Spiteri, J.	NP	Spiteri, J.	NP		NP
2			Micallef Stafrace, J.	LAB	Micallef Stafrace, J.	LAB		LAB
3	Buttigieg, A.	LAB	Cremona, D.	LAB	Micallef, F. Holland, P. Cremona, D.	LAB LAB LAB	Moran, V.	LAB
4			Micallef, F.	LAB	Holland, P. Grima, J.	LAB	Moran, V.	LAB
5			Debono Grech, J.	LAB	Muscat, P. Spiteri, L. Vella, K.	LAB LAB LAB	Moran, V.	LAB
6			Gatt, L.	NP	Gatt, L. Bonnici, E.	NP NP		

MALTA 1962-1998

Gov	Housing	Py	Agriculture	Py	Industry/Trade	Py	Environment	Py
7			Gatt, L.	NP			Falzon, M.	NP
8	Portelli, F.	LAB	Farrugia, N.	LAB	Montalto, J.A.	LAB	Vella, G.	LAB

Gov	Social Affairs (py)	Public Works (py)	Py	Other (py)	Res
0	Cachia Zammit, A. (NP)	Caruana, C. (NP) Spiteri, J. (NP)	NP	Felice, G. (NP)	0
1	Tabone, G. (NP)	Felice, G. (NP) Caruana, C. (NP)		Tabone, G. (NP) Caruana Demajo, T. (NP) Borg Olivier, P. (NP)	0
2	Cassar, J. (LAB)	Sant, L. (LAB)	LAB	Buttigieg, A. (LAB) *Barbara, A. (LAB) Micallef Stafrace, J. (LAB)	1
3	*Barabara, A. (LAB)	Abela, W. (LAB)		*Barbara, A. (LAB) Piscopo, D. (LAB) Sant, L. (LAB) Buttigieg, A. (LAB)	3
4	Sant, L. (LAB) Cremona, D. (LAB)	Vella, K. (LAB)		Cassar, J. (LAB) Sciberras Trigona, A. (LAB) Calleja, R. (LAB)	1
5	Sant, L. (LAB) Micallef, F. (LAB)	Abela, W. (LAB) Sant, L. (LAB)		Cassar, J. (LAB) Sciberras Trigona, A. (LAB) Grima, J. (LAB)	0
6	Galea, L. (NP)	Falzon, M. (NP)		Tabone, A. (NP)	2

MALTA 1962-1998

Gov	Social Affairs (py)	Public Works (py)	Other (py)	Res
7	Galea, L. (NP) Hyzler, G. (NP) Frendo, M. (NP)	Zammit Dimech, F. (NP)	Tabone, A. (NP) Frendo, M. (NP)	2
8	Farrugia, M. (LAB) Grech, E. (LAB)	Debono Grech, J. (LAB) Buhagiar, C. (LAB)	Mizzi, J. (LAB) Vella, G. (LAB) Bartolo, E. (LAB) Vella, K. (LAB)	

33. NAMIBIA

The Head of State and Government is a President directly elected for a five-year term.

The State is centralised and unitary.

Parliament is bicameral. The National Council (Upper House) has 26 members and sits for a six-year term. The National Assembly (Lower House) has 72 members elected for a five-year flexible term by proportional representation (d'Hondt) in constituencies of around 10,000 electors.

The Assembly has a quorum of 34 members. Votes are carried by a majority of votes cast. To pass a constitutional amendment, or to override a presidential veto, a two-thirds majority of all members is required. If there is insufficient parliamentary support to pass constitutional amendments, a referendum is required. The outcome is binding

Parliament has no direct power over the President, who nominates a Prime Minister and a Cabinet. No vote of investiture is required. During its lifetime, a government can face a vote of no confidence. Losing a vote of confidence always results in resignation of the government. The government is both collectively and individually responsible to parliament. Ministers are members of parliament. The Prime Minister has no dominant position in government.

There is a Constitutional Court to review legislation.

NAMIBIA 1990-1998

Gov	Begin	Dur	RfT	ToG	Py1	Seats	CPG	NoM	Prime Minister (py)
1	21.03.90	1825	1	1	SWAPO 41	72	4	18	Geingob, H. (SWAPO)
2	20.03.95		1		SWAPO 53	72	5	22	Geingob, H. (SWAPO)

- Date of Independence 21 March 1990.
- Namibia is a semi-presidential system. The popular elected president is Head of State and Head of Government and nominates a cabinet and a prime minister.
- The National Assembly has 72 elected seats plus 6 seats nominated by the President.
- Gov1, 2: Kapelwa, R. = Kapelwa-Kabajani, R.
- Gov 2: After wide spread criticism on President Nujoma (SWAPO) for taking the post Interior himself, on 15 September 1995 Edandjo, J. was appointed to this post.

Gov	Deputy PM	Py	Foreign Affairs	Py	Defence	Py	Interior	Py	Justice	Py
1			Gurirab, T.-B.	SWAPO	Mueshihange, P.	SWAPO	Pohamba, H.	SWAPO	Tjiriange, N.	SWAPO
							Witbooi, H.	SWAPO		
							*Amathila, L.	SWAPO		
2	Witbooi, H.	SWAPO	Gurirab, T.-B.	SWAPO	Malima, P.	SWAPO	Nujoma, S.	SWAPO	Tjiriange, N.	SWAPO
							*Amathila, L.	SWAPO	Hansiku, M.	SWAPO

Gov	Finance	Py	Economic Aff.	Py	Labour	Py	Education	Py	Health	Py
1	Herrigel, O.	NONA			Witbooi, H.	SWAPO	Angula, H.	SWAPO	Iyambo, N.	SWAPO
2	Angula, H.	SWAPO			Garoeb, M.	SWAPO	Angula, N.	SWAPO	Iyambo, N.	SWAPO
							Mutorwa, J.	SWAPO		

NAMIBIA 1990-1998

Gov	Housing	Py	Agriculture	Py	Industry/Trade	Py	Environment	Py
1	*Amathila, L.	SWAPO			Amathila, B.	SWAPO	Hanekom, G.	NONA
2	*Amathila, L.	SWAPO	Pohamba, H.	SWAPO	Hamutenya, H.	SWAPO	Hanekom, G.	NONA
			Mbumba, N.	SWAPO				

Gov	Social Affairs (py)	Public Works (py)	Other (py)	Res
1	Angula, H. (SWAPO)	Toivo ja Toivo, A. (SWAPO)	Angula, H. (SWAPO)	2
	Iyambo, N. (SWAPO)	Kapelwa, R. (SWAPO)	Hamutenya, H. (SWAPO)	
			Hansiku, M. (SWAPO)	
			Hanekom, G. (NONA)	
2	Iyambo, N. (SWAPO)	Toivo ja Toivo, A. (SWAPO)	Amathila, B. (SWAPO)	1
	*Ithana, P. (SWAPO)	Plichta, H. (SWAPO)	Mutorwa, J. (SWAPO)	
		Mbumba, N. (SWAPO	Hanekom, G. (NONA)	
			Kapelwa-Kabajani, R. (SWAPO)	

34. NETHERLANDS

The hereditary Head of State, the Queen or King performs largely ceremonial duties.

The Netherlands is a unitary state with a centralised organisation. Although there are features of functional autonomy, government on the sub-national level has a French (Napoleonic) flavour.

Parliament is asymmetrically bicameral; the Lower House (Tweede Kamer) of 150 seats is dominant. The Tweede Kamer is elected by proportional representation (d'Hondt) in one 150-member constituency. The Upper House (Eerste Kamer) of 75 seats is formally elected from provincial parliaments, but in fact the seats are distributed on the basis of proportionality. Parliament has a quorum of at least 50 per cent of all members Votes are carried by a majority of votes cast. Some issues require a qualified majority of two-thirds of all votes cast. Constitutional amendments require a two-thirds majority of all votes cast in both Houses. There is no referendum.

Governments are appointed by the Monarch who has some influence in directing the process of government formation (almost always by a coalition). There is no vote of investiture, nor of confidence, but governments, which lose a parliamentary majority, tend to resign. Due to strong binding agreements between government parties, governments resigning prematurely almost always call elections. Government is both collectively and individually responsible to parliament. Being a minister is not compatible with being a Member of Parliament. The Prime Minister has no dominant position in the government.

There is no judicial review since parliament is the highest power safeguarding the constitution. There is, however, an internal review by the Council of State, which is formally headed by the monarch. This council also serves as a Supreme Court for public administrative procedures. International treaties override all Dutch laws and also the constitution.

NETHERLANDS 1945–1998

Gov	Begin	Dur	RfT	ToG	Py1	Py2	Py3	Py4	Py5	Seats	CPG	NoM	Prime Minister (py)
1	03.07.46	766	1	2	KVP 32	PvdA 29				100	4	13	Beel, L.J.M. (KVP)
2	07.08.48	950	5	3	KVP 32	PvdA 27	VVD 8	CHU 9		100	3	15	Drees, W. (PvdA)
3	15.03.51	537	1	3	KVP 32	PvdA 27	VVD 8	CHU 9		100	3	15	Drees, W. (PvdA)
4	02.0.952	1502	1	3	KVP 30	PvdA 30	ARP 12	CHU 9		100	3	15	Drees, W. (PvdA)
5	13.10.56	800	5	3	KVP 49	PvdA 50	ARP 15	CHU 13		150	3	15	Drees, W. (PvdA)
6	22.12.58	148	1	6	KVP 49	ARP 15	CHU 13			150	2	10	Beel, L.J.M. (KVP)
7	19.05.59	1527	1	3	KVP 49	ARP 14	CHU 12	VVD 19		150	2	13	Quay, J.E. de (KVP)
8	24.07.63	643	4	3	KVP 50	ARP 13	CHU 13	VVD 16		150	2	13	Marijnen, V.G.M. (KVP)
9	27.04.65	574	5	3	KVP 50	PvdA 43	ARP 13			150	4	14	Cals, J.M.L.Th. (KVP)
10	22.11.66	132	1	6	KVP 50	ARP 13				150	2	13	Zijlstra, J. (ARP)
11	03.04.67	1555	1	2	KVP 42	ARP 15	CHU 12	VVD 17		150	2	14	Jong, P.J.S. de (KVP)
12	06.07.71	408	4	2	KVP 35	ARP 13	CHU 10	VVD 16	DS70 8	150	2	16	Biesheuvel, B.W. (ARP)
13	17.08.72	267	1	6	KVP 35	ARP 13	CHU 10	VVD 16		150	2	14	Biesheuvel, B.W. (ARP)
14	11.05.73	1683	4	3	KVP 27	PvdA 43	ARP 14	D66 6	PPR 7	150	4	16	Uyl, J.M. den (PvdA)
15	19.12.77	1362	1	2	CDA 49	VVD 28				150	2	16	Agt, A.A.M. van (CDA)
16	11.09.81	260	4	3	CDA 48	PvdA 44	D66 17			150	4	15	Agt, A.A.M. van (CDA)
17	29.05.82	159	1	6	CDA 48	D66 17				150	3	14	Agt, A.A.M. van (CDA)
18	04.11.82	1348	1	2	CDA 45	VVD 36				150	2	14	Lubbers, R.F.M. (CDA)
19	14.07.86	1212	5	2	CDA 54	VVD 27				150	2	14	Lubbers, R.F.M. (CDA)
20	07.11.89	1749	1	2	CDA 54	PvdA 49				150	4	14	Lubbers, R.F.M. (CDA)
21	22.08.94			2	PvdA 37	VVD 31	D66 24			150	3	14	Kok, W. (PvdA)

- The 1993 Edition contained one government (17) which has been deleted. Although it offered its resignation (03.11.81), the next government composition was exactly the same as the preceding one (16). Hence, row 17 in p. 87-89 should be deleted (without loss of information).

NETHERLANDS 1945–1998

Gov	Deputy PM	Py	Foreign Affairs	Py	Defence	Py	Interior	Py	Justice	Py
1			Boetzelaar van O., C. van	NONA	Fievez, A.H.L.J.	KVP	Beel, L.J.M.	KVP	Maarseveen, J.H. van	KVP
2	Schaik, J.R.H. v	KVP	Stikker, D.U.	VVD	Schokking, W.F.	CHU	Maarseveen, J.H. van	CHU	Wijers, Th.R.J.	KVP
3	Teulings, F.G.C.J.M.	KVP	Stikker, D.U.	VVD	Staf, C.	CHU	Maarseveen, J.H. van	KVP	Mulderije, H.	CHU
4	Beel, L.J.M.	KVP	Beijen, J.W. Luns, J.M.A.H.	NONA KVP	Staf, C.	CHU	Beel, L.J.M.	KVP	Donker, L.A.	PvdA
5	Struijken, A.A.M.	KVP	Luns, J.M.A.H.	KVP	Staf, C.	CHU	Struijken, A.A.M.	KVP	Samkalden, I.	PvdA
6	Struijken, A.A.M.	KVP	Luns, J.M.A.H.	KVP	Staf, C.	CHU	Struijken, A.A.M.	KVP	Struijken, A.A.M.	KVP
7	Korthals, H.A.	VVD	Luns, J.M.A.H.	KVP	Berg, S.J. van den	KVP	Toxopeus, E.H.	VVD	Beerman, A.C.W.	CHU
8	Biesheuvel, B.W.	ARP	Luns, J.M.A.H.	KVP	Jong, P.J.S. de	KVP	Toxopeus, E.H.	VVD	Scholten, Y.	CHU
9	Vondeling, A. Biesheuvel, B.W.	PvdA ARP	Luns, J.M.A.H.	KVP	Jong, P.J.S. de	KVP	Smallenbroek, J.	ARP	Samkalden, I.	PvdA
10	Quay, J.E. de Biesheuvel, B.W.	KVP ARP	Luns, J.M.A.H.	KVP	Jong, P.J.S. de	KVP	Verdam, P.J.	ARP	Struijcken, A.A.M.	KVP
11	Witteveen, H.J. Bakker, J.A.	VVD ARP	Luns, J.M.A.H.	KVP	Toom, W. den	VVD	Beernink, H.K.J.	CHU	Polak, C.H.F.	VVD
12	Nelissen, R.J. Geertsema, W.J.	KVP VVD	Schmelzer, W.K.N	KVP	Koster, H.J. de	VVD	Geertsema, W.J.	VVD	Agt, A.A.M. van	KVP
13	Nelissen, R.J. Geertsema, W.J.	KVP VVD	Schmelzer, W.K.N	KVP	Koster, H.J. de	VVD	Geertsema, W.J.	VVD	Agt, A.A.M. van	KVP
14	Agt, A.A.M. van	KVP	Stoel, M. van der	PvdA	Vredeling, H.	PvdA	Gaay Fortman, W.F. de	ARP	Agt, A.A.M. van	KVP
15	Wiegel, H.	VVD	Klaauw, C.A. van der	VVD	Kruisinga, R.J.H.	CDA	Wiegel, H.	VVD	Ruiter, J. de	CDA
16	Uyl, J.M. den Terlouw, J.C.	PvdA D66	Stoel, M. van der	PvdA	Mierlo, H.A.F.M.O. van	D66	Thijn, E. van	PvdA	Ruiter, J. de	CDA

Gov	Deputy PM	Py	Foreign Affairs	Py	Defence	Py	Interior	Py	Justice	Py
17	Graaf, L. de	CDA	Agt, A.A.M. van	CDA	Mierlo, H.A.F.M.O. van	D66	Rood, M.G.	D66	Ruiter, J. de	CDA
18	Aardenne, G.V.M. van	VVD	Broek, H. van den	CDA	Ruiter, J. de	CDA	Rietkerk, K.	VVD	Korthals Altes, F.	VVD
19	Korte, R. de	VVD	Broek, H. van den	CDA	Eekelen, W. van	VVD	Dijk, C. van	CDA	Korthals Altes, F.	VVD
20	Kok, W.	PvdA	Broek, H. van den	CDA	Beek, R. ter	PvdA	*Dales, I.	PvdA	Hirsch Ballin, G.	CDA
21	Dijkstal, H. Mierlo, H.A.F.M.O. van	VVD D66	Mierlo, H.A.F.M.O. van	D66	Voorhoeve, J.C.	VVD	Dijkstal, H.	VVD	*Sorgdrager, W.	D66

Gov	Finance	Py	Economic Aff.	Py	Labour	Py	Education	Py	Health	Py
1	Lieftinck, P.	PvdA	Huysmans, G.W.M.	KVP	Drees, W.	PvdA	Gielen, J.	KVP	Drees, W.	PvdA
2	Lieftinck, P.	PvdA	Brink, J.R.M. van den	KVP	Joekes,•A.M.	PvdA	Rutten, F.J.Th.	KVP	Joekes, A.M.	PvdA
3	Lieftinck, P.	PvdA	Brink, J.R.M. van den	KVP	Joekes, A.M.	PvdA	Rutten, F.J.Th.	KVP	Joekes, A.M.	PvdA
4	Kieft, J.A. van de	PvdA	Zijlstra, J.	ARP	Suurhoff, J.G.	PvdA	Cals, J.M.L.Th.	KVP	Suurhoff, J.G.	PvdA
5	Hofstra, H.J.	PvdA	Zijlstra, J.	ARP	Suurhoff, J.G.	PvdA	Cals, J.M.L.Th.	KVP	Suurhoff, J.G.	PvdA
6	Zijlstra, J.	ARP	Zijlstra, J.	ARP			Cals, J.M.L.Th.	KVP		
7	Zijlstra, J.	ARP	Pous, J.W. de	CHU	Rooy, C.J.M.A.	KVP	Cals, J.M.L.Th.	KVP	Rooy, C.J.M.A.	KVP
8	Witteveen, H.J.	VVD	Andriessen, J.E.	CHU	Veldkamp, G.M.J.	KVP	Bot, Th. H.	KVP	Veldkamp, G.M.J.	KVP
9	Vondeling, A.	PvdA	Uyl, J.M. den	PvdA	Veldkamp, G.M.J.	KVP	Diepenhorst, I.A.	ARP	Veldkamp, G.M.J.	KVP
10	Zijlstra, J.	ARP	Bakker, J.A.	ARP	Veldkamp, G.M.J	KVP	Diepenhorst, I.A.	ARP	Veldkamp, G.M.J	KVP
11	Witteveen, H.J.	VVD	Block, L. de	KVP	Roolvink, B.	ARP	Veringa, G.H.	KVP	Roolvink, B.	ARP
12	Nelissen, R.J.	KVP	Langman, H.	VVD	Boersma, J.	ARP	Veen, C. van Brauw, M.L. de	CHU DS70	Stuyt, I.B.J.	KVP
13	Nelissen, R.J.	KVP	Langman, H.	VVD	Boersma, J.	ARP	Veen, C. van	CHU	Stuyt, I.B.J.	KVP

NETHERLANDS 1945–1998

Gov	Finance	Py	Economic Aff.	Py	Labour	Py	Education	Py	Health	Py
14	Duisenberg, W.F.	PvdA	Lubbers, R.F.M.	KVP	Boersma, J.	ARP	Kemenade, J.A. / Trip, F.H.P.	PvdA / PPR	*Vorrink, I.	PvdA
15	Andriessen, F.H.J.J.	CDA	Aardenne, G.V.M. van	VVD	Albeda, W.	CDA	Pais, A. / Peynenburg, M.W.J.M.	VVD / CDA	Ginjaar, L.	VVD
16	Stee, A.P.J.M.M. van der	CDA	Terlouw, J.C.	D66	Uyl, J.M. den	PvdA	Kemenade, J.A. van	PvdA	*Gardeniers-B., M.H.M.F.	CDA
17	Stee, A.P.J.M.M. van der	CDA	Terlouw, J.C.	D66	Graaf, L. de	CDA	Deetman, W.J.	CDA	*Gardeniers-B., M.H.M.F.	CDA
18	Ruding, H.O.C.R.	VVD	Aardenne, G.V.M. van	VVD	Koning, J. de	CDA	Deetman, W.J.	CDA	Brinkman, L.C.	CDA
19	Ruding, H.O.C.R.	VVD	Korte, R. de	VVD	Koning, J. de	CDA	Deetman, W.J.	CDA	Brinkman, L.C.	CDA
20	Kok, W.	PvdA	Andriessen, J.E.	CDA	Vries, B. de	CDA	Ritzen, J.	PvdA	*Ancona, H. d'	PvdA
21	Zalm, G.	VVD	Wijers, G.J.	D66	Melkert, A.	PvdA	Ritzen, J.	PvdA	*Borst-Eilers, E.	D66

Gov	Housing	Py	Agriculture	Py	Industry/Trade	Py	Environment	Py
1	Ringers, J.A.	NONA	Mansholt, S.L.	PvdA				
2	Veld, J. in 't	PvdA	Mansholt, S.L.	PvdA				
3	Veld, J. in 't	PvdA	Mansholt, S.L.	PvdA				
4	Witte, H.B.J.	KVP	Mansholt, S.L.	PvdA	Bruijn, A.C. de	KVP		
5	Witte, H.B.J.	KVP	Mansholt, S.L.	PvdA				
6	Witte, H.B.J.	KVP	Staf, C.	CHU				
7	Aartsen, J. van	ARP	Marijnen, V.G.M.	KVP				
8	Bogaers, P.C.W.M.	KVP	Biesheuvel, B.W.	ARP				
9	Bogaers, P.C.W.M.	KVP	Biesheuvel, B.W.	ARP				
10	Witte, H.B.J.	KVP	Biesheuvel, B.W.	ARP				

NETHERLANDS 1945–1998

Gov	Housing	Py	Agriculture	Py	Industry/Trade	Py	Environment	Py
11	Schut, W.F.	ARP	Lardinois, P.J.	KVP			Stuyt, I.B.J.	KVP
12	Udink, B.J.	CHU	Lardinois, P.J.	KVP			Stuyt, I.B.J.	KVP
13	Udink, B.J.	CHU	Lardinois, P.J.	KVP			*Vorrink, I.	PvdA
14	Gruijters, J.P.A.	D66	Brouwer, T.	KVP			Ginjaar, L.	VVD
15	Beelaarts van Bl, P.A.C.	CDA	Stee, A.P.J.M.M. van der	CDA			*Gardeniers-B., M.H.M.F.	CDA
16	Dam, M.P.A. van	PvdA	Koning, J. de	CDA			*Gardeniers-B., M.H.M.F.	CDA
17	Nypels, E.	D66	Koning, J. de	CDA			Winsemius, P.	VVD
18	Winsemius, P.	VVD	Braks, G.J.M.	CDA			Nijpels, E.	VVD
19	Nijpels, E.	VVD	Braks, G.J.M.	CDA			Alders, H.	VVD
20	Alders, H.	PvdA	Braks, G.J.M.	CDA			Alders, H.	PvdA
21	*Boer, M. de	PvdA	Aartsen, J. van	VVD			*Boer, M. de	PvdA

Gov	Social Affairs (py)	Public Works (py)	Other (py)	Res
1	Drees, W. (PvdA)	Ringers, J.A. (NONA) Vos, H. (PvdA)	Jonkman, J.A. (NONA) Kleffens, E.N. (NONA)	0
2	Joekes, A.M. (PvdA)	Spitzen, J.A. (NONA)	Sassen, E.M.J.A. (KVP) Goetzen, L. (NONA) Schaik, J.R.H. van (KVP)	0
3	Joekes, A.M. (PvdA)	Wemmers, H.H. (NONA)	Peters, L.A.H. (KVP) Albregts, A.H.M. (KVP)	0
4	Suurhoff, J.G. (PvdA) Beel, L.J.M. (KVP)	Algera, J. (ARP)	Kernkamp, W.J.A. (CHU) Luns, J.M.A.H. (KVP)	0
5	Suurhoff, J.G. (PvdA) *Klompé, M.A.M. (KVP)	Algera, J.A. (ARP)	Staf, C. (CHU) *Klompé, M.A.M. (KVP)	0

NETHERLANDS 1945–1998

Gov	Social Affairs (py)	Public Works (py)	Other (py)	Res
6	Beel, L.J.M. (KVP) *Klompé, M.A.M. (KVP)	Aartsen, J. van (ARP)	*Klompé, M.A.M. (KVP) Helders, G.Ph. (CHU)	0
7	Rooy, C.J.M.A. (KVP) *Klompé, M.A.M. (KVP)	Korthals, H.A. (VVD)	*Klompé, M.A.M. (KVP)	0
8	Veldkamp, G.M.J. (KVP) *Schouwenaar-Fr., J.F. (VVD)	Aartsen, J. van (ARP)	*Schouwenaar-Fr., J.F. (VVD)	0
9	Veldkamp, G.M.J. (KVP) Vrolijk, M. (PvdA)	Suurhoff, J.G. (PvdA)	Biesheuvel, B.W. (ARP) Vrolijk, M. (PvdA) Bot, Th.H. (KVP)	0
10	Veldkamp, G.M.J. (KVP) *Klompé, M.A.M. (KVP)	Quay, J.E. de (KVP)	*Klompé, M.A.M. (KVP) Bot, Th.H. (KVP)	0
11	Roolvink, B. (ARP) *Klompé, M.A.M. (KVP)	Bakker, J.A. (ARP)	*Klompé, M.A.M. (KVP) Udink, B.J. (CHU)	0
12	Boersma, J. (ARP) Engels, P.J. (KVP)	Drees Jr., W. (DS70)	Nelissen, R.J. (KVP) Engels, P.J. (KVP) Boertien, C. (ARP)	0
13	Boersma, J. (ARP) Engels, P.J. (KVP)		Engels, P.J. (KVP) Lardinois, P.J. (KVP) Boertien, C. (ARP)	0
14	Boersma, J. (ARP) Doorn, H.W. van (PPR)	Westerterp, E. (KVP)	Gaay Fortman, W.F. de (ARP) Doorn, H.W. van (PPR) Pronk, J.P. (PvdA)	0
15	Albeda, W. (CDA) *Gardeniers-B., M.H.M.F. (CDA)	Tuynman, D.S. (VVD)	*Gardeniers-B., M.H.M.F. (CDA) Koning, J. de (CDA)	0
16	Uyl, J.M. den (PvdA) Louw, A. van der (PvdA)	Zeevalking, H.J. (D66)	Louw, A. van der (PvdA) Koning, J. de (CDA) Dijk, C. van (CDA)	0

NETHERLANDS 1945–1998

Gov	Social Affairs (py)	Public Works (py)	Other (py)	Res
17	Graaf, L. de (CDA) Boer, H.A. de (CDA)	Zeevalking, H.J. (D66)	Boer, H.A. de (CDA) Koning, J. de (CDA) Dijk, C. van (CDA)	0
18	Koning, J. de (CDA) Brinkman, L.C. (CDA)	*Smit-Kroes, N. (VVD)	Koning, J. de (CDA) Brinkman, L.C. (CDA) *Schoo, E.M. (VVD)	0
19	Koning, J. de (CDA) Brinkman, L.C. (CDA)	*Smit-Kroes, N. (VVD)	Koning, J. de (CDA) Brinkman, L.C. (CDA) Bukman, P. (CDA)	0
20	Vries, B. de (CDA) *Ancona, H. d' (PvdA)	*May-Weggen, H. (CDA)	Vries, B. de (CDA) *Ancona, H. d' (PvdA) Pronk, J. (PvdA)	0
21	Melkert, A. (PvdA) *Borst-Eilers, E. (D66)	*Jorritsma-Lebbink, A. (VVD)	Pronk, J.P. (PvdA) Aartsen, J. van (VVD) *Boer, M. de (PvdA)	0

35. NEW ZEALAND

The ceremonial Head of State is the British Monarch, represented by a Governor-General.

The State is quite strongly centralised and unitary.

Parliament is unicameral, with a three-year term between elections. There are 120 members of parliament; half of them elected by simple plurality voting in small constituencies of 15,000 to 20,000 electors. The other half have since 1995 been elected by proportional representation on party lists (d'Hondt) with a threshold of five percent. If, however, instead of the national percentage a constituency seat is obtained, the party gains access to parliament. The party composition of the parliament is adjusted to reflect the results of the PR election.

Parliament has a quorum of twenty members. Votes are carried by a majority of all votes cast. Constitutional amendments require a two-thirds majority of all votes cast. The government may call a referendum. The outcome is binding.

Prime Minister and Cabinet, who are members of parliament and leaders of the majority party or party coalition in Parliament, form the executive. No specific vote of investiture for the government is required. Nor is a vote of no confidence likely as long as the government retains the support of its relative party (coalition) majority in parliament. Losing a vote of confidence, however, always results in resignation of the government. The government is collectively responsible to parliament. Ministers are also members of parliament. The Prime Minister has a dominant position in government.

There is a Supreme Court for constitutional review of legislation.

NEW ZEALAND 1945 - 1998

Gov	Begin	Dur	RtT	ToG	Py1	Py2	Seats	CPG	NoM	Prime Minister (py)
1	20.12.46	1084	1	1	LAB 42		80	4	13	Fraser, P. (LAB)
2	08.12.49	650	1	1	NP 46		84	2	13	Holland, S.G. (NP)
3	19.09.51	1164	1	1	NP 50		84	2	13	Holland, S.G. (NP)
4	26.11.54	1035	2	1	NP 45		84	2	16	Holland, S.G. (NP)
5	26.09.57	77	1	1	NP 45		84	2	15	Holyoake, K.J. (NP)
6	12.12.57	1096	1	1	LAB 41		84	4	16	Nash, W. (LAB)
7	12.12.60	1103	1	1	NP 46		84	2	16	Holyoake, K.J. (NP)
8	20.12.63	1088	1	1	NP 45		84	2	16	Holyoake, K.J. (NP)
9	12.12.66	1106	1	1	NP 44		84	2	16	Holyoake, K.J. (NP)
10	22.12.69	779	2	1	NP 45		87	2	18	Holyoake, K.J. (NP)
11	09.02.72	303	1	1	NP 45		87	2	18	Marshall, J.R. (NP)
12	08.12.72	641	3	1	LAB 55		87	4	20	Kirk, N. (LAB)
13	10.09.74	458	1	1	LAB 55		92	4	20	Rowling, W.E. (LAB)
14	12.12.75	1097	1	1	NP 55		92	2	19	Muldoon, R.D. (NP)
15	13.12.78	1094	1	1	NP 50		92	2	19	Muldoon, R.D. (NP)
16	11.12.81	958	1	1	NP 47		95	2	19	Muldoon, R.D. (NP)
17	26.07.84	1119	1	1	LAB 56		95	4	20	Lange, D. (LAB)
18	19.08.87	723	2	1	LAB 58		95	4	19	Lange, D. (LAB)
19	11.08.89	1211	5	1	LAB 58		97	4	19	Palmer, G. (LAB)
20	14.07.86	390	2	1	LAB 58		97	4	19	Palmer, G. (LAB)
21	05.09.90	57	1	1	LAB 58		97	4	19	Moore, M. (LAB)
22	02.11.90	1102	1	1	NP 68		97	1	20	Bolger, J.B. (NP)
23	28.11.93	478	1	1	NP 50		99	2	20	Bolger, J.B. (NP)
24	30.06.95	238	7	2	NP 49	ROC 1	99	2	23	Bolger, J.B. (NP)

NEW ZEALAND 1945 - 1998

Gov	Begin	Dur	RfT	ToG	Py1	Py2	Seats	CPG	NoM	Prime Minister (py)
25	28.02.96	286	1	2	NP 43	UP 7	99	2	23	Bolger, J.B. (NP)
26	10.12.96	362	2	2	NP 44	NZF 17	120	2	20	Bolger, J.B. (NP)
27	08.12.97		2	2	NP 44	NZF 17	120	2	20	*Shipley, J. (NP)

- Gov 24: ROC is breakaway faction of NP.
- Gov 25: UP is a formation of former MP's of Labour and NP. One Cristian Democratic MP supported the government informally. Reason for Termination is elections; the first under the new mixed plural/PR system.
- Gov 26: The government was expected to be supported on most issues by ACT (8) and UP (1). Reason for Termination is resignation PM after loosing leadership contest in NP.

Gov	Deputy PM	Py	Foreign Affairs	Py	Defence	Py	Interior	Py	Justice	Py
1			Fraser, P.	LAB	Jones, F.	LAB	Parry, W.E.	LAB	Mason, H.G.R.	LAB
2	Holyoake, K.J.	NP	Doidge, F.W.	NP	MacDonald, T.L.	NP	Bodkin, W.A.	NP	Webb, T.C.	NP
3	Holyoake, K.J.	NP	Webb, T.C.	NP	MacDonald, T.L.	NP	Bodkin, W.A.	NP	Webb, T.C.	NP
4	Holyoake, K.J.	NP	MacDonald, T.L.	NP	MacDonald, T.L.; McAlpine, J.K.	NP	Smith, S.W.; Holland, S.G.	NP; NP	Marshall, J.R.	NP
5			MacDonald, T.L.		Eyre, D.G.	NP	Smith, S.W.	NP	Marshall, J.R.	NP
6	Skinner, C.F.	LAB	Nash, W.	LAB	Connolly, P.G.	LAB	Anderson, W.E.; Connolly, P.G.	LAB; LAB	Mason, H.G.R.	LAB
7	Marshall, J.R.	NP	Holyoake, K.J.	NP	Eyre, D.J.	NP	Gotz, F.L.A.; Eyre, D.J.	NP; NP	Hanan, J.R.	NP
8	Marshall, J.R.	NP	Holyoake, K.J.	NP	Eyre, D.J.	NP	Seath, D.C.	NP	Hanan, J.R.	NP
9	Marshall, J.R.	NP	Holyoake, K.J.	NP	Thomson, D.S.	NP	Seath, D.C.	NP	Hanan, J.R.	NP
10	Marshall, J.R.	NP	Holyoake, K.J.	NP	Thomson, D.S.	NP	Seath, D.C.; Thomson, D.S.	NP; NP	Riddiford, D.J.	NP

NEW ZEALAND 1945 - 1998

Gov	Deputy PM	Py	Foreign Affairs	Py	Defence	Py	Interior	Py	Justice	Py
11	Muldoon, R.D.	NP	Holyoake, K.J.	NP	McCready, A.	NP	Highet, D.A. / Allen, P.B.	NP	Jack, R.	NP / NP
12	Watt, H.	LAB	Kirk, N.	LAB	Faulkner, A.J.	LAB	May, H.L.J. / McGuigan, T.M. / Connelly, M.A.	LAB / LAB / LAB	Finlay, A.M.	LAB / LAB / LAB
13	Tizard, R.J.	LAB	Rowling, W.E.	LAB	Fraser, W.A.	LAB	May, H.L.J. / Connelly, M.A.	LAB / LAB	Finlay, A.M.	LAB
14	Talboys, B.E.	NP	Talboys, B.E.	NP	McCready, A.	NP	McCready, A. / Highet, D.A.	NP / NP	Thomson, D.S. / Wilkinson, P.I.	NP / NP
15	Talboys, B.E.	NP	Talboys, B.E.	NP	Gill, T.F.	NP	Gill, T.F. / Highet, D.A.	NP / NP	McLay, J.	NP
16	MacIntyre, D.	NP	Cooper, W.	NP	Thomson, D.	NP	Highet, D.A. / Couch, B.	NP / NP	McLay, J.	NP
17	Palmer, G.	LAB	Lange, D.	LAB	O'Flynn, F.	LAB	Tapsell, P. / *Hercus, A. / Bassett, M.	LAB / LAB / LAB	Palmer, G.	LAB / LAB / LAB
18	Palmer, G.	LAB	Marshall, R.	LAB	Tizard, B.	LAB	Bassett, M. / Goff, P. / Tapsell, P.	LAB / LAB / LAB	Palmer, G.	LAB / LAB / LAB
19	*Clark, H.	LAB	Marshall, R.	LAB	Tizard, B.	LAB	Bassett, M. / Douglas, R.	LAB / LAB	Jeffries, B.	LAB
20	*Clark, H.	LAB / LAB	Moore, M. / *Wilde, F.	LAB	Tapsell, P.	LAB	Prebble, R. / Woollaston, P. / *Austin, M.	LAB / LAB / LAB	Woollaston, P.	LAB / LAB / LAB

NEW ZEALAND 1945 - 1998

Gov	Deputy PM	Py	Foreign Affairs	Py	Defence	Py	Interior	Py	Justice	Py
21	McKinnon, D.	NP	McKinnon, D.	NP	Cooper, W.	NP	Bolger, J.B. Birch, W.F. Banks, J. Cooper, W. Creech, W.	NP	East, P. Graham, J.	NP NP
22	McKinnon, D.	NP	McKinnon, D. Burdon, P.	NP NP	Cooper, W.	NP	Banks, J. Luxton, J. Cooper, W.	NP NP NP	Graham, D.A.M. East, P.	NP NP
23	McKinnon, D.	NP	McKinnon, D.	NP	Cooper, W.	NP	Bolger, J.B. Luxton, J. Cooper, W. McCully, M. Maxwell, R.	NP NP NP NP NP	East, P. Graham, D.A.M.	NP NP
24	McKinnon, D.	NP	McKinnon, D.	NP	Cooper, W.	NP	Bolger, J.B. Luxton, J. Cooper, W. McCully, M. Maxwell, R.	NP NP NP NP NP	East, P. Graham, D.A.M.	NP NP
25	McKinnon, D.	NP	McKinnon, D. Burdon, P.	NP NP	East, P.	NP	Banks, J. Luxton, J. Dunne, P.	NP NP UP	East, P. Graham, D.A.M.	NP NP
26	Peters, W.	NZF	Birch, B. McKinnon, D.	NP NP	East, P.	NP	*Shipley, J. Elder, J. Bradford, M.	NP NZF NP	Graham, D.A.M. East, P.	NP NP

NEW ZEALAND 1945 - 1998

Gov	Deputy PM	Py	Foreign Affairs	Py	Defence	Py	Interior	Py	Justice	Py
27	Peters, W.	NZF	Birch, B.	NP	Bradford, M.	NP	*Shipley, J.	NP	Graham, D.A.M.	NP
			McKinnon, D.	NP			Williamson, M.	NP		
			Bradford, M.	NP			Bradford, M.	NP		
							Smith, N.	NP		
							Elder, J.	NZF		

Gov	Finance	Py	Economic Aff.	Py	Labour	Py	Education	Py	Health	Py
1	Nash, W.	LAB			McLagan, A.	LAB	Mason, H.G.R.	LAB	Nordmeyer, A.H.	LAB
2	Holland, S.G.	NP			Sullivan, W.	NP	Algie, R.M.	NP	Watts, J.T.	NP
3	Holland, S.G.	NP			Sullivan, W.	NP	Algie, R.M.	NP	Marshall, J.R.	NP
4	Watts, J.T.	NP			Sullivan, W.	NP	Algie, R.M.	NP	Halstead, E.H.	NP
5	Watts, J.T.	NP			McAlpine, J.K.	NP	Algie, R.M.	NP	Hanan, J.R.	NP
6	Nordmeyer, A.H.	LAB			Hackett, F.	LAB	Skoglund, P.O.S.	LAB	Mason, H.G.R.	LAB
7	Lake, H.R.	NP			Shand, T.P.	NP	Tennent, W.B.	NP	Shelton, N.L.	NP
8	Lake, H.R.	NP			Shand, T.P.	NP	Kinsella, A.E.	NP	McKay, D.N.	NP
9	Lake, H.R.	NP			Shand, T.P.	NP	Kinsella, A.E.	NP	McKay, D.N.	NP
10	Muldoon, R.D.	NP			Marshall, J.R.	NP	Talboys, B.E.	NP	McKay, D.N.	NP
11	Muldoon, R.D.	NP			Thomson, D.S.	NP	Pickering, H.E.L.	NP	Adams-Schneider, L.R.	NP
							Gandar, L.W.	NP		
12	Rowling, W.E.	LAB			Watt, H.	LAB	Amos, P.A.	LAB	Tizard, R.J.	LAB
							Moyle, C.J.	LAB		
13	Tizard, R.J.	LAB			Faulkner, A.J.	LAB	Amos, P.A.	LAB	McGuigan, T.M.	LAB
							Moyle, C.J.	LAB		
14	Muldoon, R.D.	NP			Gordon, J.B.	NP	Gandar, L.W.	NP	Gill, T.F.	NP

NEW ZEALAND 1945 - 1998

Gov	Finance	Py	Economic Aff.	Py	Labour	Py	Education	Py	Health	Py
15	Muldoon, R.D.	NP			Bolger, J.	NP	Wellington, M.	NP	Gair, G.F.	NP
16	Muldoon, R.D.	NP			Bolger, J.	NP	Wellington, M.	NP	Malcolm, A.	NP
17	Douglas, R.	LAB			Rodger, S. Burke, K.	LAB LAB	Marshall, R. Tizard, R.	LAB LAB	Bassett, M.	LAB
18	Douglas, R.	LAB			Rodger, S.	LAB	Lange, D.	LAB	Caygill, D.	LAB
19	Caygill, D.	LAB			*Clark, H. *King, A.	LAB LAB	Goff, P. Tizard, B. Tapsell, P.	LAB LAB LAB	*Clark, H.	LAB
20	Caygill, D. Neilson, P.	LAB LAB	Matthewson, C.	LAB	Matthewson, C. *King, A. Cullen, M. *Clark, H.	LAB LAB LAB AB	Goff, P. *Shields, M. Matthewson, C. *Austin, M.	LAB LAB LAB AB	Cullen, M.	LAB LAB LAB LAB
21	*Richardson, R. Creech, W.	NP NP			Birch, W.F. McTigue, M.	NP NP	Upton, S. Smith, L. Marshall, D.	NP NP NP	Upton, S.	NP NP NP
22	Birch, W.F Creech, W. McCully, M. Cliffe, B.	NP NP NP NP	Burdon, P.	NP	Kidd, D. Creech, W. Marshall, D.	NP NP NP	Upton, S. Smith, L. Luxton, J.	NP NP NP	Cliffe, B. Williamson, M. *Shipley, J. East, P.	NP NP NP
23	Birch, W.F. Creech, W.	NP NP	Maxwell, R.	NP	Kidd, D. Creech, W. Marshall, D.	NP NP NP	Upton, S. Smith, L.	NP NP	*Shipley, J.	NP NP
24	Birch, W.F. Creech, W.	NP NP	Maxwell, R.	NP	Kidd, D. Creech, W. Marshall, D.	NP NP NP	Upton, S. Smith, L.	NP NP	*Shipley, J.	NP

NEW ZEALAND 1945 - 1998

Gov	Finance	Py	Economic Aff.	Py	Labour	Py	Education	Py	Health	Py
25	Birch, W.F.	NP	Luxton, J.	NP	Kidd, D.	NP	Upton, S.	NP	*Shipley, J.	NP
	Smith, L.	NP			Creech, W.		Creech, W.	NP	Williamson, M.	NP
	McCully, M.	NP			Marshall, D.		English, B.	NP	English, B.	NP
	Dunne, P.	UP								
26	Peters, W.	NZF	Luxton, J.	NZF	McCandle, P.	NZF	Creech, W.	NZF	*Shipley, J.	NP
	East, P.	NP	Bradford, M.	NP	Bradford, M.	NP	Upton, S.	NP	English, B.	NP
	Delamere, J.	NZF					Williamson, M.			
27	Peters, W.	NZF	Luxton, J.	NZF	McCandle, P.	NP	Creech, W.	NZF	English, B.	NP
	Delamere, J.	NZF	Bradford, M.	NZF	Bradford, M.	NP	Williamson, M.	NP		
	Ryall, T.	NP					Upton, S.			

Gov	Housing	Py	Agriculture	Py	Industry/Trade	Py	Environment	Py
1			Cullen, E.L.	LAB	Sullivan, D.C.	LAB		LAB
			Skinner, C.F.	LAB				
2			Holyoake, K.J.	NP	Sullivan, W.	NP		NP
			Corbett, E.B.	NP	Bowden, C.M.	NP		NP
3			Holyoake, K.J.	NP	Sullivan, W.	NP		NP
			Corbett, E.B.	NP	Watts, J.T.	NP		NP
					Bowden, C.M.			NP
4	Sullivan, W.	NP	Holyoake, K.J.	NP	Sullivan, W.	NP		NP
			Smith, S.W.	NP	Eyre, D.J.	NP		NP
			Corbett, E.B.	NP		NP		
5	Rae, J.	NP	Smith, S.W.	NP	McAlpine, J.K.	NP		NP
			Gerard, R.G.	NP	Halstead, E.H.	NP		NP

NEW ZEALAND 1945 - 1998

Gov	Housing	Py	Agriculture	Py	Industry/Trade	Py	Environment	Py
6	Fox, W.A.	LAB	Skinner, C.F.	LAB	Hackett, F.	LAB		
			Tirikatene, E.	LAB	Holloway, P.	LAB		
					Boord, R.	LAB		
7	Rae, J.	NP	Gillespie, W.H.	NP	Marshall, J.R.	NP		
			Gerard, R.G.	NP	Shand, T.P.	NP		
8	Rae, J.	NP	Talboys, B.E.	NP	Marshall, J.R.	NP		
			Gerard, R.G.	NP	Shand, T.P.	NP		
					Shelton, N.L.	NP		
9	Rae, J.	NP	Talboys, B.E.	NP	Marshall, J.R.	NP		
			MacIntyre, D.	NP	Shand, T.P.	NP		
					Shelton, N.L.	NP		
10	Rae, J.	NP	McCready, A.	NP	Marshall, J.R.	NP		
			Carter, D.J.	NP	Shelton, N.L.	NP		
			MacIntyre, D.	NP	Adams-Schneider, L.R.	NP		
11	Holland, E.S.F.	NP	Gordon, J.B.	NP	Talboys, B.E.	NP	MacIntyre, D.	NP
			Carter, D.J.	NP	Gair, G.F.	NP		
			MacIntyre, D.	NP		NP		
12	Fraser, W.A.	LAB	Moyle, C.J.	LAB	Colman, F.M.	LAB	Walding, J.A.	LAB
					Freer, W.	LAB		
					Walding, J.A.	LAB		
13			Moyle, C.J.	LAB	Colman, F.M.	LAB	*Tirikatene-Sullivan, T.W.	LAB
					Freer, W.	LAB		
					Walding, J.A.	LAB		

NEW ZEALAND 1945 - 1998

Gov	Housing	Py	Agriculture	Py	Industry/Trade	Py	Environment	Py
14	Gair, G.F.	NP	MacIntyre, D.	NP	Holland, E.S.F.	NP	Young, V.S.	NP
			Young, V.S.	NP	Talboys, B.E.	NP		
					Adams-Schneider, L.R.	NP		
15	Quigley, D.	NP	Young, V.S.	NP	Talboys, B.E.	NP	Young, V.S.	NP
			MacIntyre, D.	NP	Adams-Schneider, L.R.	NP		
16	Quigley, D.	NP	MacIntyre, D.	NP	Cooper, W.	NP	Shearer, I.	NP
			Elworthy, J.	NP	Templeton, H.C.	NP		
17	Goff, P.	LAB	Moyle, C.	LAB	Gaygill, D.	LAB	Marshall, R.	LAB
			Wetere, K.	LAB	*Shields, M.	LAB		
					Moore, M.	LAB		
18	*Clark, H.	LAB	Tapsell, P.	LAB	Moore, M.	LAB		
			Moyle, C.	LAB	Caygill, D.	LAB		
					*Shields, M.	LAB		
19	Hunt, J.	LAB	Tapsell, P.	LAB	Moore, M.	LAB	Palmer, G.	LAB
			Moyle, C.	LAB	*Shields, M.	LAB		
20	Hunt, J.	LAB	Sutton, J.	LAB	Moore, M.	LAB	Woollaston, P.	LAB
					Prebble, R.	LAB		
					Butcher, D.	LAB		
					*Wilde, F.	LAB		
					Neilson, P.	LAB		
					Matthewson, C.	LAB		
21	Luxton, J.	NP	Falloon, J.	NP	McKinnon, D.	NP	Upton, S.	NP
			Storey, R.	NP	Kidd, D.	NP		
			Kidd, D.	NP	Burdon, P.	NP		

NEW ZEALAND 1945 - 1998

Gov	Housing	Py	Agriculture	Py	Industry/Trade	Py	Environment	Py
22	McCully, M.	NP	Kidd, D.	NP	McKinnon, D.	NP	Upton, S.	NP
			Falloon, J.	NP	Burdon, P.	NP	Marshall, D.	NP
			Marshall, D.	NP				
23	McCully, M.	NP	Kidd, D.	NP	McKinnon, D.	NP	Upton, S.	NP
			Falloon, J.	NP	Burdon, P.	NP	Marshall, D.	NP
			Marshall, D.	NP				
24	McCully, M.	NP	Kidd, D.	NP	McKinnon, D.	NP	Upton, S.	NP
			Falloon, J.	NP	Burdon, P.	NP	Marshall, D.	NP
			Marshall, D.	NP				
25	McCully, M.	NP	Kidd, D.	NP	McKinnon, D.	NP	Upton, S.	NP
			Smith, L.	NP	Burdon, P.	NP	Marshall, D.	NP
			Falloon, J.	NP	Luxton, J.	NP		
			Marshall, D.	NP				
26	McCully, M.	NP	Smith, I.	NP	McKinnon, D.	NP	Upton, S.	NP
			Luxton, J.	NP	*Shipley, J.	NP		
					Smith, L.	NP		
					Luxton, J.	NP		
27	McCully, M.	NP	Luxton, J.	NP	Luxton, J.	NP	Upton, S.	NP
			Smith, L.	NP	Ryall, T.	NP		
					McKinnon, D.	NP		
					Smith, L.	NP		

NEW ZEALAND 1945 - 1998

Gov	Social Affairs (py)	Public Works (py)	Other (py)	Res
1	Parry, W.E. (LAB) McLagan, A. (LAB)	Semple, R. (LAB) Hackett, F. (LAB) O'Brien, J. (LAB)	Fraser, P. (LAB) Nash, W. (LAB)	0
2	Sullivan, W. (NP) Watts, J.T. (NP)	Goosman, W.S. (NP) Broadfoot, W.J. (NP)	Corbett, E.B. (NP)	2
3	Bodkin, W.A. (NP) Sullivan, W. (NP)	Goosman, W.S. (NP) Broadfoot, W.J. (NP)	Corbett, E.B. (NP)	0
4	Halstead, E.H. (NP) Hanan, J.R. (NP) *Ross, G.H. (NP)	Goosman, W.S. (NP) Shand, T.P. (NP) McAlpine, J.K. (NP)	Holland, S.G. (NP) Marshall, J.R. (NP) Watts, J.T. (NP) Algie, R.M. (NP) Corbett, E.B. (NP)	2
5	*Ross, G.H. (NP)	Goosman, W.S. (NP) Shand, T.P. (NP)	Holyoake, K.J. (NP) Watts, J.T. (NP) Algie, R.M. (NP) Hanan, J.R. (NP)	0
6	Hackett, F. (LAB) *Howard, M. (LAB)	Fox, W.A. (LAB) Watt, H. (LAB) Mathison, J. (LAB) Moohan, M. (LAB)	Nash, W. (LAB) Mathison, J. (LAB)	0
7	Shand, T.P. (NP) Shelton, N.L. (NP)	Goosman, W.S. (NP) McAlpine, J.K. (NP) Hayman, T.L. (NP)	Hanan, J.R. (NP) Lake, H.R. (NP) Kinsella, A.E. (NP)	2
8	Shand, T.P. (NP) McKay, D.N. (NP)	Allen, P.B. (NP) McAlpine, J.K. (NP) Scott, W.J. (NP)	Hanan, J.R. (NP)	0

NEW ZEALAND 1945 - 1998

Gov	Social Affairs (py)	Public Works (py)	Other (py)	Res
9	Shand, T.P. (NP) McKay, D.N. (NP)	Allen, P.B. (NP) Gordon, J.B. (NP) Scott, W.J. (NP)	Hanan, J.R. (NP)	0
10	Marshall, J.R. (NP) McKay, D.N. (NP)	Allen, P.B. (NP) Gordon, J.B. (NP) McCready, A. (NP)	MacIntyre, D. (NP) Walker, H.J. (NP) Pickering, H.E.L. (NP)	0
11	Thomson, D.S. (NP) Adams-Schneider, L.R. (NP)	Allen, P.B. (NP) Gandar, L.W. (NP) Gordon, J.B. (NP) Walker, H.J. (NP)	Muldoon, R.D. (NP) Walker, H.J. (NP) MacIntyre, D. (NP) Gair, G.F. (NP)	0
12	King, N.J. (LAB) Colman, F.M. (LAB)	Watt, H. (LAB) McGuigan, T.M. (LAB) Finlay, A.M. (LAB) Tizard, R.J. (LAB) Fraser, W.A. (LAB) Arthur, B. (LAB) Douglas, R. (LAB) Freer, W. (LAB)	Watt, H. (LAB) Rowling, W.E. (LAB) Douglas, R. (LAB) Walding, J.A. (LAB) Rata, M. (LAB) *Tirikatene-Sullivan, T.W. (LAB)	0
13	King, N.J. (LAB) Colman, F.M. (LAB)	Finlay, A.M. (LAB) Faulkner, A.J. (LAB) Colman, F. (LAB) Watt, H. (LAB) Arthur, B. (LAB) Douglas, R. (LAB) Bailey, R. (LAB) Freer, W. (LAB)	Walding, J.A. (LAB) Rata, M. (LAB) *Tirikatene-Sullivan, T.W. (LAB)	0

NEW ZEALAND 1945 - 1998

Gov	Social Affairs (py)	Public Works (py)	Other (py)	Res
9	Shand, T.P. (NP) McKay, D.N. (NP)	Allen, P.B. (NP) Gordon, J.B. (NP) Scott, W.J. (NP)	Hanan, J.R. (NP)	0
10	Marshall, J.R. (NP) McKay, D.N. (NP)	Allen, P.B. (NP) Gordon, J.B. (NP) McCready, A. (NP)	MacIntyre, D. (NP) Walker, H.J. (NP) Pickering, H.E.L. (NP)	0
11	Thomson, D.S. (NP) Adams-Schneider, L.R. (NP)	Allen, P.B. (NP) Gandar, L.W. (NP) Gordon, J.B. (NP) Walker, H.J. (NP)	Muldoon, R.D. (NP) Walker, H.J. (NP) MacIntyre, D. (NP) Gair, G.F. (NP)	0
12	King, N.J. (LAB) Colman, F.M. (LAB)	Watt, H. (LAB) McGuigan, T.M. (LAB) Finlay, A.M. (LAB) Tizard, R.J. (LAB) Fraser, W.A. (LAB) Arthur, B. (LAB) Douglas, R. (LAB) Freer, W. (LAB)	Watt, H. (LAB) Rowling, W.E. (LAB) Douglas, R. (LAB) Walding, J.A. (LAB) Rata, M. (LAB) *Tirikatene-Sullivan, T.W. (LAB)	0
13	King, N.J. (LAB) Colman, F.M. (LAB)	Finlay, A.M. (LAB) Faulkner, A.J. (LAB) Colman, F. (LAB) Watt, H. (LAB) Arthur, B. (LAB) Douglas, R. (LAB) Bailey, R. (LAB) Freer, W. (LAB)	Walding, J.A. (LAB) Rata, M. (LAB) *Tirikatene-Sullivan, T.W. (LAB)	0

NEW ZEALAND 1945 - 1998

Gov	Social Affairs (py)	Public Works (py)	Other (py)	Res
17	Burke, K. (LAB) *Hercus, A. (LAB)	Rodger, S. (LAB) Burke, K. (LAB) Tizard, R. (LAB) Colman, F. (LAB) Prebble, R. (LAB) Hunt, J. (LAB)	Tapsell, P. (LAB) Tizard, R. (LAB) Goff, P. (LAB) Hunt, J. (LAB) Wetere, K. (LAB) Moore, M. (LAB)	1
18	Rodger, S. (LAB) *Shields, M. (LAB) Cullen, M. (LAB)	Prebble, R. (LAB) Jeffries, B. (LAB) Butcher, D. (LAB)	Moore, M. (LAB) Wetere, K. (LAB) Marshall, R. (LAB) *Shields, M. (LAB) *Clark, H. (LAB)	2
19	*King, A. (LAB) Cullen, M. (LAB) Douglas, R. (LAB) *Shields, M. (LAB)	Roger, S. (LAB) Jeffries, B. (LAB) Butcher, D. (LAB)	Wetere, K. (LAB) Hunt, J. (LAB) Bassett, M. (LAB) *Shields, M. (LAB) Tapsell, P. (LAB)	1
20	Cullen, M. (LAB) *Shields, M. (LAB) *King, A. (LAB)	Prebble, R. (LAB) Hunt, J. (LAB) Jeffries, W.P. (LAB) Butcher, D. (LAB) Neilson, P. (LAB) Matthewson, C. (LAB)	Prebble, R. (LAB) Wetere, K.T. (LAB) Hunt, J. (LAB) *Shields, M. (LAB) Tapsell, P. (LAB) *King, A. (LAB) *Wilde, F. (LAB) Matthewson, C. (LAB) *Austin, M. (LAB)	0

NEW ZEALAND 1945 - 1998

Gov	Social Affairs (py)	Public Works (py)	Other (py)	Res
21	Banks, J. (NP) *Shipley, J. (NP)	Kidd, D. (NP) Storey, R. (NP) Luxton, J. (NP)	East, P. (NP) Banks, J. (NP) Graham, J. (NP) Storey, R. (NP) Peters, W. (NP) Marshall, D. (NP)	0
22	*Shipley, J. (NP) Banks, J. (NP) Cooper, W. (NP) Gresham, P. (NP)	Kidd, D. (NP) Burdon, P. (NP) Williamson, M. (NP) Cliffe, B. (NP)	McKinnon, D. (NP) East, P. (NP) Burdon, P. (NP) Smith, L. (NP) Falloon, J. (NP) Graham, D.A.M. (NP) Banks, J. (NP) Marshall, D. (NP) Luxton, J. (NP) Williamson, M. (NP) McCully, M. (NP)	0
23	*Shipley, J. (NP) Cooper, W. (NP) Gresham, P. (NP) Cliffe, B. (NP) McClay, R. (NP) *O'Regan, K. (NP)	Kidd, D. (NP) Burdon, P. (NP) Williamson, M. (NP) Cliffe, B. (NP)	McKinnon, D. (NP) Graham, D.A.M. (NP) Marshall, D. (NP) Luxton, J. (NP) Williamson, M. (NP)	0

NEW ZEALAND 1945 - 1998

Gov	Social Affairs (py)	Public Works (py)	Other (py)	Res
24	*Shipley, J. (NP) Cooper, W. (NP) Gresham, P. (NP) McClay, R. (NP) *O'Regan, K. (NP)	Kidd, D. (NP) Burdon, P. (NP) Williamson, M. (NP)	McKinnon, D. (NP) Graham, D.A.M. (NP) Marshall, D. (NP) Luxton, J. (NP) Williamson, M. (NP)	0
25	East, P. (NP) *Shipley, J. (NP) Kidd, D. (NP) Banks, J. (NP) Gresham, P. (NP)	Kidd, D. (NP) Burdon, P. (NP) Upton, S. (NP) Smith, L. (NP) Williamson, M. (NP)	McKinnon, D. (NP) East, P. (NP) Falloon, J. (NP) Creech, W. (NP) Graham, D.A.M. (NP) Banks, J. (NP) Marshall, D. (NP) Luxton, J. (NP) Williamson, M. (NP) McCully, M. (NP)	0
26	Sowry, R. (NP) East, P. (NP)	*Shipley, J. (NP) Smith, L. (NP) Williamson, M. (NP) Bradford, M. (NP)	McKinnon, D. (NP) Graham, D. (NP) Henare, T. (NZF) Creech, W. (NP) Upton, S. (NP) Elder, J. (NZF) Williamson, M. (NP) Delamere, J. (NZF) McCully, M. (NP)	0

NEW ZEALAND 1945 - 1998

Gov	Social Affairs (py)	Public Works (py)	Other (py)	Res
27	Sowry, R. (NP)	Williamson, M. (NP)	*Shipley, J. (NP)	
	McCully, M. (NP)	Bradford, M. (NP)	Creech, W. (NP)	
		Ryall, T. (NP)	English, B. (NP)	
		Smith, L. (NP)	Williamson, M. (NP)	
			Sowry, R. (NP)	
			Graham, D. (NP)	
			Upton, S. (NP)	
			Delamere, J. (NZF)	
			Smith, N. (NP)	
			McCully, M. (NP)	
			Ryall, T. (NP)	
			Henare, T. (NZF)	
			Elder, J. (NZF)	
			McKinnon, D. (NP)	

36. NORWAY

The Head of State is a hereditary Monarch whose role is mostly ceremonial.

The State is unitary, with a strong tradition of devolution and decentralisation.

Parliament (Storting) is unicameral albeit of a 'hybrid' kind. Its 165 members are elected for a fixed term of four years by proportional representation (St. Lagüe) in 19 multi-member constituencies. Effectively, there is one nation-wide constituency as votes are equalised nationally. To achieve a distribution of representation that precisely reflects the spread of vote, in 1989 a scheme of 'seats at large' was adopted. Only parties that receive at least four percent of the vote may compete for the eight seats at large. After election, parliament forms an Upper House from one-quarter (41) of its members. This Upper House only plays a role in important matters touching on the national interest. In practice, however, most business is dealt with in joint sessions. Parliament cannot be dissolved during its four-year term.

There is no quorum. Votes are carried by a majority of votes cast. Some issues require a qualified majority ranging from an absolute majority to a two-thirds majority of all members present. Constitutional amendments require a two-thirds majority of all members present. A referendum is optional and may be called by the government. The outcome is binding.

The executive institution is a cabinet-government. The government does not need a vote of investiture, but must rely on a majority in parliament. Government can face a vote of no confidence. Losing a vote of confidence always results in resignation of the government. Government is both collectively and individually responsible to parliament. Ministers can not be members of parliament. The Prime Minister has no dominant position in government.

The courts are empowered to review governmental actions in terms of their constitutionality, but in practice this is left to parliament.

NORWAY 1945 - 1998

Gov	Begin	Dur	RfT	ToG	Py1	Py2	Py3	Py4	Seats	CPG	NoM	Prime Minister (py)
1	01.11.45	1439	1	1	AP 76				150	4	14	Gerhardsen, E. (AP)
2	10.10.49	766	3	1	AP 85				150	4	14	Gerhardsen, E. (AP)
3	16.11.51	695	1	1	AP 85				150	4	13	Torp, O. (AP)
4	12.10.53	466	2	1	AP 77				150	4	13	Torp, O. (AP)
5	21.01.55	990	1	1	AP 77				150	4	13	Gerhardsen, E. (AP)
6	07.10.57	1435	1	1	AP 78				150	4	15	Gerhardsen, E. (AP)
7	11.09.61	715	5	4	AP 74				150	4	15	Gerhardsen, E. (AP)
8	27.08.63	28	5	5	CP 16	CPP 15	CON 29	LIB 14	150	2	15	Lyng, J. (CON)
9	24.09.63	750	1	4	AP 74				150	4	15	Gerhardsen, E. (AP)
10	11.10.65	1426	1	2	CP 18	CPP 13	CON 31	LIB 18	150	2	15	Borten, P. (CP)
11	07.09.69	552	4	2	CP 20	CPP 14	CON 29	LIB 13	150	2	15	Borten, P. (CP)
12	13.03.71	585	2	4	AP 74				150	4	15	Brattelli, T. (AP)
13	18.10.72	363	1	5	CP 20	CPP 14	LIB 13		150	3	15	Korvald, L. (CPP)
14	16.10.73	818	2	4	AP 62				155	4	15	Brattelli, T. (AP)
15	12.01.76	609	1	4	AP 62				155	4	16	Nordli, O. (AP)
16	12.09.77	1241	3	4	AP 76				155	4	16	Nordli, O. (AP)
17	04.02.81	252	1	4	AP 76				155	4	17	*Harlem Brundtland, G. (AP)
18	14.10.81	602	2	4	CON 54				155	2	17	Willoch, K. (CON)
19	08.06.83	902	1	2	CP 11	CPP 15	CON 54		155	2	18	Willoch, K. (CON)
20	26.11.85	164	1	5	CP 12	CPP 16	CON 50		157	2	18	Willoch, K. (CON)
21	09.05.86	1256	1	4	AP 71				157	4	18	*Harlem Brundtland, G. (AP)
22	16.10.89	383	5	5	CP 11	CPP 14	CON 37		157	2	18	Syse, J. (CON)
23	03.11.90	1037	1	4	AP 63				165	4	19	*Harlem Brundtland, G. (AP)
24	07.10.93	1115	2	4	AP 67				165	4	18	*Harlem Brundtland, G. (AP)
25	25.10.96	363	1	4	AP 67				165	4	19	Jagland, T. (AP)
26	13.10.97			5	CPP 25	CP 11	LIB 6		165	3	19	Bondevik, K.M. (CPP)

NORWAY 1945 - 1998

Gov	Deputy PM	Py	Foreign Affairs	Py	Defence	Py	Interior	Py	Justice	Py
1			Lie, T.	AP	Hauge, J.C.	AP			Gundersen, O.	AP
2			Lange, H.	AP	Hauge, J.C.	AP	Olsen, J.V.	AP	Gundersen, O.	AP
3			Lange, H.	AP	Hauge, J.C.	AP	Olsen, J.V.	AP	Gundersen, O.	AP
4			Lange, H.	AP	Hauge, J.C.	AP	Olsen, J.V.	AP	Gundersen, O.	AP
5			Lange, H.	AP	Handal, N.	AP	Olsen, J.V.	AP	Hauge, J.C.	AP
6			Lange, H.	AP	Handal, N.	AP	Olsen, J.V.	AP	Haugland, J.	AP
7			Lange, H.	AP	Harlem, G.	AP	Cappelen, A.	AP	Haugland, J.	AP
8			Wikborg, E.	CPP	Kyllingmark, H.	CPP	Lyngstad, B.	LIB	Koren, P.	CPP
9			Lange, H.	AP	Harlem, G.	AP	Haugland, J.	AP	Gundersen, O.	AP
10	Lyng, J.	CON	Lyng, J.	CON	Tidemann, O.	CON	Seip, H.	LIB	*Selmer, E.S.	CON
11	Lyng, J.	CON	Lyng, J.	CON	Tidemann, O.	CON	Seip, H.	LIB	*Selmer, E.S.	CON
12			Cappelen, A.	AP	Fostervoll, A.J.	AP	Nordli, O.	AP	Berrefjord, O.	AP
13	Vaarvik, D.	CP	Vaarvik, D.	CP	Kleppe, J.	CP	*Kolstad, E.	LIB	Koren, P.	CPP
14			Frydenlund, K.	AP	Fostervoll, A.J.	AP	Aune, L.	AP	*Valle, I.L.	AP
15			Frydenlund, K.	AP	Hansen, R.	AP	*Lorentsen, A.	AP	*Valle, I.L.	AP
16			Frydenlund, K.	AP	Hansen, R.	AP	*Lorentsen, A. / Aune, L.	AP / AP	*Valle, I.L.	AP
17			Frydenlund, K.	AP	Stoltenberg, T.	AP	*Andreassen, H. / *Roenbeck, S.	AP / AP	Skau, B.	AP
18	Stray, S.	CON	Stray, S.	CON	Sjaastad, A.C.	CON	Rettedal, A. / *Gjertsen, A.	CON / CON	*Rökke, M.	CON
19	Stray, S.	CON	Stray, S.	CON	Sjaastad, A.C.	CON	Rettedal, A. / *Gjertsen, A.	CON / CON	*Rökke, M.	CON
20	Bondevik, K.	CPP	Stray, S.	CON	Sjaastad, A.C.	CON	Rettedal, A. / *Gjertsen, A.	CON / CON	*Sellæg, W.	CON
21	Frydenlund, K.	AP	Frydenlund, K.	AP	Holst, J.J.	AP	Haraldseth, L. / *Bakken, A.-L.	AP / AP	*Boesterud, H.	AP
22			Bondevik, K.	CPP	Ditlev-Simonsen, P.	CPP	Jakobson, J.	CP	*Fougner, E.	CON

NORWAY 1945 - 1998

Gov	Deputy PM	Py	Foreign Affairs	Py	Defence	Py	Interior	Py	Justice	Py
23			Stoltenberg, T.	AP	Holst, J.J.	AP	Borgen, K. *Gerhardsen, T.S.	AP AP	*Gjesteby, K.	AP
24			Holst, J.J.	AP	Kosmo, J.	AP	Berge, G. Totland, N.O.	AP AP	*Faremo, G.	AP
25			Godal, BT.	AP	Kosmo, J.	AP	Opseth, K. *Holt, A. *Brustad, S.	AP AP AP	*Holt, A.	AP
26	*Lahnstein, A.E.	CP	Vollebaek, K. *Johnson, H.F.	CPP CPP	Fjaervoll, D.J.	CPP	*Haarstad, R.Q. *Kleppa, M.M. *Aure, A.I.	CP CP CPP	*Aure, A.I.	CPP

Gov	Finance	Py	Economic Aff.	Py	Labour	Py	Education	Py	Health	Py
1	Brofoss, E.	AP			Langhelle, N.	AP	Fostervoll, K.	AP		
2	Meidalshagen, O.	AP			Langhelle, N.	AP	Moen, L.M.	AP		
3	Bratteli, T.	AP					Moen, L.M.	AP		
4	Bratteli, T.	AP					Moen, L.M.	AP		
5	Lid, M.	AP					Bergersen, B.	AP		
6	Bratteli, T.	AP	Bråthen, G.	AP			Bergersen, B.	AP		
7	Bjerve, P.	AP	Bôe, G.	AP			Sivertsen, B.	AP		
8	Vaarvik, D.	CP	Myrvoll, O.	LIB			Kortner, O.	LIB		
9	Cappelen, A.	AP	Trasti, K.	AP	Haugland, J.	AP	Sivertsen, H.	AP		
10	Myrvoll, O.	LIB	Vaarvik, D.	CP			Bondevik, K.	CPP		
11	Myrvoll, O.	LIB	Vaarvik, D.	CP			Bondevik, K.	CPP		
12	Christiansen, R.	AP	Gjærevoll, O.	AP			Gjerde, B.	AP		
13	Norbom, J.	LIB			Skipnes, J.	CPP	Skulberg, A.	CP		
14	Kleppe, P.	AP			Aune , L.	AP	Gjerde, B.	AP		

NORWAY 1945 - 1998

Gov	Finance	Py	Economic Aff.	Py	Labour	Py	Education	Py	Health	Py
15	Kleppe, P.	AP			Aune , L.	AP	Egeland, K.	AP		AP
16	Kleppe, P.	AP			Aune , L.	AP	Egeland, K.	AP		AP
17	Sand, U.	AP			*Andreassen, H.	AP	Foerde, E.	AP		AP
18	Presthus, R.	CON			Rettedal, A.	CON	Austad, T.	CON	Heløe, L.A.	CON
19	Presthus, R.	CON			Rettedal, A.	CON	Bondevik, K.M.	CPP	Heløe, L.A.	CON
20	Presthus, R.	CON			Rettedal, A.	CON	Bondevik, K.M.	CPP	Heløe, L.A.	CON
21	Berge, G.	AP			Haraldseth, L.	AP	*Groendal, K.K.	AP		
22	Skauge, A.	CON					*Bjartveit, E.	CPP	*Sellæg, W.	CON
							Steensnaes, E.	CPP		
23	Johnsen, S.	AP			*Gerhardsen, T.S.	AP	Hernes, G.	AP	*Veieroed, T.	AP
24	Johnsen, S.	AP					Hernes, G.	AP	Christie, W.	AP
25	Stoltenberg, J.	AP			Opseth, K.	AP	Sandal, R.	AP	Hernes, G.	AP
26	Restad, G.	CP	*Lower, E.	LIB	*Haarstad, R.Q.	CP	Lilletun, J.	CPP	Hoybraten, D.	CPP
	*Kleppa, M.M.	CP			*Lower, E.	LIB				

Gov	Housing	Py	Agriculture	Py	Industry/Trade	Py	Environment	Py
1			Fjeld, K.	AP	Evensen, L.	AP		
2			Fjeld, K.	AP	Evensen, L.	AP		
			Carlsen, R.	AP	Brofoss, E.	AP		
3			Nordbö, R.	AP	Evensen, L.	AP		
			Holt, P.	AP	Brofoss, E.	AP		
4			Nordbö, R.	AP	Evensen, L.	AP		
			Holt, P.	AP	Brofoss, E.	AP		
5			Meidalshagen, O.	AP	Sjaastad, G.	AP		
			Lysö, N.	AP	Skaug, A.	AP		

NORWAY 1945 - 1998

Gov	Housing	Py	Agriculture	Py	Industry/Trade	Py	Environment	Py
6			Löbak, H.	AP	Sjaastad, G.	AP		
			Lysö, N.	AP	Skaug, A.	AP		
7			Wöhni, E.	AP	Holler, K.	AP		
			Lysö, N.	AP	Skaug, A.	AP		
8			Borgen, H.	CP	Willoch, K.	CON		
			Onarheim, O.	CON	Meland, K.	CON		
9			Andersen, M.	AP	Lie, T.	AP		
			Granli, L.	AP	Himle, E.	AP		
10			Lyngstad, B.	LIB	Rostoft, S.	CON		
			Myklebust, O.	CP	Willoch, K.	CON		
11			Lyngstad, B.	LIB	Rostoft, S.	CON		
			Moxnes, E.	CP	Willoch, K.	CON		
12			Treholt, T.	AP	Lied, F.	AP		
			Hoem, K.	AP	Kleppe, P.	AP		
13			Moxnes, E.H.	CP	Braek, O.S.	LIB	Haugeland, T.	CP
			Olsen, T.	CP	Eika, H.	LIB		
14			Treholt, T.	AP	Evensen, J.	AP	Halvorsen, T.	AP
			Bolle, E.	AP	Ulveseth, I.	AP		
15			Øcksnes, O.	AP	Bakke, H.	AP	*Harlem Brundtland, G.	AP
			Bolle, E.	AP	Gjerde, B.	AP		
16			Øcksnes, O.	AP	Bakke, H.	AP	*Harlem Brundtland, G.	AP
			Bolle, E.	AP	Gjerde, B.	AP		
17			Øcksnes, O.	AP	*Gjesteby, K.	AP	Hansen, R.	AP
			Bolle, E.	AP	Kristensen, F.	AP		
					Johanson, A.	AP		
18			Löken, J.C.	CON	Haugstvedt, A.	CON	*Frogn Sellæg, W.	CON
			Listau, T.	CON	Bratz, J.H.	CON		

NORWAY 1945 - 1998

Gov	Housing	Py	Agriculture	Py	Industry/Trade	Py	Environment	Py
19			Isaksen, F.T. Listau, T.	CP CON	Haugstvedt, A. Bratz, J.H.	CON CON	*Surlien, R.	CP
20			Reiten, E. Sundsboe, S.	CP CP	Haugstvedt, A. Thomassen, P.	CPP CON	*Surlien, R.	CP
21			*Øyangen, G. Eidam, B.M.	AP AP	Mosbakk, K. Kristensen, F. Oeien, A.	AP AP AP	*Roenbeck, S.	AP
22			*Vik, A. Munkejord, S.	CP CON	*Five, K. Thomassen, P.	CON CON	*Valla, K.	CP
23			*Øyangen, G. *Pettersen, O.	AP AP	*Nordboe, E. Knapp, O. Kristensen, F.	AP AP AP	Berntsen, T.	AP
24			*Øyangen, G. Olsen, J.H.T.	AP AP	Godal, B.T. Stoltenber, J.	AP AP	Berntsen, T.	AP
25			Andersen, D.T. Schjøtt-Pedersen, K.E.	AP AP	*Knudsen, G.	AP	Berntsen, T.	AP
26			Angelsen, P. Gjonnes, K.	CP CPP	Sponheim, L.	LIB	Fjellanger, G.	LIB

Gov	Social Affairs (py)	Public Works (py)	Other (py)	Res
1	Oftedal, S. (AP)	Torp, O. (AP)	Fostervoll, K. (AP) Carlsen, R. (AP) *Aasland, A. (AP) Holt, P. (AP)	2
2	*Aasland, A. (AP)	Honsväld, N. (AP)	Moen, L.M. (AP)	0
3	*Aasland, A. (AP)	Langhelle, N. (AP)	Moen, L.M. (AP)	0

NORWAY 1945 - 1998

Gov	Social Affairs (py)	Public Works (py)	Other (py)	Res
4	*Aasland, A. (AP)	Langhelle, N. (AP)	Moen, L.M. (AP)	2
5	*Sewerin, R. (AP)	Varmann, K. (AP)	Bergersen, B. (AP)	0
6	Harlem, G. (AP) / *Bjerkholt, A. (AP)	Varmann, K. (AP)	Bergersen, B. (AP)	1
7	Bruvik, O. (AP) / *Bjerkholt, A. (AP)	Brattelli, T. (AP)	Sivertsen, B. (AP)	1
8	Bondevik. K. (CPP) / *Hagen, K.G. (CP)	Leiro, L. (CP)	Kortner, O. (LIB)	0
9	Gjaerevoll, O. (AP) / *Bjerkholt, A. (AP)	Brattelli, T. (AP)	Sivertsen, H. (AP)	1
10	Aarvik, E. (CPP) / *Skjerven, E. (CPP)	Kyllingmark, H. (CON)	Bondevik, K. (CPP)	0
11	Aarvik, E. (CPP) / *Skjerven, E. (CPP)	Kyllingmark, H. (CON)	Bondevik, K. (CPP)	0
12	Höjdahl, O. (AP) / *Valle, I.L. (AP)	Steen, R. (AP)	Gjerde, B. (AP)	0
13	*Kolstad, E. (LIB) / Fjose, B. (CPP)	Austrheim, J. (CP)	Skulberg, A. (CP)	0
14	*Ludvigsen, S. (AP) / Sagor, O. (AP)	*Lorentzen, A. (AP)	Gjerde, B. (AP)	2
15	*Ryste, R. (AP) / *Lorentsen, A. (AP)	Christiansen, R. (AP)	Egeland, K. (AP) / Evensen, J. (AP)	3
16	*Ryste, R. (AP) / *Lorentsen, A. (AP)	Christiansen, R. (AP)	Egeland, K. (AP) / Evensen, J. (AP)	0
17	*Roenbeck, S. (AP) / Nilsen, A. (AP)	Bye, R. (AP)	Foerde, E. (AP) / Kleppe, P. (AP)	0
18	Heløe, L.A. (CON) / *Gjertsen, A. (CON)	Skauge, A. (CON) / *Koppernäs, J. (CON)	Austad, T. (CON) / Langslet, L.R. (CON)	0

NORWAY 1945 - 1998

Gov	Social Affairs (py)	Public Works (py)	Other (py)	Res
19	Heløe, L.A. (CON) *Gjertsen, A. (CON)	Jakobsen, J.J. (CP) Kristiansen, K. (CPP)	Bondevik, K.M. (CCP) Langslet, L.R. (CON) *Brusletten, R. (CPP)	0
20	Heløe, L.A. (CON) *Gjertsen, A. (CON)	Jakobsen, J.J. (CP) Kristiansen, K. (CPP)	Bondevik, K.M. (CCP) Langslet, L.R. (CON) *Brusletten, R. (CPP)	0
21	*Gerhardsen, T.S. (AP) *Bakken, A.-L. (AP)	Borgen, K. (AP) Oeien, A. (AP)	*Groendal, K.K. (AP) *Vetlesen, V. (AP) Bakke, H. (AP)	1
22	*Sellæg, W. (CON) *Sollie, S. (CPP)	Reiten, E. (CP) Lie, L. (CPP)	*Sollie, S. (CPP) *Bjartveit, E. (CPP) Steensnaes, E. (CPP) Vraalsen, T. (CP)	0
23	*Veieroed, T. (AP) Sandman, M. (AP)	Opseth, K. (AP) Kristensen, F. (AP)	*Kleveland, A. (AP) *Faremo, G. (AP)	3
24	*Knudsen, G. (AP) *Berget, G. (AP)	Stoltenberg, J. (AP) Opseth, K. (AP)	*Nordheim Larsen, K. (AP) Hernes, G. (AP)	1
25	*Hill-Solberg, M. (AP) *Brustad, S. (AP)	*Faremo, G. (AP) *Rønbeck, S. (AP)	*Nordheim-Larsen, K. (AP) Sandal, R. (AP) Rød-Larsen, T. (AP) *Birkeland, T. (AP)	0
26	*Haugland, V.S. (CPP) *Kleppa, M.M. (CP)	Sponheim, L. (LIB) Dorum, O.E. (LIB) *Arnstad, M. (CP)	*Lahnstein, A.E. (CP) Restad, G. (CP) Lilletun, J. (CPP)	

37. PAKISTAN

Since independence periods of constitutional rule have alternated with Army-based regimes. This note describes the situation under constitutional governments after 1985.

The Head of State is a President who is elected indirectly for a five-year term. The President had unusually strong power over the government in that he has often dissolved governments and/or called elections when the government still had a working majority in parliament. Since the constitutional amendment of 10 April 1997, the Head of State can no longer dismiss elected governments.

Pakistan is fairly centralised even though it has a Federal structure.

Parliament is bicameral. The Upper House represents the Provinces and has 87 members. The predominant National Assembly (Lower House) has 217 members. There is a flexible term between elections of five (National Assembly) or six (Upper House) years. Elections for the National Assembly are based on plurality voting (first past the post) within constituencies of 300,000 electors approximately.

The National Assembly has a quorum of one-quarter of all members, as has the Upper House. Votes are generally carried by a simple majority of votes cast. But a vote of no confidence requires an absolute majority of all members and two-thirds of members of both Houses are required for constitutional amendments. There is no referendum.

The Head of Government is the Prime Minister who nominates his or her Cabinet from leaders of the majority party or coalition in Parliament. The Prime Minister and Cabinet are nominally appointed by the President, so no explicit vote of investiture is needed to confirm them. In practice the government rests on a relative majority in parliament. During its lifetime, government can face a vote of no confidence (see above). Losing a vote of confidence always results in the resignation of the government. The government is collectively responsible to parliament. Ministers are also members of parliament. The Prime Minister has no dominant position in government.

Because of the President's special link with the Army the government has to maintain working relationships with him, but he is not part of the government.

There is a Supreme Court for constitutional review of legislation.

PAKISTAN 1947-1998

Gov	Begin	Dur	RfT	ToG	Py1	Py2	Py3	Py4	Py5	Py6	Seats	CPG	NoM	Prime Minister (py)
1	19.07.47	1557	x	1	ML72						72		5	Khan, L.A. (ML)
2	23.10.51	542	6	1	ML72						72		10	Nazimuddin, K. (ML)
3	17.04.53	365	6	1	ML72						72		10	Ali, M. (ML)
4	24.10.54	482	1	1	ML72						72		10	Ali, M. (ML)
5	12.08.55	397	2	2	ML25	UF16					72		11	Ali, C.M. (ML)
6	12.09.56	402	4	2	AL13	RP27					72		10	Suhrawardy, H.S. (AL)
7	19.10.57	58	4	3	ML12	RP23	KrisSram 7	N-i-Islam 3			80		14	Chundrigar, I.I. (ML)
8	16.12.58	259	6	3	RP30	Diss-krisSram 2	[AL 13]	[NAP 4]	[PNC 4]	[Sched CastFed 2]	80		8	Noon, M.F.K. (RP)
9	14.08.73	1324	1	1	PPP81						117			Bhutto, Z.A. (PPP)
10	30.03.77	97	x	1	PPP155						200		23	Bhutto, Z.A. (PPP)
11	04.12.88	420	4	2	PPP93	MQM13					207			*Bhutto, B. (PPP)
12	28.01.90	191	6	1	PPP93	[IND ?]					207		27	*Bhutto, B. (PPP)
13	07.08.90	91	1	5	COP94						207		22	Jatoi, G.M. (COP)
14	06.11.90	895	6	1	IJA105						207		22	Sharif, M.M.N. (IJA)
15	19.04.93	37	x	6							207		25	Mazari, B.S.
16	26.05.93	58	2	1	IJA105						207			Sharif, M.M.N. (IJA)
17	23.07.93	88	1	6							207		13	Qureshi, M.
18	19.10.93	1113	6	2	PPP86	PML-J 6	ANP 3	[IND 26]			207		9	*Bhutto, B. (PPP)
19	05.11.96	104	1	6							207		14	Khalid, M.M.
20	17.02.97		1	1	PML-N 134						204		7	Sharif, N. (PML-N)

- Insufficient information to classify governments on CPG-scale.
- Date of Independence 15 August 1947.
- Gov 1-4: after partition parliament consisted of the 72 elected MP's of the Muslim League to the former All-(British)India Constituent Assembly. The first elections after independence took place on 21 June 1955.
- Gov 1: Reason for Termination is assassination of PM.
- Gov 4: State of Emergency proclaimed. Two representatives of the military became ministers of Defence and Interior.
- Gov 5: Reason for Termination is resignation of PM because of internal problems within Muslim League.

PAKISTAN 1947-1998

- Gov 8: Reason for Termination is intervention by Head of State after numerous attempts to form a viable parliamentary government had failed. Start of military governments under a presidential system from September 1958.
- Gov 9: First civilian parliamentary government after the general elections of 7 December 1970 wich marked the return to a parliamentary system. Due to the civil war between East- and West-Pakistan this government was postponed until 14 August 1973. The elections were held for a 313 seat parliament representing East- and West-Pakistan. After East-Pakistan declared itself independent as Bangladesh, some 117 seats for (West)Pakistan remained. The composition of the government is unknown.
- Gov 10: Reason for Termination is a military coup on 5 July 1977. The opposition boycotted parliament.
- Gov 11: This government was formed after the general elections of 16 November 1988. The new National Assembly under a semi-presidental system consisted of 207 elected Muslim members; 10 elected non-Muslim members; plus 20 seats reserved for women, chosen by the Assembly itself. The composition of the government is unknown.
- Gov 12: Four advisors to the PM were also part of the government: Ahmed, R.R.; Jafarey, V.A.; Akhund, I.; Khan, N. Reason for Termination is intervention by Head of State. National Assembly was dissolved, state of emergency imposed.
- Gov 13: COP is Combined Opposition Parties commanding 94 seats in parliament. This coalition consisted of eight parties. Which parties and how many seats per party unknown.
- Gov 14: Reason for Termination is intervention by Head of State after attempts of the PM to reduce executive powers of the president. IJA = Islami Jumhoori Iehad. IJA consisted of following parties and groups: Jamiat-e-Ulama-i-Pakistan; Jamiat-e-Islami Pakistan; National People's Party; Pakistan Muslim League; Islamic Ahle Hadith; Jamaat-ul Mashaikh; Hezb-i-Jihad/Nizam-i-Mustafa Group; Azad Group.
- Gov 15: Reason for Termination is intervention by Supreme Court, which reinstated the previous IJA government. The government was composed of representatives of 17 political parties opposing IJA, including PPP.
- Gov 16: Reason for Termination is simultanious resignation of PM and President. The composition of the government is unknown.
- Gov 18: 26 January 1994 the government was reshuffled; the Number of Ministers increased to 17.
- Gov 20: Constitution amended. As of 10 April 1997 the Head of State was no longer able to dismiss elected governments.

Gov	Deputy PM	Py	Foreign Affairs	Py	Defence	Py	Interior	Py	Justice	Py
1			Khan, L.A.	ML	Khan, L.A.	ML	Khan, G.A.	ML	Mandal, J.	Sched. Caste
2			Khan, M.Z.	ML	Nazimuddin, K.	ML	Shahabuddin, K.	ML	Sattar, P.A.	ML
3			Khan, Z.M.	ML	Ali, M.	ML	Gurmani, M.A.	ML	Brohi, A.	ML
4			Ali, M.	ML	Khan, M.A. (Gen.)	NONA	Mirza, I. (Maj.-Gen.)	NONA	Pathan, G.	ML
5	Choudhury, H.H.	UF			Ali, C.M.	ML	Huq, A.K.F.	UF	Chundigar, I.	UF
6	Noon, M.F.K.	RP			Suhrawardy, H.S.	AL	Talpur, G.A.K.	RP	Suhrawurdy, H.S.	AL

PAKISTAN 1947-1998

Gov	Deputy PM	Py	Foreign Affairs	Py	Defence	Py	Interior	Py	Justice	Py
7			Noon, M.F.K.	RP	Daultana, M.M.M.K.	ML	Talpur, G.A.K.	RP	Rahman, F.	ML
8			Noon, M.F.K.	RP	Noon, M.F.K.	RP	Talpur, G.A.K.	RP	Noon, M.F.K.	RP
9										
10			Ahmed, A.	PPP			Khan, R.M.H.	PPP	Bakhtiar, Y. Masud, S.M.	PPP PPP
11					*Bhutto, B.	PPP			Gilani, S.I.H.	PPP
12			Khan, S.Y.	PPP	*Bhutto, B.	PPP	Ahsan, A. Hayat, S.F.S. Akhund, I.	PPP PPP PPP	Gilani, S.I.H.	PPP
13			Khan, S.Y.	COP			Sarfraz, M.Z.	COP	Hussain, A.	COP
14			Khan, S.Y.	IJA	Sharif, M.M.N.	IJA	Hussain, C.S. Niazi, M.A.S.K.	IJA IJA	Imam, S.F.	IJA
15			Pirzada, S.S.		Bijarani, H.K. Sherpao, A.A.K.		Gilani, S.Y.R.			
16										
17			Sattar, A.		Bhatti, R.D.		Bandial, F.K. Junejo, A.K.		Shakurussalam, A.	
18			Leghari, F.A.K.	PPP	Mirani, A.S.	PPP	Babar, N.	PPP		
19			Khan, Y.		Hamid, S.		Afridi, U.K. Gichki, A.K.		Ibrahim, F.G.	
20			Khan, G.A.	PML-N			Hussain, C.S. *Hussain, S.A.	PML-N PML-N		

PAKISTAN 1947-1998

Gov	Finance	Py	Economic Aff.	Py	Labour	Py	Education	Py	Health	Py
1	Khan, L.A.	ML	Chundigar, I.I.	ML	Mandal, J.	Sched. Caste	Mandal, J.	Sched. Caste	Khan, G.A.	ML
2	Ali, M.	ML	Rahman, F.	ML	Malik, A.M.	ML	Rahman, F.	ML	Malik, A.M.	ML
3	+Ali, M.	ML	+Ali, M.	ML	Malik, A.M.	ML	Qureshi, H.	ML		
4	+Ali, M.	ML	+Ali, M.	ML	Malik, A.M.	ML	Talpur, G.A.K.	ML	Malik, A.M.	ML
5	Ali, C.M.	ML	Ali, C.M.	ML	Chaudry, N.H.	UF	Hussain, S.A. (Lieut.-Col.)	ML	Dutta, K.K.	UF
6	Ali, S.A.A.	RP	Suhrawardy, H.S.	AL	Khaleque, A.	AL	Zahiruddin, R.R.	AL	Zahiruddin, R.R.	AL
7	Ali, S.A.A.	RP	Chundrigar, I.I.	ML	Ahmed, F.	N-i-Islam	Khan, L.R.	KrisSram	Khan, L.R.	KrisSram
8	Ali, S.A.A.	RP	Noon, M.F.K.	RP	Aleem, A.	RP	Dutta, K.K.	RP	Dutta, K.K.	RP
9										
10	Pirzada, A.H.	PPP	Pirzada, A.H.	PPP	Gabol, A.S.	PPP	Wattu, M.Y. Vasan, N.M.	PPP PPP	Jarmali, T.M.K.	PPP
11	*Bhutto, B.	PPP								
12	*Bhutto, B. Jaffarey, V.A.	PPP NONA	Jafarey, V.A.	NONA	Awan, M.A. Maneka, G.A.	PPP PPP	Shar, S.G.I. Kazmi, S.A.H.	PPP PPP		
13	Aziz, S.	COP	Aziz, S.	COP	Mengal, N.	COP	Bajrani, H.K. *Panezi, N.J. Abid, K.A.M.	COP COP COP		
14	Aziz, S.	IJA	Aziz, S. Chatha, C.H.N.	IJA IJA	Haq, M.E.	IJA	Niazi, M.A.S.K. Imam, S.F. Chatha, C.H.N.	IJA IJA IJA	Gardezi, S.T.N.	IJA
15	Leghari, F.A.K.		Leghari, F.A.K. Chatha, C.H.N.		Jatoi, G.M. Sarfraz, Z. Gichki, M.A.		Bugti, A.N.			
16										
17	Ali, S.B.		Ali, S.B.		Balock, D.K.R.					

PAKISTAN 1947-1998

Gov	Finance	Py	Economic Aff.	Py	Labour	Py	Education	Py	Health	Py
18	*Bhutto, B.	PPP	*Bhutto, B.	PPP						
	Jafarey, V.A.	NONA	Mukhtar, C.A.	PPP						
19	Khan, M.Z.				Gichki, A.K.		*Hussain, S.A.			
20	Aziz, S.	PML-N	Aziz, S.		Hussain, C.S.	PML-N	*Hussain, S.A.	PML-N		

- Gov 3, 4: +Ali, M. no relation of PM.

Gov	Housing	Py	Agriculture	Py	Industry/Trade	Py	Environment	Py
1			Khan, G.A.	ML	Chundigar, I.I.	ML		
2			Sahar, P.A.	ML	Rahman, F.	ML		
					Nishtar, S.A.R.	ML		
3			Khan, K.A.Q.	ML	Ali, M.	ML		
					Khan, K.A.Q.	ML		
4			Pathan, G.	ML	Ispahani, M.A.	ML		
5			Biswas, A.L.	UF	Rahimtoola, H.I.	ML		
6			Ahmad, D.	AL	Ahmed, A.A.	ML		
7			Biswas, A.L.	KrisSram	Rahman, F.	ML		
					Qizilbash, M.A.K.	RP		
8			Shah, M.J.	RP	Qizilbash, M.A.K.	RP		
9								
10	Khan, A.M.J.	PPP	Rashid, M.	PPP	Gilani, S.A.R.	PPP		
			Chaudry, A.A.	PPP	Mazhari, S.F.A.	PPP		
11								
12	Gilani, Y.R.	PPP	Iqbal, R.S.	PPP	Shah, A.N.	PPP		
					Hayat, S.F.S.	PPP		

PAKISTAN 1947-1998

Gov	Housing	Py	Agriculture	Py	Industry/Trade	Py	Environment	Py
13	Nabi, I.	COP	Shah, A.H.	COP	Hussain, C.S. Raza, R. Soomro, I.B.	COP COP COP		
14	Mahmood, S.T.	IJA	Malik, A.M.	IJA	Khan, M.M.N. Nabi, I. Hussain, C.S.	IJA IJA IJA	Nasir, S.Y.K.	IJA
15			Badr, J.		Piracha, I.-u.-H. Leghari, Z.A.		Khan, A.S.	
16								
17	Junejo, A.K.		Junejo, A.K.		Balock, D.K.R. Pasha, H.			
18					Ashgar, M.	PML-J		
19			Mahmud, S.		Awan, S.M.K.		Mahmud, S.	
20					Dar, M.I.	PML-N	*Hussain, S.A.	PML-N

Gov	Social Affairs (py)	Public Works (py)	Other (py)	Res
1		Nishtar, S.A.R. (ML) Chundigar, I.I. (ML)	Khan, L.A. (ML) Nishtar, S.A.R. (ML)	2
2		Malik, A.M. (ML) Shahabuddin, K. (ML) Khan, S.B. (ML)	Gurmani, M.A. (ML)	1

PAKISTAN 1947-1998

Gov	Social Affairs (py)	Public Works (py)	Other (py)	Res
3		Khan, S.B. (ML) Malik, A.M. (ML) Qureshi, S. (ML)	Gurmani, M.A. (ML) Qureshi, H. (ML) Brohi, A. (ML) Qureshi, S. (ML)	0
4		Malik, A.M. (ML) Talpur, G.A.K. (ML) Sahib, K. (ML)	Mirza, I. (Maj.-Gen.)(NONA) Pathan, G. (ML) Khan, S.A.A. (ML)	2
5		Sahib, K. (ML) Rashidi, A.M. (ML) Chaudry, N.H. (UF)	Sahib, K. (ML) Hussain, S.A. (Lieut.-Col.)(ML) Chaudry, N.H. (UF)	3
6		Khaleque, A. (AL) Khan, S.A.A. (RP) Shah, M.J. (RP)	Suhrawardy, H.S. (AL) Khan, S.A.A. (RP)	0
7		Hussain, M.S. (KrisSram) Shah, M.J. (RP) Aleem, A. (RP)	Chundrigar, I.I. (ML) Shah, M.J. (RP) Haroon, Y. (ML)	0
8		Noon, M.F.K. (RP) Aleem, A. (RP) Ahmed, R. (Diss. KrisSram)	Noon, M.F.K. (RP) Aleem, A. (RP)	2
9				
10	Fani, R.K. (PPP)	Khan, M.A. (PPP) Bhutto, M.A. (PPP) Khan, T.M. (PPP) Khan, A.M.J. (PPP) Hamiddudin, M. (PPP) Hussain, G. (PPP)	Rashid, M. (PPP) Pirzada, A.H. (PPP) Niazi, M.K. (PPP) Khan, M.H. (PPP) Masud, S.M. (PPP) Fani, R.K. (PPP)	0

PAKISTAN 1947-1998

Gov	Social Affairs (py)	Public Works (py)	Other (py)	Res
12	Kazmi, S.A.H. (PPP) Shah, P.A. (PPP)	Leghari, S.F.A.K. (PPP) Faheem, M.A. (PPP) Laghari, Z. (PPP) Badar, J. (PPP) Gilani, Y.R. (PPP)	*Bhutto, N. (PPP) Khan, A.T. (PPP) Iqbal, R.S. (PPP) Hayat, S.F.S. (PPP) Khan, M.H. (PPP) Shah, S.Q.A. (PPP) Khan, K.B. (PPP) Rahim, K.A.T. (PPP) Maneka, G.A. (PPP) Ahmed, R.R. (PPP) Akhund, I. (PPP) Khan, N. (PPP)	0
13	*Panezi, N.J. (COP)	Khar, G.M. (COP) Khan, M.M.N. (COP) Malik, A.M. (COP) *Hussain, S.A. (COP) Nabi, I. (COP)	Sarfraz, M.Z. (COP) Khan, R. (COP) Mengal, N. (COP) Shafiquzzaman, M. (COP) Hussain, A. (COP) Shah, A.H. (COP) Zaidi, S.I.H. (COP) Azfar, K. (COP)	0

PAKISTAN 1947-1998

Gov	Social Affairs (py)	Public Works (py)	Other (py)	Res
14	Shah, S.A.G. (IJA) Niazi, M.A.S.K. (IJA)	Jatoi, G.M.K. (IJA) Bajrani, H. (IJA) Mahmood, S.T. (IJA) Khan, C.N.A. (IJA)	Singh, R.C. (IJA) Nasir, S.Y.K. (IJA) Niazi, M.A.S.K. (IJA) Imam, S.F. (IJA) Haq, M.E. (IJA) Khan, S.M.A. (IJA) Khan, R. (IJA) Zaidi, I. (IJA)	2
15	Jamote, Z.A.S. Bugti, A.N. Jogezai, W.A.K.	Qasim, M.M. Niazi, K. Khan, A.M.J. Zardari, A.A. Chatta, C.H.N.	Ali, A.A. Jadoon, A.K. Jatoi, G.M.K. Rahim, A.G. Kasuri, K.M. Khan, A.S. Gilani, S.Y.R.	0
16				0
17	Shafig, M.	Bhatti, R.D. Farouq, A. Memon, N. Junejo, A.K. Marker, K.	Bandial, F.K. Shakurussalam, A. Junejo, A.K. Pasha, H.	0
18			Niazi, S.A. (IND) Khan, M.A. (ANP)	3

438

PAKISTAN 1947-1998

Gov	Social Affairs (py)	Public Works (py)	Other (py)	Res
19	*Hussain, S.A.	Haqqani, E.A. Jabbar, J. Memon, A.J.	Hamid, S. Afridi, U.K. *Hussain, S.A. Mahmud, S. Gichki, A.K. Khan, M.F. Ibrahim, F.G.	0
20	*Hussain, S.A. (PML-N)	Khan, N.A. (PML-N) Hussain, C.S. (PML-N)	Aziz, S. (PML-N) Dar, M.I. (PML-N) Hussain, C.S. (PML-N) Khan, G.A. (PML-N) *Hussain, S.A. (PML-N)	

38. POLAND

The Head of State, the President, is directly elected for a five-year term with a maimum of two terms. He or she holds wide appointing powers and has discretionary influence over policymaking, especially in regard to military matters and foreign affairs. However, all Presidential acts require governmental endorsement. Given the powers of the President and the relatively weak position of government vis-à-vis parliament, Poland can be considered a semi-Presidential republic.

The country is a unitary state, albeit with some decentralised features.

Parliament is – like the President – a powerful body. It is bicameral. The Upper House of 100 seats represents the 47 provinces and the three main cities. The Lower House (Sejm) of 460 seats is elected by proportional representation (d'Hondt) in 52 regions of quite variable size. The election process is a complex mixture of regional and national lists. There is a threshold of five percent for individual parties and seven percent for electoral alliances. Both Houses serve a fixed term of four years.

Parliament has a quorum of at least 50 per cent of all members. Votes are carried by a majority of all votes cast. Some issues, like Bills vetoed by the President, require qualified majorities, ranging from a majority of all members present to a two-thirds majority of all members. Constitutional amendments require a two-thirds majority of all members present. A referendum is optional, and may be called by the Head of State and parliament. The outcome is binding.

The Prime Minister is nominated by the President and elected by parliament. The President on the suggestion of the Prime Minister appoints government ministers. Government is subjected to a vote of investiture and can face a vote of no confidence. Losing either vote always results in the resignation of the government. Government is both collectively and individually responsible to parliament. Individual ministers may also be members of parliament. The Prime minister has a rather prominent position in government.

There is a Constitutional Tribunal, which reviews the constitutional conformity of laws and acts. Its verdicts, however, can be modified by parliament. The Tribunal of States oversees public officials.

POLAND 1991-1998

Gov	Begin	Dur	RfT	ToG	Py1	Py2	Py3	Py4	Py5	Py6	Py7	Py8	Py9	Py10	Seats	CPG	NoM	Prime Minister (py)
1	23.12.91	166	5	5**	PC 44	WAK 49	PL 28								460	2	18	Olszewski, J. (PC)
2	06.06.92	35	x	6	PC 44	WAK 49	PL 28	UD 62							460	2	16	Pawlak, W. (PSL)
3	11.07.92	292	4	2	UD 62	ZChN 48	PChD 6	KLD 37	PL 19	SLCh 10	PPG 12	[SOL 27]	[German M 7]	[ChD 5]	460	2	25	*Suchocka, H. (UD)
4	29.04.93	180	5	5	UD 57	ZChN 44	KLD+PPG 49	KP 27	[SOL 26]	[German M 7]	[ChD 5]				460	2	22	*Suchocka, H. (UD)
5	26.10.93	496	6	3	PSL 132	SLD 171	UP 41								460	4	21	Pawlak, W. (PSL)
6	06.03.95	338	2	2	SLD 171	PSL 132									460	4	21	Oleksy, J. (SLD)
7	07.02.96	632	1	2	SLD 171	PSL 132									460	4	22	Cimoszewicz, W. (SLD)
8	31.10.97			2**	AWS 201	UW 60									460	2	24	Buzek, J. (AWS)

** = divided government

- [] Denotes party supporting the government without participating in it.
- Gov 1: WAK is Catholic Electoral Action, i.e. Christian National Union (ZChN) plus allies. Reason for Termination is adoption of a non-confidence motion in parliament wich was put forward by the President.
- Gov 2: Reason for Termination is failure to form a new government.
- Gov 4: KP is Polisch Convention; PChD plus SLCh.
- Gov 8: AWS is Solidarity Electoral Alliance, a combination of rightwing and christian parties, plus Solidarity. UW is Freedom Union (pro business).

POLAND 1991-1998

Gov	Deputy PM	Py	Foreign Affairs	Py	Defence	Py	Interior	Py	Justice	Py
1			Skubiszewski, K.	NONA	Parys, J.	NONA	Macierewicz, A.	WAK	Dyka, Z.	WAK
2			Skubiszewski, K.	NONA	Onyszkiewicz, J.	NONA	Milczanowski, A.	NONA	Dyka, Z.	WAK
3	Goryszewski, H. Łazkowski, P.	ZChN PChD	Skubiszewski, K.	NONA	Onyszkiewicz, J.	UD	Milczanowski, A.	NONA	Dyka, Z.	ZCHN
4	Goryszewski, H. Łazkowski, P.	ZChN KP-PChD	Skubiszewski, K.	NONA	Onyszkiewicz, J.	UD	Milczanowski, A.	NONA	Dyka, Z.	ZCHN
5	Borowski, M. Łuczak, A. Cimoszewicz, W.	SLD PSL SLD	Olechowski, A.	NONA	Kolodziejczyk, P.	NONA	Milczanowski, A.	NONA	Cimoszewicz, W.	SLD
6	Jagieliński, R. Kołodko, G. Łuczak, A.	PSL NONA PSL	Bartoszewski, W.	NONA	Olónski, Z.	NONA	Milczanowski, A.	NONA	Jaskiernia, J.	SLD
7	Jagieliński, R. Pietrewicz, M. Kołodko, G.	PSL PSL NONA	Rosati, D.	NONA	Dobrzánski, S.	PSL	Siemiatkowski, Z.	SLD	Kubicki, L.	NONA
8	Balcerowicz, L. Tomaszewski, J.	UW AWS	Geremek, B.	UW	Onyskiewicz, J.	UW	Tomaszewski, J.	AWS		

POLAND 1991-1998

Gov	Finance	Py	Economic Aff.	Py	Labour	Py	Education	Py	Health	Py
1	Lutkowski, K.	NONA	Eyssymontt, J. / Glapinski, A.	PC / PC	Kropiwnicki, J.	WAK	Stelmachowski, A. / Karczewski, W.	NONA / NONA	Miskiewicz, M.	NONA
2			Eyssymontt, J. / Glapinski, A.	PC / PC	Kropiwnicki, J.	WAK	Stelmachowski, A. / Karczewski, W.	NONA / NONA	Miskiewicz, M.	NONA
3	Osiatýnski, J.	UD	Goryszewski, H. / Arendarski, A. / Lewandowski, J. / Eysmont, Z. / Kropiwnicki, J.	ZChN / KLD / KLD / PPG / ZChN	Kurón, J.	UD	Flisowski, Z. / Karczewski, W.	ZChN / NONA	Wojtyla, A.	SLCh
4	Osiatýnski, J.	UD	Goryszewski, H. / Arendarski, A. / Eysmont, Z. / Kropiwnicki, J.	ZChN / KLD / PPG / ZChN	Kurón, J.	UD	Flisowski, Z. / Karczewski, W.	ZChN / NONA	Wojtyla, A.	KP-SLCh
5	Borowski, M.	SLD	Pietrewicz, M. / Podkánski, L.	PSL / PSL	Miller, L.	SLD	Łuczak, A. / Karczewski, W.	PSL / NONA	Zochowski, J.	SLD
6	Kolodko, G.	NONA	Pietrewicz, M. / Buchacz, J.	PSL / PSL	Miller, L.	SLD	Łuczak, A. / Czarny, R.	PSL / SLD	Zochowski, J.	SLD
7	Kolodko, G.	NONA	Pietrewicz, M. / Jagieliński, M. / Buchacz, J.	PSL / PSL / PSL	Bązkowski, A.	NONA	Wiatr, J. / Łuczak, A. / Karczewski, W.	SLD / PSL / NONA	Zochowski, J.	PSL
8	Balcerowicz, L. / Wasacz, E. / *Suchocka, H.	UW / AWS / UW	Balcerowicz, L. / Steinhoff, J.	UW / AWS	Komolowski, L.	AWS	Handke, M. / Wisznieuwski, A.	AWS / AWS	Maksymowicz, W.AWS	

POLAND 1991-1998

Gov	Housing	Py	Agriculture	Py	Industry/Trade	Py	Environment	Py
1			Janowski, G. / Kozłowski, S.	PL / NONA			Kozłowski, S.	NONA
2			Janowski, G. / Kozłowski, S.	PL / NONA			Kozłowski, S.	NONA
3	Bratkowski, A.	NONA	Janowski, G. / Hortmanowicz, Z.	PL / PL	Niewiarowski, W.	SLCh	Hortmanowicz, Z.	PL
4	Bratkowski, A.	NONA			Niewiarowski, W.	KP-SLCh		
5	*Blida, B.	SLD	Smietanko, A. / Zelichowski, S.	PSL / PSL	Pol, M.	UP	Zelichowski, S.	PSL
6	*Blida, B.	SLD	Jagielinski, R. / Zelichowski, S.	PSL / PSL	Scierski, K.	NONA	Zelichowski, S.	PSL
7	*Blida, B.	SLD	Jagielinski, R. / Zelichowski, S.	PSL / PSL	Scierski, K.	PSL	Zelichowski, S.	PSL
8			Janiszewski, J.	AWS			Szysko, A.	AWS

Gov	Social Affairs (py)	Public Works (py)	Other (py)	Res
1	Miskiewicz, M. (NONA) / Kropiwnicki, J. (WAK)	Waligórski, E. (NONA) / Kozłowski, S. (NONA)	Włodarczyk, K. (PC) / Sicinski, A. (NONA) / Balasz, A. (PL)	0
2	Miskiewicz, M. (NONA) / Kropiwnicki, J. (WAK)	Waligórski, E. (NONA) / Kozłowski, S. (NONA)	Łuczak, A. (PSL) / Sicinski, A. (NONA)	0

POLAND 1991-1998

Gov	Social Affairs (py)	Public Works (py)	Other (py)	Res
3	Łączkowski, P. (PChD) Kuroń, J. (UD) Wojtyła, A. (SLCH)	Hortmanowicz, Z. (PL) Jaworski, Z. (ZChN) Kilian, K. (KLD)	Łązkowski, P. (PChD) Bratkowski, A. (NONA) Kamiński, J. (PL) Bielecki, J.K. (KLD) Rokita, J.M. (UD)	0
4	Łączkowski, P. (KP-PChD) Kuroń, J. (UD) Wojtyła, A. (KP-SLCh)	Jaworski, Z. (ZChN) Kilian, K. (KLD)	Łązowski, P. (KP-PChD) Bratkowski, A. (NONA) Lewandowski, J. (KLD) Bielecki, J.K. (KLD) Rokita, J.M. (UD)	0
5	Miller, L. (SLD) Zochowski, J. (SLD)	Liberadzki, B. (NONA) Zelichowski, S. (PSL) Zieliński, A. (NONA)	Strak, M. (PSL) Dejmek, K. (PSL) Kaczmarek, W. (SLD) *Blida, B. (SLD)	0
6	Miller, L. (SLD) Zochowski, J. (SLD)	Liberadzki, B. (NONA) Zieliński, A. (NONA) Zelichowski, S. (PSL)	Borowski, M. (SLD) Kaczmarek, W. (SLD) Dejmek, K. (PSL) *Blida, B. (SLD)	1
7	Bazkowski, A. (NONA) Zochowski, J. (PSL)	Liberadzki, B. (NONA) Zieliński, A. (NONA) Zelichowski, S. (PSL)	*Blida, B. (SLD) Kaczmarek, W. (SLD) Miller, L. (SLD) Podkański, Z. (PSL)	2

446

POLAND 1991-1998

Gov	Social Affairs (py)	Public Works (py)	Other (py)	Res
8	Komolowski, L. (AWS)	Morawski, E. (UW)	*Wnuk-Nazarowa, J. (UW)	
	Kapera, L. (AWS)	Zdrojewski, M. (AWS)	Czarnecki, R. (AWS)	
			*Kaminska, T. (AWS)	
			Kropiwnicki, J. (AWS)	
			Walendziak, W. (AWS)	
			Palubicki, J. (AWS)	
			Widzyk, J. (AWS)	

39. PORTUGAL

From 1976, the Head of State has been a directly elected President with a five-year term. He or she has wide powers of appointment, and can request judicial reviews, and dissolve parliament. There is a Council of State, which serves as an advisory body to the President. This council always includes the Prime Minister, the President of the Legislature and the President of the Constitutional Court.

Portugal is a unitary and centralised state.

Parliament is unicameral, and has 250 seats elected by proportional representation (d'Hondt) for a fixed term of four years. There are 22 constituencies with approximately 360,000 electors each, although their size varies somewhat. The number of representatives is well matched to constituency size.

Parliament has a quorum of at least 50 per cent of all members. Votes are carried by a majority of all votes cast. For some issues a qualified majority of all members present is required. Constitutional amendments require either a two-thirds or a four-fifth majority of all members present, depending on the subject. A referendum is optional and may be called by the Head of State. The outcome is binding.

The government is constitutionally described as the highest organ of policy implementation and organiser of the public administration. It requires a vote of investiture and can face a vote of no confidence. Losing either vote always results in the resignation of the government. Government is collectively responsible to parliament. Ministers can not be members of parliament at the same time. The Prime Minister has no dominant position in government.

Judicial review is carried out both by the Supreme Court (in cases of appeal), and by the Constitutional Court. This latter body supervises and assesses all laws related to the political system (the electoral law and laws pertaining to political parties), and all governmental actions.

PORTUGAL 1976-1998

Gov	Begin	Dur	RfT	ToG	Py1	Py2	Seats	CPG	NoM	Prime Minister (py)
1	23.07.76	556	5	4	PSP 107		263	4	17	Soares, M.A.N.L. (PSP)
2	30.01.78	211	4	2	PSP 107	CDS 42	263	3	16	Soares, M.A.N.L. (PSP)
3	29.08.78	85	5	x			263	-	15	Nobre da Costa, A.J. (NONA)
4	22.11.78	252	5	x			263	-	16	Mota Pinto, C.A. (NONA)
5	01.08.79	155	1	6			263		17	*Pintassilgo de Lurdes, M. (NONA)
6	03.01.80	372	x	1	AD 128		250	2	15	Sá Carneiro, F.L. (AD-PSD)
7	09.01.81	238	2	1	AD 134		250	2	18	Pereira Pinto Balsemão, F.J. (AD-PSD)
8	04.09.81	643	2	1	AD 134		250	2	15	Pereira Pinto Balsemão, F.J. (AD-PSD)
9	09.06.83	881	4	2	PSP 101	PSD 75	250	3	17	Soares, M.A.N.L. (PSP)
10	06.11.85	649	5	4	PSD 88		250	2	14	Cavaco e Silva, A.A. (PSD)
11	17.08.87	1533	1	1	PSD 148		250	2	16	Cavaco e Silva, A.A. (PSD)
12	28.10.91	1462	1	1	PSD 135		250	2	16	Cavaco e Silva, A.A. (PSD)
13	29.10.95		4	4	PSP 112		230	4	17	Guterres, A. (PSP)

- MFA is the revolutionary movement of the armed forces.
- Gov 2: Reason for Termination is dismissal of PM by the president after disagreement on agricultural and health policies led to withdrawal of CDS ministers from government and withdrawal of government support by CDS in parliament.
- Gov 3-5: Government consisted of non-alligned and MFA ministers.
- Gov 6: AD is election côoperation of PSD (75); CDS (42); PPM (5) and others (6). After the elections of 5 October 1980 the PM decided not to resign and came into conflict with president Eanes. The death of the PM on 4 December 1980 resolved the conflict.
- Gov 7, 8: Reason for Termination is resignation of PM because of internal criticism and opposition. AD is election côoperation of PSD (82); CDS (46) and PPM (6).

PORTUGAL 1976-1998

Gov	Deputy PM	Py	Foreign Affairs	Py	Defence	Py	Interior	Py	Justice	Py
1			Medeiros Ferreira, J.	PSP	Miguel, M.F. (Col.)	MFA	Da Costa Brás, M. (Lieut.-Col.)	MFA	De Almeida Santos, A.	NONA
2	De Almeida Santos, A.	PSP	Nunes de Sá Machado, V.A.	CDS	Miguel, M.F. (Col.)	MFA	Gama, J. Pena, R.F.R.	PSP CDS	Dias dos Santos, J.	PSP
3			Correira Cago, C.	NONA	Miguel, M.F. (Col.)	MFA	Gonçalves Ribeiro, A. (Lieut.-Col.)	MFA	Ferreira Raposo, M.	NONA
4	Nunens, M.J.	NONA	De Freitas Cruz, J.	NONA	Loureiro dos Santos, J. (Lieut.-Col.)	MFA	Gonçalves Ribeiro, A. (Lieut.-Col.)	MFA	Correia, E.	NONA
5	Da Costa Brás, M. (Col.)	MFA	De Freitas Cruz, J.	NONA	Loureiro dos Santos, J. (Lieut.-Col.)	MFA	Da Costa Brás (Col.)	MFA	De Sousa Macedo, P.	NONA
6	Freitas do Amaral, D.	AD-CDS	Freitas do Amaral, D.	AD-CDS	Amaro da Costa, A.	AD-CDS	De Melo, E.	AD-PSD	Ferreira Raposo, M.	AD-PSD
7			Gonçalves Pereira, A.	NONA	De Azevedo Coutinho, L.	AD-CDS	Monteiro do Amaral, F. Marques de Carvalho, E.	AD-PSD NONA	Meneres Pimentel, J.	AD-PSD
8	Freitas do Amaral, D.	AD-CDS	Gonçalves Pereira, A.	NONA	Freitas do Amaral, D.	AD-CDS	Correia, A. Meneres Pimentel, J.	AD-PSD AD-PSD	Meneres Pimentel, J.	AD-PSD
9	Mota Pinto, C.A.	PSD	Gama, J.	PSP	Mota Pinto, C.A.	PSD	Ribeiro Pereira, E.	PSP	Machete, R.	PSD
10			Pires de Miranda, P.	PSD	Ribeiro de Almeida, L.	PSD	De Melo, E. Valente de Oliveira, L.	PSD PSD	Ferreira Raposo, M.	PSD
11	De Melo, E.	PSD	De Deus Pinheiro, J.	PSD	De Melo, E.	PSD	Silveira Godinho, J. Valente de Oliveira, L.	PSD PSD	Nogueira, J.F.	PSD
12			De Deus Pinheiro, J.	PSD	Nogueira, J.F.	PSD	Dias Loureiro, M. Valente de Oliveira, L.	PSD PSD	Laborinho Lúcio, A.	PSD
13			Gama, J.	PSP	Vitorino, A.	PSP	Costa, A. Cravinho, J.	PSP PSP	Vera Jardim, J.	PSP

PORTUGAL 1976-1998

Gov	Finance	Py	Economic Aff.	Py	Labour	Py	Education	Py	Health	Py
1	Medina Carreira, H.	PSP	De Sousa Gomes, A.	NONA	Curto, F.M.	PSP	Sottomayor Cardia, M. / Rosa, W.	PSP / PSP		
2	Ribeiro Constâncio, M.V.	PSP	Ribeiro Constâncio, M.V.	PSP	Maldonado Gonelha, A.	PSP	Sottomayor Cardia, M. / Melancia, C.	PSP / PSP		
3	Da Silva Lopes, J.	NONA	Da Silva Lopes, J.	NONA	Seias Costa Leal, A.	NONA	LLoyd Braga, C.A. / Santos Martins, F.	NONA / NONA		
4	Nunens, M.J.	NONA	Nunens, M.J.	NONA	Marques de Carvalho, E.	NONA	Valente de Oliveira, L. / Barreto, A.	NONA / NONA		
5	Sousa Franco, A.	NONA	Correia Cago, C.J.	NONA	Sá Borges, J.	NONA	Caldas Veiga da Cunha, L.E. / Sedas Nunes, A.	NONA / NONA		
6	Cavaco e Silva, A.A.	AD-PSD			Marques de Carvalho, E.	NONA	Pereira Crespo, V.	AD-PSD		
7	Morais Leitao, J.A.	AD-CDS	Morais Leitao, J.A.	AD-CDS	Nascimento Rodrigues, H.	AD-PSD	Pereira Crespo, V.	AD-PSD		
8	Salgueiro, J.F.	AD-PSD	Salgueiro, J.F.	AD-PSD	Queiros Martins, A.	AD-PSD	Pereira Crespo, V. / Pires, F.L.	AD-PSD / AD-CDS		
9	Lopes, E.	NONA	Lopes, E.	NONA	De Azevedo, A.	NONA	Seabra, J.A.	PSD	Maldonado Gonelha, A.	PSP
10	Ribeiro Cadilhe, M.	PSD	Valente de Oliveira, L.	PSD	Mira Amaral, L.	NONA	De Deus Pinheiro, J.	PSD	*Beleza, M.L.	PSD
11	Ribeiro Cadilhe, M.	PSD	Valente de Oliveira, L.	PSD	Da Silva Peneda, J.	PSD	Carneiro, R.	NONA	*Beleza, M.L.	PSD
12	Braga de Macedo, J.	PSD	Valente de Oliveira, L.	PSD	Da Silva Peneda, J.	PSD	Durao, D.G.	PSD	De Carvalho, A.	PSD
13	Sousa Franco, A.	PSP	Bessa, D. / Gravinho, J.	PSP / PSP	*Joao Rodrigues, M.	PSP	Grilo, M. / Cago, M.	PSP / PSP	*Belem Roseira, M.	PSP

PORTUGAL 1976-1998

Gov	Housing	Py	Agriculture	Py	Industry/Trade	Py	Environment	Py
1	Ribeiro Pereira, E.	NONA	Lopes Cardoso, A.	PSP	Rosa, W. Barreto, A.	PSP PSP		
2	De Sousa Gomes, A.	PSP	Gonçalves Saias, L.S.	NONA	Melancia, C. De Mendonça Horta da Franca, B.A.	PSP CDS		
3	Almeida Pina, J. (Lieut.-Col.)	MFA	Vaz Portugal, A.	NONA	Pires de Miranda, P.J. Santos Martins, F.	NONA NONA		
4	Almeida Pina, J. (Lieut.-Col.)	MFA	Vaz Portugal, A.	NONA	Barreto, A. Repolho Correia, A.	NONA NONA		
5			Lourenço, J.	NONA	Marques Videira, F. Pereira Mogro, A.	NONA NONA		
6			Cardoso e Cunha, A.	AD-PSD	De Medonça Horta da Franca, B.A. Barreto, A.	AD-CDS AD-PSD		
7	Da Silva Barbosa, L.E.	AD-CDS	Cardoso e Cunha, A.	AD-PSD	Vaz Pinto, A. Horta, R.	AD-PSD AD-CDS		
8	Viana Baptista, J.C.	AD-PSD	Mendonça Horta da Franca, B.A.	AD-CDS	Mendonça Horta da Franca, B.A. Baiao Horta da Franca, R.	AD-CDS AD-CDS		
9			Soares da Costa, M.	PSD	Barreto, A.	PSD		
10			Barreto, A.	PSD	Santos Martins, F.	PSD		
11			Barreto, A.	PSD	Mira Amaral, L. Ferreira do Amaral, J.	PSD PSD		
12			Cunha, A.	PSD	Mira Amaral, L. Facia de Oliveira, F.	PSD PSD	Borrego, C.	PSD
13			Da Silva, G.	PSP			*Ferreira, E.	PSP

PORTUGAL 1976-1998

Gov	Social Affairs (py)	Public Works (py)	Other (py)	Res
1	Bacelor, A. (PSP)	Da Veiga Peixoto Vilar, E.R. (PSP) Almeida Pires, J. (MFA-Lieut.-Col.) Ribeiro Pereira, E. (NONA)	Campinos, J. (PSP) Barreto, A. (PSP)	4
2	Duarte Arnaut, A. (PSP)	Ferreira de Lima, M. (PSP) De Sousa Gomes, A. (PSP)	De Mendonça Horta da Franca, B.A. (CDS)	0
3	Pereira Magro, A. (NONA)	Gouveia Marques, A.J. (NONA) Almeida Pina, J. (MFA-Lieut.-Col.)	Costas Freitas, C. (NONA) Pires de Miranda, P.J. (NONA) Lloyd Braga, C.A. (NONA)	0
4	Pereira Magro, A. (NONA) Proença de Carvalho, D. (NONA)	Marques da Costa, J. (NONA) Almeida Pina, J. (MFA-Lieut.-Col.)	Nunens, M.J. (NONA) Monjardino, A. (NONA) Repolho Correia, A. (NONA) Valente de Oliveira, L. (NONA)	0
5	Figueiredo, J. (MFA-Maj.) Bruto da Costa, A. (NONA)	Montreiro da Silva, F. (NONA) De Azevedo, M. (NONA)	Pereira Mogro, A. (NONA) Sedas Nunes, A. (NONA)	0
6	Morais Leitao, J.A. (AD-CDS)	Lopes Porto, J. (AD-CDS) Viana Baptista, J.C. (AD-PSD) Barreto, A. (AD-PSD)	Pereira Pinto Balsemão, F.J. (AD-PSD) De Mendonga Horta da Franca, B.A. (AD-CDS)	0
7	Macedo, C. (AD-PSD) Ferreiro do Amaral, A. (AD-PPM)	Da Silva Barbosa, L.E. (AD-CDS) Viana Baptista, J.C. (AD-PSD) Horta, R. (AD-CDS)	De Mendonça Horta da Franca, B.A. (AD-CDS) Vaz Pinto, A. (AD-PSD) Barreto, A. (AD-PSD)	1
8	Da Silva Barbosa, L.E. (AD-CDS)	Baiao Horta da Franca, R. (AD-CDS) Viana Baptista, J.C. (AD-PSD)	Ribeiro Teles, G. (AD-PPM) Salgueiro, J.F. (AD-PSD) Monteiro do Amaral, F. (AD-PSD) Pires, F.L. (AD-CDS)	1

PORTUGAL 1976-1998

Gov	Social Affairs (py)	Public Works (py)	Other (py)	Res
9	Correira, J.R. (PSP) Capucho, A. (PSD)	Veiga Simão, J. (PSP) Melancia, C. (PSP)	Almeida Santos, A. (PSP) Barreto, A. (PSD) Coimbra Martins, A. (PSP)	1
10	Mira Amaral, L. (NONA)	Oliveira Martins, J. (PSD)	De Melo, E. (PSD) Nogueira, J.F. (PSD) De Deus Pinheiro, J. (PSD)	0
11	Da Silva Peneda, J. (PSD) Couto dos Santos, A. (PSD)	Oliveira Martins, J. (PSD)	Nogueira, J.F. (PSD) Capucho, A. (PSD) Ferreira do Amaral, J. (PSD)	1
12	Da Silva Peneda, J. (PSD)	Mira Amaral, L. (PSD) Ferreira do Amaral, J. (PSD) Borrego, C. (PSD) De Azevedo Soares, E. (PSD)	Nogueira, J.F. (PSD) Facia de Oliveira, F. (PSD)	1
13	Rodrigues, F. (PSP)	Constantino, H. (PSP)	Carilho, M.M. (PSP)	1

40. ROMANIA

The new constitution was approved by referendum in 1991.

The Head of Sate, the President, is directly elected for a four-year term with a maximum of two terms. He or she has, apart from appointing powers, considerable influence on the executive: he or she presides over meetings of government and designates the Prime Minister. Romania is a unitary and centralised state.

Parliament is bicameral. The Upper House of 143 seats, and the Lower House of 343 seats are both elected by proportional representation (d'Hondt) in constituencies of variable sizes with approximately 415,000 electors in each, on average. The number of representatives is not well proportioned to the number of electors. Both Houses serve a fixed term of four years. There is a threshold of three percent, or eight percent when a electoral coalition of two or more parties is formed.

Parliament has a quorum of at least 50 per cent of all members. Votes are carried by a majority of all members present. Some issues require a majority of all members. Constitutional amendments require a two-thirds majority of all members in both Houses, plus a referendum. The outcome is binding. The Head of State and parliament may also call a referendum on policy matters. The outcome of these referendums is also binding.

Government is subject to a vote of investiture and can face a vote of no confidence. Losing either vote always results in resignation of the government. Government is both collectively and individually responsible to parliament. Individual ministers may also be members of parliament. The Prime Minister has no dominant position in government.

The Constitutional Court reviews the constitutionality of laws and government actions whenever requested by public bodies (including the President), but may be overruled by a two-thirds majority of all members in both Houses of parliament.

ROMANIA 1990-1998

Gov	Begin	Dur	RfT	ToG	Py1	Py2	Py3	Py4	Seats	CPG	NoM	Prime Minister (py)
1	20.06.90	483	2	1	FSN 263				400	3	21	Roman, P. (FSN)
2	16.10.91	394	1	3	FSN 263	NLP 29	REM 12	ADP 9	400	3	20	Stolojan, A. (FSN)
3	13.11.92	478	7	4	FSND 117	[PSM 13]	[Romare 16]		341	3	21	Vacaroiu, N. (NONA)
4	06.03.94	593	5	2	SDPR 117	PUNR 30	[PSM 13]	[Romare 16]	341	3	22	Vacaroiu, N. (NONA)
5	20.10.95	319	4	5	SDPR 117	PUNR 30			341	3	24	Vacaroiu, N. (SDPR)
6	03.09.96			4	SDPR 117				341	3	26	Vacaroiu, N. (SDPR)

- [] Denotes party supporting the government without participating in it.
- Gov 1: Reason for termination is resignation of PM amidst demonstration and riots by miners in Bucharest.
- Gov 4: FSND (Democratic National Savation Front) changed its name into Social Democratic Party of Romania (SDPR) on 10 July 1993. Reason for Termination is a split in coalition; PSM and Romare withdraw from coalition which lost its small majority in parliament. Type of Government is multi party minority government for SPDR and PUNR together. With support of PSM and Romare which were not represented in government it is a minimal winning coalition.

Gov	Deputy PM	Py	Foreign Affairs	Py	Defence	Py	Interior	Py	Justice	Py
1	Severin, A.	FSN	Natase, A.	FSN	Stanculescu, V.A. (Col.-Gen.)	FSN	Severin, A. Ursu, D.V.	FSN FSN	Babiuc, V.	FSN
2			Nastase, A.	FSN	Spiroiu, N. (Gen.)	FSN	Babiuc, V.	FSN	*Ionescu-Quintus, M.	NLP
3			Melescanu, T.V.	FSND	Spiroiu, N. (Lieut.-Gen.)	FSND	Danescu, G.I.	FSND	Ninosu, P.	FSND
4			Melescanu, T.V.	SDPR	Tincu, G.	SDPR	Taracila, I.D.	NONA	Chiuzbaian, I.G.	PUNR
5			Melescanu, T.V.	SDPR	Tincu, G.	SDPR	Taracila, I.D.	SDPR	Chiuzbaian, I.G.	PUNR
6			Melescanu, T.V.	SDPR	Tincu, G.	SDPR	Taracila, I.D.	SDPR	Bradescu, I.	SDPR

ROMANIA 1990-1998

Gov	Finance	Py	Economic Aff.	Py	Labour	Py	Education	Py	Health	Py
1	Stolojan, T.	FSN	Dijmarescu, E.	FSN	Zamfir, C.	FSN	George, S.	FSN	Marinescu, B.	FSN
2	Danielescu, G. / Bercea, F.	NLP / FSN	Danielescu, G.	NLP	Popescu, D.M.	FSN	Golu, M.	FSN	Mairoescu, M.	FSN
3	Georgescu, F.	FSND	Megritoiu, M.	FSND	Popescu, D.M.	FSND	Maior, L. / Palade, D.D.	FSND / FSND	Mincu, I.	FSND
4	Georgescu, F.	SDPR	Cosea, M.	SDPR	Popescu, D.M.	SDPR	Maior, L. / Palade, D.D.	SDPR / SDPR	Mincu, I.	SDPR
5	Georgescu, F.	SDPR	Cosea, M.	SDPR	Popescu, D.M.	SDPR	Maior, L. / Palade, D.D.	SDPR / SDPR	Mincu, I.	SDPR
6	Georgescu, F.	SDPR	Cosea, M.	SDPR	Popescu, D.M.	SDPR	Maior, L. / Palade, D.D.	SDPR / SDPR	Mincu, I.	SDPR

Gov	Housing	Py	Agriculture	Py	Industry/Trade	Py	Environment	Py
1			Tip, I.	FSN	Vatasescu, A. / Zisu, M. / Fota, C.	FSN / FSN / FSN	Pop, V.E.	FSN
2			Marculescu, P.	ADP	Fota, C. / Constantinescu, D.	FSN / FSN	Bleahu, M.	REM
3			Oancea, I. / Ilie, A.C.	FSND / FSND	Popescu, D.I. / Teculescu, C.	FSND / FSND	Ilie, A.C.	FSND
4			Oancea, I. / Ilie, A.C.	SDPR / SDPR	Popescu, D.I. / Ionescu, C.	SDPR / SDPR	Ilie, A.C.	SDPR

ROMANIA 1990-1998

Gov	Housing	Py	Agriculture	Py	Industry/Trade	Py	Environment	Py
5			Tabara, V. Ilie, A.C.		Popescu, D.I.	SDPR SDPR	Ilie, A.C.	SDPR
6			Lapusan, A. Ilie, A.C.		Stanescu, A. Popescu, D.I.	SDPR SDPR	Ilie, A.C.	SDPR

Gov	Social Affairs (py)	Public Works (py)	Other (py)	Res
1	Stoica, I.A. (FSN) Zamfir, C. (FSN) Niculescu Duvaz, B.N. (FSN)	Zisu, M. (FSN) Chirica, A. (FSN) Pana, D. (FSN)	Severin, A. (FSN) Fota, C. (FSN) Pana, D. (FSN) Plesu, A.G. (FSN)	1
2	Popescu, D.M. (FSN) Moldovan, I. (FSN)	Vasescu, T. (FSN) Chirica, A. (FSN) Nicolae, D. (FSN)	Fota, C. (FSN) Spiess, L. (FSN) Stoica, I.A. (FSN)	0
3	Popescu, D.M. (FSND) Angelescu, G. (FSND)	Theodoru, P. (FSND) Chirica, A. (FSND) Cristea, M. (FSND)	Dan, M.A. (FSND) Cristea, M. (FSND) Ilie, A.C. (FSND) Golu, M. (FSND) Mois, V. (FSND)	1

ROMANIA 1990-1998

Gov	Social Affairs (py)	Public Works (py)	Other (py)	Res
4	Popescu, D.M. (SDPR)	Novac, A. (PUNR)	Dan, M.A. (SDPR)	1
	Mironov, A. (SDPR)	Chirica, A. (SDPR)	Cristea, M. (SDPR)	
		Cristea, M. (SDPR)	Ilie, A.C. (SDPR)	
			Salcudeanu, P. (SDPR)	
			Mois, V. (SDPR)	
5	Popescu, D.M. (SDPR)	Novac, A. (SDPR)	Hrebrenciuc, V. (SDPR)	1
	Mironov, A. (SDPR)	Turicu, A. (SDPR)	Melescanu, T.V. (SDPR)	
		Cristea, M. (SDPR)	Popescu, D.M. (SDPR)	
			Georgescu, F. (SDPR)	
			Cosea, M. (SDPR)	
			Dorneanu, V. (PUNR)	
			Dan, M.A. (SDPR)	
			Cristea, M. (SDPR)	
			Ilie, A.C. (SDPR)	
			Sorescu, M. (SDPR)	
			Nastase, A. (SDPR)	
			Gherman, O. (SDPR)	

ROMANIA 1990-1998

Gov	Social Affairs (py)	Public Works (py)	Other (py)	Res
6	Popescu, D.M. (SDPR)	Novac, A. (SDPR)	Hrebenciuc, V. (SDPR)	0
	Mironov, A. (SDPR)	Turicu, A. (SDPR)	Melescanu, T.V. (SDPR)	
		Popescu, V. (SDPR)	Popescu, D.M. (SDPR)	
		Cristea, M. (SDPR)	Georgescu, F. (SDPR)	
			Cosea, M. (SDPR)	
			Dorneanu, V. (SDPR)	
			Dan, M.A. (SDPR)	
			Cristea, M. (SDPR)	
			Ilie, A.C. (SDPR)	
			Sorescu, M. (SDPR)	
			Nastase, A. (SDPR)	
			Gherman, O. (SDPR)	

41. SLOVAKIA

In 1993 Slovakia became an independent nation after separating from the former Czechoslovakia.

The Head of State, the President, is indirectly elected for a five-year term with a maximum of two terms. His or her powers are considerable: with regard to internal and external policymaking, and to appointing government and dissolving parliament.

The country is a unitary and centralised state.

Parliament is unicameral. Its 150 members are elected for a fixed term of four years by proportional representation (Hagenbach) in constituencies that vary considerably in size, but average around 100,000 electors. There is a threshold of five percent.

Parliament has a quorum of at least 50 percent of members. Votes are carried by a majority of all members present. Some issues require a qualified majority ranging from a majority to a three-fifth majority of all members. Constitutional amendments require a three-fifths majority of all members. A referendum is constitutionally required and may be called by the Head of State, parliament and a portion of the electorate. The outcome is binding, but within three years of the date that this outcome has become effective, parliament may legally amend or abolish it.

Governments need to win a vote of investiture by a majority of all members. Governments can also face a vote of no confidence. Losing either vote always results in resignation of the government. Government is both collectively and individually responsible to parliament. Being a minister is not compatible with being a Member of Parliament. The Prime Minister has a rather prominent position in government.

The Constitutional Court reviews and interprets laws and other measures, including public regulations. The court also reviews legislation on request.

SLOVAKIA 1992-1998

Gov	Begin	Dur	RfT	ToG	Py1	Py2	Py3	Py4	Py5	Py6	Seats	CPG	NoM	Prime Minister (py)
1	24.06.92	202	x	2	HZDS 74	SNS 15					150	3	15	Mečiar, V. (HZDS)
2	12.01.93	66	4	2	HZDS 74	SNS 15					150	3	15	Mečiar, V. (HZDS)
3	19.03.93	243	7	4	HZDS 74						150	3	16	Mečiar, V. (HZDS)
4	17.11.93	119	5	2	HZDS 66	SNS 15					150	3	18	Mečiar, V. (HZDS)
5	16.03.94	271	1	2	SDL 28	KDH 18	APR 10	AD 8	NDK 5	[MKHD 14]	150	3	18	Moravčík, J. (APR)
6	12.12.94			2	HZDS 61	ZRS 13	SNS 10				150	3	18	Mečiar, V. (HZDS)

- [] Denotes party supporting the government without participating in it.
- Gov 1: Reason for Termination is dissolution of Czech-Slovak federation.
- Gov 5: APR = Alternative of Political Realism; AD = Alliance of Democrats of the Slovak Republic; NDK = National Democratic Club. All three parties are break-away factions of HZDS and SNS

Gov	Deputy PM	Py	Foreign Affairs	Py	Defence	Py	Interior	Py	Justice	Py
1	Kováč, R.	HZDS	Knazko, M.	HZDS			Tuchynca, J.	NONA	*Tóthová, K.	HZDS
	Knazko, M.	HZDS								
2	Kováč, R.	HZDS	Knazko, M.	HZDS			Tuchynca, J.	NONA	*Tóthová, K.	HZDS
	Knazko, M.	HZDS								
3	Kováč, R.	HZDS	Moravčík, J.	HZDS	Andrejčák, I.	NONA	Tuchynca, J.	NONA	*Tóthová, K.	HZDS
4	Kováč, R.	HZDS	Moravčík, J.	HZDS	Andrejčák, I.	NONA	Tuchynca, J.		*Tóthová, K.	HZDS
	Tóth, J.	HZDS								
	Andel, M.	SNS								
	Kozlík, S.	HZDS								
	Prokeš, J.	SNS								
5	Kováč, R.	APR	Kukan, E.	APR	Kanis, P.	SDL	Pittner, L.	KDH	Šimko, I.	KDH
	*Schmögnerová, B.	SDL							Hanzel, M.	SDL
	Šimko, I.	KDH								

SLOVAKIA 1992-1998

Gov	Deputy PM	Py	Foreign Affairs	Py	Defence	Py	Interior	Py	Justice	Py
6	*Tóthová, K.	HZDS	Šhenk, J.	HZDS	Sitek, J.	SNS	Hudek, L.	HZDS	Liščák, J.	ZRS
	Kozlík, S.	HZDS								
	Kalman, J.	ZRS								

Gov	Finance	Py	Economic Aff.	Py	Labour	Py	Education	Py	Health	Py
1	Tóth, J.	HZDS	Kováč, R.	HZDS	*Keltošová, O.	HZDS	Slobodník, D.	HZDS	Sobona, V.	HZDS
			Cernak, L.	SNS			Kucera, M.	HZDS		
			Dolgos, L.	HZDS						
2	Tóth, J.	HZDS	Cernak, L.	SNS	*Keltošová, O.	HZDS	Kucera, M.	HZDS	Sobona, V.	HZDS
			Dolgos, L.	HZDS						
3	Tóth, J.	HZDS	Kubecka, J.	HZDS	*Keltošová, O.	HZDS	Kucera, M.	HZDS	Sobona, V.	HZDS
			Dolgos, L.	HZDS						
4	Tóth, J.	HZDS	Meciar, V.	HZDS	*Keltošová, O.	HZDS	Andel, M.	SNS	*Belohorská, I.	HZDS
			Tóth, J.	HZDS			Paška, J.	SNS		
			Kozlík, S.	HZDS						
			Ducký, J.	NONA						
5	Filkus, R.	AD	*Schmögnerová, B.	SDL	Brocka, J.	KDH	Harach, L.	APR	Šagát, T.	SDL
			Magvaši, P.	SDL						
			Janičina, M.	NDK						
6	Kozlík, S.	HZDS	Bisák, P.	ZRS	*Keltošová, O.	HZDS	*Slavkovská, E.	SNS	Javorský, L.	HZDS
			Ducký, J.	HZDS						

SLOVAKIA 1992-1998

Gov	Housing	Py	Agriculture	Py	Industry/Trade	Py	Environment	Py
1	Hofbauer, R.	HZDS	Baco, P.	HZDS	Cernak, L.	SNS	Zlocha, J.	HZDS
2			Baco, P.	HZDS			Zlocha, J.	HZDS
3			Baco, P.	HZDS			Zlocha, J.	HZDS
4			Baco, P.	HZDS			Zlocha, J.	HZDS
5			Končos, P.	SDL			Hraško, J.	SDL
6			Baco, P.	HZDS			Zlocha, J.	HZDS

Gov	Social Affairs (py)	Public Works (py)	Other (py)	Res
1	*Keltošová, O. (HZDS) Slobodník, D. (HZDS)	Hofbauer, R. (HZDS)	Cernak, L. (SNS) Baco, P. (HZDS) Slobodník, D. (HZDS)	0
2	*Keltošová, O. (HZDS)	Hofbauer, R. (HZDS)	Slobodník, D. (HZDS)	0
3	*Keltošová, O. (HZDS)	Hofbauer, R. (HZDS)	Slobodník, D. (HZDS)	1
4	*Keltošová, O. (HZDS) Andel, M. (SNS)	Hofbauer, R. (HZDS)	Slobodník, D. (HZDS) Prokeš, J. (SNS)	0
5	Brocka, J. (KDH)	Dzurinda, M. (KDH)	Roman, L. (KDH)	0
6	*Slavkovská, E. (SNS) *Keltošová, O. (HZDS)	Rezeš, A. (HZDS)	Hudec, I. (HZDS) Mráz, J. (ZRS)	2

42. SLOVENIA

The Head of State, the President, is directly elected for a five-year term, with a maximum of two consecutive terms. He or she may exercise certain executive powers depending on the consent of parliament.

Slovenia is a unitary state with a certain degree of local government (in particular in regions with Italian or Austrian minorities).

Parliament is bicameral. The National Assembly (the Lower House) of 90 seats is elected by proportional representation (d'Hondt) in eight 11-member constituencies of roughly 200,000 electors each. The National Council (the Upper House) of 40 seats represents socio-economic, cultural and local interests.

The National Assembly has a quorum of at least 50 per cent of all members. Votes are carried by a majority of all votes cast. For some issues a qualified majority is required, ranging from a majority of all members to either a two-thirds majority of all votes cast, or a two-thirds majority of all members. Constitutional amendments require a two-thirds majority of all members. Parliament and a portion of the electorate may call a referendum. The outcome is binding.

Government is formed by the Prime Minister–designate and has to survive a vote of investiture in the National Assembly. Government can also face a vote of no confidence during its lifetime. Losing either vote always results in resignation of the government. Government is both collectively and individually responsible to parliament. Individual ministers may also be members of parliament. The Prime Minister has a rather prominent position in government.

The Constitutional Court adjudicates the constitutionality of all public actions, but on request only.

SLOVENIA 1993-1998

Gov	Begin	Dur	RfT	ToG	Py1	Py2	Py3	Py4	Py5	Seats	CPG	NoM	Prime Minister (py)
1	12.01.93	441	4	3	LDS 22	SKD 15	ZLSD 14	ZS 5	SDSS 4	90	3	16	Drnovšek, J. (LDS)
2	29.03.94	680	4	2	LDS 27	SKD 15	ZLSD 14			90	3	17	Drnovšek, J. (LDS)
3	07.02.96	386	1	2	LDS 30	SKD 16				90	2	18	Drnovšek, J. (LDS)
4	27.02.97			2	LDS 25	SLS 19	DeSUS 5			90	2	19	Drnovšek, J. (LDS)

- Gov 1: During government 1 LDS and ZS merged into LDS. ZS ministers became LDS ministers.
- Gov 4: On 3 July 1997 the National Assembly passed a law regarding the number of ministers and ministries. The government by law consists of the PM; 16 ministers with portfolios (new ministries for Small Bussiness and Tourism and for European Affairs were created) and a non-defined number of ministers without portfolios.

Gov	Deputy PM	Py	Foreign Affairs	Py	Defence	Py	Interior	Py	Justice	Py
1	Peterle, L.	SKD	Peterle, L.	SKD	Janša, J.	SDSS	Biziak, I.	SKD	Kozinc, M.	LDS
2	Peterle, L.	SKD	Peterle, L.	SKD	Kacin, J.	LDS	Biziak, I.	SKD	Kozinc, M.	LDS
3			Thaler, Z.	LDS	Kacin, J.	LDS	Šter, A.	SKD	*Zupančič, M.	LDS
4	Podobnik, M.	SLS	Thaler, Z.	LDS	Turnšek, T.	SLS	Bandelj, M.	LDS	Marušič, T.	SLS

Gov	Finance	Py	Economic Aff.	Py	Labour	Py	Education	Py	Health	Py
1	Gaspari, M.	LDS	Kračun, D. / Tajnikar, M.	LDS / ZLSD	*Puhar, J.	ZLSD	Gaber, S. / Bohinc, R.	LDS / ZLSD	Voljč, B.	ZS
2	Gaspari, M.	LDS	Kračun, D. / Tajnikar, M.	LDS / ZLSD	*Puhar, J.	ZLSD	Gaber, S. / Bohinc, R.	LDS / ZLSD	Voljč, B.	LDS
3	Gaspari, M.	LDS	Deželak, J. / Dragonja, M.	SKD / LDS	Rop, A.	LDS	Gaber, S. / Umek, A.	LDS / SKD	Voljč, B.	LDS
4	Gaspari, M.	LDS	Dragonja, M. / Senjur, M.	LDS / SLS	Rop, A.	LDS	Gaber, S. / Marinček, L.	LDS / SLS	Jereb, M.	SLS

SLOVENIA 1993-1998

Gov	Housing	Py	Agriculture	Py	Industry/Trade	Py	Environment	Py
1			Osterc, J.	SKD			Jazbinšek, M.	ZS
2			Osterc, J.	SKD			Gantar, P.	LDS
3			Osterc, J.	SKD			Gantar, P.	LDS
4			Smrkolj, C.	SLS			Gantar, P.	LDS

Gov	Social Affairs (py)	Public Works (py)	Other (py)	Res
1	Gaber, S. (LDS) *Puhar, J. (ZLSD)	Umek, I. (SKD)	Pelhan, S. (ZLSD)	0
2	Gaber, S. (LDS) *Puhar, J. (ZLSD)	Umek, I. (SKD)	Pelhan, S. (ZLSD) Janko, A. (NONA)	0
3	Rop, A. (LDS) Gaber, S. (LDS)	Umek, I. (SKD)	Dular, J. (SKD) Janko, A. (NONA) Kovačič, B. (LDS)	0
4	Rop, A. (LDS) Gaber, S. (LDS)	Bergauer, A. (SLS)	Podobnik, M. (SLS) Gantar, P. (LDS) Školč, J. (LDS) Grafenauer, B. (SLS) Kušar, J. (DeSUS)	

43.1. SOUTH AFRICA I 1948-1984

Gov	Begin	Dur	RfT	ToG	Py1	Py2	Py3	Seats	CPG	NoM	Prime Minister (py)
1	03.06.48	1778	1	2	NP 70	AP 9		150	1	12	Malan, D.F. (NP)
2	16.04.53	230	2	1	NP 94			156	1	14	Malan, D.F. (NP)
3	02.12.53	1605	1	1	NP 94			156	1	14	Strydom, J.G. (NP)
4	25.04.58	131	x	1	NP 103			156	1	14	Strydom, J.G. (NP)
5	03.09.58	1155	1	1	NP 103			156	1	13	Verwoerd, H.F. (NP)
6	01.11.61	1615	1	1	NP 105			156	1	18	Verwoerd, H.F. (NP)
7	04.04.66	162	x	1	NP 120			166	1	18	Verwoerd, H.F. (NP)
8	13.09.66	1343	1	1	NP 120			166	1	18	Vorster, B.J. (NP)
9	18.05.70	1442	1	1	NP 118			166	1	18	Vorster, B.J. (NP)
10	29.04.74	1367	1	1	NP 123			171	1	18	Vorster, B.J. (NP)
11	25.01.78	247	3	1	NP 135			165	1	18	Vorster, B.J. (NP)
12	29.09.78	945	1	1	NP 135			165	1	17	Botha, P.W. (NP)
13	01.05.81	1234	x	1	NP 131			165	1	20	Botha, P.W. (NP)

- Between 1948 and 1984 the white community enjoyed a parliamentary democracy based on the British system.
- Gov 1-10: Seats in parliament include 6 seats for South-West Africa (later Namibia).
- Gov 1: Nationalist and Afrikaner Party merged on 23 June 1953.
- Gov 4: Reason for Termination is death of PM.
- Gov 5: On 31 May 1961 the Republic of South Africa was proclaimed which left the Commonwealth.
- Gov 7: Reason for Termination is assassination of PM.
- Gov 13: Reason for Termination is election of State President and installation of a (semi-) presidential system on 17 September 1984.

SOUTH AFRICA I 1948-1984

Gov	Deputy PM	Py	Foreign Affairs	Py	Defence	Py	Interior	Py	Justice	Py
1			Malan, D.F.	NP	Erasmus, F.C.	NP	Dönges, T.E.	NP	Swart, C.R.	NP
2			Malan, D.F.	NP	Erasmus, F.C.	NP	Dönges, T.E.	NP	Swart, C.R.	NP
3			Strydom, J.G.	NP	Erasmus, F.C.	NP	Dönges, T.E.	NP	Swart, C.R.	NP
4			Louw, E.H.	NP	Erasmus, F.C.	NP	Dönges, T.E.	NP	Swart, C.R.	NP
5			Louw, E.H.	NP	Erasmus, F.C.	NP	Dönges, T.E.	NP	Swart, C.R.	NP
6			Louw, E.H.	NP	Fouché, J.J.	NP	De Klerk, J.	NP	Vorster, B.J.	NP
7			Muller, H.	NP	Botha, P.W.	NP	Le Roux, P.M.K. / Vorster, B.J.	NP / NP	Vorster, B.J.	NP
8			Muller, H.	NP	Botha, P.W.	NP	Le Roux, P.M.K. / Vorster, B.J. / Pelser, P.C.	NP / NP / NP	Pelser, P.C.	NP
9			Muller, H.	NP	Botha, P.W.	NP	Viljoen, M. / Muller, S.L.	NP / NP	Pelser, P.C.	NP
10			Muller, H.	NP	Botha, P.W.	NP	Kruger, J.T. / Mulder, C.P.	NP / NP	Kruger, J.T.	NP
11			Botha, R.F.	NP	Botha, P.W.	NP	Schlebusch, A.L. / Kruger, J.T.	NP / NP	Kruger, J.T.	NP
12			Botha, R.F.	NP	Botha, P.W.	NP	Schlebusch, A.L. / Kruger, J.T.	NP / NP	Kruger, J.T.	NP
13			Botha, R.F.	NP	De M. Malan, M.A.	NP	Heunis, J.C. / Le Grange, L. / Treurnicht, A.P.	NP / NP / NP	Coetsee, H.J.	NP

SOUTH AFRICA I 1948-1984

Gov	Finance	Py	Economic Aff.	Py	Labour	Py	Education	Py	Health	Py
1	Havenga, N.C.	AP	Louw, E.H.	NP	Schoeman, B.J.	NP	Stals, A.J.	NP	Stals, A.J.	NP
2	Havenga, N.C.	NP	Louw, E.H.	NP	Schoeman, B.J.	NP	Viljoen, J.H.	NP	Bremer, K.	NP
3	Louw, E.H.	NP	Van Rhijn, A.J.R.	NP	De Klerk, J.	NP	Viljoen, J.H.	NP	Naudé, J.F.T.	NP
4	Naudé, J.F.T.	NP	Van Rhijn, A.J.R.	NP	De Klerk, J.	NP	De Wet Nel, M.D.C.	NP	De Wet Nel, M.D.C.	NP
5	Naudé, J.F.T.	NP	Van Rhijn, A.J.R.	NP	De Klerk, J.	NP	De Wet Nel, M.D.C.	NP	De Wet Nel, M.D.C.	
6	Dönges, T.E.	NP	Diederichs, N.	NP	Trollip, A.E.	NP	De Klerk, J. / Maree, W.A.	NP		NP / NP
7	Dönges, T.E.	NP	Diederichs, N.	NP	Viljoen, M.	NP	De Klerk, J. / Botha, M.C.	NP	Hertzog, A.	NP / NP
8	Dönges, T.E.	NP	Diederichs, N.	NP	Viljoen, M.	NP	De Klerk, J. / Botha, M.C.	NP	Hertzog, A.	NP / NP
9	Diederichs, N.	NP	Muller, S.L.	NP	Viljoen, M.	NP	Van der Spuy, J.P. / Botha, M.C.	NP	De Wet, C.	NP / NP
10	Diederichs, N.	NP	Horwood, O.P.F.	NP	Viljoen, M.	NP	Van der Spuy, J.P. / Botha, M.C.	NP	Van der Merwe, S.W.	NP / NP
11	Horwood, O.P.F.	NP	Heunis, J.C.	NP	Botha, S.P.	NP	Cruywagen, W.A. / Mulder, C.P.	NP	Van der Merwe, S.W.	NP / NP
12	Horwood, O.P.F.	NP	Heunis, J.C.	NP	Botha, S.P.	NP	Koornhof, P.G.J.	NP	Van der Merwe, S.W.	NP
13	Horwood, O.P.F.	NP			Botha, S.P.	NP	Houtzenberg, F. / Van N. Viljoen, G.	NP	Munnik, L.A.P.A.	NP / NP

SOUTH AFRICA I 1948-1984

Gov	Housing	Py	Agriculture	Py	Industry/Trade	Py	Environment	Py
1			Le Roux, S.P.	NP				
2			Le Roux, S.P.	NP				
			Schoeman, B.J.	NP				
3			Le Roux, S.P.	NP				
			Viljoen, J.H.	NP				
4			Erasmus, F.C.	NP				
			Le Roux, P.M.K.	NP				
5			Erasmus, F.C.	NP				
			Le Roux, P.M.K.	NP				
6	Botha, P.W.	NP	Sauer, P.O.	NP				
			Le Roux, P.M.K.	NP				
			Uys, D.C.H.	NP				
7			Uys, D.C.H.	NP				
			Fouché, J.J.	NP				
8			Uys, D.C.H.	NP				
			Fouché, J.J.	NP				
			Waring, F.W.	NP				
9			Uys, D.C.H.	NP				
			Botha, S.P.	NP				
10			Botha, S.P.	NP				
11			Schoeman, H.	NP			Van der Merwe, S.W.	NP
			Raubenheimer, A.J.	NP				
12			Schoeman, H.	NP			Van der Merwe, S.W.	NP
			Raubenheimer, A.J.	NP				
13			Van der Merwe, C.V.	NP	De Villiers, J.D.J.	NP	Van der Merwe, C.V.	NP
			Du Plessis, P.T.C.	NP				

SOUTH AFRICA I 1948-1984

Gov	Social Affairs (py)	Public Works (py)	Other (py)	Res
1	Stals, A.J. (NP)	Sauer, P.O. (NP) Louw, E.H. (NP) Dönges, T.E. (NP) Schoeman, B.J. (NP)	Jansen, E.G. (NP) Strydom, J.G. (NP)	1
2	Bremer, K. (NP)	Strydom, J.G. (NP) Sauer, P.O. (NP) Schoeman, B.J. (NP) Viljoen, J.H. (NP) Naudé, J.F.T. (NP)	Strydom, J.G. (NP) Verwoerd, H.F. (NP) Viljoen, J.H. (NP)	0
3	Serfontein, J.J. (NP)	Sauer, P.O. (NP) Schoeman, B.J. (NP) Van Rhijn, A.J.R. (NP) Serfontein, J.J. (NP) De Klerk, J. (NP)	Sauer, P.O. (NP) Verwoerd, H.F. (NP) Viljoen, J.H. (NP)	1
4	Serfontein, J.J. (NP)	Sauer, P.O. (NP) Schoeman, B.J. (NP) Van Rhijn, A.J.R. (NP) Serfontein, J.J. (NP) De Klerk, J. (NP)	Sauer, P.O. (NP) Verwoerd, H.F. (NP) De Wet Nel, M.D.C. (NP)	0
5	Serfontein, J.J. (NP)	Sauer, P.O. (NP) Schoeman, B.J. (NP) Van Rhijn, A.J.R. (NP) Serfontein, J.J. (NP) De Klerk, J. (NP)	Verwoerd, H.F. (NP) Sauer, P.O. (NP) De Wet Nel, M.D.C. (NP)	3

SOUTH AFRICA I 1948-1984

Gov	Social Affairs (py)	Public Works (py)	Other (py)	Res
6	Serfontein, J.J. (NP)	Sauer, P.O. (NP) Schoeman, B.J. (NP) Le Roux, P.M.K. (NP) Diederichs, N. (NP) Hertzog, A. (NP)	Sauer, P.O. (NP) De Klerk, J. (NP) De Wet Nel, M.D.C. (NP) Maree, W.A. (NP) Botha, P.W. (NP) Trollip, A.E. (NP) Waring, F.W. (NP)	1
7	Maree, W.A. (NP)	Schoeman, B.J. (NP) Maree, W.A. (NP) Hertzog, A. (NP) Haak, F.F.W. (NP)	De Klerk, J. (NP) Maree, W.A. (NP) Trollip, A.E. (NP) Waring, F.W. (NP) Haak, F.F.W. (NP) Viljoen, M. (NP) Botha, M.C. (NP)	0
8	Maree, W.A. (NP)	Schoeman, B.J. (NP) Maree, W.A. (NP) Hertzog, A. (NP) Haak, F.F.W. (NP)	De Klerk, J. (NP) Maree, W.A. (NP) Trollip, A.E. (NP) Waring, F.W. (NP) Haak, F.F.W. (NP) Viljoen, M. (NP) Botha, M.C. (NP)	3
9	Waring, F.W. (NP) Mulder, C.P. (NP)	Schoeman, B.J. (NP) De Wet, C. (NP) Van Rensburg, C.G.S. (NP) Coetsee, B. (NP)	Waring, F.W. (NP) Botha, M.C. (NP) Coetsee, B. (NP) Mulder, C.P. (NP)	2

SOUTH AFRICA I 1948-1984

Gov	Social Affairs (py)	Public Works (py) Botha, S.P. (NP)	Other (py) Loots, J.J. (NP)	Res
10	Mulder, C.P. (NP) Koornhof, P.G.J. (NP)	Viljoen, M. (NP) Muller, S.L.(NP) Botha, S.P. (NP) Du Plessis, A.H. (NP) Koornhof, P.G.J. (NP)	Botha, M.C. (NP) Mulder, C.P. (NP) Loots, J.J. (NP) Du Plessis, A.H. (NP) Koornhof, P.G.J. (NP) Van der Merwe, S.W. (NP) Heunis, J.C. (NP)	2
11	Van der Spuy, J.P. (NP) Koornhof, P.G.J. (NP)	Muller, S.L. (NP) Botha, S.P. (NP) Van der Spuy, J.P. (NP) Schlebusch, A.L. (NP) Raubenheimer, A.J. (NP)	Mulder, C.P. (NP) Van der Merwe, S.W. (NP) Steyn, S.J.M. (NP) Schlebusch, A.L. (NP) Smit, H.H. (NP)	0
12	Van der Spuy, J.P. (NP) Koornhof, P.G.J. (NP)	Muller, S.L. (NP) Botha, S.P. (NP) Van der Spuy, J.P. (NP) Schlebusch, A.L. (NP) Raubenheimer, A.J. (NP)	Mulder, C.P. (NP) Van der Merwe, S.W. (NP) Steyn, S.J.M. (NP) Schlebusch, A.L. (NP) Smit, H.H. (NP) Botha, R.F. (NP)	4
13	Munnik, L.A.P.A. (NP)	Schoeman, H. (NP) Smit, H.H. (NP) De Klerk, F.W. (NP)	Botha, S.P. Koornhoef, P.G.J. (NP) Botha, R.F. (NP) Treurnicht, A.P. (NP) Van der Merwe, C.V. (NP) De Villiers, D.J. (NP) Coetsee, H.J. (NP) Kotzé, S.F. (NP)	3

43.2. SOUTH AFRICA II 1984-1994

Gov	Begin	Dur	RfT	ToG	Py1	Py2	Py3	Seats	CPG	NoM	Prime Minister (py)
1	17.09.84	986	1	1	NP 131	LP x	NPP x	165	1	19	Botha, P.W. (NP)
2	31.05.87	843	2	1	NP 123+10	LP x	NPP x	166+12	1	19	Botha, P.W. (NP)
3	20.09.89	1538	x	1	NP 93+10			166+12	1	18	De Klerk, F.W. (NP)

- Between 1984 and 1993 the State President combined the duties of Head of State and the executive funtion of PM. The president chairs the cabinet and is commander in chief of the armed forces. Members of the cabinet were also the chairmen of the ministers councils of the House of Representatives (Coulourds) and the House of Delegates (Indians). From June 1986 until June 1990 the State of Emergency was declared.

- Gov 1, 2: LP is Labour Party of Coulourds. NPP is National Peoples Party of Indians.

- Gov 2, 3: Number of elected white seats is 166. Added are 8 seats elected by MPs according to party strength and 4 seats appointed by the president.

- Gov 3: Reason for Termination is the end of apartheid and nomination of Transitional Executive Council (TEC) on 6 December 1993 to organise first non-racial multy-party elections for a National Assembly in 1994. Technically the government ended with those general elections on 26-28 April 1994.

Gov	Deputy PM	Py	Foreign Affairs	Py	Defence	Py	Interior	Py	Justice	Py
1			Botha, R.F.	NP	Botha, P.W.	NP	De Klerk, F.W.	NP	Coetsee, H.J.	NP
					De M. Malan, M.A.		Le Grange, L.	NP	Le Grange, L.	NP
							Heunis, J.C.	NP		
2			Botha, R.F.	NP	Botha, P.W.	NP	Vlok, A.J.	NP	Coetsee, H.J.	NP
					De M. Malan, M.A.		Heunis, J.C.	NP	Vlok, A.J.	NP
							Botha, J.C.G.	NP		
3			Botha, R.F.	NP	De Klerk, F.W.	NP	Vlok, A.J.	NP	Coetsee, H.J.	NP
					De M. Malan, M.A.		Louw, W.	NP	Vlok, A.J.	NP
							De Villiers, W.J.	NP		
							Kriel, H.J.	NP		

SOUTH AFRICA II 1984-1994

Gov	Finance	Py	Economic Aff.	Py	Labour	Py	Education	Py	Health	Py
1	Du Plessis, B.J.	NP			Du Plessis, P.T.C.		De Klerk, F.W. / Van N. Viljoen, G.	NP	Van der Merwe, C.V.	NP / NP
2	Du Plessis, B.J.	NP	Steyn, D.W. / Du Plessis, B.J.	NP / NP	Du Plessis, P.T.C.		De Klerk, F.W. / Van N. Viljoen, G. / Steyn, D.W.	NP	Van Niekerk, W.A.	NP / NP / NP
3	Du Plessis, B.J.	NP			Van der M. Louw, E.		Van N. Viljoen, G. / Van der Merwe, C.J.	NP	*Venter, E.H.	NP / NP

Gov	Housing	Py	Agriculture	Py	Industry/Trade	Py	Environment	Py
1			Wentzel, J.J.G.	NP	De Villiers, D.J.	NP	Wiley, J.	NP
2			Wentzel, J.J.G.	NP			Kotzé, G.J.	NP
3			De Villiers, J.	NP	Durr, K.D.S.	NP	Kotzé, G.J.	NP

Gov	Social Affairs (py)	Public Works (py)	Other (py)	Res
1	Van der Merwe, C.V. (NP)	Schoeman, H. (NP) / Munnik, L.A.P.A. (NP) / Wentzel, J.J.G. (NP) / Steyn, D. (NP)	Heunis, J.C. (NP) / Munnik, L.A.P.A. (NP) / Van der Merwe, C.V. (NP) / Viljoen, G. (NP) / Wiley, J. (NP) / Hendrickse, H.J. (LP) / Rajbansi, A. (NPP)	2

SOUTH AFRICA II 1984-1994

Gov	Social Affairs (py)	Public Works (py)	Other (py)	Res
2		Du Plassis, P.T.C. (NP) Botha, J.C.G. (NP) Van der M. Louw, E. (NP)	Schlebusch, A.L. (NP) De Klerk, F.W. (NP) Van N. Viljoen, G. (NP) Hendrickse, H.J. (LP) Rajbansi, A. (NPP) Van Niekerk, W.A. (NP)	1
3		De Villiers, D.W. (NP) Kotzé, G.J. (NP) Bartlett, G.S. (NP)	Van N. Viljoen, G. (NP) Coetsee, H.J. (NP) Durr, K.D.S. (NP) De Villiers, W.J. (NP) *Venter, E.H. (NP) Van der Merwe, C.J. (NP) Kriel, H.J. (NP)	8

43.3. SOUTH AFRICA III

The present constitution dates from 1996.

The President is indirectly elected for a five-year term. He or she is responsible to parliament and can be forced to resign, like the government, by a vote of no confidence. In addition to the office of President there can be one or more Deputy-Presidents, to be designated by those parties in parliament that hold more than 80 seats. The President and the Deputy-Presidents are part of the government.

South Africa is a federal state with specific powers for provinces (9) and municipalities. The national and sub-national units are constitutionally bound to cooperate in lawmaking and implementation. Fiscal matters are based on the principle of subsidiarity and supervised by the Central Bank.

Parliament is bicameral and consists of the National Council of Provinces of 90 seats, representing the nine provinces, and the National Assembly of 400 seats, representing the national electorate. Provincial premiers and legislatures nominate the National Council. The National Assembly is elected by proportional representation (d'Hondt) for a fixed term of five years in nine constituencies (the provinces) which vary considerably in size round an average of approximately 2,500,000 electors.

Parliament has a quorum of at least 50 per cent of all members. Votes are carried by a majority of all members present. Some issues, like constitutional amendments, require a qualified majority of two-thirds of members present in both Houses. If there is no two-thirds majority in both Houses the matter can be settled by referendum. A referendum is optional and called by the President. The outcome is binding

The President appoints the government, which is both collectively and individually responsible to parliament. The government does not require a vote of investiture but can face a vote of no confidence. Losing a vote of confidence always results in resignation of the government. Individual ministers may also be members of parliament. The Prime Minister has no dominant position in government.

The Constitutional Court reviews legislation and also adjudicates on the fundamental rights of individuals and of groups of citizens.

SOUTH AFRICA III 1994-1998

Gov	Begin	Dur	RfT	ToG	Py1	Py2	Py3	Seats	CPG	NoM	Prime Minister (py)
0	07.12.93	154	1	x					3	15	
1	10.05.94	783	4	3	ANC 252	NP 82	Inkhata 43	400	3	26	Mandela, N.R. (ANC)
2	01.07.96		3	3	ANC 252	Inkhata 43		400	4	27	Mandela, N.R. (ANC)

- South Africa remained a (semi-) presidential system.
- Gov 0: Every political party or movement is represented in TEC except PAC and Freedom Alliance Parties. TEC does not take over the powers of government but functions in conjuction with all legislative and executive structures at all levels of government. Composition of TEC: De Villiers, D.W. (NP); Eglin, C. (DP); Gordham, P. (Indian Congress); Hendrickse, A. (LP); Mahlangu, N.J. (KwaNdebele); Meyer, R. (NP); Moeti, S.E. (Venda); Mohapi, T.J. (Dikwankwetla PSA); Ngobeni, E.E. (Ximoko PP); Rajah, D.S. (PS); Rajbansi, A. (NPP); Ramaphosa, C. (ANC); Ramodike, N. (Lebowa); Slovo, J. (SACP); Titus, Z. (Transkei).
- Gov 1: Government was a government of National Unity. All parties with 5% or more of the national vote were represented. Parties with 20% or more were represented at the deputy presidential level. Reason for Termination is withdrawal of NP from government to form an opposition.

Gov	Deputy PM	Py	Foreign Affairs	Py	Defence	Py	Interior	Py	Justice	Py
0										
1	Mbeki, T.	ANC	Nzo, A.	ANC	Mandela, N.R.	ANC	Mufumadi, S.	ANC	Omar, D.	ANC
	De Klerk, F.W.	NP			Modise, J.	ANC	Meyer, R.	NP	Mzimela, S.	Inkhata
							*Sigcau, S.	ANC		
							Buthulezi, M.	Inkhata		
2	Mbeki, T.	ANC	Nzo, A.	ANC	Modise, J.	ANC	Buthulezi, M.	Inkhata	Omar, D.	ANC
							Moosa, V.	ANC	Mzimela, S.	Inkhata
							Mufumadi, S.	ANC		
							Skweyiya, Z.	ANC		

SOUTH AFRICA III 1994-1998

Gov	Finance	Py	Economic Aff.	Py	Labour	Py	Education	Py	Health	Py
0										
1	Keys, D.	NP			Mboweni, T.	ANC	Bengu, S. Ngubane, B.	ANC Inkhata	*Zuma, N.	ANC
2	Manuel, T.	ANC			Mboweni, T.	ANC	Bengu, S. Mtshali, L.P.H.M.	ANC Inkhata	*Dlamini-Zuma, N.	ANC

Gov	Housing	Py	Agriculture	Py	Industry/Trade	Py	Environment	Py
0								
1	Slovo, J.	ANC	Van Niekerk, A.I. Asmal, K.	NP ANC	Manuel, T.	NP	De Villiers, D.	NP
2	*Mthembi-Mahanyele, S.	ANC	Asmal, K. Hanekom, D.	ANC ANC	Erwin, A. *Sigcau, S.	ANC ANC	Jordan, P.	ANC

SOUTH AFRICA III 1994-1998

Gov	Social Affairs (py)	Public Works (py)	Other (py)	Res
0				
1	Tshwete, S. (ANC) Williams, A. (ANC)	Jordan, P. (ANC) Maharaj, M. (ANC) *Sigcau, S. (ANC) Radebe, J. (ANC) Asmal, K. (ANC) Botha, R.F. (NP)	Manuel, T. (ANC) Hanekom, D. (ANC) Williams, A. (ANC) Ngubane, B. (Inkhata) Naidoo, J. (ANC)	2
2	*Fraser-Moleketi, G. (ANC) Tshwete, S. (ANC)	Asmal, K. (ANC) Maduna, P. (ANC) Maharaj, M. (ANC) Naidoo, J. (ANC) Radebe, J. (ANC)	*Fraser-Moleketi, G. (ANC) Hanekom, D. (ANC) Jordan, P. (ANC) Mtshali, L.P.H.M. (Inkhata)	

44. SPAIN

Spain is a Monarchy where the King has basically ceremonial powers.

The country is formally a unitary state, yet, in addition to the autonomous communities such as Catalonia, Galicia and the Basque country, other regions also hold powers of co-government. Hence the State format is an unusual blend of unitary and central competencies, and regional autonomy.

Parliament is a case of symmetric bicameralism, which makes the Cortes Generales a genuine countervailing power. The Upper House (Senate) of 257 seats is partly elected by plurality in the provinces and partly nominated by regional assemblies. The Lower House (Congress of Deputies) of 350 seats is elected by proportional representation (d'Hondt) in 50 constituencies (the provinces) which vary extremely in size and in the ratio of electors to representatives. This detracts from the proportionality of the electoral system. Both Houses are elected for a fixed term of four years.

Parliament has a quorum of 50 per cent of all members. Votes are carried by a majority of all members present. Some issues require a majority of all members (vote of investiture of the Prime Minister). Constitutional amendments need a majority of all members present. A referendum is constitutionally required and may be called by government and parliament. The outcome is binding.

Central government consists of a President (Prime Minister), appointed by the King, who is responsible to Parliament; a council of ministers (the cabinet) and a Council of State (an advisory body appointed by the King). The Prime Minister needs an absolute majority of all members of the Lower House before forming his government (vote of investiture). The government can also face a vote of constructive no confidence (the proposed alternative President must have an absolute majority of all members in the Lower House). However, this vote of confidence cannot be used within one year after installing the Prime Minister. Government is collectively responsible to parliament. Individual ministers may also be members of parliament. The Prime Minister has a dominant position in government.

There is a Supreme Court with wide jurisdiction, including constitutional review of legislation, violations of fundamental rights, and conflicts between state agencies, regional bodies and territories.

SPAIN 1977-1998

Gov	Begin	Dur	RfT	ToG	Py1	Py2	Py3	Py4	Seats	CPG	NoM	Prime Minister (py)
1	05.07.77	640	1	4	UCD 165				350	2	20	Suárez González, A. (UCD)
2	06.04.79	693	2	4	UCD 168				350	2	24	Suárez González, A. (UCD)
3	27.02.81	644	1	4	UCD 168				350	2	16	Calvo Sotelo y Bustelo, L. (UCD)
4	03.12.82	1331	1	1	PSOE 202				350	4	17	González Márquez, F. (PSOE)
5	26.07.86	1230	1	1	PSOE 184				350	4	17	González Márquez, F. (PSOE)
6	07.12.89	1314	1	4	PSOE 175				350	4	19	González Márquez, F. (PSOE)
7	13.07.93	1028	1	4	PSOE 159				350	4	18	González Márquez, F. (PSOE)
8	06.05.96			4	PP 156	[CiU 16]	[PNV 5]	[CC 4]	350	2	15	Aznar, J.M. (PP)

- [] Denotes party supporting the government without participating in it.
- 15 June 1977: First free elections.
- Gov 4-7: PSOE includes Catalan PSC.
- Gov 6: In October 1990 the PSOE formed a tactical alliance with CiU (18), PNV (8) and CDS (14). It was no formal coalition.
- Gov 8: The parties supporting the government did not enter into a formal coalition with the PP.

Gov	Deputy PM	Py	Foreign Affairs	Py	Defence	Py	Interior	Py	Justice	Py
1	Guttiérez Mellado, M. (Gen.), Fuentes Quintana, E., Abril Martorell, F.	NONA, UCD, UCD	Oreja Aguirre, M.	NONA	Guttiérez Mellado, M. (Gen.)	UCD	Martín Villa, R.	NONA	Lavilla Alsina, L.	UCD, UCD
2	Guttiérez Mellado, M., Abril Martorell, F.	UCD, UCD	Oreja Aguirre, M.	UCD	Guttiérez Mellado, M., Rodríguez Sahagún, A.	UCD	Ibáñez Freire, A. (Lt.-Gen.)	UCD	Cavero Lataillade, I.	NONA, UCD
3			Pérez-Llorca, J.P.	UCD	Oliant Saussol, A.	UCD	Rosón Pérez, J.J.	UCD	Fernández Ordóñez, F.	UCD, UCD
4	Guerra, A.	PSOE	Morán, F.	PSOE	Serra Serra, N.	PSC	Barrionuevo, J., Moscoso, J.	PSC	Ledesma, F.	PSOE, PSOE, PSOE

SPAIN 1977-1998

Gov	Deputy PM	Py	Foreign Affairs	Py	Defence	Py	Interior	Py	Justice	Py
5	Guerra, A.	PSOE	Fernández Ordóñez, F.	PSOE	Serra Serra, N.	PSC	Barrionuevo, J. Almunia, J.:	PSOE PSOE	Ledesma, F.	PSOE
6	Guerra, A.	PSOE	Fernández Ordóñez, F.	PSOE	Serra Serra, N.	PSC	Corcuera Cuesta, J.L. Almunia, J.	PSOE PSOE	Múgica Herzog, E.	PSOE
7	Serra Serra, N.	PSC	Solana Mandariaga, J.	PSC	García Vargas, J.	PSOE	Corcuera Cuesta, J.L. Saavedra Acevedo, J.	PSOE PSOE	Belloch Juive, J.A.	NONA
8	Cascos Fernández, F.A. De Rato y Figaredo, R.	PP PP	Matutes Juan, A.	PP	Serra Rexach, E.	NONA	Mayor Oreja, J. Rajoy Brey, M.	PP PP	*Mariscal de Gante, M.	PP

Gov	Finance	Py	Economic Aff.	Py	Labour	Py	Education	Py	Health	Py
1	Fernández Ordóñez, F.	UCD	Fuentes Quintana, E.	UCD	Jeménez de Parga, M.	UCD	Cavero Latailladé, I.	UCD	Sánchez de Léon, E.	UCD
2	García Añoveros, J.	UCD	Abril Martorell, F. Leal Maldonado, J.L.	UCD UCD	Calvo Ortega, R.	UCD	Otero Novas, J.M. González Seara, L.	UCD UCD	Rovira Tarazona, J.	UCD
3	García Añoveros, J.	UCD	García Díez, J.A.	UCD	Sancho Rof, J.	UCD	Ortega y Díaz-Ambrona, J.A.	UCD	Sancho Rof, J.	UCD
4	Boyer, M.	PSOE	Boyer, M.	PSOE	Almunia, J.	PSOE	Maravall, J.M.	PSOE	Lluch, E.	PSC
5	Solchaga Catalán, C.	PSOE	Solchaga Catalán, C.	PSOE	Chaves, M.	PSOE	Maravall, J.M.	PSOE	García Vargas, J.	PSOE
6	Solchaga Catalán, C.	PSOE	Solchaga Catalán, C.	PSOE	Chaves, M.	PSOE	Solana Madáriaga, J.	PSOE	García Vargas, J.	PSOE
7	Solbes Mira, P.	NONA	Solbes Mira, P.	NONA	Griñán Martínez, J.A.	NONA	Suárez Pertierra, G.	PSOE	*Amador Millan, A.	NONA
8	De Rato y Figaredo, R.	PP	De Rato y Figaredo, R.	PP	Arenas Bocanegra, J.	PP	*Aguirre y Gil de Biedma, E.	PP	Romay Beccaría, J.M.	PP

SPAIN 1977-1998

Gov	Housing	Py	Agriculture	Py	Industry/Trade	Py	Environment	Py
1	Garrigues Walker, J.	UCD	Martínez de Genique, E.M.	UCD	Oliant Saussol, A.	UCD		
2	Sancho Rof, J.	UCD	Lamo de Espinosa y Michels de C., J.	UCD	Bustelo y García del R., C.	UCD		
					García Díez, J.A.	UCD		
3			Lamo de Espinosa y Michels de C., J.	UCD	García Díez, J.A.	UCD		
					Bayón Mariné, I.	UCD		
4			Romero, C.	PSOE	Solchaga Catalán, C.	PSOE		
5			Romero, C.	PSOE	Croisier, L.C.	PSOE		
6			Herrera, C.R.	PSOE	Aranzadi Martínez, J.C.	PSOE		
7			Albero Sillas, V.	PSOE	Eguiagaray Ucelay, J.M.	PSOE		
					Navarro, J.G.	NONA		
8			*de Palacio de Valle-L., L.	PP	Piqué i Camps, J.	PP	*Tocino Biscarolasaga, I.	PP

Gov	Social Affairs (py)	Public Works (py)	Other (py)	Res
1	Cabanillas Gallas, P. (UCD)	Oliant Saussol, A. (UCD)	Abril Martorell, F. (UCD)	1
	Sánchez de Léon, E. (UCD)	Lladó y Fernandez Urrutia, J. (UCD)	García Díez, J.A. (UCD)	
		Garrigues Walker, J. (UCD)	Cabanillas Gallas, P. (UCD)	
			Otero Novar, M. (UCD)	
			Clavero Arévalo, M. (UCD)	
			Camuñas Solís, I. (UCD)	

SPAIN 1977-1998

Gov	Social Affairs (py)	Public Works (py)	Other (py)	Res
2	Clavero Arévalo, M. (UCD) Rovira Tarazona, J. (UCD)	Sancho Rof, J. (UCD) Sanchéz-Terán Hernández, S. (UCD)	García Díez, J.A. (UCD) Clavero Arévalo, M. (UCD) Fontán Pérez, A. (UCD) Calvo Sotelo y Bustelo, L. (UCD) Pérez-Llorca Rodríguez, J.P. (UCD) Arias Salgado Montalvo, R. (UCD) Garrigues Walker, J. (UCD)	3
3	Sancho Rof, J. (UCD)	Ortíz González, L. (UCD) Bayón Mariné, I. (UCD) Alvarez Alvarez, L. (UCD)	Martín Villa, R. (UCD) Ortiz González, L. (UCD) Cavero Lataillade, I. (UCD) Cabanillas Gallas, P. (UCD)	3
4	Almunia, J. (PSOE) Lluch, E. (PSOE)	Campo, J. (PSOE) Barón, E. (PSOE)	De la Quada Salcedo, T. (PSOE) Solana Madariaga, J. (PSOE)	1
5	García Vargas, J. (PSOE) Chaves, M. (PSOE)	Croissier, L.C. (PSOE) Sáenz de Cosculluela, J. (PSOE) Caballero Alvarez, A.R. (PSOE)	Solana Madariaga, J. (PSOE) Zapatero, V. (PSOE)	1
6	Chaves, M. (PSOE) García Vargas, J. (PSOE) *Fernández, M. (PSOE)	Aranzadi Martínez, J.C. (PSOE) Sáenz de Cosculluela, J. (PSOE) Barrionuevo, J. (PSOE)	Semprún, J. (PSOE) Zapatero, V. (PSOE) *Conde de Espina, R. (PSOE)	2
7	Griñan Martínez, J.A. (PSOE) *Amador Millan, A. (NONA) *Alberdi Alonso, C. (NONA)	Eguiagaray Ucelay, J.M. (PSOE) Borrell Fontelles, J. (PSOE)	*Alborch, C. (NONA) Navarro, J.G. (NONA) Pérez Rubalcaba, A. (PSOE)	3
8	Arenas Bocanegra, J. (PP) Romay Beccaría, J.M. (PP)	Piqué i Camps, J. (PP)	Cascos Fernández, F.A. (PP) *Aguirre y Gil de Biedma, E. (PP) Arais-Salgado y Montalvo, R. (PP)	3

45. SRI LANKA

The present constitution dates from 1978.

The Head of State is a President directly elected for a six-year term who is also Head of Government.

The State is highly centralised and unitary.

Parliament is unicameral with one House of 225 members. The maximum legislative term between elections is six years (fixed). Members are elected by proportional representation (Pref.) on a party list system with choice within large regions. There is a threshold of 12.5 percent.

The quorum is 20 members. Votes are carried with a majority of votes cast. Constitutional amendments require a majority of two-thirds of all members. A referendum can be held on any matter at the initiative of the Cabinet. The outcome is binding

The main political executive is the President, who appoints the Prime Minister and Cabinet from members of parliament to assist him or her. Parliament has no power over the President who is elected separately. As the President appoints the Prime Minister and the Cabinet no formal vote of investiture is needed. During its lifetime the government can face a vote of no confidence. Losing a vote of confidence always results in resignation of the government. The government is collectively responsible to parliament. Ministers are members of parliament. The Prime Minister has no dominant position in government; it is the President who has a casting vote in Cabinet.

There is a Supreme Court for constitutional review of legislation.

SRI LANKA 1947-1998

Gov	Begin	Dur	RfT	ToG	Py1	Py2	Py3	Py4	Py5	Seats	CPG	NoM	Prime Minister (py)
1	26.09.47	1643	x	4	UNP 42					95(+6)	3	14	Senanayake, D.S. (UNP)
2	26.03.52	68	1	4	UNP 42					95(+6)	3	15	Senanayake, D. (UNP)
3	02.06.52	498	3	3	UNP 54	TC 4	[IND 7]			95(+6)	3	14	Senanayake, D. (UNP)
4	13.10.53	912	4	3	UNP 54	TC 4				95(+6)	3	14	Kotalawala, J. (UNP)
5	12.04.56	1150	4	1	MEP 51					95(+6)	4	14	Bandaranaike, S. (MEP-SLFP)
6	06.06.59	112	x	4	SLFP 39	[IND 4]	[Nom MP 6]			95(+6)	4	16	Bandaranaike, S. (SLFP)
7	26.09.59	179	4	4	SLFP 39	[IND 4]	[Nom MP 6]			95(+6)	4	15	Dahanayake, W. (SLFP)
8	23.03.60	122	5	4	UNP 50	[CDP 4]	[Nom MP 6]			151(+6)	3	8	Senanayake, D. (UNP)
9	23.07.60	1419	7	4	SLFP 75					151(+6)	4	11	*Dias Bandaranaike, S.R. (SLFP)
10	11.06.64	289	4	2	SLFP 75	LSSP 12				151(+6)	4	15	*Dias Bandaranaike, S.R. (SLFP)
11	27.03.65	1268	4	3	UNP 66	SLFSP 5	FP 14	MEP 2		151(+6)	3	17	Senanayake, D. (UNP)
12	15.09.68	623	1	5	UNP 66	SLFSP 5	MEP 2			151(+6)	3	17	Senanayake, D. (UNP)
13	31.05.70	1935	4	3	SLFP 90	LSSP 19	CP 6			151(+6)	5	21	*Dias Bandaranaike, S.R. (SLFP)
14	17.09.75	522	4	3	SLFP 98	CP 6				151(+6)	5	19	*Dias Bandaranaike, S.R. (SLFP)
15	20.02.77	153	1	1	SLFP 93					151(+6)	4	18	*Dias Bandaranaike, S.R. (SLFP)
16	23.07.77	198	x	1	UNP 140					168	3	24	Jayawardene, J.R. (UNP)
17	06.02.78	4030	1	1	UNP 140					168	3	24	Premadasa, R. (UNP)
18	18.02.89	405	2	1	UNP 125					225	3	22	Wijetunge, D.B. (UNP)
19	30.03.90	1134	x	1	UNP 125					225	3	25	Wijetunge, D.B. (UNP)
20	07.05.93	469	1	1	UNP 125					225	3	22	Wickremansinghe, R. (UNP)
21	19.08.94	87	x	5	PA 105	SLMC 7	[TULF 5]	[DPLF 3]	[NEIG 1]	225	4	23	*Bandaranaike Kumaratunga, C. (PA-SLFP)
22	14.11.94		5	5	PA 105	SLMC 7	[TULF 5]	[DPLF 3]	[NEIG 1]	225	4	23	*Dias Bandaranaike, S.R. (PA-SLFP)

- [] Denotes party supporting the government without participating in it.
- Date of Independence 4 February 1948.
- Until 22 May 1972 the country's name was Ceylon.
- Troubles between the Tamils and the Sinhalese majority started after Sinhalese became the official government language (laws in 1956, 1958 and 1961). Between April 1961 and May 1963 the State of Emergency was declared; as was the case in 1966 and 1981. Early 1983 a full-scale guarilla war was started by the Tamil Tigers. From May 1983 in the North and East of the island the State of Emergency was in force. In 1989 Colombo was added. From 1996 it was declared nation-wide.

SRI LANKA 1947-1998

- Between March 1971 and February 1977 the left-wing JLP committed various terrorist attacks which also induced the declaration of the State of Emergency for the whole country.
- Gov 1-15: There were 95 elected seats and 6 seats nominated by the Head of State.
- Gov 1: Reason for Termination is death of PM.
- Gov 4: Reason for Termination is internal disagreement within UNP between Tamils and Sinhalese which lead to intervention by the Head of State. Parliament was dissolved and elections called.
- Gov 5: MEP = People's United Front; an election cooperation between SLFP, Viplavakari Lanka Sama Samaja, Samasta Lanka Bhasa Peramuna, plus independents. All in the favour of Sinhalese as only official government language.
- Gov 6-8: Nom MPs are the MPs nominated by the Head of State.
- Gov 6: Reason for Termination is assassination of PM.
- Gov 7: Reason for Termination is internal disagreement within SLFP. On the advise of the PM the Head of State dissolved parliament and elections were called.
- Gov 10: Reason for Termination is internal disagreement within SLFP which led 14 SLFP-MPs to cross over to opposition. As a result the government was defeated in parliament. The Head of State dissolved parliament and elections were called.
- Gov 11: Reason for Termination is resignation of FP-minister. FP continued to support the government in all matters not affecting the Tamil community.
- Gov 17ff: On 4 October 1977 a presidential system broadly based on the French model was introduced. The president was popular elected and Head of State, Government and Cabinet; assisted by a PM appointed by the president.
- Gov 17: 20 October 1982 Jayawardene, J.R. re-elected president for a term of six years. In a referendum on 22 December 1982 a majority of the population voted in favour of extending the life of parliament as it was with another six years from August 1983. In parliament the UNP had a majority of 143 of 168 seats.
- Gov 18, 19: Premadasa, R. also president.
- Gov 20, 21: Wijetunge, D.B. also president.
- Gov 21: PA = People's Alliance; election cooperation of SLFP, LSSP, DUNF, CP and Sri Lanka Workers' Congress. Reason for Termination is election of PM as president.
- Gov 22: *Bandaranaike Kumaratunga, C. also president.

Gov	Deputy PM	Py	Foreign Affairs	Py	Defence	Py	Interior	Py	Justice	Py
1			Senanayake, D.S.	UNP	Senanayake, D.S.	UNP	Goonetilleke, O.	UNP	Rajapakse, L.	UNP
							Bandaranaike, S.W.	UNP		
2			Senanayake, D.	UNP	Senanayake, D.	UNP	Goonetilleke, O.	UNP	Rajapakse, L.	UNP
							Bandaranaike, S.W.	UNP		

SRI LANKA 1947-1998

Gov	Deputy PM	Py	Foreign Affairs	Py	Defence	Py	Interior	Py	Justice	Py
3			Senanayake, D.	UNP	Senanayake, D.	UNP	Ratnayake, A. / Kannangara, C.W.W.	UNP / UNP	Rajapakse, L.	UNP
4			Kotalawala, J.	UNP	Kotalawala, J.	UNP	Ratnayaka, A. / Kannangara, C.W.W.	UNP / UNP	Rajapakse, L.	UNP
5			Bandaranaike, S.	MEP-SLFP	Bandaranaike, S.	MEP-SLFP	Jayasuriya, A.P. / Kuruppu, J.	MEP-SLFP / MEP-SLFP	De Silva, M.W.H.	MEP-SLFP
6			Bandaranaike, S.	SLFP	Bandaranaike, S.	SLFP	Illangaratne, T.B. / *Wijewardena, V.	SLFP / SLFP	De Silva, M.W.H.	SLFP
7			Dahanayake, W.	SLFP	Dahanayake, W.	SLFP	Illangaratne, T.B. / *Wijewardena, V. / Jayawickrema, V.S.	SLFP / SLFP / SLFP	Jayawickrema, V.S.	SLFP
8			Senanayake, D.	UNP	Senanayake, D.	UNP	Jayawardene, J.R. / Kaleel, M.C.M.	UNP / UNP	Cooray, E.J.	UNP
9			*Dias Bandaranaike, S.R.	SLFP	*Dias Bandaranaike, S.R.	SLFP	Samaraweera, M. / Senanayake, M.	SLFP / SLFP	Fernando, S.P.C.	SLFP
10			*Dias Bandaranaike, S.R.	SLFP	*Dias Bandaranaike, S.R.	SLFP	Jayasuriya, A.P.	SLFP	De Silva, G.C.T.A.	SLFP
11			Senanayake, D.	UNP	Senanayake, D.	UNP	Dahanayake, W. / Tiruchelvam, M.	SLFSP / FP	Wijemanne, A.F.	UNP
12			Senanayake, D.	UNP	Senanayake, D.	UNP	Premadasa, R. / Dahanayake, W.	UNP / SLFSP	Wijemanne, A.F.	UNP
13			*Dias Bandaranaike, S.R.	SLFP	*Dias Bandaranaike, S.R.	SLFP	Dias Bandaranaike, F.R.	SLFP	Jayamanne, J.F.	SLFP

SRI LANKA 1947-1998

Gov	Deputy PM	Py	Foreign Affairs	Py	Defence	Py	Interior	Py	Justice	Py
14			*Dias Bandaranaike, S.R.	SLFP	*Dias Bandaranaike, S.R.	SLFP	Illangaratne, T.B. Ariyadasa, W.P.G.	SLFP SLFP	Dias Bandaranaike, F.R.	SLFP
15			*Dias Bandaranaike, S.R.	SLFP	*Dias Bandaranaike, S.R.	SLFP	Illangaratne, T.B. Ariyadasa, W.P.G.	SLFP SLFP	Dias Bandaranaike, F.R.	SLFP
16			Hameed, A.C.S.	UNP	Jayawardene, J.R.	UNP	Montague Jayawickrema, W.G. Premadasa, R.	UNP UNP	Dewanayagam, K.W.	UNP
17			Hameed, A.C.S.	UNP	Jayawardene, J.R.	UNP	Premadasa, R. Montague Jayawickrema, W.G.	UNP UNP	Dewanayagam, K.W.	UNP
18			Wijeratne, R.	UNP	Premadasa, R.	UNP	Wijekoon, U.B.	UNP	Vincent Perera, M.	UNP
19			Herath, H.	UNP	Premadasa, R. Wijeratne, R.	UNP UNP	Perera, F.	UNP	Hameed, A.S.C.	UNP
20			Herath, H.	UNP	Wijetunge, D.B.	UNP	Perera, F.	UNP	Hameed, A.S.C.	UNP
21			Kadirgamar, L.	PA-SLFP	Wijetunge, D.B. Ratwatte, A. (Col.)	UNP PA-SLFP	Wickremanayake, R. Dodangoda, A.	PA-SLFP PA-SLFP	Peiris, G.L.	PA-SLFP
22			Kadirgamar, L.	PA-SLFP	*Bandaranaike Kumaratunga, C.	PA-SLFP	Dodangoda, A. Wickremanayake, R.	PA-SLFP PA-SLFP	Peiris, G.L.	PA-SLFP

SRI LANKA 1947-1998

Gov	Finance	Py	Economic Aff.	Py	Labour	Py	Education	Py	Health	Py
1	Jayawardene, J.R.	UNP	Suntheralingam, C.	UNP	Jayak, T.B.	UNP	Nugawela, E.A. (Maj.)	UNP	Bandaranaike, S.W.	UNP
2	Jayawardene, J.R.	UNP	Amarasuriya	UNP	Jayak, T.B.	UNP	Nugawela, E.A. (Maj.)	UNP	Bandaranaike, S.W.	UNP
3	Jayawardene, J.R.	UNP	Senanayake, R.G.	UNP	Kaleel, M.C.M.	UNP	Banda, M.D.	UNP	Nugawela, E.A.	UNP
4	Goonetilleke, O.	UNP	Senanayake, R.G.	UNP	Kaleel, M.C.M.	UNP	Banda, M.D.	UNP	Nugawela, E.A.	UNP
5	De Zoysa, S.	MEP-SLFP	Senanayake, R.G.	MEP-SLFP	Illangaratne, T.B.	MEP-SLFP	Dahanayake, W.	MEP-SLFP	*Wijewardena, V.	MEP-SLFP
6	De Zoysa, S.	SLFP	Senanayake, R.G.	SLFP	De Zoysa, M.P.	SLFP	Dahanayake, W.	SLFP	Jayasuriya, A.P.	SLFP
7	De Zoysa, S.	SLFP	Senanayake, R.G.	SLFP	De Zoysa, M.P.	SLFP	Dahanayake, W.	SLFP	Jayasuriya, A.P.	SLFP
8	Jayawardene, J.R.	UNP	Banda, M.D.	UNP	Aluwihare, B.H.	UNP	Aluwihare, B.H.	UNP	Peiris, M.V.P.	UNP
9	Dias Bandaranaike, J.R.	SLFP	Illangaratne, T.B.	SLFP	Wijesinghe, S.C.	SLFP	Mahmud, B.	SLFP	Jayasuriya, A.P.	SLFP
10	Perera, N.M.	LSSP	Perera, N.M.	LSSP	Siriwardene, M.P.de Z.	SLFP	Katugalla, I.R.P.G.	SLFP	Mahmud, B.	SLFP
11	Wanninayake, U.B.	UNP	Peiris, M.V.P.	UNP	Mohamed, M.H.	UNP	Iriyagolle, I.M.R.A.	UNP	Jayawardene, M.D.H.	UNP
12	Wanninayake, U.B.	UNP	Fernando, H.	UNP	Mohamed, M.H.	UNP	Iriyagolle, I.M.R.A.	UNP	Senanayake, E.L.	UNP
13	Perera, N.M.	LSSP	*Dias Bandaranaike, S.R.	LSSP	*Dias Bandaranaike, S.R. Siriwardene, M.P.de Z.	SLFP SLFP	Mahmud, B. Subasinghe, T.B.	SLFP SLFP	Ariyadasa, W.P.	SLFP
14	Dias Bandaranaike, F.R.	SLFP	*Dias Bandaranaike, S.R.	SLFP	Siriwardene, M.P.de Z.	SLFP	Mahmud, B. Subasinghe, T.B.	SLFP SLFP	Rajapakse, G.	SLFP
15	Dias Bandaranaike, F.R.	SLFP	*Dias Bandaranaike, S.R.	SLFP	Siriwardene, M.P.de Z.	SLFP	Mahmud, B. Subasinghe, T.B.	SLFP SLFP	Rajapakse, G.	SLFP
16	De Mel, R.	UNP	Jayawardene, J.R.	UNP	Seneviratne, C.P.J.	UNP	Wijeratna, N.P. Mathew, C.	UNP UNP	Jayasooriya, G.	UNP
17	De Mel, R.	UNP	Jayawardene, J.R.	UNP	Seneviratne, C.P.J.	UNP	Wijeratna, N.P. Mathew, C.	UNP UNP	Jayasooriya, G.	UNP
18	Wijetunge, D.B.	UNP	Wijetunge, D.B.	UNP	Atapattu, R.	UNP	Hameed, A.C.S. Lokubandara, W.J.M.	UNP UNP	*Herath, R.	UNP

SRI LANKA 1947-1998

Gov	Finance	Py	Economic Aff.	Py	Labour	Py	Education	Py	Health	Py
19	Wijetunge, D.B.	UNP	Mansoor, A.R.	UNP	Premachandra, D.M.	UNP	Athulathmudali, L. Wickremansinghe, R. Premachandra, D.M.	UNP UNP UNP	*Herath, R.	UNP
20			Mansoor, A.R.	UNP			Wijetunge, D.B. Wickremansinghe, R.	UNP UNP	*Herath, R.	UNP
21	*Bandaranaike Kumaratunga,C.	PA-SLFP	*Bandaranaike Kumaratunga,C. Wickremaratne, K.	PA-SLFP PA-SLFP	Soysa, B. Rajapakse, M.	PA-LSSP PA-SLFP	Soysa, B. Rajapakse, M. Pathirana, R.	PA-LSSP PA-SLFP PA-SLFP	Fowzie, A.H.M.	PA-SLFP
22	*Bandaranaike Kumaratunga,C.	PA-SLFP			Rajapakse, M.	PA-SLFP	Soysa, B. Rajapakse, M. Pathirana, R.	PA-LSSP PA-SLFP PA-SLFP	Fowzie, A.H.M.	PA-SLFP

Gov	Housing	Py	Agriculture	Py	Industry/Trade	Py	Environment	Py
1			Senanayake, D.	UNP	de Silva, G.E.	UNP		
2			Bulankulama, P.B. Senanayake, D.	UNP UNP	Amarasuriya de Silva, G.E.	UNP UNP		
3			Goonetilleke, O. Pannambalam, G.G.	UNP TC	Pannambalam, G.G. Senanayake, R.G.	TC UNP		
4	Vaithianathan, K.	UNP	Jayawardene, J.R. Pannambalam, G.G.	UNP TC	Senanayake, R.G. Pannambalam, G.G.	UNP TC		
5	Illangaratne, T.B.	MEP-SLFP	de Silva, P.H.W. Gunawardena, D.P.R.	MEP-Vipla MEP-Vipla	de Silva, P.H.W. Senanayake, R.G.	MEP-Vipla MEP-SLFP		

SRI LANKA 1947-1998

Gov	Housing	Py	Agriculture	Py	Industry/Trade	Py	Environment	Py
6	*Wijewardena, V.	SLFP	Bandaranaike, S. / Munesinghe, J.C.W. / de Silva, C.P.	SLFP / SLFP / SLFP	Munesinghe, J.C.W. / Senanayake, R.G.	SLFP / SLFP		
7	*Wijewardena, V.	SLFP	Senanayake, R.G. / Munesinghe, J.C.W. / de Silva, C.P.	SLFP / SLFP / SLFP	Senanayake, R.G. / Munesinghe, J.C.W.	SLFP / SLFP		
8	Jayawardene, J.R.	UNP	Aluwihare, B.H. / Banda, M.D.	UNP / UNP	Aluwihare, B.H. / Banda, M.D.	UNP / UNP		
9	Samaraweera, M.	SLFP	de Silva, C.P.	SLFP	Illangaratne, T.B. / Senanayake, M.	SLFP / SLFP		
10	Siriwardene, M.P.de Z.	SLFP	Dias Bandaraniake, F.R.	SLFP	Illangaratne, T.B. / Senanayake, M.	SLFP / SLFP		
11	Mohamed, M.H.	UNP	de Silva, C.P. / Banda, M.D. / Gunawardene, P.	SLFSP / UNP / MEP	Gunawardene, P. / Peiris, M.V.P.	MEP / UNP		
12			de Silva, C.P. / Banda, M.D. / Gunawardene, P.	SLFSP / UNP / MEP	Gunawardene, P. / Fernando, H.	MEP / UNP		
13	Kenneman, P.G.B.	CP	de Silva, C.R. / Kobbekaduwa, H.S.R.B. / Rajapakse, G.	LSSP / SLFP / SLFP	Illangaratne, T.B. / Subasinghe, T.B.	SLFP / SLFP		
14	Kenneman, P.G.B.	CP	Wickremanayake, R. / Kobbekaduwa, H.S.R.B. / Rajapakse, G. / Suriarachchi, S.K.K.	SLFP / SLFP / SLFP / SLFP	Illangaratne, T.B. / Subasinghe, T.B. / Suriarachchi, S.K.K.	SLFP / SLFP / SLFP		

SRI LANKA 1947-1998

Gov	Housing	Py	Agriculture	Py	Industry/Trade	Py	Environment	Py
15	Kumarasuriyar, C.	SLFP	Wickremanayake, R. Kobbekaduwa, H.S.R.B. Rajapakse, G. Suriarachchi, S.K.K.	SLFP SLFP SLFP SLFP	Illangaratne, T.B. Subasinghe, T.B. Suriarachchi, S.K.K.	SLFP SLFP SLFP		
16	Premadasa, R.	UNP	de Silva Jayasinghe, S. Senanayake, E.L. Jayawardene, M.D.H. Herath, S.B.	UNP UNP UNP UNP	Athulathmudali, L. Mathew, C. Mendis, W.	UNP UNP UNP		
17	Premadasa, R.	UNP	de Silva Jayasinghe, S. Senanayake, E.L. Jayawardene, M.D.H. Herath, S.B.	UNP UNP UNP UNP	Athulathmudali, L. Mathew, C. Mendis, W.	UNP UNP UNP		
18	Sirisena Cooray, B.	UNP	Dissanayake, G. Athulathmudali, L. Perera, J.M.	UNP UNP UNP	Thondaman, S. Wickremansinghe, R. Mansoor, A.R.	UNP UNP UNP		
19	Sirisena Cooray, B.	UNP	Perera, J.M. Wijeratne, D. Dharmadasa Banda, R.M.	UNP UNP UNP	Wickremansinghe, R. Mansoor, A.R. Wijekoon, U.B.	UNP UNP UNP	Vincent Perera, M.	UNP
20	Sirisena Cooray, B.	UNP	Perera, J.M. Karunatilleke, R. Dharmadasa Banda, R.M.	UNP UNP UNP	Wickremansinghe, R. Mansoor, A.R. Wijekoon, U.B.	UNP UNP UNP	Vincent Perera, M.	UNP
21	de Silva, N.S.	PA-SLFP	Wickremanayake, R. Jayaratne, D.M. Gunawardena, I.	PA-SLFP PA-SLFP PA-CP	Wickremaratne, K. Gunaratna, C.V. Peiris, G.L.	PA-SLFP PA-SLFP PA-SLFP	*Athulathmudali, S.	PA-DUNF
22	de Silva, N.S.	PA-SLFP	Jayaratne, D.M. Thondoman, S. Gunawardena, I.	PA-SLFP PA-SLWC PA-CP	Peiris, G.L. Wickremaratne, K. Gunaratna, C.V.	PA-SLFP PA-SLFP PA-SLFP		

SRI LANKA 1947-1998

Gov	Social Affairs (py)	Public Works (py)	Other (py)	Res
1		Kotalawala, J.L. (UNP)(Col.) / Sittampalam, C. (UNP)	Ratnayake, A. (UNP) / Gunawardene, R.S. (UNP)	0
2		Kotalawala, J.L. (UNP)(Col.) / Sittampalam, C. (UNP)	Bulankulame, P.B. (UNP) / Ratnayake, A. (UNP) / Gunawardene, R.S. (UNP)	0
3		Kotalawala, J. (UNP) / Nalliah, V. (UNP)	Kotalawala, J. (UNP) / Goonetilleke, O. (UNP) / Bulankulame, P.B. (UNP)	0
4	Vaithianathan, K. (UNP)	Kotalawala, J. (UNP) / Natesan, S. (UNP)	Jayawardene, J.R. (UNP) / Bulankulame, P.B. (UNP)	2
5	Illangaratne, T.B. (MEP-SLFP)	Marikkar, C.A.S. (MEP-SLFP) / Senanayake, M. (MEP-SLFP)	de Silva, C.P. (MEP-SLFP) / Kuruppu, J. (MEP-SLFP)	1
6	Kalugalle, I.R.P.G. (SLFP)	Marikkar, C.A.S. (SLFP) / Senanyake, M. (SLFP) / Wijesinghe, C. (SLFP) / Abeywickrama, H. (SLFP)	Kalugalle, I.R.P.G. (SLFP)	0
7	Kalugalle, I.R.P.G. (SLFP)	Marikkar, C.A.S. (SLFP) / Senanyake, M. (SLFP) / Wijesinghe, C. (SLFP) / Abeywickrama, H. (SLFP)	Kalugalle, I.R.P.G. (SLFP)	2
8	Peiris, M.V.P. (UNP)	Jayawardene, J.R. (UNP) / Montague Jayawickrema, W.G. (UNP)	Aluwihare, B.H. (UNP) / Banda, M.D. (UNP) / Kaleel, M.C.M. (UNP)	0

SRI LANKA 1947-1998

Gov	Social Affairs (py)	Public Works (py)	Other (py)	Res
9		de Silva, C.P. (SLFP) Illangaratne, T.B. (SLFP) Kalugalle, I.R.P.G. (SLFP) Mahmud, B. (SLFP) Wijesinghe, S.C. (SLFP)	de Silva, C.P. (SLFP) Illangaratne, T.B. (SLFP) Senanayake, M. (SLFP)	3
10	Goonesekera, D.S. (SLFP)	de Silva, C.P. (SLFP) Moonesinghe, A. (LSSP) Illangaratne, T.B. (SLFP) Goonewardene, C. (LSSP) Samaraweera, M. (SLFP)	de Silva, C.P. (SLFP) Goonesekera, D.S. (SLFP) Senanayake, M. (SLFP)	0
11	Karunaratne, N.H.A. (SLFSP)	de Silva, C.P. (SLFSP) Montague Jayawickrema, W.G. (UNP) Sugathadasa, V.A. (UNP) Hurulle, E.L.B. (UNP)	Jayawardene, J.R. (UNP) Banda, M.D. (UNP) Iriyagolle, I.M.R.A. (UNP)	1
12	Karunaratne, N.H.A. (SLFSP)	de Silva, C.P. (SLFSP) Montague Jayawickrema, W.G. (UNP) Amaratunga, J.A. (UNP) Sugathadasa, V.A. (UNP) Hurulle, E.L.B. (UNP)	Banda, M.D. (UNP) Iriyagolle, I.M.R.A. (UNP)	0
13	Temekoon, T.B. (SLFP)	Senanayake, M. (SLFP) Kalugalle, P.B.G. (SLFP) Goonewardena, L.S. (LSSP) Kenneman, P.G.B. (CP) +Kumarasurier, C. (SLFP) Perera, R.S. (SLFP)	Kalugalle, P.B.G. (SLFP) Kulatilleke, S.S. (SLFP) Ratnayake, K.B. (SLFP)	1

SRI LANKA 1947-1998

Gov	Social Affairs (py)	Public Works (py)	Other (py)	Res
14	Ratnayake, K.B. (SLFP) Kulatilleke, S.S. (SLFP)	Senanayake, M. (SLFP) Kalugalle, P.B.G. (SLFP) Ratnayake, K.B. (SLFP) Kenneman, P.G.B. (CP) +Kumarasuriyar, C. (SLFP) Perera, R.S. (SLFP)	Kalugalle, P.B.G. (SLFP) Ratnayake, K.B. (SLFP) Tennekoon, T.B. (SLFP)	1
15	Ratnayake, K.B. (SLFP) Kulatilleke, S.S. (SLFP)	Senanayake, M. (SLFP) Kalugalle, P.B.G. (SLFP) Ratnayake, K.B. (SLFP) +Kumarasuriyar, C. (SLFP) Perera, R.S. (SLFP)	Kalugalle, P.B.G. (SLFP) Ratnayake, K.B. (SLFP) Tennekoon, T.B. (SLFP)	1
16	Vincent Perera, M. (UNP) Karuratne, A. (UNP)	Dissanayake, G. (UNP) *Kannangara, W. (UNP) Premadasa, R. (UNP) Wijetunge, D.B. (UNP) Mohamed, H.M. (UNP) Shelton Jayasinghe, D. (UNP)	*Kannangara, W. (UNP) Hurulle, E.L.B. (UNP) Vincent Perera, M. (UNP)	0
17	Vincent Perera, M. (UNP) Karuratne, A. (UNP)	Dissanayake, G. (UNP) *Kannangara, W. (UNP) Premadasa, R. (UNP) Wijetunge, D.B. (UNP) Mohamed, H.M. (UNP) Shelton Jayasinghe, D. (UNP)	*Kannangara, W. (UNP) Hurulle, E.L.B. (UNP) Vincent Perera, M. (UNP)	6

SRI LANKA 1947-1998

Gov	Social Affairs (py)	Public Works (py)	Other (py)	Res
18	Atapattu, R. (UNP) Nanda Mathew, C. (UNP) *Herath, R. (UNP)	Mendis, W. (UNP) Perera, F. (UNP) Lokubandara, W.J.M. (UNP) Aluvihare, A. (UNP) Mansoor, A.R. (UNP) Sirisena Cooray, B. (UNP)	Premadasa, R. (UNP) Vincent Perera, M. (UNP) Athulathmudali, L. (UNP) Dayaratne, P. (UNP) Lokubandara, W.J.M. (UNP) Adhikari, A.M.S. (UNP)	0
19	Nanda Mathew, C. (UNP) *Herath, R. (UNP) Adhikari, A.M.S. (UNP)	Aluvihare, A. (UNP) Sirisena Cooray, B. (UNP) Lokubandara, W.J.M. (UNP) Bandara, K.D.M.C. (UNP) Karunatilleke, R. (UNP)	Premadasa, R. (UNP) Dayaratne, P. (UNP) Vincent Perera, M. (UNP) Thondaman, S. (UNP) Lokubandara, W.J.M. (UNP) Adhikari, A.M.S. (UNP) Mallimarachchi, W. (UNP)	2
20	Dayaratne, P. (UNP) Nanda Mathew, P. (UNP) *Herath, R. (UNP)	Aluvihare, A. (UNP) Sirisena Cooray, B. (UNP) Lokubandara, W.J.M. (UNP) Adhikari, A.M.S. (UNP) Bandara, K.D.M.C. (UNP)	Wijetunge, D.B. (UNP) Vincent Perera, M. (UNP) Thondaman, S. (UNP) Lokubandara, W.J.M. (UNP) Mallimarachchi, W. (UNP) Athukorale, G. (UNP)	0
21	Dissanayaka, D.S.M.B. (PA-SLFP) *Athulathmudali, S. (PA-DUNF) Fowzie, A.H.M. (PA-SLFP)	Ratwatte, A. (PA-SLFP)(Col.) Ashraff, M.H.M. (SLMC) Senanayake, D. (PA-SLFP) de Silva, N.S. (PA-SLFP) Samaraweera, M. (PA-SLFP) *Athulathmudali, S. (PA-DUNF)	Wijetunge, D.B. (UNP) *Dias Bandaranaike, S.R. (PA-SLFP) Jayakody, L. (PA-SLFP) Ashraff, M.H.M. (SLMC) Senanayake, D. (PA-SLFP) Wickremaratne, K. (PA-SLFP) Dissanayake, D.S.M.B. (PA-SLFP)	0

498

SRI LANKA 1947-1998

Gov	Social Affairs (py)	Public Works (py)	Other (py)	Res
22	Dissanayake, D.M.S.B. (PA-SLFP) Fowzie, A.H.M. (PA-SLFP)	Ashraff, M.H.M. (SLMC) Ratwatte, A. (PA-SLFP)(Col.) Senanayake, D. (PA-SLFP) Samaraweera, M. (PA-SLFP) *Athullathmudali, S. (PA-DUNF)	*Bandaranaike Kumaratunga, C. (PA-SLFP) Jayakody, L. (PA-SLFP)	

- Gov 13-15: +Kumarasurier, C. and +Kumarasuriyar, C. are the same person.

46. SWEDEN

Sweden is a Monarchy, where the King has almost no formal powers.

The country is a unitary and centralised state. However, local communities hold considerable and discretionary (including fiscal) powers.

Parliament is unicameral. The Riksdag with 349 seats is elected by proportional representation (St. Lagüe) for a fixed term of three years in 28 multi-member constituencies, with roughly 225,000 electors on average. Representation is strictly proportional to the number of electors. There is a threshold of 4 percent nationally or 12 percent in a constituency.

Parliament does not need a quorum. Votes are carried by a majority of all votes cast. Some issues require a qualified majority ranging from a majority to a two-thirds majority of all members. Constitutional amendments, however, require only a majority of all votes cast. A (consultative) referendum is optional and may be called by government and parliament. The outcome can be either binding or consultative.

Government is led by the Chancellor (Prime Minister), who forms a government if at least fifty percent of all members of the Riksdag do not vote against him or her. If the Chancellor resigns, the government as a whole resigns. The government needs a vote of investiture for the Chancellor (see above) and can, after one year in office, also face a vote of no confidence. Losing either vote results in resignation of the government. Government is both collectively and individually responsible to parliament. All governmental actions are subject to approval by the Riksdag. Ministers can not be members of parliament at the same time. The Chancellor (Prime Minister) has a rather prominent position in government.

Although the judiciary may reject state actions, these "may be set aside only if the fault is manifest" (Maddex, 1996: 268). Sweden has a constitutional Ombudsman to oversee the administration. This functionary has become an important institution in addition to the courts.

SWEDEN 1945–1998

Gov	Begin	Dur	RfT	ToG	Py1	Py2	Py3	Py4	Seats	CPG	NoM	Prime Minister (py)
1	11.10.46	748	1	1	SDA 115				380	4	16	Erlander, T. (SDA)
2	28.10.48	1066	7	4	SDA 112				380	4	19	Erlander, T. (SDA)
3	30.09.51	357	1	2	SDA 112	BF/CP 30			380	4	16	Erlander, T. (SDA)
4	21.09.52	1466	1	2	SDA 110	BF/CP 26			380	4	16	Erlander, T. (SDA)
5	26.09.56	399	4	2	SDA 106	BF/CP 19			380	4	17	Erlander, T. (SDA)
6	30.10.57	215	1	4	SDA 106				381	4	15	Erlander, T. (SDA)
7	02.06.58	852	1	4	SDA 111				381	4	15	Erlander, T. (SDA)
8	01.10.60	1464	1	4	SDA 114				382	4	14	Erlander, T. (SDA)
9	04.10.64	1456	1	4	SDA 113				383	4	16	Erlander, T. (SDA)
10	29.09.68	381	2	1	SDA 125				384	4	17	Erlander, T. (SDA)
11	15.10.69	349	1	1	SDA 125				384	4	19	Palme, O. (SDA)
12	29.09.70	1128	1	4	SDA 163				384	4	19	Palme, O. (SDA)
13	31.10.73	1072	1	4	SDA 156				350	4	18	Palme, O. (SDA)
14	04.10.76	732	4	2	CP 86	FP 39	MUP 55		349	2	20	Fälldin, T. (CP)
15	13.10.78	364	1	4	FP 39				349	3	19	Ullsten, O. (FP)
16	12.10.79	588	4	2	CP 64	FP 38	MUP 73		349	2	21	Fälldin, T. (CP)
17	22.05.81	504	1	5	FP 38	CP 64			349	3	18	Fälldin, T. (CP)
18	08.10.82	1091	1	4	SDA 166				349	4	20	Palme, O. (SDA)
19	04.10.85	148	x	4	SDA 159				349	4	21	Palme, O. (SDA)
20	01.03.86	947	1	4	SDA 159				349	4	20	Carlsson, I. (SDA)
21	04.10.88	511	5	4	SDA 156				349	4	21	Carlsson, I. (SDA)
22	27.02.90	583	1	4	SDA 156				349	4	22	Carlsson, I. (SDA)
23	03.10.91	1099	1	5	MUP 80	FP 26	KDS 26	CP 31	349	2	21	Bildt, C. (MUP)
24	06.10.94	527	2	4	SDA 161				349	4	22	Carlsson, I. (SDA)
25	17.03.96			4	SDA 161				349	4	22	Persson, G. (SDA)

- Gov 19: Reason for Termination is assassination of PM Palme.

SWEDEN 1945–1998

Gov	Deputy PM	Py	Foreign Affairs	Py	Defence	Py	Interior	Py	Justice	Py
1			Undén, O.	SDA	Vougt, A.	SDA	Mossberg, E.	SDA	Zetterberg, H.	SDA
2			Undén, O.	SDA	Vougt, A.	SDA	Mossberg, E. / Lingman, J.	SDA / SDA	Zetterberg, H.	SDA
3			Undén, O.	SDA	Nilsson, T.	SDA	Hedlund, G. / Lingman, J.	AG / SDA	Zetterberg, H.	SDA
4			Undén, O.	SDA	Nilsson, T.	SDA	Hedlund, G. / Lingman, J.	AG / SDA	Zetterberg, H.	SDA
5			Undén, O.	SDA	Nilsson, T.	SDA	Hedlund, G. / Lindholm, S.	AG / SDA	Zetterberg, H.	SDA
6			Undén, O.	SDA	Andersson, S.	SDA	Johansson, R. / Lindholm, S.	SDA / SDA	Lindell, I.	NONA
7			Undén, O.	SDA	Andersson, S.	SDA	Johansson, R. / Lindholm, S.	SDA / SDA	Lindell, I.	SDA
8			Undén, O.	SDA	Andersson, S.	SDA	Johansson, R. / Lindholm, S.	SDA / SDA	Kling, H.	SDA
9			Nilsson, T.	SDA	Andersson, S.	SDA	Johansson, R. / Lindholm, S.	SDA / SDA	Kling, H.	SDA
10			Nilsson, T.	SDA	Andersson, S.	SDA	Johansson, R. / Gustafsson, H.	SDA / SDA	Kling, H.	SDA
11			Nilsson, T.	SDA	Andersson, S.	SDA	Holmqvist, E. / Lundqvist, S.	SDA / SDA	Geijer, L.	SDA
12			Nilsson, T.	SDA	Andersson, S.	SDA	Holmqvist, E.	SDA	Geijer, L.	SDA
13	Andersson, S.		Andersson, S.	SDA	Holmqvist, E.	SDA	Gustafsson, H.	SDA	Geijer, L.	SDA
14	Ahlmark, P.	FP	*Söder, K.	CP	Krönmark, E.	CP	Antonsson, J.	CP	Romanus, S.	NONA
15			Blix, H.	FP	Geer, L. de	FP	Hansson, B.	FP	Romanus, S.	NONA
16	Ullsten, O.	FP	Ullsten, O.	FP	Krönmark, E.	FP	Boo, K.	MUP	Winberg, H.	MUP
17	Ullsten, O.	FP	Ullsten, O.	FP	Gustafsson, T.	FP	Boo, K.	CP	Petri, C.A.	NONA

SWEDEN 1945–1998

Gov	Deputy PM	Py	Foreign Affairs	Py	Defence	Py	Interior	Py	Justice	Py
18	Carlsson, I.	SDA	Bodström, L.	SDA	Andersson, B.	SDA	Holmberg, B.	SDA	Rainer, O.	SDA
19	Carlsson, I.	SDA	Andersson, S.	SDA	Carlsson, R.	SDA	Holmberg, B.	SDA	Wickbom, S.	SDA
20			Andersson, S.	SDA	Carlsson, R.	SDA	Johansson, B.	SDA	Wickbom, S.	SDA
21			Andersson, S.	SDA	Carlsson, R.	SDA	Johansson, B. Wallström, M.	SDA SDA	*Freivalds, L.	SDA
22	Engström, O.	SDA	Andersson, S.	SDA	Carlsson, R.	SDA	Johansson, B.	SDA	*Freivalds, L.	SDA
23	Westerberg, B.	FP	*Ugglas, M. af Svensson, A.	MUP CP	Björck, A.	MUP CP	*Friggebo, B. *Davidsson, I.	FP KDS	*Hellsvik, G. *Laurén, R.	MUP IND
24	*Sahlin, M.	SDA	*Hjelm-Wallén, L.	SDA	Peterson, T.G.	SDA	*Ulvskog, M. Blomberg, L.	SDA SDA	*Freivalds, L.	SDA
25			*Hjelm-Wallén, L. Schori, P.	SDA SDA	Peterson, T.G.	SDA	Andersson, J. Blomberg, L.	SDA SDA	*Freivalds, L.	SDA

Gov	Finance	Py	Economic Aff.	Py	Labour	Py	Education	Py	Health	Py
1	Wigforss, E.	SDA					Weijne, J.	SDA		
2	Wigforss, E.	SDA					Weijne, J.	SDA		
3	Sköld, P.E.	SDA					Persson, I.	BF/CP		
4	Sköld, P.E.	SDA					Persson, I.	BF/CP		
5	Sträng, G.	SDA					Persson, I.	BF/CP		
6	Sträng, G.	SDA					Edenman, R.	SDA		
7	Sträng, G.	SDA					Edenman, R.	SDA		
8	Sträng, G.	SDA					Edenman, R.	SDA		
9	Sträng, G.	SDA					Edenman, R.	SDA		

SWEDEN 1945–1998

Gov	Finance	Py	Economic Aff.	Py	Labour	Py	Education	Py	Health	Py
10	Sträng, G.	SDA					Palme, O.	SDA		
11	Sträng, G.	SDA					Carlsson, I.	SDA	Aspling, S.	SDA
12	Sträng, G.	SDA					Carlsson, I.	SDA		
13	Sträng, G.	SDA					Zachrisson, B.	SDA	Aspling, S.	SDA
14	Mundebo, I.	FP	Bohman, G.	MUP	Ahlmark, P.	FP	Wikström, J.-E.	FP	Gustavsson, R.	CP
15	Mundebo, I.	FP	Mundebo, I.	FP	Wirtén, R.	FP	Wikström, J.-E.	FP	Romanus, G.	FP
16	Mundebo, I.	FP	Bohman, G.	MUP	Wirtén, R.	FP	Wikström, J.-E.	FP	*Söder, K.	CP
17	Wirtén, R.	FP	Wirtén, R.	FP	Eliasson, I.	FP	Wikström, J.-E.	FP	*Söder, K.	CP
							*Tillander, U.	CP		
18	Feldt, K.-O.	SDA			*Leijon, A.-G.	SDA	*Hjelm-Wallén, L.	SDA		
19	Feldt, K.-O.	SDA			*Leijon, A.-G.	SDA	Bodström, L.	SDA	*Sigurdsen, G.	SDA
20	Feldt, K.-O.	SDA			*Leijon, A.-G.	SDA	Bodström, L.	SDA	*Sigurdsen, G.	SDA
									Lindqvist, B.	SDA
21	Feldt, K.-O.	SDA			*Thalen, I.	SDA	Bodström, L.	SDA	*Sigurdsen, G.	SDA
	Engström, O.	SDA					Göransson, B.	SDA	Lindqvist, B.	SDA
22	Larsson, A.	SDA			*Sahlin, M.	SDA	Göransson, B.	SDA	*Thalén, I.	SDA
	Asbrink, E.	SDA			*Lööw, M.-L.	SDA	Persson, G.	SDA		
23	*Wibble, A.	FP			Hörnlund, B.	CP	Unckel, P.	MUP	Westerberg, B.	FP
	Lundgren, B.	MUP					*Ask, B.	MUP	Könberg, B.	FP
24	Persson, G.	SDA			Sundström, A.	SDA	Tham, C.	SDA	*Thalén, I.	SDA
							*Johansson, Y.	SDA	*Hedborg, A.	SDA
25	Asbrink, E.	SDA			*Winberg, M.	SDA	Tham, C.	SDA	*Wallström, M.	SDA
	Ostros, T.	SDA			*Messing, U.	SDA	*Johansson, Y.	SDA	*Klingvall, M.-I.	SDA

SWEDEN 1945–1998

Gov	Housing	Py	Agriculture	Py	Industry/Trade	Py	Environment	Py
1			Sköld, P.E.	SDA	Myrdal, G.	SDA		
					Gjöres, A.	SDA		
2			Sträng, H.G.	SDA	Ericsson, J.	SDA		
					*Kock, K.	SDA		
3			Norup, S.B.	BF/CP	Ericsson, J.	SDA		
4			Norup, S.B.	BF/CP	Ericsson, J.	SDA		
5			Norup, S.B.	BF/CP	Lange, G.	SDA		
6			Netzén, G.	SDA	Lange, G.	SDA		
7			Netzén, G.	SDA	Lange, G.	SDA		
8			Netzén, G.	SDA	Lange, G.	SDA		
9			Holmqvist, E.	SDA	Lange, G.	SDA		
10			Holmqvist, E.	SDA	Lange, G.	SDA		
11			Bengtsson, I.	SDA	Lange, G.	SDA		
					Wickman, K.	SDA		
12	Gustafsson, H.	SDA	Bengtsson, I.	SDA	Lange, G.	SDA		
					Wickman, K.	SDA		
13	Carlsson, I.	SDA	Lundkvist, S.	SDA	Johansson, R.	SDA		
					Feldt, K.-O.	SDA		
14	*Olsson, E.	CP	Dahlgren, A.	CP	Burenstam Linder, S.	MUP		
					Aasling, N.G.	CP		
15	*Friggebo, B.	FP	Enlund, E.	FP	Cars, H.	FP		
					Huss, E.	FP		
16	*Friggebo, B.	FP	Dahlgren, A.	CP	Burenstam Linder, S.	MUP		
					Aasling, N.G.	CP		
17	*Friggebo, B.	FP	Dahlgren, A.	CP	Molin, B.	FP		
					Aasling, N.G.	CP		
18	Gustafsson, H.	SDA	Lundkvist, S.	SDA	Peterson, T.G.	SDA		

SWEDEN 1945–1998

Gov	Housing	Py	Agriculture	Py	Industry/Trade	Py	Environment	Py
19	Gustafsson, H.	SDA	Lundkvist, S.	SDA	Peterson, T.G. / Hellström, M.	SDA / SDA		
20	Gustafsson, H.	SDA	Lundkvist, S.	SDA	*Gradin, A. / Peterson, T.G.	SDA / SDA	*Dahl, B.	SDA
21	Lönnqvist, U.	SDA	Hellström, M.	SDA	*Gradin, A. / Nordberg, I.	SDA / SDA	*Dahl, B.	SDA
22	Lönnqvist, U.	SDA	Hellström, M.	SDA	Molin, R. / *Gradin, A.	SDA / SDA	*Dahl, B.	SDA
23			Olson, K.E.	CP	Westerberg, P. / Dinkelspiel, U.	MUP / MUP	Johansson, O. / *Thurdin, G.	CP / CP
24	Andersson, J.	SDA	*Winberg, M.	SDA	Heckscher, S. / Hellström, M.	SDA / SDA	*Lindh, A.	SDA
25			*Ahnberg, A.	SDA	Sundström, , A. / Sydow, B. von	SDA / SDA	*Lindh, A.	SDA

Gov	Social Affairs (py)	Public Works (py)	Other (py)	Res
1	Möller, G. (SDA)	Nilsson, T. (SDA)	Weijne, J. (SDA) / Sträng, G. (SDA) / Ericsson, J. (SDA) / Danielsson, G. (NONA) / Qvensel, N. (NONA)	1

SWEDEN 1945–1998

Gov	Social Affairs (py)	Public Works (py)	Other (py)	Res
2	Möller, G. (SDA)	Nilsson, T.(SDA)	Weijne, J. (SDA) Sköld, P.E. (SDA) Andersson, S. (SDA) Danielsson, G. (NONA) Hammarskjöld, D. (NONA) Qvensel, N. (NONA) Nilsson, H. (SDA)	0
3	Sträng, G. (SDA)	Andersson, S. (SDA)	Persson, I. (BF/CP) Danielsson, G. (NONA) Hammarskjöld, D. (NONA) Lindell, I. (NONA) Nilsson, H. (BF/CP)	0
4	Sträng, G. (SDA)	Andersson, S. (SDA)	Persson, I. (BF/CP) Danielsson, G. (NONA) Hammarskjöld, D. (NONA) Lindell, I. (NONA) Nilsson, H. (BF/CP)	0
5	Ericsson, J. (SDA)	Andersson, S. (SDA)	Persson, I. (BF/CP) Danielsson, G. (NONA) Hammarskjöld, D. (NONA) Lindell, I. (NONA) Nilsson, H. (BF/CP) Nordenstam, A. (NONA)	0
6	Nilsson, T. (SDA)	Skoglund, G. (SDA)	Edenman, R. (SDA) Kjellin, B. (NONA) Kling, H. (SDA) *Lindström, U. (SDA)	0

SWEDEN 1945–1998

Gov	Social Affairs (py)	Public Works (py)	Other (py)	Res
7	Nilsson, T. (SDA)	Skoglund, G. (SDA)	Edenman, R. (SDA) Kjellin, B. (NONA) Kling, H. (SDA) *Lindström, U. (SDA)	0
8	Nilsson, T. (SDA)	Skoglund, G. (SDA)	Edenman, R. (SDA) Af Geijenstam, S. (NONA) *Lindström, U. (SDA)	0
9	Aspling, S. (SDA)	Skoglund, G. (SDA)	Edenman, R. (SDA) *Lindström, U. (SDA) Hermansson, R. (SDA) Palme, O. (SDA) Nilsson, S.-E. (SDA)	2
10	Aspling, S. (SDA)	Lundquist, S. (SDA)	Palme , O. (SDA) Nilsson, S.-E. (SDA) *Odhnhoff, C. (SDA) Geijer, L. (SDA) *Myrdal, A. (SDA) Moberg, S. (SDA)	2
11	Aspling, S. (SDA)	Norling, B. (SDA)	Carlsson, I. (SDA) Lidbom, C. (SDA) Moberg, S. (SDA) *Odhnhoff, C. (SDA) Löfberg, B. (SDA) Nilsson, S.-E. (SDA) *Myrdal, A. (SDA)	0

SWEDEN 1945–1998

Gov	Social Affairs (py)	Public Works (py)	Other (py)	Res
12	Andersson, S. (SDA)	Norling, B. (SDA)	Lidbom, C. (SDA) Moberg, S. (SDA) *Odhnhoff, C. (SDA) Löfberg, B. (SDA) Nilsson, S.-E. (SDA) *Myrdal, A. (SDA)	1
13	Aspling, S. (SDA)	Norling, B. (SDA)	Lidbom, C. (SDA) *Leijon, A.-G. (SDA) *Sigurdsen, G. (SDA) Löfberg, B. (SDA)	1
14	Gustavsson, R. (CP)	Turesson, B. (MUP) Johansson, O. (CP)	Wikström, J.-E. (FP) *Olsson, E. (CP) Ullsten, O. (FP) *Mogård, B. (MUP) *Troedsson, I. (MUP) *Friggebo, B. (FP)	1
15	Romanus, G. (FP)	*Bondestam, A. (FP)	Wikström, J.-E. (FP) *Friggebo, B. (FP) Tham, C. (FP) *Lindahl, H. (FP) *Rodhe, B. (FP) *Wahlberg, M. (FP) *Winther, E. (FP)	0
16	*Söder, K. (CP)	Adelsohn, U. (MUP) Danell, G. (MUP)	Wikström, J.-E. (FP) Johansson, O. (CP) *Andersson, K. (CP) *Mogård, B. (MUP) *Holm, E. (MUP) Petri, C.A. (NONA)	1

SWEDEN 1945–1998

Gov	Social Affairs (py)	Public Works (py)	Other (py)	Res
17	*Söder, K. (CP)	Eliasson, I. (FP) Elmstedt, C. (CP)	Wikström, J.-E. (FP) *Tillander, U. (CP) Johansson, O. (CP) *Andersson, K. (CP) *Ahrland, K. (FP)	0
18	Andersson, S. (SDA)	Boström, C. (SDA)	Carlsson, I. (SDA) *Dahl, B. (SDA) *Gradin, A. (SDA) Göransson, B. (SDA) Hellström, M. (SDA) *Sigurdsen, G. (SDA) *Carlsson, R. (SDA)	0
19	*Sigurdsen, G. (SDA)	Hulterström, S. (SDA)	Carlsson, I. (SDA) Bodström, L. (SDA) *Dahl, B. (SDA) *Gradin, A. (SDA) Göransson, B. (SDA) Lindqvist, B. (SDA) *Hjelm-Wallén, L. (SDA) Johansson, B. (SDA)	0
20	*Sigurdsen, G. (SDA) Lindqvist, B. (SDA)	Hulterström, S. (SDA) *Dahl, B. (SDA)	Bodström, L. (SDA) Göransson, B. (SDA) Gustafsson, H. (SDA) *Hjelm-Wallén, L. (SDA) Holmberg, B. (SDA) Hellström, M. (SDA)	0

SWEDEN 1945–1998

Gov	Social Affairs (py)	Public Works (py)	Other (py)	Res
21	*Sigurdsen, G. (SDA) Lindqvist, B. (SDA)	Hulterström, S. (SDA) *Dahl, B. (SDA)	Bodström, L. (SDA) Göransson, B. (SDA) Lönnqvist, U. (SDA) Andersson, G. (SDA) *Hjelm-Wallén, L. (SDA)	1
22	*Thalén, I. (SDA) Johansson, B. (SDA) Lindqvist, B. (SDA) *Wallström, M. (SDA)	Andersson, G. (SDA)	Engström, O. (SDA) Lönnqvist, U. (SDA) Göransson, B. (SDA) *Hjelm-Wallén, L. (SDA) *Wallström, M. (SDA)	0
23	Westerberg, B. (FP) Könberg, B. (FP)	Odell, M. (KDS) Johansson, O. (CP) *Thurdin, G. (CP)	*Friggebo, B. (FP) Svensson, A. (CP) Dinkelspiel, U. (MUP)	0
24	*Thalén, I. (SDA) *Hedborg, A. (SDA)	*Uusmann, I. (SDA) Andersson, J. (SDA)	*Sahlin, M. (SDA) *Lindh, A. (SDA) *Wallström, M. (SDA) Nygren, J. (SDA) Schori, P. (SDA) Hellström, M. (SDA)	0
25	*Wallström, M. (SDA) *Klingvall, M.-I. (SDA)	*Uusmann, I. (SDA)	Pagrotsky, L. (SDA) *Ulvskog, M. (SDA)	

47. SWITZERLAND

The Swiss Confederation is a "direct democracy" in which the federal states, the cantons, as well as the people's will, expressed by means of referendum, are central features.

The Head of State is not a President or a Monarch, but the chairperson of the Federal Council, whose members alternate in the position each year.

Switzerland is not only a (con)federal state but also highly decentralised. The cantons are quite autonomous and the municipalities have considerable rights to decide and to act.

Parliament is bicameral. The Council of States represents the cantons. Its 46 members are elected by a two-ballot majority system inside cantons for a fixed term of four years. The Nationalrat represents the people. Its 200 members are elected by proportional representation (Hagenbach), also for a fixed term of four years, in constituencies varying considerably in size as each canton or half-canton must have at least one Nationalrat member. Apart from this, representation is proportional to the size of the electorate in the constituency. The constitution stipulates that parliament can involve itself with all matters relevant to the Federation, i.e. not granted to any other authority, and can settle conflicts over power with and between the cantons.

Parliament has a quorum of at least 50 per cent of all members. Votes are carried by a majority of all votes cast. Constitutional amendments are also carried by a majority of all votes cast, plus a constitutionally required referendum. The outcome is binding. Portions of the electorate may also call referendums to veto parliamentary decisions or to carry out certain policies. The outcome of these referendums is also binding.

The government, the Federal Council, is a genuine executive committee elected by the combined Houses of Parliament for a four-year term. It is the head of the federal public administration and related services and is responsible for international and military affairs. It is not subject to a vote of investiture or no confidence, and collectively responsible to parliament. The members of the Council can not be members of parliament at the same time. The President has no dominant position in government.

The Supreme Court also looks into constitutional cases, but there is no judicial review of national laws. However, the laws of the cantons are reviewed for conformity to the federal law.

SWITZERLAND 1945–1998

Gov	Begin	Dur	RfT	ToG	Py1	Py2	Py3	Py4	Seats	CPG	NoM	Prime Minister (py)
1	14.12.44	364	1	3	SVP 22	FDP 47	CVP 43	SP 55	194	3	7	Steiger, E. von (SVP)
2	13.12.45	364	1	3	SVP 22	FDP 47	CVP 43	SP 55	194	3	7	Kobelt, K. (FDP)
3	12.12.46	364	1	3	SVP 22	FDP 47	CVP 43	SP 55	194	3	7	Etter, P. (CVP)
4	11.12.47	371	1	3	SVP 21	FDP 52	CVP 44	SP 48	194	3	7	Celio, E. (CVP)
5	16.12.48	364	1	3	SVP 21	FDP 52	CVP 44	SP 48	194	3	7	Nobs, E. (SP)
6	15.12.49	364	1	3	SVP 21	FDP 52	CVP 44	SP 48	194	3	7	Petitpierre, M. (FDP)
7	14.12.50	364	1	3	SVP 21	FDP 52	CVP 44	SP 48	194	3	7	Steiger, E. von (SVP)
8	13.12.51	364	1	3	SVP 23	FDP 51	CVP 48	SP 49	196	3	7	Kobelt, K. (FDP)
9	11.12.52	376	1	3	SVP 23	FDP 51	CVP 48	SP 49	196	3	7	Etter, P. (CVP)
10	22.12.53	359	1	2	SVP 23	FDP 51	CVP 48		196	2	7	Rubattel, R. (FDP)
11	16.12.54	364	1	2	SVP 23	FDP 51	CVP 48		196	2	7	Petitpierre, M. (FDP)
12	15.12.55	364	1	2	SVP 22	FDP 50	CVP 47		196	2	7	Feldmann, M. (SVP)
13	13.12.56	364	1	2	SVP 22	FDP 50	CVP 47		196	2	7	Streuli, H. (FDP)
14	12.12.57	364	1	2	SVP 22	FDP 50	CVP 47		196	2	7	Holenstein, T. (CVP)
15	11.12.58	370	1	2	SVP 22	FDP 50	CVP 47		196	2	7	Chaudet, P. (FDP)
16	17.12.59	364	1	3	SVP 23	FDP 51	CVP 47	SP 51	196	3	7	Petitpierre, M. (FDP)
17	15.12.60	364	1	3	SVP 23	FDP 51	CVP 47	SP 51	196	3	7	Wahlen, F. (SVP)
18	14.12.61	364	1	3	SVP 23	FDP 51	CVP 47	SP 51	196	3	7	Chaudet, P. (FDP)
19	13.12.62	364	1	3	SVP 23	FDP 51	CVP 47	SP 51	196	3	7	Spühler, W. (SP)
20	12.12.63	364	1	3	SVP 22	FDP 51	CVP 48	SP 53	200	3	7	Moos, L. von (CVP)
21	10.12.64	363	1	3	SVP 22	FDP 51	CVP 48	SP 53	200	3	7	Tschudi, H.-P. (SP)
22	08.12.65	371	1	3	SVP 22	FDP 51	CVP 48	SP 53	200	3	7	Schaffner, H. (FDP)
23	14.12.66	381	1	3	SVP 22	FDP 51	CVP 48	SP 53	200	3	7	Bonvin, R. (CVP)
24	30.12.67	367	1	3	SVP 21	FDP 49	CVP 45	SP 51	200	3	7	Spühler, W. (SP)
25	31.12.68	398	1	3	SVP 21	FDP 49	CVP 45	SP 51	200	3	7	Moos, L. von (CVP)
26	02.02.70	310	1	3	SVP 21	FDP 49	CVP 45	SP 51	200	3	7	Tschudi, H.-P. (SP)
27	09.12.70	364	1	3	SVP 21	FDP 49	CVP 45	SP 51	200	3	7	Gnägi, R. (SVP)

SWITZERLAND 1945–1998

Gov	Begin	Dur	RfT	ToG	Py1	Py2	Py3	Py4	Seats	CPG	NoM	Prime Minister (py)
28	08.12.71	364	1	3	SVP 21	FDP 49	CVP 44	SP 46	200	3	7	Celio, N. (FDP)
29	06.12.72	380	1	3	SVP 21	FDP 49	CVP 44	SP 46	200	3	7	Bonvin, R. (CVP)
30	21.12.73	348	1	3	SVP 21	FDP 49	CVP 44	SP 46	200	3	7	Brugger, E. (FDP)
31	04.12.74	371	1	3	SVP 21	FDP 49	CVP 44	SP 46	200	3	7	Graber, P. (SP)
32	10.12.75	387	1	3	SVP 21	FDP 47	CVP 46	SP 55	200	3	7	Gnägi, R. (SVP)
33	31.12.76	341	1	3	SVP 21	FDP 47	CVP 46	SP 55	200	3	7	Furgler, K. (CVP)
34	07.12.77	389	1	3	SVP 21	FDP 47	CVP 46	SP 55	200	3	7	Ritschard, W. (SP)
35	31.12.78	361	1	3	SVP 21	FDP 47	CVP 46	SP 55	200	3	7	Hürlimann, H. (CVP)
36	27.12.79	370	1	3	SVP 23	FDP 51	CVP 44	SP 51	200	3	7	Chevallaz, G.-A. (FDP)
37	31.12.80	365	1	3	SVP 23	FDP 51	CVP 44	SP 51	200	3	7	Furgler, K. (CVP)
38	31.12.81	355	1	3	SVP 23	FDP 51	CVP 44	SP 51	200	3	7	Honegger, F. (FDP)
39	21.12.82	363	1	3	SVP 23	FDP 51	CVP 44	SP 51	200	3	7	Aubert, P. (SP)
40	19.12.83	352	1	3	SVP 23	FDP 54	CVP 42	SP 47	200	3	7	Schlumpf, L. (SVP)
41	05.12.84	371	1	3	SVP 23	FDP 54	CVP 42	SP 47	200	3	7	Furgler, K. (CVP)
42	11.12.85	364	1	3	SVP 23	FDP 54	CVP 42	SP 47	200	3	7	Egli, A. (CVP)
43	10.12.86	364	1	3	SVP 23	FDP 54	CVP 42	SP 47	200	3	7	Aubert, P. (SP)
44	09.12.87	364	1	3	SVP 25	FDP 51	CVP 42	SP 41	200	3	7	Stich, O. (SP)
45	07.12.88	364	1	3	SVP 25	FDP 51	CVP 42	SP 41	200	3	7	Delamuraz, J.-P. (FDP)
46	06.12.89	390	1	3	SVP 25	FDP 51	CVP 42	SP 41	200	3	7	Koller, A. (CVP)
47	31.12.90	338	1	3	SVP 25	FDP 51	CVP 42	SP 41	200	3	7	Cotti, F. (CVP)
48	04.12.91	370	1	3	SVP 25	FDP 44	CVP 36	SP 42	200	3	7	Felber, R. (SP)
49	09.12.92	363	1	3	SVP 25	FDP 44	CVP 36	SP 42	200	3	7	Ogi, A. (SVP)
50	08.12.93	363	1	3	SVP 25	FDP 44	CVP 36	SP 42	200	3	7	Stich, O. (SP)
51	07.12.94	370	1	3	SVP 25	FDP 45	CVP 36	SP 42	200	3	7	Villiger, K. (FDP)
52	13.12.95	364		3	SVP 29	FDP 45	CVP 34	SP 54	200	3	7	Delamuraz, J.-P. (FDP)
53	11.12.96	364	1	3	SVP 29	FDP 45	CVP 34	SP 54	200	3	7	Koller, A. (CVP)
54	10.12.97	364	1	3	SVP 29	FDP 45	CVP 34	SP 54	200	3	7	Cotti, F. (CVP)

- No ministers/ministries for Labour, Education, Health, Housing, Agriculture, Industry/Trade, Environment, and Social Affairs.

SWITZERLAND 1945–1998

Gov	Deputy PM	Py	Foreign Affairs	Py	Defence	Py	Interior	Py	Justice	Py
1	Kobelt, K.	FDP	Petitpierre, M.	FDP	Kobelt, K.	FDP	Etter, P.	CVP	Steiger, E. von	SVP
2	Etter, P.	CVP	Petitpierre, M.	FDP	Kobelt, K.	FDP	Etter, P.	CVP	Steiger, E. von	SVP
3	Celio, E.	CVP	Petitpierre, M.	FDP	Kobelt, K.	FDP	Etter, P.	CVP	Steiger, E. von	SVP
4	Nobs, E.	SP	Petitpierre, M.	FDP	Kobelt, K.	FDP	Etter, P.	CVP	Steiger, E. von	SVP
5	Petitpierre, M.	FDP	Petitpierre, M.	FDP	Kobelt, K.	FDP	Etter, P.	CVP	Steiger, E. von	SVP
6	Steiger, E. von	SVP	Petitpierre, M.	FDP	Kobelt, K.	FDP	Etter, P.	CVP	Steiger, E. von	SVP
7	Kobelt, K.	FDP	Petitpierre, M.	FDP	Kobelt, K.	FDP	Etter, P.	CVP	Steiger, E. von	SVP
8	Etter, P.	CVP	Petitpierre, M.	FDP	Kobelt, K.	FDP	Etter, P.	CVP	Feldmann, M.	SVP
9	Rubattel, R.	FDP	Petitpierre, M.	FDP	Kobelt, K.	FDP	Etter, P.	CVP	Feldmann, M.	SVP
10	Escher, J.	CVP	Petitpierre, M.	FDP	Kobelt, K.	FDP	Etter, P.	CVP	Feldmann, M.	SVP
11	Feldmann, M.	SVP	Petitpierre, M.	FDP	Chaudet, P.	FDP	Etter, P.	CVP	Feldmann, M.	SVP
12	Streuli, H.	FDP	Petitpierre, M.	FDP	Chaudet, P.	FDP	Etter, P.	CVP	Feldmann, M.	SVP
13	Holenstein, T.	CVP	Petitpierre, M.	FDP	Chaudet, P.	FDP	Etter, P.	CVP	Feldmann, M.	SVP
14	Chaudet, P.	FDP	Petitpierre, M.	FDP	Chaudet, P.	FDP	Etter, P.	CVP	Feldmann, M.	SVP
15	Lepori, G.	CVP	Petitpierre, M.	FDP	Chaudet, P.	FDP	Etter, P.	CVP	Wahlen, F.T.	SVP
16	Wahlen, F.T.	SVP	Petitpierre, M.	FDP	Chaudet, P.	FDP	Bourgknecht, J.	CVP	Wahlen, F.T.	SVP
17	Chaudet, P.	FDP	Petitpierre, M.	FDP	Chaudet, P.	FDP	Tschudi, H.-P.	SP	Moos, L. von	CVP
18	Bourgknecht, J.	CVP	Wahlen, F.T.	SVP	Chaudet, P.	FDP	Tschudi, H.-P.	SP	Moos, L. von	CVP
19	Moos, L. von	CVP	Wahlen, F.T.	SVP	Chaudet, P.	FDP	Tschudi, H.-P.	SP	Moos, L. von	CVP
20	Tschudi, H.-P.	SP	Wahlen, F.T.	SVP	Chaudet, P.	FDP	Tschudi, H.-P.	SP	Moos, L. von	CVP
21	Schaffner, H.	FDP	Wahlen, F.T.	SVP	Chaudet, P.	FDP	Tschudi, H.-P.	SP	Moos, L. von	CVP
22	Bonvin, R.	CVP	Spühler, W.	SP	Celio, N.	FDP	Tschudi, H.-P.	SP	Moos, L. von	CVP
23	Spühler, W.	SP	Spühler, W.	SP	Celio, N.	FDP	Tschudi, H.-P.	SP	Moos, L. von	CVP
24	Moos, L. von	CVP	Spühler, W.	SP	Gnägi, R.	SVP	Tschudi, H.-P.	SP	Moos, L. von	CVP
25	Tschudi, H.-P.	SP	Spühler, W.	SP	Gnägi, R.	SVP	Tschudi, H.-P.	SVP	Moos, L. von	CVP
26	Gnägi, R.	SVP	Graber, P.	SP	Gnägi, R.	SVP	Tschudi, H.-P.	SVP	Moos, L. von	CVP

SWITZERLAND 1945–1998

Gov	Deputy PM	Py	Foreign Affairs	Py	Defence	Py	Interior	Py	Justice	Py
27	Celio, N.	FDP	Graber, P.	SP	Gnägi, R.	SVP	Tschudi, H.-P.	SP	Moos, L. von	CVP
28	Bonvin, R.	CVP	Graber, P.	SP	Gnägi, R.	SVP	Tschudi, H.-P.	SP	Furgler, K.	CVP
29	Brugger, E.	FDP	Graber, P.	SP	Gnägi, R.	SVP	Tschudi, H.-P.	SP	Furgler, K.	CVP
30	Graber, P.	SP	Graber, P.	SP	Gnägi, R.	SVP	Hürlimann, H.	CVP	Furgler, K.	CVP
31	Gnägi, R.	SVP	Graber, P.	SP	Gnägi, R.	SVP	Hürlimann, H.	CVP	Furgler, K.	CVP
32	Furgler, K.	CVP	Graber, P.	SP	Gnägi, R.	SVP	Hürlimann, H.	CVP	Furgler, K.	CVP
33	Ritschard, W.	SP	Graber, P.	SP	Gnägi, R.	SVP	Hürlimann, H.	CVP	Furgler, K.	CVP
34	Hürlimann, H.	CVP	Graber, P.	SP	Gnägi, R.	SVP	Hürlimann, H.	CVP	Furgler, K.	CVP
35	Chevallaz, G.-A.	FDP	Aubert, P.	SP	Gnägi, R.	SVP	Hürlimann, H.	CVP	Furgler, K.	CVP
36	Furgler, K.	CVP	Aubert, P.	SP	Chevallaz, G.-A.	FDP	Hürlimann, H.	CVP	Furgler, K.	CVP
37	Honegger, F.	FDP	Aubert, P.	SP	Chevallaz, G.-A.	FDP	Hürlimann, H.	CVP	Furgler, K.	CVP
38	Aubert, P.	SP	Aubert, P.	SP	Chevallaz, G.-A.	FDP	Hürlimann, H.	CVP	Furgler, K.	CVP
39	Ritschard, W.	SP	Aubert, P.	SP	Chevallaz, G.-A.	FDP	Egli, A.	CVP	Friedrich, R.	FDP
40	Furgler, K.	CVP	Aubert, P.	SP	Delamuraz, J.-P.	FDP	Egli, A.	CVP	Friedrich, R.	FDP
41	Egli, A.	CVP	Aubert, P.	SP	Delamuraz, J.-P.	FDP	Egli, A.	CVP	*Kopp, E.	FDP
42	Aubert, P.	SP	Aubert, P.	SP	Delamuraz, J.-P.	FDP	Egli, A.	CVP	*Kopp, E.	FDP
43	Stich, O.	SP	Aubert, P.	SP	Koller, A.	CVP	Cotti, F.	CVP	*Kopp, E.	FDP
44	Delamuraz, J.-P.	FDP	Felber, R.	SP	Koller, A.	CVP	Cotti, F.	CVP	*Kopp, E.	FDP
45	*Kopp, E.	FDP	Felber, R.	SP	Koller, A.	CVP	Cotti, F.	CVP	*Kopp, E.	FDP
46	Cotti, F.	CVP	Felber, R.	SP	Villiger, K.	FDP	Cotti, F.	CVP	Koller, A.	CVP
47	Felber, R.	SP	Felber, R.	SP	Villiger, K.	FDP	Cotti, F.	CVP	Koller, A.	CVP
48	Ogi, A.	SVP	Felber, R.	SP	Villiger, K.	FDP	Cotti, F.	CVP	Koller, A.	CVP
49	Stich, O.	SP	Felber, R.	SP	Villiger, K.	FDP	Cotti, F.	CVP	Koller, A.	CVP
50	Villiger, K.	FDP	Cotti, F.	CVP	Villiger, K.	FDP	*Dreifuss, R.	SP	Koller, A.	CVP
51	Delamuraz, J.-P.	FDP	Cotti, F.	CVP	Villiger, K.	FDP	*Dreifuss, R.	SP	Koller, A.	CVP
52	Koller, A.	CVP	Cotti, F.	CVP	Ogi, A.	SVP	*Dreifuss, R.	SP	Koller, A.	CVP
53	Cotti, F.	CVP	Cotti, F.	CVP	Ogi, A.	SVP	*Dreifuss, R.	SP	Koller, A.	CVP
54	*Dreifuss, R.	SP	Cotti, F.	CVP	Ogi, A.	SVP	*Dreifuss, R.	SP	Koller A.	CVP

SWITZERLAND 1945–1998

Gov	Finance	Py	Economic Aff.	Py	Public Works	Py
1	Nobs, E.	SP	Stampfli, FDP		Celio, E.	CVP
2	Nobs, E.	SP	Stampfli, FDP		Celio, E.	CVP
3	Nobs, E.	SP	Stampfli, FDP		Celio, E.	CVP
4	Nobs, E.	SP	Rubattel, R.	FDP	Celio, E.	CVP
5	Nobs, E.	SP	Rubattel, R.	FDP	Celio, E.	CVP
6	Nobs, E.	SP	Rubattel, R.	FDP	Celio, E.	CVP
7	Nobs, E.	SP	Rubattel, R.	FDP	Escher, J.	CVP
8	Weber, M.	SP	Rubattel, R.	FDP	Escher, J.	CVP
9	Weber, M.	SP	Rubattel, R.	FDP	Escher, J.	CVP
10	Weber, M.	SP	Rubattel, R.	FDP	Escher, J.	CVP
11	Streuli, H.	FDP	Holenstein, T.	CVP	Lepori, G.	CVP
12	Streuli, H.	FDP	Holenstein, T.	CVP	Lepori, G.	CVP
13	Streuli, H.	FDP	Holenstein, T.	CVP	Lepori, G.	CVP
14	Streuli, H.	FDP	Holenstein, T.	CVP	Lepori, G.	CVP
15	Streuli, H.	FDP	Holenstein, T.	CVP	Lepori, G.	CVP
16	Spühler, W.	SP	Moos, L. von	CVP	Tschudi, H.-P.	SP
17	Bourgknecht, J.	CVP	Wahlen, F.T.	SVP	Spühler, W.	SP
18	Bourgknecht, J.	CVP	Schaffner, H.	FDP	Spühler, W.	SP
19	Bonvin, R.	CVP	Schaffner, H.	FDP	Spühler, W.	SP
20	Bonvin, R.	CVP	Schaffner, H.	FDP	Spühler, W.	SP
21	Bonvin, R.	CVP	Schaffner, H.	FDP	Spühler, W.	SP
22	Bonvin, R.	CVP	Schaffner, H.	FDP	Gnägi, R.	SVP
23	Bonvin, R.	CVP	Schaffner, H.	FDP	Gnägi, R.	SVP
24	Bonvin, R.	CVP	Schaffner, H.	FDP	Gnägi, R.	SVP
25	Celio, N.	FDP	Schaffner, H.	FDP	Bonvin, R.	CVP
26	Celio, N.	FDP	Brugger, E.	FDP	Bonvin, R.	CVP

SWITZERLAND 1945–1998

Gov	Finance	Py	Economic Aff.	Py	Public Works	Py
27	Celio, N.	FDP	Brugger, E.	FDP	Bonvin, R.	CVP
28	Celio, N.	FDP	Brugger, E.	FDP	Bonvin, R.	CVP
29	Celio, N.	FDP	Brugger, E.	FDP	Bonvin, R.	CVP
30	Chevallaz, G.-A.	FDP	Brugger, E.	FDP	Ritschard, W.	SP
31	Chevallaz, G.-A.	FDP	Brugger, E.	FDP	Ritschard, W.	SP
32	Chevallaz, G.-A.	FDP	Brugger, E.	FDP	Ritschard, W.	SP
33	Chevallaz, G.-A.	FDP	Brugger, E.	FDP	Ritschard, W.	SP
34	Chevallaz, G.-A.	FDP	Brugger, E.	FDP	Ritschard, W.	SP
35	Chevallaz, G.-A.	FDP	Honegger, F.	FDP	Ritschard, W.	SP
36	Ritschard, W.	SP	Honegger, F.	FDP	Schlumpf, L.	SVP
37	Ritschard, W.	SP	Honegger, F.	FDP	Schlumpf, L.	SVP
38	Ritschard, W.	SP	Honegger, F.	FDP	Schlumpf, L.	SVP
39	Ritschard, W.	SP	Furgler, K.	CVP	Schlumpf, L.	SVP
40	Stich, O.	SP	Furgler, K.	CVP	Schlumpf, L.	SVP
41	Stich, O.	SP	Furgler, K.	CVP	Schlumpf, L.	SVP
42	Stich, O.	SP	Furgler, K.	CVP	Schlumpf, L.	SVP
43	Stich, O.	SP	Delamuraz, J.-P.	FDP	Schlumpf, L.	SVP
44	Stich, O.	SP	Delamuraz, J.-P.	FDP	Ogi, A.	SVP
45	Stich, O.	SP	Delamuraz, J.-P.	FDP	Ogi, A.	SVP
46	Stich, O.	SP	Delamuraz, J.-P.	FDP	Ogi, A.	SVP
47	Stich, O.	SP	Delamuraz, J.-P.	FDP	Ogi, A.	SVP
48	Stich, O.	SP	Delamuraz, J.-P.	FDP	Ogi, A.	SVP
49	Stich, O.	SP	Delamuraz, J.-P.	FDP	Ogi, A.	SVP
50	Stich, O.	SP	Delamuraz, J.-P.	FDP	Ogi, A.	SVP
51	Stich, O.	SP	Delamuraz, J.-P.	FDP	Ogi, A.	SVP
52	Villiger, K.	FDP	Delamuraz, J.-P.	FDP	Leuenberger, M.	SP
53	Villiger, K.	FDP	Delamuraz, J.-P.	FDP	Leuenberger, M.	SP
54	Villiger, K.	FDP	Delamuraz, J.-P.	FDP	Leuenberger, M.	SP

48. TURKEY

The present constitution dates from 1982.

The Head of State, the President, is elected indirectly by at least a two-thirds majority of all members of the legislature for one seven year term only. The President has considerable powers but shares them with the Prime Minister and Parliament.

Turkey is a unitary state with a prefectoral system in the provinces.

Parliament is unicameral. The Grand National Assembly of 550 seats is elected by proportional representation (d'Hondt) for a fixed term of five years in constituencies that vary in size but average 500,000 electors. There is a threshold of 10 per cent of the national vote.

Parliament has a quorum of one-third of all members. Votes are carried with a majority of all votes cast. Amendments to the constitution require a three-fifths majority of all votes cast, unless the President does not assent, in which case a referendum must be held. The outcome is binding. Otherwise a referendum is optional and may be called by the Head of State. The outcome here is also binding.

The Prime Minister, who is appointed by the President, forms the government. In turn the Prime Minister selects the ministers and puts his general policy before parliament, requesting a vote of confidence, which in practice works as vote of investiture. During its lifetime the government can also face a vote of no confidence. Losing either vote always results in resignation of the government. The Prime Minister and his ministers are individually responsible to parliament. Ministers are required to be members of parliament. The Prime Minister has a dominant position in government.

The Constitutional Court adjudicates the constitutionality of laws, decrees and other policy measures taken.

TURKEY 1946-1998

Gov	Begin	Dur	RfT	ToG	Py1	Py2	Py3	Py4	Seats	CPG	NoM	Prime Minister (py)
1	07.08.46	399	3	1	PP 395				465	3	14	Peker, R. (PP)
2	10.09.47	274	5	1	PP 395				465	3	17	Saka, H. (PP)
3	10.06.48	220	4	1	PP 395				465	3	16	Saka, H. (PP)
4	16.01.49	491	1	1	PP 395				465	3	16	Günaltay, S. (PP)
5	22.05.50	292	5	1	DP 408				487	1	16	Menderes, A. (DP)
6	10.03.51	1164	1	1	DP 408				487	1	17	Menderes, A. (DP)
7	17.05.54	571	4	1	DP 503				541	1	18	Menderes, A. (DP)
8	09.12.55	707	1	1	DP 482				541	1	18	Menderes, A. (DP)
9	25.11.57	924	x	1	DP 421				602	1	20	Menderes, A. (DP)
10	20.11.61	213	4	2	CHP 173	JP 158			450	4	22	Inönü, I. (CHP)
11	21.06.62	552	4	3	CHP 173	NTP 65	RPNP 54	IND >15	450	3	23	Inönü, I. (CHP)
12	25.12.63	423	5	4	CHP 173	NTP 65	RPNP 54	NP 31	450	4	23	Inönü, I. (CHP)
13	20.02.65	249	1	3	JP 158				450	2	23	Ürgüplü, S.H. (NONA)
14	27.10.65	1478	1	1	JP 240				450	3	23	Demirel, S. (JP)
15	03.11.69	123	4	1	JP 256				450	3	25	Demirel, S. (JP)
16	06.03.70	385	x	4	JP 221				450	3	24	Demirel, S. (JP)
17	26.03.71	260	4	x	JP 221	CHP 134	NRP 15		450	4	26	Erim, N. (NONA)
18	11.12.71	163	5	x	JP 221	CHP 134	NRP 15		450	4	25	Erim, N. (NONA)
19	22.05.72	328	2	x	JP 221	CHP 134	NRP 15		450	4	25	Melen, F. (NRP)
20	15.04.73	286	1	2	JP 221	RRP 43			450	3	25	Talû, N. (NONA)
21	26.01.74	295	4	2	CHP 186	NSP 48			450	4	25	Ecevit, B. (CHP)
22	17.11.74	134	x	6					450	-	27	Irmak, S. (NONA)
23	31.03.75	82	1	5	JP 149	NSP 48	RRP 13	NAP 3	450	3	30	Demirel, S. (JP)
24	21.06.75	30	5	4	CHP 214				450	4	26	Ecevit, B. (CHP)
25	21.07.75	899	5	2	JP 189	NSP 24	NAP 16		450	3	29	Demirel, S. (JP)
26	05.01.78	676	5	2	CHP 214	RRP 3	DP 1	[IND ?]	450	4	35	Ecevit, B. (CHP)
27	12.11.79	305	x	4	JP 182	[NSP 22]	[NAP 17]		450	3	29	Demirel, S. (JP)
28	13.12.83	1469	1	1	ANAP 212				400	3	23	Özal, T. (ANAP)

TURKEY 1946-1998

Gov	Begin	Dur	RfT	ToG	Py1	Py2	Py3	Py4	Seats	CPG	NoM	Prime Minister (py)
29	21.12.87	689	2	1	ANAP 292				450	3	25	Özal, T. (ANAP)
30	09.11.89	591	2	1	ANAP 292				450	3	31	Akbulut, Y. (ANAP)
31	23.06.91	149	1	1	ANAP 292				450	3	30	Yilmaz, M. (ANAP)
32	19.11.91	584	2	2**	DYP 178	SHP 88			450	3	32	Demirel, S. (DYP)
33	25.06.93	640	x	2**	DYP 178	SHP 88			450	3	35	*Çiller, T. (DYP)
34	27.03.95	217	4	2	DYP 178	CHP 88			450	3	32	*Çiller, T. (DYP)
35	30.10.95	126	1	6	DYP 178	CHP 88			450	3	18	*Çiller, T. (DYP)
36	04.03.96	116	4	5	ANAP 132	DYP 135			550	3	33	Yilmaz, M. (ANAP)
37	28.06.96	368	4	2	Refah 158	DYP 135			550	2	37	Erkaban, N. (Refah)
38	01.07.97		2	2	ANAP 132	DYP 135	DSP 76		550	3	38	Yilmaz, M. (ANAP)

** = divided government

- [] Denotes parties supporting the government without participating in it.
- Turkey has experienced several periods of military rule, martiel law and other restrictions of political activities and liberties since 1945:

1945-1947: Martial law in the provinces Dardanelles; Istanbul and Thrace.
1954-1958: Civilian DP government severely restricted political activity and civil liberties of opposition parties.
1960-1961: Military coup, martial law and new constitution.
1961: Restoration civilian government but under new constitution. General Cürsel became Head of State.
1963-1964: Attempted military coup and subsequent martial law for the provinces Istanbul; Ankara and Izmir.
1971-1980: Martial law in a varying number (9-19) of the 67 provinces; mainly Kurdish areas.
1980-1984: Military coup and subsequent martial law in all 67 provinces.
1983: Restoration of the civilian government under new constitution. General Evren became Head of State. Four other senior Generals became members of the Presidential Council.
1983-present: Gradual relaxation of martial law to state of emergency from covering all to about 10 provinces; mainly Kurdish areas.
- Gov 1: The first direct, universal, free and secret elections in Turkey were held on 21 July 1946. This election was commonly held to be rigged, however. Reason for Termination is resignation of PM for reasons of 'ill health' after growing criticism within party ranks.
- Gov 8: 21 MPs of the 503 DP MPs formed a new party: the Freedom Party.
- Gov 9: Reason for Termination is military coup on 27 May 1960 after two months of severe tension between the government and the opposition which 'gave rise to grave fears of civil war'.
- Gov 15: Reason for Termination is split in JP. 41 MPs voted with the opposition to defeat the government on the budget.
- Gov 16: Reason for Termination is intervention by the armed forces which demanded the formation of a 'strong and credible' government capable of ending the 'anarchical situation' in the country and of realising the reforms envisaged in the 1961 constitution that was made after the military coup in 1960.

TURKEY 1946-1998

- Gov 17, 18: Type of Government is a coalition between JP (221), CHP (134) and NRP (15) plus non-parliamentory experts. PM N. Erim resigned from the CHP to become an independent. The government pledged to carry out an extensive reform program and to end political violence. A kind of national, non-political, non party government with ministers from the three last parties, non aligned MPs and non-parliamentary experts.
- Gov 19: Same Type of Government as 17+18. PM F. Melen member of NRP.
- Gov 20: Republic Reliance Party (RRP) with 43 seats in parliament is a merger between a breakaway faction of CHP and NRP under leadership of T. Feyzioğlu of the NRP.
- Gov 22: Reason for Termination is formation of a parliamentary government.
- Gov 26: Number of independent MPs supporting the government unknown. Government gained a vote of confidence on 17 January 1978.
- Gov 27: Reason for Termination is a military coup on 12 September 1980.
- Gov 30: Reason for Termination is defeat of PM in partyleadership contest and his subsequent resignation.
- Gov 32, 33: SHP includes Halkin Emek Partisi (HEP-22).
- Gov 33: Reason for Termination is merger of government party SHP with opposition party CHP (not represented in parliament) into new CHP.
- Gov 36: Type of Government is a minority coalition with alternating PM-ship.
- Gov 37: Type of Government is a minimal winning coalition with alternating PM-ship.

Gov	Deputy PM	Py	Foreign Affairs	Py	Defence	Py	Interior	Py	Justice	Py
1			Saka, H.	PP	Toydemir, C.C.	PP	Sökmensüer, Ş.	PP	Ökmen, M.	PP
2	Barutçu, F.A.	PP	Sadak, N.	PP	Birsel, M.	PP	Göle, M.H.	PP	Devrin, Ş.	.PP
3	Barutçu, F.A.	PP	Sadak, N.	PP	Çakir, H.	PP	Göle, M.H.	PP	Sirmen, F.	PP
4	Erim, N.	PP	Sadak, N.	PP	Çakir, H.	PP	Erişirgil, E.	PP	Sirmen, F.	PP
5	Ağaoğlu, S.	DP	Köprülü, F.	DP	Ince, R.S.	DP	Nasuhioğlu, R.	DP	Özyörük, H.	DP
6	Ağaoğlu, S.	DP	Köprülü, F.	DP	Köymen, H.	DP	Özyörük, H.	DP	Nasuhioğlu, R.	DP
7	Zorlu, F.R.	DP	Köprülü, F.	DP	Menderes, E.	DP	Gedik, N.	DP	Çiçekdağ, O.Ş.	DP
8			Köprülü, F.	DP	Menderes, E.	DP	Menderes, E.	DP	Göhtürk, H.A.	DP
9	İleri, T.	DP	Zorlu, F.K.	DP	Ergin, S.	DP	Gedik, N.	DP	Budakoğlu, E.	DP
10	Eyidogan, A.	JP	Sarper, S.	CHP	Sancar, I.	CHP	Topaloğlu, A.	CHP	Kurutluoğlu, S.	CHP

TURKEY 1946-1998

Gov	Deputy PM	Py	Foreign Affairs	Py	Defence	Py	Interior	Py	Justice	Py
11	Allican, E. / Dinçer, H. / Feyzioğlu, T.	NTP / RPNP / CHP	Erkin, F.C.	NONA	Sancar, I.	CHP	Kurutluoğlu, S.	CHP	Yörük, A.K.	RPNP
12	Satir, K.	CHP	Erkin, F.C.	CHP	Sancar, I.	CHP	Öztak, O.	NP	Çumrali, S.	CHP
13	Demirel, S.	JP	Işık, H.E.	NONA	Dinçer, H.	RPNP	Akdoğan, I.H.	JP	Baran, I.	RPNP
14			Çağlayangil, I.S.	JP	Topaloğlu, A.	JP	Sükan, F.	JP	Dençer, H.	JP
15			Çağlayangil, I.S.	JP	Topaloğlu, A.	JP	Menteşeoğlu, H.	JP	Önder, Y.Z.	JP
16			Çağlayangil, I.S.	JP	Topaloğlu, A.	JP	Menteşeoğlu, H.	JP	Önder, Y.Z.	JP
17	Koçaş, S. / Karaosmanoğlu, A.	CHP / NONA	Olcay, O.	NONA	Melen, F.	NRP	Ömeroğlu, H. / Kitapli, D.	NONA / JP	Arar, I.	CHP
18			Bayülken, Ü.H.	NONA	Melen, F.	NRP	Kubat, F.	NONA	Bilge, S.	NRP
19			Bayülken, Ü.H.	NONA	Izmen, M.	NONA	Kubat, F.	NONA	Alparslan, F.	NRP
20	Erkmen, N. / Satir, K.	JP / RRP	Bayülken, Ü.H.	NONA	Sancar, I.	RRP	Özetkin, M.	NONA	Mumcuoğlu, H.	NONA
21	Erbakan, N.	NSP	Güneş, T.	CHP	Işık, H.E.	CHP	Asiltürk, O.	NSP	Kazan, Ş.	NSP
22	Baykara, Z.	NONA	Esenbel, M.	NONA	Sancar, I.	RRP	Öztekin, M.	RRP	Mumcuoğlu, H.	NONA
23	Erbakan, N. / Feyzioğlu, T. / Türkeş, A.	NSP / RRP / NAP	Çağlayangil, I.S.	JP	Melen, F.	RRP	Asiltürk, O.	NSP	Müftüoğlu, I.	NSP
24	Eyüboğlu, O. / Güneş, T.	CHP / CHP	Ökçün, G.	CHP	Işık, H.E.	CHP	Uğur, N.	CHP	Elverdi, S.	CHP
25	Erbakan, N. / Türkeş, A.	NSP / NAP	Çağlayangil, I.S.	JP	Bilgiç, S.	JP	Özal, K. / Demirel, S.	NSP / JP	Cevheri, N.	JP
26	Eyüboğlu, O. / Feyzioğlu, T. / Sükan, F.	CHP / RRP / DP	Ökçün, G.	CHP	Işık, H.E.	CHP	Özaydinhi, I. / Özdemir, M.	CHP / CHP	Can, M.	CHP

TURKEY 1946-1998

Gov	Deputy PM	Py	Foreign Affairs	Py	Defence	Py	Interior	Py	Justice	Py
27			Erkmen, H.	JP	Birincioğlu, A.I.	JP	Gülcügil, M.	JP	Ucuzal, Ö.	JP
28	Erdem, K.	ANAP	Halefoğlu, V.	ANAP	Yavuztürk, Z.	ANAP	Tanriyar, A.	ANAP	Eldem, N.	ANAP
29	Erdem, K.	ANAP	Yilmaz, M.	ANAP	Vuralhan, E.	ANAP	Kalemli, M.	ANAP	Sungurlu, M.O.	ANAP
30	Bozer, A.	ANAP	Yilmaz, M.	ANAP	Giray, S.	ANAP	Aksu, A.	ANAP	Sungurlu, M.O.	ANAP
31	Pakdemitli, E.	ANAP	Giray, S.	ANAP	Doğu, H.B.	ANAP	Kalemli, M.	ANAP	Şeker, Ş.	ANAP
32	Inönü, E.	SHP	Çetin, H.	SHP	Ayaz, N.	DYP	Sezgin, I.	DYP	Oktay, M.S.	SHP
33	Inönü, E.	SHP	Çetin, H.	SHP	Ayaz, N.	DYP	Gazioğlu, B.M.	DYP	Oktay, M.S.	SHP
34	Çetin, H.	CHP	Inönü, E.	CHP	Gölhan, M.	DYP	Menteşe, N.	DYP	Moğultay, M.	CHP
35	Baykal, D.	CHP	Baykal, D.	CHP	Tanir, V.	DYP	Ünüsan, T.	NONA	Çilingiroğlu, F.	NONA
36	Menteşe, N.	DYP	Gönensay, E.	DYP	Sungurlu, M.O.	ANAP	Güney, Ü.G.	ANAP	Ağar, M.	DYP
37	*Çiller, T.	DYP	*Çiller, T.	DYP	Tayan, T.	DYP	Ağar, M.	DYP	Kazan, Ş.	Refah
38	Ecevit, B.	DSP	Cem, I.	DSP	Sezgin, I.	DSP	Maşegioğlu, M.	DYP	Sungurlu, O.	ANAP
	Sezgin, I.	DYP								

Gov	Finance	Py	Economic Aff.	Py	Labour	Py	Ediation	Py	Health	Py
1	Keşmir, H.N.	PP	Balta, T.B.	PP	Irmak, S.	PP	Sirer, R.Ş.	PP	Uz, B.	PP
2	Keşmir, H.N.	PP	Ekin, C.	PP	Balta, T.B.	PP	Sirer, R.Ş.	PP	UZ, B.	PP
	Adalan, Ş.	PP								
3	Adalan, Ş.	PP	Ekin, C.	PP	Balta, T.B.	PP	Banguoğlu, H.T.	PP	Bayazit, K.	PP
	Arişirgil, E.	PP								
4	Aksal, I.R.	PP	Boulas, C.S.	PP	Sirer, R.Ş.	PP	Banguoğlu, H.T.	PP	Bayazit, K.	PP
	Bürge, F.Ş.	PP	Sümer, N.E.	PP						

TURKEY 1946-1998

Gov	Finance	Py	Economic Aff.	Py	Labour	Py	Education	Py	Health	Py
5	Ayan, H. / Özsan, N.	DP / DP	Velibeşe, Z.	DP	Polatkan, H.	DP	Başman, A.	DP	Belger, N.R.	PP
6	Polatkan, H. / Burçak, R.S.	DP / DP	Ete, M.	DP	Özsan, N.	DP	İleri, T.	DP	Üstündağ, E.H.	DP
7	Polatkan, H. / Kalafat, E.	DP / DP	Yircali, S.	DP	Erkman, H.	DP	Yardimci, C.	DP	Uz, B.	DP
8	Ökmen, N. / Hüsman, H.	DP / DP	Ulaş, F.	DP	Tarhan, M.	DP	Özel, A.	DP	Körez, N.	DP
9	Polatkan, H. / Hüsman, H.	DP / DP	Aker, A.	DP	Erkmen, H.	DP	Yardimci, C.	DP	Kirdar, L.	DP
10	Inan, Ş. / Pulatoğlu, Ç.	CHP / JP	Gürsan, I.	JP	Ecevit, B.	CHP	Incesulu, H.	CHP	Seren, S.	JP
11	Melen, F. / Öztak, O.	CHP / CHP	Ete, M.	RPNP	Ecevit, B.	CHP	Hatipoğlu, S.R.	CHP	Azizoğlu, Y.	NTP
12	Melen, F. / Yüceler, M.	CHP / NONA	Islimyeh, F. / Göğus, A.I.	CHP / CHP	Ecevit, B.	CHP	Öktem, I.	CHP	Demir, K.	CHP
13	Gürsan, I. / Topaloğu, A.	JP / JP			Cağlayangil, I.S.	JP	Bilgehan, C.	JP	Sükan, F.	JP
14	Gürsan, I. / Tekin, I.	JP / JP			Erdem, A.N.	JP	Dengiz, O.	JP	Somunoğlu, O.E.	JP
15	Erez, M. / Birincioğlu, A.I.	JP / JP			Öztürk, S.	JP	Oğuz, O.	JP	Özkan, V.A.	JP
16	Erez, M. / Birincioğlu, A.I.	JP / JP			Öztürk, S.	JP	Oğuz, O.	JP	Özkan, V.A.	JP

TURKEY 1946-1998

Gov	Finance	Py	Economic Aff.	Py	Labour	Py	Education	Py	Health	Py
17	Ergin, S.N. / Özalp, H.	NONA / NONA		NONA / NONA	Sav, A.	NONA	Orel, Ş.	NONA	*Akyd, T.	NONA
18	Ergin, S.N. / Özalp, H.	NONA / JP			Uzuner, A.R.	CHP	Arar, I. / Erez, M.	CHP / JP	Aykan, C.	NONA
19	Müezzinoğlu, Z. / Ozalp, H.	NONA / JP	Talü N.	NONA / JP	Uzuner, A.R.	CHP	Özbek, S. / Erez, M.	NONA / JP	Demir, K.	CHP
20	Müftüoğlu, S.T. / Çelikbaş, F.	JP / NONA	Türkel, A.	JP / NONA	Erdem, A.N.	JP	Dengiz, O. / Bayar, N.	JP / JP	Tanir, V.	RRP
21	Baykal, D. / Türkmenoğlu, M.	CHP / CHP	Adak, F.	CHP / CHP	Sav, Ö.	NSP	Üstündağ, M. / Doğru, A.	CHP / NSP		
22	Gürsay, B. / Tuncer, B.	NONA / NONA	Cillov, H.	NONA / NONA	Essener, T.	NONA	Reisoğlu, S. / Gölhan, M.	NONA / NONA	Demir, K.	RRP
23	Egenekon, Y. / Öztak, O.	JP / RRP	Başol, H.	JP / RRP	Paksu, A.T.	NSP	Erdem, A.N. / Doğru, A.	JP / NSP	Demir, K.	RRP
24	Üstünel, B. / Can, M.	CHP / CHP	Müezzinoğlu, Z.	CHP / CHP	Ersoy, B.	CHP	Üstündağ, M. / Erdem, T.	CHP / CHP	Ertuğ, C.	CHP
25	Bilgehan, C. / Sazak, G.	JP / NAP		JP / NAP	Cumalioğlu, I.F.	NSP	Menteşe, N. / Asiltürk, O.	JP / NSP	Gölkçek, C.	NAP
26	Müezzinoğlu, Z. / Mataraci, T.	CHP / NONA	Köprülüler, T.	CHP / NONA	Ersoy, B.	CHP	Uğur, N. / Alp, O.	CHP / NONA	Tan, M.	NONA
27	Sezgin, I. / Çakmak, A.	JP / JP	Başol, H.	JP / JP	Erdemir, C.	JP	Fersoy, O.C. / Bayar, N.	JP / JP	Islamoğlu, M.	JP
28	Arikan, V.	ANAP		ANAP	Kalemli, M.	ANAP	Dinçerler, V.	ANAP	Aydin, M.	ANAP
29	Özal, Y.B. / Alptemocin, A.K.	ANAP / ANAP	Özal, Y.B.	ANAP / ANAP	*Aykut, I.	ANAP	Güzel, H.C.	ANAP	Akarcali, B.	ANAP
30	Pakdemirli, E.	ANAP		ANAP	*Aykut, I.	ANAP	Akyol, A.	ANAP	Şivgin, H.	ANAP

TURKEY 1946-1998

Gov	Finance	Py	Economic Aff.	Py	Labour	Py	Ediation	Py	Health	Py
31	Kahveci, A.	ANAP			Emiroğlu, M.	ANAP	Akyol, A.	ANAP	Eryilmaz, Y.	ANAP
32	Oral, S.	DYP	*Çiller, T.	DYP	Moğultay, M.	DYP	Toptan, K.	DYP	Aktuna, Y.	DYP
33	Attila, I.	DYP			Moğultay, M.	DYP	Menteşe, N.	DYP	Serdaroğlu, R.	DYP
34	Attila, I.	DYP			Gürkan, A.G.	CHP	Ayaz, N.	CHP	Baran, D.	DYP
35	Attila, I.	DYP			Kul, M.	CHP	Tayan, T.	CHP	Baran, D.	DYP
36	Kayalar, L.	ANAP			Kul, E.	ANAP	Tayan, T.	ANAP	Aktuna, Y.	DYP
37	Şener, A.	Refah			Çelik, N.	Refah	Sağlam, M.	Refah	Aktuna, Y.	DYP
38	Temizel, Z.	DSP			Çağan, N.	DSP	Uluğbay, H.	DSP	Özsoy, H.I.	ANAP

Gov	Housing	Py	Agriculture	Py	Industry/Trade	Py	Environment	Py
1			Kurdoglu, F.	PP	Inan, A.	PP		
2			Coşkan, T.	PP	Gündüzalp, M.N.	PP		
3			Oral, C.	PP	Barlas, C.S.	PP		
4			Oral, C.	PP	Barlas, C.S.	PP		
5			İriboz, N.	DP	Velibeşe, Z. Ete, M.	DP		
6			Ökmen, N.	DP	Ete, M. Gedik, H.	DP		
7			Ökmen, N.	DP	Yircali, S. Çelikbaş, F.	DP		
8			Budakoğlu, E.	DP	Ulaş, F. Ağaoğlu, S.	DP		
9			Ökmen, N.	DP	Ağaoğlu, S.	DP		

TURKEY 1946-1998

Gov	Housing	Py	Agriculture	Py	Industry/Trade	Py	Environment	Py
10	Güven, M.	JP	Oral, C.	JP	Çelikbaş, F.	CHP		
11	Gökay, F.K.	NTP	Izmen, M.	NTP	Ete, M.	RPNP		
12			Şahin, T.	CHP	Erten, M.	CHP		
13	İskenderoğlu, R.	NTP	Kapanli, T.	NTP	Zeren, M.	JP		
					Erdem, A.N.	JP		
14	Mentesoğlu, H.	JP	Deağdaş, B.	JP	Zeren, M.	JP		
					Turgut, M.	JP		
15	Nakipoğlu, H.	JP	Ertem, I.	JP	Dalli, A.	JP		
			Özalp, H.	JP	Kiliç, S.	JP		
16	Nakipoğlu, H.	JP	Ertem, I.	JP	Kiliç, S.	JP		
			Özalp, H.	JP				
17	Babüroğlu, S.	NONA	Dikmen, O.	NONA	Derbil, Ö.	NONA		
			Inal, S.	NONA	Çilingiroğlu, A.	NONA		
18	Bingöl, S.	NONA	Dikmen, O.	NONA	Talü N.	NONA		
			Inal, S.	NONA	Erez, M.	JP		
19	Toker, T.	JP	Karaöz, T.	JP	Erez, M.	JP		
			Inal, S.	NONA				
20	Oktay, M.N.	RRP	Tuna, A.N.	JP	Bayar, N.	JP		
			Bingöl, I.	JP				
21	Topuz, A.	CHP	Özal, K.	NSP	Doğru, A.	NSP		
			Şener, A.	CHP				
22	Babüroğlu, S.	RRP	Aktan, R.	NONA	Gölhan, M.	NONA		
			Saatçioğlu, F.	NONA				
23	Ok, N.	JP	Özal, K.	NSP	Doğru, A.	NSP		
			Kapanli, T.	JP				

TURKEY 1946-1998

Gov	Housing	Py	Agriculture	Py	Industry/Trade	Py	Environment	Py
24	Tüer, E.	CHP	Gündoğan, F. / İlhan, V.	CHP / CHP	Erdem, T.	CHP		
25	Kutan, M.R.	NSP	Adak, F. / Savli, S.	NSP / NSP	Güner, A.O. / Asiltürk, O.	JP / NSP		
26	Karaaslan, A.	NONA	Yüceler, M. / İlhan, V.	CHP / CHP	Alp, O. / Bulutoğlu, K.	NONA / CHP		
27	Toker, T.	JP	Külahli, C. / Ekinci, H.	JP / JP	Bayar, N.	JP		
28	Giray, S.	ANAP	Doğan, H.	ANAP	Aral, C.	ANAP		
29	Giray, S.	ANAP	Doğan, H.	ANAP	Yürür, Ş.	ANAP		
30	Altinkaya, C.	ANAP	Kayalar, L.	ANAP	Yürür, Ş.	ANAP		
31	Örüç, H.	ANAP	Tuncay, İ.	ANAP	Yücelen, R.K.	ANAP		
32	Kumbaracibasi, O.	SHP	Cevheri, N.	DYP	Köse, M.T.	SHP	Akyürek, B.D.	DYP
33	Kumbaracibasi, O.	SHP	Şahin, R.	DYP	Köse, M.T.	SHP	Akçali, R.	DYP
34	Şahin, E.	CHP	Şahin, R. / Ekinå, H.	DYP / DYP	Akyoe, H.	CHP	Akçali, R.	DYP
35	Keskin, A.	CHP	Kurt, N. / Ekinci, H.	DYP / DYP	Çay, F.	CHP	Üçpinarlar, A.H.	DYP
36	Keçeciler, M.	ANAP	Attila, İ. / Ercan, N.	DYP / DYP	Erez, Y.	DYP	Taşar, M.R.	ANAP
37	Ayhan, C.	Refah	Demirci, M. / Dağli, M.H.	Refah / DYP	Erez, Y.	DYP	Tokar, Z.	Refah
38	Topçu, Y.	ANAP	Taşar, M. / Taranoğlu, E.	ANAP / ANAP	Erez, Y.	IND	*Aykut, İ.	ANAP

TURKEY 1946-1998

Gov	Social Affairs (py)	Public Works (py)	Other (py)	Res
1		İncedayı, C.K. (PP) Koçak, Ş. (PP)		1
2		Gülek, K. (PP) Koçak, Ş. (PP)	Bacutçu, F.A. (PP) Renda, M.A. (PP)	0
3		Gülek, K. (PP) Erim, N. (PP)	Barutçu, F.A. (PP)	0
4		Adalan, Ş. (PP) Satir, K. (PP)		1
5	Belger, N.R. (DP)	Belen, F. (DP) İleri, T. (DP)	Ağaoğlu, S. (DP)	1
6	Üstündağ, E.H. (DP)	Zeytinoğlu, K. (DP) Kurtbek, S. (DP)	İnce, R.Ş. (DP)	4
7	Uz, B. (DP)	Zeytinoğlu, K. (DP) Çavuşoğlu, M. (DP)	Zorlu, F.R. (DP) Sarol, M. (DP) Kapani, O. (DP)	3
8		Çavuşoğlu, M. (DP) Demirer, A. (DP)	Bengü, M.C. (DP) Kalafat, E. (DP) Ergin, Ş. (DP) Yardimci, C. (DP)	5
9	Kirdar, L. (DP)	Menderes, E. (DP) Uçaner, F. (DP) Yircali, S. (DP) Berk, M. (DP)	İleri, T. (DP) Kalafat, E. (DP) Kurbanoğlu, M. (DP) Yircali, S. (DP)	6

TURKEY 1946-1998

Gov	Social Affairs (py)	Public Works (py)	Other (py)	Res
10		Paksüt, E. (CHP) Evyaoğlu, K. (JP) Akyar, C. (JP) Güven, M. (JP)	Feyzioğlu, T. (CHP) Doğan, A. (CHP) Ökten, N. (JP) Su, N. (JP) Evliyaoğlu, K. (JP)	0
11	Azizoğlu, Y. (NTP)	Seçkin, I. (CHP) Karasapan, C. (RPNP) Öçten, R. (NTP) Gökay, F.K. (NTP)	Aybar, R. (NTP) Bekata, H.O. (CHP) Ökten, N. (NONA) Karasapan, C. (RPNP)	3
12		Onat, A.H. (CHP) Alpiskender, F. (NONA) Uzer, C. (CHP) Oral, H. (CHP)	Satir, K. (CHP) Yolaç, M. (NONA) Omay, I.S. (CHP) Pirinçcioğlu, V. (CHP) Goçguş, A.T. (CHP) Yurdoğlu, L. (CHP)	1
13	Sükan, F. (JP)	Alp, O. (NONA) San, M. (NTP) Turgut, M. (JP) Iskenderoğlu, R. (NTP)	Ataman, H. (NP) Altinsoy, M. (RPNP) Inal, Ş. (NTP) Dorman, Ö.Z. (NP) Öztürk, S. (RPNP)	1
14	Smunoğlu, O.E. (JP)	Erdinç, E. (JP) Öztürk, S. (JP) Deriner, I. (JP) Menteşoğlu, H. (JP)	Bilgehan, C. (JP) Sezgin, R. (JP) Ocak, K. (JP) Alişan, A.F. (JP) Kürşad, N. (JP) Avcı, S.O. (JP)	4

532

TURKEY 1946-1998

Gov	Social Affairs (py)	Public Works (py)	Other (py)	Res
15	Özkan, V.A. (JP) Sezgin, I. (JP)	Gülez, T. (JP) Menteşe, N. (JP) Avcı, S.O. (JP) Nakipoğlu, H. (JP)	Titrek, G. (JP) Atabeyli, H. (JP) Bilgin, T. (JP) Sezgin, R. (JP) Cevheri, N. (JP) Kapanli, T. (JP)	0
16	Özkan, V.A. (JP) Sezgin, I. (JP)	Gülez, T. (JP) Menteşe, N. (JP) Avcı, S.O. (JP) Nakipoğlu, H. (JP)	Titrek, G. (JP) Atabeyli, H. (JP) Bilgin, T. (JP) Sezgin, R. (JP) Cevheri, N. (JP) Kapanli, T. (JP)	0
17	*Akyol, T. (NONA) Ergun, S. (JP)	Karakaş, C. (JP) Arik, H. (NONA) Topaloğlu, I. (CHP) Babüroğlu, S. (NONA)	Koçaş, S. (CHP) Karaosmanoğlu, A. (NONA) Özgunes, M. (NONA) Kitapli, D. (JP) Akçal, E.Y. (JP) Aykan, C. (NONA) Halan, T. (NONA)	1
18	Aykan, C. (NONA) Karaküçük, A. (JP)	Öztekin, M. (CHP) Danişman, R. (JP) Devres, N. (NONA) Bingöl, S. (NONA)	Kitapli, D. (JP) Göğüs, A.T. (CHP) Karagöz, I. (JP) Öztak, I. (NONA) Akçal, E.Y. (JP) Sönmez, N. (NONA)	0

TURKEY 1946-1998

Gov	Social Affairs (py)	Public Works (py)	Other (py)	Res
19	Demir, K. (CHP) Karakücük, A. (JP)	Öztekin, M. (CHP) Danişman, R. (JP) Kodamanoğlu, N. (CHP) Toker, T. (JP)	Kitapli, D. (JP) Arrar, I. (CHP) Baykara, Z. (NONA) Öztak, I. (NONA) Akçal, E.Y. (JP) Sönmez, N. (NONA)	0
20	Tanir, V. (RRP) Coşkun, C. (JP)	Ok, N. (JP) Özbek, S. (NONA) Demir, K. (RRP) Oktay, M.N. (RRP)	Erkmen, N. (JP) Satir, K. (RRP) Tekinel, I.H. (JP) Öztak, I. (NONA) Kirimli, A.I. (JP) Kürümoğlu, O. (JP)	0
21	Cizrelioğlu, S. (CHP) Mele, M.Y. (CHP)	Çevikçe, E. (CHP) Güley, F. (CHP) Kayra, C. (CHP) Topuz, A. (CHP)	Erbakan, N. (NSP) Eyüboğlu, O. (CHP) Birler, I.H. (CHP) Emne, S.A. (NSP) Birgit, O. (CHP) Ok, M. (CHP)	0
22	Demir, K. (RRP) Baloğlu, Z. (RRP) Şide, S. (RRP)	Tanir, V. (NONA) Özbek, S. (NONA) Işil, E. (NONA) Babüroğlu, S. (RRP)	Baykara, Z. (NONA) Özgüneş, M. (NONA) Fer, M. (NONA) Yildiz, S. (NONA) Evliyaoğlu, I.H. (NONA) *Neftçi, N. (RRP)	0

TURKEY 1946-1998

Gov	Social Affairs (py)	Public Works (py)	Other (py)	Res
23	Demir, K. (RRP) Erek, A.Ş. (JP) Ablum, A.M. (JP)	Adak, F. (NSP) Menteşe, N. (JP) Kiliç, S. (JP) Ok, N. (JP)	Öztürk, S. (JP) Aksay, H. (NSP) Erkovan, M.K. (NAP) Karaca, G. (JP) Tokoğlu, L. (JP) Poyraz, V. (JP) Danişman, R. (JP)	1
24	Ertuğ, C. (CHP) Çakmur, Y. (CHP) Uysal, H. (CHP)	Zilan, A.K. (NONA) Çevikçe, E. (CHP) Akmandor, N. (CHP) Tuncer, E. (CHP)	Eyüboğlu, O. (CHP) Güneş, T. (CHP) Doğan, L. (CHP) Bulutoğlu, K. (CHP) Üstündağ, M. (CHP) Öymen, A. (CHP) Topuz, A. (CHP)	0
25	Gökçek, C. (NAP) Şakar, Ö. (JP) Kapanlí, T. (JP)	Kuliç, S. (JP) Ergenekon, Y. (JP) Inan, K. (JP) Kutan, M.R. (NSP)	Erbakan, N. (NSP) Türkeş, A. (NAP) Öztürk, S. (JP) Emre, S.A. (NSP) Somuncoğlu, S. (NAP) Erek, A.S. (JP) Ege, A.S. (JP) Yücel, T. (JP) Akyol, A. (JP)	2

TURKEY 1946-1998

Gov	Social Affairs (py)	Public Works (py)	Other (py)	Res
26	Tan, M. (NONA)	Elçi, Ş. (NONA)	Eyüboğlu, O. (CHP)	6
	Çakmur, Y. (CHP)	Öngüt, G. (NONA)	Feyzioğlu, T. (RRP)	
	İşgüzar, H. (NONA)	Baykal, D. (CHP)	Sükan, F. (DP)	
		Karaaslan, A. (NONA)	Akova, E. (NONA)	
			Yıldız, S. (RRP)	
			Doğan, L. (CHP)	
			Septioğlu, A.R. (NONA)	
			Kiliç, M. (NONA)	
			Şener, A. (CHP)	
			Çetin, H. (CHP)	
			Coşkun, A. (CHP)	
			Topuz, A. (CHP)	
			Kişlaki, A.T. (CHP)	
27	İslamoğlu, M. (JP)	Kiliç, S. (JP)	Eren, O. (JP)	0
	Asal, T. (JP)	Özalp, H. (JP)	Ceyhun, E. (JP)	
	Oral, S. (JP)	Kiratlioğlu, E. (JP)	Kelleci, M. (JP)	
		Toker, T. (JP)	Karahan, A. (JP)	
			Musoğlu, M. (JP)	
			Toptan, K. (JP)	
			Küntay, B. (JP)	
			Koraltan, T. (JP)	

TURKEY 1946-1998

Gov	Social Affairs (py)	Public Works (py)	Other (py)	Res
28	Dinçerler, V. (ANAP) Aydın, M. (ANAP) Kalemli, M. (ANAP)	Giray, S. (ANAP) Atasoy, V. (ANAP) Büyükbaş, C. (ANAP)	Erdem, K. (ANAP) Oksay, K. (ANAP) Yılmaz, M. (ANAP) Türel, S.N. (ANAP) Teneci, A. (ANAP) Özdağlar, I. (ANAP) Alptemoçin, A.K. (ANAP) Doğan, H. (ANAP) Taşıoğlu, M. (ANAP) Bozer, A. (ANAP)	5
29	Güzel, H.C. (ANAP) Akarcali, B. (ANAP) *Aykut, I. (ANAP)	Giray, S. (ANAP) Pakdemirki, E. (ANAP) Kurt, F. (ANAP)	Erdem, K. (ANAP) Oksay, K. (ANAP) Tenekeci, A. (ANAP) Atasoy, V. (ANAP) Bozer, A. (ANAP) Özal, Y.B. (ANAP) Kahveci, A. (ANAP) Yazar, M. (ANAP) Çiçek, C. (ANAP) Doğan, H. (ANAP) Titiz, M.T. (ANAP)	2

TURKEY 1946-1998

Gov	Social Affairs (py)	Public Works (py)	Other (py)	Res
30	Akyol, A. (ANAP)	Altinkaya, C. (ANAP)	Bozer, A. (ANAP)	0
	Sivgin, H. (ANAP)	Tuncer, C. (ANAP	Taner, G. (ANAP)	
	*Aykut, I. (ANAP)	Kurt, F. (ANAP)	Özarslan, I. (ANAP)	
			Inan, K. (ANAP)	
			Konukman, E. (ANAP)	
			Yazar, M. (ANAP)	
			Çiçek, C. (ANAP)	
			Kayalar, L. (ANAP)	
			Zaybek, N.K. (ANAP)	
			Aküzüm, I. (ANAP)	
			Keçeciler, M. (ANAP)	
			Taşar, M.R. (ANAP)	
			Doğvan, M.R. (ANAP)	
			Çelebi, I. (ANAP)	
			Dinçerder, V.M. (ANAP)	
			Özdemir, I. (ANAP)	
			Akkrayd, K. (ANAP)	
			Örüç, H. (ANAP)	

TURKEY 1946-1998

Gov	Social Affairs (py)	Public Works (py)	Other (py)	Res
31	Emiroğlu, M. (ANAP)	Örüç, H. (ANAP) Özdemir, I. (ANAP) Arici, M. (ANAP)	Pakdemirli, E. (ANAP) Kurt, F. (ANAP) Taşar, M.R. (ANAP) *Aykut, I. (ANAP) Dinçerler, V.M. (ANAP) Inan, K. (ANAP) Aküzüm, I. (ANAP) Tuncer, C. (ANAP) Aras, S. (ANAP) Koçak, E. (ANAP) Çevik, M. (ANAP) Gülpinar, E.C. (ANAP) Sönmez, B. (ANAP) Özdemir, A.T. (ANAP) Tuncay, I. (ANAP) Maraş, G. (ANAP) Akarcali, B. (ANAP)	1

TURKEY 1946-1998

Gov	Social Affairs (py)	Public Works (py)	Other (py)	Res
32	Moğultay, M. (DYP)	Kumbaracıbaşı, O. (SHP)	*Çiller, T. (DYP)	0
		Topçu, Y. (DYP)	Cevheri, N. (DYP)	
		Faralyalí, E. (DYP)	Sağlar, D.F. (SHP)	
			Ateş, A. (SHP)	
			Kahraman, M. (SHP)	
			Çağlar, C. (DYP)	
			Ceyhun, E.E. (DYP)	
			Tez, I. (SHP)	
			Gönen, A. (SHP)	
			Ergenekon, G. (DYP)	
			Kilercioğlu, O.S. (DYP)	
			Barutçu, Ö. (DYP)	
			Yılmaz, M.A. (DYP)	
			Şahlin, E. (SHP)	
			Ercan, Ş. (DYP)	
			Batalli, M. (DYP)	
			Tanír, V. (DYP)	

TURKEY 1946-1998

Gov	Social Affairs (py)	Public Works (py)	Other (py)	Res
33	Moğultay, M. (SHP)	Kumbaracıbasi, O. (SHP)	İnönü, E. (SHP)	5
		Köstepen, M. (DYP)	Alagöz, B. (SHP)	
		Atasoy, V. (DYP)	Cevheri, N. (DYP)	
			Aktuna, Y. (DYP)	
			Gölhan, M. (DYP)	
			Tez, I. (SHP)	
			Daçe, B.S. (DYP)	
			Akyol, T. (SHP)	
			Müftüoğlu, G. (DYP)	
			Kurt, N. (DYP)	
			Kahraman, M. (SHP)	
			Erhan, C. (DYP)	
			Çiloğlu, M. (DYP)	
			Şahin, E. (SHP)	
			Şanal, A. (DYP)	
			Erdem, Ş. (DYP)	
			Şahin, R. (DYP)	
			Sağlar, D.F. (SHP)	
			Ateş, A. (SHP)	

TURKEY 1946-1998

Gov	Social Affairs (py)	Public Works (py)	Other (py)	Res
34	Gürkan, A.G. (CHP)	Şahin, E. (CHP)	Çetin, H. (CHP)	1
		Köstepen, M. (DYP)	Cevheri, N. (DYP)	
		Atasoy, V. (DYP)	Aktuna, Y. (DYP)	
			Erek, A.Ş. (DYP)	
			Kumbaracibaşi, O. (CHP)	
			Baykal, A. (CHP)	
			Gökdemir, A. (DYP)	
			Kurt, N. (DYP)	
			Hacaloğlu, A. (CHP)	
			Doğan, A.A. (DYP)	
			Ataç, A. (DYP)	
			Halis, Z. (CHP)	
			Kiratlioğlu, E. (DYP)	
			Erdem, Ş. (DYP)	
			Şahin, R. (DYP)	
			Karakaş, E. (CHP)	
			Gürpinar, I. (CHP)	

TURKEY 1946-1998

Gov	Social Affairs (py)	Public Works (py)	Other (py)	Res
35	Kul, M. (CHP)	Keskin, A. (CHP)	Cevheri, N. (DYP)	0
		Tezmen, O. (NONA)	Çağlar, C. (DYP)	
		Altiner, Ş. (NONA)	Ateş, A. (CHP)	
			Doğan, A.A. (DYP)	
			Dinçer, A. (CHP)	
			Gökdemir, A. (DYP)	
			Islamoğlu, A.M. (DYP)	
			Ekmen, M.A. (CHP)	
			Kirca, A.C. (DYP)	
			Banitçu, Ö. (DYP)	
			Sevigen, M. (CHP)	
			*Saygin, I. (DYP)	
			Alp, M. (CHP)	
			Ensarioğlu, M.S. (DYP)	
			Daçe, B.S. (DYP)	
			Kurt, N. (DYP)	
			Sağlar, D.F. (CHP)	
			Gürpinar, I. (CHP)	

TURKEY 1946-1998

Gov	Social Affairs (py)	Public Works (py)	Other (py)	Res
36	Kul, E. (ANAP)	Keçeciler, M. (ANAP)	Menteşe, N. (DYP)	0
		Barutçu, Ö. (DYP)	Saracoğlu, R. (ANAP)	
		Doğan, H. (ANAP)	Yılmaz, A. (DYP)	
			Aksu, A. (ANAP)	
			Söylemez, U. (DYP)	
			Aşik, E. (ANAP)	
			Törüner, Y. (DYP)	
			*Aykut, I. (ANAP)	
			Gökdemir, A. (DYP)	
			Çiçek, C. (ANAP)	
			Dedelek, I.Y. (DYP)	
			Özdemir, A.T. (ANAP)	
			Erkan, Ü. (DYP)	
			Taranoğlu, E. (ANAP)	
			Dağli, M.H. (DYP)	
			Attila, I. (DYP)	
			Güner, A.O. (ANAP)	
			*Saygin, I. (DYP)	

TURKEY 1946-1998

Gov	Social Affairs (py)	Public Works (py)	Other (py)	Res
37	Çelik, N. (Refah)	Ayham, C. (Refah) Barutçu, Ö. (DYP) Kutan, M.R. (Refah)	Adak, F. (Refah) Ercan, N. (DYP) Gül, A. (Refah) *Saygin, I. (DYP) Tekir, S. (Refah) Kurt, N. (DYP) Altimsoy, M. (Refah) Zeybek, N.K. (DYP) Esengün, L. (Refah) Ensarioğlu, M.S. (DYP) Tunç, A.C. (Refah) Aksoy, B. (DYP) Dağdaş, G. (Refah) Söylemez, U. (DYP) Güneri, T.R. (Refah) Yilmaz, A. (DYP) Günbey, S. (Refah) Şeker, B. (DYP) Demircan, A. (Refah) Demirci, M. (Refah) Kahraman, I. (Refah) Yücel, B. (DYP)	0

TURKEY 1946-1998

Gov	Social Affairs (py)	Public Works (py)	Other (py)	Res
38	Çağan, N. (DSP)	Topçu, Y. (ANAP)	Taner, G. (ANAP)	
		Menzir, N. (DYP)	Özkan, H. (DSP)	
		Ersümer, C. (ANAP)	Seçkiner, Y. (ANAP)	
			Saygin, Y. (ANAP)	
			Türk, B.S. (DSP)	
			Yildirim, S. (ANAP)	
			Serdaroğlu, R. (DYP)	
			Gürdere, M. (ANAP)	
			Gürel, S.S. (DSP)	
			Andican, A. (ANAP)	
			Çelebi, I. (ANAP)	
			Yilmaz, M. (DSP)	
			Şahin, R. (DYP)	
			Kara, B. (ANAP)	
			Kavak, C. (ANAP)	
			Aşik, E. (ANAP)	
			Yücelen, R.K. (ANAP)	
			Gemici, H. (DSP)	
			Batalli, M. (DYP)	
			Talay, I. (DSP)	
			Gürdal, I. (ANAP)	

49. UNITED KINGDOM

The United Kingdom of Great Britain and Northern Ireland is a constitutional Monarchy, albeit without a written constitution.

The State is unitary, legislatively very centralised, but administratively very decentralised.

Parliament is bi-cameral, but with a weak unelected Upper House (House of Lords). The membership of the House of Lords is around 1200 at present, but plans for reform are under way.

The House of Commons has 650 seats, and sits for a flexible term of a maximum of five years. Elections are by plurality voting in single member constituencies of about 60,000 electors.

The House of Commons has a quorum of 40 members, the House of Lords of 30 members. Votes, also on constitutional amendments, are carried by a majority of all votes cast. A consultative referendum is optional and may be called by the government.

The main political executive is the Prime Minister and the Cabinet who dominate the majority party in the House of Commons through strong internal discipline. The government party usually rests on an absolute majority in the House of Commons, but it can get by with a relative majority as well, depending on the divisions between the main opposition party and the others. No special vote of investiture is needed to confirm the government. During its lifetime a government may face a vote of no confidence. Losing a vote of confidence always results in resignation of the government and probably a new General Election, which the Prime Minister can call at any time. The government is very large: over 100 members. It is co-ordinated and directed by the Cabinet, averaging about twenty Ministers. The government is both collectively and individually responsible to parliament. Ministers have to be either MPs or Peers (Members of the House of Lords). The Prime Minister has a dominant position in Cabinet and government.

There is no Constitutional Court as such. However, judges often informally reinterpret legislation in terms of what Parliament 'must have' intended. British courts accept decisions of the European Court of Justice as binding, when it rules that British legislation or government decisions go against the founding treaties. In that sense the European Court of Justice is a constitutional court for Britain.

UNITED KINGDOM 1945–1998

Gov	Begin	Dur	RfT	ToG	Py1	Seats	CPG	NoM	Prime Minister (py)
1	26.07.45	1678	1	1	LAB 392	640	4	33	Atlee, C.R. (LAB)
2	28.02.50	605	1	1	LAB 315	625	4	18	Atlee, C.R. (LAB)
3	26.10.51	1258	2	1	CON 321	625	2	16	Churchill, W. (CON)
4	06.04.55	51	1	1	CON 345	630	2	17	Eden, A. (CON)
5	27.05.55	594	3	1	CON 345	630	2	17	Eden, A. (CON)
6	10.01.57	1008	1	1	CON 365	630	2	18	MacMillan, H. (CON)
7	15.10.59	1465	3	1	CON 365	630	2	19	Macmillan, H. (CON)
8	19.10.63	364	1	1	CON 365	630	2	23	Douglas-Home, A. (CON)
9	17.10.64	536	1	1	LAB 317	630	4	23	Wilson, H. (LAB)
10	06.04.66	1536	1	1	LAB 363	630	4	23	Wilson, H. (LAB)
11	20.06.70	1354	1	1	CON 330	630	2	18	Heath, E. (CON)
12	05.03.74	227	1	4	LAB 301	635	4	20	Wilson, H. (LAB)
13	18.10.74	536	2	1	LAB 319	635	4	23	Wilson, H. (LAB)
14	06.04.76	1124	1	1	LAB 319	635	4	16	Callaghan, J. (LAB)
15	05.05.79	1499	1	1	CON 339	635	2	22	*Thatcher, M. (CON)
16	12.06.83	1462	1	1	CON 397	650	2	21	*Thatcher, M. (CON)
17	13.06.87	1264	2	1	CON 367	650	2	21	*Thatcher, M. (CON)
18	28.11.90	500	1	1	CON 376	650	2	22	Major, J. (CON)
19	11.04.92		1	1	CON 336	651	2	23	Major, J. (CON)
20	07.05.97		1	1	LAB 418	659	4	22	Blair, T. (LAB)

- Gov 20: Key non-cabinet posts were occupied by Brown, N. (Parliamentary Secretary to the Treasury and Government Chief Whip), Mandelson, P. (Minister without portfolio in the Cabinet Office) and Morris, J. (Attorney General).

UNITED KINGDOM 1945-1998

Gov	Deputy PM	Py	Foreign Affairs	Py	Defence	Py	Interior	Py	Justice	Py
1			Bevin, E.	LAB	Lawson, J.J.	LAB	Chutor Ede, J.	LAB	Jowitt, W.	LAB
					Alexander, A.V.	LAB			Shawcross, H.	LAB
					Stansgate, Visc.	LAB			Soskice, F.	LAB
					Barns, A.	LAB				
					Atlee, C.R.	LAB				
2			Bevin, E.	LAB	Shinwell, E.	LAB	Chutor Ede, J.	LAB	Jowitt, Visc.	LAB
3			Eden, A.	CON	Churchill, W.	CON	Maxwell Fyfe, D.	CON	Simonds, Lord	CON
							MacMillan, H.	CON		
4			MacMillan, H.	CON	Lloyd, J.S.	CON	Lloyd-George, G.	CON	Kilmuir, Visc.	CON
							Sandys, D.	CON		
5			MacMillan, H.	CON	Lloyd, J.S.	CON	Lloyd-George, G.	CON	Kilmuir, Visc.	CON
							Sandys, D.	CON		
6			Lloyd, J.S.	CON	Sandys, D.	CON	Butler, R.A.	CON	Kilmuir, Visc.	CON
							Brooke, H.	CON		
7			Lloyd, J.S.	CON	Watkinson, H.	CON	Butler, R.A.	CON	Kilmuir, Lord	CON
							Brooke, H.	CON		
8			Butler, R.A.	CON	Thorneycroft, P.	CON	Brooke, H.	CON	Dilhorne, Lord	CON
							Joseph, K.	CON		
9			Gordon Walker, P.	LAB	Healey, D.	LAB	Soskice, F.	LAB	Gardiner, Lord	LAB
							Crossman, R.	LAB		
10			Stewart, M.	LAB	Healey, D.	LAB	Jenkins, R.	LAB	Gardiner, Lord	LAB
							Crossman, R.	LAB		
11			Douglas-Home, A.	CON	Carrington, Lord	CON	Maudling, R.	CON	Hogg, Q.	CON
							Walker, P.	CON		
12			Calaghan, J.	LAB	Mason, R.	LAB	Short, E.	LAB	Jones, E.	LAB
13			Calaghan, J.	LAB	Mason, R.	LAB	Shepherd, Lord	LAB	Jones, E.	LAB
							Silkin, J.	LAB		

UNITED KINGDOM 1945–1998

Gov	Deputy PM	Py	Foreign Affairs	Py	Defence	Py	Interior	Py	Justice	Py
14			Crosland, A.	LAB	Mason, R.	LAB	Jenkins, R.	LAB	Jones, E.	LAB
15			Carrington, Lord	CON	Pym, F.	CON	Whitelaw, W.	CON	Hailsham of M., Lord	CON
16			Howe, G.	CON	Heseltine, M.	CON	Brittan, L. *Thatcher, M.	CON CON	Hailsham of M., Lord	CON
17			Howe, G.	CON	Younger, G.	CON	Hurd, D. *Thatcher, M.	CON CON	Havers, Lord	CON
18			Hurd, D.	CON	King, T.	CON	Baker, K. Major, J.	CON CON	Mackay of Glashfern, Lord	CON
19			Hurd, D.	CON	Rifkind, M.	CON	Clarke, K. Major, J.	CON CON	Mackay of Glashfern, Lord	CON
20	Prescott, J.	LAB	Cook, R.	LAB	Robertson, G.	LAB	Straw, J. Blair, T.	LAB LAB	Irvine of Lairg, Lord	LAB

Gov	Finance	Py	Economic Aff.	Py	Labour	Py	Education	Py	Health	Py
1	Dalton, H. Atlee, C.R.	LAB LAB			Isaacs, G.	LAB	*Wilkinson, E.	LAB	Bevan, A.	LAB
2	Cripps, S.	LAB			Isaacs, G.	LAB	Tomlinson, G.	LAB	Bevan, A.	LAB
3	Butler, R.A.	CON			Monckton, W.	CON			Crookshank, H.F.C.	CON
4	Butler, R.A.	CON			Monckton, W.	CON	Eccles, D.	CON		
5	Butler, R.A.	CON			Monckton, W.	CON	Eccles, D.	CON		
6	Thorneycroft, P.	CON			MacLeod, I.	CON	Hailsham, Lord	CON		
7	Heathcoat A., D. Mills, Lord Macmillan, H.	CON CON CON	Heath, E.	CON	Eccles, D. Hailsham, Lord	CON CON				

UNITED KINGDOM 1945–1998

Gov	Finance	Py	Economic Aff.	Py	Labour	Py	Education	Py	Health	Py
8	Maudling, R. Boyd-Carpenter, J.	CON CON	Godber, J.	CON	Boyle, E. Barber, A.	CON				
9	Callaghan, J.	LAB	Brown, G.	LAB	Gunter, R.	LAB	Stewart, M. Cousins, F.	LAB LAB		
10	Callaghan, J.	LAB	Brown, G.	LAB	Gunter, R.	LAB	Crosland, A. Cousins, F.	LAB LAB		
11	MacLeod, I.	CON			Carr, R.	CON	*Thatcher, M. Rippon, G.	CON CON		
12	Jenkins, R.	LAB			Foot, M.	LAB	Prentice, R.	LAB		
13	Jenkins, R.	LAB			Foot, M.	LAB	Prentice, R.	LAB		
14	Healey, D.	LAB			Booth, A.	LAB	Mulley, F.	LAB		
15	Howe, G. Biffen, J.	CON CON			Prior, J.	CON	Carlisle, M.	CON		
16	Lawson, N. Rees, P. *Thatcher, M.	CON CON CON			Tebbit, N.	CON	Joseph, K.	CON		
17	Lawson, N. Major, J. *Thatcher, M.	CON CON CON			Fowler, N.	CON	Baker, K.	CON		
18	Lamont, N. Mellor, D. Major, J.	CON CON CON			Howard, M.	CON	Clarke, K.	CON	Waldegrave, W.	CON
19	Lamont, N. Major, J. Portillo, M.	CON CON CON			*Shephard, G.	CON	Patten, J.	CON	*Bottomley, V.	CON
20	Brown, G. Blair, T. Darling, A.	LAB LAB LAB			Blunkett, D.	LAB	Blunkett, D.	LAB	Dobson, F.	LAB

UNITED KINGDOM 1945–1998

Gov	Housing	Py	Agriculture	Py	Industry/Trade	Py	Environment	Py
1			Williams, T.	LAB	Cripps, S.	LAB		
			Smith, B.	LAB				
2	Dalton, H.	LAB	Williams, T.	LAB	Wilson, H.	LAB		
3	MacMillan, H.	CON			Thorneycroft, P.	CON		
4	Sandys, D.	CON	Heathcoat Amory, D.	CON	Thorneycroft, P.	CON		
5	Sandys, D.	CON	Heathcoat Amory, D.	CON	Thorneycroft, P.	CON		
6	Brooke, H.	CON	Heathcoat Amory, D.	CON	Eccles, D.	CON		
7	Brooke, H.	CON	Hare, J.	CON	Maudling, R.	CON		
8	Joseph, K.	CON	Soames, C.	CON	Heath, E.	CON		
9	Crossman, R.	LAB	Peart, F.	LAB	Jay, D.	LAB		
10	Crossman, R.	LAB	Peart, F.	LAB	Jay, D.	LAB		
11	Walker, P.	CON	Prior, J.	CON	Noble, M.	CON		
12			Peart, F.	LAB	Shore, P.	LAB	Crosland, A.	LAB
					Wedgewood Benn, A.	LAB		
13			Peart, F.	LAB	Shore, P.	LAB	Crosland, A.	LAB
					Wedgewood Benn, A.	LAB		
14	Shore, P.	LAB	Peart, F.	LAB	Dell, E.	LAB		
					Varley, E.	LAB		
15			Walker, P.	CON	Joseph, K.	CON		
					Nott, J.	CON		
16			Jopling, M.	CON	Parkinson, C.	CON	Jenkin, P.	CON
17			MacGregor, J.	CON	Young of Graffham, Lord	CON	Ridley, N.	CON
					Clarke, K.	CON		
18			Gummer, J.	CON	Lilley, P.	CON	Heseltine, M.	CON
19			Gummer, J.	CON	Hesseltine, M.	CON	Howard, M.	CON
20			Cunningham, J.	LAB	*Beckett, M.	LAB	Prescott, J.	LAB

UNITED KINGDOM 1945–1998

Gov	Social Affairs (py)	Public Works (py)	Other (py)	Res
1	Griffiths, J. (LAB) Paling, W. (LAB)	Shinwell, E. (LAB) Silkin, L. (LAB) Tomlinson, G. (LAB) Winster, Lord (LAB) Williams, E.J. (LAB) Listowel, Lord (LAB)	Westwood, J. (LAB) Morrison, H.S. (LAB) Greenwood, A. (LAB) Addison, Visc. (LAB) Hall, G.H. (LAB) Pethick-Lawrence, F.W. (LAB) Noel-Baker, P. (LAB) Hynd, J.B. (LAB)	7
2			McNeil, H. (LAB) Morrison, H. (LAB) Addison, Viscount (LAB) Alexander of Hillsborough, Visc. (LAB) Jowitt, Visc. (LAB) Griffiths, J. (LAB) Gordon Walker, P. (LAB)	4
3			Crookshank, H.F.C. (CON) Maxwell Fyfe, D. (CON) Stuart, J. (CON) Woolton, Lord (CON) Salisbury, Marq. of (CON) Ismay, Lord (CON) Lyttelton, O. (CON) Leathers, Lord (CON) Cherwell, Lord (CON)	4

UNITED KINGDOM 1945–1998

Gov	Social Affairs (py)	Public Works (py)	Other (py)	Res
4	Peake, O. (CON)		Eden, A. (CON) Lloyd-George, G. (CON) Stuart, J. (CON) Salisbury, Marquess of (CON) Crookshank, H.F.C. (CON) Woolton, Visc. (CON) Lennox-Boyd, A.T. (CON)	0
5	Peake, O. (CON)		Eden, A. (CON) Lloyd-George, G. (CON) Stuart, J. (CON) Salisbury, Marq. of (CON) Crookshank, H.F.C. (CON) Woolton, Visc. (CON) Lennox-Boyd, A.T. (CON)	0
6		Mills, P. (CON) Watkinson, H. (CON)	Butler, R.A. (CON) Brooke, H. (CON) MacLay, J.S. (CON) Salisbury, Lord (CON) Hill, C. (CON) Lennox-Boyd, A.T. (CON) Home, Lord (CON)	3
7		Sandys, D. (CON) Marples, E. (CON)	Mills, Lord (CON) Hailsham, Lord (CON) Brooke, H. (CON) Home, Lord (CON) MacLeod, I. (CON) MacLay, J. (CON) Hill, C. (CON)	4

UNITED KINGDOM 1945–1998

Gov	Social Affairs (py)	Public Works (py)	Other (py)	Res
8		Marples, E. (CON) Erroll, F. (CON) Rippon, G. (CON)	Joseph, K. (CON) Noble, M. (CON) Hailsham, Lord (CON) Lloyd, J.S. (CON) Blakenham, Lord (CON) Deedes, W. (CON) Carrington, Lord (CON) Sandys, D. (CON)	1
9		Fraser, T. (LAB) Lee, F. (LAB)	Brown, G. (LAB) Ross, W. (LAB) Bowden, H. (LAB) Longford, Earl of (LAB) Houghton, D. (LAB) Bottomley, A. (LAB) Griffiths, J. (LAB) Greenwood, A. (LAB) *Castle, B. (LAB)	2
10		*Castle, B. (LAB) Marsh, R. (LAB)	Brown, G. (LAB) Bowden, H. (LAB) Bottomley, A. (LAB) Ross, W. (LAB) Houghton, D. (LAB) Greenwood, A. (LAB) Longford, Earl of (LAB) Hughes, C. (LAB) Lee, F. (LAB)	9

UNITED KINGDOM 1945–1998

Gov	Social Affairs (py)	Public Works (py)	Other (py)	Res
11	Joseph, K. (CON)		Campbell, G. (CON) Whitelaw, W. (CON) Jellicoe, Earl (CON) Barber, A. (CON) Thomas, P. (CON)	7
12	*Castle, B. (LAB) *Williams, S. (LAB)		Ross, W. (LAB) Short, E. (LAB) Shepherd, Lord (LAB) Lever, H. (LAB) Rees, M. (LAB) Morris, J. (LAB)	0
13	*Castle, B. (LAB) *Williams, S. (LAB)	Silkin, J. (LAB)	Ross, W. (LAB) Short, E. (LAB) Shepherd, Lord (LAB) Lever, H. (LAB) Rees, M. (LAB) Morris, J. (LAB) Mellish, R. (LAB, *Hart, J. (LAB)	1
14			Millan, B. (LAB) Foot, M. (LAB) Shepherd, Lord (LAB) Lever, H. (LAB)	3
15	Jenkins, P. (CON)	Howell, D. (CON)	Carrington, Lord (CON) Maude, A. (CON) St John Stevas, N. (CON) Atkins, H. (CON) Edwards, N. (CON) Younger, G. (CON) Soames, Lord (CON) Gilmour, I. (CON)	4

UNITED KINGDOM 1945–1998

Gov	Social Affairs (py)	Public Works (py)	Other (py)	Res
16	Fowler, N. (CON)	Walker, P. (CON) King, T. (CON)	Whitelaw, W. (CON) Prior, J. (CON) Younger, G. (CON) Edwards, N. (CON) Biffen, J. (CON) Cockfield, Lord (CON)	5
17	Moore, J. (CON)	Channon, P. (CON) Parkinson, C. (CON)	Clarke, K. (CON) Whitelaw, W. (CON) Walker, P. (CON) King, T. (CON) Rifkind, M. (CON) Wakeham, J. (CON)	4
18	Newton, A. (CON)	Rifkind, M. (CON) Wakeham, J. (CON)	Waddington, Lord (CON) MacGregor, J. (CON) Patten, C. (CON) Brooke, P. (CON) Hunt, D. (CON) Lang, I. (CON)	0
19	Lilley, P. (CON)	MacGregor, J. (CON)	Wakeham, Lord (CON) Newton, T. (CON) Hunt, D. (CON) Waldegrave, W. (CON) Lang, I. (CON) Mellor, D. (CON) Mayhew, Sir P. (CON)	3

UNITED KINGDOM 1945–1998

Gov	Social Affairs (py)	Public Works (py)	Other (py)	Res
20	*Harman, H. (LAB)	Prescott, J. (LAB) Clark, D. (LAB) Strang, G. (LAB)	Prescott, J. (LAB) Dewar, D. (LAB) *Taylor, A. (LAB) Smith, C. (LAB) *Mowlam, M. (LAB) Davies, R. (LAB) *Short, C. (LAB) Richard, Lord (LAB) Clark, D. (LAB)	

50. RUSSIAN FEDERATION

Russia is a presidential republic whose constitution is strongly influenced by those of France and the USA. The Head of State, the President, is a dominant actor within the executive. He or she is directly elected for a four-year term, with a maximum of two consecutive terms. In addition to wide appointing powers the president is responsible for directing state action, in particular in foreign and military matters.

Parliament is bicameral. The legislature and the executive of the 89 constituent members (federal territorial units) of the Federation appoint the Upper House (Federal Assembly) of 178 seats. The Lower House (Duma) of 450 seats represents the population of the whole Federation, and is elected for a fixed term of four years by a mixed system of proportional representation (d'Hondt) and plurality voting. 225 Members are elected by simple majority in single-member constituencies of varying size with on average 500,000 electors each; 225 members are elected on the basis of party-list PR in one nation-wide constituency with a threshold of five per cent.

Parliament has a quorum if the absolute majority of members is present. Votes are carried by a majority of all members present. Some issues require qualified majorities, ranging from an absolute majority to a three-fifths majority of all members. Constitutional amendments require between two-thirds and three-fifths support from all members in both Houses. A referendum is constitutionally required and may be called by the Head of State. The outcome is binding.

The President nominates the Prime Minister and appoints ministers. The government is mainly responsible for implementing presidential policies. The Prime Minister needs a vote of investiture in the Duma, a majority of all votes cast. The government can also face a vote of no confidence, which, however, can be ignored. Government is collectively responsible to parliament. Being a minister is not compatible with being a Member of Parliament. The Prime Minister has a rather prominent position in government.

The Constitutional Court supervises and adjudicates federal laws, presidential decrees and acts, as well as the actions of Federation members. On the request of the President, or the Government, or one-fifth of the members of the Federal Assembly or the Duma, the Court will review the constitutionality of legislation and government actions.

RUSSIAN FEDERATION 1991 - 1998

On 12 June 1990, the Russian Federation was declared a sovereign state by the Congress of People's Deputies (1,068).

COMPOSITION OF FEDERAL ASSEMBLY
On 12 December 1993 the first post-communist elections for the bicameral Federal Assembly took place (Federation Council - 178 seats (2 for each of the 89 components which make up the Russian Federation); Duma - 450 seats). Election results vary according to source. Part of the difference can be explained by the very volatile and embrionic nature of the party system.

12 December 1993 DUMA elections	Keesing's	Sakwa
Russia's Choice	96	70
Liberal Democratic Party of Russia	70	64
Communist Party	65	48
Agrarian Party	47	33
Women of Russia	25	23
Yabloko	33	23
Party of Russian Unity and Accord	27	19
Democratic Party of Russia	21	15
Civic Union for Stabilization, Justice and Progress	18	1
Movement for Democratic Reforms	8	4
Dignity and Mercy	3	2
Others		31
Vacant (Chechnya)		6
New Names		1
Independents		141
Total seats	450	450

17 December 1995 DUMA elections	Keesing's	Sakwa
Communist Party	157	157
Our Home is Russia	55	55
Liberal Democratic Party of Russia	51	51
Yabloko	45	45
Agrarian Party of Russia	20	20
Russia's Democratic Choice	9	
Power to the People	9	
Congress of Russian Communities		5
Women of Russia		3
Others	96	45
Independents		97
Total seats	450	450

RUSSIAN FEDERATION 1991 - 1998

The first elections for the 178 seat strong Federal Council were conducted in open competition between independents. There was no organisation of candidates on partylists.

Since 5 December 1995 a new law covering the composition of the Federation Council is in force. As of that date the Council consists of the heads of administration (governors) and heads of the legislative branch of the 89 components of the Russian Federation. In toto 178 members.

Sources:
Keesing's Record of World Events
Richard Sakwa, *Russian Politics and Society*, 2nd edition, Routledge, London & NY, 1996

RUSSIAN FEDERATION 1991 - 1998

Yeltsin Administration	2 June 1991 Yeltsin, B. elected President; 10 July 1991 sworn in
	3 July 1996 Yeltsin, B. reelected President; 9 August 1996 sworn in
President	10 Jly 1991 - : Yeltsin, B.
Vice-President	10 Jly 1991 - 1 Sep 1993: Rutskoi, A. ('suspendend' by President)
Prime Minister	6 Nov 1991 - 15 Jne 1992: Yeltsin, B.
	15 Jne 1992 - 14 Dec 1992: Gaidar, Y. (acting)
	14 Dec 1992 - : Chernomyrdin, V.
First Deputy Prime Minister	6 Nov 1991 - 3 Apr 1992: Burbulis, G.
	6 Nov 1991 - 15 Jne 1992: Gaidar, Y. (responsible for Economy until 24 Feb 1992; Finance 24 Feb 1992 - 2 Apr 1992)
	15 May 1992 - 19 Jan 1994: Shumeiko, V. (responsible for Management of the Economy from 23 Dec 1992; temporarily 'suspended' by President between 1 and 22 Sep 1993; from 22 Sep 1993 responsible for Press and Information)
	15 Apr 1993 - 18 Sep 1993: Lobov, O.
	18 Sep 1993 - 16 Jan 1994: Gaidar, Y.
	Apr 1993 - 20 Jne 1996: Soskovets, O.
	20 Jne 1996 - 22 Aug 1996: Lobov, O.
	5 Nov 1994 - 16 Jan 1996: Chubais, A. (responsible for Economic Policy)
	25 Jan 1996 - : Kadannikov, V. (responsible for Economic Policy)
	22 Aug 1996 - 17 Mar 1997: Bolshakov, A. (PM's Deputy)
	22 Aug 1996 - 17 Mar 1997: Ilyushin, V.
	22 Aug 1996 - 17 Mar 1997: Potanin, V.
	17 Mar 1997 - : Nemtsov, B. (responsible for Utilities Reform, Housing, Reform of Monopolies, Payment of Wages and Pensions)
	17 Mar 1997 - : Chubais, A. (Finance Minister and responsible for day-to-day Economic Management, Relations with the Media and with International Financial Organisations)
Deputy Prime Minister	6 Nov 1991 - 26 Nov 1992: Poltoranin, M.
	6 Nov 1991 - 30 May 1992: Lopukhin, V. (responsible for Energy)
	30 May 1992 - 15 dec 1992: Chernomyrdin, V. (responsible for Energy)
	6 Nov 1991 - May 1992: Titkin, A. (responsible for Industry)
	May 1992 - : Khizha, G. (responsible for Industry)
	May 1992 - 5 Nov 1994: Chubais, A. (responsible for privatization from 20 Jan 1994)
	8 Nov 1991 - 14 Jne 1992: Shokhin, A. (responsible for Social Policy)
	30 May 1992 - : Chernomyrdin, V. (responsible for Energy)
	14 Jne 1992 - 20 Jan 1994: Shokhin, A. (responsible for Foreign Economic Relations until 23 Dec 1992)
	4 Nov 1992 - 20 Jan 1994: Shakhrai, S.
	15 Jne 1992 - 26 Mar 1993: Saltykov, B.
	23 Dec 1992 - 20 Jan 1994: Shafranik, Y.
	23 Dec 1992 - 26 Jan 1994: Fedorov, B. (responsible for Finance and Economy)
	23 Dec 1992 - : Yarov, Y.

RUSSIAN FEDERATION 1991 - 1998

20 Jan 1994 - 17 Mar 1997: Zaveryukha, A. (responsible for
Agriculture)

24 Mar 1994 - 4 Nov 1994: Shokhin, A. (responsible for the Economy
and Relations with CIS-Members)

17 Apr 1994 - 5 Jan 1996: Shakhrai, S.

15 Nov 1994 - 24 Jan 1994: Polevanov, V.

15 Nov 1994 - 25 Jan 1996: Bolshakov, A. (responsible for Relations
with CIS-Members)

9 Nov 1994 - 17 Mar 1997: Davydov, O. from 22 Aug 1996
(responsible for Foreign Economic Relations)

1 Jne 1995 - 17 Mar 1997: Ignatenko, V. (responsible for the Media)

16 Jan 1996 - : Kinelev, V. (responsible for Education, Science and
Culture)

25 Jan 1996 - : Kazakov, A.

- 12 Mar 1996: Gusev, V.

12 Mar 1996 - : Artynkhov, V.

22 Aug 1996 - : Babichev, V.

22 Aug 1996 - 17 Mar 1997: Livshits, A. (responsible for Finance)

22 Aug 1996 - 17 Mar 1997: Lobov, O.

22 Aug 1996 - : Serov, V. (from 17 Mar 1997 responsible for National
and Regional Policies, CIS, and Local Government)

22 Aug 1996 - : Fortov, V.

17 Mar 1997 - : Urinson, Y. (Minister for Economic Reform,
responsible for Industrial Policy and Conversion, Foreign Economic
Relations, Agriculture))

17 Mar 1997 - : Kokh, A. (Head of State Property Cttee, Tax and
Customs Policy, Alcohol Revenue)

17 Mar 1997 - : Sysuyev, O. (responsible for Housing, Utility Reform)

17 Mar 1997 - : Bulgak, V. (responsible for Science and Technology,
Communications, Transport)

17 Mar 1997 - : Kulikov, A. (responsible for Law Enforcement, Anti-
Corruption Policy, Natural Disasters)

Foreign Affairs	(11 Oct 1990) 6 Nov 1991 - 5 Jan 1996: Kozyrev, A.
	9 Jan 1996 - : Primakov, Y.
CIS Affairs	22 Aug 1996 - : Tuleyev, A.
Defence	16 Mar 1992 - 18 May 1992 : Yeltsin, B.
	18 May 1992 - 18 Jne 1996: Grachev, P. (Marshal)
	18 Jne 1996 - 17 Jly 1996: Kolesnikov, M. (Gen.) (acting)
	17 Jly 1996 - : Rodionov, I. (Col.-Gen.)
Defence Industry	- 17 Mar 1997: Pak, Z.
	(merged with Industry and Economy on 17 Mar 1997)
Security Service (abolished 21 Dec 1993)	23 Dec 1992 - : Barannikov, V. (Col.-Gen.)
	18 Sep 1993 - 21 Dec 1993: Golushko, N.
National Security Advisor and	15 Jne 1993 - 10 Aug 1993: Shaposnikov, Y.I. (Marshal)
Secretary of Security Council	18 Sep 1993 - : Lobov, O
	17 Jne 1996 - Jly 1996: Lebed, A.
Interior	23 Dec 1992 - 29 Jne 1995: Yerin, V. (Lt.-Gen.)
	6 Jly 1995 - : Kulikov, A. (Gen.)

RUSSIAN FEDERATION 1991 - 1998

Civil Defence, Emergencies, Natural Disasters	20 Jan 1994 - : Shoigu, S.
Justice	23 Dec 1992 - Apr 1993: Fyodorov, N.
	5 Aug 1993 - 9 Dec 1994: Kalmykov, Y.
	5 Jan 1995 - : Kovalyov, V.
Finance	24 Feb 1992 - 2 Apr 1992: Gaidar, Y.
	2 Apr 1992 - 26 Mar 1993: Barchuk, V.
	26 Mar 1993 - 26 Jan 1994: Fedorov B.
	26 Jan 1994 - 4 Nov 1994: Dubinin, S. (acting)
	4 Nov 1994 - 17 Mar 1997: Panskov, V.
	17 Mar 1997 - : Chubais, A.
Chair Central Bank	28 Nov 1995 - : Dubinin, S. (from 28 Nov 1995 status Federal Minister)
Economy	24 Feb 1992 - 26 Mar 1993: Nechayev, A.
(merged with (Defence) Industry on 17 Mar 1997)	
	26 Mar 1993 - : Shapovalyants, A.
	- 16 Sep 1993: Lobov, O.
	16 Sep 1993 - 16 Jan 1994: Gaidar, Y.
	20 Jan 1994 - 4 Nov 1994: Shokhin, A.
	8 Nov 1994 - 17 Mar 1997: Yassin, Y.
	17 Mar 1997 - : Urinson, Y.
Foreign Economic Relations	6 Nov 1991 - 23 Dec 1992: Aven, P.
	23 Dec 1992 - 2 Sep 1993: Glazyev, S.
	22 Aug 1994 - 17 Mar 1997: Davydov, O.
	17 Mar 1997 - : Fradkov, M.
Labour	15 Jne 1992 - Apr 1997: Melikyan, G.
(& Social Development from 22 Aug 1996)	
Education	23 dec 1992 - : Tkachenko, Y.
General and Vocational Education	22 Aug 1996 - : Kinelev, V.
Science and Technology	6 Nov 1991 - : Saltykov, B.
Science, Higher Education and Technology	26 Mar 1993 - : Saltykov, B.
Director Russian Academy of Sciences	28 Nov 1995 - : Osipov, Y. (from 28 Nov 1995 status Federal Minister)
Health (& Medical Industries from 20 Jan 1994)	23 Dec 1992 - 28 Nov 1995: Nechayev, E.
	28 Nov 1995 - 22 Aug 1996: Tsaregorodtsev, A.
	22 Aug 1996 - : *Dimitriyeva, T.
Agriculture (& Food from 20 Jan 1994)	23 Dec 1992 - 26 Oct 1994:Khlystun, V.
	26 Oct 1994 - 12 Jan 1996: Nazarchuk, A. (Agrarian Bloc)
	12 Jan 1996 - 14 May 1996: Zaveryukha, A. (acting)
	14 May 1996 - : Khlystun, V.
Industry	22 Aug 1996 - 17 Mar 1997: Bespalov, Y.
(merged with Defence Industry and Economy on 17 Mar 1997)	
Social Security	23 Dec 1992 - : *Pamfilova, E.
Construction (abolished 17 Mar 1997)	12 Jly 1994 - 17 Mar 1997: Basin, Y.
Transport	23 Dec 1992 - 10 Jan 1996: Yefimov, V.
	12 Jan 1996 - : Tsakh, N.
Railways	23 dec 1992 - 22 Aug 1996: Fadeev, G.
	22 Aug 1996 - : Zaytsev, A.
Fuel and Energy	23 Dec 1992 - 22 Aug 1996: Shafranik, Y.
	22 Aug 1996 - 23 Apr 1997: Rodionov, P.
	23 Apr 1997 - : Nemtsov, B.

RUSSIAN FEDERATION 1991 - 1998

Atomic Energy	23 Dec 1992 - : Mikhailov, Victor
Energy and Natural Resources	23 Dec 1992 - 22 Aug 1996: Danilov-Danilyan, V.
Natural Resources (from 22 Aug 1996)	22 Aug 1996 - : Orlov, V.
Communications	23 dec 1992 - :Bulgak, V.
Press and Information	6 Nov 1991 - 29 Dec 1992: Poltoranin, M.
(abolished 22 Dec 1993)	23 Dec 1992 - 20 Aug 1993: Fedotov, M.
	22 Sep 1993 - 22 Dec 1993: Shumeiko, V. (acting)
Culture (& Tourism until 22 Aug 1996)	23 Dec 1992 - : Sidorov, Y.
Affairs of Nationalities & Regional Policies	20 Jan 1994 - 16 May 1994: Shakrai, S.
Nationalities & Federal Relations	16 May 1994 - 29 Jne 1995: Yegorov, N.
(from 22 Aug 1996)	5 Jly 1995 - : Mikhailov, V.
Without Portfolio	6 May 1994 - 5 Jan 1996: Travkin, N. (Democratic Party of Russia)
	17 Mar 1997 - : Yasin, Y.
Russian State Secretary	3 Apr 1992 - : Burbulis, G.
State Secretary under Russian President	14 Jne 1992 - 25 Nov 1992: Burbulis, G.
State Counsellor for Legal Affairs	6 Nov 1991 - 7 May 1992: Shakhrai, S.
Chair of State Duma	20 Jan 1994 - : Rybkin, I.
Chair of Federation Council	20 Jan 1994 - : Shumeiko, V.
Head of Government Apparatus	8 Nov 1994 - : Babichev, V.

Chairs of State Committees with the rank of minister

Nationalities Policy	6 Nov 1991 - 19 Oct 1992: Tishkov, V.
(from 20 Jan 1994 a Ministry)	4 Nov 1992 - 20 Jan 1994: Shakhrai, S.
(Management of State) Property	6 Nov 1991 - 5 Nov 1994: Chubais, A.
	15 Nov 1994 - 24 Jan 1995: Polevanov, V.
	26 Jan 1995 - 8 Feb 1995: Mostovoi, P. (acting)
	8 Feb 1995 - 25 Jan 1996: Belyayev, S.
	25 Jan 1996 - 17 Mar 1997: Kazakov, A.
	17 Mar 1997 - : Kokh, A.
Architecture and Construction	23 Dec 1992 - 12 Jly 1994: Basim, Y.
(from 12 Jly 1994 a Ministry)	
Antimonopoly Policies	23 Dec 1992 - : Bochin, L.
State Customs	23 Dec 1992 - : Kruglov, A.
Socioeconomic Development of Northern Regions	23 Dec 1992 - : Kuramin, V.
Economic Cooperation with CIS-Members	23 Dec 1992 - : Mashits, V.
Civil Defence and Emergency Situations	23 Dec 1992 - 20 Jan 1994: Shoigu, S.
(from 20 Jan 1994 a Ministry)	
Social Security and Rehabilitation of Territories affected by Chernobyl and other Radioactive Catastrophes	23 Dec 1992 - : Voznyak, V.
State Taxation Service	- 12 Mar 1996 : Gusev, V.
	12 Mar 1996 - : Artynkhov, V.
Science and Technology	22 Aug 1996 - : Fortov, V.

51. UNITED STATES OF AMERICA

The Head of State and of Government is the President, elected directly for a fixed four-year term, with a maximum of two consecutive terms.

The State is federal and administratively fairly decentralised, with a division of power between the Federal Government and the States. Nevertheless, the Federal government has its own administration across the country, and many joint programmes with State governments, particularly in health and welfare areas.

Parliament (Congress) is bicameral. The 100 members of the Upper House (Senate) are directly elected within States by plurality voting for a six-year term. Plurality voting directly elects the 435 members of the Lower House (House of Representatives) for a two-year term from constituencies of 400-500,000 electors, also.

Congress has a quorum of at least 50 per cent of all members. Votes are carried by a majority of all votes cast. For some issues a qualified majority of two-thirds of all votes cast is required. Constitutional amendments require a majority of all votes cast but are subject to a complicated ratification procedure by states. There is no national referendum.

The President appoints his own Cabinet whose members do not serve in Congress. Special Advisers or Envoys have a special position outside the Cabinet and may even come from the party not holding the Presidency. Congress has no power of removal, other than formal impeachment, over the President. Legislation is subject to its approval and it can initiate its own, subject to presidential veto. The Cabinet and Government are entirely dependent on the President and do not need a congressional vote of investiture. Neither is a vote of no confidence possible. In the last resort the Cabinet is advisory to the President and can be over-ruled by him.

There is a Supreme Court for the constitutional review of legislation.

UNITED STATES of AMERICA 1945 - 1998

Composition of Congress

1946				
House of Representatives	Dem 188	Rep 246	American Labor 1	total seats 435
Senate	Dem 54	Rep 42		total seats 96
1948				
House of Representatives	Dem 264	Rep 170	American Labor 1	total seats 435
Senate	Dem 54	Rep 42		total seats 96
1950				
House of Representatives	Dem 235	Rep 199	Ind 1	total seats 435
Senate	Dem 49	Rep 46	Ind 1	total seats 96
1952				
House of Representatives	Dem 213	Rep 221	Ind 1	total seats 435
Senate	Dem 47	Rep 48	Ind 1	total seats 96
1954				
House of Representatives	Dem 232	Rep 203		total seats 435
Senate	Dem 48	Rep 47	Ind 1	total seats 96
1956				
House of Representatives	Dem 235	Rep 200		total seats 435
Senate	Dem 49	Rep 47		total seats 96
1958				
House of Representatives	Dem 283	Rep 153		total seats 436
Senate	Dem 64	Rep 34		total seats 98
1960				
House of Representatives	Dem 259	Rep 178		total seats 437
Senate	Dem 64	Rep 36		total seats 100
1962				
House of Representatives	Dem 259	Rep 176		total seats 435
Senate	Dem 68	Rep 32		total seats 100
1964				
House of Representatives	Dem 295	Rep 140		total seats 435
Senate	Dem 68	Rep 32		total seats 100
1966				
House of Representatives	Dem 248	Rep 187		total seats 435
Senate	Dem 64	Rep 36		total seats 100
1968				
House of Representatives	Dem 243	Rep 192		total seats 435
Senate	Dem 58	Rep 42		total seats 100
1970				
House of Representatives	Dem 255	Rep 180		total seats 435
Senate	Dem 55	Rep 45		total seats 100
1972				
House of Representatives	Dem 244	Rep 191		total seats 435
Senate	Dem 57	Rep 43		total seats 100
1974				
House of Representatives	Dem 291	Rep 144		total seats 435
Senate	Dem 62	Rep 37	Ind 1	total seats 100
1976				
House of Representatives	Dem 292	Rep 143		total seats 435
Senate	Dem 61	Rep 38	Ind 1	total seats 100

UNITED STATES of AMERICA 1945 - 1998

1978				
House of Representatives	Dem 277	Rep 158		total seats 435
Senate	Dem 58	Rep 41	Ind 1	total seats 100
1980				
House of Representatives	Dem 242	Rep 192	Ind	total seats 435
Senate	Dem 46	Rep 53	Ind 1	total seats 100
1982				
House of Representatives	Dem 269	Rep 166		total seats 435
Senate	Dem 46	Rep 54		total seats 100
1984				
House of Representatives	Dem 253	Rep 182		total seats 435
Senate	Dem 47	Rep 53		total seats 100
1986				
House of Representatives	Dem 258	Rep 173	Undecided 4	total seats 435
Senate	Dem 54	Rep 46		total seats 100
1988				
House of Representatives	Dem 262	Rep 173		total seats 435
Senate	Dem 55	Rep 45		total seats 100
1990				
House of Representatives	Dem 267	Rep 167	Ind 1	total seats 435
Senate	Dem 57	Rep 43		total seats 100
1992				
House of Representatives	Dem 259	Rep 175	Ind 1	total seats 435
Senate	Dem 57	Rep 43		total seats 100
1994				
House of Representatives	Dem 204	Rep 230	Ind 1	total seats 435
Senate	Dem 47	Rep 53		total seats 100
1996				
House of Representatives	Dem 207	Rep 207	Ind 1	total seats 435
Senate	Dem 45	Rep 55		total seats 100
1998				
House of Representatives	Dem 211	Rep 223	Ind 1	total seats 435
Senate	Dem 45	Rep 55		total seats 100

UNITED STATES of AMERICA 1945 - 1998

Truman Administration: 12 April 1945 - 20 January 1953
(1946 and 1952 Republican majority in both Houses)

President	12 Apr 1945 - 20 Jan 1953: Truman, H. S (Dem)
Vice-President	20 Jan 1949 - 20 Jan 1953: Barkley, A.W. (Dem)
Secretary of State	1 Dec 1944 - 3 Jly 1945: Stettinius, E. (Dem)
	3 Jly 1945 - 21 Jan 1947: Byrnes, J.F. (Dem)
	21 Jan 1947 - 20 Jan 1949: Marshall, G.C. (NONA)
	20 Jan 1949 - 20 Jan 1953: Acheson, D.G. (Dem)
Treasury	1 Jan 1934 - 23 Jly 1945: Morgenthau jr., H. (Dem)
	23 Jly 1945 - 25 Jne 1946: Vinson, F.M. (Dem)
	25 Jne 1946 - 20 Jan 1953: Snyder, J.W. (Dem)
Defense	17 Sep 1947 - 28 Mar 1949: Forrestal, J.V. (Dem)
	28 Mar 1949 - 21 Sep 1950: Johnson, L.A. (Dem)
	21 Sep 1950 - 17 Sep 1951: Marshall, G.C. (NONA)
	17 Sep 1951 - 20 Jan 1953: Lovett, R.A. (Rep)
Interior	4 Mar 1933 - 18 Mar 1946: Ickes, H.L.C. (Dem)
	18 Mar 1946 - 1 Dec 1949: Krug, J.A. (Dem)
	1 Dec 1949 - 20 Jan 1953: Chapman, O.L. (Dem)
Postmaster General	10 Sep 1940 - 1 Jly 1945: Walker, F.C. (Dem)
	1 Jly 1945 - 16 Dec 1947: Hannegan, R.E. (Dem)
	16 Dec 1947 - 20 Jan 1953: Donaldson, J.M. (Dem)
Attorney-General	5 Sep 1941 - 1 Jly 1945: Biddle, F. (Dem)
	1 Jly 1945 - 24 Aug 1949: Clark, T.C. (Dem)
	24 Aug 1949 - 27 May 1952: McGrath, J.H. (Dem)
	27 May 1952 - 20 Jan 1953: McGranery, J.P. (Dem)
Agriculture	5 Sep 1940 - 30 Jne 1945: Wickard, C.R. (Dem)
	30 Jne 1945 - 2 Jne 1948: Anderson, C.P. (Dem)
	2 Jne 1948 - 20 Jan: Brannan, C.F. (Dem)
Commerce (Trade)	19 Sep 1940 - 2 Mar 1945: Jones, J.H. (Dem)
	2 Mar 1945 - 28 Sep 1946: Wallace, H.A. (Dem)
	28 Sep 1946 - 6 May 1947: Harriman, W.A. (Dem)
	6 May 1948 - 20 Jan 1953: Sawyer, C. (Dem)
Labor	4 Mar 1933 - 1 Jly 1945: Perkins, F. (Dem)
	1 Jly 1945 - 10 Jne 1948: Schwellenbach, L.B. (Dem)
	13 Aug 1948 - 20 Jan 1953: Tobin, M.J. (Dem)
European Aid	9 Apr 1948 - 30 Sep 1950: Hoffman, P.G. (Rep)
	1 Oct 1950 - 20 Jan 1953: Foster, W.C. (Rep)

Eisenhower Administration: 20 January 1953 - 20 January 1961
(1954, 1956, 1958, and 1960 Democratic majority in both Houses)

President	20 Jan 1953 - 20 Jan 1961: Eisenhower, D.D. (Rep)
Vice-President	20 Jan 1953 - 20 Jan 1961: Nixon, R.M. (Rep)
Secretary of State	21 Jan 1953 - 15 Apr 1959: Dulles, J.F. (Rep)
	22 Apr 1959 - 20 Jan 1961: Herter, C.A. (Rep)
Treasury	21 Jan 1953 - 29 Jly 1957: Humphrey, G.M. (Rep)
	29 Jly 1957 - 20 Jan 1961: Anderson, R.B. (Dem)
Defense	28 Jan 1953 - 9 Oct 1957: Wilson, C.E. (Rep)
	9 Oct 1957 - 1 Dec 1959: McElroy, N.H. (Rep)
	1 dec 1959 - 20 Jan 1961: Gates, T.S. (Rep)
Interior	21 Jan 1953 - 8 Jne 1956: McKay, D. (Rep)
	8 Jne 1956 - 20 Jan 1961: Seaton, F.A. (Rep)
Postmaster General	21 Jan 1953 - 20 Jan 1961: Summerfield, A.E. (Rep)
Attorney-General	21 Jan 1953 - 8 Nov 1957: Brownell jr., H. (Rep)
	8 Nov 1957 - 20 Jan 1961: Rogers, W.P. (Rep)

UNITED STATES of AMERICA 1945 - 1998

Agriculture	21 Jan 1953 - 20 Jan 1961: Benson, E.T. (Rep)
Commerce (Trade)	21 Jan 1953 - 13 Nov 1958: Weeks, S. (Rep)
	13 Nov 1958 - 27 Jne 1959: Strauss, L.L. (Rep) (confirmation refused by Senate)
	21 Jly 1959 - 20 Jan 1961: Mueller, F.H. (Rep)
Labor	21 Jan 1953 - 9 Oct 1953: Durkin, M.P. (Dem)
	9 Oct 1953 - 20 Jan 1961: Mitchell, J.P. (Rep)
Health, Education & Welfare	11 Apr 1953 - 1 Aug 1955: *Hobby, O.C. (Rep)
	1 Aug 1955 - 1 Aug 1958: Folsom, M.B. (Rep)
	1 Aug 1958 - 20 Jan 1961: Flemming, A.S. (Rep)
Disarmament	19 Mar 1955 - 14 Feb 1958: Stassen, H.E. (Rep)
Participating in cabinet meetings were:	
Director of Budget	20 Jan 1953 - 15 Apr 1954; Dodge, J.M. (Rep)
	15 Apr 1954 - 20 Jan 1956: Hughes R.B. (Rep)
	20 Jan 1956 - 13 Mar 1958: Brundage, P.E. (Rep)
	13 Mar 1958 - 20 Jan 1961: Stans, M.A. (Rep)
Administrator Federal Secretary	20 Jan 1953 - 10 Apr 1953: *Hobby, O.C. (Rep)

Kennedy Administration: 20 January 1961 - 22 November 1963

President	20 Jan 1961 - 22 Nov 1963: Kennedy, J.F. (Dem)
Vice-President	20 Jan 1961 - 22 Nov 1963: Johnson, J.B. (Dem)
Secretary of State	20 Jan 1961 - 22 Nov 1963: Rusk, D. (Dem)
Treasury	20 Jan 1961 - 22 Nov 1963: Dillon, D. (Dem)
Defense	20 jan 1961 - 22 Nov 1963: McNamara, R.S. (Rep)
Interior	20 Jan 1961 - 22 Nov 1963: Udall, S. (Dem)
Postmaster General	20 Jan 1961 - 10 Sep 1963: Day, J.E. (Dem)
	10 Sep 1963 - 22 Nov 1963: Gronouski, J.A. (Dem)
Attorney-General	20 Jan 1961 - 22 Nov 1963: Kennedy, R.F. (Dem)
Agriculture	20 Jan 1961 - 22 Nov 1963: Freeman, O.L. (Dem)
Commerce (Trade)	20 Jan 1961 - 22 Nov 1963: Hodges, L.H. (Dem)
Labor	20 Jan 1961 - 20 Sep 1962: Goldberg, A.J. (Dem)
	25 Sep 1962 - 22 Nov 1963: Wirtz, W.W. (Dem)
Healt, Education & Welfare	20 Jan 1961 - 13 Jly 1962: Ribicoff, A.A. (Dem)
	31 Jly 1962 - 22 Nov 1963: Celebresse, A.J. (Dem)
Housing & Town Planning	18 Jan 1966 - 22 Nov 1963: Weaver, R.C. (Dem)
	(Urban Development) (est. 9 Sep 1965)
Sollicitor-General	20 Jan 1961 - 22 Nov 1963: Cox, A. (Dem)
Ambassador to the United Nations	20 Jan 1961 - 2 Nov 1963: Stevenson, A.E. (Dem)

Johnson Administration: 22 Nov 1963 - 20 January 1969

President	22 Nov 1963 - 20 Jan 1969: Johnson, L.B. (Dem)
Vice-President	20 Jan 1965 - 20 Jan 1969: Humphrey, H.H. (Dem)
Secretary of State	22 Nov 1963 - 20 Jan 1969: Rusk, D. (Dem)
Treasury	22 Nov 1963 - 1 Apr 1965: Dillon, D. (Dem)
	1 Apr 1965 - 20 Dec 1968: Fowler, H.H. (Rep)
	21 dec 1968 - 20 Jan 1969: Barr, J.W. (Dem)
Defense	22 Nov 1963 - 29 Feb 1968: McNamara, R.S. (Rep)
	1 Mar 1968 - 20 Jan 1969: Clifford, C.M. (Dem)
Interior	22 Nov 1963 - 20 Jan 1969: Udall, S. (Dem)
Postmaster General	22 Nov 1963 - 30 Aug 1965: Gronouski, J.A. (Dem)
	3 Nov 1965 - 26 Apr 1968: O'Brien, L.F. (Dem)
	26 Apr 1968 - 22 Jan 1969: Watson, M.M. (Dem)
Attorney-General	22 Nov 1963 - 3 Sep 1964: Kennedy, R.F. (Dem)
	4 Sep 1964 - 2 Oct 1966: Katzenbach, N. de B. (Dem)

UNITED STATES of AMERICA 1945 - 1998

	3 Oct 1966 - 20 Jan 1969: Clark, R. (Dem)
Agriculture	22 Nov 1963 - 20 Jan 1969: Freeman, O.L. (Dem)
Commerce (Trade)	22 Nov 1963 - 15 Jan 1965: Hodges, L.H. (Dem)
	18 Jan 1965 - 31 Jan 1967: Connor, J.T. (Dem)
	14 Jne 1967 - 1 Mar 1968: Trowbridge, A.B. (Dem)
	6 Mar 1968 - 19 Jan 1969: Smith, C.R. (Dem)
Labor	22 Nov 1963 - 20 Jan 1969: Wirtz, W.W. (Dem)
Transportation	12 Jan 1967 - 20 Jan 1969: Boyd, A.C. (Dem)
Healt, Education & Welfare	22 Nov 1963 - 17 Aug 1965: Celebresse, A.J. (Dem)
	18 Aug 1965 - 1 Mar 1968: Gardner, J.W. (Rep)
	1 Mar 1968 - 20 Jan 1969: Cohen, W.J. (Dem)
Housing & Town Planning	18 Jan 1966 - 31 Dec 1968 1969: Weaver, R.C. (Dem)
	(Urban Development) 2 Jan 1969 - 20 Jan 1969: Wood, R.C. (Dem)
	(est. 9 Sep 1965)
Sollicitor-General	22 Nov 1963 - 20 Jan 1969: Cox, A. (Dem)
Ambassador to the United Nations	22 Nov 1963 - 14 Jly 1965: Stevenson, A.E. (Dem)
	28 Jly 1965 - 25 Apr 1968: Goldberg, A.J. (Dem)

Nixon Administration: 20 January 1969 - 9 August 1974
(1970, 1972 Democratic majority in both Houses)

President	20 Jan 1969 - 9 Aug 1974: Nixon, R.M. (Rep)
Vice-President	20 Jan 1969 - 10 Oct 1973: Agnew, S.T. (Rep)
	20 Jan 1969 - 9 Aug 1974: Ford, G.R. (Rep)
Secretary of State	22 Jan 1969 - 3 Sep 1973: Rogers, W.P. (Rep)
	30 Sep 1973 - 9 Aug 1974: Kissinger, H.A. (NONA)
Treasury	22 Jan 1969 - 1 Feb 1971: Kennedy, D.M. (Rep)
	11 Feb 1970 - 12 Jne 1972: Connally, J.B. (Dem -> Rep)
	12 Jne 1972 - 8 May 1974: Shultz, G.P. (Rep)
	8 May 1974 - 9 Aug 1977: Simon, W.E. (Rep)
Defense	20 Jan 1969 - 20 Jan 1973: Laird, M.R. (Rep)
	29 Jan 1973 - 30 April 1973: Richardson, E.L. (Rep)
	2 Jly 1973 - 9 Aug 1974: Schlesinger, J.R. (Rep)
Interior	24 Jan 1969 - 25 Nov 1970: Hickel, W.J. (Rep)
	29 Jan 1971 - 9 Aug 1974 Morton, R.C.B. (Rep)
Postmaster General	22 jan 1969 - 30 Jne 1970: Blount, W.M. (Rep)
	1 Jly 1970: no longer cabinet post
Attorney-General	21 Jan 1969 - 1 Mar 1972: Mitchell, J.N. (Rep)
	2 Mar 1972 - 24 May 1973: Kleindienst, R.G. (Rep)
	25 May 1973 - 20 Oct 1973: Richardson, E.L. (Rep)
	20 Oct 1973 - 4 Jan 1974: Bork, R.H. (acting)
	4 Jan 1974 - 9 Aug 1974: Saxbe, W.B. (Rep)
Agriculture	21 Jan 1969 - 17 Nov 1971: Hardin, C. (Rep)
	2 Dec 1971 - 9 Aug 1974: Butz, E.L. (Rep)
Commerce (Trade)	21 Jan 1969 - 15 Feb 1972: Stans, M.H. (Rep)
	29 Feb 1972 - 1 Feb 1973: Peterson, P.G. (Rep)
	2 Feb 1973 - 9 Aug 1974: Dent, F.B. (Rep)
Labor	22 Jan 1969 - 1 Jly 1970: Shultz, G.P. (Rep)
	2 Jly 1970 - 1 Feb 1973: Hodgson, J.D. (Rep)
	2 Feb 1973 - 9 Aug 1974: Brennan, P.J. (Dem)
Healt, Education & Welfare	21 Jan 1969 - 23 Jne 1970: Finch, R.H. (Rep)
	24 Jne 1970 - 29 Jan 1973: Richardson, E.L. (Rep)
	12 Feb 1973 - 9 Aug 1974: Weinberg, C.W. (Rep)
Housing & Urban Development	21 Jan 1969 - 2 Feb 1973: Romney, G.W. (Rep)
	2 Feb 1973 - 9 Aug 1974: Lynn, J.T. (Rep)

UNITED STATES of AMERICA 1945 - 1998

Transportation   22 Jan 1969 - 20 Jan 1973: Volpe, J.A. (Rep)
                              2 Feb 1973 - 9 Aug 1974: Brinegar, C.S. (Rep)

Ford Administration: 9 August 1974 - 20 January 1977
(1974, 1976 Democratic majority in both Houses)
President   9 Aug 1974 - 20 Jan 1977: Ford, G.R. (Rep)
Vice-President   9 Aug 1974 - 20 Jan 1977: Rockefeller, N.A. (Rep)
Secretary of State   9 Aug 1974 - 20 Jan 1977: Kissinger, H.A. (NONA)
Treasury   9 Aug 1974 - 20 Jan 1977: Simon, W.E. (Rep)
Defense   9 Aug 1974 - 20 Nov 1975: Schlesinger, J.R. (Rep)
                              20 Nov 1975 - 20 Jan 1977: Rumsfeld, D. (Rep)
Interior   9 Aug 1974 - 30 April 1975: Morton, R.C.B. (Rep)
                              13 Jne 1975 - 9 Oct 1975: Hathaway, S.K. (Rep)
                              17 Oct 1975 - 20 Jan 1977: Kleppe, T.S. (Rep)
Attorney-General   9 Aug 1974 - 3 Feb 1975: Saxbe, W.B. (Rep)
                              7 Feb 1975 - 20 Jan 1977: Levi, E.H. (Dem)
Agriculture   9 Aug 1974 - 4 Oct 1976: Butz, E.L. (Rep)
                              5 Nov 1976 - 20 Jan 1977: Knebel, J.A. (Rep)
                              (served as interim; not submitted to Senate)
Commerce (Trade)   9 Aug 1974 - 26 Mar 1975: Dent, F.B. (Rep)
                              1 May 1975 - 30 Jan 1976: Morton, R.C.B. (Rep)
                              2 feb 1976 - 20 Jan 1977: Richardson, E.L. (Rep)
Labor   9 Aug 1974 - 5 Mar 1975: Brennan, P.J. (Dem)
                              18 Mar 1975 - 31 Jan 1976: Dunlop, J.T. (Dem)
                              10 Feb 1976 - 20 Jan 1977: Usery, W.J. (Dem)
Healt, Education & Welfare   9 Aug 1974 - 8 Aug 1975: Weinberg, C.W. (Rep)
                              8 Aug 1975 - 20 Jan 1977: Mathews, F.D. (Dem)
Housing & Urban Development   9 Aug 1974 - 9 Feb 1975: Lynn, J.T. (Rep)
                              10 Mar 1975 - 20 Jan 1977: * Anderson Hills, C. (Rep)
Transportation   9 Aug 1974 - 6 Mar 1975: Brinegar, C.S. (Rep)
                              7 Mar 1975 - 20 jan 1977: Coleman, W.T. (Rep)

Carter Administration: 20 January 1977 - 20 January 1981
(1980 Republican majority in the Senate)
President   20 Jan 1977 - 20 Jan 1981: Carter, J. (Dem)
Vice-President   20 Jan 1977 - 20 Jan 1981: Mondale, W. (Dem)
Secretary of State   23 Jan 1977 - 28 Apr 1980: Vance, C.R. (Dem)
                              8 May 1980 - 20 jan 1981: Muskie, E.S. (Dem)
Treasury   23 Jan 1977 - 4 Aug 1979: Blumenthal, W.M. (Dem)
                              6 Aug 1979 - 20 Jan 1981: Miller, G.W. (Dem)
Defense   21 Jan 1977 - 20 Jan 1981: Brown, H. (Dem)
Interior   23 Jan 1977 - 20 Jan 1981: Andrews, C.D. (Dem)
Attorney-General   26 Jan 1977 - 16 Aug 1979: Bell, G.B. (Dem)
                              16 Aug 1979 - 20 jan 1981: Civiletti, B.R. (Dem)
Agriculture   23 Jan 1977 - 20 Jan 1981: Bergland, R. (Dem)
Commerce   23 Jan 1977 - 2 Nov 1979: *Kreps, J.M. (Dem)
Commerce & Industry   9 Jan 1979 - 20 Jan 1981: Klutznick, P.M. (Dem)
Labor   27 Jan 1977 - 20 Jan 1981: Marshall, F.R. (Dem)
Health, Education & Welfare   21 Jan 1977 - 3 Aug 1979: Califano, J.A. (Dem)
                              3 Aug 1979 - 17 Oct 1979: *Harris, P.R. (Dem)
Health & Human Services   17 Oct 1979 - 20 Jan 1981: *Harris, P.R. (Dem)
Education   30 Oct 1979 - 20 Jan 1981: *Hufstedler, S.M. (Dem)
Housing & Urban Development   23 Jan 1977 - 3 Aug 1979: *Harris, P.R. (Dem)
                              3 Aug 1979 - 20 Jan 1981: Landrieu, M. (Dem)

UNITED STATES of AMERICA 1945 - 1998

Transportation	23 Jan 1977 - 20 Jly 1979: Adams, B. (Dem)
	15 Aug 1979 - 20 Jan 1981: Goldschmidt, N.E. (Dem)
Energy	5 Aug 1977 - 24 Aug 1979: Schlesinger, J.R. (Rep)
	24 Aug 1979 - 20 Jan 1981: Duncan Jr., C.W. (NONA)

Reagan Administration: 20 January 1981 - 20 January 1989
(1982, 1984 Democratic majority in House of Representatives; 1986, 1988 Democratic majority in both Houses)

President	20 Jan 1981 - 20 Jan 1989: Reagan, R. (Rep)
Vice-President	20 Jan 1981 - 20 Jan 1989: Bush, G.H.W. (Rep)
Secretary of State	20 jan 1981 - 16 Jly 1982: Haig. A.M. (Rep)
	16 Jly 1982 - 20 Jan 1989: Shultz, G.P. (Rep)
Treasury	20 Jan 1981 - 20 Jan 1985: Regan, D.T. (Rep)
	20 jan 1985 - 5 Aug 1988: Baker III, J.A. (Rep)
	5 Aug 1988 - 20 Jan 1989: Brady, N. (Rep)
Defense	20 Jan 1981 - 20 Nov 1987: Weinberger, C.W. (Rep)
	20 Nov 1987 - 20 Jan 1989: Carlucci, F. (Rep)
Interior	20 Jan 1981 - 21 Nov 1983: Watt, J.G. (Rep)
	21 Nov 1983 - 20 Jan 1985: Clark, W. (Rep)
	20 Jan 1985 - 20 Jan 1989: Hodel, O.P. (Rep)
Attorney-General	20 Jan 1981 - 23 Jan 1984: Smith, W.F. (Rep)
	23 Jan 1984 - 11 Aug 1988: Meese III, E. (Rep)
	11 Aug 1988 - 20 Jan 1989: Thornburgh, R. (Rep)
Agriculture	20 Jan 1981 - 14 Feb/6 Mar 1986: Block, J. (Rep)
	29 Jan/6 Mar 1986 - 20 Jan 1989: Lyng, R. (Rep)
Commerce	20 Jan 1981 - 25 Jly 1987: Baldrige, M. (Rep)
	10 Aug/13 Oct 1987 - 20 Jan 1989: Verity, C.W. (Rep)
Labor	20 Jan 1981 - 2 Oct 1984: Donovan, R.J. (Rep)
	2 Oct 1984 - 20 Jan 1985: Ford, F.B. (acting)
	20 Jan 1985 - 14 Oct 1987: Brock, W.E. (Rep)
	3 Nov/11 Dec 1987 - 20 Jan 1989: *McLaughlin, A.D. (Rep)
Health & Human Services	20 Jan 1981 - 11 Jan 1983: Schweiker, R.S. (Rep)
	12 Jan 1983 - 20 Jan 1989: *Heckler, M.M. (Rep)
Education	20 Jan 1981 - 20 Jan 1985: Bell, J.T. (Rep)
	20 Jan 1985 - 9 Aug 1988: Bennett, W.J. (Rep)
	9 Aug 1988 - 20 Jan 1989: Cavazos, L. (Rep)
Housing & Urban Development	20 Jan 1981 - 20 Jan 1989: Pierce, S.R. (Rep)
Transportation	20 Jan 1981 - 1 Feb 1983: Lewis, A.L. (Rep)
	1 Feb 1983 - 1 Oct 1987: *Dole, E.H. (Rep)
	30 Nov 1987 - 20 Jan 1989: Burnley IV, J.H. (Rep)
Energy	20 Jan 1981 - 5 Nov 1982: Edwards, J.B. (Rep)
	5 Nov 1982 - 20 Jan 1985: Hodel, D.P. (Rep)
	20 Jan 1985 - 20 Jan 1989: Herrington, J.S. (Rep)
Cabinet level appointments:	
Director of Budget	20 Jan 1981 - 20 Jan 1989: Stockman, D.A. (Rep)
Director of CIA	20 Jan 1981 - 2 Feb 1987: Casey, W.J. (Rep)
	3/19 Mar 1987 - 20 jan 1989: Webster, W.H. (Rep)
Ambassador to the United Nations	20 Jan 1981 - 20 Jan 1985: *Kirkpatrick, J. (Rep)
	20 Jan 1985 - 20 Jan 1989: Walters, V.A. (Rep)
Special Trade Representative	20 Jan 1981 - 20 Jan 1985: Brock, W.E. (Rep)
Chairman of Council of Economic Advisers to the President	29 Oct 1987 - 20 Jan 1989: Sprinkel, B. (Rep)

UNITED STATES of AMERICA 1945 - 1998

Bush Administration: 20 January 1989 - 20 January 1993
(1990, 1992 Democratic majority in both Houses)

President	20 Jan 1989 - 20 Jan 1993: Bush, G.H.W. (Rep)
Vice-President	20 Jan 1989 - 20 Jan 1993: Quayle, J.D. (Rep)
Secretary of State	20 Jan 1989 - 13 Aug 1992: Baker III, J.A. (Rep)
	13 Aug 1992 - 20 Jan 1993: Eagleburger, L. (acting) (Rep)
Treasury	20 Jan 1989 - 20 Jan 1993: Brady, N. (Rep)
Defense	20 Jan 1989 - 9 Mar 1989: Tower, J. (rejected by Senate)
	9/16 Mar 1989 - 20 Jan 1993: Cheney, R. (Rep)
Interior	20 Jan 1989 - 20 Jan 1993: Lujan, M. (Rep)
Attorney-General	20 Jan 1989 - 9 Aug 1991: Thornburgh, R. (Rep)
	16 oct/15 nov 1991 - 20 Jan 1993: Barr, W.R. (Rep)
Agriculture	20 Jan 1989 - 20 Jan 1993: Yeutter, C. (Rep)
Commerce	20 Jan 1989 - 5 Dec 1991: Mosbacher, R. (Rep)
	5 Dec 1991 - 20 Jan 1993: *Franklin, B.H. (Rep)
Labor	20 Jan 1989 - 24 Oct 1990: *Dole, E.H. (Rep)
	14 Dec 1991 - 20 Jan 1993: *Martin, L. (Rep)
Health & Human Services	20 Jan 1989 - 20 Jan 1993: Sullivan, L. (Rep)
Education	20 Jan 1989 - 12 Dec 1990: Cavazos, L. (Rep)
	17 Dec 1990 - 20 Jan 1993: Alexander, L. (Rep)
Housing & Urban Development	20 Jan 1989 - 20 Jan 1993: Kemp, J. (Rep)
Transportation	20 Jan 1989 - 5 Dec 1991: Skinner, S.K. (Rep)
	22 Jan 1992 - 20 Jan 1993: Card, W.H. (Rep)
Energy	20 Jan 1989 - 20 Jan 1993: Watkins, J. (Rep)
Veterans Affairs	20 Jan 1989 - 20 Jan 1993: Derwinsky, E. (Rep)

Clinton Administration: 20 January 1993 -
(1994, 1996 Republican majority in both Houses)

President	20 Jan 1993 - : Clinton, W.J. (Dem)
Vice-President	20 Jan 1993 - : Gore, A. (Dem)
Secretary of State	20 Jan 1993 - 21 Jan 1997: Christopher, W.M. (Dem)
	22 Jan 1997 - : *Albright, M.K. (Dem)
Treasury	20 Jan 1993 - 6 Dec 1994: Bentsen, L. (Dem)
	6 Dec 1994 - : Rubin, R.E. (Dem)
Defense	20 Jan 1993 - 15 Dec 1993/20 Jan 1994: Aspin, L. (Dem)
	16 Dec 1993 - 18 Jan 1993: Inman, B.R. (nominated but withdrew)
	25 Jan/ 3 Feb 1994 - 23 Jan 1997: Perry, W.J. (Dem)
	24 Jan 1997 - : Cohen, W.S. (Rep)
Interior	20 Jan 1993 - : Babbit, B. (Dem)
Attorney-General	24 Dec 1992 - 22 Jan 1993: *Baird, Z. (nominated but withdrawn)
	11 Feb 1993 - : *Reno, J. (Dem)
Agriculture	20 Jan 1993 - 3 Oct 1994: Espy, M. (Dem)
	28 Dec 1994 - : Glickman, D. (Dem)
Commerce	20 Jan 1993 - 3 Apr 1996: Brown, R.H. (Dem)
	12 Apr 1996 - 29 Jan 1997: Kantor, M. (Dem)
	30 Jan 1997 - : Daley, W.J. (Dem)
Labor	20 Jan 1993 - ??: Reich, R.R. (Dem)
	?? - : Herman, A. (Dem)
Health & Human Services	20 Jan 1993 - : *Shalala, D.E. (Dem)
Education	20 Jan 1993 - : Riley, R.W. (Dem)
Housing & Urban Development	20 Jan 1993 - 26 Jan 1997: Cisneros, H.G. (Dem)
	27 Jan 1997 - : Cuomo, A.M. (Dem)
Transportation	20 Jan 1993 - 5 Feb 1997: Pena, F.F. (Dem)
	6 Feb 1997 - : Slater, R. (Dem)

UNITED STATES of AMERICA 1945 - 1998

Energy	20 Jan 1993 - ? Mar 1997: *O'Leary, H.R. (Dem)
	? Mar 1997 - : Pena, F.F. (Dem)
Veterans Affairs	20 jan 1993 - : Brown, J. (Dem)
Director Office of Management and Budget	20 Jan 1993 - 28 Jne 1994: Panetta, L.E. (Dem)
	28 Jne 1994 - : *Rivlin, A.M. (Dem)
US Trade Representative	21 Jan 1994 - 11 Apr 1996: Kantor, M. (Dem)
	12 Apr 1996 - : *Barshefsky, C. (acting) (Dem)

SOURCES: LITERATURE AND INTERNET SITES

LITERATURE

Constitutions of the World, edited by A. Blaustein & G. Flanz, New York, Oceana Publications, 1972 ff.

Constitutions of the World, compiled by Robert L. Maddex, London, Routledge 1996.

Keesing's Contemporary Archives/Record of World Events, 1945-1998.

Parliaments of the World. A Reference Compendium, edited by the Inter-Parliamentary Union, London, MacMillan 1976.

Parliaments of the World. A Reference Compendium, edited by the Inter-Parliamentary Union, London, Gower House 1986.

Political Handbook of the World 1998, edited by A.S. Banks, A.J. Day & T.C. Muller, Binghamton NY, CSA Publications, 1999.

Referendums around the World. The Growing Use of Direct Democracy, edited by D. Butler & A. Ranney, Washington DC, the AEI Press 1994.

The Statesman's Yearbook. A Statistical and Historical Annual of the State of the World, London, MacMillan, 1997.

INTERNET SITES

1. General Sites

http://www.freedomhouse.org/ranking.pdf/

Contains indicators on civil and human rights of most countries in the world, including those represented in this databook

http://www.gksoft.com/govt

Comprehensive dataset of governmental institutions and parliaments, ministries, offices, and political parties. Organised as a central linkage website around individual countries (N=220) and institutional categories like Heads of State, Parliaments, Political Parties, and Elections. The information offered varies from complete to quite fragmented.

http://www.agora.stm.it/ politic/

This website lists available political resources sorted by country around parties and governments. It is an open website and therefore contains a lot of superfluous material. The general information is from the CIA-Factbook (see next entry).

http://www.odci.gov/cia/publications/factbook/

This is the well-known *CIA-Factbook* and contains useful information of almost all countries of the world (N=191). Most of this is socio-economic, demographic and geographic in nature. Political data concern: the constitution, diplomatic relations, the Head of State, cabinet structure and leadership, regime-type, the legislature, and political parties. All countries in this databook are represented.

http://www.phw.binghamton.edu/handbook.html

Website of the well-known '*Political Handbook of the World*' edited by Arthur S. Banks and others. Contains all countries in this databook.

http://www.idea.int

Website of the International Institute for Democracy and Electoral Assistance. Very useful links to various other sites with information on elections, parliaments and governments.

Constitutions

http://lcweb2.loc.gov/glin/x-icl-lk.html

http://www.uni-wuerzburg.de/law/index.html

http://www.uni-wuerzburg.de/law/home.html

International Constitutional Law project (ICL)

These links give access to the mirror site at Cornell University of the International Constitutional Law project originated in Hamburg. The same information is provided by the original Hamburg (Wuerzburg) site. Most documents are inofficial translations provided by the information offices of the embassies. Indispensible website for constitutional information across many of the countries of the world (N=130). Comprehensive but not well organised.

http://star.hsrc.ac.za/modcon.html

MODCON

In 1990 the Centre for Constitutional Analysis of the Human Sciences Research Council (South Africa) started compiling an exhaustive set of questions which could serve as a tool for analyzing different constitutions. The questionnaire, which was discussed with a wide range of local and international scholars, culminated in a document with more than 700 questions. Modern constitutions - a comparative analysis (MODCON) is aimed at assisting researchers and practitioners throughout the world to analyze and compare various democratic constitutions.

Relevant countries included: Australia, Belgium, Canada, Germany, India, South Africa, Switzerland, United States of America.

Inter Parliamentary Union

http://www.ipu.org/

Official website of the Inter-Parliamentary Union with much information on the organisation of government and parliament and their rules of operation. Contains almost all countries of the world. All countries in this databook are represented.

Electoral Information

http://www.agora.stm.it/elections

Contains data on national elections, candidates, and results for individual parties.

http://www.idea.int/turnout

This site covers 1,129 parliamentary elections, and 360 presidential elections, in 171 countries since 1945.

Political Parties

http://www.agora.stm.it/elections/parties.htm

Contains data on all parties in the world if represented in parliament, with the number of seats they have. Includes all countries in this databook.

Heads of State

http://www.geocities.com/athens/1058/rulers.html

Contains lists of Heads of State and of Government, and sometimes the 'de facto' leaders. All countries in this databook are included.

2. Country Sites

http://www.centraleurope.com/

This site offers valuable information on countries in Central Europe.

Australia	http://gov.info.au
Austria	http://gov.austria-info.at
Bangladesh	http://www.un.int/Bangladesh/
Belgium	http://belgium.fgov.be
Botswana	http://www.gov.bw
Bulgaria	http://www.bulgaria.govrn.bg
Canada	http://canada.gc.ca
Czech Republic	http://www.czech.cz
Denmark	http://www.um.dk
Estonia	http://www.rk.ee
	http://www.ibs.ee/State/index.html.en
Finland	http://www.vn.fi
France	http://www.france.diplomatie.fr
Germany	http://www.bundesregierung.de
Greece	http://www.mfa.gr
Guyana	http://www.guyana.org/cabinet_members.html
Hungary	http://www.meh.hu
Iceland	http://www.stjr.is
India	http://india.indiagov.org
Ireland	http://www.irlgov.ie
Israel	http://www.parliament.gov.il/israel.htm
Italy	http://www.palazzochigi.it
Jamaica	http://www.jamaica_info.com(/contacts.html)
Japan	http://www.mofa.go.jp
Latvia	http://www.mfa.bkc.lv
Lithuania	http://www.lrs.lt (not in english)
	http://neris.mii.lt (not official)
Luxembourg	http://www.restena.lu
Macedonia	http://www.gov.mk
Malta	http://www.magnet.mt
Namibia	http://www.republicofnamibia.com/
The Netherlands	http://www.minbuza.nl
New Zealand	http://www.govt.nz
Norway	http://odin.dep.no
Pakistan	http://www.pak.gov.pk/govt(/information(desk).htm)
Poland	http://www.urm.gov.pl
Portugal	http://infocid.sma.pt
Romania	http://www.guv.ro
Russian Federation	http://www.gov.ru
Slovakia	http://www.government.gov.sk/
Slovenia	http://www.sigov.si
South Africa	http://www.southafrica.co.za/govt/
Spain	http://www.la-moncloa.es
Sri Lanka	http://www.lk/national/ministry.html
Sweden	http://www.sb.gov.se

Switzerland   http://www.admin.ch
Turkey   http://www.mfa.gov.tr
United Kingdom   http://www.open.gov.uk
United States of America
                     http://www.whitehouse.gov/WH/Welcome.html

Jaap Woldendorp (1952) is lecturer in the department of Political Science and Public Administration of the *Vrije Universiteit* Amsterdam. His research interests are 'neo-corporatism in the Netherlands since 1965' and 'government formation in parliamentary democracies'.

His recent publications include 'Neo-corporatism as a Strategy for Conflict Regulation in The Netherlands (1970-1990)' in *Acta Politica* (1995); 'Corporatism and Socioeconomic Conflict Regulation', in H. Keman (ed.), *The Politics of Problem Solving in Democracies; Institutionalising Conflict and Consensus* (1997); and 'Neo-corporatism and Macroeconomic Performance' in *Acta Politica* (1997).

On government formation his publications include 'Political Data 1945-1990. Party Government in 20 Democracies' in *European Journal of Political Research* (1993; with Hans Keman and Ian Budge), which was also published as *Handbook of Democratic Government. Party Government in 20 Democracies (1945-1990)* (1993). And 'Party Government in 20 democracies: an update (1990-1995)' in *European Journal of Political Research* (1998; also with Hans Keman and Ian Budge).

Hans Keman (1948) holds the Chair in Political Science at the *Vrije Universiteit* Amsterdam. Before that he held positions at the University of Amsterdam and Leyden. In addition he was research fellow at the European University Institute (Florence), the University of Nairobi (Kenya), the Australian National University (Canberra) and at the Netherlands Institute of Advanced Studies (NIAS). He has been Editor of the *European Political Science Book Series* between 1994-1999, published by Routledge. At present he is Editor of the *European Journal of Political Science.*

He has published numerous articles and book contributions. Among his book publications are: *Coping with the Crisis* (1987; co-editor); *The Development Toward Surplus Welfare* (1988); *Parties and Democracy* (1990; with Ian Budge); *Comparative Politics*: New Directions in Theory and Method (1993; edited); *Politics in Europe:* From the Atlantic to the Urals (1996; co-authored); *The Politics of Problem-Solving in Postwar Europe* (1997); *Institutions and Political Choice* (1998; co-editor); *Doing Research in Political Science* (1999; with Paul Pennings and Jan Kleinnijenhuis).

Ian Budge (1936) is full professor of Government at the *University of Essex.* He read history at Edinburgh and received his PhD at Harvard with Robert Dahl. He has held positions at the European University Institute (Florence), the University of Barcelona, the State University of New York (Binghamton) and California (Denver). He has also been Fellow at the Netherlands Institute of Advanced Studies (NIAS) and the Wissenschaftzentrum Berlin (WZB). He is a former director of the *European Consortium for Political Research* and one of the founders of the Essex Summer School in Statistical Data Analysis. Ian Budge has also founded the Manisto Research Group, the first and most comprehensive data bank on party programmes and government declarations.

He has published numerous books, articles and book contributions. Among his books are *Explaining and Predicting Elections* (1983, with R. Farlie); *Ideology, Strategy and Party Change* (1987; with D. Hearl and D. Robertson - editors); *Parties and Democracy* (1990, with Hans Keman); *Party, Policy and Government Programmes* (1992, with M. Laver - editors); *Parties, Policies and Democracy* (1994, with H.-D. Klingemann and R. Hofferbert et al.); *The New Challenge of Direct Democracy* (1996); and *The Politics of the New Europe* (1997, with K. Newton et al.).